Reading   presents a new departure in Herodotean scholarship: it i **Martial F** lti-authored collection of scholarly essays to focus
on a sing **Tel: 019** erodotus' *Histories*. Each chapter covers a separate
logos in I   proposes an original thesis about the political, historical, a   significance of the subjects that Herodotus treats
in this se   ie narrative. In addition, each chapter analyses the
connectic   ontinuities between its *logos* and the overarching
structure   otus' narrative. This collection of twelve essays by
internatic   owned scholars represents an important contribution to ex: iolarship on Herodotus and will serve as an essential
research t   ll those interested in Book 5 of the *Histories*, the
interpreta   Ierodotean narrative, and the historiography of the
Ionian Re

ELIZABE   VIN is Assistant Professor of Classics at Columbia
University   : the author of *Solon and Early Greek Poetry. The
Politics of I   tion* (2005).

EMILY GI   VOOD is Lecturer in Greek at the University of
St Andrev ..   ; the author of *Thucydides and the Shaping of History*
(2006) and c   tor, with Barbara Graziosi, of *Homer in the Twentieth
Century. Bett   World Literature and the Western Canon* (2007).

READING HERODOTUS

A Study of the logoi *in Book 5 of Herodotus'* Histories

EDITED BY

ELIZABETH IRWIN

Columbia University

and

EMILY GREENWOOD

University of St Andrews

CAMBRIDGE
UNIVERSITY PRESS

CAMBRIDGE UNIVERSITY PRESS
Cambridge, New York, Melbourne, Madrid, Cape Town,
Singapore, São Paulo, Delhi, Tokyo, Mexico City

Cambridge University Press
The Edinburgh Building, Cambridge CB2 8RU, UK

Published in the United States of America by Cambridge University Press, New York

www.cambridge.org
Information on this title: www.cambridge.org/9780521201025

First published 2007
First paperback edition 2011

A catalogue record for this publication is available from the British Library

ISBN 978-0-521-87630-8 Hardback
ISBN978-0-521-20102-5 Paperback

To those who have helped
us read Herodotus

Contents

Acknowledgements

The editors have incurred many fortunate debts in the preparation of this volume. The Colloquium on which this volume is based was held in the Faculty of Classics at Cambridge University (July 2002) and was made possible by a generous grant from the Faculty of Classics. We would like to thank the then Faculty Board for supporting the Colloquium. Liz Irwin would like to thank the AHRB-sponsored project 'The Anatomy of a Cultural Revolution: 430–380 BC', directed by Robin Osborne, for supporting her decision to organize a Colloquium on Herodotus and to undertake joint editorship of the subsequent volume. She would also like to thank Girton College, which was her home from the Colloquium's conception to its realization as an edited volume. Emily Greenwood would like to thank St Catharine's College, Cambridge, where she was a research fellow at the time of the Colloquium, and the School of Classics at the University of St Andrews. Both editors are indebted to the Classics Department of Columbia University for the generosity of the Lodge Fund in helping to defray some of the costs involved in the publication of this volume.

All of the speakers at the Colloquium benefited from an astute and engaging audience composed of members of the Faculty of Classics at Cambridge; we regret that we cannot name participants individually but would like to thank those who took part for their contribution to *Reading Herodotus*. We would also like to record particular thanks to Tom Harrison, Rosalind Thomas, and Hans van Wees, who acted as general respondents to the papers and helped us to articulate themes and questions.

We happily acknowledge how much we owe to our contributors; without them we could not have realized this experiment of reading Herodotus in the round. On a practical level they have made our work easy in submitting chapters so expertly, promptly and graciously. It is a privilege to have the opportunity to publish their work in this volume.

As editors we have been blessed with unstinting criticism, advice and encouragement from Paul Cartledge, Pat Easterling, Robin Osborne, and

John Henderson. They have shown us great generosity in commenting on successive drafts.

In the final stages of preparing this volume we were fortunate to work with Mr Bernard Dod, who has been an astute and congenial copy-editor in spite of being confronted with a bulky typescript. We would like to express our gratitude for the benefit of his editorial expertise, which has saved us from many errors and oversights. Alan Fishbone was also of great assistance in ridding the typescript of errors, and to him we offer our thanks. We have been very lucky to have Rosina di Marzo as our production editor and thank her for her patience and support. After all the help that we have received, we bear responsibility for any errors that remain.

Last but by no means least, we are especially grateful to Michael Sharp who has been a patient and judicious adviser throughout the development of this volume. We have had the benefit of no fewer than five different anonymous readers whose rigorous criticism and tough questioning has improved the final volume.

Contributors

DAVID FEARN is P. S. Allen Junior Post-Doctoral Research Fellow in Classics at Corpus Christi College, Oxford. His first book, *Bacchylides: Politics, Performance, Poetic Tradition* is forthcoming with Oxford University Press (2007). His research interests include the cultural and political contexts of choral lyric in the early fifth century BC, papyrology and the discovery of classical texts in the context of nineteenth-century imperialism in Egypt and the Middle East.

VIVIENNE GRAY is Professor of Classics and Ancient History at the University of Auckland. She has published extensively on Herodotus and Xenophon, and her commentary entitled *Xenophon on Government* (on Xenophon's *Hiero* and *Lacedaemoniorum Respublica* and the anonymous *Atheniensium Respublica*) was published in April 2007 in the Cambridge Greek and Latin Classics series. Her recent publications on Herodotus include 'Herodotus' Short Stories', in Egbert J. Bakker, Irene de Jong and Hans van Wees (eds.) *Brill's Companion to Herodotus* (Leiden, 2002), and 'Herodotus in two minds', in John Davidson (ed.) *Theatres of Action*, (Auckland, 2003). She is currently writing a monograph entitled *Xenophon Reassessed*.

EMILY GREENWOOD is Lecturer in Greek at the University of St Andrews. Her recent publications include *Thucydides and the Shaping of History* (London, 2006) and articles on Greek historiography and the reception of Classics in the Caribbean. She is co-editor, with Barbara Graziosi, of *Homer in the Twentieth Century: between World Literature and the Western Canon* (Oxford, 2007), and is also writing a book entitled *Afro-Greeks: Dialogues between Classics and Caribbean Literature*.

JOHANNES HAUBOLD is Leverhulme Lecturer in Greek Literature at the University of Durham. He is the author of *Homer's People: Epic Poetry and Social Formation* (Cambridge, 2000) and co-author, with Barbara

Graziosi, of *Homer: The Resonance of Epic* (London, 2005). He is currently working on a commentary on *Iliad* 6.

JOHN HENDERSON is Professor of Classics at the University of Cambridge. His most recent books are *The Triumph of Art at Thorvaldsens Museum: Love in Copenhagen* (Museum Tusculanum Press, Copenhagen, 2005), *The Medieval World of Isidore of Seville: Truth from Words* (Cambridge, 2006), *Oxford Reds: Classic Commentaries on Latin Classics* (London, 2006), and *Plautus, Asinaria: The One About the Asses* (Madison, 2006). He is currently working on the following books: *Sculpture and People in Vigeland Park at Frogner: Oslo's Monster, Brothers Keepers: Cicero's Letters to Cicero*, and *Terence, Getting Your Own Back on Yourself (Hautontimorumenus)*.

SIMON HORNBLOWER teaches at University College London, where he is Grote Professor of Ancient History and Professor of Classics. His most recent book is *Thucydides and Pindar: Historical Narrative and the World of Epinikian Poetry* (Oxford, 2004). He is now working on the third volume of a large-scale Thucydides commentary for Oxford University Press (previous volumes 1991 and 1996). This will include books 6 and 7, the Sicilian Expedition.

ELIZABETH IRWIN is Assistant Professor of Classics at Columbia University. She has published mainly on archaic Greek poetry, including her recent book, *Solon and Early Greek Poetry: the Politics of Exhortation* (Cambridge, 2005). She is now devoted to political readings of fifth-century literature.

JOHN MOLES is Professor of Latin at the University of Newcastle-upon-Tyne. His most recent publication is 'The Thirteenth Oration of Dio Chrysostom', *JHS* 125 (2005) 112–38. He has published extensively on Greek and Latin literature and Greek philosophy and is currently preparing articles on Virgil and the Acts of the Apostles and a commentary on Plutarch's *Life of Brutus*.

ROSARIA MUNSON is Professor of Classics at Swarthmore College. She is the author of numerous articles on Herodotus and two books: *Telling Wonders: Ethnographic and Political Discourse in the Work of Herodotus* (Ann Arbor, 2001) and *Black Doves Speak: Herodotus and the Languages of Barbarians* (Cambridge, Mass., 2005). She is currently co-authoring (with Carolyn Dewald) a commentary to Book I of Herodotus' *Histories* to be published by Cambridge University Press.

ROBIN OSBORNE is Professor of Ancient History in the University of Cambridge, and Fellow of King's College. His recent books include *Greek History* in the Classical Foundations series (London, 2004), *The Old Oligarch: Ps.-Xenophon's Constitution of the Athenians, Introduction, Translation and Commentary* (LACTOR 2, 2nd edition, 2004), (ed. with B. Cunliffe) *Mediterranean Urbanization 800–600 BC* (London and Oxford, 2005), (ed. with E. M. Atkins) *Poverty in the Roman World* (Cambridge, 2006), and (ed. with S. D. Goldhill) *Rethinking Revolutions through Classical Greece* (Cambridge, 2006), and (ed. with J. J. Tanner) *Art's Agency: Anthropological Explorations in the History of Art* (Oxford, 2007). He is currently working on the social and political significance of iconographic choices in Athenian vase painting.

CHRISTOPHER PELLING is Regius Professor of Greek at the University of Oxford. His most recent books are *Literary Texts and the Greek Historian* (London, 2000) and *Plutarch and History* (Swansea and London, 2002). He is currently working on a commentary on Plutarch's *Life of Caesar* and on a number of papers on Herodotus and other Greek historians; his next project will be a work on ideas of historical explanation in Greek historiography.

ANASTASIA SERGHIDOU is Lecturer in Greek History at the Department of History and Archaeology at the University of Crete and an associate member of the research division Phécie EA 3563 at the University of Paris I and VII. She specializes in Greek cultural history with a particular focus on social, cultural and affective dependencies. Her current research project is 'Aspects of affective and social dependencies in Herodotus'. She is also editing a volume entitled *Fear of Slaves–Fear of Enslavement in the Ancient Mediterranean*, based on the Proceedings of the 29th Conference of the Groupement International de Recherches sur l'Esclavage Antique that she organized in Rethymnon in November 2004 (forthcoming in 2007, Presses Universitaires de Franche-Comté).

Abbreviations

All Greek passages quoted in this volume are taken from the latest Oxford Classical Texts edition of each author or, occasionally, the latest Teubner edition (where the Teubner edition is used, this is mentioned in the text).

The following abbreviations are used in this work:

AAA	*Archaiologika Analekta ex Athenon*
AAntHung.	*Acta Antiqua Academiae Scientiarum Hungaricae*
ABSA	*Annual of the British School at Athens*
AION	*Annali dell'Istituto Orientale di Napoli*
AJPh	*American Journal of Philology*
AncSoc	*Ancient Society*
AncW	*Ancient World*
ASNP	*Annali della Scuola Normale Superiore di Pisa*
ATL	B. D. Merritt, H. T. Wade-Gery and M. F. McGregor, *The Athenian Tribute Lists* (Cambridge, Mass. (vol. I) and Princeton (vols. II–IV), 1939–53)
BCH	*Bulletin de correspondance hellénique*
BICS	*Bulletin of the Institute of Classical Studies*
CAH	*Cambridge Ancient History*
ClAnt	*Classical Antiquity*
CJ	*Classical Journal*
CPh	*Classical Philology*
CQ	*Classical Quarterly*
CR	*Classical Review*
DK	H. Diels and W. Kranz (eds.) *Die Fragmente der Vorsokratiker* (Berlin, 1952)
EMC	*Echos du monde classique*
FGrH	F. Jacoby, *Die Fragmente der griechischen Historiker*, 15 vols. (Berlin and Leiden, 1923–58)
GRBS	*Greek, Roman and Byzantine Studies*

G&R	*Greece and Rome*
HCT	A.W. Gomme, A. Andrewes, and K. J. Dover, *A Historical Commentary on Thucydides*, 5 vols. (Oxford, 1945–81)
HSCPh	*Harvard Studies in Classical Philology*
ICS	*Illinois Classical Studies*
IG	*Inscriptiones Graecae*
JHS	*Journal of Hellenic Studies*
JRS	*Journal of Roman Studies*
K–A	R. Kassel and C. Austin (eds.) *Poetae Comici Graeci* (Berlin and New York, 1983–95)
LGPN	*A Lexicon of Greek Personal Names*, currently 4 vols. (Oxford, 1987–2005)
LSJ	H.G. Liddell, R. Scott, and H.S. Jones, *A Greek–English Lexicon*, 9th edition with supplement (Oxford, 1968)
MH	*Museum Helveticum*
ML	R. Meiggs and D. Lewis, *A Selection of Greek Historical Inscriptions*, revised edition (Oxford, 1988)
M–W	R. Merkelbach and M. L. West (eds.) *Hesiodi Theogonia; Opera et dies; Fragmenta selecta*, 3rd edn. (Oxford, 1990)
PAPS	*Proceedings of the American Philosophical Society*
PBA	*Proceedings of the British Academy*
PCA	*Proceedings of the Classical Association*
PCPS	*Proceedings of the Cambridge Philological Society*
PLLS	*Proceedings of the Leeds Latin Seminar*
PMG	D. L. Page, *Poetae Melici Graeci* (Oxford, 1962)
QUCC	*Quaderni urbinati di cultura classica*
RDAC	*Report of the Department of Antiquities, Cyprus* (Nicosia)
REA	*Real-Encyclopädie der classischen Altertumswissenschaft*
REG	*Revue des études grecques*
RhM	*Rheinisches Museum für Philologie*
SEG	*Supplementum Epigraphicum Graecum*
SIMA	*Studies in Mediterranean Archaeology*
TAPhA	*Transactions of the American Philological Association*
YCS	*Yale Classical Studies*
ZPE	*Zeitschrift für Papyrologie und Epigraphik*

Introduction
Reading Herodotus, reading Book 5

Elizabeth Irwin and Emily Greenwood

I. BACKGROUND

This volume is devoted to the *logoi* of a single Book of Herodotus' *Histories* (Book 5). It derives from a Colloquium entitled 'Reading Herodotus' held at the Faculty of Classics, Cambridge University in July 2002. The rationale behind the Colloquium was to gather together a group of Herodotean readers to explore the texture of individual *logoi*, their place in the structure of Herodotus' narrative, and their significance for interpreting the history that he offers us. To this end, each contributor undertook to focus on a *logos* in Book 5, examining not only its content, but also its logic and language. We hoped that the project of bringing together different readers to address the same book in concert, but with distinctive voices and guided by different *logoi*, would provide an apt demonstration of just how much may be required to read Herodotus in all his complexity.

When we took the decision to publish the papers that had been presented at the Colloquium, we were keen to preserve the spirit of the conference and the tone of the original papers, which varied in approach and took the kind of interpretative risks that are associated with exploratory reading and debate. We have tried to give the reader a sense of publication as conversation by throwing open our original discussions to a larger audience. To some extent this has already begun to happen in the published volume, as new voices have joined the original discussion and have opened it up in different directions. Three of the scholars (Carolyn Dewald, Alan Griffiths and Tim Rood) who took part in the original Colloquium decided not to publish their papers and we regret not having had the opportunity to include them here. However, some traces of the discussion that they initiated are visible in footnotes to the present volume. In the interest of achieving more extensive coverage of Book 5, we solicited additional essays from David Fearn, Vivienne Gray, Johannes Haubold, John Henderson, Rosaria Munson and Anastasia Serghidou. Of this second wave of contributors,

John Henderson was a discussant at the original Colloquium; the others read written versions of the original papers. We can truly claim that our volume speaks with many voices. By offering twelve different contributions on a single book, we have tried to produce a graphic picture of the challenges entailed in reading and interpreting Herodotus, based on a dialogue between the different *logoi* in his work. The purpose of this Introduction is to explain what sense it makes to deal with Herodotus' work in this way, and to foreground broader themes and connections between the *logoi* of Book 5.

II. WAYS OF READING

Since there is no obvious precedent for this volume, we begin by explaining how it relates to other studies of Herodotus. Several book-length studies of Herodotus have already appeared in this young millennium; these studies include single-authored monographs, edited volumes, conference proceedings, and commentaries, to say nothing of the numerous articles published in journals and edited volumes.[1] The current volume is a hybrid of these different types of publication. It is, incidentally, an 'edited volume' – to use a term with minimal descriptive value – and, like other edited volumes on Herodotus, it boasts a diversity of subjects and approaches to Herodotus, pursuing many different lines of interpretation simultaneously. A common phenomenon in conventional edited volumes, which typically have their origins in conferences or colloquia, is that the unity provided by the occasion of the conference disappears in the conference proceedings, in which debates that may have taken place between the speakers fall out of sight. Correspondingly, in these volumes contributors' essays go their separate ways, with little or no continuity or dialogue.[2] The reader ends up knowing both more and less than he or she would learn from a good

---

[1] In the Anglophone field, these studies include two landmark monographs: Thomas (2000) and Munson (2001b), as well as several important edited volumes (Luraghi (ed.) (2001a); Bakker *et al.* (eds.) (2002); Derow and Parker (eds.) (2003); Karageorghis and Taifacos (eds.) (2004) and Dewald and Marincola (eds.) (2006)). In the same period a commentary on Book 9 appeared in the Cambridge Greek and Latin Classics Series (Flower and Marincola (2002)), and further commentaries on Herodotus have been commissioned for the same series. There is also a new commentary on Book 6 by Lionel Scott (Leiden, 2005) and the first volume of the English translation of the Italian commentary series on Herodotus (*Erodoto: le storie*) will be published by Oxford University Press in 2007 (*A Commentary on Herodotus Books 1–iv*, by Asheri, Lloyd and Corcella).

[2] See, for instance, Flory (2004) who identifies this divergence as a feature of a recent collection of conference proceedings on Herodotus: 'I have attempted here to make at least some of the widely-divergent essays in this volume enter into conversation with one another, a conversation not explicitly intended by the authors or their editors.'

single-authored monograph: more, because the volume covers more angles with more contexts and intertexts, but less because the knowledge on display is divergent rather than convergent. The reader is left to reflect on the questions that the respective essays pose for each other: can they all be true of the same text at the same time? How do you reconcile essays that start with Herodotus' text, with those that start with grand historical narratives and apply them to Herodotus' text? As editors we have confronted this problematic head-on by putting Herodotus' text and the exercise of 'reading Herodotus' in the foreground. By focusing on a single book, both we and our contributors have been compelled to think about connections across adjacent *logoi* and, consequently, between the interpretations offered in adjacent chapters.[3]

In contrast to the edited volume, the single-authored monograph is necessarily single-minded. Granted, single-mindedness does not preclude open-mindedness, but by its very nature this type of book cannot possess the many-mindedness of an edited volume, or a book by two or more authors. The author's commitment to a single thesis means that questions are pursued and resolved as s/he attempts to square Herodotus' text with her/his own understanding of it. In this sense the reader may emerge from the book knowing more in the form of a portable thesis, but ultimately knowing less since the exposition of a single thesis has suppressed other lines of enquiry in order to reach its conclusion. While there are many different ways of reading the conventional monograph and it is certainly possible for an author to sustain parallel narratives or even counter-arguments in footnotes, a single narrative and thesis must usually prevail. What this volume lacks in terms of single-minded unity, it makes up for through the richness of interpretation supplied by many intelligent and distinctive voices.

To turn to yet another genre of academic interpretation, insofar as it resembles any genre of publication, this volume is perhaps most akin to the conventional Commentary. Like the commentary, it addresses a single Book of Herodotus' *Histories* and is intended to be read alongside the text in question: if the volume achieves its aims, the readings offered here will send the reader back to Herodotus, rather than stand in as a substitute for his text. We cannot pretend to offer readers comprehensive coverage of Book 5, nor do we claim to present a definitive study: this is beyond the scope of any scholarly volume. Even in the case of the Commentary

---

[3] This formulation is indebted to Griffiths (2001), a study that examines the logic that binds together 'adjacent material' in Herodotus.

form, which is coextensive with the text and in principle covers every line or chapter of the work in question, total coverage is as much a fantasy as Borges' total library. A Commentary does not gloss all of the words in a given text and, more significantly, it cannot account for all of the conjunctions of words and their potential significance, both those imputed to the author and to readers/audiences. In addition, much is made of the tendency of commentaries to atomize texts into disconnected fragments (*lemmata*). Indeed, this is almost an inevitable consequence of the genre. Problems arise in trying to determine what constitutes an atom of text and where the lines of division occur. We have faced similar challenges with the anatomy of the *Histories*, but unlike many commentaries we have tried to make these challenges an explicit topic of interpretation.[4]

Whereas the conventional commentary can accommodate the needs of the 'hit-and-run' user,[5] this volume expects from its readers engagement with Herodotus' narrative in all its complexity. Readers who are tempted to use the indices to finger passages of text or discussions of specific subjects (tyranny, contingency in history, Aristagoras, Medism, onomastics . . .) will miss the point of this volume. With each successive chapter, the process of reading Book 5 should become increasingly dynamic and interactive, as successive contributors alert the reader to different aspects of Herodotus' narrative. For instance, the chapters on the Ionian Revolt acquire an additional dimension from those chapters that highlight the importance of the theme of revolutions of power in the *Histories* (Gray, Henderson, Moles, Munson, Pelling). To give another example, questions of aetiology and onomastics feed into broader debates about contingency and the way in which Herodotus constructs webs of causation (Henderson, Hornblower, Irwin, Osborne). The question of Greek relations with Persia is informed by the broader field of Herodotean ethnography, which includes competing myths of origins (Fearn, Haubold, Serghidou). Then there are essays which focus on apparent geographical detours in Herodotus' narrative (Fearn, Greenwood, Hornblower, Serghidou). Each of our contributors brings a *logos* into the foreground, and the fact that we all do this in concert counterbalances the selective vision of the single reader who privileges those aspects of the narrative from which s/he can make meaning, leaving others to the side. What our multiple voices bring out in relation to Book 5 is that

---

[4] For the anatomical metaphor applied to the organization of Thucydides' and Herodotus' narratives, see Dionysius of Halicarnassus *Letter to Gnaeus Pompeius* 3 (cited at the beginning of de Jong (2002)). See also Munson (2001b) 2 on the (analytic) tradition of treating the ethnographies in Herodotus as *disiecta membra*.

[5] For the 'hit-and-run' user see Kraus (2002) 11.

no other book so challenges an audience to decide on where its dominant narrative lies. Ostensibly the dominant narrative is the Ionian Revolt, but Herodotus uses the Revolt as an occasion for narrating histories of mainland Greece, past and present, playing intricate games with geography and temporality as he does so.

Insofar as this volume comments on Book 5, it does so in discursive mode. Firstly, our approach is discursive in that we explore the work fully in relation to its contexts: religion, history, politics, geography, intertextuality. Secondly, individual contributors all enter into discussion with other interpretative studies of the work in question. Thirdly, and this is something that is seldom attempted in edited volumes, our approach to Book 5 is discursive because it is conducted as a dialogue between different readers and offers an overview of a single book that comprises different points of view. Finally, through the intervention of the reader, this volume seeks further discussion and dialogue and invites repeated re-readings of the *Histories*. At the same time, the parallel readings of Book 5 put forward by different scholars provide for readers a suggestive if implicit commentary on the breadth of academic reception of Herodotus at the beginning of the twenty-first century.

III. THE READER'S AUTOPSY

Scholars are familiar with the conflicting pull of unitarian and analytic approaches to Herodotus,[6] a distinction further complicated by the study of traces of oral performance in the written text;[7] however, as an interpretative community, we seldom stop to ask how the form in which we read and interpret Herodotus affects the kind of text that emerges.[8] The unique format of this volume has made us acutely aware of the ways in which patterns of academic engagement tend to delimit a text's potential meaning.

Readers will note that the title of this volume refers to the '*logoi*' of 'Book' 5, signalling two different units into which one might divide Herodotus' narrative. We will address the question of Herodotean book divisions below (pp. 14–19), but at this point in our discussion it seems pertinent to define how we use the terms *logos* and *logoi* in this work. By evoking the explanatory power of *logoi* we are not attempting to carve up the narrative into different parts, but rather to focus on connections and continuities between the *logoi*

---

[6] See, e.g., Lateiner (1989) 3–5, Munson (2001b) 1–19, and de Jong (2002).
[7] See Thomas (1993) and (2000) 249–69, and Munson (2001b) 14–17.
[8] See Kraus (2002) 10: 'what divisions, structural and thematic, do we impose on the text when we read?' See also Griffiths (2001) 178: 'of which reading are you guilty?'

and the overarching *logos*. Contributors were all given free rein to define the formal beginning and end of our *logoi*, and to respond individually as readers to the gestures by which the narrative punctuates itself. At the same time, each contributor was invited to trace the relevance of his/her *logos* in ever-widening narrative contexts, the widest being the entire *Histories* itself. Each accepted the text's several invitations at given junctures to pause, to mark a beginning and a *telos* to which to look. And yet we all acknowledge how provisional these *termini* must be, embedded in the text as staging-posts at which the reader may choose to rest, even reflect, or simply drive on.[9]

Our title also alludes to the problem of defining *logoi* on another, implicit level. What constitutes a *logos* is subject to ongoing debate in Herodotean scholarship. As several recent studies have emphasized, there is a discrepancy between the way in which Herodotus uses this term self-reflexively, in reference to his own work,[10] and the way in which scholars have appropriated the term to categorize different sections of the *Histories*.[11] In the case of the latter, *logos* is used loosely to refer to (a) the work as a whole; (b) individual sections within the larger story; and (c) discernible patterns or themes that run throughout the narrative. While we take the point that the term *logos* is used loosely in the secondary literature, this looseness reflects the complex and loose-weave narrative structure of Herodotus' *Histories*, a work in which individual units of narrative work both independently and in concert.

The essays here embody the view that Herodotus' *logos* always comprises several different *logoi* (arguments, accounts, versions) about history both more remote and recent. There are the individual *logoi*, which need to be read within the overarching narrative(s) to which they belong and which, indeed, they constitute when taken together. But there are also those *logoi* – 'accounts', but also 'reasons' – that are external to the text, but implied every time Herodotus tells us that one group or another chooses to tell the version of the past that they do: these are the contemporary fifth-century contexts, and audiences, for which the *logoi* had their meaning, and those which

---

[9] We owe the metaphor of staging-posts to John Henderson.

[10] For an example of the self-reflexive use of *logos* in Book 5, see 5.36.4, where Herodotus reminds the reader that he has already illustrated the substance of Croesus' dedications to the oracle at Branchidae 'in the first of my *logoi*' – using *logos* here in the sense of an extended stretch of narrative on Croesus' dealings with Persians and Greeks.

[11] For recent bibliographical discussions of the use of *logos* as a construct in Herodotean scholarship see de Jong (2002) 255, who comments on variations in the use of the term and concludes that it is time for an in-depth study of the term *logos*; see also Gray (2002) 291 with n. 5; and Brock (2003) 8. All of these works refer back to Immerwahr (1966) 79–147 ('chapter 3: The units of the work').

we as scholars can only attempt to reconstruct. While their extradiegetic status makes it precarious to involve these contexts in interpretation, it is no less dangerous to exclude them. Moreover, such extratextual comparison can in fact claim to be an intrinsic dimension of the text: namely, the intellectual process promoted by the narrator of the *Histories* and conveyed by the verb συμβάλλειν, 'to throw things together', 'bring information to bear on a situation', 'to engage with something', and (in the middle voice: συμβάλλεσθαι) 'to conjecture/infer knowledge from diverse sources of information', 'to comprehend a situation by being able to apply this knowledge'.[12] Herodotus' text sends us back and forth as readers, trying to establish the significance that a *logos* holds within the narrative, the significance it might have held for his contemporary audiences, and the metahistoriographical significance it holds for us as interpreters. To put these different tiers together is to begin to comprehend the structure of Herodotus' narrative.

It is only through this process of paying close attention to Herodotus' text and relating it to its due contexts, that we can hope to counteract – if never avoid – our own biases as readers and those of the scholarship upon which we draw, and only through such a process that we are able to confront the inevitability that our own writing will be no less a product of its cultural, political and historical context than that of Herodotus. We have left our approaches open to examination and have tried to offset our individual angles of interpretation through continual recourse to Herodotus' own commentary on ways of seeing and their significance.

It is here that the centrality of autopsy in Herodotus' work must come into play. Like the narrator-researcher who has undertaken the travels, interviews, and reasoning processes that underlie the narrative, readers of the *Histories* have to negotiate their way through a text which travels to the frontiers of what is and can be known about other lands and peoples, and the near and distant past. However, whereas the Herodotean narrator claims autopsy for much of the information in the text, or direct engagement with his sources, what the reader sees and hears recounted in Herodotus' text is only ever virtual. We see and hear Herodotus' *logos*, as opposed to the objects, phenomena, and first-hand accounts which he claims to have experienced himself. For us as readers, the object of our autopsy is Herodotus' text. The primary challenge for the reader is not therefore to achieve an authentic account of the customs of the Sigynnae (5.9),[13] the

---

[12] See Hohti (1977), passim; and Munson (2001b) 83–5. For further discussion see Irwin's chapter, pp. 47–56 below.

[13] Still defying scholars see Irwin, pp. 83–6 below.

statistics about the road and journey-time to Susa (5.52–4), or the fate of Dorieus in Sicily (5.45). Instead, the reader's project is to construct an authentic account of Herodotus' *logos* on the basis of what he or she has seen on the page and in the work; everything that we claim to know about this book emerges from our reading of it.

When we leave the text and attempt to describe it, as we are doing here, we ourselves begin to create and spread *logoi* about the text, transforming our own readers into consumers of *akoē* (evidence from hearsay) about Herodotus' *Histories*. Our reading may conflict with their own autopsy of Herodotus' work, or with what is said (λέγεται) in the scholarly literature. In his first extended *logos* (1.8–12), Herodotus warns the reader of the disparity between seeing for oneself and hearing from others (*akoē*). Candaules may be foolish to urge Gyges to view his beautiful wife on the grounds that 'for men ears are less trustworthy than eyes' (1.8.2),[14] but his statement flags up the epistemological hierarchy that operates in the *Histories*, and poses a challenge to the external audience of the text: will we as voyeurs of the *logos* about the beauty of Candaules' naked wife remember that we are only *hearing* about this woman and everything else on offer in Herodotus' text – and for how long? As Candaules makes clear and as the ensuing consequences of Gyges' autopsy confirm, the experience of hearing is qualitatively different from seeing. The point has implications for us as audiences who only *hear* about the events and wonders that the *Histories* will narrate. Herodotus' style of attributing his *logoi* to various sources makes one thing clear: it is not enough to know a story and the information that it contains; one must also notice who is telling it, and grasp their motivation. Will we forget this when it comes to the grand story, and its master narrator?

This is not the whole story: arguably Herodotus encourages us to see his text both as an event and as a monument, as an object of reflection in its own right. If we immerse ourselves unguardedly in the aesthetic enjoyment of the deeds, monuments, and sights that are narrated in the text, we may fail to notice the all-important contexts in which we encounter them.[15] It is not easy to separate the events within the narrative from the *logoi* about them, for sure, and it is also not easy to divorce these *logoi* from the interpretative frame supplied by the rest of the work. The closer the reading, the more one becomes aware that *logoi* have been designed to be read in concert, and are separated from each other at a price. This brings

---

[14] ὦτα γὰρ τυγχάνει ἀνθρώποισι ἐόντα ἀπιστότερα ὀφθαλμῶν. Only an audience can determine whether this is heard as 'commonplace' (cf. Austin and Olson (2004) 53–4 (*ad* Ar. *Thesmo.* 5–6)) or seen as embedded philosophy (Heraclitus DK 101a and 55, with Robb (1991), Kurd (1991)).

[15] On the 'aesthetic enjoyment' of monuments in the *Histories*, see Immerwahr (1960) 270.

us back to the way in which the interpretative choices that we make, and the academic genres that we employ, (re)configure the text. The potential for partial, myopic readings, or oversights, is starkly illustrated in the case of the commentary form, where unlemmatized text slips out of view and falls through gaps in scholarly debates. This phenomenon of the vanishing text has been discussed elegantly by Christina Kraus:

> As a reflection of someone else's reading, lemmata can guide our interpretation – but if we are responsible readers, they are also an open invitation to challenge the commentator's articulation. If 'looking' is at the root of theory (θεωρία), then the processes of selection and lemmatization are fundamental to theorizing, as they put a pattern onto a text which shows it in a different light. A lemmatized text literally looks different, and the reader in turn sees the text differently. Unlemmatized text is absent, unmarked, invisible, whether literally (if one does not return from commentary to text) or figuratively, as it is disregarded by the cumulative authority of the commentary tradition to date.[16]

Our volume was conceived in the joint knowledge that readers see different patterns in Herodotus, and that the subject of *theōria* is at the heart of his work. Since our contributors all come at the same book from different angles of vision, and from the perspectives afforded them by their different sections, this volume constitutes a many-sided reading. And although a panoramic view of the *Histories* is beyond the scope of a single academic work, the juxtaposition of different readings presented here means that we cover some of each other's blind spots. We believe that this volume offers an important experiment in reading Herodotus discursively and in dialogue with the interpretations of others, and hope that it will stimulate new debates.

IV. CHOOSING BOOK 5

Beginning with the middle, looking to the end

The notion of 'beginning at the beginning' is a powerful literary fiction that derives its authority from the claim that one's point of departure is somehow natural. It is, of course, always an artifice, the choice of a narrator; and narrators can be more or less candid about revealing the artificiality of their beginning. Consider Thucydides: in the first sentence of the work Thucydides informs the reader that he began to write down the Atheno-Peloponnesian war, beginning (ἀρξάμενος) at a 'natural' beginning,

---

[16] Kraus (2002) 13–14.

as soon as it broke out (1.1.1), only to spend the first Book on material that constitutes a 'pre-beginning' by way of explanation for the conflict that is his subject. Then both the war and the work (insofar as Thucydides encourages us to view the war and his work as a unity) begin again at the start of the second Book: ἄρχεται δὲ ὁ πόλεμος ἐνθένδε ('the war begins at this point' – 2.1). At a symbolic level, there is yet another beginning at 2.12.3–4, with a statement by the Spartan Melesippus that 'this day will be the beginning of great evils for the Hellenes' (μεγάλων κακῶν ἄρξει), a passage that resonates with our own Book 5 (5.97, see below). Whereas Thucydides' staggered beginnings are understated, Herodotus' account of the Persian War draws full attention to his choices as narrator, the subjectivity and particularity of his chosen beginning, '*I* am not going to say how thus or otherwise these [past mythic] events happened, but *I* know who first perpetrated unjust acts against the Greeks, and telling this *I* will proceed . . . Croesus was the first of those we know . . .' (1.5.3–6.1). And in contrast to Thucydides' one-book beginning which denies almost all its past events any meaningful status as *aitiai*,[17] Herodotus will provide some two centuries of context in which to begin to understand the cause of his war, focusing intently and extensively precisely on those fifty-odd years that precede it.

Our volume begins, artificially enough, at the middle of Herodotus' work, but we too can claim this artificial beginning is not entirely unnatural from the text's point of view. The narrative of Book 5 builds up to a beginning, the twenty ships that the Athenians sent to Ionia in c. 499 BC that constitute a symbolic 'beginning of evils' (ἀρχὴ κακῶν – 5.97.3) heralded from the very first paragraph of the work.[18] Herodotus' *archē kakōn* screams artifice. The phrase not only looks back intertextually to Homer and forward to the events of 431 BC, if not also to Thucydides,[19] but it also punningly gestures towards a meaning that it will only acquire after the events narrated in the *Histories* with the arrival of Athenian *archē* ('empire') – an 'evil' that is already in force in real time for Herodotus' contemporary audiences, but has yet to begin in narrative time.[20] Book 5 presents us

---

[17] Only the most recent events, Epidamnus, Corcyra, Potidaea can be called 'causes', but never the truest cause (1.23.6).

[18] See Pelling, p. 187 below, and Munson, p. 146 below, on the way in which Book 5 echoes themes from the beginning of the work.

[19] On the intertextual link between Herodotus (5.97.3) and Homer *Iliad* 5.63 and 11.604, see Munson, p. 153 with n. 34, Hornblower, pp. 171–2, Pelling, p. 186, and Haubold, p. 234 below.

[20] The 'evil' of Athenian *archē* is a matter of perspective, depending on the different audiences that we posit for the *Histories*. For the pun on *archē* (beginning) to *archē* (empire), see Irwin (p. 47, n. 16), Munson (p. 155), Pelling (p. 182), and Henderson (p. 305) below.

with the moments leading up to, and those immediately following, the 'beginning of ills', highlighting the role of Aristagoras as a character who precipitates Athenian involvement in the revolt and whose death closes a chapter of 'the Ionian Revolt' and indeed Book 5 itself. At the point where Herodotus marks his beginning, how that *archē* came about, what it in fact began, and where (if) it should be seen to end, are less than clear. In 5.97 all that is specified is its source – Athenian ships – and its recipients – Greeks *and* barbarians: αὗται δὲ αἱ νέες ἀρχὴ κακῶν ἐγένοντο Ἕλλησί τε καὶ βαρβάροισι ('These very ships were to become the *archē* of evils for Greeks and barbarians').[21] By the time readers reach the similarly portentous and analogously timed passage in Book 6 (6.98), describing the future-present ills (κακά) for Greece betokened by the Delian earthquake that extend down to the late 420s, the makings of an answer may start to emerge. But as always in Herodotus, it matters crucially what an audience will bring to bear on the text.[22]

If Herodotus' beginnings always encompass what has come before, they also look to the end, and our approach to Book 5 will follow suit in not distancing itself from the wider narrative context of the *Histories*. Even as the essays in this volume all focus on a single moment in the *Histories*, they are also sensitive to the wider frame of the *Histories* in its entirety. At the same time, they also look beyond the literal temporal confines of the narrative to an extratextual frame, as does Herodotus. This frame encompasses the decades prior to the narration of the *Histories*, and the broader contemporary context surrounding the hazy date at which Herodotus' text began to circulate. Indeed, the historical context of Herodotus' readers supplies the ultimate *telos* to which the text looks, evoked every time the narrator says 'in my day' or reports what one or another group *says* (present tense). Book 5 marks a discernible shift in the narrative, where that end comes into view more sharply than in preceding books as Athenian democracy comes on stage, introducing with it mounting tensions with Sparta and involvement in Ionia.[23]

---

[21] As Paul Cartledge pointed out to us, the phrase Ἕλλησί τε καὶ βαρβάροισι echoes the preface of the *Histories* (τὰ μὲν Ἕλλησι, τὰ δὲ βαρβάροισι) in which the crossings of ships between between Greek and Barbarian lands act as a false start for the aetiology of Graeco-Persian geopolitical conflict.

[22] For further discussion of these *kaka* see Munson, pp. 149–59 below. The analogous content of these passages is met by analogous placement within the narratives of each book, immediately prior to the Ionian and Athenian sacking of Sardis and the Persians' retaliatory invasion of mainland Greece. On the complementarity of theme and structure of Books 5 and 6 see below.

[23] Indeed Hippias' prophecy of the suffering Corinth will experience at the hands of Athens (5.93) takes the audience into the world of Book 1 of Thucydides (see Moles, Ch. 10 below), as does mention of the Cylonian curse (5.70–2, cf. Thuc. 1.126).

At this point in the *Histories* the reader arrives at the centre of the work where concepts of text, geography and time converge: the centre of the nine-book narrative, the centre of the known world in Thrace – the midpoint between Europe and Asia – and indeed even the temporal centre, if one recognizes that the events around 490 BC constitute a midpoint between the first wrong done by barbarians to Greeks (c. 560–546 BC according to Herodotus – 1.6) and audiences of the 420s BC who are inscribed in Herodotus' text by the absence of any explicit reference to post-430 BC events.[24] Book 5 marks the start of the Persian War narrative, the one that he has kept his audience waiting for all this time. But what follows is in fact a particular, Herodotean, telling of events that will compete with whatever versions are already in the minds of each member of the audience.[25] Book 5 heralds one of the most exciting aspects of this text's endgame, namely how Herodotus anticipates those present-day responses in his reconstruction of past (and present) history.

Books 5 and 6 together serve as 'bridging' books containing *logoi* about Greeks in transition.[26] Herodotus turns his critical eye to the cultural and political development of the many Greek *poleis*, as well as to a new phase in Graeco-Persian relations defined by the outbreak and rapid escalation of hostilities between them. There is a discernible change of focus: instead of the heavily ethnographic account of non-Greek peoples presented in earlier books, the narrative becomes more historical and moves closer to home, geographically, historically, and politically. But if Book 5 turns our attention towards the text's end – the main Persian War narrative – and the extra-textual *telos* of contemporary events, in doing so it requires readers to review what they have already read in Books 1–4 and to re-evaluate the pertinence and proximity of what may have passed – on first reading – for foreign history.[27]

---

[24] Whenever the text of Herodotus was circulated as a written text and in the form in which we have it, the text constructs an *inferred* audience of the 420s by making the last certainly datable events in the *Histories* belong to the period immediately preceding: Plataea, spring 431 BC (7.233; cf. Thuc. 2.2–6) and the reference to Talthybius' anger, 430 BC (7.137 cf. Thuc. 2.67), while 6.98 may gesture to the death of Artaxerxes I in 425/4 BC: Fornara (1971a) and (1981).

[25] For discussion of these versions as sources see Murray (1988) and Thomas (2004); that Herodotus is our only surviving literary source (Murray (1988) 466) suggests the degree to which his master narrative eclipsed others. For the tension between a *logopoios'* account and local – oral – traditions, see the reappearance of Hecataeus at the close of Book 6 (137–9) in an account that pits his written authority against Athenian tradition.

[26] On the salience of the metaphor of the bridge see Greenwood, Ch. 4 below. On political and ethnic change, see pp. 25–33 below.

[27] The reference to the 'telos' of the *Histories* is to 1.32.9, where Solon advises Croesus that he should 'look to the end (*telos*) of all things'. Many critics see a meta-narrative statement in this utterance: the

Beginning not at *the* beginning of the *Histories*, but with Book 5 – as well as ending not at its end – does require some explanation of our decision to focus on this single book. While any book would have presented its own reasons, the challenges posed by the narrative of Book 5 rendered it a particularly appropriate choice to engage a community of readers. As Murray acknowledges, the dominant narrative of Book 5, the Ionian Revolt, is notorious as 'one of the most problematical sections' of the *Histories* and one that invariably leads to selective readings of Herodotus' text: 'Inevitably the desire to teach Herodotus what he ought to have said leads to "substituting for the Herodotean reconstruction one which is completely personal, more rational perhaps, but not necessarily more true"'.[28] Moreover, the influential model that Murray put forward in that same article in which he understood Herodotus' bewildering Revolt narrative as the synthesis of many competing voices, suggested our assembly of diverse readers as its appropriate academic counterpart.[29] However, our volume will not focus solely on the Ionian Revolt, but rather on Book 5 for the reasons that we present below.

While the remarks of Murray above provide an astute critique of those attempting to extract the causes of the Ionian Revolt from the account Herodotus provides, the same critique of selectivity and subjectivity might equally be levelled against those who choose to engage with Herodotus' narrative of Book 5 (and parts of Book 6) narrowly as the account of the Revolt. While such a conflation of narrative with the event it narrates is understandable, it may nevertheless be seen as arbitrary from the point of view of the text. In truth, no other section of the *Histories* proves so obstructive to readers who are desirous of reducing it to a single, dominant narrative.[30] Given the way that Herodotus has constructed his text, it is

---

denouement of events is only visible at the end of Herodotus' text and the reader, in order to fulfil Solon's instructions, will have to read to the end. However, the end of the text is only a provisional *telos*, since the text ends in 479 BC, but brings events up to 430 BC within its purview. As Moles points out, there is a heavy Athenian framing for Solon's warnings to Croesus – not least because Solon is an Athenian – making this a warning (that will inevitably be unheeded) about a *telos* that eludes the Athenians of Herodotus' day: Moles (2002) 36. See also Moles (1996) 267–9.

[28] Murray (1988) 466, quoting Tozzi (1978).

[29] Murray (1988); on the influence of his importation of anthropological models to the study of Herodotus see the volume of Luraghi (2001a) and, on the Ionian Revolt, see most recently Thomas (2004). This model of the reconciliation of competing oral traditions ultimately derives its strength from Herodotus' claim that he is unable to provide a full account of the final naval defeat of the Revolt, 'because everyone blames everyone else' (6.14). On the causes of the Revolt, and the nuances of the tone of Herodotus' narrative, see Munson, Ch. 5 below.

[30] Those so inclined are forced to produce their own selective editions: see, for instance, such late nineteenth-century British school editions as Tancock (1897), *The Story of the Ionic Revolt and Persian War as Told by Herodotus*, with the subtitle, 'Selections from the translation of Canon Rawlinson,

only through wilfulness or myopia that readers can keep focused on the ostensibly dominant narrative, the Revolt, while so many other 'diversions' vie to occupy centre-stage. Our volume engages with the interpretative choices that confront the reader in the shifting, fragmented, 'problematic' narrative of Book 5. Faced with such a diverse narrative, we have relied on multiple focalizations to trace and illuminate this diversity.

The question, however, remains why choose the book *qua* book as a meaningful unit of focus, given that the evidence for the existence of our traditional book divisions remains later than the composition of the *Histories*?[31] Despite the argument above, the decision to focus on a 'book' rather than a continuous stretch of narrative defined by a single historical event, like the Ionian Revolt, may call for defence, particularly when the book in question not only displays less obvious unity than the stretches of narrative coextensive with some other book divisions (e.g. 1, 2, 4), but also can be read in conjunction with Book 6 as a single narrative unit.[32] The question of the *termini* of this volume is a valid one (why end with Book 5,

---

revised and adapted to the purposes of the present work'. The first line of Tancock's preface (v) – 'Few words are necessary in explanation of this book' – epitomizes the sensibilities at play in those who, he continues, have from 'long experience . . . felt the *want* of a *continuous* narrative, in a *convenient* form, of the *simple* story of the Persian War as told by Herodotus' [our italics]. Our volume will counter such sensibilities, which still persist, albeit to a lesser extent, in many contemporary responses to Herodotus.

[31] On the division at Book 5 see Nenci (1994) 151; the earliest attestation of our book divisions is a commentary of Aristarchus (*P. Amherst* II.11), followed by Diodorus (11.37.6) and Lucian (*de conscribenda historia* 42; *Herodotus sive Aetion* 1). For a modern attempt to subdivide the *Histories* into constituent *logoi* see Cagnazzi (1975), nine of whose 28 *logoi* begin, nevertheless, with our traditional book divisions (each book containing three *logoi*, save Book 5 to which she ascribes four, treating as significant a division that many, including Gray, Ch. 8 below, would ignore). It must be noted that although the modern orthodoxy asserts the divisions to be *post*-Herodotean, there is no positive evidence that they are not Herodotus', and in contrast to the case with Thucydides no evidence for readers generating competing book divisions (Marcellin. *Thuc.* 58, Diod. Sic. 12.37, cf. 13.42; see Johnson (2004) 17). There is, however, room to challenge the orthodoxy: as there was no radical change in book production from the Classical to Hellenistic period, to assume that considerations of the format by which this monumental work would appear and, of necessity, be divided had no part in its ultimate design as a written text may be unduly naive; such *a priori* assumptions may occlude deeper appreciation of the structure and unity of Herodotus' narrative. An in-depth study of book divisions in Herodotus is beyond the scope of this introduction. In our role as editors we maintain that the book divisions, whether originating with Herodotus or otherwise, serve to make more visible and reify transitions in the text that have already been embedded in the narrative, even as these transitions have been constructed in such a way as to defy any total commitment to segmentation. In other words, a book does not cease to be a unit just because there is a major through-flow of content from one book to another, any more than a theme is interrupted by book division – it must always be a two-way street. Herodotean or otherwise, the book division is a 'dimension' for narrative organization that at once creates a discrete unit even as it asserts that unit's cohesion within a larger whole. This position owes much to discussions with John Henderson.

[32] E.g. Dewald (1998) 664; see also Murray (1988) 472 who notes that 'with one major exception', the stories which concern Histiaeus, the narrative of 5 and 6 'is unified and coherent, without obvious changes in source or approach.'

rather than 6?), and in true Herodotean form we offer several kinds of explanations (*logoi*).

To start with an obvious explanation, 5.1 is universally recognized as the start of something new, the book division itself representing of course an ancient assessment of a narrative break. In terms of plot, while the figure of Histiaeus has been introduced in Book 4 (in passing, but with great moment, see below, 'Starting out', p. 21), in terms of both length and subject the Libyan *logos* (4.145-end) marks a resounding break in the narrative, allowing all readers – ancient and modern – to sense here a new beginning even as the better readers know that such beginnings in Herodotus' narrative – even *the* beginning –[33] are never detached from what has come before. The Libyan *logos* functioned as a pause in the text, creating an interval before the resumption of what is to become *the* Persian War narrative.

Our decision to end at the division between Books 5 and 6 is, however, somewhat less obvious, given that this is perhaps one of the easiest of book divisions to ignore:[34] Books 5 and 6 recount together a narrative event, the Ionian Revolt, but do so in a characteristically Herodotean fashion: readers are given not just the event itself, but also the circumstances leading up to and the consequences ensuing from it, that is, an extended *logos* that includes all manner of 'digressions' providing the background – whether necessary or not – to individual characters, collectivities (political and ethnic) and geography that audiences will find embroiled in the ensuing plot. The succession of stories is deceptively natural – the narrative equivalent of the *lexis eiromenē*: Megabazus' campaign on the Thracian coast beginning in 5.1 explains his failure to stop Darius from granting Histiaeus a colony in the same area, which in turn leads to Histiaeus' unwanted sojourn in Susa causing him to incite Aristagoras to revolt, the latter then becoming the engine of the Revolt until his death in the last chapter of Book 5; at the opening of Book 6 Histiaeus returns to Sardis, the site of the initial gift, to forward the Revolt, which ends in failure, his death and the fall of Miletus, closing the second phase in the course of the Revolt as Book 6 then moves on to narrate its repercussions, culminating in the battle of Marathon. In so many ways the narrative of Book 6 draws on and complements the material presented in Book 5, narrating the end of the Revolt and its wider

---

[33] See, for instance, the story of Croesus: Herodotus claims that he will begin with Croesus as the man who did the first wrong to the Greeks, only to embark on a *logos* that occurred four generations earlier (1.5, 7–14), the 'relevance' of which is to be revealed only at the point of Croesus' near-death (1.91.1–3). See pp. 19–25 below on how the narrative of 5.1–10 resumes that broken off at 4.144.

[34] As demonstrated by a commentary such as that of Abbott (1893).

consequences, including where the mainland Greeks whose circumstances have been introduced in Book 5 are left in its aftermath.[35]

In light of these continuities across books 5 and 6, the decision to dedicate a volume solely to Book 5 requires explanation. There are of course the practical reasons: just as Herodotus himself could hardly have been unaware of the format – its ambitions and constraints – in which his own work would be circulated, so too, *mutatis mutandis*, the format of an academic volume is marked by its own aspirations and constraints. Clearly, close engagement with a continuous stretch of narrative requires a limit to be placed on the amount of text that can be covered, particularly with a narrative like Book 5 in which tracing the contours of the many diverse *logoi* on offer requires the participation of many voices. But there are less pragmatic reasons for defending the selection of Book 5 as a meaningful unit. Within the wider unit formed by 5 and 6, Book 5 is itself a clearly defined unit. As Murray notes, the existing book division does correspond to two distinct blocks: 'the period from the outbreak of the Revolt to the failure of the first Persian counter-offensive in Caria and the flight of Aristagoras in Thrace, and the period which begins with the preparations for the battle of Lade and continues beyond the Revolt into the Marathon campaign and the main wars'.[36] Book 5 opens with conquest on the Thracian coast, and progresses to the Ionian Revolt as set in motion by the figure of Aristagoras. It ends with that figure dying in an attempt at conquest in the very same region; one might even refer to this stretch of narrative as 'the Aristagorean leg' of the Ionian Revolt. The narrative is united by means of character, through the figure of Aristagoras,[37] and through the ring composition provided by the geographical setting of Thrace.[38]

But it is not just the life of Aristagoras and the return to the Thracian coast that lends unity to Book 5 in the midst of the wider narrative represented by Books 5 and 6. As a unit Books 5 and 6 provide the wider frame around the destructions of the two cities that mark the beginning and end of the Revolt, the destruction of Sardis (5.99–102) and Miletus (6.18–22) – the destruction of these cities uncannily equidistant from the

---

[35] See Munson, Ch. 5 below on the flow-through from 5 to 6 and their thematic continuities; see also Hornblower, Ch. 6 below on the explicit link that Herodotus' narrative forges between the destruction of Miletus (6.21) and Sybaris (5.44). The complementarity of the narratives presented in 5 and 6 is extensive, and would require a study in its own right.

[36] Murray (1988) 472.

[37] And recapitulated in his textual double, the instigator of the Cypriot Revolt, Onesilus (5.104). See further n. 45 below.

[38] Within the frame provided by Thrace occur repeated narrative sequences that frame the *logoi* of mainland Greece: the uprooting and return of the Paeonians (5.12–17, 5.98), Histiaeus in Susa (5.24 and 35, 106–8), and the twice rejected advice of Hecataeus (5.36, 125).

book division.[39] Seen this way, the respective focus of each book becomes clear: Book 5 represents the cause and outbreak (Sardis) of the Revolt, while Book 6 depicts its quashing (Miletus) and consequences. A further structural parallelism reinforces this characterization: each unit is punctuated by its similarly portentous utterances – 5.97 describing the beginning of evils for Greeks and Barbarians, and 6.98 the consequent evils to come for Greece.

The first chapters of Book 6 seem to confirm Book 5 as focused on causes. In 6.1 Histiaeus returns to Sardis, where the Ionian Revolt narrative began, that is, where Darius' fateful gift of Myrcinus precipitated the Ionian tyrant's distasteful sojourn in Susa that was to last the entirety of Book 5. It is precisely at this moment that Herodotus induces reflection on the narrative of Book 5 through the question of a character who has not been privy to its content. The Persian Satrap Artaphrenes asks Histiaeus the very question that has plagued historians of the Ionian Revolt forced to depend on Herodotus as our only surviving literary source, namely what in his opinion caused the Ionian Revolt. As Artaphrenes demands from Histiaeus, so too have we demanded the same answer from Herodotus' text, and given the elegance of the parallelism we might well ask whether Herodotus the master narrator has left the audience of Book 5 any closer to an answer than Histiaeus, as the figure who stitched the boot (τοῦτο τὸ ὑπόδημα ἔρραψας μὲν σύ) that is the Revolt?[40] Or has Herodotus' narrative placed his own audience in the same position as the intradiegetic Artaphrenes, asking 'why', and suspecting much? But for us as the audience of a text, not an event, the question can no longer concern solely what caused the Revolt, but must also explore what has caused such a narration of it.

Murray lists 'modern dissatisfaction' with 'the signs of incoherence between episodes, lack of motivation for events, and implausibility of moral explanations'.[41] He finds a solution grounded in a certain understanding of oral tradition – reflecting a trend in anthropology – which in effect functioned to render the apparent 'idiosyncrasies and weaknesses' of the narrative unintentional, a reflection of a proto-historian's inability to reconcile

---

[39] In terms of the wider structure of Books 5 and 6, one may also note how Hecataeus closes both books as the figure who provides the segue into the final *logos* of each (at 5.125 and 6.137 respectively).

[40] The verb ῥάπτω can, of course, be reflexive and evoke composition: see Nagy (1996) Ch. 3 with bibliography. If one presses further, the audience may also find themselves configured as Aristagoras. How Aristagoras 'put on' the injunction to revolt is, at the level of meta-narrative, the analogue of how an audience will choose to 'put on' the *logos* describing it, that is, how they will make sense of what Herodotus has stitched out of the many *logoi* at his disposal.

[41] Murray (1988) 471.

irreconcilable narratives.[42] Murray was surely right to draw our attention
to the oral traditions, loosely conceived as *akoē*, that must have provided
material for Herodotus' account. His insistence, however, on orality as the
explanation for the quirks of the account may overlook the insistence with
which our author has posed the question of 'why' at the juncture in the
Revolt narrative that is the start of Book 6: so pressing is that question of
why, that the text stages its characters once again posing a related question:
this time it is the Ionians who ask Histiaeus why he had been so anxious to
encourage the Revolt (6.3).[43] The repetition of the question 'why' prompts
us to consider what the apparently diffuse narrative of Book 5 was about –
its very unity – namely the 'cause(s)' of the Revolt. In contrast, Book 6 will
narrate the continued course of the Revolt and its consequences, which
result in Persia's reciprocal attack on Athens, an event that coincides with
the Delian earthquake forecasting the *kaka* to come; but Book 5 has been
about 'why' and 'how' the Revolt came to take place, its beginning and
the beginning of *kaka*, the full reverberations of which, typified by those
of the Delian earthquake, will be clarified only in 6.98.[44] And indeed even
after the Revolt has officially begun, with the destruction of Sardis (5.99–
102), Herodotus delays its end by exploring the anatomy of Revolt using
Cyprus as a microtheme, enabling the failure of the Cypriot Revolt to foreshadow that of the Ionians, while also inviting audiences to compare and
contrast.[45]

   If Book 5 narrates the cause of the Revolt, consonant with Herodotean-
style historiography, he supplies no 'truest cause', but rather a puzzle for
those who would seek one, his success at which is well attested by modern

---

[42] Murray (1988) 466–75; cf. Thomas (2004).
[43] For the significance of the Ionians' question as representing an interdiegetic audience see Munson,
      p. 152 below. On the level of meta-narrative, the answers that Histiaeus gives are somewhat worrying:
      to the Persian question of why the Ionians revolted he claims ignorance, to that of the Ionians he
      fabricates a lie; but as an audience, the only basis on which we can evaluate the truth status of his
      answers is in fact the narrative of Book 5. It should also be noted that the only sources for Histiaeus
      are those manifestly dependent on Herodotus' account of him (e.g. Polyaen. 1.24, Aen. Tact. 31.28.1),
      unlike the situation for Aristagoras who is attested as early as Thucydides (4.102.2). The claim that
      'much of the story must be true' as 'Histiaeus is indeed a recognizable type' (Murray (1988) 486)
      must be called into question, not least because it is precisely our *logopoios* who is to thank for making
      this type so recognizable.
[44] On which see Munson, pp. 153–4 below.
[45] Hdt. 5.104, 108–16. For the return of the earliest motifs of Book 5 in the Cyprus story see Serghidou,
      pp. 271, 277, 280 below. The parallels are striking: Onesilus, the instigator of a revolt of ambiguous
      motivation, functions as a miniature of Aristagoras; the immediate and total abandonment of
      the Cypriot cause by the Ionians (5.115) recapitulates that just performed by the mother of Ionia,
      Athens (5.103); even their speaking names, 'best in speech' and 'beneficial one', demonstrates an
      analogous ambiguity in relation to their respective narratives: was Aristagoras best in speech? was
      Onesilus beneficial? On the character of Aristagoras see Pelling, Ch. 7 below; on that of Onesilus
      see Serghidou, Ch. 11 below. On speaking names, see Irwin, Ch. 1 below.

scholarship. Like Thucydides' 'truest cause' it *may* be the one least said in the narrative, but most implicit and universal: a desire for autonomy. Between Megabazus' (successful) and Aristagoras' (failed) conquests of the Thracian coast that frame Book 5, an underlying cause – and thereby a source of unity – emerges through its narrative as it depicts a host of different groups attempting to resist subjugation by an external enemy – Perinthians, lake-dwelling Paeonians, Ionians, Carians, Cypriots, and finally again the Thracians, though the enemy has changed – or even subjugation to a native tyrant, imposed, as so often, by external means;[46] this is not to maintain that these themes are not explored further in Book 6, and indeed the rest of the *Histories*, but rather to recognize how Herodotus' narrative frames them here in Book 5, with a frame that can only be tentative, relying as it does on the willingness of the reader to discern certain patterns in the narrative.[47] In short, we fully acknowledge that the narrative of Book 5 is no island, set apart from the rest of the *Histories*, and yet maintain the value of engaging with it as a unit, if only provisionally as we experiment with what such a focalization has to offer.

V. READING BOOK 5

With the nature of our study defined, we now embark on the narrative of Book 5. This section sets the stage for the opening of Book 5, while the next section provides a summary overview of the subtle yet persistent themes connecting its constituent *logoi*.

Starting out

That Chapter 1 of Book 5 marks a significant break from the preceding extended narrative about Libyan affairs (4.145–205) is uniformly recognised as such by commentators:[48]

οἱ δὲ ἐν τῇ Εὐρώπῃ τῶν Περσέων καταλειφθέντες ὑπὸ Δαρείου, τῶν ὁ Μεγάβαζος ἦρχε, πρώτους μὲν Περινθίους Ἑλλησποντίων οὐ βουλομένους ὑπηκόους εἶναι Δαρείου κατεστρέψαντο

Those of the Persians left behind by Darius in Europe under the command of Megabazus subdued first of the Hellespontines the Perinthians who refused to be made subjects of Darius. (5.1.1)

---

[46] See pp. 25–9 below.
[47] A frame which some reader (not excluding Herodotus himself) at some time marked formally by a book division and which subsequent readers have recognized as meaningful enough to retain.
[48] Widely recognized: e.g. Asheri (1990) 132, 'in direct continuation of IV 144, 3'; How and Wells (1912) 1; Macan (1895) 153.

Chapter 1 puts all that is needed in place for the ensuing Thracian campaign narrated in the subsequent chapters, the Ionian Revolt of Books 5 and 6, and indeed the big war against the mainland that brings Persia to a halt at Athens' door and Herodotus' narrative to its end on the Hellespont:[49] the *Persians* are in *Europe*; against their will *Greeks* are being made *subject* to Darius; the Perinthians are only the *first*.

But this beginning is simultaneously a continuation of the linear historical narrative. 5.1 portrays Megabazus as resuming and forwarding the imperial agenda of Darius just as he advances Herodotus' master narrative, which was left suspended in Scythia. At the close of 4.144, Darius and Herodotus' text left Megabazus in Europe, conquering those peoples in the region of the Hellespont who refused to medize:

οὗτος δὴ ὦν τότε ὁ Μεγάβαζος στρατηγὸς λειφθεὶς ἐν τῇ χώρῃ Ἑλλησποντίων τοὺς μὴ μηδίζοντας κατεστρέφετο.

'This Megabazus was the general left in the territory of the Hellespontines and he began conquering whoever was not medizing.'

The fact that 5.1 contains a verbal echo of 4.144 serves not only to reorient an audience, after a disorienting excursion to north Africa, but also to link what has transpired before to what is occurring now in the text: characters, plot, and themes introduced in the last chapters of the Scythian campaign will exert their influence in and on the narrative of Book 5.[50]

This linking is done with sophistication. Although some sixty chapters have intervened between Megabazus assuming his command and executing Darius' orders, Herodotus has carefully laid the groundwork in Book 4 for the resumption of the dominant narrative: two stories told back to back there make Megabazus 'memorable' when he begins subjugating Europe in Book 5. Herodotus records the γέρας that he received from Darius, which took the form of a superlative evaluation of his character. When asked what he would wish to have as many of as the seeds of a pomegranate, he answered that he would prefer to have as many men of Megabazus' quality rather than to have Greece subject [to him] (μᾶλλον ἢ τὴν Ἑλλάδα ὑπήκοον).[51] We are told that Darius' evaluation extended beyond a chance wish uttered among his entourage, but rather translated more concretely into the forces that he assigned to Megabazus' control: 'Saying this among an audience of Persians,

---

[49] See Henderson, Ch. 12 below.
[50] Histiaeus, Megabazus, and evaluations of the Ionians are some of the elements of the later narrative planted in 4.137–44.
[51] 4.143.1–3.

Darius was paying a compliment to Megabazus, and at the time in question he left him in command of an army of 80,000 men' (4.143.3–144.1). These 80,000 will of course prove to be the army whose actions are first encountered in 5.1. And Book 5 will introduce us to the Hellas whose mastery has been valued, unflatteringly, as not worth a Persian general multiplied by the number of a pomegranate's seeds. However, cynical readers may suspect that Darius performs an implicit calculation whereby Megabazuses (or other wise counsellors) cash out in terms of conquest of Greeks and other peoples. And since of course Darius has only one Megabazus, not many, conquest of Greece seems the inevitable consequence of such a calculus.

But it is not only Megabazus who is worth remembering, but also the 'memorable' utterance that he left behind at 4.143: an ἀθάνατος μνήμη ('immortal memorial'), directed at the Hellespontine Greeks but reaching a wider audience, when he said that the founders of Chalcedon must have been blind when they overlooked Byzantium and settled another land first. Here Herodotus' text both perpetuates the immortality of Megabazus' μνήμη by recording it, and thereby also creates an immortal *aide-mémoire* for the resumption of his narrative. No audience could fail to recall a character to whom an utterance that has gained the status of an immortal monument has been attributed, particularly when Herodotus has pitched in, ascribing a *bon mot* originally attributed to the Delphic oracle – a *mnēma* differently 'immortal' – to a Persian general.[52]

But this earlier moment, where Herodotus interrupts one narrative to begin another, impacts still further on the narrative that resumes in Book 5. The Scythian *logos* is brought to a close with the Persians' escape from the Scythians, owing to the intrigues of Histiaeus, both of which are introduced in 4.137 and prove instrumental to the plot of the Ionian Revolt as Herodotus constructs it in Books 5 and 6. At the point where Herodotus abandons this ethnographic and historical interlude, the Scythians are made to fire one last parting shot in the form of an evaluation of the Ionians. The trajectory of their remark will become apparent only in the narrative that begins in Book 5, and the impact of the blow it delivers will depend entirely on the mindset of its readers. In the Scythians' estimation, Histiaeus' act is emblematic of the Ionian people:

---

[52] Strabo 320. The transfer of this remark to a *Persian general* would have served to draw attention both to Megabazus and to Herodotus' text: the implicit denial of one kind of immortality to the utterance, and the (potential) conferral of another. One cannot, of course, be sure who the source was, but Macan's comments (1895: 98) show just what is at stake in the decision: 'The *bon mot* was afterwards appropriated by the Delphic oracle (for one cannot suppose that Herodotus would have transferred an immortal witticism from the god to a barbarian).'

καὶ τοῦτο μέν, ὡς ἐόντας Ἴωνας ἐλευθέρους, κακίστους τε καὶ ἀνανδροτάτους
κρίνουσι εἶναι ἀπάντων ἀνθρώπων, τοῦτο δέ, ὡς δούλων Ἰώνων τὸν λόγον
ποιεύμενοι, ἀνδράποδα φιλοδέσποτά φασι εἶναι καὶ ἄδρηστα μάλιστα. ταῦτα
μὲν δὴ Σκύθησι ἐς Ἴωνας ἀπέρριπται.

On the one hand, inasmuch as Ionians are free, the Scythians judge them to be the
most cowardly and least manly of all mankind, but, conversely, when they speak
about (τὸν λόγον ποιεύμενοι) the Ionians as slaves, they say they are captives
most loving their masters and least likely to run away. So then these are the insults
hurled at Ionians by Scythians. (4.142)

In anticipation of the *logos* of the Ionian Revolt, the Scythians are made
to offer two perspectives on the Ionians, neither flattering, that anticipate
their re-entrance as protagonists in Herodotus' account:[53] if they are considered as free men then they are the most cowardly of all mankind; but
when viewed as slaves, they emerge in a more 'positive' light – as loving their masters and least likely to run away.[54] From the perspective of the
Scythians presented in Book 4, the forthcoming Ionian Revolt seems deeply
improbable, its outcome destined to failure. The Scythians' comparative
perspective presents the Ionians in a synchronic frame as free men or as
slaves, but the text also invites an implicit diachronic comparison since the
insults that have been levelled at them in the past invariably engage with
those that are or have been levelled against them in more recent times.
The Scythian insults hover between the status of a timeless utterance, what
they judge and say in the present (κρίνουσι and φασι, present tense), and
insults already spoken that nevertheless have some purchase on the present
(ταῦτα . . . ἀπέρριπται, 'these aspersions have been cast', perfect tense).
Contemporary audiences may well here share the Scythians' evaluation of
the Ionians, whether considering them to be ἐλεύθεροι, 'free' from Persian
overlordship and 'free' as living under democracy, a status afforded them
by their alliance with Athens; or when they talk about them as slaves, an
evaluation closer to what could be imagined from Athens' enemies (largely
Dorians), despairing of the possibility of a collective Ionian Revolt and even
exhibiting a disdain that extends to Athenians *qua* Ionians.[55]

---

[53] While the Ionians were introduced in Book 1, and Samian politics and history have been a subject of
   Book 3, here in Book 5 they step into the limelight as a collective, influencing the course of history
   and Herodotus' narrative: see Munson, p. 146 below.
[54] See Thomas (2004) 29 for a discussion of this passage and the significance of the fact that Herodotus
   attributes this view to the Scythians. Thomas suggests that the fact that Herodotus does not vouch
   for this perspective complicates the ensuing narrative of the Ionian Revolt and the question of where
   responsibility for its failure lies.
[55] Cf. the views expressed about the Ionians by Athens' enemies in Thucydides: Thuc. 5.9.1, 6.77.1,
   etc.; see Munson, p. 149 below, n. 17. For the enslavement of late fifth-century Ionians see Thuc.

From either of these perspectives revolt seems unlikely, at least if the Scythians' evaluation is to be taken as valid. But understanding what this evaluation means is far from simple. As a remark that Herodotus reports as attributed to the Scythians when they are creating their *logos* (τὸν λόγον ποιεύμενοι) about the Ionians, it *should* require more than a little audience participation to go away secure in the truth value of what is being claimed about Ionians. How exactly readers understand the Scythian remark, whether they agree and just how they agree, not only reflects back on their own perceptions of the Ionians, but also exposes conflicts in their own identities. Just why does Herodotus attribute this evaluation to the Scythians? Why does he choose to tell their *logos*?

In hearing their own views expressed, an audience may be induced to forget a Herodotean *dictum* that they must judge not only what is said, but who is saying it and why, questions that apply equally to the Scythians as to Herodotus the master narrator who tells their *logos* in telling his own. As Herodotus has introduced this comment, several questions are raised. Who are the Scythians to judge the Ionians? Who is an audience to agree with them, and who do they become in agreeing? When Thucydides calls the Scythians below average in *sunesis* and *euboulia* (Thuc. 2.97.6), he reflects what is likely to have been a popular and current Greek view of Scythians, if not a view distinctive to Athenians for whom a taste for the ethnographic was combined with political interests in northern Europe.[56] For a reader who shares this view of Scythians, and also shares the Scythian view of Ionians, the text places them in an uncomfortable position. For while an audience may construe their agreement with Scythians as Scythians agreeing with *them*, revealing something universally recognized and therefore true about Ionians, the sharing of this view may equally say something true about that audience, who emerge as being Scythian in their evaluations, no better than those who as a people are wanting *sunesis* and *euboulia*.[57]

1.69.1,139.3; cf. Aristagoras' failed attempt to get the Spartans on side by convincing them that the prospect of the political enslavement of the Ionians would be a source of *shame* and *grief* to them (5.49.2–3), on which see Serghidou (2004) 189.

[56] Witness the context in which Thucydides makes this comment and note also Pericles' Pontic expedition, Plut. *Per.* 20 and Surikov (2001). On the misapplication in Herodotean terms of Thucydides' criticism see Braund (2004) 39. On the possibility of a more positive Spartan reception of the Scythians in Herodotus, cf. Cleomenes' reception of the Scythian embassy (6.84) with that of Aristagoras with Braund (2004) 38.

[57] Compare the text's effect on the (Athenian) audience with the recurrent analogies between Scythians and Athenians constructed in the Scythian *logos* identified by Hartog (1988), esp. ch. 2 and 198–204, who, however, fails to comment adequately how these analogies might have struck contemporary audiences. See, however, Munson (2001b) 107–18.

But that is, of course, if one subscribes to this derogatory view of Scythians. There is, however, an alternative, Herodotean, view of the Scythians that an audience might have been encouraged to formulate in response to the earlier Scythian *logos*. Herodotus evaluates the Scythians as superlative in one respect, as the most autonomous of all people, knowing the single most important thing, how to retain their independence (4.46).[58] As the limit case of autonomy, where will the narrator's/Herodotus' perspective on Scythians leave the Ionians? When uttered from the status that Herodotus grants his Scythians, can their vantage point on Ionians as slaves or free men possibly have any universal meaning? Who could be in a position to agree with this evaluation? And from their unique vantage point one might wonder how other peoples look, and even – more pointedly – which Greeks would look most similar to the Ionians from that Scythian perspective. On the terms set by Herodotus' text no one can be in a position to agree with the Scythians,[59] and, for those who fail to realize that, unexamined agreement – grasping for the assurances that come from having one's own view endorsed by others – comes at a cost: one distances oneself from slavish Ionians (whether *qua* Greeks or *qua* kin) at the expense of becoming the Scythian 'other'. Herodotus' Scythians emerge as less the ethnographic mirror than a lens that burns the careless viewer.[60]

The complexity of how readers will situate themselves in relation to Herodotus' account of the Scythians' view of Ionians is a prelude to the complexity of assessing the narrative of the Ionian Revolt to come. Based on the Scythian evaluation, how confident can one be that the failure of the Revolt was a foregone conclusion? How a reader evaluates the Scythians' *logos*, recognizing it as the particular privilege of a superlatively free people or uncritically accepting it as a universal given, anticipates how s/he will evaluate the Ionian Revolt in Books 5 and 6, the events and characters involved in its failure: will it be the result of self-interested leadership (a theme of Book 5) and a 'universally' recognized Ionian slavishness (a topic of Book 6)? Or will there be yet another, Herodotean, explanation that will test its audiences' *sunesis* and *euboulia*? For those who look to history through the eyes of medicine, seeking prognoses for the future, just what

---

[58] On the admiration expressed in this passage see Braund (2004) 28–9. On Herodotus' presentation of Scythian nomadism as a strategy see Hartog (1988) 202–4. On the relationship of this strategy to Scythian freedom cf. 4.128 with Braund (2004) 37.

[59] Some may, however, be in a better position than others: see Braund (2004) on the analogies between Spartans and Scythians constructed in Book 4.

[60] For the image of the mirror, see of course Hartog (1988), whose model of textual engagement with its (many) Greek readers needs, however, considerable nuancing. For a similar critique of the mirror image see Pelling (2002) 155.

value can this (or any?) narrative of the past have for predicting Ionian behaviour and success in the future, that is, in the 'present' of Herodotus and his Greek audiences, when Ionians – at least individual cities – certainly do revolt?

VI. THEMES IN BOOK 5

Greek political history, internal politics and external policies

As each city and each *ethnos* in Thrace is subjugated indiscriminately to the Persian monarch (5.2), and the Greeks of Ionia make overtures to the mainland Greeks to deliver them from an enslavement that brings shame to all the Greeks, a narrative of the events contained in Book 5 could easily have lived up to the simplest of conceptual polarities – Greek autonomy vs. barbarian slavery. In fact, the content proves surprising. It transpires that Greek freedom is anything but a self-evident and unifying entity that binds the Greek *poleis* to a shared ideal. An insistent theme in the *logoi* of Book 5 is the diverse and changing political organization of its many Greek cities who will ultimately – if temporarily – play their part in rallying together in the war for Greek freedom.

Book 5 represents its many Greeks in political flux: simply put, following the Herodotean dictum, Greek cities change over time (1.5.3–4); some more than others. At this moment when Graeco-Persian hostilities find their beginnings, Herodotus chooses to provide his audiences with more than a comparative constitutional 'history' of Greece of the late sixth and early fifth centuries. Instead, he supplies an elaborate study of the dynamic interplay of internal political change and external relations in the history of the many Greek cities. The theme begins with Naxos and Miletus at the height of their power, the Milesians only recently so: Parian mediation transformed their ailing city (νοσήσασα) into one at its peak (ἀκμάσασα).[61] Their solution involved the transfer of power to a land-based elite whose care for their own affairs suggested an ability to take care of the city (τὴν πόλιν νέμειν, 5.28–9). Here the introduction of an oligarchy leads to prosperity; but it apparently led to tyranny as well, as the mention of Histiaeus and Aristagoras reminds us (5.30). The text does not explain the origins of this tyranny. But Book 5 presents two models of the inception of tyranny: one model is that which took place in Corinth, the excesses of an oligarchy that lead to a home-grown tyrant (a process abstractly formulated by 'Darius'

---

[61] See Munson, p. 156 below.

in 3.82), and another represented by the (failed) attempts to secure tyranny by Coes, the Paeonian brothers, and Hippias.[62]

Political change is also afoot in Naxos. But this time the elite are removed from power, by the demos, and ironically it is the prosperity brought about by political change in Miletus which puts Milesians in a position to attempt to stem the tide of revolution in Naxos by backing their oligarchic refugees (5.30). The internal stability of one city leads to and enables its interference in another city's instability. Again we find a precursor to the *logoi* to come – if not also to much of fifth-century politics: Sparta becomes embroiled in Athenian constitutional upheaval (5.63–5, 70–5, 90–4), and for its part a new and improved Athens capitalizes on the Ionian Revolt (5.97), a revolt which itself had already necessitated political changes, namely the deposition of the Ionian tyrants (5.37–8), if it was ever to have got off the ground. Here the highly evocative political term, *isonomiē*, puts in one of its rare appearances in Herodotus' text,[63] inviting enigmatic comparison with Athenian *isēgoriē*, a concept yet to be introduced textually (5.78), despite its inception being historically prior.[64]

Things are hardly more stable in mainland Greece, whether in the city of long-standing *eunomiē* (cf. 1.65.2), or in the one recently made strong by *isēgoriē*. In Sparta there are problems with kingly succession: first a lack of heirs, then too many, and an apparent flaw in the system that privileges the order of birth over inborn excellence (5.39–43).[65] The (temporary) stability arrived at by Cleomenes turns the Spartan gaze outwards, to intervention in the political affairs of another city (Athens), but ironically it also leads to disputes in foreign policy: on the one hand, internal conflicts between the Spartan kings precipitating constitutional change regarding their military roles (5.75) and, on the other hand and more seriously, a near-rupture with League allies (5.91–3) that reveals the contingency of Spartan hegemony.[66]

---

[62] The text does not make us aware of how Histiaeus became tyrant, only of his claim that Persia supports the continuation of the Ionian tyrannies (4.137, but apparently not on principle as 6.43 shows). On Hippias, backed alternately by Sparta and then Persia, see 5.90–4 (cf. Isagoras at 5.70–4) and 5.96. On the Paeonian brothers and Coes, see Osborne, Ch. 2 below.

[63] 3.80.6, 3.83.1, 3.142.3.

[64] As in the Constitutional Debate of 3.80, Herodotus once again anticipates Athenian *isonomiē* by another group, generating comparisons and inferences which some in his audience would no doubt hardly find flattering. Interestingly, Herodotus never attributes *isonomiē* to democratic Athens, despite its central importance in Athenian tradition surrounding the tyrannicides: *PMG* 893 (though apparently contested, see the alternative lines in *PMG* 895.3–4) and 896. See Moles, p. 246 below, and cf. his n. 12.

[65] See Hornblower (pp. 170–1 below) on the difficulties of Herodotus' account.

[66] See Moles, pp. 251–2 below. See also Pelling (2000) 102–3.

Such crises of leadership are brought to the fore by the most dramatic of constitutional changes in Book 5, that of Athens. Herodotus' narrative provides a bewildering account of just how Athens was liberated from tyranny, by whom and why, with a range of explanations on offer: Phoenician tyrannicides, Spartan piety, and Alcmaeonid machinations; with little mention, notably, of *eleutheriē*. Democracy emerges as the result of elite competition, with a strong whiff of its tyrannical origins. The benefits of *isēgoriē* are extolled (5.78), but only if one is undisturbed by the aggression that inevitably seems to arise from stability and prosperity;[67] that will, of course, depend on who the audience is – and not least on whether they are on the receiving end of this aggression. Athens and Sparta are comically juxtaposed according to popular (Athenian) stereotype: Athens totally transforms herself politically, while Sparta 'radically' limits the number of kings on military campaign to one (5.75); but those laughing may find themselves doing so on the wrong side of their faces when 30,000 Athenians (i.e. a democracy) prove easier to dupe than one Spartan king (i.e. constitutional kingship, 5.97). There also seem to be other provocations that look further ahead in Athenian political history: Herodotus depicts an Epidaurus (implausibly) anticipating Athenian *archē* in exerting the same legal controls over a dependent Aegina, and, moreover, portrays this relationship as one from which the dependency successfully revolts.[68]

All such comparisons and contrasts that have been narrated so obliquely across the *logoi* of Book 5, embedded in its narratives, are formulated more acutely in the Socles episode, where his just-so story about Corinthian tyranny documents the process whereby constitutional change occurs:[69] a tyrant comes to power through the abuses and weaknesses of an oligarchy (conveyed fabulistically in the command to murder a baby, and the ineptitude and buck-passing of the would-be murderers); he performs the violent, but no doubt popular measures advocated by a Thrasybulus; and inevitably after one generation (as in the case of the Peisistratids, though *not* as Herodotus tells it) the tyranny becomes debased and is overthrown.

---

[67] And, only if one is undisturbed by a syntactical parallelism that renders every Athenian his own overlord: ἐθελοκάκεον ὡς δεσπότῃ ἐργαζόμενοι, ἐλευθερωθέντων δὲ αὐτὸς ἕκαστος ἑωυτῷ προεθυμέετο κατεργάζεσθαι ('They fought badly on purpose inasmuch as they laboured for an overlord, but when they were free each man was eager to achieve for himself'). This formulation no doubt draws on the discourse of slavery used in philosophical discussions about individuals enslaved by their desires, while revealing such discussions to be at base political (e.g. Xen. *Mem.* 4.5).

[68] 5.83.1. One may infer the unprecedented nature of this aspect of Athens' relationship to her allies from [Xen.] *Ath. Pol.* 1.16 and from the Athenian defence of this practice in Thuc. 1.77. On (lack of) autonomy as particularly vexing to Aegina of the late 430s see Thuc.1.67.2.

[69] On this *logos* see Moles, Ch. 10 below.

A question is raised by the juxtaposition of Athenian and Corinthian versions of tyranny: do the stories convey something true, or believed to be true, about the timeless nature of tyranny *per se*, its inception, course, and inevitable downfall, or rather about the historical moment of the late sixth century when tyranny becomes *passé*?[70] A contemporary audience may have read one or the other view reflected in Herodotus' *logoi*, or may indeed have understood both, but by communicating such political reflections through characters narrating *logoi*, the text evades simple access to their meaning and involves the audience in formulating answers that can only be as good as the readers they prove themselves to be.

Together, these multiple *logoi* on the varieties of Greek autonomy, and on their inherent instability, constitute a political study. The *logoi* narrate the causes and dynamics of political change. They explore how these changes emerge as products of internal pressures within cities, external intervention,[71] or, most commonly, a mixture of both. They recount the fate of political ideals in the hands of the individuals who interpret and exploit them (i.e. Aristagoras removing tyrannies, 5.37; Cleisthenes' reforms, 5.66.2, 69.2). They also depict how certain constitutional solutions work, or rather turn out not to work, in given environments (the oligarchies of Miletus, Naxos, Corinth), and how apparently mutually exclusive constitutions may, or may come to, display inherent similarities (tyrants and the tyranny of the demos), or share the same descriptive language. All in all, as Herodotus recounts the past, and as it engages with the present, no constitution seems to emerge as inherently better than any other; and even tyranny, universally hated, may be found to be lurking under other names. They all have their shelf-life, and all, given enough time, are capable of injustices and excesses. Whether such views are Herodotean provocation or Herodotean belief, or both, is of course another question, and one that should not be overlooked even if, or rather precisely because, it cannot be answered. If Socles' extended speech has been seen by many to evoke the constitutional debate of Book 3.80–2, one might also observe that the narrative of the events of Book 5 contributes to that debate by providing multiple narratives of concrete complex historical enactments and refractions of those earlier abstract formulations.

---

[70] Cf. Aristagoras' manoeuvre of deposing tyrants and even that of the Persians in 6.43.

[71] E.g. the apparently neutral Parian-mediated imposition of elite rule (29), the opportunistic move by Aristagoras with the Naxian oligarchs against their inchoate democracy (30), the apparently pious Spartan deposing of Hippias (63), or the mixed motivations of a Sparta imposing Hippias on the new Athenian democracy and of Corinthian opposition (90–4); on the last see Moles, Ch. 10 below.

Greek ethnicity

If the diversity, flux and historical contingency of Greek autonomy are a consistent theme of Book 5, the concept of what being *Greek* means is rendered no less problematic. Standing at the fore of the Book, the Paeonians demonstrate principles that will be played out in the *logoi* to follow (5.15–16). Here two peoples with vastly different cultural practices go under the same collective name, and as such they are paradigmatic of the Greeks who will be encountered in Book 5.[72] These Paeonians also demonstrate two kinds of cultural change: revolution as the Paeonian brothers solicit Persian-backed tyranny; and evolution as the former socio-economic equality of the land-dwelling Paeonians has been replaced by a stratified society.[73]

Following these Paeonians are the first appearances of the category of Greek, shown to prove almost meaningless except in the mouth of those of contested Greek status (Alexander), Persian detractors (Megabazus), and those obviously playing an angle (Aristagoras, 5.49).[74] Here the micro-categories of Ionian and Dorian, dispassionately explained by our narrator in Book 1 (56–7), are put into action by historical agents, mobilized for the sake of political ends and demonstrated to be far from stable. As the Graeco-Persian conflict begins to take shape it does so in a textual environment that seems to maximize the diversity of the Greek players, potentially shattering the unity of Greekness, even as this concept is supposedly taking form (surely making attentive readers cynical by the time we reach the only apparently glorifying, and no less motivated, 8.144).[75] If characters within the text are constructing and mobilizing their Greek identity, or rather identities, for their audiences internal to the narrative, we should recognize that Herodotus' text is also engaged in an analogous process before his own audiences. Amid the complexity of Herodotus' study of Greek micro-ethnicities in Book 5, lies perhaps a historical reality more fundamental

---

[72] This comparison arises not least because Herodotus describes them in ways tantalizingly evocative of the two dominant, yet contrasting, city-states: see Osborne, pp. 94, 96 below. The counterpart to the widely differing yet single-named Paeonians are the multiply-named yet virtually identical Thracians of 5.3–7: see Irwin, p. 58 below.

[73] On which see Osborne, pp. 94–6 below.

[74] On the Macedonians see Fearn, Ch. 3, below; on Aristagoras see Pelling, Ch. 7. Megabazus demonstrates the relativity of cultural categories when he complains about what a Myrcinus founded by Histiaeus will lead to: ὅμιλός τε πολλὸς μὲν Ἕλλην περιοικέει, πολλὸς δὲ βάρβαρος (5.23.2) – the Persians are depicted as having their own barbarians.

[75] αὖτις δὲ τὸ Ἑλληνικὸν, ἐὸν ὅμαιμόν τε καὶ ὁμόγλωσσον καὶ θεῶν ἱδρύματά τε κοινὰ καὶ θυσίαι ἤθεά τε ὁμότροπα, τῶν προδότας γενέσθαι Ἀθηναίους οὐκ ἂν εὖ ἔχοι. This would be particularly true for contemporaries for whom the political realities offered little that would not induce cynicism. For a contextualization of this passage see Cartledge (1993) 155–6. On its ironies see Fearn, p. 125 with n. 66 below; and see Thomas (2001a) 213–15. On the manipulative use of cultural identity by characters within the *Histories* see Thomas (2000) 113.

and basic, a persistent subtext which, although lost on modern readers,[76] was a crucial reality for fifth-century Athenians: Ionians revolt and Dorians invade.

The narrative of Book 5 opens with Thracians who are ambiguously barbarian and, conversely, Macedonians who are ambiguously Greek. It draws to a close with the Cypriots, another people at the margins of the Greek world who are also ambiguous Greeks, at least in so far as their actions show them to be divided in their response to Persia.[77] It is at the eastern edge of the Greek world that the first battles of the Ionian Revolt will be waged, and there and later in mainland Ionia it will be Carians who are shown meeting their deaths, resisting the Persians to the end, just as Greeks in the text have done (5.2) and are yet to do, and in an account that evokes the Carian origin of the quintessential instrument of Greek warfare, the hoplite shield.[78] Finally, the Aristagorean leg of the Ionian Revolt closes as the narrative of Book 5 began, with attempts at conquest in Thrace and the all-important Myrcinus, an account which recounts the death of Aristagoras at the hands of Thracians as not a particularly barbarous act, but rather an apparently rational response to the intransigence of a (Greek) figure who is hell-bent on their subjugation and a figure who has been utterly compromised by the preceding narrative.[79]

Between these extremes, cultural and textual, Greeks are found contracting with Persians, sometimes even to the detriment of one another: some solicit moderate advantage from their personal relationships with the Persian king (Histiaeus, Coes, 5.11 and 24), but there are also those with more ambitious political designs (Aristagoras, 5.31–2). The prelude to Greek unity and resistance to Persian opposition is anything but glorious. Book 5 conveys deep ironies; not only does Aristagoras tantalizingly offer to deliver up his fellow-Greeks to Persian rule, which some may too hastily construe as typically Ionian, but Athens will also solicit Persian help against Sparta

---

[76] But recovered by Henderson, Ch. 12 below.

[77] On the collapsing of self and other in the Thracian ethnography see Irwin, Ch. 1 below; on the Greek evocations of the Paeonians see Osborne, Ch. 2 below; on Herodotus' provocative study of Macedonian Hellenism see Fearn, Ch. 3 below; and on the Greek origins of the many Cypriot kingdoms see Serghidou, Ch. 11 below.

[78] 5.119: συνέβαλόν τε τοῖσι Πέρσῃσι οἱ Κᾶρες καὶ μάχην ἐμαχέσαντο ἰσχυρὴν καὶ ἐπὶ χρόνον πολλόν, τέλος δὲ ἐσσώθησαν διὰ πλῆθος. The Persian *plethos* sends us back to the first *logos* of Book 5, the Perinthians of 5.2 who died for their freedom defeated by numbers (οἱ Πέρσαι . . . ἐπεκράτησαν πλήθεϊ). On the Carian Onesilus' shield – an aetiological *logos* for the superiority of hoplite warfare over the cavalry – see 5.112, with Hdt. 1.171.4, and Irwin (2007). Herodotus himself was from Caria, and the emphasis on Carian resistance to the Persians perhaps hints at a sense of local allegiance; see Dewald (2002) 267 with n. 2.

[79] See Greenwood, p. 142 below.

some forty chapters later:[80] this is not just the act of a tyrant, Hippias, but the decision of a new democracy, even if the terms offered were later to be rejected. A parting shot of the narrative is the re-enactment of a similar pattern of conflicting and shifting allegiances among Cypriots (5.113). It is only by the end of Book 5 that one understands fully the significance of the Perinthian *logos* of the first two chapters. The otherwise minor characters of the Perinthians introduce a theme variously played out among Greeks and even non-Greeks in Book 5, the desire to be free. But the negative formulation used of them, 'not wishing to be subject to Darius' (οὐ βουλομένους ὑπηκόους εἶναι Δαρείου, 5.1.1), imports into the text the idea of its opposite, namely those who *were* willing. Book 5 will begin to narrate what is to become a central question for the rest of the *Histories*, namely, who is willing to become, or remain, aligned with Persia, and who will oppose it, and why. Lurking in the formulation 'not wishing to be subject to Darius' is, however, a question with the potential to reach beyond the historical narrative, namely whether what is so objectionable is subjection to *Darius* or more fundamentally the status of being ὑπήκοοι. This is a question that will resonate with Herodotus' own day, particularly as the narrative of Book 6 will go on to recall for readers the origin of the tribute divisions still operative 'in my day' (αἰεὶ ἔτι καὶ ἐς ἐμέ, 6.42.2).

While crossings of the Greek–Persian divide undermine a coherent concept of Greekness, this concept is also undermined from within the collective Greek entity, as Herodotus shows both individual characters and communities choosing how they will define themselves ethnically against other Greeks. When Cleomenes asserts that he is not *d/Dorieus*, but Achaean, he kledonically rejects Dorian ethnicity (5.72),[81] a disdain already attributed to the elder Cleisthenes, tyrant of Sicyon (5.67–8). Whether this reflects historical reality or a Herodotean invention that plays to and with audience expectations, the subtext is clear: it seems it just wasn't hip to be Dorian around the turn of the sixth century BC – not in Athens, at any rate. Cleomenes' Acropolis incident presents an irony that will take some three books to appreciate, barred as he is from one of the soon to be burnt temples of gods that the Athenians adduce as the basis of their commitment to the Greek cause (8.144.2).[82] And there is, of course, a more proximate irony: a

---

[80] Aristagoras and the Naxian oligarchs with Artaphrenes (5.30–1), Athenian delegates and Artaphrenes (5.73). The narration of the Athenian attempt gives particular salience to Herodotus' comment in 7.152 on Argos' medizing as protection against Sparta, as of course does the presence in the Persian court of the Athenian Callias.

[81] See already Macan (1895) I.217 and 183.

[82] There is a nice Athenian equivocation in 8.144.2 where there are clearly limits to which of the θεῶν ἱδρύματα ('temples of the gods') really are κοινά ('shared').

mere twenty-five chapters later, these same post-Cleisthenic reformed Athenians with their new non-Ionian tribes (a product of disdain for Ionians, 5.69) will embrace the Ionian cause, solicited on the basis of their shared Ionian bond (5.97); but even so, these kindred ties will be shown to have their limits as Athens withdraws her support soon after (5.103).[83]

Meanwhile Herodotus makes us aware of how contingent, politically, such ethnic self-definition is, and how unreliable the indicators of ethnicity are, in stories such as that of Athens' rejection of Dorian dress in favour of Ionian garb, the latter itself not strictly speaking Ionian but Carian.[84] Herodotus' conclusion that all Greeks *used to* wear Dorian clothing can become a symbol of the fractured and fracturing Greek collectivity on display in his text (and a reality for his contemporary audience). Of course, whether such aggressive oppositional self-definition among Greek *poleis* along ethnic lines should be regarded as a historical fact of the late sixth and early fifth centuries, or as a retrojection from their prominence in Herodotus' time, remains unclear; either way, one may consider Herodotus to be using this material both to maximize the unexpectedness of Greek victory over the Persians in the past, as well as to engage with how these shifting identities were drawn on and exploited in his present day.

And yet the study of Greek ethnicity and history that he provides runs deeper than the intratextual ironies that we have stressed. Sparta chooses not to avenge the death of Dorieus ('the Dorian') in Sicily.[85] The Thebans receive their oracle to ally with those 'nearest' and are shown deliberating on just *whom* they will consider near, and indeed on the very basis on which proximity is to be constructed.[86] Meanwhile, the theme culminates in an Athens whose citizens choose to allow an argument of kinship ties with Ionia to draw them into a military venture. Herodotus' *logoi* not only depict the active choice of participants in defining themselves ethnically, but also provide an allusive meta-narrative on the consequences of such choices for Herodotus' contemporary audience. The Athenians capitalize on Ionianism in the east, albeit Herodotus has undercut the sincerity of their affinity by imputing disdain for the Ionians to Cleisthenes' democratic reforms. In contrast, the Spartans miss the boat with Dorianism in the

---

[83] See 6.21 with its back-reference to the narrative of 5.44–5 (on which see Hornblower, pp. 175–7 below) for an elegant coda that implicitly reflects (critically) on the strength of such (Ionian) ties.

[84] 5.87.3, on this change see Haubold, pp. 242–4 below. See also Herodotus' comments on the Sigynnae's Median dress and their claim to Median descent (5.9) with Irwin, pp. 83–7 below. On the constructedness of ethnic identity and the variable and arbitrary indices of ethnicity see Hall (1997) and (2002), on Hellenic ethnicity.

[85] As Hornblower, pp. 173–5 below points out, a choice made explicit in 7.158.

[86] See Haubold, Ch. 9 below, and Irwin, pp. 52–3 below.

west – opting for an epic, Achaean, identity – [87]while the Thebans fail to play the Boeotian card by neglecting to ally with those so obviously nearest to them (the Plataeans), instead preferring a tenuous and mythical sororal tie with Aegina, with tragi-comic results.[88] The political topography of the late fifth century would have looked very different had Sparta and Thebes consolidated their power bases on ethnic lines as Athens had done: but perhaps Plataea was too near, and Sicily too far away.[89] One might infer that Herodotus is demonstrating the meaninglessness of such ethnic claims as they come to the fore through the opportunistic intrigues of individuals like Aristagoras who tries to engage the Spartans as 'Greeks' and the Athenians as 'Ionians', through the political machinations of other figures (the two Cleistheneses, Cleomenes), and through political hostilities between cities (Thebes and Aegina vs. Athens). Yet the narrative of Book 5 demonstrates such an inference to be premature and profoundly wrong: these *nomoi* exist precisely because they are *nomizomenoi*, and therefore the use that historical agents make of them, *pace* Thucydides, must render them an inextricable part of any account of historical causation.[90]

Writing the Ionian Revolt, writing history

It is in the context of a book cross-examining Greek ethnicity and its mode of oppositional self-definition that Herodotus chooses to remind his audience that his entire work is dependent upon a non-Greek invention, namely the Phoenician invention of writing (5.58). There is a neat irony in the fact that Herodotus emphasizes the barbarian origins of the technology that enables his audience to view the contingencies of their variously constructed political and ethnic identities. For an audience who accept the premise of Thucydidean developmental ethnography in seeing Greeks as the vanguard of cultural development (1.6.6), and the Athens his Pericles presents as its forefront (2.41.1), Herodotus' carnivalesque excursus is disconcerting. It implies, ironically, that Greek superiority is propped up

---

[87] Here Cleomenes is said not to have observed the *klēdon* (τῇ κληηδόνι οὐδὲν χρεώμενος, 5.72), but what would it mean if he had; what would he have done then? The text invites the attuned audience to contemplate what this *klēdon* means.

[88] 5.81.1.

[89] See Hornblower (pp. 172–3 below) for this excellent observation on Sparta and the counterfactual histories of Book 5, and see Irwin, p. 52, n. 3 below, for a similar missed opportunity in Thebes. See Haubold, p. 228 below, on the Theban interpretation of their oracle.

[90] For a critique of the scholarship following Thucydides in discounting the emotive force of ethnic ties see Alty (1982). See also Sahlins (2004), Ch. 1, for a study of the 'ethnographic history' that Thucydides chose not to write.

by barbarian technology, a manoeuvre that renders, in this crucial respect at least, present-day Greeks like barbarians of the past, rather than the reverse.[91] But the excursus also implicitly draws attention to a wider theme presented in the *logoi* of Book 5, the self-consciousness of Herodotus' historiographic enterprise, and – specifically – of the writing of an account of the Ionian Revolt.

Book 5 makes us aware of the role of writing in making accessible and even creating knowledge about diverse lands and times, that would otherwise be lost to an audience eager to consume it. What is more, Herodotus demonstrates how this knowledge, once created and disseminated, constitutes a historical phenomenon in its own right that has the potential to influence historical agents. The text stages the ethnographic writer as character: Hecataeus attempts to influence the course of the Ionian Revolt in an account that reflexively writes Herodotus' own endeavour into the narrative. Herodotus imports the first four books of his *Histories* into this *logos*: in 'cataloguing all the peoples who were under Darius' *archē* and his *dunamis*' (5.36.2), Hecataeus illustrates the relevance of Herodotus' past narrative to this moment in the *logos*. It is relevant to the Ionians who might have fared better following this advice, and it is also relevant to the audience if they are listening, who may find in Hecataeus' words, which summarize the content of Herodotus' earlier books, the truest *aitiē* for the Revolt's failure: not so much bad leadership or slavish Ionians, but rather the magnitude of the opponent; his is an *aitiē* that may otherwise be obscured as much by the complex and distracting details of Herodotus' account as by the audiences' own views about Ionians. Herodotus makes it clear that an audience should contemplate the link between Hecataeus' *logos* and his own by inserting one of the precious few references to his own work at the end of the *logos*. When Hecataeus advises his peers to confiscate the treasury of the oracle at Branchidae, Herodotus confirms the basis of Hecataeus' advice, if not also its viability, by reminding his audience of his coverage of this topic back in Book 1:[92] τὰ δὲ χρήματα ἦν ταῦτα μεγάλα, ὡς δεδήλωταί μοι ἐν τῷ πρώτῳ τῶν λόγων ('And this wealth was great,

---

[91] Herodotus' attribution of the alphabet to the Phoenicians suppresses the extent of Greek invention and innovation in the development and application of their alphabet. If the irony is to be pushed, Herodotus renders the Phoenicians ultimately responsible for the text they are reading. On the Phoenicians and writing see Pelling, pp. 197–8 below, and Gray, pp. 211–12 below. In Herodotus' narrative, Phoenicians also emerge as responsible for freeing the Athenians of one Peisistratid, on which see Gray, pp. 212–18 below.

[92] One may wonder how this advice interacted with an Athenian audience whose appropriation of the League treasuries in Delos may be anticipated by the general idea of Hecataeus' advice, if not by the specific location.

as I have made clear in the first of my *logoi*', 5.36.4).[93] The text directs us back to its very beginning, enacting the narrator's control over his text, over the knowledge it wields *and* the influence it exerts over the attention of his audience.

If Herodotus has staged Hecataeus, writer of ethnography performing his knowledge, as his textual double, another character is made to adopt his role as raconteur of history.[94] Socles' history of early Corinthian tyranny, which both complements and contrasts with Herodotus' own account in Book 3, provides a case-study of how and why ἔργα become λόγοι. Socles' speech demonstrates how a particular occasion gives rise to the narration, if not the creation, of historical *logos*, inducing reflections on how the rhetorical requirements of that performance may shape the telling of *erga*.[95] If Herodotus' *Histories* is an *apodexis* of research into an *aitiē*, Socles also demonstrates that there are *aitiai* ('reasons') behind such *apodexeis* – a point the careless audience may forget amid the pleasure of listening to Herodotus' own *apodexis*.[96] In the case of Socles' *logos*, while an audience watches the Peloponnesian League pass judgement on the relevance of the Corinthians' *logos* to the course they will take, the Herodotean *logos* engages their knowledge of the present day by framing it as the consequence of the course it describes as taken, and inevitably also engages their own respective political vantage points.[97]

While Book 5 stages its characters as purveyors of ethnography (Hecataeus, Aristagoras) and history (Socles) attempting to influence the course of events, it is also self-conscious about its project in other ways. A pervasive feature of the narrative is the demonstration of the conscious choices involved in, and an inevitable part of, history as *logos*: whether it is the 'beginning of ills' or the 'Fourth Dorian Invasion',[98] attention is called to the narrator's punctuation, even manipulation, of events,[99] and his capacity to impart a greater significance to these events than may have been, or even could have been, apparent to the agents themselves. But history

[93] The map of Aristagoras likewise provides a graphic representation of the world, and its use similarly invites a meta-narrative on the Herodotean enterprise and writing, see Pelling, pp. 195–7 below.

[94] See Moles, Ch. 10 below.

[95] This shaping can be independent of the truth value of the narrowly defined content of the account, though the difficulty in extricating content from form is a Herodotean preoccupation and a central problematic addressed in this volume.

[96] This point should not be forgotten when considering Thucydides' own *apodeixis*, of the *archē* of Athens (1.97.2).

[97] For the sophistication of the engagement of Socles' *logos* with the audience of the *Histories* see Moles, Ch. 10 below.

[98] See Munson, Ch. 5 below and especially Henderson, Ch. 12 below.

[99] Socles' history of Corinthian tyranny provides the defining example of this, see Moles, Ch. 10 below.

can do this: in creating an *apodexis* of *historiē*, Herodotus wields a power that can not only re-create the past as *logos* in ways that are necessarily different from the *erga* experienced by the actors and contemporaries of those events, but one that can also re-create these same *erga* in ways vastly different from how his own contemporary audiences may have chosen to tell them.[100] Here simplistic debates over whether Herodotus is an inaccurate historian or a liar elide issues of historiography that Herodotus' narrative addresses implicitly.[101] There are multiple levels of consideration, not only as to whether the 'facts' he presents are true, or whether it was his aim to present 'facts' that are true, but equally as to whether the facts he presents are those recognized as true by (all) his audiences. Even granted the credibility of these facts in the opinion of his audiences (and the correctness of their opinions), we might wonder if his audiences (all, some or any) would ever have put these 'facts' together to create a narrative of causation, an *aitiē*, in the way Herodotus does here. And finally, there remains the question of whether an audience would have been willing to *approve* of his account, and what such approval would have meant: belief in its historical accuracy, agreement with a truth it may seem to convey that is not narrowly historical, or simply pleasure. Audiences may differ, and these types of approval are not mutually exclusive.

Herodotus' study goes beyond simply calling attention to how one may highlight events as they occurred in their natural linear succession. In creating *logos* from *erga*, the narrator must provide the connectives between past events that are by their very nature often irretrievable and for the most part unverifiable by his audiences. It is Herodotus' *logos* that has the power to mould those events into a chain of causation which has meaning for his audiences. The study of this power is an underlying preoccupation of the narrative of Book 5. Herodotus creates a narrative dense with coincidences and contingencies. The Ionian Revolt was the product of coincidences, Histiaeus' discontent and Aristagoras' difficulties: συνέπιπτε τοῦ αὐτοῦ χρόνου πάντα ταῦτα συνελθόντα ('all these things converging occurred during the same time' – 5.36.1).[102] Athens' freedom from tyranny was similarly coincidental: οὐδέν τι πάντως ἂν ἐξεῖλον τοὺς Πεισιστρατίδας οἱ Λακεδαιμόνιοι . . . νῦν δὲ συντυχίῃ τοῖσι μὲν κακὴ ἐπεγένετο, τοῖσι δὲ

---

[100] Herodotus' use of the first-person stance, particularly when used with the verb of discovery, can mark his narrative as unique: 'I have discovered' = 'no one else says'; on Herodotus' use of the first person singular, see Dewald (1987).

[101] It is time to review the debate on the veracity and rhetoric of Herodotus' source citations, opened up by Fehling (1989) and developed in the counter-thesis of Pritchett (1993), by focusing on the putative audiences for Herodotus' different *logoi* and their stake in the truth/falsity of a given *logos*.

[102] On this phrase see Pelling, p. 185 below.

ἡ αὐτὴ αὕτη σύμμαχος ('There is no way that the Spartans would have captured the Peisistratids . . . but now a chance occurrence happened that was unfortunate for the latter, but of assistance to the Spartans' – 5.65.1).[103] In the case of Corinth, tyranny owed itself to chance: θείη τύχη προσεγέλασε τὸ παιδίον ('by a stroke of divine chance, the child smiled' – 5.92.γ3).[104] And finally, Athenian participation in the Ionian Revolt itself was the result of an Aristagorean *kairos*, the arrival of the Milesian at the moment when the Athenians likewise consider their hostility to Persia to have become open (5.96.2). If the historian 'succeeds' in his task, his role in constructing explanations from events goes unnoticed; the contingencies he re-creates appear plausible, natural and true. However, the degree to which the narrative of Book 5 contrives to make such contingencies conspicuous suggests that Herodotus is drawing attention not just to how things happened in the past, but how his narrative constructs their happening and its power to influence the reception of past events, while still seeming to provide a plausible explanatory account of the failure of the Revolt. Of course, the more one delves into the events as Herodotus presents them, the more difficulties emerge with the narrative as a representation of historical *erga*, as scholarship on the Revolt well demonstrates.[105] But the degree to which recognition of the flaws of the account leads to engagement with the events as Herodotus presents them, rather than with wider meta-narrative concerning the creation of historiographical *logos*, is testimony to the success of the narrator's stance: when the narrative has left us asking the same questions as its characters, perhaps the appropriate response should be that of admiration. Here the warning expressed above about the dangers of excerpting *logoi* from their wider context to create an account that we find historically plausible is particularly salient.[106]

The contingencies witnessed in Book 5 can be otherwise framed: one might stress instead how such formulations make the audience aware of just what *could* have happened . . . but did not. It could all have been so different: this need not be a shocking concept in itself, but as it is played out in particular instances, it may well be. That unfulfilled potential, once uttered, is capable of introducing instability and fear into an otherwise stable present: for now, too, things could have been very different (what if the children of the Peisistratids had not been captured? what if Socles had not persuaded the Spartans . . .?). If Solon's advice to Croesus emphasized how each human's life is dependent on the day and focused primarily on

[103] On this depiction see Gray, pp. 218–19 below. [104] See Moles, pp. 258–9 below.
[105] E.g. Murray (1988) 466; see discussion above.
[106] See the discussion (pp. 13–19) above with Murray's quotation of Tozzi (n. 28).

the individual and his future-oriented *telos*, Book 5 writes such dependency into the life of the collective as recorded by the backward-looking genre of history, and invites his audience to look also to these would-be (would-have-been) τέλη, and to evaluate them against what did happen and the present as they believe it to have ensued therefrom. Counterfactual histories dominate Book 5 as many of the contributors will observe repeatedly in their discussions of individual *logoi*.[107] The narrator of the past has enormous power to create alternative worlds, worlds whose only ontological status is that of *logos* (no matter how 'true' these evaluations of what could have been may be felt to be) residing in the minds of an audience willing to accept them as plausible: what would have happened if . . .? what would that mean now?

Though nebulous and unreal, nevertheless such constructions can exert influence: a tension arises between their non-existence as *erga* and their existence as *logos*, which may in fact give rise to *erga* for those who accept or impose the acceptance of their plausibility, who ordain or allow them to influence the efforts in the present to control the future. Inasmuch as a study of history might proclaim itself as useful, as offering the prospect of future security based on the patterns it claims to recognize in the past, the only security that we are offered – by Herodotus' Solon – is the warning that things could have been very different given the precariousness of human life (πᾶν ἐστι ἄνθρωπος ξυμφορή, 1.32.4). In many ways the 'Ionian Revolt' is the perfect case through which to explore these themes. As a historical event it allows readers to explore just how many ways one can account for an event that has failed, and also raises the interesting (if academic) question for its audience: what would have happened had it succeeded? What might that mean now?[108] But as a historical event that may be repeated, its existence as *logos* raises other questions, such as, just who is remembering this *logos* of failure, and why? This must have been a pressing question in the late fifth century BC, a period in which Ionian revolts were being attempted, and where *logoi* of the Ionian Revolt were no doubt circulating, not least because

---

[107] See below, Irwin, pp. 78–83 on 5.3, Hornblower, pp. 172–3, Pelling, pp. 190–1, Moles, pp. 262–3. We thank Paul Cartledge for drawing our attention to a similar point in Gibbon: ('Marginalia in Herodotus', in Craddock (1972) 367–8) on 1.170: 'Had the Ionians removed to Sardinia, that fertile island (obscure and barbarous in every age) might have become the seat of arts, of freedom, and perhaps of Empire. Such a powerful colony might have oppressed the infant fortune of Rome, and changed the history of mankind.'

[108] The question would be academic to some either on historical grounds (it did not happen), or on ethnographical grounds (the Ionians' slavish nature would mean the Revolt could never not have failed, and even if it succeeded they would nevertheless still be (Athenian) subjects now).

they could be used to comment on the present and forecast the future.[109] Perhaps failure was not due to any of the distracting and contradictory features of Herodotus' narrative – the weakness of the Ionians, or the poor leadership – that may have been so constructed to warn the careful reader off accepting them as explanations, while pleasing those who see, as in the Scythians' words of 4.143, their own low opinion of Ionians reflected back at them.[110] The explanation may be more simple: failure was due to what Hecataeus catalogued at the very start, and what every reader has experienced for four books, the magnitude and *dunamis* of the Persian empire. In which case, as prognosis of the failure of future revolts history might prove to be less than reassuring. The important question might then become somewhat different: how does Athenian *dunamis* of the present measure up to that of the Persians of the past?[111]

But if the historian can bring counterfactual history into existence through the power of his written word, introducing a negative influence that will control, shade and frame the reception of what did in fact happen, Book 5 may also engage provocatively with the power of the written historical text to bring into existence non-existent events, and to cause to happen that which may not have, demonstrating the power of history as written text. Book 5 contains a worrying number of 'vanishing' events: events asserted to have occurred but which leave, and are capable of leaving, no mark on the historical record apart from that constituted by Herodotus' narrative, events that because of their very nature as Herodotus narrates them are entirely unverifiable, remembered only as Herodotean *logoi*. The relocation of the Paeonians (brought back in 5.98, therefore in Herodotus' time where they always were); Macedonian resistance to Persia (luggage and pack animals vanish without a trace, all that is left is a Macedonian marriage alliance with Persia, 5.21);[112] the gift of Myrcinus (given and taken in the space of a few chapters, 5.11, 5.23–4); the elder Cleisthenes' renaming of the Sicyonian tribes (after sixty years the old ones are there as they always were before, 5.68.2), the Spartan attempts to make Isagoras tyrant (5.74–6)

---

[109] This point is overlooked by even the most recent scholarship on the Revolt (e.g. Thomas (2004)), which focuses on the Ionian sources for the Revolt, and the blame game.

[110] Scholarship sees the contradictions as a function of Ionian tradition, fragmented by recriminations: see Thomas (2004) 27–8, 37–8 with bibliography. This is to render Herodotus far too passive a reporter and fails to take into account the many *logoi* that are encompassed by, and in turn shading, the Ionian Revolt narrative. See Munson, Ch. 5 below, for an analysis of the Revolt that engages with the nuances of its narrative.

[111] See Irwin, pp. 68–70 and 77–9 below, for discussion of the importance of relative *kratos* in the Thracian *logos*.

[112] Fearn, p. 115 below.

and to reinstate Hippias (5.90–3),[113] the 'freedom' of Cyprus lasting for a
single year (5.116).[114]

The narrative of Dorieus assisting the Crotoniates in their war against
Sybaris is conspicuous for what it offers and takes away.[115] The incon-
clusiveness of the 'evidence' to which each side appeals in support of their
mutually exclusive accounts leaves the historical status of this 'event' deeply
uncertain, as does Herodotus' frank invitation to his audience to choose
the version they find persuasive: ταῦτα μέν νυν ἑκάτεροι αὐτῶν μαρτύρια
ἀποφαίνονται, καὶ πάρεστι· ὁκοτέροισί τις πείθεται αὐτῶν, τούτοισι
προσχωρέειν ('This is the evidence that each side puts forward, and one
may side with whichever of them they are persuaded by', 5.45.2). The
reminder of persuasion at work should make us aware of how many factors
influence our decisions about how to constitute the past, factors that may
lie outside pure considerations of plausibility, which become all the more
apparent the less sufficient the adduced evidence is. And even the notion of
plausibility has its limits, grounded in the inter-subjectivity of a community of interpreters. As Herodotus comments again in Book 5, on the *logoi*
belonging to another inter-Greek conflict that admits no consensus: ἐμοὶ
μὲν οὐ πιστὰ λέγοντες, ἄλλῳ δέ τεῳ ('To me what they say is unbelievable,
but to someone else . . .', 5.86.3).[116] If Herodotus abstains from committing
himself on whether or not this past event happened, it is worth asking if
he may be encouraging his audience to realize that, at any point, they too
must not accept indiscriminately the *logoi* of events that his account will
present.

Similarly, readers of the many voices of this volume must choose whether
or not to accept our versions of Herodotus' *logoi*, but we hope that these
versions will serve as an incitement, even provocation, to re-view Herodotus'
work again for themselves. As Herodotus' Candaules understood – if only
imperfectly – there can be no substitute for autopsy.

---

[113] See Moles, pp. 264–5 below, on the historicity of Socles.   [114] See Serghidou, Ch. 11 below.
[115] See Hornblower, pp. 172, 175 below on the unusual appearance of this story here.
[116] The reference is to the Aeginetan account of what happened when Athens tried to remove the
statues of Damia and Auxesia; but the Athenian account requires just as much willingness on the
part of the audience. On this story see Haubold, Ch. 9 below.

CHAPTER I

'What's in a name?' and exploring the comparable: onomastics, ethnography, and kratos in Thrace, (5.1–2 and 3–10)

Elizabeth Irwin

INTRODUCTION

What we now call Herodotus' 'Book 5' begins with a historical anecdote about the Paeonian defeat of the Perinthians (5.1–2), followed by a description of Thracian customs (5.3–10). The two *logoi* are seemingly inconsequential, aside from the fact that they share a focus on Thrace and that they both seem, in the opinion of most people, to make a rather unpromising contribution to their respective genres of history and ethnography. However, this cursory evaluation may prove misleading: the prominent position of these *logoi* in the wider narrative and the geopolitical significance of the Thracian coast – the location they narrate – in Herodotus' time, recommend a closer look. In the analysis that follows, I will be concerned with four general aspects of the *logoi* that are at the same time central to Herodotean studies:

(1) the textual and conceptual interplay between these seemingly disparate *logoi*;

(2) the function of these chapters in the *Histories* as a transition to a narrative of Persian engagement with mainland Greeks in Books 5–9 and as a prelude to Herodotus' account of the Ionian Revolt;

(3) the possibility that they provide programmatic reading strategies in miniature for the ensuing (and preceding) narrative; and

(4) the implications that interpretation of these *logoi* has for the meaning of the *Histories* in their wider contemporary (political) context.

I adopt two premises in what follows: namely that it is meaningful to consider these stories as the beginning of Book 5 and also to discuss them together. The first is not difficult to defend: despite our concerns about whether the book divisions of the *Histories* are Herodotus' own, without a doubt chapter one of Book 5 provides a marked break from the preceding extended narrative of Libyan affairs (4.145–205) and resumes the account, only summarily introduced in 4.144, of Megabazus' conquest of the Hellespontine Greeks.[1] More questionable is the assumption that the two initial *logoi* of Book 5 (represented by chapters 1–2 and 3–10) can and should be treated together in one discussion, not least because the wider narrative to which these chapters belong suggests other ways of grouping them. The anecdote about the Paeonian defeat of the Perinthians (5.1–2) provides the introduction of the Paeonians who will almost immediately become the subject of their own *logos* in 11–17, and whose appearances will punctuate the events of Book 5 (5.23.1, 5.98). As for the Thracian ethnography (5.3–10), the general of the Thracian conquest, Megabazus, will continue to be a presence in the narrative until chapter 26, when he hands over command to Otanes and Herodotus begins the slow start-up to the Ionian Revolt.

Those other ways of viewing the narrative units acknowledged, there are surface reasons for pausing at the end of chapter 10. The dramatic entrance of Darius at chapter 11, as he returns from Herodotus' Scythian *logos*, marks a new phase in the narrative.[2] At the same time, chapters 1–10 display their own internal unity: they both belong to the Persian conquest of τὰ παραθαλάσσια of Thrace, the region adjoining Asia and Europe; hence they are Thracian *logoi*. There is a marked progression from 5.1.1 to 5.2.2 that comes to a (temporary) rest in 5.10, as the first stage of Thracian conquest is completed:

οἱ δὲ ἐν τῇ Εὐρώπῃ τῶν Περσέων καταλειφθέντες ὑπὸ Δαρείου, τῶν ὁ Μεγάβαζος ἦρχε, πρώτους μὲν Περινθίους Ἑλλησποντίων οὐ βουλομένους ὑπηκόους εἶναι Δαρείου κατεστρέψαντο.

Those of the Persians left behind by Darius in Europe, whom Megabazus led, subdued first of the Hellespontines the Perinthians who refused to be made subjects of Darius. (5.1.1)

ὡς δὲ ἐχειρώθη ἡ Πέρινθος, ἤλαυνε τὸν στρατὸν ὁ Μεγάβαζος διὰ τῆς Θρηίκης, πᾶσαν πόλιν καὶ πᾶν ἔθνος τῶν ταύτῃ οἰκημένων ἡμερούμενος βασιλέϊ· ταῦτα γάρ οἱ ἐνετέταλτο ἐκ Δαρείου, Θρηίκην καταστρέφεσθαι.

In this way Perinthus was subdued; Megabazus drove his army through Thrace subjugating to the king every city and tribe that inhabited it; for this is what had been commanded by Darius: conquer Thrace. (5.2.2)

ταῦτα μέν νυν τῆς χώρης ταύτης πέρι λέγεται, τὰ παραθαλάσσια δ' ὧν αὐτῆς Μεγάβαζος Περσέων κατήκοα ἐποίεε.

This then is what's said about this land, and it's the coastal region of it that Megabazus was in the process of making subject to the Persians. (5.10)

[1] See Introduction, pp. 13–21.
[2] On Darius' entrance as a new beginning see Osborne, pp. 88–9 below.

Perinthus is the first Hellespontine *and* the first Thracian city to be conquered: geographic divisions contend with ethnic ones, while ultimately such ethnic and geographic divisions will be suborned to political ones, as Darius' imperial agenda subsumes πᾶσα πόλις (Hellenic) and πᾶν ἔθνος (non-Hellenic) alike (5.2).[3] Here Herodotus juxtaposes the geographic, ethnic and political divisions of the space between Europe and Asia, between Greek and barbarian, between autonomous Greeks and Persian empire, all significant dichotomies in Book 5, even as the narrative to come will challenge the security of these stark oppositions.[4] Text and geography likewise merge in these *logoi*: the space where the Paeonians from Strymon cross to overpower the Perinthians will be precisely that crossed by Megabazus in subjecting the *parathalassia* of Thrace, but in reverse. But this is not all: it is similarly the imaginative space that Greek mainland readers must cross to meet Darius (crossing the Hellespont) and arrive with him in Sardis (ch. 11) to meet a new group of Paeonians who have once again crossed that self-same distance: narrative is configured as topography, a trope that places the audience of the text in a position analogous to, if also differing from, that of its characters.[5]

And yet the relationship between the two *logoi* may be more complex than this. The Thracian ethnography pulls back to Book 4, while the Perinthian/Paeonian *logos* looks forward to the historical narrative of Book 5. Together they construct a bridge between the two halves of the *Histories*, the overwhelmingly ethnographical and the predominantly historical, through a structure at once described as an alternation of these differing narrative modes, and as chiasmus, where *logoi* of diminutive size are flanked by the more extensive historic and ethographic narratives that ensue and precede. Diminutive, insignificant, yet pivotally positioned, these *logoi* seem as unnaturally situated within Herodotus' narrative as those man-made structures contrived by his characters to cross natural boundaries. What kind of crossing will audiences make to the narrative ahead? And how will the manner in which they make this crossing affect what they find on the other side?

An important reason for taking these *logoi* together is the possibility that at this midpoint of the *Histories* at the exchange of the largely ethnographic for the predominantly historic, we may come to understand better the perfect unity of these two aims, and a key to the end to which they were

---

[3] See Macan (1895) I.154.   [4] See Introduction, pp. 12, 19.
[5] I am indebted to Emily Greenwood's contribution below (Ch. 4) for making me more sensitive to the textual geography of Herodotus' Thracian *logoi*.

united.[6] At the same time, we may obtain a deeper appreciation of the degree to which Herodotus has created meaning through the structuring of his *logoi*, realizing the truth in Immerwahr's claim, 'The study of how Herodotus organizes must be the main basis in answering the many other questions which may be put to the work, such as its general purpose, the audience for which it was written, its sources, its reliability as a source, or the historiographic and philosophic principles embodied in it.'[7]

In what follows, I will examine how the historical and ethnographical are joined by the injunction the text lays on the reader to construct their own bridges across time and across cultures, to survey the different events, cultural practices, and even language on display and from these to make inferences, συμβάλλεσθαι. The injunction is, however, implicit, only to be heard by those audiences who can make inferences from the prominence of the position given to these seemingly inconsequential *logoi*. But for those who pay close heed to their disparate and selective details, a sophisticated study emerges on three dominant fifth-century intellectual preoccupations and their discourses, and on the interrelationship between them: onomastics and linguistic theory; comparativism and ethnography; and, pervading both, κράτος.

PART I: HISTORY – THE PERINTHIAN *LOGOS* (5.1–2)

Chapter 1 resumes the main historical narrative by bringing to the fore the players and themes necessary for what is to come in the narrative of Book 5 and beyond,[8] and it does so, paradoxically, by introducing a seemingly tangential, if not irrelevant, narrative of apparently only local interest, or at best a banal demonstration of history repeating itself: while Perinthians might have been the *first* (πρώτους) of the Hellespontines made subject to the Persians, a similar sort of thing actually happened to them *before* (πρότερον). The strong statement of what is first is moderated by the comparative adverb, in a manoeuvre that demonstrates how a framing of the past in absolute terms may always be rendered relative: 'Of the Hellespontines, the Persians subdued the Perinthians first, who were unwilling to be subject to Darius; on a previous occasion they had been treated badly by the Paeonians,' and off the narrative goes.[9] At some indefinite time in

[6] On the unity of these aims, see Munson (2001b).
[7] Immerwahr (1957) 312, (1966); see already Jacoby *REA* Suppl. II.380.
[8] See Introduction, pp. 19–20.
[9] Here, by comparison with Herodotus' text one might observe how a reader's (my) autopsy invariably corrupts its discourse, transmitting it as *akoē*; on this process, see Introduction, pp. 5–9. The language of the oracle will be examined in more depth below.

the past, as it seems, the Paeonians from Strymon received an oracle pertaining to a campaign against the Perinthians. The oracle provides what seem simple alternatives: the Paeonians are to attack if the Perinthians call on them 'by name' (ὀνομαστί), but are not to if the Perinthians do not. During what is apparently the resulting absence of military engagement, the armies divert themselves by a *monomachia* of men, horses and dogs. Having won in two contests, the Perinthians sing a *paeon* in joy, whereupon the Paeonians consider, συνεβάλοντο (more on this verb below), that this singing is itself the oracle (χρηστήριον αὐτὸ τοῦτο εἶναι). They say (it seems – κου) to one another, 'Now the oracle could be fulfilled, now the deed is ours (νῦν ἡμέτερον τὸ ἔργον)!' And on this basis they attack the 'paeonizing' Perinthians (Περινθίοισι παιωνίσασι) and vastly overpower them (πολλὸν ἐκράτησαν). This is what happened to them πρότερον. But τότε Megabazus conquered the Perinthians (ἐπεκράτησεν) by sheer numerical force.

Like so many of Herodotus' *logoi* this one could vanish without great consequence to the *Histories* if their subject is narrowly (and erroneously) defined as the Persian Wars; but to account for its inclusion by evoking the observable habits of Herodotean style is to confuse description with explanation. The effectiveness of Herodotus' casual style is borne out by the degree to which secondary literature has almost uniformly ignored this story. The seemingly superficial transition, 'a similar thing happened before', masks perfectly the literary artifice by which Herodotus introduces elements that his ensuing narrative will exploit, the most immediate being the introduction of the Paeonians who will dominate the next historical *logos* and punctuate the narrative of Book 5 as they are transplanted and returned in its course (5.98). The apparently otiose nature of the *logos* could engender two responses to it: literalist, that is, this is just an event that Herodotus may or may not be right to think had happened, but one providing a convenient introduction to his next *logos*; or analogical, the recognition that Herodotus' words may yield more meaning than first appears. The choice is the audience's, but as the Paeonian capacity to interpret on another level brought them *kratos*, so the potential for other, greater, interpretations lies in Herodotus' narrative for those who choose to engage with it.

On closer examination, this apparently simple *logos* emerges as studiously vague. Questions arise for which there are no ready answers. On the Paeonian side: why are the Paeonians from *Strymon* attacking Perinthians in the *Hellespont*? Did the oracle tell them to conduct this campaign, or merely advise them on a decision already undertaken? Did the oracle actually *mean* what the Paeonians take it to mean? The answers are perhaps all too obvious from the perspective of *Realpolitik* and that of the Paeonians: the correct-ness of the interpretation is an imputation based on the Paeonians' desire and confirmed, to them at least, by their success. On the Perinthian side, one is left asking: what were the terms of the contest (did they cheer at their overall victory, two out of three, or were their cries premature), or – more literally – which contests did they win? A cultured audience may infer that the Perinthians' optimism was based on upset victories in those contests in which the Paeonians – famous for their dogs and horses – should excel,[10] an irony that must hover at the level of urbane inference, but one that must point to the decisive contest as being that between men.[11]

A victory in that contest, however, may be for different reasons: the Persians gained *kratos* over the Perinthians by their numbers (πλήθεϊ), but for the Paeonians it all seems to have depended on being able to see a pun, or, less flippantly, on their ability to manipulate language and to recognize a less obvious meaning inherent in the oracle's words. The Paeonians' response may be understood in more traditional, religious terms as a response to a *klēdēn* ('numinous utterance'), or more in line with contemporary fifth-century linguistic theorizing about the inherent meaning of *onomata*, par-ticular proper nouns.[12] Either way (and Herodotus leaves this vague, κου), the Paeonians respond by considering (συνεβάλοντο) the singing of the *paeon* 'to be itself the oracle' (τὸ χρηστήριον αὐτὸ τοῦτο εἶναι). Their response and its success points to the Perinthian *logos*' function as foreshad-owing another unifying, but implicit, feature of Book 5, the prevalence of paronomasia and the significance of names.[13]

Herodotus exploits names throughout his *Histories*, but nowhere is it more pervasive than in Book 5. I simply list some examples: the meaning-ful renaming of the Sicyonian tribes by Cleisthenes (5.68);[14] the contrast between the Isagoras the Spartans intend to impose on Athens, and its

---

[10] Paeonian dogs, Pollux 5.46, 47; horses, Mimn. 17.

[11] Battle is of course the contest of men *par excellence*. See Osborne, p. 89 below.

[12] These choices are hardly exclusive, with figures like Heraclitus hovering between religious and philo-sophic conceptualizations of language (see Stanford (1972) 117–19), and such linguistic theorizing often focused on religious matters, such as the gods' names: see Baxter (1992) 107–63. On kledo-mancy see Peradotto (1969), Cameron (1970) and Steiner (1994) 13. For discussion of *orthoepeia* and *orthotēs onomatōn* among the sophists, see Kerferd (1981) ch. 7; and see also de Romilly (1986). For the contemporary importance of, and ironic observations on, the subject see Plato's *Cratylus* with Woodhead (1928) and Sedley (2003).

[13] I follow O'Hara (1996) (cf. Woodhead (1928) 36, 72) in treating the several varieties of wordplay as related: 'strenuous efforts to distinguish or separate . . . are not useful, and probably not true' to practice. On the varieties of wordplay in Herodotus, see Powell (1937); Immerwahr (1966) *s.v.* etymologies; Fowler (1996) 72–3, and now Lateiner (2005) whose accounts are overly primitivizing; in Greek literature more generally, see Woodhead (1928) and O'Hara (1994) 7–18, with bibliography.

[14] See Gray, Ch. 8 below.

new-found *isēgoriē*, the result of the time when one Cleisthenes 'imitated Cleisthenes of the same name' (τὸν ὁμώνυμον Κλεισθένεα ἐμιμήσατο, 5.69.1); Cleomenes failing to observe the *klēdōn* (τῇ κληηδόνι οὐδὲν χρεώμενος (5.72.4) when he asserts to the priestess of the Acropolis, ἀλλ' οὐ Δωριεύς εἰμι ('I am not Dorian/Dorieus); Cypselus, whose father Ἤετίων ὁ Ἐχεκράτεος ('Eëtion, son of Echecrates') from a deme called *Petrē* ('Rock') received an oracle, αἰετὸς ἐν πέτρῃσι κύει . . . ('An eagle is pregnant among the rocks', 92β.3) ultimately and apparently about how his son would – true to *his* grandfather's name – 'hold *kratos*', because of which the rulers of Corinth 'sought (αἴτεον) the child of Eetion (Ἠετίωνος) (5.92.γ.2), whom his mother hid in a κυψέλη (chest, 5.92ε.1), whereby he derived his name (ἐπωνυμίη).[15] At the same time, the bold advice of Thrasybulus can lurk in his actions, ἐκόλευε αἰεὶ ὅκως τινὰ ἴδοι τῶν ἀσταχύων ὑπερέχοντα ('he was continually docking any of the ears of corn he saw holding itself above the others', 92.ζ.2), unintelligible to some, but clear to another tyrant: ὥς οἱ ὑπετίθετο Θρασύβουλος τοὺς ὑπερόχους τῶν ἀστῶν φονεύειν ('in this way Thrasybulus was advising him to murder those outstanding among the citizens', 92.η.1). And to return to where Book 5 begins, the ἀνάσπαστοι ('deported', 12.1) Paeonians ἀσπαστὸν ἐποιήσαντο ('are delighted', 98.3) at the prospect of being returned home, that is, rendered 'not' ἀν-ἀσπάστοι.[16]

Once recognized, one might account for the pervasive wordplay of Book 5 as yet another narrative device providing a stylistic unity across the disparate *logoi* of Book 5; and this it certainly does. Yet such a casual reading does no justice to the function of the *logos* that introduces this unity, and the implicit advice that it gives to its audiences (particularly contemporary audiences) on how they will need to engage with the ensuing narrative. For the denouement of the story, Paeonian victory, depends on an interpretative act, συμβάλλεσθαι, whose power is able to overturn the results

---

[15] In this story other puns abound: e.g. ἔδωκε φέρουσα ἡ Λάβδα, τὸν λαβόντα . . . (92.γ.3).

[16] See also Macan (1895) I.256, Munson and Henderson, Chs. 5 and 12 below, on Histiaeus' promise of Sardo for Sardis in (5.106.6). The most flagged play on words in all of Book 5, however, must be in 5.97, when Athenian ships (αὗται δὲ αἱ νέες) are said to *become* the ἀρχὴ κακῶν ('beginning of ills' or 'empire of evils') for both Greeks and barbarians. Whether Herodotus' audiences would have appreciated this play on words would likely have depended on their orientation in relation to that *archē*, and their own understanding of history. For the pun elsewhere see esp. Isoc. 4.119 but also Isoc. 3.28, 8.101 and 5.61. One might also consider the meaning of the cult statue Auxesia which Athens in the 490s attempts to wrest from her then naval superior, Aegina (θαλασσοκράτορες, 5.83.2). As with so many of Book 5's aspects – themes, characters, style – wordplay continues throughout Book 6 (see Introduction, pp. 15–18). With all the accumulated meaning from its earlier use: see the more explicit instances in 6.50 and esp. 6.98 when Herodotus 'translates' the names of the Persian kings.

of threefold *monomachia*.[17] What the Paeonians 'reckoned', 'considered', 'conjectured', literally, 'threw together for themselves' (συνεβάλοντο), out-does what each side brought against the other when the Perinthians and Paeonians 'matched' (συνέβαλον) dogs, horses and men. συμβάλλω in the middle as 'consider', 'conjecture', is marked as rare outside of Herodotus, not appearing in other historians and attested prior to Herodotus only in Heraclitus.[18] As Hohti notes, 'The συμβάλλεσθαι conclusion is based on the recognition that two existing parts belong together' – such as, but not limited to, an oracle and a real situation.[19] And according to Herodotean usage, these parts, these facts, 'can be similar, identical, symmetrical, ana-logous, or supplementary'.[20] The Paeonians bring together the Perinthians' singing of the *paeon* with the oracle's condition that they be called on by name (ὀνομαστί), draw a conclusion, attack and successfully overpower the Perinthians.

συμβάλλεσθαι conclusions are not, however, confined to the characters within Herodotus' narrative. It is a word that Herodotus uses frequently of his own activities in composing his *Histories*; that is, Herodotean usage makes no formal distinction between the activities of the text's narrator and those of his characters.[21] In turn, the extradiegetic usage of the term implies that the audience of the narration, its 'we', can also make *sumballesthai* con-clusions. Indeed, the audience's role in the process is fostered by the logic of the Perinthian *logos* itself. The Paeonians engage with the situation at hand on another level than that of its other participants, and, by considering a less obvious relationship between an *onoma* and reality, they gain *kratos*. The possibility arises that in the context of a book teeming with wordplay, homophony, shared names, puns – Herodotus may be enjoining his readers (or at least those who want a different kind of *kratos*, mastery of the text) to do the same. Indeed, the very modalities of the *logos*' narration facilitate

---

[17] On the recognition of the importance of this word in Herodotus, see Hohti (1977) and Munson (2001b) 83–4; cf. Immerwahr (1966) 5 n. 11.

[18] As Hohti (1977) 5 notes, LSJ provide only a single other case of this use of συμβάλλω in the middle, Heraclitus DK 47: μὴ εἰκῆ περὶ τῶν μεγίστων συμβαλλώμεθα ('let us not draw conclusions randomly about the greatest matters'). If this verb is enough to posit Heraclitean allusion, it would likely function as an implicit warning to the reader about the interpretations they might put together (συμβάλλεσθαι) when reading this tale about μέγιστα, war. For Heraclitus' own oracular style see Stanford (1972) 117–19. Heraclitus is also relevant in this discussion as 'le père de l'étymologie populaire' (Collart (1954) 258–62).

[19] Hohti (1977) 12. He comments, as the σύμβολον consists of two complementary parts, so the conclusion with συμβάλλεσθαι is formed on the basis of two existing complementary parts 'whose combination results in an intelligible whole which has a significance of its own and is more than the total of its parts'.

[20] Hohti (1977) 13.   [21] See Immerwahr (1966) 5 n. 11 and Hohti (1977).

this conclusion: in contrast to the oracle told in indirect speech, the Paeo-nians' solution is given in direct speech. The tentativeness expressed by the word κου marks their words as authorial creation, its presentation entirely a function of authorial choice. While within the narrative, the contrast emphasizes the role of the interpretative community, allowing it to vie with the oracular pronouncement over responsibility for the ἔργον, the first-person utterance draws the audience into the interpretative community: 'Now the task is ours' (νῦν ἡμέτερον τὸ ἔργον) signals to an alert audience that there is a task in front of us, too, *now*: it will be *ours* to determine (or fail to determine) what we are to bring to the *onomata* of the narrative to come, and what we are to conclude (συμβάλλεσθαι).

The Perinthian *logos* anticipates future invitations to draw συμβάλ-λεσθαι conclusions in Book 5 which cannot be dealt with here in detail: will an audience hear the story of Cleisthenes bringing the *demos* into his *hetaireia*, and rejoice in the birth of democracy, or will they consider precisely what might be in a name, and see the democratic reforms of Cleis-thenes as a tyrannical inheritance from his grandfather of the same name?[22] Will they see beneath the pun of Isagoras and *isēgoriē* to find at the level of meta-narrative an opportunity to reflect on competing conceptions of political equality, Spartan and Athenian, or, broadly speaking, oligarchic and democratic?[23] The identical *onomata* of the Cleistheneses, on the one hand, and *adnominatio* of *isēgoriē*/Isagoras, on the other, might lead, for example, to considering whether there is a tyrannical element to Athenian democracy, or how it may have been born out of the conflict of competing conceptions of *isēgoriē*.[24] The elements are there to be brought together, but the decision to do so, and the conclusions that they understand as following, are the audience's own.[25]

But this is to dwell on only one aspect of the *logos'* function in the wider narrative of Book 5. In Herodotus' narrative of chapters 1 and 2, the Paeonians are given alternative courses of action predicated upon whether they hear themselves called on, and can recognize the potential to equate the *paeon* of the Perinthians with themselves; in Herodotus' meta-narrative,

[22] See Munson (2001b) 52–7, Irwin (2005a). And will the reader go farther and see disdain for the Ionians (5.69.1) as a constituent element of Athens' democracy, and draw any conclusions for the present?

[23] 5.78 provides the single use of *isēgoriē* in Herodotus; for the general recognition of the apparent *non sequitur* of its occurrence here (as opposed to e.g. *isonomia*) see Yoshio (1988). On this passage, see Gray, Ch. 8 below.

[24] See Munson (2001b) 58; Ehrenberg (1946) 89.

[25] But there is of course textual encouragement to draw conclusions, as when Herodotus brings together the reactions to Aristagoras of the one Spartan King and the Athenian assembly (5.97, and see Hornblower, Ch. 6 below).

where the analogue of the apparently straightforward oracular utterance is the apparently straightforward *logos*, an audience will choose whether and how they hear themselves called upon by ἡμέτερον ('our'), the first-person utterance facilitating a connection between intra- and extradiegetic audiences. If the *paeon* could be equated by a part of its audience with calling on the Paeonians, the audience of this *logos* may be invoked to make their own equation from Herodotus' evocation of the Paeonians at this juncture in his *Histories* and in this manner. The potential is open for the extradiegetic audience to read Herodotus' words as an oracle, and to find in it new meaning should they consider the *logos* in the light of the circumstances they find themselves in (συμβάλλεσθαι). The logic of the oracular *logos* cannot be contained within the bounds of the *logos* any more than the Paeonian interpretation could be circumscribed by a literal response to the circumstances in which they found themselves. The question then arises, with whom or what will an audience be induced to equate the Paeonians, that is, to make a Paeonian-like conjecture? Several types of evidence will point to a single identification, that is, of Athenians with Paeonians.

The *logos* is itself almost oracular; its peculiar events (a contest pitting dog against dog, horse against horse, man against man) and the tendentiousness of its presence in the narrative (the shared subject of conquered Perinthians) merely underscore the lack of explicit motivation for its inclusion; its presence, no less than the oracle, poses an interpretative challenge. Yet, like an oracle, how the significance of this *logos* is construed will interpret its reader. To describe the Perinthians as 'dying bravely for their freedom' (ἀγαθῶν περὶ τῆς ἐλευθερίης γινομένων), and to have them defeated by Persian numbers (ἐπεκράτησαν πλήθεϊ) could elicit opposing responses: on the one hand, some may be more sympathetically disposed to the Perinthians, keeping the Perinthian defeats as distinct as Herodotus' text does, and even identify with the valiant attempt of the Perinthians to maintain autonomy and die for their freedom, just as their own forebears may have done; on the other hand, some may be inclined less generously to see instead in such apparent historical repetition something distinctive about Perinthians – perhaps even *qua* Ionians –[26] and feel confirmed in their own difference and superiority as belonging to a collective who did withstand the Persian *plēthos*; and perhaps (some of) this group will also be the ones who

[26] A timely subject given that (1) one of the last points made in Book 4.142 before breaking for the Libyan *logos* is the Scythian evaluation of Ionians as slavish, (2) the story we are about to embark on is of the botched Ionian Revolt, and (3), closer to (one audience's) home, Herodotus will assert in the chapters to come that disdain for the Ionians was an inherent feature of the birth of Athenian *isēgoriē* (5.69); see Introduction, pp. 19–25.

particularly pride themselves on being like the Paeonians, knowing how to interpret an oracle to their own advantage, a story which they are primed to anticipate as Herodotus' narrative drives ever onwards (7.142–4).[27] To take this view of the events of the *logos*, and its Perinthians, is to adopt a Paeonian perspective; and I would maintain it is a perspective that (some) Athenians might be more inclined to adopt than others.

The potential association of the Paeonians with an Athenian audience is appropriately also fostered via wordplay. In chapters 11–13, the attempt of two Paeonians at tyranny through a deceptive ploy with a tall, beautiful girl (μεγάλην τε καὶ εὐειδέα, 5.12.1) might lead one to recall a similar tyrannical story from Athens, and consider (συμβάλλεσθαι) how it involved a big, beautiful girl from *Paeania*: 'a women in the deme of Paeania, whose name was Phye, in height three fingers short of four cubits and indeed altogether beautiful' (ἐν τῷ δήμῳ τῷ Παιανιέϊ ἦν γυνή, τῇ οὔνομα ἦν Φύη, μέγαθος ἀπὸ τεσσέρων πήχεων ἀπολείπουσα τρεῖς δακτύλους καὶ ἄλλως εὐειδής, 1.60.4). And these Paeonians emerge – individually – as shifty solicitors of Persian tyranny and – collectively – as a group who take to the sea intending to abandon their city in the face of the Persians.[28]

It is far more significant when, later in the context of Book 5 (and nowhere else),[29] a second Paeonia appears in the *Histories*, this time located firmly in Athens in a gloss Herodotus provides for the stronghold which the Alcmaeonids took when they failed to make Athens 'free': Λειψύδριον τὸ ὑπὲρ Παιονίης τειχίσαντες ('fortifying Leipsydrion which is up beyond Paeonia', 62.2). It can hardly be coincidence for there is in fact no deme called Paeonia, only Paeonidae, and a passage of the *Ath. Pol.* (19.3), otherwise highly derivative from Herodotus, provides a correction of Parnes for Paeonia (τειχίσαντες ἐν τῇ χώρᾳ Λειψύδριον τὸ ὑπὲρ Πάρνηθος). To say Herodotus has made a mistake – 'has given the deme name in an incorrect form (which a non-Athenian might have done)' –[30] overlooks the widespread use of wordplay in Herodotus' narrative: Herodotus chooses to place a Paeonia in Athens, framed by references to Thracian Paeonians, an 'error' especially noticeable to (at least) an Athenian audience. If Herodotus causes the name Paeonia to denote two different places, Thracian and Athenian, will his Paeonians correspondingly denote these two peoples? And if audiences can bring these elements together to mean more than

---

[27] Hdt. 7.142–4.

[28] For the Athenian connotations of these Paeonians see Osborne, p. 92 below; cf. Thuc. 1.18.2.

[29] This single appearance of an *Attic* Paeonia is matched by the single use of παιωνίζω in the entire *Histories*.

[30] Rhodes (1981) 235.

Herodotean error, what might they conclude? As Heraclitus advised, 'let us not draw conclusions (συμβαλλώμεθα) randomly about the greatest of matters': to answer that one must go back to the oracular element of the story and its foreshadowing of another oracular *logos* of Book 5.

The Paeonian decision to read the Perinthians' *paeon* as an invocation of themselves imputes ambiguity to the oracle's meaning even as it promises its solution. νῦν ἂν εἴη ὁ χρησμὸς ἐπιτελεόμενος ἡμῖν, νῦν ἡμέτερον τὸ ἔργον ('Now the oracle would be fulfilled for us, now it is ours to act'): the dative of reference with the optative marks this solution to be tentative and interested, finalized by the assertion of agency in the declaration that the deed is 'ours', all amounting to retrospective religious endorsement based on proactive interpretation. Herodotus' choice to give the oracle in indirect speech and its interpretation in direct speech stresses the human agency – it is most certainly their choice to act on the conclusion they have made.

This strategy of using indirect and direct speech in an oracular *logos* antic-ipates that employed with more elaboration in the Theban *logos* later in Book 5 (5.79–81): both stress the role of an interpretative community ('they said to one another', 5.1.3; 'they called an assembly', 5.79.2), who simultane-ously create and resolve ambiguity from an otherwise clearly stated oracle (ὀνομαστὶ βώσαντες, 'calling on them by name', 5.1.2; ἄγχιστα, 'near-est', 5.79.2);[31] the tentativeness of interpretation (νῦν ἂν εἴη ὁ χρησμὸς ἐπιτελεόμενος ἡμῖν, 5.1.3; καὶ οὐ γάρ τις ταύτης ἀμείνων γνώμη ἐδόκεε φαίνεσθαι, 'and since no interpretation was considered to be better than this', 5.80.2); and play on words (ἐπαιώνιζον as singing the *paeon* and calling on the Paeonians; 'nearest' as geographical proximity and as mytho-logical kinship, 5.79.2–80.1, Aeacidae as cult statues and men, 5.80.2–81.1).[32]

But further parallels in the denouement of the Thebans' interpretative act impact on how the earlier story is to be understood and render the Perinthian *logos* itself an oracle that attains its full meaning as an act of our interpretation (ἡμέτερον ἔργον), if we bring these *logoi* together (συμβάλ-λεσθαι) to find an ἀμείνων γνώμη ('better interpretation') for why what we have read appears in Herodotus' narrative.

And since no interpretation seemed to appear better than this, straightaway they sent a request to the Aeginetans, calling on them to help as allies in accordance with the oracle (ἐπικαλεόμενοι κατὰ τὸ χρηστήριόν σφι βοηθέειν), because they were

---

[31] Of course, an obvious interpretation would have been the Plataeans, who were ethnically among the nearest, geographically closer than Aegina, *and* not allies; but no Theban would then have found this interpretation ἀμείνων.

[32] Cf. Cypselus' response to the χρηστήριον of 92.ε.1, called ἀμφιδέξιον. See also Haubold, p. 228 below.

nearest (ὡς ἐόντων ἀγχιστέων); and in answer to the request of the Thebans for military support, the Aeginetans said they were sending the Aeacidae. But when the Thebans attacked, acting on their alliance with/of the Aeacidae and were badly beaten by the Athenians (τρηχέως περιεφθέντων ὑπὸ τῶν Ἀθηναίων), in response they sent the Aeacidae back to Aegina and returned them, and asked for men instead.

Verbal repetition attends the thematic and structural parallelism between the two oracular *logoi*. The Athenian 'rough handling' of the Thebans (τρηχέως περιεφθέντων ὑπὸ τῶν Ἀθηναίων) repeats the formulation used of the Paeonians' treatment of the Perinthians (περιεφθέντας πρότερον καὶ ὑπὸ Παιόνων τρηχέως, 'earlier they had been roughly handled also by the Paeonians'),[33] and may raise some qualms over the identity of the characters in that earlier story. At the same time, the repeated appearance of the verb ἐπικαλέομαι in the context of an oracle points to another way of understanding the clever interpretation of the apparently god-sanctioned Paeonians. A careless reading may have erroneously understood ἐπικαλέσωνται in the oracle's condition, 'if when they are sitting opposite you they call on you', as meaning an invitation to battle, a challenge, synonymous with προκαλέεσθαι ('call out to battle, challenge'). Unfortunately, this is a meaning ἐπικαλέομαι never has in extant literature. Herodotus seems to underscore the difference a prefix makes with the use of πρόκλησις ('challenge') a few lines later.[34] The two most common meanings in Herodotus of the word are 'to invoke' a god, or to 'summon' allies, and indeed of the twelve appearances of this latter meaning, a full half are packed into Book 5.

The Theban passage, pointing back to the Perinthian *logos* thematically with its more critical examination of the process of oracular interpretation and verbally with its repetition of τρηχέως περιεφθέντων and ἐπικαλέομαι, may induce reconsideration of the oracle received by the Paeonians, a different act of συμβάλλεσθαι that will add a sinister tone to their interpretative act. For more accurately the transmitted oracle reads, 'if they summon you [as allies], calling on you by name, attack them, if they don't, do not.'[35] And as the events of the peculiar contests play out, the two meanings of ἐπικαλέομαι are simultaneously evoked – in singing the *paeon*, the

[33] This phrase for the results of military conflict is used eight times in Herodotus, overwhelmingly at the hands of Persians (only one other time of Greeks, Phocians, 8.27.2).

[34] See Creuzer (1869), Stein (1874), Abbott (1893) and Nenci (1994) *ad loc*. The juxtaposition with πρόκλησις suggests underlying Prodicean technique (DK 84A13 and Kerferd (1981) 70; cf. μισθὸν δωρεήν of 5.23.1 with Greenwood, pp. 138–41 below).

[35] Immerwahr's single comment (1966) 243 n. 17 on this *logos*: 'Trickery may develop into treachery, e.g . . . the Paeonians at Perinthus (5.1.1–2).'

Perinthians 'invoke' the god, but in calling on the god to celebrate their victories, they summon the Paeonians as allies, or worse, call on their Paeonian allies; that is, they *'paeonize'*, an act which leads to them becoming subject to Paeonian *kratos* (οἱ Παίονες καὶ πολλόν τε ἐκράτησαν, 'the Paeonians greatly overpowered them') and renders an equivalence between Paeonians and Persians (οἱ Πέρσαι τε καὶ ὁ Μεγάβαζος ἐπεκράτησαν πλήθεϊ, 'The Persians and Megabazus prevailed by their numbers'). Any who inferred at first reading that the Perinthian *logos* conveyed an inherent similarity between Perinthians at two different periods may be faced with the truth that what the story really conveyed was an inherent similarity between two other distinct peoples at different times, 'Paeonians' and Persians.

With this change of focus, the unanswered questions raised by the narrative become different from those asked above (p. 45): as they enjoyed their contests, did the Perinthians actually know that the Paeonians had come with intent to attack? were the two sides (for the Perinthians at least) sitting literally opposite, rather than opposed to, one another? Should an audience engage in the oracular logic performed within the *logos* (and by its Paeonians), stepping outside of the confines of the reading which on the surface the narrative *seems* to expect, they might wonder whether there was another time when a group of people (perhaps Athenians) sat opposite (ἀντικατιζόμενοι) the Perinthians,[36] and waited to be called on (for assistance, that is, when the Ionians called on Athens to replace Sparta as their leader)[37] – a moment that coincided with the Perinthians (and all the other Greeks) celebrating their victories (over the Persians) – a singing of the *paeon* that led to 'Paeonian' *kratos* over them (or Athenian *archē*)?[38] The Perinthians 'Paeonized' (Περινθίοισι παιωνίσασι) then, like so many others of the Ionian Greeks, and, like so many by the time of Herodotus' audience, they had been treated roughly for it.

---

[36] When the Paeonians become divided into two different groups in the next *logos*, the group evocative of Athenians will in fact move (temporally) to a location opposite Perinthus, in Phrygia (5.98). The question Darius will ask them – τίνες δὲ οἱ Παίονες ἄνθρωποί εἰσι καὶ κοῦ γῆς οἰκημένοι ('Who are these Paeonian men and where do they live', 13.2 – the question is metatextual, just *who* are these Paeonians?) – is the very same question asked of the Athenians – τίνες ἐόντες ἄνθρωποι καὶ κοῦ γῆς οἰκημένοι (73.2) – with identical phraseology used nowhere else in the *Histories*, in a similar context of attempting to ally with Persia, and in both cases backfiring.

[37] This is a scenario described by Plut. *Arist.* 23.3–4; if only we knew where in the Propontis Aristeides' negotiations were carried out: opposite Perinthus? At any rate, Herodotus may be exploiting dialect affinities – Athenians have more in common with *paeon*-singing Ionians than the *paean*-singing Spartans did. The exploitation of Athens' Ionian ties is of course central to Book 5, see Aristagoras in 5.97.

[38] On this reading Herodotus has exploited another meaning of πρότερον, not prior in time, but rather prior in his narrative: he will tell of the Paeonians' use of *kratos* before he narrates the Persian one; no less that ἡμέτερον, the νῦν of the direct speech would then activate a contemporary frame.

If this identification should be considered correct, one might then ask why should Paeonians be chosen to stand for Athenians, to which there would be several kinds of answers, depending on whether one evokes the 'deep' meaning of the name that involves the *paeon*, or a more ethnographic and historic explanation involving what the signifier more prosaically denotes, a tribe of Thracians. As for the former, although the paean has several associations, the logic of these stories narrows them down to two, a feature that belongs to both the start of military engagement and to its end in the celebration of victory. As such the Paeonians' speaking name would reveal them as a people characterized as simultaneously warlike and victorious, while the collapsing of the distinct meanings belonging to the start and end of military ventures would itself be entirely consonant with Thucydides' characterizations of Athens.[39] As to the latter, while it is of course useful that according to Thucydides (2.97) Paeonians are *autonomoi*, a quality particularly valued in Athenian political discourse, the answer to why a Thracian people at all may be best explained by Athens' long-standing Thracian ties: on the one hand, the location of these Paeonians vaguely ἀπὸ Στρυμόνος ('from the river Strymon') may well evoke the place on the Strymon most familiar to audiences, the Athenian colony Amphipolis (and, more darkly, its predecessor *Ennea Hodoi*); on the other, not only did Athens have long-standing ties with Thrace (dating back to Peisistratus), but the granting of citizenship to the son of Sitalces in 431 BC from the point of view of detractors at least might have made the identification of *these* particular Greeks with *those* barbarians unproblematic and pointed, as might also Athenian use of Thracian mercenaries to fight other Greeks (cf. Aristoph. *Ach.* 133–73, esp. 167–72, and Thuc. 2.101.4).[40]

But if an audience has been induced to consider whether the Thracians they encounter in the story are the Athenians of the present, there are a few subtle indications that the *logos* was tending this way. The first lies in the

[39] For the Athenians as a people who cause the multiple functions of the paean to collapse into one, assuming victory at the start of every undertaking, see Thuc. 1.70.7 and cf. 4.65.3. *Paeon*-play in the historians is suggestively intertextual: the only time Athenians sing the paean in Thucydides occurs in an event for which Thucydides will engage in his own wordplay involving the dangers of a single term's multiple meanings: at the start of the Sicilian expedition the Athenians sing paeans (παιωνίσαντες, 6.32.2) that are later remembered with rue (7.75.7), as if they had sung a *victory* paean before they began; and doubly pointed given the consequences of their failure to understand what the *Dorian* paean of 7.44.6 actually meant. Certainly relevant here is Aristoph. *Knights* (1316–20) where an injunction to the theatre παιωνίζειν leads the chorus (otherwise unmotivated, cf. Sommerstein (1981) 215) to call on the sausage-seller/Athens in the capacity of *epikouros* of the islands.

[40] On the substantial Thracian presence, cultural and literal, in Athens of at least the 430s onwards, see Parker (1996) 170–5, esp. 174 and n. 74; Simms (1988); and see below. Cf. Thuc. 1.82 for anxiety about engaging barbarians as allies in war against Greeks.

classification of the Perinthians as belonging to the *Hellespontine* Greeks, an appellation that one has to understand 'in the wide sense', as How and Wells comment, given the Perinthians' location in the Propontis, but such an understanding is not at all difficult from an Athenian (imperial) perspective at least since this *onoma* is identical to that employed in the Athenian Tribute Lists: in using this 'naturalized' classification of Thracian geography here Herodotus may well allude to and activate a rather different historical narrative about the power of names to shape the world as well as the ability to name as a demonstration of power.[41]

More obviously, language points to another sign that this *logos* is not as straightforward as it might at first glance seem. The event that Herodotus has narrated presumes a shared language between Paeonians and Perinthians. As Asheri comments: 'The amusing anecdote narrated in this chapter (VI) is entirely built around a pun (Παίονες–παιωνίζω) under-standable of course only by Greeks, and hence a pure Greek fiction.'[42] But the fiction is also purely Herodotean, as is made clear to the alert reader by the κου attending his reported speech: the Paeonians are not presented as Thracians who have mistaken the singing of the Greek *paeon* as invoking them by name, but rather as people from Strymon for whom the question of a different language is never raised. This is nothing other than Herodotus' dog that didn't bark in the night: has anyone in the audience been so carried along by the easy style as not to ask about the question of language? If they have been, what might their failure to notice serve to demonstrate; and if they did notice, what conclusion did they draw (συνεβάλοντο) from Thra-cians who have been presented in a manner that minimizes their differences from these 'Hellespontine' Greeks?

PART II: ETHNOGRAPHY – THE THRACIAN *ETHNOS* (5.3–10)

Introduction: bridging the logoi – extraneous narratives, relative κράτος *and onomastics*

The ethnographic interlude of chs. 3–10 raises the same questions as that of its historical neighbour: why is it here and why in this form? Herodotus is

---

[41] How and Wells (1912) *ad* 5.1 and Abbott (1893). On the usual correspondence of Herodotean usage with that familiar from the Tribute Lists see How and Wells (1912) *ad* 4.38. An innovation, these geographic categories in the Tribute Lists seem not to have appeared before List 12 (443/2 BC), see *ATL*. The heated ancient debates (e.g. Strabo vii *fr.* 58) on the application of the label of 'Hellespontine' to the Propontis may well find their origin here.

[42] Asheri (1990) 155.

hardly *compelled* to describe these Thracians here: his own explicit reference
to his earlier *logos* on the Getae – εἴρηταί μοι, 'I have said' (5.4.1) – draws
attention to the choices he has exercised in the selection and placement
of the content of his narrative. Moreover, the ethnography promises a historical *logos* that will in fact never be told. In 5.3 the wholesale conquest
of Thrace hovers tantalizingly, a command by Darius 'to subdue Thrace'
(Θρηίκην καταστρέφεσθαι, 5.2.2), conditionally entertained ('if it should
be ruled by one', εἰ δὲ ὑπ' ἑνὸς ἄρχοιτο, 5.3.1), and distant from what was in
fact more modestly attained by Megabazus: the subjugation of the maritime
regions (τὰ παραθαλάσσια . . . κατήκοα, 5.10). Finally, the ethnography
is unique in its brevity.[43] For how much ends up being known about the
Thracians beyond their being all much of a muchness? One has to look
instead to Thucydides for greater elaboration in his famous 'Herodotean'
excursus on Thrace.[44] Vague, brief and casually placed, Herodotus' Thracian *logos* stands in an analogous relationship to his ethnographies as the
Paeonian defeat of the Perinthians does to the overarching historical narrative. The questions I wish to pose are these: how and why has Herodotus
brought these Thracian narratives together (συμβάλλειν); and what should
one conclude (συμβάλλεσθαι) from that choice? But first, we must consider the more obvious bridges that Herodotus constructs between the *logoi*
and then the details of his Thracian account.

If the Perinthians were the 'first' in a historical series, the Thracians are
the 'biggest' in an ethnographic frame – that is, both superlative, albeit each
with some qualification: 'of the Hellespontians' (5.1.1); 'after the Indians'
(5.3.1). And as the Perinthian *logos* was predicated upon comparison (of
similar events, but at different times and with different agents), so too
comparison functions at every level in this ethnographic *logos*, even extend-
ing to the very relationship the Thracian *logos* strikes with its Perinthian
predecessor: for if the κράτος of Persians and Paeonians is implicitly (though
inconclusively) compared by the similarity of the act they performed, mastery of Perinthus (ἐπεκράτησαν), the κράτος of the Thracian *ethnos* is
evaluated in the assertion that under certain circumstances they would
(future time) be superlative on a more absolute scale (κράτιστον πάντων
ἐθνέων, 'of all peoples'), and as such (whether actual or potential) it vies
with these preceding (historical and textual) demonstrations of strength.
But how these κράτη compare now, under the present circumstances, what
hierarchy might exist between these three groups, is left indeterminate – a

---

[43] On which see Asheri (1990).
[44] Thuc. 2.95–101: on its 'Herodotean' style see Hornblower (1991) *ad loc.*; cf. Westlake (1969) 14–15;
   and below.

disappointment for any audience who may have wished history to provide some coordinates against which to measure Thracian strength of the present. As it is, Herodotus' *Histories* never narrate an engagement between the Thracian *ethnos* and the Persians.

Herodotus creates a further bridge between these *logoi* of Thracian κράτος in terms of structure: the conditional circumstances necessary for superlative Thracian κράτος (εἰ δὲ . . . ἢ, 5.3.1) replays the conditional scenario of the oracular utterance involving Paeonian κράτος (ἢν μὲν . . .ἢν δὲ μὴ, 5.1.2). Qualified as it is by the subjective opinion of the narrator (κατὰ γνώμην τὴν ἐμήν, 'in my judgement'), that evaluation of Thracian potential leaves itself open for interpretation by interested parties, no less than the oracle did. Of course, the stakes involved in Paeonian κράτος are much higher: the potential inherent in future, πολλῷ κράτιστον πάντων ἐθνέων ('most powerful by far of all peoples'), would dwarf what is past and actual, πολλόν τε ἐκράτησαν ('they hugely overpowered them'), if, that is, it ever would happen.

Nor have onomastics been left behind. The subject of naming unites the narrative units of these ten chapters – ὀνομαστί ('by name', 5.1.2), οὐνόματα ('names', 5.3.2), οὔνομα ('name', 5.9.1) – and each appearance introduces a study on the relationship of language to the world it denotes. While for the Paeonians the capacity to manipulate *onomata*, to exploit the relationships that language can strike with reality, was a source of their *kratos*, the Thracian ethnography provides another kind of exploration of the relationship between language, reality and κράτος. The Thracian *ethnos* would be strongest if they should find unity in leadership or thought, but that lack of unity finds its analogue in onomastics: for if they are a people divided in thought, they are also a people divided in name ('they have many names, each taking their name from their lands, but they all use practically the same (παραπλησίοισι) customs in relation to everything'). While their individual names may derive meaning from their lands, a deeper, collective, 'meaning' may seem to lie elsewhere: having chosen to define themselves – literally name themselves – by their different territories (χῶραι) rather than by shared custom (νόμοι), this nearly homogeneous *ethnos* is found to be – at least, at present – 'without strength' (ἀσθενέες) – a result that is anything but nominal.

To judge from Thucydides, this sort of inference from names seems indeed topical, underlying as it does a central claim of his history. His war, he argues, is greater than all that have come before, even Troy, as one can tell from the strengthlessness (ἀσθενεία) of early Greeks, somehow epitomized by their lack of a collective *name*:

Also it is clear to me not least from what follows that the ancients had no strength (*astheneia*): for Greece does not yet seem to have undertaken anything in common before the Trojan war; and it seems to me that the whole of Hellas did not even have this name (*onoma*); on the contrary, before the time of Hellen son of Deucalion, the name (*epiclēsis*) itself did not even exist, but it went by the name (*epónumia*) of the different tribes, in particular of the Pelasgians. (Th. 1.3.1–2)

While Thucydides seems satisfied to draw such conclusions drawn from onomastics, for Herodotus, any causal connection between the absence of a collective Thracian name and overall capacity is, as between the Perinthian defeats, left at the level of inference. Thucydides or his audience may draw such a conclusion from these 'facts', but should a Herodotean audience? That question can only be answered once we examine what it means for Herodotus to narrate the existence of, *without* actually naming, these many Thracians, and consider the contemporary resonances of his Thracian *logos*.

But one final study of onomastics is carried out in chs. 9–10: in the first person, the narrator claims the ability to learn of only a single people beyond the Ister, knowledge that consists largely in knowing a single name: μούνους δὲ δύναμαι πυθέσθαι οἰκέοντας πέρην τοῦ Ἴστρου ἀνθρώπους τοῖσι οὔνομα εἶναι Σιγύννας ('Only a single people living beyond the Ister have I been able to learn of; their name is the Sigynnae', 5.9.1). He cites a single custom, their Median clothing, and their claim to be colonists of the Medes. Here is a case where name and geography provide no insight into these people; the only knowledge may come from a νόμος, a custom of clothing, that one might infer to be the basis of the descent they claim to have, though Herodotus neither makes such a claim explicit nor ascribes any evidential value to the clothing.[45]

Almost the only thing interesting about these Sigynnae seems to be their name: 'The Ligurians who live above Massalia call retail merchants (καπήλους) "sigynnae", but the Cypriots use this word for spears (τὰ δόρατα).' One *onoma*, so many meanings; 'Sigynnae' signifies three classes of nouns – a people, retailers, or spears. But what is meant by this display of meanings? A display of erudition, to be sure, but it also demonstrates a point about relativity: what σιγύνναι means is entirely dependent on where you happen to be, the very point that Aristotle uses the word to make when he singles out *sigunon* to demonstrate that the 'same' word can be both exotic (γλῶττα) and common (κύριον), but not in relation to the same people: 'For *sigunon* is a common word to the Cypriots, but to us it

---

[45] On the instability of clothing as an indicator of ethnicity cf. 5.87.3–90. On the claims and use of colonial ties: Aristagoras at 5.97.2 with Macan (1895) I.246. See below.

is exotic' (*Poetics* 21). Its appearance in Aristotle and Herodotus suggests that it was a stock example from language theory, *the* γλῶττα. But if so, the addition of the Massalian traders – yet another meaning in yet another place – may point to a particular linguistic debate of the late fifth century: the juxtaposition of referents (συμβάλλειν) gestures towards a conclusion (συμβάλλεσθαι) about the inherent meaninglessness of *onomata*, that is, the arbitrariness of the sign.[46]

Names could be made to mean all too much in the Perinthian *logos*, but they seem to mean less and less through the trajectory of the Thracian *logos*: the unity of an *ethnos* can be belied by its many names; and knowing a name may not be knowing much when its meaning is entirely dependent upon the context in which it is used. Taken together Herodotus' onomastic narrative might induce a series of cursory inferences in his audience: one might infer from the Paeonians that a clever use of *onomata* will lead to the successful exercise of κράτος; from the Thracians that their polyonymous state stands in some inverse relationship to the unity that would give them superlative κράτος; from the Sigynnae the relativity of meanings, if not also the inherent meaninglessness of words. A spectrum of contemporary responses to language are on offer in these chapters, but if the Sigynnae demonstrate the importance of context for the meaning of words, we must examine the wider context in which Herodotus' onomastics operates. After journeying to the end of this 'digression', and to the extra-textual intertexts beyond – Sophocles, Aristophanes and above all Thucydides – we may be led to draw other conclusions about Herodotus' implicit excursus on the meaning of *onomata* and their relationship to *kratos* in the context of Thrace.

Ethnographic comparison

The ethnographic comparison of the *logos* must be the first concern. The Perinthian *logos* juxtaposed comparable historical situations, leaving the significance of the juxtaposition to be construed by its audience. Here in the ethnographic frame, comparison is an explicit feature in the presentation of the νόμοι of the Thracians. *Nomoi* of distinct groups of Thracians are compared against the norm which the collective *ethnos* constitutes as a single, yet polyonymous, entity, and against all other *anthrōpoi* and *ethnea*: and once again the meaning of this Thracian *logos* in context – textual, cultural, political – is left for the audience to construe, now doubly enjoined

---

[46] The *locus classicus* for the conventionalist view of language is Plat. *Crat.* 383–4.

to do so by the discourse of comparison inscribed within the ethnography of the Thracian *logos* itself and by the model of inference based on comparison (συμβάλλεσθαι) established by the preceding *logos*.

The brevity of Herodotus' Thracian ethnography – unique among his ethnographic excursuses – belies its significance.[47] In what follows an explanation for this minimalist treatment will be found to lie in contemporary discourse and politics surrounding Thrace. If brief, the ethnography is also deceptively simple. Its dynamics are constructed to assay repeatedly the distance between the subject of the ethnographic *logos* and its viewer. At the outset, the text configures the audience of this ethnography as belonging to the universalizing categories of all mankind, all peoples. That is, they are subsumed into categories that minimize their difference from others, among whom the Thracians emerge as not different in essence, but rather in quantitative terms – (almost) biggest and (potentially) strongest – that as such presuppose similarity in kind. This manoeuvre is the ethnographic equivalent of the strategy of the Perinthian *logos* inviting the audience to engage with the *logos'* subject in terms that induce them to bring themselves into comparison with – even possibly identifying with – its Thracians, the Paeonians. At the same time, the highly selective account of Thracian *nomoi*, organized through comparative terms – three exceptional *nomoi*, each practised uniquely by a single group of Thracians (5.3.2–5), and three *nomoi* common to the whole *ethnos* that are called *epiphanestatoi* (5.6–8) – is designed to exploit the comparative frame it constructs in order to place the audience in an ambiguous relationship with the ethnography they are consuming.

This culturally uniform *ethnos* is introduced, paradoxically, by its exceptional tribes (νόμοισι δὲ οὗτοι παραπλησίοισι πάντες χρέωνται κατὰ πάντα, πλὴν . . . 5.3.2). The choice to present the exceptional Thracian *nomoi* before the collective Thracian customs has consequences for an audience's reception of the former. The irregular sequencing creates a 'comparative vacuum': from what position will the audience view these Thracians, and against what are these exceptional *nomoi* to be compared? In the absence of explicit textual *comparanda*, the audience is forced to step in, either with what they 'know' about Thrace or, as is common with ethnographic engagement, with *comparanda* that include especially themselves.[48] If these exceptional Thracians are defined negatively, as unlike their ἔθνος, it is left

---

[47] Asheri (1990).

[48] These choices may amount to the same thing if the audience with the most 'knowledge' about Thrace is the one that from other Greek perspectives seems most Thracian by their policies and *nomoi*: on Athens' relationship to Thrace in the fifth century see below.

open-ended whom they may be like: if my enemy's enemy is my friend, is my other's other me?

The practices that Herodotus highlights will raise precisely these questions, enjoining the reader to bring what they find comparable to the passage and to make inferences (συμβάλλεσθαι). Trausic joy (5.4) at funerals and sadness at births may at first seem peculiar:

> The Trausi perform all other practices in the same way as other Thracians, but with respect to a birth among them or a death they do the following things. All the relations sit around the new-born and lament the many ills he will have to endure now that he is alive, recounting all the sufferings that are part and parcel of being a human. But at someone's death, they rejoice and are happy burying him, giving as an explanation that since he is free from so much misery he is now in complete happiness. (ἐν πάσῃ εὐδαιμονίῃ).

Modern commentators attest to the capacity of this passage to evoke two contrary responses, difference from and identity with the Greeks: while How and Wells contextualize the practice as Thracian, calling the belief in the afterlife 'primitive [!] and widespread', they admit that 'the pessimistic view of the present life (cf. Soph. *Oed. Col.* 1225; Theogn. 425) is in accord with one side of Hellenic sentiment . . . and with H.'s own oft-repeated opinion.'[49] Macan captures the balance the passage strikes, tempering his comparisons from anthropology with the recognition that 'the pessimistic vein is, however, anything but un-Hellenic.'[50] While not acknowledging it as such, both scholars point to the choice that was likely to have faced contemporary audiences, namely to register extreme 'otherness' in this practice, or instead to recognize in it an exaggerated version of their own beliefs, albeit taken to their logical (ἐπιλέγοντες) conclusion – extreme alterity or similarity in the extreme. As Herodotus constructs the comparison, however, the choice is less clear-cut: if Trausic practice is exceptional among the Thracians, it indicates nothing about general Thracian belief, unless that the Thracian norm was a more moderate version; and if so, this would be nothing if not also Greek, with Athenian tragedy a dominant contemporary purveyor.

The exceptional practice of the Thracians north of Crestonia, polygamy, leads to a similar inference. As Macan notes, there is a 'temptation to see the exceptional polygamy ascribed by this passage to certain Thracians as

---

[49] See also Eur. *Cresph.* fr. 449 N; on its relationship with Hdt. 5.4.2, see Browning (1961) and Harder (1985) 93–4.

[50] Macan (1895) *ad loc.*: 'This Trausic view of life as "not worth living" is by no means uncommon, specially when a higher culture intrudes. Wholesale cases of voluntary extinction by barbarous nations are not unknown'.

implying monogamy to be the Thracian norm.'[51] Such an inference flies in the face of popular stereotypes of barbarians reflected on the Attic stage, and potentially renders the unspoken Thracian norm to be (similar to the) Greek.[52] Closer to Book 5, the competitive practice in which the families of a man's wives compete for the dubious honour of having their member die on her husband's pyre, and celebrate her victory – a 'barbaric' custom – has apparently no Greek equivalent, but the ensuing chapters will reveal a Spartan King practising bigamy, and one of his wives, the one more loved, will have to give birth before an audience because of the *invidia* of the relations of the other wife (5.40.2), a competition that continues between their issue. It may be argued that Anaxandrides did οὐδαμῶς Σπαρτιητικά ('nothing at all Spartan') in this, but neither do these exceptional Thracians do what is Θρηίκια ('Thracian').[53]

When the text turns from the exceptional *nomoi* of the Thracians to those shared (νόμος τῶν ἄλλων Θρηίκων, 5.6.1), each example raises questions about its specificity or uniqueness to the Thracians. Herodotus presents three νόμοι that he concludes by calling ἐπιφανέστατοι ('most notable'): (in reverse order) contempt for manual work, tattooing, and practices involving the exchange of children, particularly daughters, for money. Contempt for manual work (6.2) is by no means distinctly Thracian; it is a νόμος prevalent throughout the whole of Greece, as Asheri well notes, and already marked in the *Histories* as almost universal (2.167).[54] In a different way, the νόμος that considers tattooing as elevated, its absence as coarse, is marked: it belongs to a 'repertoire' of 'ethnological examples illustrating the relativism of social conventions', apparent from the *Dissoi Logoi*:[55] 'It is cosmetic for the Thracians to tattoo their daughters, but for others tattoos are

---

[51] Macan (1895) *ad loc.*

[52] E.g. Eur. *Andr.* 170–6; see also Asheri (1990) 145. Cf. Hdt. 3.31 for an analogous challenge to popular stereotypes.

[53] And sometimes 'kings', whether Spartan or Thracian, can be like a different tribe: οἱ δὲ βασιλέες αὐτῶν, πάρεξ τῶν ἄλλων πολιητέων, σέβονται ... ('Their kings, separate from the other citizens, worship ...', 5.7); the designation πολιητέων facilitates cross-cultural comparison ('curious', Abbott (1893); 'looks like a *lapsus calami*', Macan (1895) I.156). On polygamy and Sparta see also 6.61; cf. 5.16.2–3 with Osborne, pp. 95–7 below.

[54] Asheri (1990) 143–4. τὸ ζῆν ἀπὸ πολέμου καὶ ληιστύος κάλλιστον ('living from war and booty is the finest thing') would in a Greek context even unite Spartans and Athenians, though their form of practising this νόμος would differ: the shared disdain for farming would be inferred from different practices – the use of helots, on the one hand, or the choice to abandon the countryside and live off the produce of others through naval *archē*, on the other.

[55] τοῖς δὲ Θραξὶ κόσμος τὰς κόρας στίζεσθαι, τοῖς δ' ἄλλοις τιμωρία τὰ στίγματα τοῖς ἀδικέοντι (DK 90 fr. 2.13). Asheri (1990) 142–3. Asheri points out that for the sake of paradox Herodotus puts on the same level ornamental and penal tattooing, exploiting the fact that in Greek these very *different* practices are denoted by the *same* verb, στίζειν.

for criminals.' While illustrating the difference of Thracians in contrast to others (ἄλλοι), in contemporary theorizing tattooing was a stock example for illustrating what was – paradoxically – universal: the relativity of *nomoi*. Again, Greeks of Book 5 are foreshadowed by this νόμος: tattooing will emerge as a crucial feature in the instigation of the Ionian Revolt (5.35).[56]

More striking, and locally relevant, is perhaps the passage that introduces this section on the *nomos* of the other Thracians: 'They sell their children for export . . . they buy their wives from their parents for a lot of money' (πῶλευσι τὰ τέκνα ἐπ' ἐξαγωγῇ . . . ὠνέονται τὰς γυναῖκας παρὰ τῶν γονέων χρημάτων μεγάλων, 5.6.1). The passage allows for ambiguity: is marrying daughters off for money a subset of the sale of children, or does it specify what was meant in the first statement? It cannot be told; but following the sale of children by references to marriage practice, the former practice (which may or may not be distinct from the second) is associated with the second, and capable of normalizing what at first is outlandish by evoking a practice far from alien to Greek audiences.[57] This particular *nomos* may have further resonance closer to home and to Thrace. Sophocles' *Tereus*, set in Thrace, stages such a cultural practice, but performed by *Greeks*, and more specifically by *Athenians*. The subject of Procne's lament (*fr.* 583) is precisely such sale and export:

> ὅταν δ' ἐς ἥβην ἐξικώμεθ' ἔμφρονες,
> ὠθούμεθ' ἔξω καὶ διεμπολώμεθα
> θεῶν πατρῴων τῶν τε φυσάντων ἄπο,
> αἱ μὲν ξένους πρὸς ἄνδρας, αἱ δὲ βαρβάρους.

When we come of age and reach maturity, we are pushed out away from paternal gods and the parents who begot us, and peddled to different buyers, some to strangers, and some to barbarians.

And this complaint finds itself couched not as a specific ethnic problem, but rather as a universal one, a consequence of γυναικεία φύσις ('woman's nature').[58] But if there is a general intertextuality between Herodotus' and Sophocles *logoi* here, in the next section it will be considered whether it is significant that both authors situate these reflections in Thrace.

---

[56] See Munson, Ch. 5 below.

[57] The peddling of female relations (involving figures ambiguously 'barbarian') is a motif of the first *logoi* of Book 5: the Paeonians (5.12–13) and Alexander (5.21.2), in both cases sisters. On contemporary resonances in Thrace, see Thuc. 2.101 and discussion below.

[58] The universality of this female condition belongs to a wider theme of the play, the shared human condition: see the ἓν φῦλον ἀνθρώπων of fr. 591; cf. the θνητὴ φύσις ('mortal nature') of fr. 590, and fr. 592.4, and as explored against the alterity of the Thracians, e.g. fr. 587. See also the bold comparison of Procne's and Tereus' crimes in fr. 589. For a cogent discussion of the reconstruction of the play see Fitzpatrick (2001).

According to Herodotus, these three customs are ἐπιφανέστατοι (5.6.2), but one might wonder what this *onoma* actually means, since it presupposes a comparative framework that is nevertheless left unspecified. What makes these *nomoi* 'most conspicuous'? Is it by comparison with Thracian *nomoi* or Greek? And if the latter, are they *epiphanestatoi* because the narrator and the audience find them 'most recognizable' as Thracian – or rather 'most remarkable' because they are so like their own?[59] It is a question that becomes more pressing as Herodotus continues by listing the gods that they worship by their Greek names (5.7) – Ares, Dionysus, Artemis, Hermes[60] – and concludes by describing their elaborate funeral celebrations (5.8) in terms overwhelmingly evocative of the most famous of Greek funerals in that most Hellenic of texts, that of Patroclus.[61]

Thracian logoi and Herodotus' audience

Sophocles' *Tereus* suggests another *comparandum* for Herodotus' Thracian *logos*, that of contemporary *logoi* and experience of Thrace. Here the relationship between ethnography and onomastics in Herodotus' opening chapters becomes salient. It is in the context of Thrace that Thucydides famously tries to prevent the inferences that might arise from paronomasia. His vehement claim that *Teres*, the father of the Thracian king with whom Athens had dealings in 429/8, BC was no relation to *Tereus*, the mythic husband of Athenian Procne – they do not have the 'same name' and are not from the 'same Thrace' –[62] reveals not only the degree of influence of such wordplay (and by extension the purveyors of it) in contemporary

---

[59] Herodotus' only other use of the superlative of ἐπιφανής is to qualify ἔθνεα (9.32.1) in a context that similarly elides the distinction between whether the peoples deployed by the Persians are worthy of note absolutely or rather because they are likely to be already known to the audience. Compare Thucydides' marked use of ἐπιφανέστατα with the σημεῖα (1.21.1) that render a version of τὰ παλαιά in terms most familiar and recognizable to his own audience.

[60] Artemis is particularly pointed as Athens is already likely to have started celebrating the Thracian Artemis, Bendis; the cult was officially recognized by 429/8 (*IG* I³.383, line 143).

[61] See Petropoulou (1986–7); cf. Abbott (1893) 6. Homeric allusion may explain the awkwardness of κατὰ λόγον (variously taken, 'as is reasonable', 'in proportion to', 'according to the norms of single combat', 'on account of its importance', etc.; see Nenci (1994) 163 and Asheri (1990) 147 n. 21) as Herodotean double-meaning, simultaneously gesturing outside his *logos* to its model: 'in accord with (Homer's) *logos*', or 'as the story goes'. μουνομαχίη may also carry significance: it is a word used in Herodotus only in the Perinthian *logos*, *supra*, and in 6.92 about the successful Athenian *monomachist* Sophanes, who will later die fighting for Athenian possession of the goldmines in *Thrace* (9.75), usually identified with the Athenian disaster at Drabescus (Thuc. 1.100.3).

[62] Τήρει δὲ τῷ Πρόκνην τὴν Πανδίονος ἀπ᾽ Ἀθηνῶν σχόντι γυναῖκα προσήκει ὁ Τήρης οὗτος οὐδέν, οὐδὲ τῆς αὐτῆς Θρᾴκης ἐγένοντο . . . Τήρης δὲ οὐδὲ τὸ αὐτὸ ὄνομα ἔχων (Thuc. 2.29.3). Hornblower (2004) 310: 'Thucydides issues a pedantic surface denial on onomastic grounds . . .' See also Zacharia (2001) 102 and Rusten (1989) 133–4.

discourse, but also lets on that one simply cannot speak about Thrace without factoring in what an audience might import from elsewhere, no doubt
from drama.[63] Thucydides' reaction both provides a contemporary context
through which to see Herodotus' own onomastics, and should remind us
that such audience responses would have likewise registered with Herodotus
when composing his own Thracian *logos*. In contrast to Thucydides,
Herodotus seems likely to have favoured the anonymous source in seeing
such conflations and what one might be led to conclude (συμβάλλεσθαι)
from them as desired.[64] And even if in this instance the contours of the
appropriations and counter-appropriations of mythic Tereus in relation
to the historic Teres elude us, it is difficult to avoid the conclusion that
such mythic ties (and their denial) would have been exploited in debates
surrounding Athenian negotiations with Thrace.[65]

    Beyond revealing the contemporary salience of Thracian onomastics –
a context for our Paeonian *logos* – Thucydides proves instructive for recon-
structing the expectations of Herodotus' audiences in further respects.
Beneath the manifest intertextuality between the two authors, it is possible to construct a shared contemporary discourse of ethnic comparison in
which they participate. Thucydides digresses from his historical narrative
to describe the Odrysian *archē* with which Athens had dealings in 429/8
(2.96–101), and to include some comparative ethnography of his own:

For it is the greatest kingdom (βασιλεία) of those in Europe between the Ionian
Gulf and the Black Sea in revenue (χρημάτων προσόδῳ) and in other good
fortune (τῇ ἄλλῃ εὐδαιμονίᾳ), but in their battle strength and size of their army
they are much the second (πολὺ δευτέρα) to the kingdom of the Scythians. It is not
just that it is impossible for the nations of Europe to match strength against it, but
even in Asia, nation (ἔθνος) against nation, they would not be able to make a stand

[63] It must have been so important to refute this view that he risked making known forever what he
seems to have hoped to eradicate in the present; on this irony see Hornblower (1991) 288. The
strength of Thucydides' refutation might suggest the proponent is sooner Sophocles (enforced by
Aristophanes) than Hellanicus. And, unless one believes Thucydides' fiction that the text we have is
exactly contemporary with the events it describes, Sophocles' *Tereus* certainly predates Thucydides'
text, and its Thracian setting is precisely what so vexed Thucydides (likely a Sophoclean innovation:
Wilamowitz (1931) 52 n. 2; Parsons (1974) 46–50; Fitzpatrick (2001) 91; Zacharia (2001) 102). On
the influence of Sophocles' play see Ar. *Birds* with Dobrov (1993) esp. 214–15. For the abundance of
audience 'knowledge' about Thrace, see Asheri (1990) 133–4; for musing on the dynamics of Thracian
'knowledge' in the assembly, see Garland (1990) 85 n. 28, (1992) 113–14 and its comic portrayal in
Ar. *Ach.* 133–73.
[64] For Thucydides' general antipathy towards exploiting the significance of names in contrast to
Herodotus, see Hornblower (1996) 134–6.
[65] For recognition of the manifest political import of a play concerned with Athenian–Thracian relations
(albeit loosely defined), see Zacharia (2001). See also Marchant (1891) 163 and Rusten (1989) 133–
4. On ambivalence among Athenians about negotiations with Thrace to wage their war (against
Greeks) see Ar. *Ach.* 133–73.

against the Scythians if they all acted in concert (Σκύθαις ὁμογνωμονοῦσι πᾶσιν ἀντιστῆναι). But in terms of the other good counsel (εὐβουλία) and intelligence (ξύνεσις) about the things that enrich one's life they do not match up with other peoples. (2.97.5–6)

The similarities with Herodotus are striking. When Thucydides ranks the Thracians as second by far after the Scythians, commenting on the superlative strength of that latter group should they unite, it is hard not to perform our own comparison of Herodotus' own evaluation that Thracians are indeed second, but after the *Indians*,[66] and recognize a deeper similarity underlying their differing opinions about just which northern people would be superlative should they unite.[67] In contrast to Thucydides' objective style, Herodotus' κατὰ γνώμην τὴν ἐμήν ('in my judgement') makes explicit the contest of opinion in which the one he calls his *own* competes. Aristotle offers yet another view, demonstrating that even Greeks could be placed into the fray:

But the race of the Greeks, as they are geographically positioned in the middle, they share of both these qualities. For they are spirited and intelligent; and therefore they continue free, both being governed in the best fashion and able to rule all, if they could attain a single *politeia*. (*Politics* 1327b27–33)

These competing assertions point to contemporary contexts of ethnic comparison, revealing particular tropes of the discourse ('which people might be capable of ruling all?', 'what qualities, what circumstances, would make that (im)possible?'). But their juxtaposition likewise helps bring into relief the claim the Herodotean narrator marks as distinctly his. First, Aristotle's description of the Greeks in terms akin to Herodotus' Thracians may remind us now that the *Histories* begin to be dominated for the first time by Greeks of differing names but παραπλήσιοι νόμοι ('customs that are very nearly the same'), the potential superlative strength of the Thracians εἰ δὲ ὑπ' ἑνὸς ἄρχοιτο ἢ φρονέοι κατὰ τὠυτό ('if it should be ruled by one person, or it should become unanimous') could just as easily describe the Greeks of Herodotus Book 5, some of whom will in the course of the *Histories* for the most fleeting of moments think κατὰ τὠυτό. And it could just as easily describe his present-day audience. To describe Thracians in

---

[66] Cf. Hdt. 3.94 and 98. Why should Herodotus and Thucydides differ on this point? The answer is likely to lie in an Athenian perspective that preferred to elevate (however backhandedly) a people the Persians did not subsume to avoid the implications of elevating a people that the Persian empire possessed, an explanation perhaps confirmed by Ctesias' rare agreement with Herodotus (*FGrH* 688 F 45a2; cf. Asheri (1990) 137).

[67] The intertextuality with Hdt.'s πᾶσα εὐδαιμονίη (5.4.2) and εὐδαίμονες of the Thracians (5.8) is also worth noting.

terms evocative of Greeks parallels the effect described above of Herodotus'
choice to present first and more prominently the Thracians with the exceptional *nomoi*: there articulation of internal differences between Thracians
in the (temporary) absence of a Thracian norm (minimally described when
it does finally come) facilitated positive comparison with Greeks. It also
corresponds to the dynamic at play in the Perinthian *logos* where a specific
group of Thracians (Paeonians) might also be read as a specific group of
Greeks (Athenians).

One might also note, by comparison, that Herodotus' text does not
demonstrate the overt signs of the cultural supremacy of the Greeks implicit
in Thucydides, and flagrant in Aristotle.[68] In contrast to Thucydides'
negative appraisal of Scythian ξύνεσις περὶ τῶν παρόντων ἐς τὸν βίον
('intelligence about the things that enrich one's life'), Herodotus elsewhere
grants them superlative status precisely in what he calls the single matter
most important in human life (τῷ δὲ Σκυθικῷ γένεϊ ἓν μὲν τὸ μέγιστον
τῶν ἀνθρωπηίων πρηγμάτων σοφώτατα πάντων ἐξεύρηται τῶν ἡμεῖς
ἴδμεν, 'the Scythian race have come up with the cleverest solution – better
than any we know – to the single matter most important to human affairs'),
while rendering his negative evaluation as one that is confessedly subjective (τὰ μέντοι ἄλλα οὐκ ἄγαμαι, 'I don't however admire them in other
respects', 4.46).[69] Plutarch would call this Herodotus' 'philobarbarism' (the
result of his own συμβάλλεσθαι), but in the context of these chapters we
might choose (for the moment) to forgo our own conclusions and rather
flag such passages as an invitation for his audience to compare, an exercise in which Herodotus as narrator (unlike Thucydides and Aristotle) has
explicitly implicated himself, and one that operates within a contemporary
context where such ethnographic comparison is the currency.[70]

Beyond the shared mode of comparison in Thucydides' and Herodotus'
Thracian *logoi*, Thucydides' excursus on Thrace has more generally seemed
to demonstrate a distinctively 'Herodotean' quality.[71] This quality is seen

---

[68] Macan (1895) I.154 comments, 'Aristotle leaves no obscurity about the implicit moral.' See also
Croiset (1886) 457. In fact, on the surface at least the Perinthian *logos* shows Thracians outwitting
Greeks.

[69] See Henderson, Ch. 12 below, n. 20.

[70] The constraints of space force me to leave out the important dimension provided by the Hippocratic
writers. On Herodotus' polemical stance against several of their theses, see Thomas (2000).

[71] See Hornblower (1991, 1997²) 372 on for instance ἀνὴρ εὔζωνος ('a man travelling light'): a
'Herodotean' expression found in Thucydides only in 2.97.1–2. As Hornblower (2004) 310 now
recognizes, the term need not be distinctly 'Herodotean', but rather ethnographic. See also Marchant
(1891) 234 (*ad* 2.97.1) for Thucydides' omission of the article with the name of a river when ποταμός
is inserted, a practice common in Herodotus but attested in Attic outside Thucydides only a single
time (Isocr. 7.80).

to reside in the digressive detail of the passage: 'In this section the amount of information Thuc. gives perhaps goes a little beyond the needs of the narrative . . . nor is by any means all of the detail, valuable though it is to us, essential for the understanding of later episodes. These chapters are a shining exception to the rule that there is little ethnography in Thuc. for its own sake.'[72] More startling is that on Thrace Thucydides actually emerges as more 'Herodotean' than even Herodotus: his extensive list of tribe names and topography reveals Herodotus' excursus by comparison to be highly selective, idiosyncratic and disproportionately brief – Herodotus for instance provides few names here.[73] A biographical explanation would suggest that Thucydides is elaborating on a gap left by his predecessor,[74] exploiting his audience's knowledge that he, Thucydides (unlike, for instance, a Herodotus), should *know* about Thrace.[75] Such a point is valid as far as it goes, but more may be had by looking beyond the narrow model of allusion, to the ethnographic genre and discourse presupposed by the two Thracian excursuses.

Herodotus and Thucydides on Thrace presuppose a discourse in which their ethnographies of Thrace participate, that of politics, or what, in the spirit of our Herodotus chapters, we might call relative κράτος. The details Thucydides chooses to focus on in his Thracian *logos* speak volumes: the extent of Sitalces' *archē* (2.96.1, 96.3), the amount of *phoros* (2.97.3) and the particular Thracian *nomos* of taking that resulted in its strength (ὥστε ἐπὶ μέγα ἡ βασιλεία ἦλθεν ἰσχύος), rendering it 'greatest' (μεγίστη) in πρόσοδος χρημάτων and ἄλλη εὐδαιμονία. If Herodotus' Thracian ethnography ended up seeming uncannily Greek, Thucydides' presents his Thracians in terms no less Greek, if not also specifically Athenian. His account reflects Athenian standards of evaluation *and* his own conception of historical causation, the importance of πρόσοδοι, χρήματα and the securing thereof (cf. 1.19; and πρόσοδοι 1.4, 1.13):[76] this is what Thucydides thinks is important for his audience to know, and is no doubt in part a function of knowing his audience all too well. Thucydides demonstrates the degree to which the ethnographic 'other' emerges as a version of oneself, a function of the very *language* which one uses to describe them. The Thucydidean treatment of Thrace offers its (Athenian) audiences a host of its own (largely flattering)

---

[72] Hornblower (1991) 371.
[73] See Asheri (1990) esp. 135 and 162. Herodotus does eventually provide the names of 23 tribes, but his choice to integrate them so diffusely into the narrative is significant. See Nenci (1994) 158.
[74] Even if this is in some sense true, the filling of a gap may not be a simply academic exercise.
[75] On this view see Westlake (1969) 15; see also Hornblower (1996) 22–3 quoting 4.103.5 and 5.11.1.
[76] See Kallet-Marx (1993).

implications. The first stresses difference: though the Odrysians possess, like Athens, *archē*, they were also markedly inferior: Thucydides/Athens supplies the standard of measure, *phoros*, and theirs was only 400 talents. The second lies in their similarity: in demonstrating something universal about the drive to possess *archē*, Thracian *archē* justifies Athenian *archē*, not barbarian (as some Greek critics of Athens may assert), but rather human.

But this Thucydidean ethnography not only demonstrates how the perspective and values of the viewer and audience are embedded in the ethnographic exercise; it points also to a source of the ethnographic impulse: Thucydides waxes ethnographic precisely in those contexts in which he treats subjects of Athenian imperial interest, Thrace and Sicily. Such material was no doubt topical for his narrative,[77] but this does not entirely account for the extent of his detail. Here one might turn to the affective quality of ethnography, its capacity to stoke an audience's interest in what is far away: interest in and desire for all that is offered by distant lands spiral out of control as cause becomes effect, effect cause, particularly when the desire for knowledge of faraway places is met by the capacity to acquire both the knowledge and the places. Herodotus demonstrates throughout his narrative that the desire for knowledge and the desire to possess are never far from one another for an imperial power.[78]

At the same time, Book 5 introduces another dynamic surrounding ethnographic knowledge: its use to further particular aims. Both Hecataeus and Aristagoras demonstrate in their own ways the fact that agenda may lie behind the promulgation of such knowledge. Hecataeus *may* originally have catalogued peoples and places for their own sake, but Herodotus casts him as performing this knowledge ('cataloguing – καταλέγων – all the tribes which Darius ruled and the strength (δύναμιν) of him', 5.36.2) for anything but disinterested reasons. Furthermore, this knowledge, once constituted as such, gains through writing an independence from its creator and becomes available for appropriation by others, not least as a means of persuasion to pursue their own ends. When Aristagoras describes the Persian *nomoi* and their extensive sources of wealth (5.49 and 97), the subtext is clear: they are rich and weak. It is significant that Herodotus explicitly notes – not leaving it to inference – just how well this kind of ethnography goes down in the context of the Athenian assembly.[79] Thucydides' ethnographies of

---

[77] Interweaving ethnography with history, presenting ethnographic information at historically salient moments, is of course Herodotean, but, if distinctly so, Thucydides' use of this convention in relation to Athens would place her in a very Persian light.

[78] See Osborne, p. 93 below, on Darius' curiosity; cf. 3.17–23 and 4.44 with Christ (1994).

[79] On this *logos* see Pelling, Ch. 7 below.

Thrace and Sicily are often considered as motivated by a desire to fill in what Herodotus has left out, but from a Herodotean perspective it may be that Thucydides' text indulges certain audiences, purveying those ethnographies of interest to contemporary Athenian imperial ambitions which were no doubt at home in the assembly; by contrast, the ethnographies that Herodotus provides, those of Egypt, India and Scythia, were safely in another league.

Here one might therefore challenge the notion expressed above of Thucydides providing 'ethnography for ethnography's sake', and wonder whether this noble fiction was any more possible in the late fifth century than now. Thucydides' Thracian ethnography serves important functions in his text: while the opportunities and events he describes may have passed by the time of his narration, his detailed narrative can re-create the moment when such material was current and eagerly consumed by audiences because of the promise of conquest that it seemed to offer. The interest in Thrace that his narrative generates in its audience serves an important explanatory function: if such ethnography succeeds in enamouring its reading audience of distant lands (and their subjection), it thereby furnishes an implicit historical explanation/justification for the events which transpired, explaining why it was entirely reasonable for the Athenians to pursue the relationship they did with the Odrysians, and ultimately why it was no reflection on them that this policy yielded no advantage to them (2.101.6).[80]

Thucydides' handling of the Odrysians is, however, telling of greater tensions. He employs the comparative discourse to distinguish Odrysians in three distinctive ways: from other Thracians by virtue of their greater strength, size and wealth; from Persians by virtue of differing *nomoi* with respect to taking and giving; and from the Scythians, next to whom they are πολὺ δευτέρα ('a clear second'). The first distinction serves as an implicit answer to the question of what could have induced Athens to have had dealings with Thracians given their past experiences (Drabescus) and in face of his audiences' historical hindsight: on the one hand, their wealth made them desirable allies, and, on the other, not all Thracians are the same.[81] The final distinction – against the numerous and warlike Scythians – might allay fears by dwarfing the Odrysian kingdom, implying that although powerful, it was nevertheless no threat, certainly not the one that was feared by Athens' enemies (2.101.2–4). At the same time, and more cynically, the

---

[80] The emphasis would be that the machinations of Seuthes were to blame, *not* Sitalces, with whom the Athenians had their relationship.

[81] This differentiation implicitly invites an audience to bracket the events at Drabescus (Th. 1.100.3) and the slaughter at Mycalessus (7.29).

richness of the ethnographic detail so overwhelming and distracting has an amazing capacity to obscure otherwise more obvious motivations behind the provision of such lavish narration.[82]

The second distinction of these Thracians – from Persia – is more sophisticated in its aims. If both Herodotus' and Thucydides' Thracian ethnographies consist in contrasting exceptional Thracians against the collective *ethnos*, they also share in providing a minimal treatment of *nomoi* common to all Thracians. Herodotus has been discussed above, but for Thucydides the single shared *nomos* is that of taking rather than giving, which he emphasizes twice and compares, irrelevantly, to the opposite *nomos* of the Persians, apparently a case of ethnographical detail for its own sake:

κατεστήσαντο γὰρ τοὐναντίον τῆς Περσῶν βασιλείας τὸν νόμον, ὄντα μὲν καὶ τοῖς ἄλλοις Θρᾳξί, λαμβάνειν μᾶλλον ἢ διδόναι (καὶ αἴσχιον ἦν αἰτηθέντα μὴ δοῦναι ἢ αἰτήσαντα μὴ τυχεῖν), ὅμως δὲ κατὰ τὸ δύνασθαι ἐπὶ πλέον αὐτῷ ἐχρήσαντο· οὐ γὰρ ἦν πρᾶξαι οὐδὲν μὴ διδόντα δῶρα. ὥστε ἐπὶ μέγα ἡ βασιλεία ἦλθεν ἰσχύος.

For they have established for themselves a custom that is the opposite of that of the Persian monarchy, a custom that also exists for other Thracians, namely to take, rather than to give (indeed it was more shameful for a person asked not to give, than for one asking not to receive what he asked for), but nevertheless the Odrysians practised this custom more extensively in accord with their capacity to do so – for it was impossible to get anything done if one wasn't prepared to give gifts. Consequently their kingdom reached a position of strength.

Is this ethnography for its own sake? Irrelevant for elucidating Thracian practice, the inclusion of this Persian custom does serve other purposes. First, it conveys a dual message: namely that (in) dealing with Thracians (it) is *not* like (Athens was) dealing with the Persian *basileia*. Second, in adopting the comparativist manoeuvre, Thucydides implicitly asserts his expertise in making this claim – *he* is in the position to compare – and such expertise will facilitate the persuasiveness of his account. Third, the focus on the Thracian custom itself, of *taking*, is significant. The logic of Thucydides' argument is somewhat awkward here: in a context that will ultimately differentiate Odrysians as superlative among the other Thracians, he invokes as explanation – almost oxymoronically – a *common* practice (τὸν νόμον, ὄντα μὲν καὶ τοῖς ἄλλοις Θρᾳξι, λαμβάνειν μᾶλλον ἢ διδόναι, 'the custom existing also among other Thracians of taking rather than giving', 2.97.4), which in turn he is then forced to qualify in order to

---

[82] E.g. Thucydides' 'irrelevant' comparison of the *nomos* of the Thracians with that of Persian monarchy (2.97.4). See below. For the label of 'irrelevant' see Westlake (1969).

explain how by using a custom common to Thracians Odrysians could attain a distinctive status (ὅμως δὲ κατὰ τὸ δύνασθαι ἐπὶ πλέον αὐτῷ ἐχρήσαντο· οὐ γὰρ ἦν πρᾶξαι οὐδὲν μὴ διδόντα δῶρα. ὥστε ἐπὶ μέγα ἡ βασιλεία ἦλθεν ἰσχύος, 'all the same they used the custom to a greater degree corresponding to their ability to do so. For it was impossible to get anywhere if one didn't give gifts. The result was that the kingdom attained great strength', 2.97.4–5). A question is of course begged as to whence their capacity to exploit the *nomos* so extensively arose; but, more importantly, as Thucydides makes the argument, *nomos* as such is insufficient to explain their superlative status: what emerges as more salient is their greater ability to practise it, κατὰ τὸ δύνασθαι ἐπὶ πλέον, their *dunamis*.[83] The γάρ clause separating the two claims interrupts the sequence of thought and makes less apparent a claim that may ungenerously be read as 'they became strong because they were able'.

But why not then leave aside the *nomos* and just simply say they were strongest? Why invoke *nomos* at all? The answer is twofold. Thucydides admits here, but only at the level of inference, what is indeed confirmed later, δῶρα passed from Athens to Sitalces (2.101.1): in apparently elaborating on ἐπὶ πλέον qualifying the previous sentence, the γάρ clause in fact tacitly admits to a certain relationship between Athens and the Odrysians. But how should that relationship be characterized? Thucydides is at pains to make it seem nonchalant: he claims later that the Athenians never had any expectations from Sitalces, though the use of negation in the statement may itself belie the claim (ἀπιστοῦντες αὐτὸν μὴ ἥξειν, 'placing no trust in the idea he would come' 2.101.1). Without Thucydides' invocation of *nomos*, and the framework that it provides of δῶρα, the relationship could easily be (and may have been) described as (and possibly was) payment for military service: monies passed from Athens to Sitalces for him to fulfil what Thucydides calls ὑποσχέσεις; and indeed if that was the relationship (with the aim being that understood by Athens' enemies, 2.101.4), then Athens was quite simply shafted, when in the end Sitalces fulfilled none of his promises and opted for a marriage deal with Macedon.

Thucydides' further elaboration of the Thracian custom would serve to diminish Athenian discomfort: καὶ αἴσχιον ἦν αἰτηθέντα μὴ δοῦναι ἢ αἰτήσαντα μὴ τυχεῖν ('indeed it was more shameful not to give if asked,

---

[83] Thucydides obscures the cause of their greatness, creating an ostentatious correlation with the *nomos* of gift-receipt, when the actual path of causation is *dunamis*. See Classen (1914) *ad loc.* 'infolge der grösseren Macht . . . übten sie um so mehr diese Erpressungen'; Shilleto (1880) *ad loc.* comments on the 'obscurity' of κατὰ τὸ δύνασθαι; for *dunamis* as a key concept in Thucydides see Kallet-Marx (1993) 3 with n. 6 and passim.

than, asking, not to meet with success') provides a way of seeing how Athens' avoided what was αἴσχιον in giving what they did as asked, and getting nothing in return for what they asked. The evocation of *nomos* allows Thucydides to control the framework through which Athens' negotiations with the Odrysians should be seen, that is as one of gift exchange (δῶρα 2.101.1, their *nomos*) rather than payment;[84] and indeed by the time Thucydides explicitly admits to this transaction, his audience has already been primed to accept it in his ('Thracian') terms. *A fortiori* it becomes preposterous to subscribe to the *logos* of Athens' enemies regarding Athens' intentions in 'giving gifts' to the Odrysians (2.101.4; but cf. *Ach.* 159–60).[85] This interpretation of course must remain conjecture, but adopting as it does Thucydides' own more typical and cynical mode of analysis, an explanation emerges for just what is at stake in his adopting an anomalous style: ethnography becomes a means of masking (and perhaps flagging for select readers) events both unflattering to Athens, and ones that in occurring too soon might upset the grand narrative of Athenian degeneration over time of which Thucydides' overall account attempts to persuade. But there is a cost to his strategy for the reader: it involves inducing his readers to see the events not as Greeks would, but rather as Thracians do (*if* Thucydides' account of their *nomos* is to be believed), to see Athens' actions through the eyes of Thracian *nomos* rather than Greek.

Thracians and Athenians

Thucydides' use of Thracian *nomos* shares another feature with Herodotus' selection and presentation of Thracian *nomoi*, namely the configuration of Thracians in familiar terms. For if nothing can be done in Thrace without giving, the same may be said of Athens. Or so it is characterized by the Old Oligarch whose bias, however, configures the *nomos* in those very terms Thucydides avoids, χρήματα rather than δῶρα:[86]

But some say, 'If someone with money approaches the *boulē* or the demos, he gets his business done.' And I would agree with them that a lot can be accomplished in Athens with money (ἀπὸ χρημάτων), and even more could be accomplished,

---

[84] Cf. the μισθὸς δωρέη ('payment gift') of 5.23.1 with Greenwood, Ch. 4 below.

[85] Did the Athenians' fleet not arrive because they ἀπιστοῦντες μὴ ἥξειν, or did that rather reflect political tensions in Athens about this particular policy (an inference one might make from Aristophanes *Acharnians*, esp. 169–71)? Comedy may be a difficult historical source, but, unlike Thucydides, it was almost exactly contemporary with the events it parodies and aware that some 20,000 contemporary viewers would moderate and scrutinize its claims.

[86] [Xen.] *Ath. Pol.* 3.3; see Shilleto (1880) 330.

if even more people gave money (ἀργύριον). This, however, I know well, the city is not capable of completing the business of all those making demands, not even should someone offer to them any amount of money (χρυσίον καὶ ἀργύριον).

The Athenian sheen that Thucydides gives his Thracians through *nomos* is effective: it helps explain Athens' choice to negotiate with the superlative *archē* among them, while making dealing with *these* barbarians *not* the same as dealing with Persia. But the historians are not alone in collapsing Athenian and Thracian identity: the *Acharnians*, near-contemporary with the events Thucydides describes, performs this strategy in action in the assembly.

When Theorus reports to the assembly on his visit to the court of Sitalces (141–50), attempting to curry favour for the Thracian alliance, it is precisely in terms of shared *nomoi* that his claim is made:

> Τοῦτον μετὰ Σιτάλκους ἔπινον τὸν χρόνον.
> Καὶ δῆτα φιλαθήναιος ἦν ὑπερφυῶς
> ὑμῶν τ' ἐραστὴς ὡς ἀληθῶς, ὥστε καὶ
> ἐν τοῖσι τοίχοις ἔγραφ', «Ἀθηναῖοι καλοί».
> Ὁ δ' υἱός, ὃν Ἀθηναῖον ἐπεποιήμεθα,
> ἦρα φαγεῖν ἀλλᾶντας ἐξ Ἀπατουρίων,
> καὶ τὸν πατέρ' ἠντεβόλει βοηθεῖν τῇ πάτρᾳ·
> ὁ δ' ὤμοσε σπένδων βοηθήσειν ἔχων
> στρατιὰν τοσαύτην ὥστ' Ἀθηναίους ἐρεῖν·
> «Ὅσον τὸ χρῆμα παρνόπων προσέρχεται».

I was all this time drinking with Sitacles. Indeed he is exceedingly pro-Athenian, and a lover of you in the truest sense of the word: he writes on walls, 'Athenians are beautiful'. And his son, whom we have made Athenian, is longing to eat sausages from the Apatouria, and he beseeches his father to help his *father*land; and making an agreement he has sworn to help us having so big an army the Athenians will say, 'what a swarm of locusts is coming'.

The speaker's rhetoric configures the Thracian king in familiar terms designed to minimize the cultural differences between the Thracians and his audience (both intradiegetic, the assembly, and extradiegetic, the theatre): Theorus has been drinking with the king; he is described in the common currency of a political catchphrase φιλαθήναιος ὑπερφυῶς;[87] he is, in good Periclean terms, an ἐραστής of the Athenian collective (ὑμῶν),[88] a phrase whose connotations are played out with the addition of a sympotic, that is cultured Greek, practice of inscribing his beloved's name, Ἀθηναῖοι

---

[87] See Starkie (1909) *ad loc.*, Olson (2002) 117.
[88] Thuc. 2.43.1; cf. *Knights* 1341 and Plato, *Alc. I* 132a.

καλοί.[89] Meanwhile his son,[90] who was made an Athenian citizen, wishes to celebrate the Apatouria – a festival at which one is initiated into citizenship and one said by Herodotus to be definitive of Ionianism.[91]

The diminishing of cultural difference between Thracians and Greeks/Athenians is evocative of Herodotus' Thracian *logos*. But this scene has added resonance for Herodotus' Thracian *logos*: Aristophanes makes his assembly speaker employ etymologizing wordplay to tell how Sitalces' son begs his father (πατήρ) to help his fatherland (πάτρα).[92] The wordplay, both of the character and poet, runs even deeper: Aristophanes' Theorus may also exploit an etymology of Apatouria from ἁ-copulative and πατήρ.[93] At the same time, the poet portrays the Thracians as involved in the same game over the same word – Apatouria is the perfect festival because, as the scholiasts note, what the Thracians want is to deceive (ἀπατᾶν) the Athenians.[94] And of course, given that πάτρα for Sitalces' son is now one word that refers to two places, the statement is as difficult to interpret as the 'empire' of Croesus' oracle; and, in Book 5, Herodotus' Paeonia.

The scene is, to be sure, parody, but what it demonstrates, however exaggerated, are the strategies of persuasion in the assembly in relation to Thracians salient to Herodotus' Thracian *logoi*: emphasis on similarity of *nomoi* (5.3–8) *and* a rhetoric that exploits wordplay (5.1–2).[95] Dicaeopolis underscores the double-talk of this embassy by his comment, τοῦτο μέν

---

[89] The scholiast uses the language of *nomos* to explain this passage, saying it is ἴδιον ἐραστῶν ('specific to lovers') to inscribe the beloved's name; cf. *Wasps* 97–9. It is telling that the characterization of the Macedonians as Greek in subsequent chapters uses the correct practice of the symposium as the standard: 5.18–22 and Fearn, Ch. 3 below. Cf. Eur. *Cycl.* 503–95.

[90] The *scholia vetera* comment: '[The son] is said to be Teres. But some say he had the same name (ὁμώνυμος) as his father Sitalces who was an ally of the Athenians. Thucydides mentions him but ascribes to him a different name (ἄλλο ὄνομα) . . .' If Thucydides is to be believed, the scholium may be read as further demonstrating Athenian hellenizing reception of Sitalces by attributing to him the Greek practice of naming his son after his father; the fact that Sadocus was popularly called Teres would also explain why Thucydides would go to such lengths to separate this name (and the person who goes by it, rather than his grandfather) from the mythic Tereus; it would also lead one to appreciate the degree to which Thucydides dissembles in 2.29 and later, selectively acknowledges one popular misnomer of the father of Sitalces to the exclusion of his son.

[91] Hdt. 1.147.2 and Hall (1997) 39–40.

[92] Starkie (1909) 42 sees further humour in use of πάτρα as an old Ionic word. On ὡς ἀληθῶς as common to etymologicizing passages, see Woodhead (1928) Appendix.

[93] See Starkie (1909) 42 on the implication of this origin in Xen. *Hell.* 1.7.8.

[94] χαριέντως ὡς ἐξαπατωμένων τῶν Ἀθηναίων ('this is a really fine joke because the Athenians are being deceived'). On the currency of this folk etymology see Olson (2002) 118 quoting Hellanic. *FGrH* 4 F 125 and cf. Ephor. *FGrH* 70 F 22.

[95] On the extensive punning in this scene (beginning with Theognis and χιών) see Rennie (1909) 112–15 and Starkie (1909) 44 on Θρᾳκές and ἀποτεθρίακεν. On another note, lines 137–8 demonstrate the efficacy of topographical knowledge, such as the rivers of Thrace, in the assembly.

γ᾽ ἤδη σαφές ('This then will be clear'), in response to the apparently unequivocal, yet soon to be belied, claim that the Odomantians are the μαχιμώτατον Θρᾳκῶν ἔθνος ('most warlike people of the Thracians') – notice the superlative as a mark of ethnographic discourse.[96] Exactly how distinctive this characterization of the assembly is to the topic of Thrace, is unclear, but in the *Acharnians* at least such punning and emphasis on affinity are portrayed as markedly different from the previous encounter involving Persians, a difference which seems reflected in Thucydides' own attempt to contrast Thracian and Persian *nomoi*. And it seems too coincidental that such features should characterize each of these Thracian *logoi*, Herodotus', Thucydides' and Aristophanes': together they may well gesture towards a historical reality – the shape Thracian debates of the late 430s and 420s took – even if one or more of these authors should be deemed to have influenced the other(s).[97]

Herodotus and Thucydides and the meaning of second-best

Now we may return to Herodotus and the Herodotean Thucydides, and examine their apparent consensus on one point, that whichever ἔθνος may be superlative, the Thracians are the *clear* second. The agreement will prove deceptive, obscuring the dissimilarities lurking beneath the 'same' claim.[98] A lexical point should first be noted: in contrast, Thucydides never actually speaks of a Thracian *ethnos* as such; instead he slips between talking explicitly about the Odrysian *archē* or *basileia* (employing one or the other for their different connotations).[99] At the same time, an ambiguity exists in his evaluation of 'second-best' status: πολὺ δευτέρα – 'certainly second'

---

[96] The scholiast was not fooled: 'most warlike: this is a lie, because they are weak (ἀσθενῶν) or few'. Aristophanes, of course, will undermine that σαφές claim by bringing on the Thracians themselves and thereby staging the gap that exists between the claims of the discourse as it is mobilized in the assembly, and the actuality. He is, however, engaged in the 'same' activity as Theorus, that of representing Thracians before the gathered Athenians, albeit in another genre and to the opposite political end, but no less distorting: cf. Aristophanes' (mis)representation of Thracians as circumcised (Olson (2002) 121).

[97] Of course, more generally the *Acharnians*' intertextual, if not also allusive, relationship with the *Histories* has long been recognized, and for some forms a criterion for dating the *Histories*, though such a basis for dating fails to recognize that even if Aristophanes is alluding to Herodotus, this need not be to the written text in our possession. On models of publication, see Thomas (2000).

[98] See Gomme's futile efforts (1956) 245–6 to reconcile the accounts of Herodotus and Thucydides.

[99] The progression of his excursus seems linguistically to 'other' his subjects: first, Odrysians have an *archē* (in 2.96.3 and 2.97.1), then it becomes a *basileia* (2.97.4), and as such (the *nearest* feminine antecedent for μεγίστη, but less frequently used than *archē*) is compared to that [*sic*] of the Scythians (μετὰ τὴν Σκυθῶν, 2.97.5); then the Thracians drop away leaving the Scythians to become an *ethnos* (2.97.6).

or 'second by a mile'[100] – raises questions about what comparative frame is implied: πολὺ δευτέρα when compared to all those that come after, or πολὺ δευτέρα in comparison with the superlative? The wider context Thucydides supplies, the manifest superiority of the Scythians in war, seems to favour the latter, more disparaging reading, but this is at odds with more common usage: just what kind of second are the Thracians?[101] The tension between usage and context is quickly placed to the side by a description of the superlative Scythians, who, though admittedly unequalled in strength and number, are also unequalled in the degree to which they lack those qualities which could translate their strength and numbers into *kratos*; and ultimately, for Scythians to be superlative by any of the relative criteria that Thucydides allows them serves only to confirm the standard constituted by his own (Greek-reading, if not also Athenian) audience as absolute (e.g. ξύνεσις, εὐβουλία).

Herodotus' second place is not only less equivocal, but also, we will see, more so. Herodotus introduces the Thracian *ethnos* quite simply as 'biggest of all mankind, after the Indians' (Θρηίκων δὲ ἔθνος μέγιστόν ἐστι μετά γε Ἰνδοὺς πάντων ἀνθρώπων 3.1). In contrast to Thucydides' μεγίστη, little qualifies Herodotus' μέγιστον, not geography (τῶν γὰρ ἐν τῇ Εὐρώπῃ ὅσαι μεταξὺ τοῦ Ἰωνίου κόλπου καὶ τοῦ Εὐξείνου πόντου, 'of those who are in Europe between the Ionian gulf and the Black Sea') nor economics (χρημάτων προσόδῳ καὶ τῇ ἄλλῃ εὐδαιμονίᾳ, 'in revenue and in other kinds of prosperity'); or rather nothing qualifies the Thracians' second place short of all mankind (πάντων ἀνθρώπων). And even those in first place, the Indians, are likewise minimally described and similarly absolute. But more equivocal in that, albeit conditionally and subjectively assessed, Herodotus does admit the possibility that these second-place Thracians could become κράτιστον: εἰ δὲ ὑπ᾽ ἑνὸς ἄρχοιτο ἢ φρονέοι κατὰ τώυτό, ἄμαχόν τ᾽ ἂν εἴη καὶ πολλῷ κράτιστον πάντων ἐθνέων κατὰ γνώμην τὴν ἐμήν ('if it should be ruled by one or be unanimous, it would be unbeatable and have the most *kratos* of all races in my opinion'). And in becoming so, presumably they would trump Thucydides' Scythians both in strength *and* in having those other qualities the Scythians lack, for what else should superlative κράτος imply if not also εὐβουλία and ξύνεσις? If Thucydides introduces his Scythians to undermine the threat of the (πολὺ δευτέρα) *archē* of the Odrysians only to dismiss them as lacking those skills

[100] See Shilleto (1880) 330–1; the former view is Arnold's (1830), based on Soph. *OC* 1228. Most, however, opt for the latter interpretation.
[101] See Jebb (1885) 193 on the phrase, who however interprets Thucydides' usage to be the same as Sophocles'.

(possessed by Athenians in abundance) that would enable them to realize fully the potential of the unrivalled aspects of their *ethnos*, Herodotus' Thracian ethnography, by contrast, offers no such unambiguous security.

The passage is characterized by double-talk that is almost oracular: how will an audience read Herodotus' conditional utterance? Like Croesus they might hear in it precisely what they wish to hear: very definitely *only* potential (and inconceivable that it come about); or perhaps they might even go so far as dreaming of becoming the 'one' that might rule them. But the conditional alternative, εἰ δὲ ὑπ' ἑνὸς ἄρχοιτο ἢ φρονέοι κατὰ τὼυτό, in reality offers no such securities: the scenarios it entertains are not so terribly unlikely in the great expanse of time (whose force will be felt in 5.9), particularly if Thracians are in some important ways 'like' (some) Greeks, as one strand of Athenian imperial rhetoric represented in Aristophanes and by Thucydides seems to reflect: after all the Greeks did in the Persian Wars roughly (albeit briefly) 'think the same way', and Athens with her *archē* is now 'the one' by which other Greeks are ruled (and compelled to think the same way), the latter a situation that Herodotus' narrative renders particularly amazing, given that her inauspicious earlier 'silliness' (Hdt. 1.60) gave no sign of her future ξύνεσις. The passage must be seen as extremely provocative, granting the possibility of this absolute superlative status to *Thracians*, hampered only by what hampers Greeks: for if both could attain like-mindedness or be ruled by one, just who would become second-best?

The ambiguities become more apparent in the irregular syntax that concludes Herodotus' evaluation: ἀλλὰ γὰρ τοῦτο ἄπορόν σφι καὶ ἀμήχανον μή κοτε ἐγγένηται· εἰσὶ δὴ κατὰ τοῦτο ἀσθενέες. On the surface, the meaning that the context seems to require is something like this: 'But really this is impossible for them and inconceivable/impossible that it would ever happen; and indeed on account of this they are weak.' But on closer inspection, the apparently simple statement of impossibility may be seen to harbour deeper uncertainties about its claim. First of all, it is less than apparent that the subjectivity of Herodotus' previous claim (κατὰ γνώμην τὴν ἐμήν) ought also to be imported to this claim, an uncertainty that may allow a gap to emerge between the personally attested conditional possibility and the emphatic denial that may reflect only popular opinion.[102] Moreover, the future construction, optatives rather than indicatives, renders the scenarios he describes as possible rather than excluded out

---

[102] ἀλλὰ γάρ is no less ambiguous. In Herodotean usage (18 times) ἀλλὰ (οὐ) γάρ does not in itself compromise the validity of what has been previously expressed or described (1.147.1, 4.83.2, 9.27.4, 9.27.6), but merely indicates that other considerations (9.27.6), circumstances (2.120.5, 7.4.2,

of hand, leaving it up to the readers to supply their own belief as to its likelihood.[103]

More important is the construction in which Herodotus uses ἀμήχανον: had Herodotus used the standard construction, an infinitive dependent on ἀμήχανον,[104] any uncertainty would have vanished, the absolute claim of the impossibility of the proceeding conditional would stand, and the subjectivity of the narrator would vanish as surely as Thucydides' has in the analogous passage. But the clause μή κοτε ἐγγένηται deprives us of that security, and indeed of security in our very understanding of the language used: Herodotus' use of ἀμήχανον is the *single* appearance in all of Greek literature of such a clause dependent on ἀμήχανον; elsewhere ἀμήχανον never governs anything other than a complementary infinitive, a construction that admits little ambiguity.[105] Instead, the resulting expression may be simply construed in ways that on the level of connotation at least yield meanings at odds with one another: a strong assertion of impossibility, or a tacit admission of possibility, which expressly (syntactically) involves a stance of fear; or rather surfaces in and hereby belies the strength of the denial. The former is read by taking the approach of Stein in supplying an οὐ, presumably to be inferred from the alpha-privative, and reading in the utterance emphatic denial: 'Ein Attiker hätte gesagt τοῦτο οὐ μή ποτε αὐτοῖς ἐγγένηται,

---

9.113.2), or *other perspectives* (1.147.1, 4.83.2, 9.109.3, 9.113.2) may render the content of what has been previously expressed as in some way immaterial to the current situation (8.8.2, 9.27.4, 9.27.6, Athenian *praeteritio*), discussion or *audience* (4.83.2, 9.106), a state that may be only temporary (9.46.6). Moreover, the view expressed in the ἀλλὰ γάρ statement might be flawed, or less valid than that which it denies, representing a difference of opinion from the narrator: see 1.147.1 (with 146.1 μωρίη πολλὴ λέγειν), 6.124.1, 4.83.6.

[103] See Goodwin (1889) §455–6 on the future-less-vivid conditional. Cf. Pl. *La.* 200d for ἀλλὰ γάρ following the future-less-vivid conditional where Nicias clearly still entertains a hope that Socrates might teach his son, though we the readers know otherwise.

[104] Kühner-Gertz (1904) II.35d and 44.

[105] The fact that elsewhere Herodotus uses the common construction of ἀμήχανον plus the infinitive renders this passage all the more striking. It is, however, worth noting that, when Hdt. uses ἀμήχανον elsewhere (with the infinitive construction), he does so in contexts that compromise its certainty: both Croesus and Cyrus are mistaken about what is ἀμήχανον when the former tests the oracles with something he thinks is ἀμήχανον (1.48), and the latter attacks the Massagetae on the mistaken premise that whenever he drove his army 'it was impossible (ἀμήχανον) for that tribe (ἔθνος) to escape him' (1.205.1). By contrast, the final appearance occurs in a context that belongs to a different, more absolute, frame of reference, the human condition vis-à-vis the divine: ὅ τι δεῖ γένεσθαι ἐκ τοῦ θεοῦ, ἀμήχανον ἀποτρέψαι ἀνθρώπῳ ('what must needs happen from the god, it is impossible for a man to avert', 9.16.4). This usage is likely to reflect Herodotus' philosophy about the human condition that by its nature does not allow for such absolute assertions: neither more generally (5.9.3), nor for the individual human (1.32.4). The collocation of ἀπορ- and ἀμήχαν- is deserving of greater discussion than is possible here: it is interesting that in classical authors outside Herodotus the ontological status of what is asserted as such is often denied or in some other way belied by the wider context: see Thuc. 7.48.5, Hippocr. *Sacred Disease* 21, Xen. *Anab.* 2.5.25; cf. Dion. Hal. *Dem.* 51, Plut. *Mor.* 165d3.

'dahin werden sie gewiss niemals kommen.'[106] The second is to assimilate the μή clause into a final clause introduced by ἀμήχανον as if this adjective functions as an expression of fear or caution,[107] and the fear-inducing premise (i.e. the Thracians becoming κράτιστον) leading then to the expression of the situation feared even as it appears to be excluded.

Herein lies the dichotomy: a syntactical construction that denies easy classification. Readers must choose what they will hear in these words: will it be emphatic denial, a process of attraction to οὐ μή, a choice which implicitly suggests the self-satisfied security offered by Thucydides' characterization of the second-place Thracians; or will latent fear be detected as motivating the assertion that for the Thracians to attain superlative κράτος is ἀμήχανον, its very obliqueness of expression giving voice to the fear that the words seem on surface to deny – in a sense, a 'lurking fear clause' that articulates lurking fear?[108] That all depends: Attic listeners would be confronted with a choice (if subconscious). They might hear emphatic denial, and that would reveal something about them, their evaluations of the Thracians; and these perhaps would be the same people who might have entertained the possibility that their own *archē* might one day be the 'one' to rule the Thracian ἔθνος. But without the οὐ the syntax might induce other responses. What if the Thracian ἔθνος did become united in thought, what if one entity did rule them? Like an oracle, Herodotus' utterance will interpret its interpreter.[109]

---

[106] Stein (1874) 6. Cf. Stahl (1907) 367 §2, Smyth (1956) §1804, Goodwin (1889) §295–6; this might be justified by seeing the negation in ἀμήχανον as adopting the function of οὐ, but again this unparalleled use of ἀμήχηνον would imply the reader's choice (conscious or otherwise) in this construal.

[107] Classified as such by Cooper and Krüger (2002) 2435 (§2.54.8.9A); cf. Hdt. 7.157.2. On this construction see, for instance, Goodwin (1889) §307–9, Smyth (1920) §2222 and §2224, Kühner-Gertz, 553b.

[108] Asheri (1990) 137 sees Herodotus here as 'significantly troubled by the huge number of the people and its potential might'. The passage *is* constructed to be significantly troubling, but its tone need not reflect Herodotus' state of mind, so much as his attempt to elicit that response in his readers.

[109] It is worth noting that on traditional understandings of Attic οὐ μή some apprehension is already implicit, though assuredly emphatically denied, whether one sees it as deriving from an elision (cf. οὐχι δέος μή σε φιλήσῃ, Ar. *Eccl.* 650; Xen. *Mem.* 2.1.25) or as a negative form of the independent subjunctive with μή, which had come already to express apprehension with a desire to avert its object; see Goodwin (1889) Appendix II. Thucydides suggests contemporary salience for Herodotus' play with the syntax of fear. By using the rare construction of the infinitive with φοβοῦμαι (5.105.3), his Athenians demonstrate their total absence of fear by the absence of a traditional fear clause (οὐ φοβούμεθα ἐλασσώσεσθαι (see Goodwin (1889) §372): to replace the independent clause with an infinitive is the logical corollary of the denial of the existence of any fear. The unconventional syntax gives the statement a particular irony: it asserts that the basis of Athenian fearlessness is the adherence to *nomos* with respect to the gods at that very moment when they are defying those conventions – both moral and *linguistic* – that pertain to humans; and here the genre in which this formulation occurs, the dialogue (5.85), is significant.

The text provides one final chance for an audience to consider the basis of the security of this denial: εἰσι δὴ κατὰ τοῦτο ἀσθενέες, 'Indeed *for this reason* they are weak.' But what is that reason? It is, in fact, the conditional expression whose impossibility has been by no means unequivocally demonstrated, an impossibility due as much to an incapacity of the Thracians (ἄπορόν σφι) as to that of an audience for whom it may be ἀμήχανον to contemplate the alternative – for *this* reason they are weak. If Herodotus' conditional functioned as an oracle, ambiguously offering potential, what potential will its audience hear? Will they be enamoured of the possibility of being the 'one' (ὑπ' ἑνός) and of exercising *archē* over those who could have had superlative κράτος, or will they instead hear a warning and correspondingly feel fear that if the Thracians should 'think the same' the superlative κράτος would be the Thracians' to wield, one that might be like that which had once already been wielded against them when indeed the Thracians did seem to have the same opinion: 'They were destroyed in Edonian Drabescus by the Thracians *en masse* for whom the colonizing of this land was an act of hostility' (ὑπὸ τῶν Θρᾳκῶν ξυμπάντων οἷς πολέμιον ἦν τὸ χωρίον κτιζόμενον, Thuc. 1.100.3)? But perhaps such scenarios are all too much to contemplate; much more comfortable to stick with beliefs in one's own cultural supremacy, regardless of what history may have already demonstrated by the time one reads this text, if not yet fully apparent at the time of its publication in the form we now have.[110]

Macan laconically comments on chs. 3–8, 'For the Greeks, esp. Athenians of the Periclean age, the interest in Thrace and its inhabitants was doubtless augmented by the fresh settlements there (cf. 9.75)'. This is no doubt true, but the question is just what Herodotus' text is doing with that interest. Herodotus may himself be tantalizing his audience when in just a few chapters he refers to boundaries of Macedonia that correspond anachronistically to those of his own time, refering to the mines 'which in later times than these yielded Alexander a talent of silver every day' (5.17.2), or when he describes the desirability of Myrcinus and the threat of it falling in Greek hands (5.23.2).[111] But if Thucydides indulges his audiences' (past? current? future?) imperial ambitions with his ethnography, Herodotus denies them such indulgences, saving his extended ethnographies (Egypt, Scythia, India) for what they are with certainty (from his vantage point at least) never likely to possess. And there is a darker

[110] Of course, it must be noted that fearful connotations of Thracian strength at the start of Book 5 are met by a realization at its end with an event unpleasantly reminiscent for some audiences: the death of Aristagoras at the hands of Thracians in Myrcinus (5.126).
[111] See Osborne, Fearn and Greenwood, Chs. 2, 3 and 4 below. Cf. [Xen.] *Ath. Pol.* 2.11.

element to his Thracian *logos*,[112] one in direct conflict with the apparent security and vision of the past offered by Thucydides' own Thracian *logos* and the narrow temporal confines of Thucydidean history.

CONCLUSION: BEYOND THE ISTER, AND BACK TO THE NARRATIVE, THE MEANING(S) OF SIGYNNAE – 5.9–10

But if such lurking fears and ὑπόνοιαι are not to overwhelm the narrative, and make it obviously other than it seems on the surface, some ethnographic wandering is badly needed; this time, all the way beyond the Ister. Relief comes in the simplicity of the lack of knowledge, lack of people: an ἔρημος χώρη and ἄπειρος ('empty land', 'boundless'); a single people, a single name; their culturally different, but nevertheless easily visualized clothing (Median); short, shaggy, flat-nosed horses, which no man can ride, but which are paradoxically swiftest (ὀξύτατοι – the ethnographic superlative); an implicit urbane irony of geography that these funny ponies are neighbours of the Adriatic Eneti (famous for their horses);[113] a comfortable lack of rigour when it comes to interrogating colonial claims – a polite use of aphorism worthy of Sophocles, 'anything can happen given some time'; a name, Sigynnae, that seems to mean all too much, but only by comparison, and therefore apparently not much in absolute terms right here; and a demonstration at the Thracians' expense of what is οἰκότα – the *presence* of bees does not, as Thracians maintain, explain why this area is uninhabited, but rather it is their *absence* that *points* to the explanation – it's too cold![114] From here – a quick visit – an audience may happily resume the historical narrative that will constitute Book 5.

The ethnography that Herodotus' narrative claims expertise of even as – or because – Herodotus paradoxically stresses its limits, reaches its limits

---

[112] One he reminds his audience of with the prominence of Sophanes, 6.92 and 9.73–5; and of course the last dated event of the *Histories* takes place in Thrace: 7.133, 137.

[113] Herodotus significantly stipulates 'Adriatic' Eneti because there are *two* peoples that have the *same* name: according to Homer there are Eneti also located in Paphlagonia in north-west Asia Minor (*Il.* 2.852): Myres (1907) 258. On the Adriatic Eneti and their horses see already Alcm. 1.51; urbane cultural knowledge here parallels that of 5.1.2–3 (see above n. 10), and together provides a structure: Greek cultural knowledge frames the Thracian excursus.

[114] Herodotus is punster to the end: ἐμοὶ μέν νυν ταῦτα λέγοντες δοκέουσι λέγειν οὐκ οἰκότα ... ἀλλά μοι τὰ ὑπὸ τὴν ἄρκτον ἀοίκητα δοκέει εἶναι διὰ τὰ ψύχεα ('In my opinion when they say these things they are not saying what is plausible . . . but to me the area above the Bear is uninhabited because of the cold'); note the exchange of οὐκ for the α-privative. But he makes a more serious point, demonstrating how such rhetorical finesse aids the persuasiveness of an εἰκός argument, while undermining the opposing view by locating it in the realm of speech (λέγοντες . . . λέγειν) not 'reality' (εἶναι), and by moving from the personal to the impersonal use of δοκεῖν.

with a natural boundary,[115] supplying what an audience experience as so 'natural' a transition as for them not to dwell upon what the presence of these apparently (or at least relatively) meaningless Sigynnae might mean. If, however, they do, two dimensions are revealed that speak to the ensuing narrative of Book 5 and to contemporary politics. The first relates to the Sigynnae's claim to be colonists of the Medes. Herodotus describes these Sigynnae's clothing as Median and cites their claim to be Median colonists. Herodotus, however, refrains from using the clothing as evidence for the claim, instead throwing up his hands by evoking the explanatory power of time as rendering anything possible. An audience may well passively choose to go no further in their enquiry, and see the inclusion of these details as ethnography for ethnography's sake. But the course of Book 5 will bring these issues closer to home, when the Athenian change from Dorian to Ionian garb in 5.87.3–90 might induce a realization about the instability of clothing as an indicator of ethnicity (rather than evidence of it), and when the claim to be colonists finds itself mobilized in the rhetoric of an Aristagoras desperate for an alliance (5.97.2).[116] The truism, 'anything can happen in the course of time', masks ambiguity: while ostensibly facilitating 'understanding' about the past (i.e. Sigynnae could have settled beyond the Ister from Media),[117] its gnomic quality allows it to look forward as well as backwards, transcending specific application to a particular past event to encompass such events as may lie in the future. And what may take place is likewise ambiguous, not necessarily limited to surprising colonial ventures (*erga*), but rather stretching also to surprising *claims* (*logoi*) about colonial status. How these Sigynnae became (γεγόνασι) Median colonists Herodotus cannot say: was it an act of history or an act of political rhetoric? Anything can happen given enough time, as Book 5 and perhaps Aristagoras' rhetoric – will soon show.[118]

There is a final twist in this Median tale: the most comprehensive scholarly accounts of these elusive Sigynnae see their claim of descent reported here as the product of paronomasia, a 'mistaken' inference from the name of a tribe attested in this region, the Maedi, and their clothing, broadly

---

[115] Limits: μούνους δὲ δύναμαι πυθέσθαι ('I am able to learn of only these', 5.9.1); ἐγὼ μὲν οὐκ ἔχω ἐπιφράσασθαι ('I am not able to guess', 5.9.3). Note the prevalence of his 'I' here and its relation to Thracian sources.

[116] See Macan (1895) I.246.

[117] This is how Myres (1907) 260 takes it, and then demonstrates how Assyrian records of the Medes show that (past) time renders it impossible: 'Herodotus is inclined [*sic*] to admit a Median origin, only if time will allow it. But this is precisely what time will not allow . . .'

[118] See Introduction, p. 33.

similar to that of the Medes.[119] The question then arises, whose mistake is this? In a passage rife with wordplay, we should not conclude too quickly that the mistake is Herodotus' or that he reports the mistake of others unawares. Given its context, we might recognize rather how Herodotus has created a narrative with the potential to entrap an audience carried along by its ethnographic stance – its claim to expertise – to accept a persuasive narrative, predicated on an implicit case of paronomasia and a visual referent of apparently the 'same' clothing, and to be induced to make the same easy conclusion (συμβάλλεσθαι) that the Sigynnae are insinuated to have made, descent as demonstrated by clothing.

But that leaves it to ask the meaning(s) of the name, Sigynnae. Aristotle's use of σίγυνον as the paradigmatic loan word, proof that a word can be 'ordinary' and 'rare' but not in relation to the same people, does more than suggest the currency of this word in Greek linguistic theorizing.[120] It may also point to Herodotean engagement with such theory. That Aristotle's account omits the Ligurian word (and indeed the Sigynnae) could be significant: had it too belonged to the stock *exempla* in linguistic theory, Ligurian *sigynnae* would have further proved Aristotle's point; its absence in his account might suggest Herodotean innovation on a *trope* (independent of whether this word with this meaning had actually belonged to the region above Massalia). This cannot of course be proved. Instead, we may move to safer ground and remember the injunction that words have their meanings in context, and that context may be defined as not only geographical, but textual. What, then, would the 'meanings' of Sigynnae be in the context of Herodotus' *Histories*, and in the context of his contemporary audiences?

If one fails to pause and reflect, Herodotus' furnishing of multiple meanings functions as a display of erudition – dazzling, but otherwise meaningless, though whether one notices and what one's reaction to it will be if one

---

[119] Myres (1907) 260: 'the *Maedi* (Μαιδοί) in Western Thrace, who may have been kinsmen of the Sigynnae, and may well have been confused, in local speech, with the *Medi* whose name would suggest itself at once to Greek observers, to account for the Sigynnae trousers'. See also Macan (1895) I.157. Thuc. 2.98.2 shows Greek knowledge of the Maedi. As for the Sigynnae, Ctesias locates a *Sigynni* in Egypt, *FGrH* 688 F 55, and is followed by Herodian and Steph. Byz. *s.v.* Sigynnos. Only Apollonius seems to follow Herodotus when he links Sigynni with Thracians (4.320), likewise revelling in the rare *sigynnoi* for spears (2.99). On the Sigynnae see Myres' article (1907), 'yet to be surpassed' according to the more recent Barrett (1979). There is a lovely irony that Herodotus' mysteriously named Sigynnae have generated their own onomastic folklore in the erroneous attempts to connect them with gypsies (Germ. *Zigeuner*, Hung. *cigany*): see Barrett's survey (1979).

[120] *Poetics* 21. See pp. 59–60 above. The spelling and gender of this rare noun (and its meaning) vary in its few appearances in the ancient sources. Herodotus alone gives σιγύνναι, otherwise it is overwhelmingly masculine, with a single or double *nu*.

should, will be a matter of ability and/or taste.[121] If, however, one engages more closely with the apparent randomness of the facts Herodotus seems interested to espouse, one might recognize what is reflected in the two meanings of this word, shopkeepers or spears. The two lifestyles reflected in this single word tap into a *topos* of the *Histories*, the contrast between 'soft' and 'hard' lifestyles, introduced in Book 1 when Croesus advises Cyrus to take the Lydians' weapons and make them shopkeepers (1.155.4), and implicit in the comparison of the warlike Great King, Cyrus, with his successor, Darius (3.89.3). In either of those cases, an implicit point is that cultures do not remain the same: 'hard' peoples become 'soft' over time. Here Herodotus allows the single word with different meanings in two different places at the same time to provide a spatial analogue for how at different times (and 'in the course of time') a single people in the same place may (come to) be characterized in two different ways.

But beyond the thematics of Herodotus' text, there is another context for understanding the function of this polysemous word in Herodotus' narrative, or rather a solution to how these multiple meanings may have proved more interesting to certain audiences than they have to modern readers; and this time the answer lies in socio-political linguistics. How indeed does a γλῶττα enter one language from another? And more particularly, why would Athenians of the fifth century have been familiar with the Cypriot word for spears? Why would (some) audiences' ears have pricked up at the word for traders beyond Marseilles? One *onoma*, also a *nomos*, furnishes an answer to all these questions: *archē*.[122]

The Paeonians (in the 'past'), the Thracians (of the ethnographic present), and the Sigynnae (far away) emerge as three different (Thracian) ways to talk about the same thing, contemporary Athens. And this they do in *logoi* that interweave three intellectual discourses, those of history, ethnography, and linguistic theory, and challenge an audience to contemplate the equivalences that may obtain across time, space and language, and between viewer and subject. How will the reading strategies of these first chapters apply to the rest of Book 5?

Such close examination will always raise the question of whether a text can have (had) so much meaning (for its contemporary audiences)? But perhaps the more salient question is this: will modern audiences let it? While it is unlikely the reading proposed here will persuade in each of its

---

[121] On the rhetoric of expertise, see Thomas (2000) Chs. 7–8.
[122] On Athenian efforts to gain Cyprus, see Meiggs (1972) 92–3, 477–86, and, Serghidou, pp. 272 and 285 below. On Athens' obsession with the wealth of the west see Aristoph. *Kn.* 173–6, *Wasps* 700; Plut. *Nic.* 12, *Per.* 20.3–4.

details, it is hoped that what it does persuade of is this, that any analysis of Herodotus' *logoi* would do well to take the advice of two of his most respectful readers: 'The difficulties in appreciating Herodotus lie not in his lack of organisation, but in an excess of relatedness . . . it is possible in one and the same story, for several different meanings to appear simultaneously or one after another', and 'there is little in Herodotus that is irrelevant.'[123]

[123] Immerwahr (1957) 312; Wood (1972) 19. Many thanks to the participants of the original Cambridge Colloquium, and the 'Anatomy of a Cultural Revolution' Seminar for commenting on versions of this paper; thanks also to Paul Cartledge, Pat Easterling, John Henderson, Rosaria Munson, Robin Osborne, Rob Tordoff for their helpful comments and corrections, and above all to Emily Greenwood, the ideal interlocutor.

CHAPTER 2

The Paeonians (5.11–16)

Robin Osborne

That a new *logos* begins at 5.11 is clear.[1] At 4.143–4 Darius left Megabazus in Thrace, reached Sestos and crossed the Hellespont. Megabazus went into action against those who did not medize. And then we moved to Libya. At 5.1 we rejoined Megabazus but not Darius. Now at 5.11 we rejoin Darius. There is no messing about here: in a familiar enough Herodotean technique, a new section begins with the name, no article, of the prime protagonist.[2] We know from this first word what we are in for: Darius resumes control. If the reader thought that Megabazus had been left to determine for himself the precise contours of a mission that was only generally defined and that Darius had no further personal interest west of the Hellespont, s/he is about to discover otherwise. If Darius has scurried off extremely fast (*tachista*) that is not so much to get out of it, as to get back into it, to pick up the reins of power.[3]

The opening chapters of Book 5 have highlighted a number of issues about power. A concern with the nature of power, with what makes one city powerful and another weak, with how and why cities and peoples that were once powerful cease to be powerful, and those who were not previously powerful become powerful, is central to the whole Herodotean endeavour, from the proem to the final sentence. The first four books have, in a sense, constituted a description of the contours of power within the Persian empire, and the final four books will describe how the power game played out when that empire came face to face with the Greek world. When Thucydides comes to make his assessment of power he will concentrate very heavily, from the 'archaeology' onwards, on resources.[4] Herodotus

---

[1] My reading here has been enriched by discussions with the editors, for whose invitation to participate in this project reading Herodotus Book 5 I am most grateful.

[2] Compare Nenci (1994) *ad loc.* 'tipica formula di transizione . . .'

[3] Compare Megabazus' haste to get to Sardis at 5.23: for the Persians, access to the nodes of power is urgently important.

[4] This has all been illuminatingly explored by Kallet (1993, 2001).

does not neglect those aspects of resources that can be counted – even if his own counting, as of the Persians themselves, cannot be trusted – but he repeatedly makes his readers aware both that resources take many different forms, and that questions of power cannot be reduced simply to questions of resources.

Herodotus has already re-alerted us to problems of assessing resources in the first chapters of Book 5. When the Perinthians and Paeonians make their first attempt (5.1.2–3) to settle who is best by the triple single combat, I take the man, horse, and dog to symbolize pitting the resources of one place against the resources of another. That is what all conflict does, and what better way to avoid squandering one's resources in conflict than to find some way independently to measure the competing resources? In an ideal world we would be able to identify the eventual victors of a war by knowing who had the greater resources. But what happens when the resources are pitted against each other in this triple competition is that we find that resources are not straightforwardly commensurable, and that if two sides have not agreed in advance on how the resources are to be compared the competition will be in vain. If two of the three Perinthian single combatants win, does that mean defeat for the Paeonians, or does it matter in which combats they are successful, and in which unsuccessful? The Paeonians defeat the Perinthians because they take superiority in numbers of victories not to be everything, and bring other signs (specifically oracular, in this case) into consideration.

But if numerical superiority is not everything in Herodotus it is certainly something: the Persians defeat the Perinthians by number (5.2.1). Nevertheless the Thracian numbers turn out not to count because the Thracians are not sufficiently united to mobilize those numbers (5.3.1). And here we meet a second aspect of power. To know whether a city or *ethnos* (5.3.1) is powerful or not we need to know not only the resources but also the *nomoi*.

At 5.11.1 Darius reaches the seat of delegated power, Sardis, and questions of power, its possession, exercise, and loss, become more complicated. They also become more personalized. They become more complicated because we re-enter a world of alliances and dependencies: how powerful a city, people, or person is may depend on who his friends are. But they also become more complicated because power, like friendship, is a two-way process: those over whom power is exercised are themselves in a position to affect the exercise of that power. Darius, immediately on his return, remembers, or is reminded of, some particular individuals to whom power has been delegated and whose decisions with regard to his own power have exercised power over him, Histiaeus and Coes. We have not met Coes since 4.97, when he advised Darius not to destroy his Danube bridge behind him and was promised by Darius a return in good deeds for his good advice (*sumboulië*). We have not met Histiaeus since 4.141 when, after he had pointed out to his fellow rulers that their power was entirely dependent on their relationship to Darius (4.137), he repaired the same bridge, enabled Darius' army to re-cross successfully, and earned for the Ionians a reputation among the Scythians whom he deceived as cowardly freemen and subservient slaves. Herodotus reminds us of all this when he tells us that Darius recalled Coes' advice and Histiaeus' benefaction to him. Darius will remain faithful to the end to his perception of Histiaeus as benefactor (6.30.2).

Darius sends for Histiaeus and Coes to come to him in Sardis and offers them the chance to choose (5.11.1). Moments of choice in Herodotus are never trivial, from the moment that the wife of Candaules offers a choice to Gyges (kill or be killed) (1.11.2) to the moment that Xerxes offers a choice to his brother Masistes (divorce your wife or . . .) at the end of Book 9 (9.111.2–5). With Cyrus' final apothegm that 'soft lands breed soft men' (9.122.3) Herodotus leaves his reader reflecting on the enormous implications of choices and of the difficulty of measuring up advantages and disadvantages. In this passage both choices turn out to be a source of trouble for the person choosing: they both get their *telos*.

Histiaeus, we are told, 'because he was tyrant of Miletus did not ask for any tyranny'. Why are we told this? Because power over others was the greatest gift to be had from a Persian king? Because it prepares us for Coes' choice? Or are we to remember Archilochus 19 and Charon the carpenter and think of all that a cultured man will put before tyranny? If we do think of Charon then Histiaeus' choice reveals how exclusively political his world has become. The man who knows all about bridges chooses to have a place on the other side of the unbridged Hellespont put in his power, a base in Europe, to complement (or is it potentially to replace?) his base in Asia. Histiaeus chooses 'Myrcinus the city of the (H)edonians' (5.11.2), a place between Amphipolis and Drabescus, a place which the Athenians lost to Brasidas in 424 BC (Th. 4.107.3).

In 5.124 to 126 Aristagoras will take refuge in Myrcinus when things get too hot for comfort in Ionia (only to be slaughtered by the Thracians), but we must not allow this to prevent us seeing how odd a choice of place this is for Histiaeus. This is the first that the modern reader, dependent on Herodotus, has heard of the Edonoi/Hedonoi, but it would not be the first that an ancient Athenian reader had heard of them. Obsession with securing a base among the Hedonians was something from which Athenians too suffered (Thuc. 1.100.3), and, as Herodotus himself will remind us at

9.75, what the Athenians were prepared to fight and die for was the gold mines.[5] Herodotus never offers a Histiaean justification; what we will get in 5.23 is Megabazus' interpretation of the choice.[6] That interpretation turns not simply on the mines (at 5.23 silver mines) and on timber suitable to build ships and make oars but on the resources of men, both Greek and barbarian. All these resourceful people need, Megabazus will suggest, is a leader. If Histiaeus is not searching for tyranny, the inhabitants of Myrcinus and the area around turn out, at least in Megabazus' view, to be searching for a leader. Put together the resources of Thrace and the leadership qualities – which are precisely what has drawn Histiaeus to Darius' attention – and Darius must expect trouble.

Coes offers a counterpoint to Histiaeus. If Histiaeus is a man who understands power as Herodotus understands it, as dependent upon resources and unity of purpose, Coes has a much more limited purview. Coes, Herodotus tells us, chose tyranny at his native city of Mytilene 'being a man of the people' (*dēmotēs*). The rarity of the word *dēmotēs* in Herodotus underlines the paradoxical force of this observation. Herodotus only otherwise uses *dēmotēs* of Amasis, king of Egypt, explaining at 2.172 that Amasis' having originally been a 'commoner' led the Egyptians at first to despise him. Coes, the implication here seems to be, only rates being a tyrant because he has not previously tasted power. He acts here as if the story Histiaeus tells the other tyrants at the Strymon bridge is the whole story: if you have the support of Darius you can be tyrant. Coes will soon discover that this is only part of the story. Being a tyrant will turn out to depend equally on pleasing that city. When the Ionian Revolt comes, Coes will be the one tyrant killed, stoned, by his people (5.38). Once we have appreciated Coes' limitations we can appreciate the wisdom of Histiaeus' choice. Not that it will bring him joy. But for now both Histiaeus and Coes have their wishes granted.

If we haven't guessed at this point that Coes' choice will be fatal, we are immediately given a strong hint to that effect. Darius' attention is at this point distracted. In a remarkable piece of storytelling technique Herodotus finishes one story and not only starts but also reveals the conclusion of his next story in the next sentence (5.12.1). Darius, in three successive words sees for himself, desires, orders. And as we know from the conclusion of the last story, Darius' orders are carried out. We have just had Histiaeus

[5] Herodotus' decision to comment at 9.114 on Persian behaviour when they learn the name of the place Ennea Hodoi is unlikely to be independent of that being the site of a later defeat for the Athenians. On the evocations of this later history, see Irwin, pp. 81–3 above.
[6] On 5.23 see further Greenwood, pp. 129–32 below.

and Coes remembered by Darius with the result that each of them gains a new power base, with Histiaeus adding Europe to Asia, Coes turning commonership into tyranny. Now provoking Darius' attention leads to the Paeonians being uprooted from Europe and transplanted to Asia. Darius causes not just individuals but whole peoples to change places.

Movement back and forth between Europe and Asia is very much put in the foreground in this story: far from being content to see Darius cross back to Asia, two Paeonians voluntarily follow him to Sardis, wanting to become tyrants over the Paeonians. What they want Darius to do for them is what Coes has got Darius to do for him. What they succeed in getting Darius to do is very much the mirror image of what Histiaeus has had done for him. Power, we are reminded, works both ways, and the exercise of power never loses its arbitrariness. Manuscripts do not agree on the form of the names Herodotus uses here: Pigres or Tigres or Tugres; Mastues or Masties or Mantues. Any which way, these do not seem to be speaking names, though they lend an air of specificity to a story with a familiar pattern. For the 'charming story' that follows is found also in Nikolaos where it concerns Thracians and Alyattes (*FGrH* 90 F 71). But what does it do for us here?

This is a story about men parading a woman who is a wonder for another man to see. The two Paeonians intend that the man who sees the woman should draw conclusions about the men to whom the woman belongs, and in particular about their power. No reader of Herodotus can miss this pattern, which starts with Candaules parading his naked wife for Gyges and continues through Peisistratus. Peisistratus parades Phye from Paeania, like this Paeonian woman described as *eueidēs*, before the Athenians and gets tyranny for it (1.60.4).[7] The Paeonian brothers try the same trick. But as Aristagoras will find, it is easier to fool 30,000 than one man (5.97.2; cf. 1.60.3). That it is not by chance that Paeonians, Athenians, tyranny, Aristagoras and Persian power are linked together by the resonances of this story emerges from the juxtaposition of Paeonians and Athenians that occurs when Aristagoras' visit to Athens at 5.97 is immediately followed by his sending a message to the Paeonians in 5.98, inviting them to take advantage of the Ionian Revolt in order to return home.[8]

The basic plot in the story at 5.12–13 turns out, however, to be rather different from the expectation that the opening of the narrative sets up. We

---

[7] Almost whenever Herodotus notes handsome appearance in the course of a narrative it turns out that there is trouble in the air for someone! Cf. e.g. 1.112.1, 3.1.3, 5.56.2, 6.32, 7.12.1; beauty may be noted in ethnographic descriptions without associated dire effects, cf. 1.196.2, 2.89.

[8] For Athenians and Paeonians cf. Irwin, pp. 50–6 above.

have the fine upstanding and good-looking sister, and we expect it to be her good looks that win the King over, so that the King's desire to possess the woman brings rewards for her family. But here it is not her beauty that is the focus of attention. For her beauty is supplemented by her industry, and the King, whom we have already met at 3.38 as the great observer of cultural difference, is amazed, and gets intrigued by the different *nomoi* of her people.[9] Making claims about the industry of the Paeonian women is, Herodotus tells us, the point of bringing the women to Darius' attention in the first place (5.13.3). Why that was supposed to lead to their tyranny is never spelt out, we are left ourselves to realize that if resources are an important source of power, that does not mean that those who have power will distribute it to those who have resources – very far from it.

Contrary to the expectations of the story motif, the beauty of the woman turns out in this case to be merely a means of attracting attention to her industry, and the woman turns out to be paraded not for her individual virtues but as a member of a class. And if the conclusion we expect for the individual outstanding woman is to be acquired by the viewing man (with positive or negative results for the man who sets up the viewing), we cannot be surprised if, when this woman is revealed as one of a class, Darius decides to acquire the lot. The desire of the Great King is not here for outstanding women but for outstanding habits: imperial powers collect peoples with different customs; the threat posed by difference can only be countered by domesticating it. The brothers turn out not to have learned the lesson from Histiaeus and Coes that tyranny comes from thinking the same, not thinking differently.

What is at issue with the Paeonians, however, is not simply their difference but their resources. The behaviour of the woman in wearing finery, filling waterpots, leading a horse, and spinning at the same time (that is, acquiring basic sustenance, maintaining the transport infrastructure, and manufacturing the clothes needed for survival) is explicitly identified as not Persian behaviour, not Lydian behaviour, and not the behaviour to be found in any part of Asia. They suggest a land whose resources are its people. They suggest indeed a land where what the land holds is of little moment: this is a people who could be anywhere. Where they are in fact, on their own description, is not just anywhere, but on the river Strymon and not far from the Hellespont, and they claim to be settled in cities (*poleis*). And the Strymon valley is actually a place whose resources are special. This emerges from what happens at the end of this story. Megabazus

---

[9] Nenci (1994) 171–2 is surely right to see here an echo of the *erga megala kai thōmasta* of the proem.

brings the Paeonians from Paeonia to Asia on Darius' written instructions, and immediately tells Darius (5.23) that he has been mad to give Myrcinus to Histiaeus since it has endless supplies of timber, metals and men. But that this is a place whose resources are special we have already had cause to note, for the (H)edonians too have led us to the Strymon, and at the Strymon we have met the Athenians. Like the Paeonians, Histiaeus will have to be moved out (*anaspastoi*, 5.12.1; *anaspastos*, 5.106.4). Imperialist powers cannot afford to overlook resourceful people or resourceful places.

The Paeonians are moved out, Herodotus twice repeats (5.14.1, 15.3), *ex etheōn* – from their native land but also from their habits. It will be habits as well as natural resources that end up defeating the Persians in Greece, and the Paeonians offer a foreshadowing of the Greeks. It will be the resources of the (Athenian) silver mines, and the number of ships and oars, that end up crucial to defeating the Persians: on that occasion getting people out of their native land proves to be not enough. Greeks win through because of the sort of people they are then found to be: *nomos* proves to be king in more senses than one. But I anticipate Herodotus' story.

In this story Megabazus invades, but not by the route the Paeonians expect. The Thermopylae trick of the path round the back is carried out on a large scale, cities are taken deserted of men, and when the cities are taken the people surrender (but we will meet them again, restored, at 8.115.3). These are a people who in the end do not trust in their own industry at all, who cannot survive without their cities – even though to surrender is to be deprived of them in any case. Herodotus spells out that once their cities are captured the Paeonians are unable to maintain their unity, but scatter (5.15.3). Whether when their cities are threatened a people can maintain their unity will turn out to be crucial not just in this instance but in the great narratives of the Ionian Revolt and Persian wars. The Paeonians introduce us to the dynamics of power within a people, not merely the dynamics of the power of individual rulers.

But not all the Paeonians are captured. There are some more who prove invulnerable. The Paeonians who resist capture are precisely the ones close to Mount Pangaeon (the mountain of the mines) and Lake Prasias, which the Barrington Atlas places on the Strymon river and less than five miles upstream (west) of Myrcinus. When Megabazus takes those Paeonians he has managed to get hold of to Darius, no wonder he complains about the prospect of having Histiaeus established in this place. Both the locals and other Greeks would come to feel the same about Athenian attempts to establish themselves in this area.

But what the Paeonians in this place turn out to use the timber for is not ships, but houses on stilts (5.16.1–2). Their 'city' turns out to be a wooden platform on which individuals then build themselves houses. The platform has a narrow entrance and so is easy of defence. The food comes from below the platform: the supply of fish is sufficient to meet the needs of horses and cattle. Here we have a self-sufficient (is)land, 'digging' for victory, invulnerable to attack. If Megabazus taking the back route is reminiscent of Thermopylae, this platform is reminiscent of the Peloponnese.

But Herodotus wants to tell us rather more about the lifestyle than simply this fact of self-sufficiency and islandness. The Paeonians in the past acted as a community: the citizens together set up the platform. But now they use a different *nomos* according to which each man adds three stakes when he marries a wife 'and each marries many wives' (5.16.2). Common activity is replaced by individual endeavour, but individual endeavour where what is contributed conforms to the individual's needs, or is it capacity? Given how industrious those women are supposed to be . . . Each man now has power over his own part of the platform and is in a position to have his own direct access to the resources of the water beneath. Then, in what appears to be the addition of a merely gratuitous ethnographic detail, Herodotus tells us that the dangers of the water to infants are solved by tying them with a rope (*spartōi*, the only occurrence of this word in Herodotus) round their feet so they cannot roll in (5.16.3).

What are we to make of this strange combination of collaboration and self-help? The choices, collaboration or going it alone, are precisely the choices that the cities and peoples face. It is the fellow Paeonians who have just been unable to resist the Persians because they cannot maintain unity, and we are once more reminded of the Thracians who are unable to realize their strength because they cannot unite (5.3.1). But given that this issue of unity is already raised by the very narrative, we need to pay attention here not simply to the united past and the independent present, but also to the many wives and the tied-up infants.

Wives and children have a consistent place in Herodotean ethnography; already in Book 5 we have met the dutiful Thracian wives and their saleable children (5.6.1). But this particular story reads in an unusually transparent way: the city of the Paeonians is built upon wives, and its future depends on taking special measures to keep safe the next generation. Unlike their neighbours, who abandon their cities and leave the Persians to discover them 'deserted of men' and take them, these Paeonians know how fundamental wives and children are. The multi-tasking Paeonian woman who does three

things at once leads not to the acquisition of power but to its displacement. These Paeonians on Lake Prasias know one thing: that their greatest
resources lie in the element beneath them; it is just a matter of fishing it
up.

Appealing as this analogical reading of the lake-dwellers' habits is, it falls
short of accounting for Herodotus' ethnographic details here. Not only
are we told that not simply the men but also the horses and cattle are
fed on fish, we are told how exactly they are fished up and that there are
two varieties (5.16.4). That the people of this area fed their cattle on fish
caught the attention of Athenaeus (*Deipnosophistai* 345e) and it should also
attract ours: fish are hardly the natural diet of horses or cattle. The extent
of the dependence of these people on a single resource (if the two otherwise
unheard of species of fish can be treated as one) could hardly be more
strongly stressed. By contrast to their fellow Paeonians, who are equipped
to live anywhere, these particular Paeonians are firmly rooted in a single
place and entirely dependent on a single resource. They have adopted a
manner of living which demands extraordinary treatment of their children
and an extraordinary diet for all. And when it comes to outside threats they
are impregnable themselves but useless in protecting their fellow Paeonians.

This *logos* about the Paeonians has been framed by issues of power and
choice. Herodotus' narrative construction at 5.11.2–12.1 has ensured that
the account of the Paeonians cannot be divorced from the choices offered
to Coes and to Histiaeus. As Histiaeus' choice underlines, not least when
interpreted by Megabazus at 5.23.2–3, issues of the power of Darius over
Ionian Greeks are bound up with issues of power over Thrace. But power
in Thrace turns out itself to reveal men who have made different choices.
There are those who rely on transferable skills, and those who rely on one
local resource. In this story the skills prove all too transferable, and, unable
to maintain their unity, the Paeonians who rely on them find themselves
transferred. But are we to understand the lake-dwellers to have made a
better choice? Does it constitute success for the Paeonians to be divided?
Has Herodotus flagged up the links between disunity and weakness in the
case of the Thracians for nothing?

Among the Greeks too there will prove to be those who, in the face of
Persian attack, display multi-tasking abilities and those who will be keen
to rely instead on natural defence. Among the Greeks too there are those
whose treatment of wives and children attracts attention (e.g. Hdt. 5.39–
42, 6.51–5, 61–70) and those in whose story beautiful women play a part
(1.60). If the reader's mind drifts from the lake-dwelling Paeonians, securing
their children with *sparton*, to the Spartans, powerful through the peculiar

resource of helot labour but condemned by it not to stray too far from their dwellings, not to help the Ionians in their revolt, and condemned also to adopt dietary limitations and some curious marriage conventions, the considerations of these Paeonian chapters on where power lies and on the choices that different individuals and people make of how to secure and maintain power will seem pregnant with questions which the succeeding narrative will do nothing to make less pertinent.[10]

---

[10] For puns on Sparta and *sparton* see Dunbar (1995) in Aristophanes *Birds* 813–15.

CHAPTER 3

Narrating ambiguity:
murder and Macedonian allegiance (5.17–22)

David Fearn

In Herodotus 5.17–21, Amyntas receives the Persian ambassadors sent to demand submission to Darius, accepts their offer, and gives a banquet to welcome the Persians.[1] The youthful Alexander, outraged at the Persians' treatment of Macedonian women during the after-dinner drinking, assassinates the ambassadors by replacing the endangered women with young men carrying knives, who kill the Persians; Alexander then manages to keep the affair secret, by handing over his sister Gygaea to Bubares, the leader of the Persian search party and son of Megabazus. An account is then given in chapter 22 of Alexander's demonstration of Greekness at Olympia, and his victory in the *stadion* there.

Herodotus' treatment of Alexander and his father Amyntas has an important place in Book 5. Chapters 17–21 form a bridge between Darius' failed invasion of Scythia in Book 4 and the Ionian Revolt and subsequent Persian invasion of Greece in Books 5 and following; they follow immediately on from Megabazus' deportation of the Paeonians of Thrace to Persia on Darius' instruction in the first sixteen chapters. The Macedonian ruling family is thus introduced in a way that focuses on relations with Persia. Alexander's political and strategic actions then tie in with Herodotus' concern with medism, and the question of the allegiance by Greek *poleis* to the cause against Persia in Books 8 and 9.

Herodotus' engagement with Alexander here has been explored in some important work.[2] My aim will be to see how the precise details of Herodotus' narrative in chapters 17–22 of Book 5 square with the presentation of Macedon throughout the *Histories*, and add colour and further complexity to the interactions between the Greek world and the East.

---

[1] Many thanks to Liz Irwin for the initial invitation to take part in this endeavour, and for her detailed comments and constant encouragement; also to Kathleen McLaughlin for Homeric inspiration and for reading and commenting on earlier drafts.

[2] I would single out the contributions by Borza, Errington, Scaife, and in particular Badian.

The story that Herodotus tells here is one that requires different levels of reading. We are invited to read the story in some senses historically, conveying information about Macedon's Greekness, but then to recognize ways in which that story is undercut by Herodotus' method of exposition and by details within the story which jar: most importantly, the way the story of the rejection of the Persians' advances on the Macedonian women at a quasi-Greek symposium, and Alexander's demonstration of his Greek ethnicity at Olympia, conflict with the detail concerning Alexander's alliance with the Persians through the marriage of his sister to a Persian. The text also encourages us to recognize a plausible construct of Macedonian propaganda, which we can support from some other sources (Bacchylides, for example). But at the same time we cannot be sure that Herodotus' account here is actually a piece of such propaganda, rather than a story invented by Herodotus that could be passed off, at least superficially, as plausible pro-Macedonian propaganda.

Moreover, as we shall see, 5.17–22 encourage us to think not only about the surface sense of the narrative, as a story about Macedonian cunning in their dealings with the Persians, but also much more deeply. We are invited to take the long view, and consider Alexander's interactions with not only Persians but also Greeks (at Olympia) within the context of Alexander's broader actions and interactions throughout the course of Herodotus' work. This leads to the question of whether we can read the ambiguity of Alexander's Macedon as a symbol of, or aetiological background for, the political interactions of states at the time of Herodotus' writing. Alexander and Macedon, then, are no mere sideshow to the events dealt with more extensively in Book 5; they serve to remind Herodotus' audiences and readers of exactly the kinds of political problems besetting Greece towards the end of the fifth century, and shed unexpected, ironic, and occasionally cynical light upon them.

My discussion will be in six parts. In the first, I shall discuss how the *logos* of Book 5 sets up for investigation the nature of Alexander's rise to the throne and the form of his rule. In the second, I shall look at ways in which Herodotus' treatment of the Macedonian banquet challenges preconceptions about the ethnic associations of sympotic practice. In section three, I shall trace the ways in which the Macedonian *logos* uses differing mythological models that might act as a guide to understanding the behaviour and actions of Alexander. In the fourth, I shall explore the effects of Herodotus' keenness to add vividness to the account of the Persians' murder. In the fifth, I shall look at 5.22, and discuss how the claim that Alexander won an Olympic victory works within the structure of the *logos*. Finally, I shall show how 5.17–22 fits with Herodotus' overall picture of Alexander and Macedon, and, taking the characteristically Herodotean 'long view', how this overall portrayal invites critical comparison with political and strategic engagements with Macedon at the time of Herodotus' own work.

I. MACEDONIAN QUESTIONS

Our first introduction to Alexander of Macedon in Herodotus presents his power and rule as a *fait accompli*. Amyntas, Alexander's father, is the target of the Persian embassy to request earth and water (17.1), but the narrator then continues with a very brief account of the geographical location of Macedon, in which Amyntas' son is presented as the man in power. As Carolyn Dewald has recently observed, such 'helpful' linking sections, even where, as in this case, the Herodotean 'I' is absent, actually serve to modify 'the narrator's insistence that Herodotus-the-author is merely at base telling the *logoi* of others'.[3] However, this seemingly insignificant opening presents to us an essential, though unexplained, detail: the silver mines next to lake Prasias which in future time amassed for *Alexander* as much as a talent per day. The temporal complexity of this section is striking: 'next to the lake *is* the mine from which *in future time* a talent of silver *came* each day to Alexander', πρῶτα μὲν γὰρ ἔχεται τῆς λίμνης τὸ μέταλλον ἐξ οὗ ὕστερον τούτων τάλαντον ἀργυρίου Ἀλεξάνδρῳ ἡμέρης ἑκάστης ἐφοίτα (17.2). Reference to present, future, and past time invites consideration by Herodotus' audiences of the connection between incipient Macedonian power and its link with Persia, and the future experience of Macedon in their own later fifth-century world. How exactly was it that Alexander came to rule seemingly independently in an open territory near lake Prasias, when Macedon itself was provided with no protection of the kind that the lake provided – however precariously – to its Paeonian inhabitants? The ethnographic and geographical focus of this introductory passage sets up the major question surrounding Herodotus' engagement with Alexander, not only in the *logos* here at the start of Book 5 but elsewhere throughout the *Histories*: the nature and source of Macedonian power. The extraordinary wealth of Alexander engenders within Herodotus' audiences a desire to learn more about this man, and, perhaps more interestingly, to bring into consideration their knowledge of, and stories about, Macedon.[4] The seemingly gratuitous detail about the silver mines activates in Herodotus' audiences knowledge that they already possess about Macedon, in terms of

---

[3] Dewald (2002) 285.   [4] For more detail here, see section VI.

the political history of the later fifth century. This is a subtly Herodotean way of connecting the past with the present, allowing audiences to think about power and wealth more broadly in a Macedonian context.

The 'helpfulness' of the narrator's detail about how *easy* the route between Paeonia and Macedon is figures and traces the invasive route taken by the Persians here.[5] The juxtaposition of this detail with the details of Alexander's subsequent wealth raises a number of questions: How did Alexander come to be ruling Macedon? How did Macedon go from a position of imminent subservience to Persia under Amyntas, to one of seeming self-sufficiency and financial independence under Alexander? And exactly how independent *was* Alexander's Macedon?

In the following sections I want to investigate how chapters 5.17–22 explore these questions, and *perform* the abdication of Amyntas and Alexander's succession.

II. MACEDONIAN HOSPITALITY: GREEKNESS AT ITS *MAGNIFICENT* BEST?

All the action of the *logos* takes place within a Macedonian symposium, after the eating is over but while the wine is still going round.[6] It has been suggested by one critic recently that the murder enacts Alexander's restoration of the normative rules of conduct that go together with the Greek symposium (that wives and female relatives be absent), and symbolizes the progressive establishment of his own regal power.[7]

It is clear that this entire section is likely to have its origins, at least, in Macedonian propaganda: Herodotus offers us a view of Amyntas', and hence Macedonian, opposition to Persian behaviour when dining; and the opposition in small details implies opposition in general. The opening dialogue between the Persians and Amyntas between 18.2 and 3 is structured around opposing *nomoi*. First, the Persians: Ξεῖνε Μακεδών, ἡμῖν νόμος ἐστὶ τοῖσι Πέρσῃσι, ἐπεὰν δεῖπνον προτιθώμεθα μέγα, τότε καὶ τὰς

---

[5] σύντομος κάρτα, 'extremely short': 17.2.

[6] Hdt. 5.18.2. The relatively rare word διαπίνω, seemingly with the sense 'to take it in turns to drink', refers to sympotic practice: see Pl. *Rep.* 420e4; Plut. *Quaest. Conv.* 711d5; cf. Poll. *Onom.* 6.19, juxtaposing διαπίνειν with διαμιλλᾶσθαι ἐν πότῳ, 'to be competitive in one's drinking'. The verb occurs in Herodotus only here and at 9.16.7. In the latter the symposium held for Thebans and Persians at Thebes frames the prophecy of Persian destruction and subordination to their rulers told by a Persian to Thersander of Orchomenus, and marks an implicit contrast between Persian subordination and Greek ideals of freedom and equality (see Bowie (2003) 106–7). But it is of further significance that in both cases the archetypally Greek act of shared drinking is set up by individuals (Amyntas; Attaginus of Thebes) whose allegiance to the *Persian* cause is at issue.

[7] Bowie (2003) 107.

παλλακὰς καὶ τὰς κουριδίας γυναῖκας ἐσάγεσθαι παρέδρους· . . . ἔπεο νόμῳ τῷ ἡμετέρῳ 'Macedonian host, it is a custom among us Persians that, when we lay out a great dinner, to bring in to sit by our sides our concubines and wives . . . follow our custom.' Second, Amyntas' response: Ὦ Πέρσαι, νόμος μὲν ἡμῖν γέ ἐστι οὐκ οὗτος, ἀλλὰ κεχωρίσθαι ἄνδρας γυναικῶν, 'Persians, our custom at least is not like this: we keep our men and women separated.'

Moreover, as Errington and Badian have shown, the episode has its origin in a Macedonian invention to disguise the historical fact of previous submission to Persia under Amyntas and the establishment of subsequent subservience in the marriage of Alexander's sister to a notable Persian.[8] Alexander's father is referred to here at 5.20.4 as ὕπαρχος, Herodotus' usual term for satrap;[9] Herodotus mentions later at 8.136 that the offspring of the union received the name of his maternal grandfather, Amyntas, and this child is likely to have been the intended successor of Alexander as satrap-king after Xerxes' conquest of Greece, though, obviously, things turned out rather differently.[10]

However, there are other factors in play that make such a straightforward reading untenable. Herodotus' presentation of the symposium here raises questions that seem to be at odds with the notion of Alexander as a restorer of normative Greek civilized conduct. Even though Alexander claims to have killed these ambassadors, they are dining on the specific invitation of Alexander's father. The Persian quoted above continues: σύ νυν, ἐπεί περ προθύμως μὲν ἐδέξαο, μεγάλως δὲ ξεινίζεις, διδοῖς τε βασιλέϊ Δαρείῳ γῆν τε καὶ ὕδωρ, ἔπεο νόμῳ τῷ ἡμετέρῳ, 'so now, since you eagerly received us, and are entertaining us greatly, and are offering earth and water to King Darius, follow our custom.' From a Persian perspective, Persian *nomoi* are merely the natural adjunct to Amyntas' lavish hospitality towards the Persians and his willing submission to them. When Amyntas ultimately gives way to the Persians' wishes, and says that he does so because they are now his *despotai* (18.3), we are left to worry about how Herodotus' narrative juxtaposes Amyntas' expression of helplessness here (i.e. 'since you're our masters now, I have no choice') with his earlier willingness to submit to the Persians and offer them such lavish hospitality.

It might be argued that the presentation of the *logos* is motivated primarily by the presentation of Alexander as a man of action and resistance, in direct opposition to his father. Alexander's involvement here performs his accession to the throne and the abdication of his father in his abdication

---

[8] Errington (1981); Badian (1994).   [9] See Badian (1994) 114.   [10] Badian (1994) 115–16.

of responsibility. However, the fact that Alexander becomes, as a man of action, a more proactive and threatening figure than his father surely works against any notion that Alexander's rise to power is a straightforward projection of normatively civilized, non-tyrannical Greek values. On the contrary, in its location as a bridging narrative between Persian expansion in the East and Persian expansion into the West, the episode suggests that any such straightforward polarity between East and West, or between tyrannical and free, is always insufficient: insufficient to the complexity of the developing political and strategic situation, and insufficient to the complexity of evolving reconstructions and re-performances of *logoi* about the past which involve Macedon, when it becomes expedient to various parties to emphasize or diminish Macedonian claims to Greekness. Herodotus' account of Macedon introduces, and indeed establishes, a third category lying indeterminately between East and West, challenging and deconstructing that opposition at the moment when we might have expected it to have been established, at the start of Persian approaches to Greece and in what might initially appear to be the first dramatized rejection of medism.

The key term of the whole banqueting passage is *xenia*, an idea that encapsulates the 'friend or foe?' ambivalence of the relations between Macedonian and Persians here.[11] The hospitality of Amyntas is continued by his son, when he calls the Persians *xenoi*. But since Alexander's *xenia* replaces the forced prostitution of female Macedonian royalty with murder, we must recognize that Alexander's actions cannot be interpreted as a straightforward re-establishment of Greek *nomoi* subsequent to the Persians' perversions of them. So what kind of *xenos* is Alexander?

Alexander's invitation to the Persians to have their wicked way with his female relatives is noteworthy: γυναικῶν τουτέων, ὦ ξεῖνοι, ἔστι ὑμῖν πολλὴ εὐπετείη, he says at 20.1 (very loosely to be translated, 'Guests, these women are entirely at your disposal'). This statement figures possible Persian rape, and its rejection by Alexander, in a direct though symbolic relation to military and political rape: elsewhere in Herodotus, εὐπετείη, 'ease', is a quality attached to the ease by which cities, territories, or political power, may be taken possession of, or overcome.[12] In addition, this fits with the Homeric analogy linking the rape of women with the rape of cities.[13] Understood in these terms, Alexander's subsequent protection of his

[11] *Xenia*-cognates in 5.18–20: ἐπὶ ξείνια, 18.1; ξεῖνε Μακεδών, ξεινίζεις 18.2; τοῖσι ξείνοισι, 19.2; ὦ ξεῖνοι, 20.1. More on this below in section III in relation to Homer's *Odyssey*.
[12] Some examples: 3.120, 3.143 (Samos); 5.49 (projected) Ionian rejection of Persian power. See Munson (pp. 158–9), and Pelling (pp. 179–83) below.
[13] *Il.* 16.100; *Od.* 14.388; *Il.* 22.460–72; cf. *HHDem.* 151. See Nagler (1974) 44–60; Friedrich (1977) 295–6.

women does indeed appear as a symbolic rejection of imperial subjugation by Persian power. When, however, we hear Herodotus tell us later of how Alexander gave his sister to a Persian (21.2), the disparity in his actions is surely noteworthy. Whether or not Herodotus had any idea that the story was a cover for earlier Macedonian submission to Persia, if we can read the women in the symposium as symbols of political power and Macedonian autonomy, then Alexander's subsequent gift of his sister to the Persian Bubares symbolizes a strategic sell-out. Alexander seems initially to show that Macedonian women, and Macedon itself, are not 'easy', but this may be thought to change when he seems able to smooth over relations with the Persians on his own terms through the arranged marriage of his sister, a detail that Herodotus places on a par with what is effectively a large bribe (χρήματά τε δοὺς πολλὰ καὶ τὴν ἑωυτοῦ ἀδελφεὴν, 'having given a good deal of money and his own sister'): a bride and a bribe, then.

However, it would also be possible to read Alexander's final gift of his sister to a Persian as the culmination of his own implicit submission to the Persian *nomoi*. After all, the *logos* has the Persians state how well-suited their own practices are to the Macedonians. The autonomy which seems to result from Alexander's subsequent appeasement of the Persians, with any Persian presence in Macedon now literally invisible (ἠφάνιστο: 'they vanished', 21.1) subtly, but not too subtly, hides Alexander's own Persian acculturation. Of course, the most significant of all Persian *nomoi* is *monarchiē*, for which see Darius in the constitution debate at 3.82.5: Alexander's dealings with women ultimately symbolize his inherent closeness to the Persians in cultural and constitutional terms.

We also have to consider Persian drinking and drunkenness here. Although we are perhaps made to recall Herodotus' earlier observations on Persian drinking practices at 1.133, in the Persian ethnography, to account for Persian drunkenness here, it is not made clear in the narrative of the *logos* whether or not this drunkenness is caused by the Persians' own *nomoi*, or those of the Macedonians.

Nomos itself occurs three times in the *logos*, in 18.2 and 18.3. The episode focuses on the conventions surrounding the treatment of women at the feast, with Alexander's intervention appearing to be a reinstatement of Greek *nomoi*; but we have already seen how Alexander's rejection of Persian rape is severely undercut. A further point worth emphasizing is that we never get a fully realized or clear picture of exactly what constitutes the *nomos* of Macedonian drinking, and whether it is intrinsically Greek. We never know, because we are never told, whether this banquet is laid on especially for the Persians or whether this *is* an illustration of the *nomos* of Macedonian royal dining. The fact that the Persians seem happy enough with the banquet may actually point away from thinking in Greek terms here. In the Persian ethnography of 1.133, Greek dining practices are characterized as being strange to the Persians because the Greeks seem to run out of proper food after the first course (1.133.2); there is no sign of this concern here.

Moreover, the narrator's characterization of the banquet as 'magnificent' (δεῖπνον μεγαλοπρεπές, 18.1) raises the stakes. Whether or not we read this as focalizing Amyntas' aims or the Persians' enjoyment, it is clear that such terminology directly characterizes the feast itself as tyrannical.[14] Alexander's deceitful rhetoric there also makes it impossible to determine the extent to which he himself subscribes to such strongly excessive and tyrannical characterizations of feasting. Furthermore, Herodotus' treatment of the way the murder is carried out distances it from *logos*: in the invitation to the Persians to have their way with the women, we know that these women are not really women at all, ὡς γυναῖκα τῷ λόγῳ, 'a woman in word only', 20.5. This creates extra distance between the supposed sequence of events, and Herodotus' own narrative *logos* about them.

Though the focus of the narrative appears to be on the opposed *nomoi* of Macedonians (as good Greeks) and the Persians in their treatment of women, these other details serve to confuse the picture and suggest that Macedonian conventions may themselves be tyrannical; whether this makes Macedon seem Greek or Persian is a question whose openness reveals the arbitrariness and provisionality of such categories.

On the surface, Alexander successfully sees off the threat of Persian imperial domination under Darius; but, as we read more closely, we can see that the narrative is a lot more complex.

III. MYTHOLOGICAL ARCHETYPES

To consider the nature and symbolism of Alexander further, we have to place this *logos* in the context of literary and mythological representations of father and son relationships and of revenge. We will see that the presentation of Alexander here recalls a number of contradictory models, and this can only

---

[14] *Megaloprepeia* and tyranny, esp. Polycrates at 3.125.2–3, the hospitality of Cleisthenes of Sicyon at 6.128.1, and the magnificent dining arrangements in Xerxes' tent at Plataea at 9.82; Kurke (1999) 119–20. Note also Alexander's use of the exotic terms πανδαισίη, 'luxurious feast', and ἐπιδαψιλευόμεθα, 'we lavish upon you', at 20.4: these two terms, in context, suggest the abundance and luxury only elsewhere associated in Herodotus with tyranny. Herodotus' only two uses elsewhere of the cognate δαψιλής 'plentiful', 'abundant', are in the context of tyranny: first, at 2.121δ in the run-up to Rhampsinitus' offering to the thief of his daughter in marriage in honour of his cleverness; second, at 3.130.5, used to characterize Darius' gift to Democedes.

serve to highlight the inherent contradictions in Alexander's presentation in the narrative.

The theme of revenge is central to Alexander's succession in Herodotus' narrative. The *logos* fits in with the reciprocal revenge theme treated at length before being dismissed in the prologue of Book 1. Immediately we think of Paris' rape of Helen, inspired by stories of earlier Greeks' theft of Medea, for which Greek revenge is sought through the Trojan War. Another non-Herodotean source, generally ignored, highlights Alexander's connections with this Trojan mythology: Pindar fr. 120, the opening two lines of an encomium for Alexander, refer to him as follows:

> ὀλβίων ὁμώνυμε Δαρδανιδᾶν
> παῖ θρασύμηδες Ἀμύντα
>
> Namesake of the blessed offspring of Dardanus,
> Bold-counselling son of Amyntas . . .[15]

Immediately we are faced with multiple ironies. Alexander, namesake of Trojan Alexander = Paris, is now punishing Persians for their behaviour towards his own female kin. This reverses the mythological background, according to which it is the eastern Paris who is punished for his rape of a foreign woman.[16] This whole issue of revenge puts into even sharper focus the nature of Alexander's behaviour towards the Persians here: we are now entitled to ask how well the view of justified revenge for rape present in the epic tradition concerning Alexander/Paris squares with the view here in Herodotus' narrative of Alexander's treatment of these Persians. Given that we have already observed that the Persians quite naturally expect Amyntas to conform to their own *nomoi*, following his already lavish, and indeed Persian-like, hospitality; given that the Persians are under the influence of Macedonian alcohol; given that the Persians are nowhere told, even by Alexander himself, that their behaviour is outrageous; and, finally, given that it is Amyntas, and not the Persians, who orders the women to sit with the Persians, we are to wonder whether Alexander's murder of the Persians is in fact an understandable reaction to the maltreatment of his female relatives. Altogether, then, Alexander's act cannot be made out as a clear-cut case of revenge.

---

[15] For more on this text, in relation to Bacchylides fr. 20B, another rather more complete sympotic *enkomion* on Alexander, see Fearn (forthcoming) Ch. 2.

[16] A mythological background which, as a result of the Persian Wars, had elsewhere been panhellenically politicized, especially by Simonides in his *Plataea Elegy*: on Paris specifically as a morally degenerate model for the Persians, see Sim. fr. 11.11–12 W² (with West's supplements *exempli gratia*), [εἵνεκ' Ἀλεξά]νδροιο κακόφρ[ονο]ς, ὡς τὸν [ἀλιτρόν] | [ἀλλὰ χρόνω]ι θείης ἅρμα καθεῖλε δίκ[ης], 'for the sake of wicked Paris, since in time the chariot of swift justices catches the sinner'.

The theme of hospitality and its perversions should also take us straight to the *Odyssey*. We might choose to read Alexander's 'revenge' as a replaying of Odyssean revenge against the suitors besetting Odysseus' *oikos*. This model provides a neat background highlighting the complexity of judging correctness in *xenia*, when Odysseus' methods are presented in ways that occasionally make him appear as savage and morally questionable as his opponents. However, Amyntas and Alexander do not precisely reflect the father–son dynamic of the *Odyssey*. Whereas Odysseus is the dominant figure, Herodotus' *logos* presents in Amyntas a father who is incapable of action, despite displeasure and distress (δυσφορέων, 'in distress', 19.1), and whose departure from the scene in an abdication of responsibility performs his abdication from the throne. See in particular Alexander's words to Amyntas at 19.1: Σὺ μέν, ὦ πάτερ, εἶκε τῇ ἡλικίῃ ἀπιών τε ἀναπαύεο μηδὲ λιπάρεε τῇ πόσι· ἐγὼ δὲ προσμένων αὐτοῦ τῇδε πάντα τὰ ἐπιτήδεα παρέξω τοῖσι ξείνοισιν, 'Father, give in to your years: go and rest, and do not carry on with the drinking. I shall stay here and see to all the needs of our guests.' Indeed, the only way in which we are able to read Alexander as 'ventriloquizing' Telemachus is by feminizing Amyntas and making him into a Penelope-figure. Alexander's words just quoted work directly in relation to Telemachus' words to Penelope about power in the *oikos* on two separate occasions in the *Odyssey*, at 1.356–9 and 19.344–53. But on neither of these occasions is Telemachus actually able to do away with the suitors, and in fact he is implicitly humouring them; and in the second of the two passages Telemachus' words have an ironic ring about them given his knowledge of his father's disguise and the imminence of Odysseus' reinstatement of his own authority. The only alternative Odyssean model for this father–son dynamic would be Laertes and Odysseus.

Perhaps a more successful procedure would be to see Herodotus' *logos* as an inversion or extrapolation of the Odyssean model: Alexander now becomes the son Telemachus never was, by taking on the characteristics of the Odyssean father-figure in his cunning deception of the drunken Persians.

We can see elsewhere the extent to which Herodotus seems keen to disrupt the straightforward application of Greek heroic cunning from the epic tradition to Greeks within his own narrative: see for example the Persian Zopyrus of 3.154ff. operating as a Persian Sinon/Odysseus-character in the sack of Babylon (with δόλον at 3.158.1). *Dolos* is a feature of Cyrus' character condemned by Tomyris at the close of Book 1, at 1.214; and the story that matches Alexander's revenge most closely in Herodotus is that of the *dolos* invented by Queen Nitocris of Egypt, who invented a subterranean chamber in which to drown the men responsible for the death of her brother, during a banquet held in their honour: 2.100. Another close parallel of a story proceeding through drink and trickery is that involving the thief-son of Rhampsinitus' treasurer, at 2.121a–b, who manages to rescue the body of his brother and escape punishment, and is subsequently dubbed the cleverest man in all the world, gaining the king's daughter in marriage as a reward. *Dolos* here is an activity once again associated with characters who are not exclusively Greek.

Compare also Herodotus' characterization of Alexander's actions as σοφίη, 'cleverness': his cover-up of the murder of the Persians is so described, at 21.2. Yet this characterization further aligns Alexander with the Persians. For just a little earlier it is the Persian ambassadors who have the authority to pronounce upon *sophiē*, when they berate Amyntas for a lack of this quality in bringing out the Macedonian women only to refuse to let the Persians get their hands on them: τὸ ποιηθὲν τοῦτο οὐδὲν εἶναι σοφόν, 'what he had done made no sense', 18.4. When we consider the substance of Alexander's *sophiē*, namely his bribery of a Persian official, and in particular the sell-off of his sister, within the context of this *logos* we may have to read this from a Persian perspective, given that, before now, they have been the only arbiters of *sophiē* in the *logos*. In the broader context of Book 5, claims to *sophiē* fit within the overall ambiguity of the interface between Ionia and Persia; such *sophiē* is as much a characteristic of the Persians in this Book as it is of the Greeks, or quasi-Greeks, who make deals with them; but such *sophiē* is not unambiguously positive, and can, in Alexander's case, be taken to represent the unscrupulous nature of his character.[17]

If Herodotus provides two Homeric models for Alexander, neither fits his situation exactly. On the one hand Herodotus shows Alexander outdoing the Odyssean model. On the other hand, an Iliadic model is to be seen as deeply ironic given the way it clashes directly with Alexander's Trojan eponym. Yet these two alternative mythological analogues for Alexander do important work for Herodotus. They provide a deeply ambivalent basis for Alexander as a man whose actions throughout the narrative characterize him neither as obviously Greek, nor as entirely Eastern either: he continues to hover somewhere in the middle.

The problem we face when we unearth these connections with mythological archetypes is that of determining whether or not they represent

---

[17] See further Greenwood, p. 144 below, on Histiaeus' and Darius' *sophiē*: Munson (2001b) 43 n. 67.

Herodotus' use of epic *topoi* to fill out his representation of Alexander's character, or whether they signify Alexander's own self-representation. It seems clear that the truth lies somewhere in between.

We have seen already that Pindar in an encomium of Alexander flagged up explicitly the connection between the Macedonian and Trojan Alexanders; as I discuss in detail elsewhere, we can see Bacchylides, in another encomium, also using mythological, and specifically Homeric, *topoi* in order to investigate the nature of his patron.[18] Bacchylides' encomium of Alexander has at its heart a musing on the power of the symposium to produce fantastic thoughts in its participants (including, amongst other things, thoughts about destroying cities; about monarchic rule over all men; and about wealth from Egypt).[19] This can be read as a construction of the Greekness of Alexander's *nomoi* as well as an implicit warning concerning the dangers of the East and the trappings of wealth that might seem, from a Greek perspective, worryingly Eastern-looking.

It seems plausible that this, and other occasional pieces composed for Alexander, provided the background against which Herodotus set his own *logos* about Alexander, the symposium, and the interface with the East. Herodotus can thus, to some degree at least, be seen as the natural successor of such poets, investigating, as well as portraying and memorializing Alexander. Of course, we have no way of telling the extent to which Herodotus constructed his view of Macedonian politics out of such sources, but my suspicion is that texts like these provided rather more for Herodotus to work with than any other more directly historical accounts of events originating in Macedon itself.

However, Bacchylides and Pindar, and the other praise-poets, were able ultimately only to offer a relatively limited and circumscribed view of men who were, after all, their clients. The fundamental difference in Herodotus' case is that the wealth and variety of his *logoi* which the scope of his *Histories* permits invite a range of different readings and a range of different comparisons between one another that have the power to shed even more ironic light on such individuals as Alexander. Though poets such as Bacchylides and Pindar were also able to invite deep thinking about parallels between

---

[18] Again, see Fearn (forthcoming, 2007) Ch. 1, on Bacchylides fr. 20B; cf. Most (1994), esp. 145–6, on Simonides' *Ode to Skopas* (*PMG* 542) and the delicate task of the encomiast, balanced between the demands of different audiences, and between praise and blame.

[19] Bacchylides fr. 20B.11–16: αὐτίκα μὲν πολίων κράδεμνα λύει, | πᾶσι δ' ἀνθρώποις μοναρχήσειν δοκεῖ· | χρυσῷ δ' ἐλέφαντί τε μαρμαίρουσιν οἶκοι, | πυροφόροι δὲ κατ' αἰγλάεντα πόντον | νᾶες ἄγουσιν ἀπ' Αἰγύπτου μέγιστον | πλοῦτον· ὡς πίνοντος ὁρμαίνει κέαρ, 'for instance, a man is undoing the veils of cities, and fancies he will be monarch over all men. Halls gleam with gold and ivory, and, bearing their wheat over a glittering sea, ships carry from Egypt vast wealth.'

mythological and historical figures, the relatively limited scope and conventions of their compositions did not allow those poets to have quite the same degree of breadth and depth of potential comparison as Herodotus does.

There is a final detail worth consideration in relation to mythical archetypes. We are told at the start of the *logos* of a certain mountain over which one passes to enter Macedon from the East. This mountain is called Dysoron: μετὰ δὲ τὸ μέταλλον Δύσωρον καλεόμενον ὄρος ὑπερβάντα εἶναι ἐν Μακεδονίῃ, 'and after the mine, once you've crossed a mountain named Dysoron you're in Macedonia', 17.2. The fact that Herodotus takes pains to tell us the unusual name of this mountain is surely significant. For in addition to the remarkable fact that it seems that this is the only reference to this mountain in all of Greek literature,[20] the name of the mountain has an interesting etymology: it seems to mean something like 'difficult to keep watch over'.[21] This sense takes its reference point from a single usage in Homer, in a simile figuring anxious vigilance among the Greeks, watching the Trojan encampment out on the plain:

> ὡς δὲ κύνες περὶ μῆλα δυσωρήσωνται ἐν αὐλῇ
> θηρὸς ἀκούσαντες κρατερόφρονος, ὅς τε καθ' ὕλην
> ἔρχηται δι' ὄρεσφι, πολὺς δ' ὀρυμαγδὸς ἐπ' αὐτῷ
> ἀνδρῶν ἠδὲ κυνῶν, ἀπό τέ σφισιν ὕπνος ὄλωλεν,
> ὡς τῶν νήδυμος ὕπνος ἀπὸ βλεφάροιιν ὀλώλει
> νύκτα φυλασσομένοισι κακήν· πεδίον δὲ γὰρ αἰεὶ
> τετράφαθ', ὁππότ' ἐπὶ Τρώων ἀΐοιεν ἰόντων.

> Like dogs about the sheep in a yard have trouble on their watch
> as they hear a mighty-hearted beast, who roams the woods
> in the mountains, and much clamour about him
> of men and of dogs, and their sleep is taken from them,
> so the sleep of those men was ended, taken from their eyelids
> as they kept watch that terrible night; for always towards the plain
> they turned, whenever they heard the Trojans coming and going.
>
> (*Iliad* 10.183–9)

Bryan Hainsworth, in comment on the usage δυσωρήσωνται, could allow himself to state that this is 'a "precious" linguistic invention . . . that found no imitators'.[22] But this is to reckon without Herodotus.

---

[20] With the exception of a single *Suda* entry (Δύσωρον· ὄνομα ὄρους· δ 1680) which can be understood to be a straightforward reference to Herodotus' naming of the mountain.

[21] E.g. Hesychius, *Lex.* δ 2697, glossing δυσωρήσωνται as δυσφυλακτήσωσι, κακὴν νύκτα διαγάγωσι, 'they have a difficult watch; they spend a bad night on guard'. See also Pollux 5.109.6 for δύσωρον as a word for describing a particular locality in negative terms.

[22] Hainsworth (1993) 171.

On a basic reading, the name's meaning of 'difficult to keep watch' matches its transgression and crossing by the Herodotean narrator.[23] In turn, this acts as a model for the way the Persian embassy is able swiftly and easily to arrive in the Macedonian court. 'Hard to guard' is the equivalent of saying 'easy to invade'. The name thus figures the boundaries of Greece and the north-eastern approaches to the Greek world as essentially porous and easy to enter; this establishes a subtle precedent for the future Persian invasions. We might also recognize some dialectal slippage in the interpretation of the omega, so that the name can also be understood as not only a bad ὤρος/ὄρος, 'mountain' (*qua* easily crossed), but also, ultimately, as a bad, or difficult, ὤρος/ὄρος, '*boundary*'. As a prelude to the Macedonian *logos*, this would suitably prefigure as potentially porous the categorizations and distinctions that that *logos* contains.

We might also be able to explore the Iliadic context of the usage a little more widely. At this point in the narrative the Greeks are suffering an uneasy night after Trojan advances. However, instead of enduring their uneasy watch, they proactively seek out a response to the Trojan threat. This, initially at least, maps onto Alexander's own awareness of the Persian threat symbolized in a mountain that is dangerously easy to cross. The Greeks, Odysseus and Diomedes, ultimately take advantage of their reconnaissance mission to murder the recently arrived Thracian contingent under the leadership of Rhesus. It would be difficult to push a parallel with Alexander's action too far, but there may be some connection in the recent arrival and vulnerability of both sets of victims, and in the timely advantage taken of this by the cunning actors who appeared at first to be on the weaker side.

However, there is another possible etymology: Δύσωρον might be taken to have a sense of 'bad or inauspicious timing', formed from δύσ+ὤρη. This sense of the mountain's name can indeed be seen to stand prophetically at the head of this *logos*, since, as it will pan out, the Persians' timing is all wrong: their arrival causes the young heir to usurp his father's authority, and the naming of the mountain is ironically replayed in Alexander's guileful suggestion to his Persian *xenoi* that now it's their bedtime: νῦν δέ, σχεδὸν γὰρ ἤδη τῆς κοίτης ὤρη προσέρχεται ὑμῖν ('now, since the time for you to go to bed is now here'), at 20.2. This is clearly an ill-omened ὤρη

---

[23] ὑπερβάντα, the verb used for the ease of 'crossing' the mountain, has far more connotations than simply travel: in a Herodotean context it fits more generally into the crossing of boundaries, and the breakdown of distinctions, territorial and cultural: see for instance its usage at 3.89.6, symbolizing Darius' new-found power to ignore regional boundaries in the collection of *phoros*; also the Athenians' crossing of the river Asopus at 6.108 (a sign of their alliance and support of Plataea), one of the most symbolic territorial boundaries in all of Herodotus (6.108 to be read against 9.36 in the immediate run-up to the battle of Plataea).

('time') for these Persians, because it marks the moment of their death. We must also, however, factor in the strong likelihood that, despite the vividness with which Herodotus constructs this *logos* through details such as this, the events that he narrates never actually happened. Herodotus' insinuation of bad or inauspicious time here starting with the etymological play on the name of the mountain may in fact also operate as a device to flag up the artificiality and constructedness of this elaborate and memorable narrative. The narrative gains a timeless quality in Herodotus' telling, but an additional implication is that it was always timeless in that the events described never happened.

IV. SEX, ROLE-PLAY, AND THE STAGINESS OF DEATH

We now have to consider the nature of Alexander's act of cunning in doing away with the ambassadors. A fruitful approach may be to think in terms of spectacle. For the episode seems to involve a continued focus on the language of seeing: initially, the Persians had an audience, technically a 'seeing', ὄψιν, with Amyntas, at which their request for earth and water is accepted: 18.1. Subsequently, the Macedonian royal women are, for the Persians, 'pains on their eyes', ἀλγηδόνας σφίσι ὀφθαλμῶν (18.4), if they are only able to look but not touch. When Amyntas cedes to the Persians' wishes for closer contact, the differing reactions of both Amyntas and Alexander to the sight of Persian maltreatment are given: Ἀμύντης μὲν δὴ ταῦτα ὀρέων ἀτρέμας εἶχε, καίπερ δυσφορέων, οἷα ὑπερδειμαίνων τοὺς Πέρσας· Ἀλέξανδρος δὲ ὁ Ἀμύντεω παρεών τε καὶ ὀρέων ταῦτα, ἅτε νέος τε ἐὼν καὶ κακῶν ἀπαθής, οὐδαμῶς ἔτι κατέχειν οἷός τε ἦν . . ., 'Amyntas, seeing these things, kept himself unmoved, despite his distress, because of his great fear of the Persians. But Alexander, Amyntas' son, was also there and able to see what was happening; he was young, with no experience of trouble, and was no longer at all able to restrain himself', 19.1. Amyntas subsequently urges his son to restrain himself under such provocation, again referring to the maltreatment visually: ἀλλὰ ἀνέχευ ὀρέων τὰ ποιεύμενα, 'bear up, though you see what they are doing', 19.2. Alexander then can claim that he can 'see', ὁρῶ, that the Persians are well-lubricated with wine, 20.2. And, climactically, the episode turns on the Persians themselves not being able to spot the difference between the Persian royal women and the smooth-faced youths with daggers that Alexander has substituted for them, 20.3–5. We are thus invited throughout to think of the episode in dramatic terms, despite its status as narrative *logos*. Moreover, we are invited to consider the irony for Amyntas: having the Persians come into his presence, ὄψιν, as though he were the *Persian* king,[24] means that he has to suffer the consequences of the characteristically Persian behaviour of his guests. The notion that Amyntas put up with the sight of his female relatives being maltreated, and so would Alexander if he were older, is also worthy of comment. For this does not bode well for Alexander's activities later in the *Histories*: the idea that Amyntas, as an adviser-figure, proposes to his son foreshadows the character that Alexander will explicitly become as Herodotus' text moves to its culmination and shows us Alexander's involvement in later Books.[25]

The inherent implausibility of the way Alexander achieves his goal in the *logos* does not lessen the significance of the episode in symbolic terms. For the way in which the *logos* has led us to consider its culmination in dramatic terms is significant if we read the killing as the piece of theatre that it is: the Macedonian youths essentially become actors in Alexander's power game, donning female costumes, and hoodwinking their entranced audience, who are already under the Dionysiac spell of drink; this parallels in an obvious way the fact that female roles were played by men in the theatre. The Persians' failure here is, ironically for them, a representational success: through the effects of drunkenness they are unable to tell the difference between mimetic and real Macedonian women. There may be more than a hint here that this *logos* has something to say to the Athenians, for whom both the tyranny of empire and the institution of theatre were central concerns.[26]

What are we to make of this deception? This can be read as an ironic enactment and test of the claim made in the Persian ethnography of Book 1 that the Persians make their best decisions when they are drunk, and that the master of the house in which the decision is made submits for reconsideration the decision on the following day when they are sober (1.133.3). Here in Book 5 this notion of Persian decision-making is dismantled: here the influence of wine leads them to want to assault sexually the Macedonian women; and the master of the house, who is now Alexander, makes sure that they do not live to sober-up the following day.

However, the theatricality and cross-dressing of the Macedonians here do not entirely redound to their credit. For in dressing up like women, the

---

[24] Compare ἐλθόντες ἐς ὄψιν τὴν Ἀμύντεω, 'having come into Amyntas' presence' at 18.1 with, for instance, 5.106, where Histiaeus is summoned into Darius' presence, ὄψιν.
[25] More on this in section VI.
[26] Tyranny in Herodotus as a potential model for Athenian power: Moles (2002); cf. Pelling (2002); Athenian imperial power and the theatre: Goldhill (1990); tyranny in tragedy: Seaford (2003).

Macedonians seem like Herodotus' Lydians after their subjugation by Cyrus (1.155.4), or at least like Athenian *ludopatheis*, those aristocratic Eastern-looking men who destabilize by themselves the boundaries between Greece and the East. The connection between Greeks (and Athenians in particular) and Lydians through the Macedonians here is also hinted at through Alexander's treatment of his sister subsequent to the killing of the ambassadors. It is of course ironic that Alexander ends up repeating, to all intents and purposes, especially from a female perspective, the behaviour of the drunken Persians in handing Gygaea over to the Persian Bubares, leader of the search party. But in proffering his nearest female kin as a bribe/bride, he looks rather like a Lydian, for the Lydians, as Herodotus tells us in Book 1, are similar to the Greeks *except* in so far as they prostitute their daughters: 1.94.1. Moreover, in the ethnography of 5.6.1 the selling of children for export is a Thracian hallmark. So despite all Alexander's claims to Greekness, when read in the broader context of the opening of Book 5, what his culminating action here may suggest is that he is all too close to his Thracian neighbours, not his Greek ones; and such social, geographic, and textual proximity may also suggest the Persian subjugation (through analogy with, for instance, 5.2.2) which the narrative of his actions seems ostensibly to reject. Let's now return to those smooth-chinned Macedonians: seated among their Persian *erastai*, they surely remind us of aristocratic Greek pederasty. But if we think that the narrative is pointing to a characteristically Greek *nomos* here in the Macedonians' rejection of Persian sexual abuse of female kin, Herodotus again evades such easy polarities: for, according to the Persian ethnography the Persians themselves enjoy pederasty, a practice which, so the narrative claims, they learnt from the Greeks (1.135). If we think, then, about the general discourse of 5.17–22 on sex, cultural practice, and geopolitics, we become aware that two different strands are inextricably entwined in the narrative. First, the episode raises questions and problems concerning the ambivalence of Macedonian cultural practices, sympotic and sexual – inviting analogies with Greeks, Thracians, Lydians, and Persians. Second, the episode also suggests a complex interrelationship between sexual domination or subjugation – in terms of pederasty, prostitution, and marriage – and military or political domination, in the context of medism and the Persian invasions. The problems we face in pinning down Alexander's *nomoi* regarding sex and the treatment of his kin and his Macedonian associates map directly onto the problems we face in attempting to pin Alexander down politically.

It is no surprise, then, that in the end the theatricality of the murder of the ambassadors makes the presentation of the Macedonians, and the nature and power of Alexander himself, seem more ambivalent and more contrived, not less so. Though the professed aim of the narrative is to present Alexander as anti-Persian and philhellenic, the details of the narrative itself undermine and challenge that aim at almost every turn.

Perhaps the vivid and visual quality of the text here suggests that we could look for a 'real' event behind the propaganda: that we should suspend belief in a narrative that so conspicuously serves Alexander's Philhellenic interests, and reconstruct an occasion in which Persians did in fact come to Macedon, and enjoy a 'Greek' symposium, in which young members of the Macedonian elite were dressed up in exotic Lydian style. Such an event could then be interpreted as the Macedonians' symbolic paying of homage to Darius under Amyntas by aping, and thus already buying into, Eastern culture. If we were to go down this line, a view of Macedonian *nomos* would emerge that was rather sponge-like, in its capacity to appropriate and adopt for its own pragmatic purposes the *nomoi* of other *ethnē*; and this would still leave us unable to offer any more enlightening view of Macedonian *nomoi* at any stage before we hear anything about their engagement with the *nomoi* of others.

However, it is more likely that Herodotus' account of the Persian ambassadors' murder is an account of an event which never actually took place. It is not insignificant that Herodotus tells us at 21.1 that with the Persians all evidence disappeared without a trace. In the context of Book 5, this fits with other historically unverifiable accounts that Herodotus gives,[27] and it does seem to have its origins in a Macedonian story constructed in order to explain away, and exculpate themselves from, later accusations of medism.[28] But this is not the whole story, as the structure of Herodotus' narrative shows. By framing it with the earth and water at the start and Alexander's marrying-off of his sister at the end, he undermines its Macedonian propaganda-value as a way of fending off claims of medism. For a *logos* which continually emphasizes display, perception, and appearance, it is ironic that the only historical, visible survival from the whole episode we are left with (after the disappearance of the entire Persian entourage along with their pack animals) is the marriage of Gygaea and Bubares, the token of Persian–Macedonian alliance in the years leading up to the Persians' full-scale invasion of Greece.

The very name of Alexander's sister Gygaea is significant. First, the tradition of a 'Gygaean Lake' in Maeonia goes back as far as the catalogue

---

[27] Darius' gift of Myrcinus to Histiaieus (11, taken away at 23–4); Spartan attempts to install tyrants in Athens (Isagoras: 74–6; Hippias: 90–3). See Introduction, pp. 39–40 above.

[28] For which see Badian (1994).

of Trojan allies at *Iliad* 2.865, according to which the local eponymous nymph generated the lineages of local rulers.[29] Secondly, and more signifi- cantly, at 1.93.5, Herodotus tells us of a lake which the Lydians call Gygaea close to the tomb of Alyattes near Sardis; and it is precisely at this point that Herodotus then chooses to tell us about Lydian child-prostitution:[30] λίμνη δὲ ἔχεται τοῦ σήματος μεγάλη, τὴν λέγουσι Λυδοὶ ἀένναον εἶναι· καλέεται δὲ αὕτη Γυγαίη. τοῦτο μὲν δὴ τοιοῦτό ἐστι. Λυδοὶ δὲ νόμοισι μὲν παραπλησίοισι χρέωνται καὶ Ἕλληνες, χωρὶς ἢ ὅτι τὰ θήλεα τέκνα καταπορνεύουσι, 'Next to the tomb there is a large lake, which the Lydi- ans say is ever-flowing. Its name is Gygaea. Such, then, is this tomb. The Lydians share almost all their customs with the Greeks, except for the fact that they prostitute their female offspring.'[31] In Herodotus' telling, then, Gygaea's name is another element speaking for an Eastern-looking Mace- don, extremely well connected with Lydian/Persian *nomoi* and governance. But these details are only the *coup de grâce* in a narrative that has systemat- ically exposed and undermined Macedonian claims to Greekness.

V. ALEXANDER AT THE OLYMPICS?

In the concluding section of the *logos*, Herodotus goes out of his way in chapter 22 to refer to his later treatment of the Hellenic descent of the Macedonian kings at 8.137.[32] To justify this claim, he brings in the notorious account of Alexander's competition at Olympia, according to which Alexander proved his Argive descent to the *hellanodikai*, and came joint first in the Olympic *stadion*:

Ἀλεξάνδρου γὰρ ἀεθλεύειν ἑλομένου καὶ καταβάντος ἐπ᾽ αὐτὸ τοῦτο οἱ ἀντιθευσόμενοι Ἑλλήνων ἔξεργόν μιν, φάμενοι οὐ βαρβάρων ἀγωνιστέων εἶναι τὸν ἀγῶνα ἀλλὰ Ἑλλήνων. Ἀλέξανδρος δὲ ἐπειδὴ ἀπέδεξε ὡς εἴη Ἀργ- εῖος, ἐκρίθη τε εἶναι Ἕλλην καὶ ἀγωνιζόμενος στάδιον συνεξέπιπτε τῷ πρώτῳ. ταῦτα μέν νυν οὕτω κη ἐγένετο.

For when Alexander had elected to compete, his opposing Greek competitors tried to exclude him, saying that the games could only be contested by Greeks, not barbarians. But Alexander demonstrated his Argive descent, and was judged to be a Greek; in competition he came equal first in the *stadion*. The events took place in something like the way I described them. (5.22.2)

---

[29] See Kirk (1985) 260 *ad loc.*
[30] See already p. 114 above for the importance of this detail in relation to Alexander and his sister.
[31] That Herodotus has the Lydians say that the lake is 'ever-flowing' seems to me a (metapoetic) nod to the Homeric source, given that ἀένναον is also an epithet which is used metaphorically to refer to κλέος (e.g. Sim. *PMG* 531.9; Heraclit. 97 DK).
[32] For which see section VI below.

Given the essential fact that no record of Alexander's victory survives on the Olympic list or anywhere else,[33] the veracity of Herodotus' extraordinary claim must be questioned; and indeed, Herodotus' use of κη, 'somehow', in the concluding sentence, seems to cast a pall of doubt over the entire Macedonian *logos*, before Herodotus takes up once more Megabazus' dealings with the Paeonians.[34] It seems doubtful that historians will ever get to the bottom of the nature of Herodotus' claim about Alexander's athletic success, but its surface function in the context of Herodotus' narrative seems relatively clear.[35] The use of the symposium and Olympic competition, two touchstones of Greekness, does seem to represent, at least to some extent, Macedonian philhellene propaganda in the face of charges of medism in the period of the Persian Wars. Moreover, we have epigraphic testimony from the middle of the century to the effect that Macedonian royalty were allowed to compete at the Argive Heraia: a bronze tripod found in the Macedonian royal tombs at Vergina, dating to 460–450 BC, bears, in Argive lettering, 'I am a prize from Argive Hera.'[36] Thus it might seem possible that Alexander could have competed as a Greek at Olympia through his claim to Temenid Argive lineage. Even here I suspect that competing at Argos was rather less significant and controversial than competing at Olympia, though for Alexander the former might have helped as a stepping-stone to the latter. Yet the claim to an Olympic victory is, of itself, unverifiable, and remains suspicious.

Of course, Herodotus is rather more interested in Alexander's involvement with Olympia on a political level. His focus on Alexander's dealings with Greeks at Olympia forms a natural coda to the doubts he has raised throughout the *logos* as a whole as to the nature of Alexander's power

[33] See Badian (1982) 45–6 n. 15 for Hammond's failure to check the complete list in Eusebius.

[34] Borza (1990b) 113 is correctly suspicious; Crowther (2000) 137–8 seems to assume that Herodotus' evidence points to an actual competition, but he states in conclusion (p. 139) that no clear-cut evidence for joint athletic victories is found before the imperial period. It does seem that ties were possible in other competitions of the classical period (in the citharoidic competition at the Great Panathenaea in 402/1: Shear (2003) 95 n. 33, with epigraphic detail – on the dedication of the victor's crown to the god); no evidence is forthcoming to explain adequately the abnormal situation involving Alexander and Olympia. I note that Posid. AB 74 seems to refer to the miraculous equal first place achieved by an important Alexandrian official in the Pythian chariot race, but it seems quite possible that details of this 'miraculous' event are themselves derived from a combination of Herodotus' account in Book 3 of Darius' 'miraculous' succession to the Persian throne (3.86) and Alexander's joint first place here.

[35] Sourvinou-Inwood (2002) relies too strongly on the historicity of the verdict by the *hellanodikai* in her argument for the Greek ethnicity of the Macedonians; cf. Maehler (2004) 244; Hall (2001) 168 and (2002) 154–6 accepts it, but is, rightly, rather more interested in the propaganda value of the claim to Greek origins than the historicity of the athletic victory associated with it.

[36] *SEG* xxix (1979) no. 652: παρ' hέρας Ἀργείας ἐμὶ τὸν ἄϝεθλον; Hornblower (1991) 375 *ad loc*. Thuc. 2.99.3.

and his allegiances.[37] Herodotus elsewhere gives us good reason elsewhere to be critical of claims to the objectivity of the *hellanodikai* at Olympia: at 2.160 a delegation from Elis arrives in Egypt, boasting of the fairness and objectivity of their organization of the Olympic games; but these proud Greeks are roundly criticized by the pharaoh for the self-interested bias that was made inevitable by Elean involvement in the organization of games in which their own citizens (or, implied, individuals with political connections with Elis) were also able to compete.[38] By mentioning the positive verdict of the *hellanodikai* here at 5.22 immediately after he himself has already exposed significant doubts concerning Alexander's Greek ethnicity, Herodotus invites further questions among his Greek audiences about why the *hellanodikai* were willing to accept his Greekness. Moving forward a few decades to the time of the Peloponnesian War and of Herodotus' composition, we hear from Thucydides that competing at the Olympics was, again, a controversial business. During the Olympic festival of 420, the Eleans, now allied with the Athenians, interdict the Spartans for not paying a fine as punishment for their alleged breaking of the sacred truce; a Spartan, Lichas, was flogged by the officials because, when his team won and was announced as a communal Boeotian entry, he came up and personally crowned the charioteer, to indicate that the chariot belonged to him: Thucydides 5.49–51, especially 51.[39] For our concerns, this indicates two things. First is the difficulty involved in staking claims to political affiliation within Olympic competition: we may, perhaps, read into Herodotus' account of Alexander's victory, this kind of political complexity (for instance, Alexander may have tried to compete under an Argive 'flag of convenience'). Second is the possibility that Herodotus' audiences are, in the context of later fifth-century politics, being tempted cynically to read back into Alexander's claim to victory their own experiences of the way the supposed impartiality of the Olympic competitions had been attracted into political squabbling and power-plays. The end result is that the Elean officials and Greeks in general come out of this no better off than Alexander himself.

---

[37] Cf. Hall (2001) 156, on the claim to Greekness at Olympia: 'The credibility of the claim may be less significant than its articulation – a case of form overriding content . . . what mattered was that Alexander had played the genealogical game *à la grecque* and played it well, perhaps even excessively.'

[38] See Lloyd (1975–88) III.167 *ad loc.*: 'We can only conclude that, in Herodotus' time, observers were already voicing reservations about the conduct of the games and the propriety of making excessive claims for them.' See Plut. *Apoth. Lac.* 215F (Agis II).

[39] See also Paus. 6.2.2–3. For detailed discussion of the Lichas episode in its Thucydidean context, see Hornblower (2004) 273–86.

VI. ALEXANDER'S TRAJECTORY

I want now to trace how our introduction to Alexander here in this *logos* relates to and in fact underwrites all of Herodotus' subsequent dealings with Alexander; and secondly, to explore some ways in which Herodotus' treatment of Alexander as a whole may intersect with views about Macedon current among Herodotus' audiences later in the century.

Alexander's next appearances are somewhat later, in the build-up to Thermopylae and Plataea. At 7.173.3 messengers from Alexander come to the Greek forces who are massing to defend Tempe; they suggest that the army withdraw, so as not to be trampled underfoot by the invading Persians, about the size of whose force they also provide some detail (information perhaps garnered from his Persian brother-in-law, Bubares, now one of the commanders of the Athos canal project: 7.22). Herodotus *seems* intent on asserting the pro-Greek nature of Alexander's advice, and he goes as far as to state that the Greeks heeded it.[40] But he immediately counters this with his own thought that the Greeks actually withdrew out of a fear that there was another way into Thessaly through upper Macedon, the way that Xerxes' army did in fact come in, as Herodotus reminds us;[41] and as Badian has pointed out, Herodotus' narrative here thus overtly offers kind words for Alexander's advice, whilst undercutting it with a personal perspective borne out by fact, therefore suggesting disingenuousness on Alexander's part.[42] Herodotus' Greeks at the Isthmus at 7.175 recall the warnings given by Alexander about Tempe in their consideration of the proposal to guard the pass of Thermopylae.[43] But this should not blind us to the fact that the main narrator has interspersed his Greeks' acceptance of the advice with his own questioning of it.

Alexander and his actions feature a further four times in Herodotus' narrative. At 8.34 we are told that Alexander had garrisoned the medizing cities of Boeotia and saved them by making it clear to Xerxes that the Boeotians

---

[40] ὡς δὲ οὗτοί σφι ταῦτα συνεβούλευον (χρηστὰ γὰρ ἐδόκεον συμβουλεύειν, καί σφι εὔνοος ἐφαίνετο ἐὼν ὁ Μακεδών), ἐπείθοντο, 'they discussed the matter amongst themselves (for they thought the advice was good, and the Macedonian appeared to be well disposed towards them), and were persuaded'.

[41] 173.4: δοκέειν δέ μοι, ἀρρωδίη ἦν τὸ πεῖθον, ὡς ἐπύθοντο καὶ ἄλλην ἐοῦσαν ἐσβολὴν . . ., τῇ περ δὴ καὶ ἐσέβαλε ἡ στρατιὴ ἡ Ξέρξεω, 'it seems to me that fear was what persuaded them, when they found out that there was another way in . . . , the way, in fact, by which Xerxes' army invaded.'

[42] Badian (1994) 117. A Herodotean subtlety overlooked by Hall (2001) 174.

[43] Hdt. 7.175.1: οἱ δὲ Ἕλληνες ἐπείτε ἀπίκατο ἐς τὸν Ἰσθμόν, ἐβουλεύοντο πρὸς τὰ λεχθέντα ἐξ Ἀλεξάνδρου, 'the Greeks, when they arrived at the Isthmus, held a discussion, in view of Alexander's words . . .'

were friends to the Medes just as he himself was; the unusually emphatic phraseology at this point makes clear the involvement of Alexander here.[44] At 8.121.2 a gold statue of Alexander is mentioned at Delphi, next to which the monument to the Greek victory by the allied states was erected after Salamis. This minor detail on the position of two dedications again situates Alexander in a discursive relation to the conflict between Greeks and Persians. The mention of a dedication by Alexander at Delphi is partly a sign of Macedonian propaganda;[45] but its mention at precisely this moment is a sign also of the subtlety of Herodotus' narrative; a link with Croesus, and thus to the ethnic and political character of Delphic dedications may also be suggested by the parallel positioning of the Aeginetan dedication next to the great bowl of Croesus only a chapter later at 8.122. We are invited by the narrator to compare and contrast these dedications, their inspiration, and their aspirations.[46] The juxtaposition of Alexander's and Croesus' dedications may be a point about their shared but tenuous status as quasi-naturalized 'Greeks'; Alexander therefore looks more like a barbarian king who recognizes Greek sanctuaries than a native Greek worshipper. Moreover, in a Delphic context, and, specifically one that celebrates Greek unity in the Persian Wars, Alexander's presence reminds Herodotus' audience not only to be cynical and suspicious about Macedonian claims to Greekness and philhellenism, but also to note how much times had changed. For Herodotus' contemporary audiences, it was no longer actually possible neatly to separate off Greek unity on the one hand from the East and from Macedon on the other: the geopolitical intrigues of the later century had transformed everything; and Aegina was now an Athenian cleruchy.[47]

8.136–43 is the climax of Herodotus' treatment of Alexander, one which implicitly points to the fact that Alexander has been for some time an ally of, and subject to, the Persian king.[48] Herodotus places his exposition

---

[44] Hdt. 8.34 as follows, with Badian (1994) 117–18: Βοιωτῶν δὲ πᾶν τὸ πλῆθος ἐμήδιζε, τὰς δὲ πόλις αὐτῶν ἄνδρες Μακεδόνες διατεταγμένοι ἔσωζον, ὑπὸ Ἀλεξάνδρου ἀποπεμφθέντες. ἔσωζον δὲ τῇδε, δῆλον βουλόμενοι ποιέειν Ξέρξῃ ὅτι τὰ Μήδων Βοιωτοὶ φρονέοιεν, 'all the Boeotians had medized, and their cities were under the special protection of Macedonians dispatched by Alexander. *They were protecting them for the following reason*: they wanted to make it clear to Xerxes that the Boeotians were well-disposed to the Medes.'

[45] Borza (1990b) 130.

[46] Errington (1990) 12 fails to read Herodotus correctly at this point.

[47] See further below for more on Thucydides and Macedon; for more of Herodotus' view of Aegina, see, in addition to the work of Haubold in Ch. 9 below, his account at 6.91 of the Nicodromus affair, which is significantly coloured by the later history of the island and the Athenian establishment of the cleruchy at the start of the Peloponnesian War in 431 (Thuc. 2.27).

[48] See, with Badian (1994) 116–17, Hdt. 6.44 for Mardonius' addition of the Macedonians to the list of Darius' subjects c. 492 BC: another detail covered over by the story of the murder of the Persian ambassadors.

of Alexander's Temenid ancestry, promised since 5.22, in chapters 137–9 just before one of Alexander's most conspicuous act of medism, his role as Mardonius' ambassador to Athens to propose alliance with Persia (140). As Badian has pointed out, Herodotus uses this placement to offer implicit crit-icism of Alexander's duplicity whilst avoiding overt offence to the Temenid dynasty as a whole, and in particular to Perdiccas II, son of Alexander and with Athenian connections, on the Macedonian throne at the time of Herodotus' writing.[49]

Herodotus' last look at Alexander is at 9.44–5. On the eve of Plataea he has him ride up to the Athenian lines opposite – for the Macedonians are on the right wing of the *Persian* army.[50] Alexander reveals Mardonius' plans to the Athenian generals, and asks them to remember him in their concern for freedom, if the Greeks win the day.[51] This has, reasonably, been read as Alexander hedging his bets on his own future, in view of a now probable Greek victory, and likely Greek retaliation against medizers.[52]

Despite the amount of work done on the above passages by other schol-ars, what has been overlooked is the way in which these passages address Alexander's status as ruler, and the full implications of how they develop Alexander's connections with Greece, and Athens in particular. Herodotus is increasingly specific about this, in a way that matches his treatment of

---

[49] Badian (1994) 119–21. See also Hall (2001) 171 for the possibility of Herodotus' shedding ironic light on the later fifth-century relations between Athens, Sparta, Persia, and the Macedonian monarchy.

[50] The Macedonians are posted by Mardonius on the right wing facing the Athenians (whose rejection of Alexander's embassy we recall from the previous book): Hdt. 9.31.5.

[51] See in particular 9.45.1–2, 3: οὐ γὰρ ἂν ἔλεγον, εἰ μὴ μεγάλως ἐκηδόμην συναπάσης τῆς Ἑλλάδος. αὐτός τε γὰρ Ἕλλην γένος εἰμὶ τώρχαῖον καὶ ἀντ' ἐλευθέρης δεδουλωμένην οὐκ ἂν ἐθέλοιμι ὁρᾶν τὴν Ἑλλάδα . . . ἢν δὲ ὑμῖν ὁ πόλεμος ὅδε κατὰ νόον τελευτήσῃ, μνησθῆναί τινα χρὴ καὶ ἐμεῦ ἐλευθερώσιος πέρι, ὃς Ἑλλήνων εἵνεκα ἔργον οὕτω παράβολον ἔργασμαι ὑπὸ προθυμίης . . . εἰμὶ δὲ Ἀλέξανδρος ὁ Μακεδών, 'I would not be speaking to you now unless I cared deeply for the whole of Greece. I am myself a Greek by descent: my family goes back a long way. Moreover, I have no wish to see Greece exchange her freedom for slavery . . . If this war turns out for you the way you intend it, you must remember me, and have thought for my own freedom; for the sake of Greece I have taken an enormous risk in my eagerness . . . I am Alexander of Macedon.' We should note that Alexander's plea to be remembered here is contained within a Herodotean master-narrative of *kleos* (cf. preface to Bk. 1). Alexander's deeds are therefore memorialized, but on rather different terms than he would himself have dictated.

[52] Badian (1994) 118–19; Flower and Marincola (2002) 188 *ad* 9.44–5. Badian, who notes that Alexander's words are again insincere, also observes that Herodotus tells us little about the Persian retreat through Macedon at 9.89 after their defeat *except that* Artabazus passed through Macedon by the shortest route and was not attacked until he reached Thrace, though in the same chapter he does dwell on Artabazus' hospitable reception in Thessaly. The Macedonian embarrassment at continued medism and Alexander's duplicity is now palpable here. A later tradition recorded in the anti-Macedonian rhetoric of Demosthenes has Alexander's son, anachronistically, destroy the barbarians retreating from Plataea: Dem. 13.24, 23.200; cf. Ps.-Dem. 12.21 for the dedication of a gold statue of Alexander at Delphi with the spoils from the Persian defeat, subsequent to occupation of Amphipolis. There is no trace of this in Herodotus, as Flower and Marincola (2002) *ad* 9.89.4 rightly observe.

Macedon during the Persian invasions. But the revelation of Alexander's status as leader is delayed. In the proleptic reference in 5.17.2 to his future silver mines, he is merely 'Alexander'. As we shall see shortly in more detail, at 5.19.1 he is simply his father's outraged son, ignorant of the harsh ways of the world: Ἀλέξανδρος δὲ ὁ Ἀμύντεω . . ., ἅτε νέος τε ἐὼν καὶ κακῶν ἀπαθής, 'Alexander, Amyntas' son . . . ; he was young, with no experience of trouble' (though not for long! See my earlier discussion). At 7.173.3 he is Ἀλεξάνδρου τοῦ Ἀμύντεω ἀνδρὸς Μακεδόνος, 'Alexander son of Amyntas the man from Macedon', and ὁ Μακεδών, 'the Macedonian'; at 7.175.1 he is 'Alexander'. At 8.34 he is simply 'Alexander' again; at 8.121.2 ὁ Μακεδὼν Ἀλέξανδρος, 'the Macedonian Alexander' (with ὁ χρύσεος, 'golden', indicating that this is the statue of him).

All this begins to change at 8.136. When Mardonius chooses him to go to Athens, he is again simply Ἀλέξανδρον τὸν Ἀμύντεω ἄνδρα Μακεδόνα, 'Alexander son of Amyntas, the man from Macedon'. But when at 137.1 Herodotus gives his Hellenic genealogy of the Temenid house, he uses the term τυραννίς, 'power', but also 'tyranny', to refer to the nature of the rule: τοῦ δὲ Ἀλεξάνδρου τούτου ἕβδομος γενέτωρ Περδίκκης ἐστὶ ὁ κτησάμενος τῶν Μακεδόνων τὴν τυραννίδα τρόπῳ τοιῷδε, 'Alexander was descended in the seventh generation from Perdiccas, who won *turannis* ('power'/'tyranny') for the Macedonians, in the following way.' Though the narrator's terminology may seem neutral, the precision of Herodotus' diction must be loaded in view of his earlier engagement with Alexander and Macedonian rule in Book 5, and the fact that τυραννίς has received full treatment more widely. Book 3 interweaves the Greek tyrants Polycrates and Periander with the Persian monarchs Cambyses and Darius; and in the context of Book 5, the important presence of a number of Greek tyrants – Histiaeus, Coes, Aristagoras, among others, serves to challenge preconceptions current at the time of Herodotus' writing concerning straightforward associations of tyranny with Persia (in the earlier century at least); but these are associations which, ironically, Herodotus' text sometimes seems to support.[53] Herodotus is developing his account with an eye on an extremely rich, but more contemporary, Greek political landscape; in this context, it can only be unsatisfactory for states and individuals within Herodotus' discrete *logoi* to criticize others: such accusers end up looking, at best, radically naive or short-sighted, and, at worst, hypocritical and dangerous.

---

[53] See e.g. Dewald (2003) 33–4. But see also Thuc. 1.69 for the Corinthians' view of Athens as the natural successor of the Medes as a tyrannical force of invasion. In general see also Hall (1989) for the construction of tyranny as Eastern in tragedy.

Herodotus has the Spartans, in their rejection of submission, state that his advice is not at all surprising coming from a man the nature of whose power made him a natural ally of the enemy. Here again the terminology is specifically that of tyranny. Alexander's actions are entirely predictable: as a tyrant he is a natural collaborator with a tyrant.[54] However, as well as reflecting badly on Macedonian governance, in the context of Herodotus' ongoing narrative, the Spartans and the Athenians come off badly. It is felt to be extremely unwise of them to criticize Athens for involvement with Macedonian 'tyranny' when it is they who, back in Book 5, attempted to install first Isagoras and then Hippias as tyrants in Athens.[55] Furthermore, as discussed by John Moles below, it is tempting to see Socles' speech at 5.92, at least in part, as a commentary on Sparta's own tyrannical foreign policy against a tyrannically imperialist Athens during the Peloponnesian War.[56]

Athens does ultimately cede to the Spartans' appeal, and rejects Alexander's advances. But in the context of Herodotus' detailed account of Alexander's descent from Perdiccas I, even historically unaware audiences would be able to read in here popular controversy in Athens concerning Athens' unstable alliance during the Peloponnesian War with Alexander's son, Perdiccas II. Herodotus' audiences would detect a particularly hollow ring in Athens' rejection of Macedonian advances; moreover, it appears ironic in relation to the parallel between Macedonian trickery at the start of the Persian War and Macedonian trickery at the start of the Peloponnesian War.[57] Athens' ongoing involvement with Macedonian political intrigue later in the century would, in fact, make the Spartans' comment about Alexander's tyrannical involvement with the tyrannical Persians, quoted above, fit perfectly as a model or aetiology for Athens'

---

[54] Hdt. 8.142.4–5: μηδὲ ὑμέας Ἀλέξανδρος ὁ Μακεδὼν ἀναγνώσῃ, λεήνας τὸν Μαρδονίου λόγον· τούτῳ μὲν γὰρ ταῦτα ποιητέα ἐστί· τύραννος γὰρ ἐὼν τυράννῳ συγκατεργάζεται, 'Don't let Alexander the Macedonian change your minds, with his smooth-talking version of Mardonius' proposal. This kind of thing is what you should expect from him: as a tyrant he collaborates with a tyrant.'

[55] Hdt. 5.70–6 (including the fourth, but, as Herodotus' audience would know only too well, not the last, invasion of Attic soil by Spartans; see above all Henderson, pp. 300–6 below.

[56] See Moles, pp. 250–3 below.

[57] See esp. Thuc. 1.56–9. Hermippus fr. 63 K-A, part of a catalogue of the good things which Athens imports, contains the following lines (8–9): καὶ παρὰ Σιτάλκου ψώραν Λακεδαιμονίοισι, | καὶ παρὰ Περδίκκου ψεύδη ναυσὶν πάνυ πόλλαις, '. . . and from Sitalces an itch to plague the Spartans, and from Perdiccas lies in a great fleet of ships.' Whereas Sitalces king of Thrace is here viewed as a nuisance for Sparta, Macedonians, and Perdiccas in particular, have become stereotypically untrustworthy. This is to be read in conjunction with Thucydides' own critical account of Perdiccas' involvement with Athens, for which see Badian (1993) Ch. 6. See also Borza (1990b) Ch. 6.

own subsequent (imperial, even tyrannical) involvement with the tyrannical Perdiccas.[58]

The fullest description of Alexander's status is reserved for his night mission to the Athenian line before Plataea. Although Alexander is made to refer to himself simply as Ἀλέξανδρος ὁ Μακεδών, 'Alexander the Macedonian', at 9.45.3, the narrator introduces him at 44.1 as Ἀλέξανδρος ὁ Ἀμύντεω, στρατηγός τε ἐὼν καὶ βασιλεὺς Μακεδόνων, 'Alexander son of Amyntas, general and king of the Macedonians'. In the very act of telling the Athenians of Mardonius' plans, and pledging allegiance to the Greek cause, metamorphosing into 'a spokesperson for the ideal of Greek liberty',[59] Alexander's rhetoric is undercut not only by his lining up on the opposing side in the battle, but also by the Herodotean narrator's culminating statement on Alexander's power. By reserving the foreign-sounding appellation of *basileus* for him at precisely this moment, in combination with the term 'general', which makes him sound quite Greek, Herodotus here neatly recapitulates the overall problem with Alexander: whatever he claims in his own *logoi*, it is his independently verifiable actions, such as his marrying-off of his sister, on which he must be judged; and these actions always align him with the Persians.[60] Note further irony redounding against the Athenians: it does not work to their credit that they later attempted alliances with the son of the very man who formed up against them in the Persian Wars; Alexander also therefore provides a neat aetiology of subsequent Macedonian untrustworthiness, which, for political and imperial expediency, the Athenians ended up accepting.

Herodotus has it both ways with Alexander. He is keen to present his Greek *credentials*, but offers a very different take on his *actions*. For Jonathan Hall this is all of a part with Herodotus' questioning of the usefulness of ethnic definitions of Greekness: '[Herodotus's questioning of the validity of the ethnic criterion in the definition of *to Hellēnikon*] . . . allows us to understand why two passages in which Herodotus unreservedly accepts the claims of the Macedonian monarchy to Greek descent are appended

[58] Athens' tyrannical *archē*: esp. Thuc. 1.23, for 'the increasing greatness' (always a loaded term in Thuc.) of Athens as part of the *alēthestatēn prophasin* for the Peloponnesian War; Thuc. 2.65.9 (with Hornblower (1996) 346 *ad loc.*, highlighting the similarity with Darius' argument in the constitution debate at Hdt. 3.82.4); and, of course, Thuc. 2.63.2, read against 3.37.2; cf. also the anti-Athenian rhetoric of Thuc. 1.122.2 and 2.8.4. See also Ar. *Kn.* 1111–15; for more detail on the implications of Athens' tyrannical *dēmos*, see Kallet (2003); see also Munson (2001b) 58. For parallels between Athens and Herodotus' tyrants elsewhere in Book 5 see especially the discussion by Moles (pp. 262–3 below) of the baby Cypselus as model for newborn Athenian democracy.

[59] Flower and Marincola (2002) 189 *ad* 9.44–5.

[60] As Pelling (2002) 148 points out, Herodotus makes Darius in his speech in the Constitutional Debate of Hdt. 3 avoid using the term *basileia* precisely because of its overly narrow associations with the archetypally Persian form of government, deficient in resonance for Herodotus' Hellenic reception.

without explicit comment to medizing actions on the part of Alexander I. Alexander's alleged Hellenic descent is no guarantee that he will *act* like a Greek.'[61] Herodotus' muddying of the waters here is, however, challenging not only for our thinking on Alexander and the Persians. That it under- mines some certainties is significant also for Greek thinking on power and governance, inviting Greek audiences to examine carefully the actions of individuals and groups who were generally accepted to be Greek. Although Herodotus' treatment of Alexander offers implicit criticism of duplicity in the realms of international politics and military strategy, it also serves to put additional pressure on the supposed fixity of oppositions between Greeks and barbarians.[62]

Alexander's trajectory links him more and more with Athens. We might then ask what might happen if we take up this association in terms of eth- nicity. Now that the association between claiming Greekness and acting in a Greek way has been severed in Herodotus' Macedonian *logoi*, the implica- tions for Athens are stark. The tyrannical nature of Athens' own imperialist activities is well documented after the Persian wars: for Herodotus, these begin explicitly with Xanthippus' crucifixion of Persians in his own final (but open-endedly allusive) *logos*;[63] and they continue with their collection of tribute from the same Ionian states who suffered likewise from Croesus' own imperialist ambitions.[64] Earlier, at 8.142, the Spartans had emphasized the idealizing Greekness of Athens as a guide to how she must or should act in resisting the Persians and Macedonians;[65] and Athens, of course, claims that she will act according to shared Greek standards.[66] But if a claim to ethnic Greekness cannot any longer be taken as an accurate guide to how

---

[61] Hall (2001) 170 (original italics).
[62] This matches in many ways the approach of Pelling (2002), on the implications of the Persian Constitutional Debate for Greeks and Greek governance.
[63] 9.114-end; cf. Moles (2002) 48–9.
[64] See 1.5.3 (Croesus as the first man known to Herodotus as having committed acts of injustice against the Greeks); cf. 1.26.
[65] οὔτε γὰρ δίκαιον οὐδαμῶς οὔτε κόσμον φέρον οὔτε γε ἄλλοισι Ἑλλήνων οὐδαμοῖσι, ὑμῖν δὲ δὴ καὶ διὰ πάντων ἥκιστα πολλῶν εἵνεκα, 'it would in no way be consistent with justice or decency for any other of the Greeks [to side with Persia], and you least of all, for many reasons'; ἄλλως τε τούτων ἁπάντων αἰτίους γενέσθαι δουλοσύνης τοῖσι Ἕλλησι Ἀθηναίους οὐδαμῶς ἀνασχετόν, οἵτινες αἰεὶ καὶ τὸ πάλαι φαίνεσθε πολλοὺς ἐλευθερώσαντες ἀνθρώπων, 'Moreover, it would be unbearable for you Athenians, who always, particularly in the past, seem so often to have been men's liberators, to be responsible for the enslavement of the Greeks.'
[66] This culminates in the famous chapter at 8.144. In context with Herodotus' overall view of Alexander, and his likely awareness of Athenian involvement with the Macedonians, it is to be felt now ironic that it is the Athenians who give voice to the shared customs of the Greeks at 8.144, so often claimed as Herodotus' touchstone for Greekness (Thomas (2001a) for instance makes no connection between this passage, cited at the start of her discussion, and the Macedonians she discusses later, where she notes (219): 'It is curious that at this supreme moment of Medizing in Book 8 Herodotus chooses to stress their [the Macedonians'] Argive, and therefore Greek, ancestry'). Making these connections would add an extra strand to the argument of Hall (2002) 189ff.

Alexander will act, nor can it in the case of the Athenians themselves, whose subsequent affiliations with the Macedonians are suggested and implicitly criticized through the dynamic trajectory of Herodotus' accounts of the behaviour of Alexander.

Let us now return, in conclusion, to chapter 19 of Book 5, Herodotus' introduction of Alexander to us. This highly allusive and temporally complex introduction invites us to read in our own fuller knowledge of Alexander and Macedon, and fill out our view of Alexander with Herodotus' accounts in later books: this is, in fact, what we are asked to do explicitly at the start of 5.22, on the question of Macedonian ethnicity. As we have seen, these later accounts in turn encourage us to read and think critically and discursively about tyranny, ethnicity, and interactions between Macedon and the Greek world, and Athens in particular. Herodotus' overall opacity on the issue of the Macedonians' *nomoi* prevents us from giving any full account of their cultural or ethnic identity. As such, the possibility remains open for audiences to consider Macedonian ethnicity as merely an exceptional case, or as providing a limit-case for Greekness. But Herodotus, rather more interestingly, also provides us, through the structuring and detail of his Macedonian *logos*, sufficient scope to read more discursively, allowing us to read his portrayal of the complex, duplicitous, and highly ambiguous actions of Alexander as paradigmatic for the political history of Greece beyond the terminus of his *Histories*.

One final point: Alexander 'demonstrated', ἀπέδεξε, his Greekness to the *hellanodikai* at Olympia, and is allowed to compete (22.2); as we have seen, even in its assertion of Alexander's Greekness, Herodotus' account calls it into question. It seems at least plausible that we are allowed to read this panhellenic 'demonstration' against Herodotus' own such project of 'demonstration' as set out in the opening words of the preface of the *Histories*: Ἡροδότου Ἁλικαρνησσέος ἱστορίης ἀπόδεξις, 'the demonstration of the inquiries of Herodotus of Halicarnassus'. We thus have two acts of demonstration, one incorporating the other within itself.[67]

What may we take from this parallelism? After all, both men present their credentials as Greeks on the margins, Herodotus doing so in his first sentence.[68] But the upshot is that Herodotus' own act of demonstration (whether oral or literary) is more effective than that of Alexander: in any case, the contest is ultimately unfair, given that the latter is reported in and subsumed by the former. The richness of Herodotus' narrative tapestry

---

[67] Herodotus, of course, is too savvy to give us his own genealogy: see 2.143.1, with Dewald (2002).
[68] Cf. e.g. Goldhill (2002) 11 on the proem: 'The location "of Halicarnassus" signals a position – writing on the boundary between Greece and its enemy.'

radically outdoes and overcomes the claims which Alexander makes, and ultimately offers a rather more open-hearted version of political history and cultural/ethnic identity. Herodotus' account is, overall, no less ambiguous, but transforms the partisan and propagandist claims often voiced in individual *logoi* by individuals such as Alexander, allowing the multiplicity of such *logoi* to impose themselves upon our minds, in order for us to work through for ourselves their seemingly boundless implications and interconnectedness. Herodotus' own ambiguities are ultimately rather more munificent.

CHAPTER 4

Bridging the narrative (5.23–7)

Emily Greenwood [1]

The image of the bridge is germane to the spirit of a volume that seeks to identify and explain connections between different *logoi* in Herodotus' *Histories*. The bridges in Herodotus' work have the potential to reveal the constructedness of the narrative and the transitions between different sections within this narrative. Bridging can also represent the historical operation that twenty-first-century readers are obliged to perform as we attempt to read historically and to make connections with the work's implied audiences. [2]

The transition between Books 4 and 5 of the *Histories* coincides, neatly, with the interstitial space of the Hellespont and marks a shift in subject matter as Herodotus links the acts of conquest undertaken by foreign rulers in distant lands (narrated in Books 1–4) with the extension of conquest into the Greek arena (narrated in Books 6–9). In the following discussion of chapters 23–7, I will examine how the geographical gulf of the Hellespont serves to highlight cultural gaps and differences and, as a marker that features in several significant campaigns, highlights gaps in understanding on the part of different agents in the *Histories*. As a symbolic space between two continents that has geographical, ethnographical, and historical significance, the Hellespont represents the kinds of repeated crossings that the reader of Herodotus has to make in order to comprehend the significance of the different dimensions of the narrative.

The idea that the Hellespont, as a landmark, might serve as a metaphor that conveys meaning between different continents and peoples, and between different sections of the *Histories*, reflects a pattern that other readers have detected in Herodotus' text. At several points in the *Histories*, Herodotus seems to envisage his work as a space or territory unto itself, which subsumes the literal geographical territories that he surveys in the

---

[1] I have enjoyed discussing the ideas expressed in this Chapter with Elizabeth Irwin, and would like to thank her for the improving suggestions that she has made at every stage of its development.

[2] Cf. Munson (2001b) 18 for the idea of 'bridging our distance from the intended audience'.

course of his historical enquiry and enables the reader to travel through the text.[3] David Chamberlain calls this Herodotus' 'narrative geography', and writes that 'Herodotus presents us with a world whose social and topographical boundaries are conceptually equivalent to the internal structures and borders of the text; we can't understand one independently of the other.'[4] Finally, the bridge also enables us to negotiate our way around what Thomas Harrison has called the 'landscape of causation' in the *Histories*, enabling us to comprehend the connections between apparently disparate historical actions.[5]

CROSSING THE HELLESPONT

Μεγάβαζος δὲ ἄγων τοὺς Παίονας ἀπίκετο ἐπὶ τὸν Ἑλλήσποντον, ἐνθεῦτεν δὲ διαπεραιωθεὶς ἀπίκετο ἐς τὰς Σάρδις.

Megabazus arrived at the Hellespont with the Paeonians in tow, and once he had made the crossing from there came to Sardis. (5.23.1)

The first sentence in chapter 23 exemplifies the importance of the bridge as a narrative construct in the *Histories*. At 5.23.1 Megabazus crosses the Hellespont (διαπεραιωθείς: lit. 'was conveyed across') and arrives in Sardis. At the same time this sentence acts as a bridge with the preceding narrative: Megabazus arrives at the Hellespont with the Paeonians in tow (ἄγων τοὺς Παίονας). This reference to the Paeonians takes us back to chapters 12–17 of Book 5, where the Paeonians entered the narrative as an enthralling ethnographic sideshow. In fact, there is a faint verbal echo of 5.17.1 (ἤγοντο . . . Μεγάβαζος δέ) at the beginning of 5.23.1 (Μεγάβαζος δὲ ἄγων). Rather than take this echo as an indication that the intervening chapters are an insertion, as does Macan,[6] we should see it as a prompt to examine the implicit connections between the different *logoi* at the beginning of Book 5. The Thracian *logos* (5.3–10) develops a brief ethnography of Thrace through the lens of contemporary Greek history, specifically the role of Thrace in the geopolitics of the Greek world in the late 430s/420s (see Irwin, pp. 79–83

---

[3] This 'spatial-geographical' interpretation of Herodotus' text has been expounded chiefly by French scholars. In *The Mirror of Herodotus* François Hartog proposed a model of Herodotus' text as a work that constructs actual geographical space (*l'espace concret*) in the space of its own narrative (*l'espace du discours*) according to his way of conceptualizing space (*l'espace du savoir*), which is in its turn determined by language (*l'espace de la langue*). Cf. Hartog (1988) 354–5. Inspired by Hartog, Pascal Payen has taken this spatial metaphor in a different direction by examining Herodotus' text as a territory that resists conquest and colonization: Payen (1997); cf. especially chapter 3, 'Usages de l'espace du récit'. See also Darbo-Peschanski (1987) section 2.3 'Le Territoire de l'enquête'. On Herodotus' narrative as a metaphorical journey, see Munson (2001b) 33 with nn. 31–4.

[4] Chamberlain (2001) 7.   [5] Harrison (2003) 240.   [6] See Macan (1895) I. 167.

above). Next, the Paeonian *logos* (5.11–17) explores the relationship between ethnographic knowledge and the conquest of other *ethnē* against the backdrop of cultural and geographical displacement. As Robin Osborne notes, the detail that the Paeonians are being uprooted ἐξ ἠθέων (from their land and customs) occurs twice in the Paeonian *logos* (see p. 94 above). The theme of cultural displacement and geographical transition then recurs in the Macedonian *logos* (5.17–22), where Macedonian and Persian customs are narrated in such a way that they are mutually transformative: aspects of the Persians' behaviour look quite Greek, and Macedonian customs look quite Persian (see Fearn, Ch. 3 above). The Macedonian *logos* also suggests that the Hellespont constitutes a tricky geographical crossing, which is never without difficult consequences for those who cross. These themes continue to resonate in the present *logos*, as Herodotus focuses on interpersonal relations between Ionian Greeks and the court of Darius. These relations are characterized by ambiguity and precariousness, illustrating the difficulty of crossing cultures in the *Histories*. The historian crosses back and forwards between cultures continually, but for the characters in his *Histories* and for agents in history, such crossings are hard to make since geography and ethnography are founded on complicated ideological constructions.

Immediately before the digression on the Paeonians, Darius had been reminded of the benefaction (*euergesia*) done to him by Histiaeus tyrant of Miletus and the profitable advice rendered by Coes of Mytilene, both of which related to the Hellespont.[7]

As for Darius, as soon as he had crossed the Hellespont (Δαρεῖος δὲ ὡς διαβὰς τάχιστα τὸν Ἑλλήσποντον) and come to Sardis, he remembered the good service (εὐεργεσίης) done him by Histiacus of Miletus and the counsel (παραινέσιος) of Coes the Mytilenean, . . . (5.11.1)

This passage points backwards in the narrative to 4.97 where Coes' advice had prevented Darius from breaking up the bridge over the Danube during his invasion of Scythia, and to 4.137 where Histiaeus opposed the proposal of the Athenian Miltiades to destroy this same bridge. So at 5.11.1 as Darius crosses the Hellespont, Herodotus bridges the narrative and puts Darius' dealings with the Ionian Greeks in the context of his recent attempts at conquest (of the Scythians), as well as his son Xerxes' future attempt at the conquest of Greece.[8] The politics of Darius' cross-cultural negotiations with Histiaeus are the focus in these chapters. As with the preceding Macedonian *logos*, this section of the narrative explores the gaps and potential for

---

[7] For Persian kings rewarding benefactions, see Lewis (1989) 228; and Braund (1998) 301 with n. 51.
[8] See Xerxes' bridging of the Hellespont at 7.33–7.

misunderstandings in the cross-cultural dealings that result, ultimately, in an all-out act of cross-cultural and geopolitical transgression – the Persian invasions of Greece.

READING BACKWARDS AND FORWARDS

τειχέοντος ἤδη Ἱστιαίου τοῦ Μιλησίου τὴν παρὰ Δαρείου αἰτήσας ἔτυχε μισθὸν δωρεὴν φυλακῆς τῆς σχεδίης, ἐόντος δὲ τοῦ χώρου τούτου παρὰ Στρυμόνα ποταμόν, τῷ οὔνομά ἐστι Μύρκινος, μαθὼν ὁ Μεγάβαζος τὸ ποιεύμενον ἐκ τοῦ Ἱστιαίου, ὡς ἦλθε τάχιστα ἐς τὰς Σάρδις ἄγων τοὺς Παίονας, ἔλεγε Δαρείῳ τάδε·

Histiaeus of Miletus was already fortifying the [land] which he had received from Darius as a gift-payment for his custody of the bridge (this region, whose name is Myrcinus, is on the river Strymon); Megabazus learned of Histiaeus' actions and as soon as he came to Sardis, leading the Paeonians, he spoke to Darius as follows: . . . (5.23.1–2)

At 5.23.1 the adverb ἤδη – 'already' – alerts us to the fact of time passing in the space of twelve chapters (between 5.11 and 5.23), during which 'time' Megabazus has been waylaid by the campaign against the Paeonians, and Histiaeus has already begun to fortify the strategic city of Myrcinus. The link between Histiaeus' current status and his actions at 4.137 is made explicit at 5.23.1, where we are told that Megabazus encountered Histiaeus who was already fortifying the city which he had got as his μισθὸν δωρεήν ('gift-payment') for guarding the bridge across the Hellespont (φυλακῆς τῆς σχεδίης). The second sentence in chapter 23 (cited above) is notably circumambient: two genitive absolute constructions (τειχέοντος . . . ἐόντος) and two further subordinate clauses defer the main verb ἔλεγε. The fact that the sentence structure is so indirect perhaps reflects the fact of Megabazus being bypassed (while stuck in a digression) and having to learn of the gift of Myrcinus indirectly, after the event, as opposed to having been consulted before the event. Since we have been told that Megabazus was leading the Paeonians in the first sentence, the repetition of the same phrase – ἄγων τοὺς Παίονας – is marked. Megabazus has been saddled with a dead-end campaign that wastes time and resources, while Histiaeus, one of Megabazus' rivals in the contest for influence with Darius, has obtained one of the most sought-after cities in Thrace.[9] The inappropriateness of

---

[9] This reading is influenced by Pericles Georges' interpretation of the outbreak of the Ionian Revolt as a product of the rivalry among influential Persians and Ionian Greeks for the Great King's favour and patronage. See Georges (2000) 12 and 15. Herodotus refers to this rivalry at 6.30.1 (see p. 143 below), and his representation of Megabazus' resentment of Histiaeus supports Georges' interpretation.

this arrangement is compounded by the fact that Megabazus was Darius'
military commander in Thrace and his rival Histiaeus is not even a Persian. Megabazus himself quantifies the honour paid to Histiaeus when
he describes Myrcinus' natural resources at 5.23.2: ἤδη ναυπηγήσιμος
ἄφθονος ('abundant timber for shipbuilding'), πολλοὶ κωπέες ('wood to
build many oars'), and μέταλλα ἀργύρεα ('silver mines').[10] As Macan suggests, Megabazus' protest about the danger of allowing a clever Greek to
control this strategic city in Thrace, prompted (allegedly) by the fear that he
might establish an independent kingdom, has an anachronistic colouring,
calling to mind the importance of Thrace in the Pentekontaëtia and the
Second Peloponnesian War.[11]

   Still sticking with the theme of 'bridging the narrative', Megabazus'
speech to Darius, warning him not to trust Histiaeus (5.23.2–24.1)
prompts us to make forward-reaching connections. At 5.24.1, Herodotus
writes that Megabazus easily persuaded Darius that he had a good grasp of
what would happen in the future (ταῦτα λέγων ὁ Μεγάβαζος εὐπετέως[12]
ἔπειθε τὸν Δαρεῖον ὡς εὖ προορῶν τὸ μέλλον γίνεσθαι).[13] In one sense
Megabazus does foresee the future, but his foresight is self-fulfilling. For
at 5.35.1, the motivation attributed to Histiaeus' sending a signal (the tattooed slave) to provoke the Ionian Revolt, is his distress at being detained
in Susa against his will,[14] which is a direct result of Megabazus' supposedly prescient advice.[15] So Megabazus 'sees the future', but at the level of
one who anticipates how events will unfold and yet unwittingly facilitates
their denouement. If Megabazus had been better informed, then his knowledge of the past – for instance the case of the Greek doctor Democedes
detained against his will at the court of Darius in Susa (cf. 3.132ff.) – might
have made him advise Darius otherwise. This is tantamount to suggesting
that Megabazus would have offered Darius better advice if he had read
Herodotus' *Histories*.

   The 'bridge' between Histiaeus and Democedes is made at 5.24.4, where
Darius tells Histiaeus: 'follow me to Susa. All I have will there be yours. You

---

[10] As Elizabeth Irwin has pointed out to me, these natural resources were crucial to the Athenian empire.
The adjective ναυπηγήσιμος evokes the theme of naval *archē*. Cf. Ps.-Xenophon, *Constitution of
the Athenians* 2.11–12.

[11] Macan (1895) I.168 (*ad loc.*). See Irwin, pp. 82–3 above.

[12] For the idea that εὐπετής, εὐπετέως and εὐπετείη sound notes of caution that things are not as easy
as they seem, see Pelling (pp. 179–83 below), Fearn (p. 103 above) and Munson (pp. 158–9 below).

[13] An analogy can be drawn here with the different types of anticipatory constructions discussed by
Brock (2003).

[14] 5.35.4: ταῦτα δὲ ὁ Ἱστιαῖος ἐποίεε συμφορὴν ποιεύμενος μεγάλην τὴν ἑωυτοῦ κατοχὴν τὴν ἐν
Σούσοισι ('what prompted Histiaeus to do this was his distress at being detained in Susa').

[15] I thank Rob Tordoff for pointing this out to me.

will eat at my table and be my counsellor' (σὺ δέ μοι ἑπόμενος ἐς Σοῦσα ἔχε τά περ ἂν ἐγὼ ἔχω, ἐμός τε σύσσιτος ἐὼν καὶ σύμβουλος). The noun σύσσιτος (table companion, messmate) recalls the honorific status of ὁμοτράπεζος ('sharing the same table') accorded to Democedes at the court of Darius (3.132.1).[16] Darius' proposition to Histiaeus should trouble the reader on several levels. I will return to the theme of commensality below, but first there is the question of the discrepancies between what Darius proposes to Histiaeus in his letter (5.24.1–2) and what he proposes to his face (5.24.3–4).

DARIUS' LETTER AND SPEECH (5.23–4)

Darius' letter is encouraging, but vague. He commends Histiaeus' proven goodwill towards him and his affairs and mentions that he is contemplating πρήγματα μεγάλα ('great matters') and wants to set them before Histiaeus. The letter is a plausible, if not a historical document: the explicit acknowledgement of Histiaeus' goodwill towards Darius and the implication of his trustworthiness is in keeping with the qualities in their benefactors that Achaemenid kings record and reward in surviving documents,[17] and the opening phrase echoes an official formula.[18] The letter is thus doubly plausible: both intratextually from the point of view of the recipient of the letter, and also extratextually from the point of view Herodotus' Greek audiences – these are the kind of sentiments and terms, and this is the tone that one would expect in a communiqué from the King of Persia.[19]

The terms that Darius puts to Histiaeus in person are subtly different. The speech is more elaborate, occupying ten lines of text in contrast to the five lines occupied by the letter. Macan argued that the discrepancies between the letter and the speech expose the fact that they are invented by Herodotus, observing that Histiaeus would have been disconcerted by

[16] Herodotus uses various terms to refer to 'dining companions' of the Persian King; in addition to the terms *homotrapezos* and *sussitos*, cited here, at 7.119.3 he uses the plural noun *homositoi*. The hierarchical relationship, if any, between these terms is not clear. For discussion see Briant (1996) 319–22.

[17] The adjective *eunous* (benevolent, showing goodwill) used here is linked with the adjectives *pistos* (faithful, trustworthy), and *bebaios* (dependable) in a passage of Xenophon's *Anabasis* describing the qualities possessed by those in the circle of the younger Cyrus (I.9.30). I owe this reference to Briant (1996) 335; see ibid. 335–7 for a discussion of the Greek and Persian terms for the moral qualities attributed to the King's benefactors.

[18] Robert Fowler (2001) 110 points out that the format of this letter ('thus says X' followed by a statement in the first person, as here) follows a formula used in official edicts issued by the King of Persia.

[19] It is important to stress that here we are dealing with a *Greek* view of the Achaemenid kings, their system of government and their moral and cultural world. Moreover, this is the highly nuanced and idiosyncratic view of a particular Greek author.

these discrepancies had they actually existed.[20] However, if we grant the plausibility, although not necessarily the historicity of the letter and the speech, then we can concentrate on the function that these discrepancies serve in Herodotus' narrative.

Essentially, the letter conveys an order (the imperative ἀπικνέο ('come') – 5.24.2), prefaced by the flattering statement that Darius acknowledges Histiaeus' benevolence and the enticement that he wants Histiaeus to be party to the matters of great importance that he is contemplating. This reflects Megabazus' recommendation that he should employ a gentle tone (τρόπῳ ἠπίῳ). In the next sentence the narrative is focalized through Histiaeus, and we are shown the letter achieving its desired effect. Two participles, πιστεύσας and (μέγα) ποιεύμενος, signal his credulous and ambitious outlook. This is important for the face-to-face speech that follows: the letter has done its work and primed Histiaeus to be a suggestible recipient, and this psychological realism helps to establish the plausibility of Herodotus' account. Although the speech departs from the words of the letter, its perlocutionary force is the same and Darius elaborates on the same themes. Rather than disconcerting Histiaeus and putting him on his guard, the speech is calculated to give him an even greater sense of his status with the king and the security of his position. Darius lays it on thick, stating that he cannot stand to have Histiaeus out of his sight and that Histiaeus is the most valued of all his possessions. The speech is cleverly crafted to sound different notes with the internal audience (Histiaeus) and the external audience of Herodotus' text. The external audience can see the ambiguity in Darius' statement that he cannot bear to have Histiaeus out of his sight, since we know that he is being brought to Susa precisely so that they can keep an eye on him. Another difference between the reader's perspective and that of Histiaeus, is that the reader has just 'heard' Megabazus refer to Histiaeus negatively as *deinos te kai sophos* ('(too) clever and sagacious', 5.23.2), whereas Darius modifies this in his speech and instead Histiaeus hears the complimentary description '*sunetos te kai eunoos*' ('intelligent and benevolent' – 5.24.3).[21] The peroration of Darius' speech is similarly equivocal, from the reader's point of view, but calculated to keep Histiaeus sweet. Darius instructs him, again using an imperative, to leave Miletus and Myrcinus (Μίλητον μὲν ἔα καὶ τὴν νεόκτιστον ἐν Θρηίκῃ πόλιν, 5.24.4),

---

[20] Macan (1895) I.168: 'The contrast between the message and the speech of Darius had they been genuine would have opened the eyes of Histiaeus. The μεγάλα πρήγματα of the despatch disappear in the speech.'

[21] See n. 58 below.

but the verb is vague enough to hide the fact that effectively Histiaeus is being dispossessed of this territory. Besides, this detail is eclipsed by the second clause in which Darius elevates Histiaeus, promising him 'whatever I have' and inviting him to share his table and to be his adviser. Again, from the perspective of the reader, the ostensibly cosy invitation to join the king's table is undermined by the fact that the invitation is prompted by suspicion as opposed to trust.

Furthermore, the concept of such cross-cultural dining is unsettling in view of the curious cross-cultural symposium in the preceding *logos*. As David Fearn has shown in his discussion of the 'quasi-Greek' symposium in Macedon (5.18–20; see pp. 104–5 above), it is hard for different cultures to preserve their customs when dining together, leading to ambiguity and confusion. Ambiguity is present in the very language in which Darius' proposition is couched: he summons Histiaeus to be his *sussitos* – a term that evokes the Spartan system of communal dining.[22]

This proposal from the King of Persia to an ambitious Greek, with its curious Spartan colouring, may call Pausanias into the minds of some of Herodotus' readers. If we turn to Thucydides' *History*, we find Pausanias, like Histiaeus before him in Herodotus, securing the gratitude of the King of Persia (in this case with Xerxes – Darius' son) through *euergesia* (Thuc. 1.128.4). Thucydides also reports that Pausanias underwent a process of Persian acculturation, which included adopting Persian dining habits (τράπεζαν περσικήν, 1.130.1).[23] If this analogy seems far-fetched, consider the pointed insertion of Pausanias into the narrative at 5.32 in the context of a passage about Aristagoras' cooperation with the royal house of Persia.[24] Arguably Herodotus associates Histiaeus' dealings with Darius with future Greek–Persian relations both within the text and beyond it.

Another connection that links this section of text with the later books of the *Histories* is that Histiaeus serves as a precursor for Themistocles: another cunning, opportunistic, influential Greek who ingratiates himself with the Persian king. As we have just seen, Megabazus refers to Histiaeus as *deinos te kai sophos*. In his *CAH* article on the Ionian Revolt, Oswyn Murray links Histiaeus with Themistocles as archetypal cunning tricksters,

---

[22] The only other instance of this word group in the *Histories* is at 1.65.5, in a passage where Herodotus mentions the Spartan institution of communal messes (συσσίτια), whose introduction he attributes to Lycurgus.

[23] Cf. Pelling at p. 194 below. We can contrast Pausanias' austere 'Laconian meal' in Herodotus (9.82.2–3; on which see Pelling, p. 189 n. 36 below), with his 'Persian table' in Thucydides.

[24] 5.32: 'Megabates' daughter – if there is any truth in the report – was later betrothed to Pausanias son of Cleombrotus, when he conceived a desire to become tyrant of Greece.' See also n. 34 below.

in the mould of Odysseus.[25] In his *Life of Themistocles*, Plutarch records
the tradition that Persian kings after Artaxerxes – the Persian king at whose
court Themistocles achieved greatest influence – used Themistocles' name
as a byword for high status and influence at the Persian court (29.9):

Λέγεται δὲ καὶ τοὺς ὕστερον βασιλεῖς, ἐφ' ὧν μᾶλλον αἱ Περσικαὶ πράξεις ταῖς
Ἑλληνικαῖς ἀνεκράθησαν, ὁσάκις δεηθεῖεν ἀνδρὸς Ἕλληνος, ἐπαγγέλλεσθαι καὶ
γράφειν ἕκαστον, ὡς μείζων ἔσοιτο παρ' αὐτῷ Θεμιστοκλέους.

It is said that subsequent kings, in whose time Persian and Greek affairs were
mingled to a greater extent, whenever there was need for a Greek, would each
write and promise that this man's influence in his court would be greater than
Themistocles'. (Greek text and translation cited from B. Perrin's Loeb edn. (1914),
vol. II)

And yet Themistocles' rise to prominence at the court of the Artaxerxes
belongs to a larger tradition of influential Greeks ingratiating themselves
with Persian kings. In certain respects, Themistocles' career in the *Histories*
mimics Histiaeus' earlier example.[26] Whereas Histiaeus did genuinely prevent some of his fellow Ionian Greeks from pulling down Darius' bridge
across the Danube, Themistocles lied (to Xerxes) about his role vis-à-vis the
bridge across the Hellespont. In fact, his role constitutes a reversal of Histiaeus' position. At 4.137.2 Histiaeus counsels preserving the bridge across the
Danube in opposition to Miltiades' proposal to break it up. In contrast, at
8.108 Themistocles proposes to break Xerxes' bridge across the Hellespont
and to trap the Persians in Europe. He is opposed by Eurybiades, who is in
favour of letting the Persians get back to Asia. When he realizes that Eurybiades' advice is popular, he appropriates it as his own. Herodotus describes
this tactic as setting up a 'store', or 'deposit' (ἀποθήκη) – of favour with
the Persian king, in case he should fall foul of the Greeks (8.109.5).

ταῦτα ἔλεγε ἀποθήκην μέλλων ποιήσεσθαι ἐς τὸν Πέρσην, ἵνα ἢν ἄρα τί μιν
καταλαμβάνῃ πρὸς Ἀθηναίων πάθος, ἔχῃ ἀποστροφήν·

Themistocles said these things with the intention of setting up a store of favours
with the Persian King, so that if his relations with the Athenians should suffer, he
would have somewhere to turn to.

The noun ἀποστροφή – 'turning back', 'escape', 'refuge', 'recourse' – might
remind us of the noun ἄποδος at 4.97.4, where Coes advises Darius not to

---

[25] Murray (1988) 486. For Themistocles as a 'fifth-century Odysseus', see also Fornara (1971b) 72;
echoed by Moles (2002) 48 who terms Themistocles as an 'Odyssean or Promethean figure'.
[26] See Munson (2001b) 52 for the idea that in the *Histories*, 'the responsibility for bringing two disparate
actions together lies not with the collector of the *logoi* but with the historical agents who chose to
play someone else's role.'

take down the bridge across the Danube, on the grounds that it will provide an ἄποδος for them: a way out/a retreat/an escape. The existence
of these precarious bridges – the bridge across the Hellespont in particular – provides opportunities for crossings backwards and forwards, for
reversals, and for going back on previous commitments. At the same time,
they serve a historiographical function, alerting us to connections and patterns between characters and their actions in the *Histories*. In this case they
encourage the reader to see Themistocles' behaviour in light of the career
of Histiaeus, and vice versa.[27] The double-dealing practised by Histiaeus
and Themistocles blurs the ideological boundaries between Greeks and Persians. Both characters display intellectual virtues that are tarnished by the
contexts in which they use them. Histiaeus' *sophiē* is self-serving and serves
the Persian King, effectively undermining the cause of Ionian freedom.
For his part, Themistocles is proclaimed the wisest Greek (ἀνὴρ σοφώτα-
τος – 8.124.1–2) for his role in orchestrating the battle of Salamis and is
awarded an olive crown by the Spartans for his wisdom and intelligence
(σοφίης δὲ καὶ δεξιότητος – 8.124.2). The honours paid to Themistocles
at Sparta are described as both ἀριστήια ('prizes', 8.124.2) and γέρεα
('honours', 8.125.1). However, the veneer of heroic glory is undermined by
a corrupt streak, since Themistocles deceived both Greeks and Persians (see
8.108–10), and exploited his enhanced reputation after the battle of Salamis
to extort money from the islands in the Aegean (8.112). Wolfgang Blösel
has argued for an analogy between Themistocles' transformation in the
Histories from 'champion of Greek liberty' to an increasingly greedy and
opportunistic broker of his own interests, and the imperialistic and 'greedy'
Athens of Pericles.[28] Herodotus is forthright in diagnosing Themistocles'
motivation as *pleonexia* (οὐ γὰρ ἐπαύετο πλεονεκτέων, 8.112.1), evoking
in the minds of contemporary audiences a trait commonly ascribed to the
Athenians.[29] The introduction of the slogan of *pleonexia* tightens the association between Themistocles and the Athenians and blurs the direction of
influence: the two become like each other through diachronic analogy.[30]
The man who was to be perceived subsequently as the architect of Athenian

---

[27] Histiaeus is not unique. Book 5 gives other hints of 'Greeks' who trade favours with the Persians.
Alexander I of Macedon, who double-crosses the Persian envoys at 5.17–21, is another example. In
fact, Alexander is even better placed for such double dealing and reversible loyalties, given that his
Greekness is fluid (Fearn, Ch. 3 above).

[28] Blösel (2001) 181.

[29] On Themistocles' *pleonexia*, see Blösel (2001) 190 with n. 46 and 196. More generally, on *pleonexia*
and Athenian imperialism in the *Histories* see Raaflaub (1987) 227–43; Konstan (1987) 70–2; and
Moles (2002) 47–8. All three scholars refer back to Fornara (1971b) 66–72.

[30] See Munson (2001b) 52 and 73 on 'diachronic analogy'.

imperialism already bears the signs of this imperialism in the 470s BC. Through the same process, the Athenians of the present are cast in the image of the opportunist Themistocles, and are consequently not a world away from the Persian king who supposedly embodies the antithesis of Athenian ideology and government.[31] Writing the history of the Ionian Revolt through the retrospective filter of Greek resistance to Persia followed by Greek overtures to Persia, Herodotus contests the binary opposition that pitted Greek freedom against the slavishness of the Persian Monarchical system. Instead, he portrays Greeks who succumb to the lure of tyranny and the wealth to be gained from services rendered to the Persian King.[32] The spectre of Athens the would-be tyrant[33] is already hinted at in the career of Histiaeus the puppet tyrant, who tries to reconcile tyrannical ambitions with Greek ideals of freedom.[34]

DARIUS' ECONOMY AND THE COMMODIFICATION OF ADVICE

At 5.23.1, the city of Myrcinus is described as the place which Histiaeus 'had asked Darius to give him as a "gift payment" for guarding the bridge': τὴν παρὰ Δαρείου αἰτήσας ἔτυχε μισθὸν δωρεὴν φυλακῆς τῆς σχεδίης. Some editors delete the adverb δωρεήν (adverbial accusative), on the grounds that it is tautologous after μισθόν. Nenci argues that δωρεήν should be retained, since two different ideas are at stake: on the one hand the king's gift (denoted by δωρεήν), and on the other hand a reward (μισθός) for action.[35] The syntax of this sentence, which juxtaposes two nouns, whose meaning is apparently either tautologous or contradictory, requires the reader to reflect on the relationship between the two words: how can a *payment* be a *gift*, and vice versa? Sitta Von Reden's discussion of the connotations of *misthos* in networks of social and economic exchange throws light on this passage.[36] She argues that the bestowal of *misthos* always denotes an unequal or asymmetrical relationship, but that this relationship could be construed positively in the Greek context if a city (or citizen community) was the donor. In cases where a supposedly free Greek is receiving

---

[31] See Moles' list of the salient elements of the Herodotean Themistocles: 'bribery, rapacity, incipient medism, proto-imperialist bully-boy tactics' (2002) 48.
[32] See Wohl (2002) 220 on the tyrant as a 'saturated locus of fantasy' in Athenian ideology: 'what is hated at the level of "official policy". . . may appear in fantasy in the form of identification and desire.'
[33] Cf. Thucydides' Pericles on Athens' *archē* as 'like a tyranny' (2.63.2–3), and Thucydides' Cleon on Athens' tyrannical *archē* (3.37.2).
[34] The liberation struggle espoused by tyrants such as Histiaeus and Aristagoras is cut down to size by the reference to the Spartan King Pausanias at 5.32, ἔρωτα σχὼν τῆς Ἑλλάδος τύραννος γενέσθαι ('having a passionate desire to be master of Greece').
[35] Nenci (1994) *ad loc.*   [36] Von Reden (1995) 89–92 ('Symbolic loss: gaining a *misthos*').

misthos from the Persian king, the connotations of *misthos* are negative and imply servility. However, von Reden also explains how a coinage like μισθὸν δωρεήν ('gift payment') might arise: 'since every *dōron* had tied the recipient to its donor, the effects of receiving a *dōron* could be tantamount to receiving a *misthos*'.[37]

The jarring juxtaposition of μισθόν and δωρεήν invites the reader to reflect upon the strings attached to this 'gift payment', which is simultaneously part of a contract between Darius and the dependent tyrant Histiaeus. Perhaps there is also a hint of ἄδωρα δῶρα[38] – gifts that are no gifts. The contradictoriness of the phrase may also convey a clash of different cultures.[39] The juxtaposition of the terms μισθόν and δωρεήν might have sounded odd to some of Herodotus' Greek audiences, for whom the conflation of δῶρον and μισθός suggests corruption, although perfectly logical from a Persian perspective.[40] In rendering Darius a service, Histiaeus has entered into a vast symbolic economy within which the Persian King distributes and redistributes gifts as payments for past services and (implied) down payment for future services. As Pierre Briant notes, the retraction of Myrcinus – Darius' gift to Histiaeus – demonstrates the conditionality of the King's gifts, which remain his to repossess depending on the behaviour of the recipient.[41]

That the *misthos* for services rendered to the King might entail negative reciprocity is seen at 7.11.1, where Xerxes threatens his uncle Artabanus – who has just spoken against his proposal to invade Greece at a conference of the leading Persians – by saying that their close family relationship is all that protects him from receiving the *misthos* ('payback' = punishment) that he deserves for such vain words:

Ἀρτάβανος μὲν ταῦτα ἔλεξε, Ξέρξης δὲ θυμωθεὶς ἀμείβεται τοισίδε· Ἀρτάβανε, πατρὸς εἶς τοῦ ἐμοῦ ἀδελφεός· τοῦτό σε ῥύσεται μηδένα ἄξιον μισθὸν λαβεῖν ἐπέων ματαίων.[42]

For his part Artabanus said these things, and Xerxes, who was irate, replied as follows: 'Artabanus, you are my father's brother and this saves you from receiving a worthy payback for your irreverent words.'

---

[37] Von Reden (1995) 93.   [38] Sophocles, *Ajax* 665.

[39] On the problematics of gift-giving and exchanging favours across cultural boundaries see Braund (1998) passim and 162: 'How much more uncertain is reciprocity when it crosses cultural boundaries and operates between radically different world-views . . . as in the programme of Herodotus' *Histories*'.

[40] See Lewis (1989) 229: 'there are therefore transactions which may look different from the Persian side and the Greek side'. Von Reden (1995) 101 n. 43 notes, 'the discrepancy between Persian gift exchange and Greek descriptions of it needs further investigation'. See also Fisher (2002) 204, 209, and 214 on the broader themes of moral reciprocity and (loss of) freedom in Greek–Persian interaction.

[41] Briant (1996) 331.   [42] For comment on this passage see Gould (2001) 297.

Here the gift economy practised by the Persian kings turns debate into a marketplace. Artabanus himself acknowledges the economic motif that underlies the debate when he prefaces his advice by comparing the testing of ideas in debate to testing the purity of gold (7.10α.1).[43] Xerxes later repents and acknowledges that Artabanus was offering χρηστῆς . . . συμβουλῆς (7.15.2). This recalls Darius' guarantee to Coes at 4.97.6, where he promises that he will give Coes a fitting exchange for his good advice when he returns to Asia: like Xerxes in the passage just cited, he uses the phrase χρηστῆς συμβουλῆς.[44] At 5.24.2, Herodotus suggests that one of the factors that makes Histiaeus less circumspect than he should be, is because he is flattered by the prospect (and profit) of being the *sumboulos* of the king of Persia: μέγα ποιεύμενος βασιλέος σύμβουλος γενέσθαι.

The symbolic gift economy of the Persian King (as seen through Greek eyes) runs into confusion when it operates across cultures. Notice that when Darius puts his deceitful proposal to Histiaeus, he says that he realizes that an intelligent and well-disposed friend is the most highly valued of all possessions: ἐγνωκὼς ὅτι κτημάτων πάντων ἐστὶ τιμιώτατον ἀνὴρ φίλος συνετός τε καὶ εὔνοος (5.24.3). The context suggests that we should interpret this proverbial maxim literally when spoken by Darius: intelligence, goodwill and friendship are treated as commodities. The potential for confusion of moral and material values is particularly evident in contexts of advising and judgement, where the outcome seems preconditioned by the intrusion of rewards. Darius' statement is echoed by his brother Artabanus in the debate in Xerxes' court referred to above, where the latter articulates the materialism of debate in the Achaemenid court by saying that good counsel is the best source of profit: κέρδος μέγιστον (7.10δ.2). The commodification of advice is not exclusive to the Persians: another prominent non-Greek example in the *Histories* is Croesus king of Lydia, who attempts to form some kind of contract with the Delphic oracle through gift-giving (1.53.2, 1.54.1, and 1.90–1).[45] However, Croesus is subsequently

---

[43] 7.10α.1: Ὦ βασιλεῦ, μὴ λεχθεισέων μὲν γνωμέων ἀντιέων ἀλλήλῃσι οὐκ ἔστι τὴν ἀμείνω αἱρεόμενον ἑλέσθαι, ἀλλὰ δεῖ τῇ εἰρημένῃ χρᾶσθαι, λεχθεισέων δὲ ἔστι, ὥσπερ τὸν χρυσὸν τὸν ἀκήρατον αὐτὸν μὲν ἐπ' ἑωυτοῦ οὐ διαγινώσκομεν, ἐπεὰν δὲ παρατρίψωμεν ἄλλῳ χρυσῷ, διαγινώσκομεν τὸν ἀμείνω.

'O King, if conflicting judgements are not spoken, then it is not possible to choose the better judgement, and instead one has to use the opinion that has been spoken, but it is possible if they are spoken. Similarly, we cannot distinguish pure gold in relation to itself, but when we rub it against gold, we distinguish which is better.'

[44] 4.97.6: Ξεῖνε Λέσβιε, σωθέντος ἐμεῦ ὀπίσω ἐς οἶκον τὸν ἐμὸν ἐπιφάνηθί μοι πάντως, ἵνα σε ἀντὶ χρηστῆς συμβουλίης χρηστοῖσι ἔργοισι ἀμείψωμαι. 'Friend from Lesbos, when I am safely home again, make sure that you put in an appearance at my house, so that I can reciprocate your good advice with good deeds.'

[45] See Kurke (1999) chapter 4 ('Kroisos and the oracular economy').

converted, albeit too late, by Solon's ethical calculus (1.29.3–32.9), revealing to Cyrus that he would 'have considered it more valuable than vast sums of money to set up dialogues between this man [Solon] and all kings': τὸν ἂν ἐγὼ πᾶσι τυράννοισι προετίμησα μεγάλων χρημάτων ἐς λόγους ἐλθεῖν (1.86.4).

Although feigned, the terms that Darius puts to Histiaeus reveal the king's economic calculus encompassing all his dealings. This is hard to square with the anecdote about Sisamnes in the next chapter (5.25). Herodotus records that Darius appointed Otanes, son of Sisamnes, to be in charge of the coastal region, and mentions that Cambyses had put Sisamnes to death by flaying as a punishment for corrupting justice with bribes: ἐπὶ χρήμασι δίκην ἄδικον ἐδίκασε (5.25.1), and then made Otanes give his judgements sitting on a chair made from his father's skin. Leslie Kurke comments that 'Herodotus' horrified fascination with Sisamnes' punishment clogs up his narrative: he simply can't get past the image of the son sitting on his father's flayed skin as he renders judgement.'[46] However, as she acknowledges, the detail of Sisamnes' skin is rich in thematic resonances. This reminder of another Persian king's apparent concern for the integrity of judgement jars with both the immediate context, and the broader context of the actions of Persian kings in the *Histories* – not least Cambyses.[47] In Book 3 Herodotus records an anecdote about Cambyses – the same Cambyses who punished Sisamnes for 'judicial' corruption – intimidating the royal judges into falsifying ancestral custom and overriding established law (3.31). Cambyses does not exactly bribe them into interpreting the laws in his favour, but his kingly power inspires sufficient fear (δείσαντες Καμβύσεα – 3.31.5) to influence their judgement. In the anecdote about Sisamnes, it is hard to reconcile the Persian kings' insistence on the impartiality of justice, given their practice of a gift economy that introduces material interest into every action.

READING TO THE END

In the context of Herodotus' *Histories*, this symbolic economy is itself subsumed in the broader scheme of historical causation, which, as John Gould argued, is influenced by the principle that 'historical action is . . . repayment of what is owed'.[48] The payment/gift that Coes asks for in return for his advice at 5.11 – tyranny over Mytilene – leads to his death at 5.37–8. It is notable that when Herodotus recounts the names of the commanders who

---

[46] Kurke (1999) 83.   [47] For Herodotus' portrayal of the Persian royal judges, see Kurke (1999) 81–3.
[48] Gould (2001) 302.

fell into the hands of the Ionian rebels, he lists Coes as 'the one to whom Darius had given Mytilene as a gift' (τῷ Δαρεῖος Μυτιλήνην ἐδωρήσατο – 5.37.1). It is as though an initial act of reciprocity that was marked by gift-giving ultimately manifests itself in historical payback.[49] This is seen even more starkly in Histiaeus' case, where the receipt of Myrcinus as a 'gift payment' from Darius sets up a trajectory that results in violence at the end of the Book. Book 5 closes with Aristagoras looking for a settlement to serve as a refuge in case he should lose Miletus. He sets his sights on Myrcinus against the advice of Hecataeus, who counsels a quiet retreat to the island of Leros (5.125). We are reminded, quite pointedly, that Myrci-nus was the territory that Histiaeus had received as a 'gift' (δωρεή, 5.124.2, repeated from 5.23.1) from Darius. So here we see Aristagoras, following Histiaeus' trajectory (set in motion when he acted on Histiaeus' fateful order to revolt, 5.35–6) and ignoring Hecataeus' good advice, which he has already ignored once before (5.36.2–4); he gains possession of Myrcinus, but dies while laying siege to one of the neighbouring Thracian towns (5.126.2).[50] Herodotus underscores the fact that his death was avoidable: firstly, he might have avoided it by taking Hecataeus' advice and secondly, because the Thracians who killed him had wanted to make a truce and end the siege (βουλομένων τῶν Θρηίκων ὑποσπόνδων ἐξιέναι). Aristago-ras' fate represents an ironic inversion of Herodotus' comment about the Thracians at 5.3.1: '*if* the Thracians were governed by a single man, or were to have have a common cause, in my opinion they would be unbeatable and by far the most powerful of all peoples.'[51] As Herodotus goes on to comment, these conditions are impossible and consequently the Thracians are weak. But it is these 'weak' Thracians who kill Aristagoras and whose actions highlight, albeit incidentally, one of the flaws of the Ionian Revolt – its lack of a common cause.

   The suggestion of historical payback is also present in Herodotus' account of the fate of Histiaeus, which is similarly laden with irony. When Histiaeus is captured by the Persian commander Harpagus, while launching an attack on Atarneus, he reveals his identity, confident that his relation-ship with Darius will save him (6.29.2). Herodotus remarks that this was

---

[49] See Gould (2001) 297–8 on negative reciprocities and revenge. See also Braund (1998) 165 on the association of reciprocity and justice. Coes' acquisition of Mytilene is framed in terms of reciprocity at 4.97.6, where Darius states that he will reciprocate (ἀμείψωμαι – from ἀμείβομαι) with good works in return for Coes' good advice.

[50] With the qualification that Hecataeus' advice looks 'good' because it was the advice that was not taken. It is the advice of a commentator-figure, like Herodotus himself, who seems to share the historian's privilege of retrospective foresight. See Introduction, pp. 34–5 above.

[51] See Introduction, p. 78 above.

a reasonable assumption, but explains that it was actually because of his relationship and his former influence with Darius, that Harpagus and Artaphernes – the governor of Sardis – had him killed (6.30.1). While Histiaeus counts on his past actions (and benefactions) to Darius to save his life, these actions unwittingly bring about his death owing to the resentment of high-ranking Persians.[52] But there is further – and more savage – irony in Herodotus' account. When Harpagus and Artaphrenes deliver Histiaeus' mummified head to Darius in Susa, Darius blames them for not bringing Histiaeus to him alive, and then instructs them to wash, wrap and bury the head 'as that of a man who was a great benefactor to himself and the Persians' (ὡς ἀνδρὸς μεγάλως ἑωυτῷ τε καὶ Πέρσῃσι εὐεργέτεω, 6.30.2). Hence ultimately the payback for Histiaeus' benefaction occurs in death.

In these chapters we see the symbolic economy framed by Herodotus' historiographical account in which the real cost and rewards of actions are seldom evident to their agents at the time. Similarly, through the way in which acts of advising are framed in the narrative, Herodotus gives us clues as to the quality of the advice offered by a Croesus, a Histiaeus, or a Mardonius in the longer term. Even Megabazus, who convinces Darius that his forecast of events is accurate, does not foresee the consequences of his advice, with disastrous results. It is the forward- and backward-looking narrative of Herodotus that enables readers to see shortcomings in what sounds like good advice. If Megabazus half-sees the future (see p. 132 above), then Herodotus sees the future fully because he writes the future.

The ironic contrast between Darius' consultations with his advisers and the fuller knowledge of the historian is apparent in the text of Darius' summons to Histiaeus (5.24; see p. 133 nn. 17–19 above): Ἱστιαῖε, βασιλεὺς Δαρεῖος τάδε λέγει . . . ('King Darius writes the following things . . .'). It is tempting to posit an additional irony: Herodotus the good *histōr* showing his knowledge of the style of official Persian edicts, and at the same time exposing the Persian king as a bad *histōr*. Darius employs intellectual vocabulary that echoes the vocabulary used elsewhere by Herodotus in first-person statements about his historical research.[53] For example, Darius' letter contains the phrases: φροντίζων εὑρίσκω ('thinking it over I find', 5.24.1)

[52] See n. 9 above.
[53] For a discussion of the overlap between the vocabulary that Herodotus uses of his own *historiē*, and that used by kingly enquirers in the *Histories*, see Christ (1994), especially 168 with n. 6. Christ does not examine this particular passage, but he describes Darius' interest in the Paeonians as an inept attempt at *historiē* in which the terms and the methods of the enquiry are ill-conceived (ibid. 169–71).

and οἶδα μαθών ('I know from learning', ibid.).[54] David Chamberlain points out that only two 'speakers' in the *Histories* say οἶδα and thereby make a bold claim to self-guaranteed knowledge.[55] Aside from Darius' words in this passage, the other instance is the Delphic oracle (1.47.3).[56] Darius' authoritative rhetoric is *not* backed up by authoritative research; the king's claims to knowledge continue in his speech to Histiaeus at 5.24.3: συνειδώς . . . ἔχω μαρτυρέειν ('having knowledge, I can bear witness').[57] Perversely, Darius makes these claims to discernment in statements that are knowingly false, since Megabazus has persuaded him that Histiaeus is not to be trusted; Darius is dissembling what he knows in order to set a decoy.

By sending this letter and by detaining Histiaeus in Susa, Darius motivates Histiaeus to betray him, albeit inadvertently. Hence the letter gains further irony when read in light of the denouement of the *Histories*. Darius thinks he is being smart, but he is not smart enough. He may have superior resources of power, but he is pitted against Greeks with greater resources of *sophiē*. However, this is not to suggest that Herodotus is endorsing the easy ethnographic stereotype of the dim Barbarian. As Rosaria Munson observes, in Herodotus *sophiē* does not necessarily convey moral approval.[58] Artaphrenes is a far-better intratextual historiographer, in that he sees through Histiaeus' deceit (ὁρῶν αὐτὸν τεχνάζοντα – 'observing him scheming', 6.1.2) and is credited with accurate knowledge about the Ionian Revolt, after the style of Herodotus: 'εἰδὼς τὴν ἀτρεκείην τῆς ἀποστάσιος . . .' ('knowing the truth about the revolt' – 6.1.2). But it is significant that this insight is deferred and belated.

The significance of Histiaeus' influence with Darius still reverberates in Book 7, when Artabanus tries to put Xerxes off invading Greece by pointing out that his plan to convey forces via a bridge over the Hellespont will make him vulnerable. He reminds Xerxes how Darius' retreat from

---

[54] Compare the authorial statements: ὡς ἐγὼ εὑρίσκω ('as I discover', 1.60.3); ὡς ἐγὼ πυνθανόμενος εὑρίσκω ('as I have found out', 1.105.3).

[55] I treat the text of the letter as an example of reported discourse and, as such, comparable to the speeches.

[56] Chamberlain (2001) 13 with n. 26.

[57] For the legalistic vocabulary see Book 2, where Herodotus cites various pieces of information to bear witness to the correctness of his judgements about (a) the extent of the territory of Egypt (μαρτυρέει, 2.18.1), and (b) the causes of the flooding of the Nile (μαρτύριον, 2.22.2).

[58] Munson (2001b) 43 with n. 67. There are different hierarchies of approbation in Herodotus' text that coexist in tension with each other. Aspects of the *sophiē* of Themistocles and Histiaeus correspond to the historiographical values promoted in Herodotus' text; however, the fact that they end badly suggests that they lack full control over their resources of cunning intelligence, and certainly lack the farsightedness of Herodotus.

Scythia depended upon the whim of one man, Histiaeus (7.10γ.2), which led, through a sequence of historical contingencies, to the Ionian Revolt.

In the *Histories* the largest obstacle to insight on the part of kings such as Darius is failure of memory, or failure of historical knowledge. There are several details in this section of narrative (5.23–7) that recall the experience of previous kings (Croesus, Cyrus, and Cambyses), and anticipate the experience of Xerxes. Yet Cyrus, Cambyses, Darius, and Xerxes overlook important lessons learned by other Persian kings. Artabanus tries to provide this historical continuity for Xerxes at 7.18.2–3, drawing on his memory of previous campaigns (μεμνημένος ('remembering') . . . μεμνημένος), but is overruled by a dream. As the *Histories* unfolds, the challenge of remembering what we have read, and making connections between different (and distant) *logoi*, is one of the most demanding aspects of reading Herodotus. Unlike the kings in Herodotus' text, we can read to the end and span or 'bridge' the entire narrative, crossing backwards and forwards between *logoi*.[59] However, at the end of the *Histories* extratextual history is poised to replay patterns familiar from Herodotus' text. Consequently, reading to the end is a never-ending occupation.[60]

---

[59] Cf. Christ (1994) 199: 'If Herodotus' kings reveal a great deal about themselves through the investigations they carry out, the historian, through his portrayal of them, also reveals something of himself and his view of inquiry. Herodotus' exploration of regal investigation helps both to define and to lend authority to the inquiry that he undertakes in the *Histories*.'

[60] Cf. Henderson, p. 290 below, on history 'echoing through the endzone – at, and past, the very end of the *Histories*'.

CHAPTER 5

The trouble with the Ionians:
Herodotus and the beginning of the Ionian
Revolt (5.28–38.1)

Rosaria Vignolo Munson[1]

THE LARGER CONTEXT

Placed at the very centre of Herodotus' work (5.28–6.42), the Ionian Revolt
of 499–494 BC plays a pivotal role, both chronologically and causally, linking
the Persians' Eastern campaigns to their invasions of Greece.[2] It also represents a crucial moment in Herodotus' history of the Ionians, which spans the
whole work from beginning to end. The Ionians jump-start the *Histories*,
one might say, and they do so because they find themselves at the receiving
end of the first known Eastern aggressions against Greeks (1.5.3, 6.2–3).
Croesus of Lydia completes 'the first subjection of Ionia', as the narrator
summarizes at the end of the Croesus *logos*.[3] The second is called 'enslavement', when Cyrus defeats Croesus and conquers his possessions.[4] And so
is the third, which occurs after the failure of the revolt we are examining:

οὕτω δὴ τὸ τρίτον Ἴωνες κατεδουλώθησαν, πρῶτον μὲν ὑπὸ Λυδῶν, δὶς δὲ
ἐπεξῆς τότε ὑπὸ Περσέων

In this way the Ionians were enslaved for the third time, [having been conquered]
first by the Lydians and twice in a row by the Persians. (6.32)

The Ionians become free from Persian domination after the Greek victory
at the time of Xerxes' invasion. But the 1-2-3 count in the statement above
proleptically alludes to a fourth subjection, beyond the chronological range

---

[1] I thank Carolyn Dewald and Donald Lateiner for reading earlier drafts of this paper and offering
suggestions. All errors that remain are of course mine.
[2] Many narratives in Book 5 can be described as 'bridges' between larger or smaller units. The entire
book is transitional, between East and West. On bridges in the *Histories*, both narrative and spatial,
see Greenwood, Ch. 4 above.
[3] 1.92.1; cf. 1.26. For less systematic attacks by the Lydian kings from Gyges to Alyattes, see 1.14.4–19.
[4] First conquest: 1.92.1 (κατὰ μὲ δὴ . . . Ἰωνίης τὴν πρώτην καταστροφὴν ἔσχε οὕτω 'this is how
it happened with respect to the first subjection of Ionia'). Second conquest: 1.169.2 (οὕτω δὴ τὸ
δεύτερον Ἰωνίη ἐδεδούλωτο, 'and so it was that Ionia was enslaved for the second time').

of the *Histories* and not explicitly mentioned in our text.[5] At the time of narration the Ionians are the tributary subjects of Athens.[6]

Herodotus' history of the Ionians is a narrative about being conquered. Its fragmented but ongoing structure mirrors both the marginality of the Greeks of Asia and, at the same time, their nagging long-range involvement in the causality of events bigger than them. 'Outside of Athens and Sparta, no other Greek nation is followed with such consistency in the work as are the Ionians.'[7] They keep reappearing in the *logos*, though only to be upstaged at every turn by other agents or groups. They tend to trigger or suffer circumstances without determining them. They are capable of bouts of heroism and endurance,[8] but they are also divided,[9] and therefore weak,[10] not sufficiently committed to the goal of liberty,[11] conflicted in their allegiances, and generally requiring the oversight or support of a larger power – first Lydia or Persia, then Persia or the mainland Greeks, and finally Athens or Persia (or Sparta) in Herodotus' time.

The narrative of the Ionian Revolt, which stretches across Books 5 and 6 of the *Histories*, is shaped like a dumbbell, narrow in the middle and bulkier at the two ends, namely, the *aitiē* section (5.28–35) – which represents the focus of our discussion – and the account of the preliminaries, course and aftermath of the Ionian defeat at Lade (6.6–33).[12] This final battle, from the point of view of the text, is both analogous and antithetical to the battle of Salamis, just as the entire Ionian Revolt comes across as a sort of botched-up preliminary of the Persian Wars.[13] In both cases a partial and fragile coalition

---

[5] On counting see Henderson, Ch. 12 below.

[6] On the different meanings of the term 'Ionian', see the appendix in Tozzi (1978) 227–30. Herodotus exploits its fluidity to discuss the past in the light of the present. In its broader sense 'Ionian' denotes the Ionian stock (including, e.g., the Athenians themselves), regardless of geography. In its narrowest sense 'Ionians' are the Greeks of the twelve Ionian cities of the Asian coast (1.142), as opposed to Aeolians to the north and the Dorians to the south of them. In between these two meanings, Herodotus also uses 'Ionians' to refer to the Greeks of Asia in general (as at 1.92.1, 1.169.2 and 6.32 cited above), sometimes with the addition of the islands closer to the coast. But the Ionian subjects of Athens also include islands of the Aegean that were never part of a Persian satrapy.

[7] Immerwahr (1966) 230. Cf. Neville (1979) 269–70; Stadter (1992) 803.

[8] See p. 151 and n. 27 below.

[9] 1.142.3–4: they speak different languages. 1.146–7: they have diverse ethnic origins. 1.18, 141.4, 143.1, 168–9: they follow different policies. 1.170, 5.36: they receive and disregard advice to unite politically.

[10] Largely as a cause of disunity: see Neville (1979) 269, who cites 1.170 with 5.3. But see also 1.143.2–3; and softness is a factor at 6.12.

[11] The Samians 'did not want to be free' (3.143.2, narrator's gloss); the Ionians are cowardly as free men, but the best of slaves (4.142, opinion of the Scythians); they prefer slavery to hardships (6.11–12, reported speech of the Ionians themselves).

[12] '*Aitiē* section' and 'preparation section' (below) are terms coined by Immerwahr (1966) in reference to the patterned subdivisions of campaign *logoi* in Herodotus. See ibid. 345–6 for his schematic outline of the Ionian Revolt narrative.

[13] On the parallel between Lade and Salamis, see Tozzi (1978) 43–4.

of Greek city-states follows the initiative of their most dynamic member (Miletus/Athens) and fights to achieve/defend their autonomy. This time, however, the leadership is bad, its strategic decisions misguided, and the commitment to the cause uneven. The coalition disintegrates and Miletus, unlike Athens, leads all to enslavement (6.32) instead of freedom, even though that freedom will in turn be viewed as another form of enslavement (see Thuc. 1.122.3).

The two fat ends of the Ionian Revolt narrative are in some respects the opposite of one another. The *aitiē* section is comic, the one on Lade tragic. At Lade, the Ionians reject the (valiant) Dionysius of Phocaea and end up with no leaders. The *aitiē* section is all about the doings of (rascally) leaders, while 'the Ionians' as a people do not appear at all beyond the introductory sentence, either as subject or object. But these contrasting extremes emphasize the motif of Ionian helplessness, which goes hand in hand with the Ionians' relative lack of importance conveyed in the thin narrative middle. Thus, in the preparation *logos*, Aristagoras' one-man mission to Sparta and Athens (5.36–97)[14] is overwhelmed by two lengthy analeptic insertions that contribute to explaining, among other things, why the second city, and not the first, agreed to send aid. Here the main narrative becomes subordinate to the digressions, just as Ionian affairs (now and later) are viewed in terms of their effects on the free Greek world. The military operations of the revolt begin with the exploits of Athenians and Eretrians, who are the real protagonists of an attack on Sardis, cause a fire that burns the temple of Cybebe, suffer a defeat at Ephesus, and then withdraw (5.97.3–103.1). In the next phase (5.103–6.5), one third of the way through the narrative, we finally find the Ionians, acting on their own and as a group.[15] They enlist the participation of the cities of the Hellespont as well as parts of Cyprus and Caria and achieve a short-lived success. But even here Herodotus frequently turns away from their actions to talk of something else: of Aristagoras, who flees to Thrace and dies, of Histiaeus' whereabouts, of Darius' angry reaction to the news of Sardis devastated by fire. The king makes a fuss about the Athenians but, somewhat like the narrator, pays little attention to the Ionians (5.105).

Herodotus' entire Ionian Revolt *logos* bears signs of being founded on oral traditions influenced both by the unsuccessful outcome of the revolt itself

---

[14] See Pelling, Ch. 7 below.
[15] See Ἴωνες at 5.108.2, 109.3, etc. We find the expression τὸ κοινὸν τῶν Ἰωνίων ('the common-wealth of the Ionians') at 109.3 in the speech of the Ionians at Cyprus, where there seems to be no commander.

and by later political circumstances in Ionia and the mainland.[16] Different agents had different biases and/or the need to justify their actions, both then and now. The Ionians, who failed so miserably, would skirt responsibility and 'accuse one another' in Herodotus' time (see 6.14.1). The other Asiatic Greeks (including, presumably, those of Herodotus' Dorian birthplace, Halicarnassus) had not participated in the effort. The Spartans, too, had declined their support and were, at any rate, contemptuous of anything 'Ionian', in the broadest sense of the term.[17] Delphi, of course, condemned all resistance to Persia and the outcome of this one, at least, validated its position (see 6.19). Finally, the Athenians of Herodotus' day had particular cause for downplaying Ionian courage and competence. They were not very helpful to the Ionians at their initial revolt, but were victorious against Persia later. After the Persian Wars they proceeded to hold sway over those Ionians they had liberated (and other cities as well) – some of whom were now eager to revolt from *them*.[18] Herodotus has both absorbed and transcended these viewpoints.[19] He has produced a narrative that is entirely his, and an apologia for no one. Modern historians consider it unreliable on a number of levels, but it communicates this historian's interpretation of the role of the Ionians in the history of the Greeks.[20]

THE RENEWAL OF EVILS: WHAT EVILS?

Before examining the *aitiē* narrative, let us look at how it ends and compare its end with its beginning. Several Ionian cities depose their Persian-supported tyrants and formally secede from Persia (5.37–8). This double event, in the words of Murray, 'marks a decisive step in the creation of [the]

---

[16] See most recently Thomas (2004); Murray (1988) 471–2. On Herodotus' use of oral traditions, see Murray (2001a), esp. 32–3 for the Ionian Revolt, and (2001b). For various discussions of the biases of different groups of Greeks underlying Herodotus' account, see especially Tozzi (1978) 38–41, Evans (1976), Wallinga (1984). Brown (1981) argues for the existence of more positive versions of the revolt which have not survived.

[17] See above, n. 6. On Dorian beliefs about Ionian inferiority, see Thuc. 1.124.1, 5.9.1, 6.76–80, 7.5.4. See also Alty (1982) 3–4. See also Introduction, p. 24 and n. 59 above.

[18] See Thuc. 6.82–83.2. Fornara and Samons (1991) 106–7. Stadter (1992) 806–7 suggests that Herodotus' narrative of the Ionian Revolt against Persia would have reminded the audience of the Samian Revolt from Athens in 441 (Thuc.1.115.2–117.3; Diod. 12.27–8; Plut. *Per.* 25–8). The Athenians appealed to common Ionianism for the purpose of imperial propaganda even while harbouring contempt for other Ionians and rejecting their own Ionian identity. See Alty (1982) 8–11 with Hdt. 1.143.3. Already Cleisthenes, according to Herodotus, renamed the Athenian tribes in order to distance Athens from the Ionians (5.69). See Introduction, pp. 25, 29–30 above.

[19] Tozzi (1978) 41.

[20] Herodotus is our only source for the Ionian Revolt and modern attempts to derive from him a plausible reconstruction are innumerable. See especially Lang (1968), Tozzi (1978), Lateiner (1982a), Murray (1988), Osborne (1996) 322–5, Cawkwell (2005) 61–86. See Introduction, p. 13 above.

polarity between despotic Persia and Greek democracy; freedom from Persia and freedom from tyranny become identified.'[21] This could be sustained as a convincing historical interpretation, one that aligns the Greeks of Asia on the same side of the ideological divide as the mainland Greeks. It would also have suited Herodotus' overarching reconstruction (at least) of the Persian Wars past. It is not, however, Herodotus' interpretation. In his account of the outbreak of the Ionian revolt so far, the notion and vocabulary of freedom play no role.[22] The narrator indicates instead that an 'interruption of tyranny' in Ionia (τυράννων . . . κατάπαυσις, in the concluding statement at 5.38.2) coincides with a 'resumption of evils' for the Ionians.[23] He proclaims this evaluation at the outset, in the summary that serves to introduce the *aitiē* section and the entire *logos*:

μετὰ δὲ οὐ πολλὸν χρόνον ἀνανέωσις κακῶν ἦν καὶ ἤρχετο τὸ δεύτερον ἐκ Νάξου τε καὶ Μιλήτου Ἴωσι γίνεσθαι κακά.

After a short time there was a *resumption of misfortunes*, and it was from Naxos and Miletus that *misfortunes began again for the Ionians*. (5.28)

And he repeats it again resumptively, after a brief analeptic insertion on the background of the cities involved:

Τότε δὲ ἐκ τουτέων τῶν πολίων ὧδε ἤρχετο κακὰ γίνεσθαι τῇ Ἰωνίῃ

At that time from these cities *misfortunes began for Ionia* in the following way. (5.30.1)

This is a remarkable set of introductions, since in the inserted Athenian narrative of Book 5 (inserted, that is, precisely within the Ionian Revolt *logos*) both the narrator and his characters agree that tyranny itself is a very bad thing, while liberation from tyranny and *isēgoriē* (cf. *isonomiē* in Ionia at 5.37.2) are precious assets, at least in Athens.[24] The Ionian Revolt, of course, is a war, and Herodotus calls war in general a *kakon*.[25] But when

[21] Murray (1988) 475.

[22] The notion of freedom occurs for the first time in the discredited speech of Aristagoras at Sparta (5.49.2). Von Fritz (1967) I T 341, 344, 347 (cited by Tozzi (1978) 44 n. 53) remarks on the rarity of words of the ἐλευθερία family in Herodotus' account of the Ionian Revolt as a whole. See p. 151 below for passages in the *Histories* where the notion of freedom is prominent.

[23] I am grateful to Liz Irwin for this insight. I follow Nenci and accept ἀνανέωσις. Stein, Hude, Legrand adopt the reading ἄνεσις ('relief'), but that requires doing violence to the grammar. See Nenci (1994) 188.

[24] See the narrator's interpretative gloss on the establishment of democracy in Athens (5.78) and the speech of the Corinthian Socles at Sparta on the evils of tyranny (5.92); on the latter see Moles, Ch. 10 below.

[25] See the narrator's generalization at 8.3.1: 'Internal struggle (στάσις) is a greater evil than a war (πόλεμος) fought in agreement by as much as war is a greater evil than peace.' At 1.87.1 Croesus says that 'no one would choose war over peace; for in peace, children bury their fathers, and in war fathers bury their children.' For Herodotus on the evils of war, see Munson (2001b) 211–17.

defence or liberation is at stake, the narrator normally likes to emphasize the valour of those who resist oppression. The entire narrative of the
mainland Greeks' resistance to the Persians centres on that theme. Even
beyond the Greek world the Medes, for example, are praised for being the
first to revolt against the Assyrians (πρῶτοι . . . ἤρξαντο ἀπίστασθαι):
they fought for their freedom (ἐλευθερίης), they were brave men (ἄνδρες
ἀγαθοί), and they shook off servitude (δουλοσύνην, 1.95.2). The resistance
of the Ionians themselves against Cyrus receives a celebratory nod (1.169.1).
On that occasion, some of the Ionians left their cities rather than tol-
erate enslavement (δουλοσύνη). The others succumbed to their attacker
but nevertheless 'behaved with valour each fighting for his city' (ἄνδρες
ἐγένοντο ἀγαθοὶ περὶ τῆς ἑωυτοῦ ἕκαστος μαχόμενοι). A few chapters
before the Ionian Revolt *logos*, the Perinthians, already defeated once by the
Paeonians, were unsuccessful again when attacked by the Persians, but they
fought like brave men for the cause of freedom (ἀνδρῶν ἀγαθῶν περὶ τῆς
ἐλευθερίης γινομένων).[26]

Language of this sort, whether in speeches or in the narrator's own voice,
occurs only sporadically in the account of the Ionian Revolt, and only in
the battle narratives.[27] Ambivalent or negative judgements overwhelm the
positive ones, and pervasive throughout, as nowhere else in the *Histories*, is
the notion of *kakon* and *kaka*, both in a passive and in an active sense.[28] In
response to Dionysius' attempt to enforce military discipline, Herodotus
reports an extraordinary collective direct speech in which the Ionians declare
that they prefer slavery to their present hardships (κακῶν, 6.12.3). As he
attempts to report the battle, the narrator is unable to say who was *agathos*
or who was *kakos* because current reports amount to nothing more than
mutual accusations by different groups of Ionians (6.14.1). To the Chians
alone he attributes splendid deeds (ἔργα λαμπρά). They refused to play
the coward (οὐκ ἐθελο-κακέοντες) or to descend to the level of most of
their allies, who betrayed the cause and were *kakoi* (6.15.1–2). Here again
the majority of the Ionians are quite different from the newly democratic

---

[26] 5.2.1; cf. 5.1.1. On the repercussions of this evaluation of the Perinthians for our interpretation of the
Ionians in the Revolt narrative, see Irwin, pp. 50–1 above.

[27] 5.112.1: At Cyprus the Ionians overcome the Phoenician navy fighting at the peak of their form
(ἄκροι γενόμενοι), and the Samians are especially brave (ἠρίστευσαν). 5.109.2–3: Cyprians and
Ionians exhort one another to pursue the goal of freedom and be men of valour. 6.10.1–11.2: before
Lade the Ionians display 'stubbornness' in refusing the overtures of their former tyrants. Dionysius
of Phocaea urges them to be free rather than slaves. In this last passage the term ἀγνωμοσύνη is
somewhat more ambivalent than other praise terms in Herodotus. We find it describing the stiff but
unsuccessful resistance of the Getae to Darius (4.93) and the *revolt* (ἀπέστησαν) of Aegina from
Epidaurus (5.83.1).

[28] For the ambiguity of the term *kaka* (misfortunes or bad actions?), see 7.152.2, discussed by Munson
(2001b) 225–30.

Athenians of the inserted narrative, since the latter no longer fought badly on purpose (ἐθελοκάκεον) after their liberation from tyranny, but went on to become first on the battlefield (5.78). Unfortunately the Chians, most valorous of the Ionians, also suffered a disproportionate amount of *kaka*, both during and after the battle (6.15–16; 26–7). So did Miletus, which the Persians destroyed, killing the male inhabitants and selling the women and children into slavery: this catastrophic outcome fulfilled an oracle that addressed the city of Miletus as 'perpetrator of evil actions' (κακῶν ἐπιμήχανε ἔργων, 6.19).

These and other disasters of the revolt are obviously the *kaka* said to begin for the Ionians in the summary introductions at 5.28. Even before the final defeat, the intradiegetic Ionians themselves echo the narrator and ask their former ruler Histiaeus why he had 'caused them such a great evil' (κακὸν τοσοῦτον ἐξεργασμένος, 6.3.1). But at one point in the narrative Herodotus projects the evil of the revolt both in time and in space. This happens at the moment of the Athenian intervention in support of the Ionians. If the beginning of the Ionian Revolt was the beginning of evil for the Ionians, the ships that Athens sent to Ionia turned out to be the 'beginning of misfortunes for both Greeks and barbarians':

αὗται δὲ αἱ νέες ἀρχὴ κακῶν ἐγένοντο Ἕλλησί τε καὶ βαρβάροισι. (5.97.3)

This proleptic reference to the Persian invasions of mainland Greece is soon re-emphasized within the narrative: when Phrynicus' *Capture of Miletus* caused distress among the audience, its author was publicly punished with a fine for reminding the Athenians of *their own* misfortunes (6.21.2). Here the phrase οἰκήϊα κακά seems to have a broader meaning than simply 'family troubles'.[29]

The Ionian Revolt plays a role in the causality of the Persian Wars because the support that the Athenians and Eretrians gave the rebels 'woke up the war' against the Persian king.[30] From the 'beginning of evil' statement at 5.97.3 to the section on deliberations for Xerxes' campaign in Book 7, Herodotus keeps reminding us of the connection, both in his own voice and in character text.[31] But Herodotus' notion of the Ionian Revolt as

---

[29] Cf. Alty (1982) 13 and Nenci (1998) 188 who interpret it strictly as a reference to the ties of kinship between Athenians and the Ionians of Miletus.

[30] Cf. the Spartan to the Athenians at 8.142.2: ἠγείρατε γὰρ τόνδε τὸν πόλεμον ὑμεῖς ('It was you who woke up this war').

[31] The accidental burning of the local sanctuary of Cybebe later served as a pretext for the Persians to set fire to Greek sanctuaries (narrator's conclusion, 5.102.1). When Darius hears the news, he shoots an arrow in the air, prays to Zeus for revenge, and instructs a slave to remind him of the Athenians three times a day (5.105). The slave continues to do his job for nine years and eventually Darius dispatches two expeditions at least nominally for the purpose of punishing Athens and Eretria

an origin of misfortunes means both something less and something more than the fact that it led to the Persian Wars. Something less, because the narrative makes clear that imperialism is its own cause and the Ionian Revolt – or the participation in it by the mainland Greeks – was more a pretext than a cause of Persian aggression.[32] Something more, because the proleptic range of the announcement 'beginning of misfortunes for Greeks and barbarians' at 5.97.3 turns out to have greater *amplitude* than the span of time occupied by the Persian invasions and Greek resistance.[33] Herodotus' Homeric quotation, as it happens, was also used in his time in reference to the outbreak of the Peloponnesian War, and this correspondence agrees with Herodotus' next mention of *kaka*.[34] In his interpretation of the earthquake of Delos, an event that occurred when the Persian fleet first sailed across the Aegean against Greece, the narrator's prophecy of evils extends beyond the narrative range of the *Histories* and covers wars of the time of narration:

This [earthquake] was no doubt a portent that the god made manifest to men as a sign of *the evils that were going to happen* (τῶν μελλόντων ἔσεσθαι κακῶν). For in the time of Darius, the son of Hystaspes, Xerxes, the son of Darius, and Artaxerxes, the son of Xerxes, during these three consecutive generations, more *evils* (κακά) happened to Greece than during the previous twenty generations, some deriving to Greece from the Persians and some from the leading cities themselves fighting for the hegemony/rule/empire (ἀρχή). (6.98.1–3)

From West to East and from East to West: the two crossings are almost equivalent. At 5.97.3 Athenian ships cross over to Asia marking 'the beginning of evils for both Greeks and barbarians'. At 6.98, the Persian crossing to Europe begins long-term future misfortunes for Greece.[35] In this second

---

(6.43.4 and 6.94.1–2). Xerxes mentions the need to exact revenge from the Athenians for initiating the hostilities by joining the Ionian cause (7.8β.2–3). See also the allusion cited in the preceding note. De Jong (2001) 101–5.

[32] 5.102.1: σκηπτόμενοι. 6.43.4: πρόσχημα. 6.94.1: προφάσιος. 7.138.1: οὔνομα. Immerwahr (1956) esp. 253. Already Darius had set his eyes on Greece much before the time of the Ionian Revolt: 3.134; cf. 5.73, 97.2. For a full representation of the causality of Xerxes' expedition, see 7.5–19. By then the motive of revenge was complicated by the ditching of Darius' heralds and the Athenian victory at Marathon.

[33] The term is used by de Jong (1998) 235 in reference to this very passage.

[34] The phrase 'beginning of evils' is ultimately from *Iliad* 1.6, 5.63, 11.604 and refers to the disproportion between cause and result in the case of the Trojan War. But the latter is the Greek paradigm of all wars and in Thucydides 2.12.3 the last Spartan herald, expelled by the Athenians from Attica, exclaims that 'this day will be the beginning of great evils for the Greeks' (ἥδε ἡ ἡμέρα τοῖς Ἕλλησι μεγάλων κακῶν ἄρξει). Correspondingly, in Aristophanes' *Peace* 435–6 Trygaeus prays that this day may bring the 'beginning of many good things'.

[35] The connection between the two passages is noted by Evans (1976) 35–6, de Jong (1998) 235, and Stadter (1992) 790–1, who draws a parallel between the two crossings. Cf. also Munson (2001b) 201–5. Liz Irwin has remarked to me on the analogy with the first five chapters of the *Histories*, with crossings for the purpose of abducting women. There barbarians begin, whereas here the Athenians go first.

case, however, the barbarians, though they are en route against Hellas, have paradoxically become less central because the most striking idea in the passage is that the *kaka* of the Persian Wars are followed, with no interruption, by those of the wars of Greeks against Greeks, including the Peloponnesian War. The narrative of the *Histories* focuses on the first conflict, but it elsewhere indicates that the transition to the second passes through an offensive stage against Persia, at the moment when the Greeks turn the war of resistance into one 'about the King's own country'. It is in close proximity to a proleptic reference to this second phase of the conflict, incidentally, that we find Herodotus' generalization that war is a *kakon*.[36]

In the transition between defence and offence, between a war for freedom and one of conquest, the Ionians are a major factor. The Revolt of 499, as we shall see, is presented, through the words of Aristagoras, as a war with both aims. With its failure, the Ionians are again the subjects of Persia, and during the Persian invasions they fight against the Greeks on the Persian side.[37] After Salamis, however, they embrace the Greek cause in what Herodotus calls the second Ionian Revolt.[38] With the battle of Mycale the Ionians are definitively free from Persian domination, but Herodotus' narrative encodes the suggestion that that they will continue to represent a cause for Greek activism, both immediately and in the long term. This is due to their uncomfortable geographical situation and to their endemic inability to provide for their own defence. The Spartans are in favour of eliminating the problem by means of a radical measure:

Once they arrived at Samos the Greeks deliberated about an evacuation (ἀναστά-σιος) of Ionia and how it was necessary to settle the Ionians in a region of Greece that was under their (i.e., the mainland Greeks') control and leave Ionia to the barbarians. For it seemed impossible to them that they sit in guard of the Ionians until the end of time. If they did not do that the Ionians had no hope to be happily rid of the Persians. (9.106.2)

The notion of a resettlement of the Ionians as the *conditio sine qua non* of their freedom emerges intermittently in the *Histories*.[39] Here, however,

---

[36] 8.3.1–2; cf. 8.108.4.   [37] 6.98.1; 7.51–2; 8.10, 19, 22, 85, 90.

[38] 9.90–2 (Samians appeal to Leotychides and the Greek fleet to free the Ionians); 9.98–9 (Leotychides writes messages urging the Ionians to defect; the Persians suspect their loyalty); 9.103–4 (Samians and Milesians help the Greeks at Mycale); 9.104: οὕτω δὴ τὸ δεύτερον Ἰωνίη ἀπὸ Περσέων ἀπέστη ('and so it was that Ionia revolted from the Persians for the second time'). The third Ionian Revolt, in 412, was against Athens (see Thucydides 8.5–17).

[39] During the Ionian resistance to Cyrus, Phocaeans and Teians migrated to Italy and Thrace respectively (1.164–9); Bias of Priene urged all the Ionians to move to Sardinia (1.170.2). See also the resettlement of the Samian oligarchs (6.22–4) and the migration of Byzantians and Chalcedonians after Lade (6.33.2).

transplantation appears engineered from the outside, in a way more appropriate to subject states. The measure would in turn entail evacuating the territories of the medizing Greek states (ἐξαναστήσαντας).[40] The Athenians step in to veto the proposal, making clear that the Ionians are their affair. 'They thought that Ionia should absolutely not be evacuated and that the Peloponnesians had no business deliberating about their colonies' (9.106.3). Soon after this time the Spartans will abandon, or be excluded from, the war effort and Athens will assume the leadership of the anti-Persian operations.[41] Her alliance with the Ionians will become the empire over which the Greeks will fight with one another the wars Herodotus mentions at 6.98.[42] Athens' involvement with the Ionians and her entitlement to provide for her 'colonies' (ἀποικιέων, 9.106.3) begins precisely at the time of the Ionian Revolt, when Aristagoras 'reminds' the assembly that the Milesians were Athenian *apoikoi* and Athens was obliged to protect them.[43] For Herodotus, in other words, the ships that sail for Ionia at 5.97.3 become both the beginning (*archē*) of evils and, as at 6.93 quoted above, an empire (*archē*) of evils – the evils of war deriving from the Athenian empire.[44] Even without doing anything in particular, the Ionians are the occasion of both.

EVILS IN THE BEGINNING

Herodotus' interpretation of the role of the Ionians in the formation of the Athenian empire and in the embattled state of Greece in his own time is connected to his view of the Revolt of 499–494 BC. Sandwiched between

---

[40] 9.106.3. For the Persian King's wholesale deportations within, or in the neighbourhood of, the first Ionian Revolt narrative, see 6.119 (Eretrians) and 5.12–15 (Paeonians). It is the threat of deportation by the Persian king, says Histiaeus, that induced him to urge the Revolt (6.3). Herodotus also reports deportation in Sicily by the tyrant Gelon (7.156). Demand (1988) and (1990).

[41] Hdt. 8.3.2; Thuc. 1.75.2; 95.1–2; Arist. *Ath. Pol.* 23.4.

[42] These events fall outside the chronological range of the *Histories*, but Herodotus alludes or refers to them by external prolepsis. Thus the inclusion of Samians, Chians, Lesbians and other islanders in the Greek League, sanctified by an oath (9.106.4), and the departure of the Peloponnesians from the Hellespont while the Athenians remain in charge (9.114.2) foreshadow respectively the formation of the Delian League and the withdrawal of the Spartans after the Pausanias incident (8.3.2). For the historical reality of an early transformation of the Delian League into Athenian empire, see Fornara and Samons (1991) 104–5.

[43] 5.97.2. This argument, according to Herodotus, is the only one that differentiates Aristagoras' Athenian from his Spartan speech. It is uncertain whether the fiction of the Attic origin of the Ionians of Asia may not have antedated the time of the Ionian Revolt. Sakellariou (1990); Connor (1993) 198–200; Hall (1997) 52–6.

[44] I agree with Liz Irwin (p. 47 n. 16 above), Christopher Pelling (p. 182 below) and John Henderson (p. 305 below), that Herodotus plays with different meanings of the word. See also the somewhat mischievous use of the adverb ἀρχήν ('in the first place', 'at all') at 9.106.3, which is immediately followed by (the accusative noun) Ἰωνίην, suggesting 'Ionian province', or something of the sort.

the two 'beginning of evils' introductions to the *aitiē* section is a brief
analeptic passage about the situation of Naxos and Miletus before the misfortunes that began 'from' them. The narrative is elliptical, but it manages
to make two preliminary points. The first is that both cities were then at
the peak of their prosperity. The terms used to describe this wealth (*eudai-
moniē, akmasasa,* and *proschēma tēs Ioniēs*) serve to reinforce the surrounding
announcements of imminent *kaka*.[45] In Herodotus, however, prosperity is
not an automatic cause of subsequent ruin. Reversals of fortune are more
often than not the result of culpable or misguided human behaviour, represented in this case by the Milesian initiative to attack Naxos. This brings
us to the second point of the insertion. Before becoming prosperous the
Milesians were suffering from internal struggle (*stasis*), until they invited the
Parians to reconcile them (κατήλλαξαν, 5.28) and the latter set things in
order for them (κατήρτισαν, καταρτιστῆρας, 5.28; κατήρτισαν, 5.30.1).
The Milesians' request for arbitration and the benign Parian intervention
provide a positive model for Greek cities helping each other recover from
stasis. This contrasts with the Naxian oligarchs' partisan request in the *aitiē*
narrative and Aristagoras' willingness, as regent of Miletus, to invest Naxos.
Both magnify an intra-city *stasis* into a conflict between Greek city-states,
of the sort that Herodotus also calls *stasis* (8.3.1). With the participation of
Persia, Naxos' problems will include *polemos*, an external war.

The mutual exacerbation of internal party struggle and war is a very
Thucydidean scenario, familiar to mid-fifth-century Greeks.[46] Herodotus'
most original contribution to the history of the Ionian Revolt is perhaps, as
we have seen, the view that it began a long new series of aggressive actions
perpetrated by Greeks for the sake of *archē* (6.98). First it provides the
opportunity for an intervention of Athens and Eretria across the Aegean.
This intervention, as the speech of Aristagoras shows (see below), is implicitly motivated by imperialism as well as liberation, just as the Persian attacks
on Greece that follow are for the sake of conquest no less than revenge. The
mainland Greeks' resistance to the Persian invasions then turns into the

---

[45] Lateiner (1982b) shows how Herodotus habitually restricts his employment of terms denoting prosperity to foreshadow future calamities. For Herodotus' generalization on the instability of human
fortune, see 1.5.3. Simon Hornblower (pp. 175–7 below) most particularly notices the parallelism
between Miletus and her close friend and Western counterpart, Sybaris, whose prosperity is described
in similar terms at 6.127.1 and whose fall is mentioned in connection with the fall of Miletus at 6.21.

[46] The *Musterbeispiel* is of course represented by the events involving Corcyra before (and as the
immediate cause of) the outbreak of the Peloponnesian War as well as after (Thuc. 1.24–55; 3.70–
85). Just as in this and other cases a hostile faction or city brings the Athenians in against their
enemies, in Herodotus it may bring in the Persians. See e.g. the episode of the flashing of the shields
at Marathon (6.115) and the story of Argive medism (7.152.3), the latter notable for the attached
discussion of *kaka* (n. 28 above).

operations of Athens and her allies in the King's territory and the aggressions by Athens against Greek allies and rivals. The final chapter includes the Spartan invasions of Attica and the various inter-Greek hostilities in the Peloponnesian War. Accordingly, the beginning of all this, the Ionian Revolt, is in turn described as the direct result of what Herodotus considers the ultimate *kakon*, a Greek war of aggression against other Greeks.[47] This analogy with present conflicts was likely to resonate deeply with contemporary audiences and apparently it goes both ways. Recently, in fact, Lisa Kallet has made a powerful if surprising argument that *Thucydides* imitates Herodotus by modelling his narrative of the Sicilian expedition on his predecessor's account of the Ionian Revolt.[48]

Herodotus' narrative is here all about conquest. The protagonists, aside from the Naxian 'Fats Cats' (ἄνδρες τῶν παχέων) who request help against their fellow citizens, are Greek or Persian individuals in power, subordinate to the Persian king.[49] Aristagoras, regent in Miletus (ἐπίτροπος, 5.30.1), is the nephew of the city's absent tyrant Histiaeus, the poster-child for Persian-supported Ionian tyranny.[50] Aristagoras also boasts that he is a *philos* of Artaphrenes, who is the satrap of Sardis and brother of Darius (5.30.5), and he embraces his uncle's relationship of *xenia* to the Naxian oligarchs (5.30.2–3). Finally, the kinship and guest-friendship network includes the Persian general Megabates, an Achaemenid cousin of Darius in charge of military operations against Naxos (5.32). A gloss of identification informs us that this Megabates is the man

to whose daughter, if the story is true, the Spartan Pausanias, the son of Cleombrotus, became betrothed when he fell in love with the idea of becoming tyrant of Greece. (5.32)

The appearance of Pausanias in this group creates a link between the events of the narrative and a later time, between Asiatic Greece and mainland Greece: all Greeks in love with power are in bed with Persia, in one way or another.[51]

---

[47] 8.3. Munson (2001b) 211–17.
[48] Kallet (2001) 85–97. Early parallels are represented by the appeal of the Naxian exiles to Miletus and the Egestans' request for help from Athens; Naxian and Egestan promise of *chrēmata* for the expedition; and by the roles of Aristagoras (both vis-à-vis Artaphrenes and at Sparta/Athens) and Alcibiades. For other parallels, see nn. 54, 55 and 62 below.
[49] Herodotus appears to have described accurately the network of Darius' Greek and Persian retainers and their mutual rivalries. See Georges (2000) 12–18.
[50] 4.137; 5.11, 23–25.1. On Persian policy towards Greek tyrants, see Austin (1990).
[51] David Fearn, Ch. 3 above, makes a similar point concerning Alexander of Macedon, a *turannos* who hands over his sister to a Persian noble (5.21.2); on Pausanias see also Greenwood, p. 135 above and Pelling, pp. 189 n. 36 and 194 below.

The narrative of the expedition against Naxos is rich in unmarked attribution of motives, direct or indirect speeches and narrator glosses that leave no doubt that *archē* is the intended aim. Aristagoras is inclined to support the Naxian exiles with the pretext (σκῆψιν) of their guest-friendship with Histiaeus, but his real motive is the calculation (ἐπιλεξάμενος) that this is for him an opportunity to establish his rule (ἄρξει) in Naxos (5.30.3). Pretexts of this sort, based on reciprocity, are standard for expansionistic projects – one need only recall the Persian expeditions against Greece or, for favours returned, the one against Libya.[52] The Naxian exiles, for their part, are in on the deal: they claim to be sure that as soon as Milesians and Persians showed up, the Naxians would do their bidding, and so would the neighbouring islanders. For none of those islands, explains the narrator, was yet subject to Darius (5.30.6). A similar negative gloss, anticipating an attempt to conquer, occurs in the passage, already cited, at the beginning of Herodotus' narrative of the Persians' venture in Libya.[53] To persuade Artaphrenes to give him a force for attacking Naxos, Aristagoras describes the real estate: the island is not large but beautiful and fertile, close to Ionia, and containing much wealth. Artaphrenes will acquire for the King not only Naxos itself, but also its neighbours, Paros (the old friend of 5.28), Andros and the other Cyclades (5.31.1–2); from there he 'will easily (εὐπετέως) attack Euboea, which is vast and prosperous, no smaller than Cyprus and exceedingly easy to capture' (εὐπετέϊ αἱρεθῆναι, 31.3). This speech establishes the pattern for Aristagoras' later attempts to enlist Spartan and Athenian help for the Ionian Revolt, where the alleged cakewalk is to go in the opposite direction and all the way to Susa. Also on those occasions he will use the discourse of conquest to advertise the fertility of the land, the types of wealth it contains and the opportunity for easy (εὐπετής) conquest beyond the immediate occasion.[54] As later the Athenians, so now

---

[52] On 'pretexts' for a Persian invasion of Greece, see pp. 152–3 and nn. 31 and 32 above. See also 4.167.3: the Persians attack Barca under the πρόσχημα τοῦ λόγου ('specious claim') of helping Pheretime achieve revenge, but the expedition was really for the sake of conquering Libya. On reciprocity in Herodotus, see Gould (1989) 63–7.

[53] 4.163.3: 'Many and diverse are indeed the peoples of Libya, and only few of them were then subject to the king.'

[54] 5.49.3–9, esp. 4 (εὐπετέες χειρωθῆναι, 'easy to conquer'); cf. 5.97.1–2, esp. 1 (εὐπετέες . . . χειρωθ-ῆναι). Solmsen (1943) 199. For terms of the εὐπετ- family as Aristagoras' 'signature tune', see Pelling, pp. 179–83 below. Also Ceccarelli (1996) 51. David Fearn, p. 103 above, notices Herodotus' use of the term εὐπετείη in the Macedonian narrative (5.20.1). In Thucydides, Alcibiades promises the Athenians an easy conquest of Sicily (Thuc. 6.17). See Kallet (2001) 91. The advertisement of assets is in Herodotus especially a feature of the discourse of *Persian conquest of Greece*, the paradigm for conquest *tout court*. See 3.134.5 (Atossa to Darius); 7.5.3 (Mardonius to Xerxes). Michael Flower,

Artaphrenes is easily persuaded. Two hundred ships sail for Naxos, double the number Aristagoras had requested.⁵⁵

What Aristagoras essentially promises to Artaphrenes is – from the Cyclades to Euboea – the subjection of Greece, just as in Sparta and Athens he proposes the subjection of Persia. East to West or West to East – it is, once again, all the same, with Aristagoras as the embodiment of the tedious predictability of the pattern of conquest. Aristagoras' attack on Naxos, in fact, specifically anticipates Darius' expedition of 490, which sails across the Aegean, proceeding 'from island to island' (διὰ νήσων), because 'Naxos still uncaptured obliged them to do so' (this is a back-reference).⁵⁶ The Naxians flee, remembering 'what had happened before' (another back-reference), but the Persians enslave all those they can capture, burn the place, and then move on 'to other islands'. Herodotus' next entries are the Persian stop at Delos with his interpretation of the earthquake as omen of future *kaka*, where he explicitly lumps together the conflict with Persia and the subsequent inter-Greek wars (6.97–8). Naxos is both the origin of *kaka* at the time of the Ionian Revolt (5.28) and the marker of their continuation. She represents the first target of Aristagoras and Artaphrenes, and the first target of Artaphrenes and Datis on their way to Greece. Closer to Herodotus' day, the same island makes the front page for a third time. According to Thucydides, Naxos is the first member of the Athenian league to *revolt* and, more importantly, 'the first Athenian ally to be enslaved against the established rule'.⁵⁷ Aristagoras failed against Naxos, and the narrator introduces the narrative of how that happened with a summary statement that is proleptic at multiple levels: 'It was not to be that the Naxians would perish with *this* expedition' (5.33.2). But Naxos is squeezed between Persia and Athens, and to both she will eventually succumb.⁵⁸

however, has persuasively argued that Aristagoras' speeches at Sparta and Athens in favour of a *Greek conquest of Persia* reflect a panhellenist notion of a Greek invasion of Asia, which greatly developed in the fourth century but originated after Plataea. Needless to say, Herodotus is equally opposed to both. Flower (2000) 70–6.
⁵⁵ This increase, which maximizes the damage when the expedition fails, is parallel to the increase of Athenian forces at the time of the Sicilian expedition (Thuc. 6.24). Kallet (2001) 91; also Lang (1968) 26.
⁵⁶ 6.95.2. Ceccarelli (1996) 52–3.
⁵⁷ Thuc. 1.98. Concerning Aristagoras' plan to conquer from Naxos to Euboea, Payen suggests that Herodotus is offering 'une évocation ramassée des événements' which from the Athenian enslavement of Naxos between 475 and 470 led to Pericles' subjection of Euboea in 446. Payen (1997) 213.
⁵⁸ 6.95–6; Thucydides 1.98.4.

TATTOOED IN THE HEAD

When the operations against Naxos come to nothing, Aristagoras organizes the Revolt of Ionia to avoid the consequences of his fall from grace with respect to the Persian king. The Ionians' liberation from Persia, in other words, and the concomitant end of tyranny in Ionia represent a default plan after an Ionian tyrant's attempt to bring a free and democratic Greek state under Persian rule. As his first action of open revolt, Aristagoras sends an envoy to arrest the pro-Persian Ionian tyrants accompanying the fleet. Next he sets aside his own tyrannical power and establishes in Miletus a nominal *isonomiē*. He does the same in the rest of Ionia: he banishes some of the tyrants while turning in those he had captured to their respective cities, which for the most part let them go. He also orders each of the cities to establish *stratēgoi*, and then leaves for Sparta and Athens in search of support (5.37–8). And so, the narrator concludes, 'the deposition of tyrants happened in the cities'.[59]

   All the singular verbs in this section and the passive form of the conclusion beg the question: what do *the Ionians* stand for, at this point? We should compare this account with two parallel narratives where collectivities play a more substantial role. The first is the inserted narrative of the liberation of Athens. Here the Spartans depose the tyrants, but Cleisthenes 'befriends the *demos*', and the Athenians respond by claiming and defending their freedom.[60] On a later occasion, the Athenians hold a public debate over whether and how to resist Xerxes, and Themistocles exercises his leadership in the context of the democratic assembly (7.143). The comparison between Miletus and Athens is implicitly encouraged by the presence in the Ionian Revolt narrative of Hecataeus. On one level Hecataeus, who at first objects to the rebellion, is an intradiegetic analogue of Herodotus and the polar opposite of Aristagoras.[61] But when he settles for military success in a war he cannot prevent, he gives strategic advice worthy of Themistocles or, for that matter, of Pericles and others in Thucydides: obtain mastery of the sea and use the Branchidae treasure (5.36.2–3).[62] But this is not Athens, there is no capable leader (unscrupulous or not) and there is no *demos*, either. The only collectivity that deliberates anything in Miletus is the apparently

---

[59] 5.38.2: τυράννων μέν νυν κατάπαυσις ἐγίνετο ἀνὰ τὰς πόλιας. See p. 150 above.

[60] 5.62–6, 69–70, 72–5. See Ober (1993). On the parallel between Aristagoras and Cleisthenes, see Georges (2000) 19.

[61] Hecataeus uses the reverse of the geo-ethnographic cakewalk argument Aristagoras will take to Sparta and Athens. Armayor (2004) 324. For the practical wisdom here displayed by Hecataeus, and dear to both Herodotus and Thucydides, see Dewald (1985).

[62] See Kallet (2001) 92 for a parallel with Thucydides 6.70, 71. See also Lateiner (1982a) 147.

narrow circle of Aristagoras' *stasiotai*, rather analogous to the Naxian oligarchs of the previous section. Indeed, we find indications in the *Histories*
that the Ionian masses disliked their pro-Persian tyrants and yearned for
a constitutional form of government.[63] But Herodotus has structured this
account in terms least likely to suggest popular participation.[64] In Ionia at
this time freedom – or something of the sort – seems to come from the top
and from the outside.[65] After the suppression of the revolt, democracies in
the re-subjected Ionian cities will be established by Persia (6.43.3), and later
by Athens.

More important to Herodotus than the theoretical and short-lived liberation of Ionia is the chain of events leading from the aggression at Naxos to
the Revolt from Persia, in an absurd sequence that again only emphasizes
individual agents (5.33.2–35). The expedition against Naxos fails because of
a quarrel between Aristagoras and the Persian general Megabates. During a
stop of the force at Chios, we are told, Megabates discovers a ship of Myndos
unattended and proceeds to punish the negligent captain by tying him up
with his head sticking out of the oar hole of his ship. This is too much for
Aristagoras, since this Myndian fellow happens to be – wouldn't you guess –
another *xeinos* of his. A shouting match ensues, and Aristagoras rails against
Megabates: 'What business is this of yours? Didn't Artaphrenes send you to
do my bidding and sail where I tell you to? What are you *doing*?' (5.33.4).[66]
What is everyone doing indeed: it is hard to fathom why Herodotus has
even chosen to report this speech, unless he is specifically signalling the
triviality of the scene.[67] But trivial or not, Megabates is furious and warns

---

[63] This is implicit in the statement that the establishment of *isonomiē* was designed to induce the
Milesians to support the revolt (5.37.2). Outside of this narrative, see especially 4.137: Histiaeus says
that every Ionian city would opt for a democratic government if Darius' power should wane. 5.106.5:
Histiaeus says that by revolting the Ionians have taken advantage of his absence to do what they had
wanted to do for a long time. 6.5.1: the Milesians decline to receive Histiaeus because they are not
eager for another tyrant, 'having tasted freedom'. Forrest (1979) 316.

[64] See p. 148 and n. 15 above, for the first appearances of the Ionians in Herodotus' narrative of the
revolt. Cf. Burn (1984) 192: 'But the question which Herodotus frequently, as here, fails to ask,
is not why the leaders acted as they did, but why people were ready to follow them.' We may
forget about Burn's generalization ('frequently'); we should rather notice that what happens 'here'
is deliberate and implies a judgement about the Ionians. Burns, like most other modern historians,
then proceeds to supplement Herodotus' narrative by listing the factors that induced the Ionians to
revolt: discontent with tribute, commerce, pro-Ionian tyrants and so on. But see Forrest (1979), who
criticizes this approach, and Cawkwell (2005) 71–4, who does not accept most of the usual motives
except for the simple desire to be free from foreign domination.

[65] Cf. the Greeks' proposal to transplant the Ionians (9.106; see pp. 154–5 above). Aristagoras' mission
to Athens and Sparta contrasts with the Ionians' dispatch of an envoy to Sparta at the time of Cyrus
(1.141.1, 152).

[66] τὶ πολλὰ πράσσεις lit. 'Why are you doing many things?' Nenci (1994) 199 notes that this is an
expression of the *sermo quotidianus* that adds vividness to the exchange.

[67] Solmsen (1943) ignores this speech.

the Naxians, who have time to prepare to withstand the attack. After four months of an inconclusive siege, Aristagoras' plans of conquest have come to an end (5.33.4–34).

Disagreement between Greek and Persian retainers of the Great King is of course plausible,[68] but modern historians tend to be especially sceptical with regard to this narrative.[69] Some argue that it reveals the existence in Herodotus' time of two different traditions: certain sources, perhaps even Persian, would have blamed the failure of the Naxian expedition on Ionian or Carian lack of discipline (*à la* Lade: cf. 6.12), while the Ionians attributed the fault to the Persian commander.[70] If this is true, Herodotus has accepted both versions and by combining them he has reconciled (so to speak) a modern quarrel and projected it onto the past.[71] The result is hardly credible, but that may be precisely the point. It is a ridiculous scene that hits a new register and draws attention to the element of comedy, which was present throughout the narrative and which we are no longer allowed to ignore. The wheeler-dealer, super well-connected, fast-talking Aristagoras differs, as it turns out, from most, if by no means all, other actual or aspiring kings and tyrants in Herodotus because he is a character of comedy, a *miles gloriosus*, and a trickster *manqué*.[72] After his Naxian blunder, he makes a mess in Ionia to get out of trouble with the king, but stays in Miletus during the campaign of Sardis (5.99.2). Being 'not a champion of courage' (ψυχὴν οὐκ ἄκρος), he runs for his life as soon as things get tough, leaving the Ionians behind to do what they can and fight like champions (ἄκροι γενόμενοι).[73]

Equally ludicrous is the figure of Histiaeus, who is about to enter the narrative as the second instigator of the Ionian Revolt. Histiaeus' mobility and thief-in the-night *modus operandi* makes him a more ambiguous figure,

---

[68] Forrest (1979) 318–19 and see n. 49 above. Compare, earlier in the narrative (5.23–4), the rivalry between Megabazus and Histiaeus, another powerful cause of the Ionian Revolt (5.35.4): see Greenwood, Ch. 4 above.

[69] It is unlikely that Megabates would shoot himself in the foot in this way. See How and Wells (1912) II.13; Lang (1968) 28. The Naxians, moreover, would not have needed intelligence from Megabates to figure out that they would shortly be under attack. Murray (1988) 473.

[70] Tozzi (1978) 132; see also Burn (1984) 196.

[71] On past and present quarrels in Herodotus, see Munson (2001b) 217–31.

[72] For the pattern of kingship, see Dewald (2003). There are plenty of successful tricksters in Herodotus: e.g., Democedes, Themistocles (both especially analogous to Histiaeus: see Greenwood, pp. 132, 135–7 above), Amasis and Artemisia, to name just a few. Several use trickery to gain tyrannical power (Deioces, Peisistratus). See Dewald (1985), Lateiner (1990).

[73] Compare 5.124.1, referring to Aristagoras, with 5.112.1, of the Ionians fighting in the waters of Cyprus. Both are, once again, colloquial expressions. Of only two references to the Ionian Revolt in Thucydides (4.102.2 and 6.4–5), both having to do with flight, one mentions the flight of Aristagoras to Thrace (and the other the flight of the Samian oligarchs to Zancle after Lade).

but he too, like Aristagoras, is a con artist with big pretensions and a disastrous career.[74] When Darius in Susa accuses him of having caused the outbreak of the Revolt, he deceives the king into sending him back to Ionia to set things in order. From there, he swears, he will not change his undergarment before he has subjected *Sardinia* 'the largest of islands' (5.106.6), just as Aristagoras has promised Naxos and Euboea, 'a large and prosperous island' (5.31.3).[75] He actually gets only as far as *Sardis*,[76] where he clashes with Artaphrenes, attempts to take on the leadership of the Revolt, is rejected by several Ionian cities who have had enough of tyrants, and sets up his own semi-piratical operations in the Hellespont and Ionia, not without causing considerable damage to his fellow Greeks along the way (6.1–5, 26).[77] Eventually he is killed by his Persian captors, who are jealous of his ties to the king and unimpressed by his language skills (6.29–30). It is perhaps significant that although they impale his body, they embalm his *head* and send it to the king. We have already seen one manhandled head in this narrative. A second is coming up soon.[78]

If we view the Ionian Revolt as a bungled version of the Greek resistance against Persia, Aristagoras and Histiaeus are degraded versions of the brilliant trickster Themistocles who, self-serving or not, does save Greece from enslavement instead of almost doing the opposite. But the closest analogues for this clownish duo appear only a few chapters earlier in Book 5. Here two Paeonian brothers 'wishing to rule the Paeonians as tyrants', dress their sister in her best clothes and parade her in front of Darius at Sardis as she carries water on her head, leads a horse to the fountain, and spins flax – all at the same time.[79] Darius is amazed and asks from which people they come, who are the Paeonians, where they live, and what are they doing in Sardis. The brothers respond that they have come to offer their submission and that the Paeonians are Trojan colonists who inhabit a settled land on the river Strymon, near the Hellespont. After learning

---

[74] Histiaeus' tendency to operate at night (6.2.1; 6.5.2) is noted by Tozzi (1978) 30.

[75] Ceccarelli (1996) 49–50. Sardinia is where the Ionians, according to Bias, should have founded their unified and autonomous city (1.170.1–2). By promising Sardinia to Darius, says Ceccarelli, Histiaeus is offering him 'l'essence du désir d'indépendance des Ioniens'.

[76] 5.106.6; cf. 6.1, 2. The joke Σαρδώ/Σάρδιες is noted by Macan (1895) I.256 and will be used to good effect by Henderson, p. 297 below. Sardinia is also a prospective place of refuge for Aristagoras, who, however, ends up preferring Myrcinus, the stronghold in Thrace Histiaeus had fortified (5.11, 23–4): two more elements thematically connecting Aristagoras and Histiaeus.

[77] Especially the Chians, the recipient of greatest *kaka* at the time of Lade (6.26–7; cf. 6.15).

[78] See p. 164 below. Cf. also the strange fate of Onesilus of Salamis, the instigator of the revolt in Cyprus (5.114) with Serghidou, pp. 282–5 below.

[79] The parallel is only noticed, as far as I know, by Dewald (2003) 37–8. In a broader sense, of course, the Paeonian rustics provide a paradigm for all aspiring tyrants and tyrannies. See Irwin and Osborne, Chs. 1 and 2 above.

in addition that all Paeonian women can multi-task as well as these men's sister, Darius sends word to Megabazus and orders that the Paeonians be deported to Asia (5.12–13). Darius' questions to the Paeonians anticipate his later enquiry about the Athenians.[80] The answer of the brothers and the commercial starring the sister match Aristagoras' advertisement of the Naxian venture (5.31.1). The forced deportation of the Paeonians to Phrygia anticipates that of the Eretrians to Cissia (6.119.4) at the time of Darius' Marathon campaign. Just as the Paeonian brothers attract the attention of Darius to their people, so Aristagoras and Histiaeus help to direct Persian imperialistic efforts toward Greece.[81] The thematic connection between the Revolt and the Paeonian narrative is emphasized by a factual one: Darius deports the Paeonians from Europe to Asia, and Aristagoras re-transplants them back home to annoy the king (5.98).

Unlike the Paeonian brothers, Aristagoras and Histiaeus are mutually complementary and play their respective roles in turn: the death of the first leader marks a major break, what is now, at any rate, the end of Book 5. After that the narrative begins again centred around the second leader and repeating some of the earlier themes.[82] Aristagoras and Histiaeus converge in the narrative only once and from a distance, precisely at the point of transition between the (failed) expedition against Naxos and the beginning of the (doomed) Revolt in Ionia, in a passage where we also find the very first occurrence of the term 'revolt' (ἀπόστασις). In a spectacular comic scene, Aristagoras is surveying the quagmire he has produced when an extraordinary messenger bursts upon the stage:

Aristagoras was unable to fulfill his promise to Artaphrenes. At the same time, what irked him was the expense the expedition required, and he was upset that the army had done badly and that Megabates had slandered him, and he thought he would be stripped of his kingship in Miletus. Upset by each of these things, he deliberated a revolt. And it just so happened that the man with the tattooed head (τὸν ἐστιγμένον τὴν κεφαλήν) arrived from Susa. He was sent by Histiaeus, with a message bidding him to revolt against the king. (5.35.1–2)

Aristagoras' position in Miletus is focalized through the megalomaniac Aristagoras himself, which is the only conceivable reason (but a very good reason) why it is termed a kingship (βασιληίη).[83] But the perspective soon

---

[80] 105.7. Nenci (1994) 172. Cf. Irwin, p. 54 n. 36 above.

[81] See Dewald (2003) 38: 'The Ionian Revolt . . . is, in some respects, the story of the Paeonians writ large, with Aristagoras and Histiaeus cast in the role of the two rustics, Pigres and Mastyes.'

[82] 6.1–6, with another secret message and requests for forces.

[83] Ferrill (1978) 391 finds this explanation unconvincing, but we must imagine it as part of Aristagoras' monologue. See also Georges (2000) 23, who remarks that the anomalous use of the term points to the Ionian tyrants' satrapal style.

changes to that of narrator and audience with the definite article that enhances the proleptic force of *the* (evidently notorious) man with the tattooed head.[84] The emphasis on coincidence (συνέπιπτε) agrees with the fatally haphazard progress of events so far:[85] the message is, again, that if a couple of adventurers had not found themselves in a tight spot, the revolt would not have happened, nor the 'beginning of evils', nor perhaps the Persian invasions of Greece, at least not at the time when they did.[86] But, Herodotus proceeds to explain, Histiaeus was languishing as a virtual prisoner at Darius' court and thought that destabilizing Ionia would provide him with his only chance for being sent back to Miletus (5.35.3–4). He therefore inscribed the secret message for Aristagoras on the shaved head of one of his slaves and let the man's hair grow back before sending him on his way. To summarize the causes of the Ionian Revolt: the head of some Carian stuck in an oarlock *and* an inscribed skinhead.[87]

The tattooed communication that travels from East to West, from Histiaeus to Aristagoras, stands at the intersection of writing and mutilation, two means by which despots exercise their dominance.[88] In the Greek view, as in the text of Herodotus, tattooing and branding are Persian punitive practices for prisoners of war and wrongdoers.[89] At the level of performance, however, this pathetic envoy also recalls the stereotypical slaves or loser figures of Old Comedy. The beaten-up Xanthias of Aristophanes' *Wasps* howls that he is being 'tattooed to death by a stick'.[90] In the *Frogs*, Pluto threatens Cleophon and others with tattoos (στίξας) and fetters; the *Birds* contains a

---

[84] I can only think of 'the path' at 7.212.2 as an approximate (non-comic) parallel. Sudden and vivid introductory images are otherwise Herodotus' specialty; see e.g. Arion on the dolphin in the introductory statement at 1.23.

[85] Wood (1972) 117 n. 6. Cf. 5.30.2, ἐτύγχανε (bis); 5.33.2, ἔτυχε; also 5.36.1, συνέπιπτε. On convergences and coincidences see also Pelling, p. 185 below.

[86] Hornblower (2004) 301. On the role of the Ionian Revolt in the causality of the Persian Wars, see pp. 152–3 above.

[87] Steiner (1994) 158 and n. 83 remarks that the latter makes literal the Ionians' linguistic use of calling paper 'skins' (5.58.3).

[88] Steiner (1994) esp. 154–9. An inorganic version of Histiaeus' message is represented by Demaratus' waxed-over tablet (7.239.3). See also the message of Harpagus urging Cyrus to persuade the Persians to revolt (ἀπίστασθαι) from Astyages, a letter sown up in a the belly of a hare (1.123.4–124). For a survey and discussion of all written messages in Herodotus, see Ceccarelli 2005.

[89] 7.35: Xerxes brands the Hellespont (verb στίζειν). 7.233.2: the Persians 'branded with royal marks' (ἔστιξαν στίγματα βασιλήια) the Thebans who deserted from the Greek side at Thermopylae, beginning with their general Leontiades whose son Eurymachus, Herodotus specifies, participated in the attack of Plataea that began the Peloponnesian War (cf. Thuc. 2.2–5). There is a difference between branding (with hot irons) and tattooing (with ink and needles), and according to Jones (1987) στίζειν more properly denotes the second procedure.

[90] *Wasps* 1296: ἀπόλωλα στιζόμενος βακτηρίᾳ ('I am dead tattooed by a stick!')

mention of a 'tattooed runaway' (δραπέτης ἐστιγμένος).[91] Prisoners of war at the time of the Samian war were apparently marked with symbols on their forehead. Plutarch, who tells this story, quotes two lines of the *Babylonians* about the *demos* of Samos being 'much lettered' (πολυγράμματος), that is to say, both 'inscribed' and 'learned', two Ionian stereotypes combined in one word.[92] The figure of the runaway slave is a recurrent metaphor also in Herodotus' representation of the Ionians. The Scythians call them 'master-loving chattel least likely to flee' (ἀνδράποδα φιλοδέσποτα . . . καὶ ἄδρηστα μάλιστα, 4.142).[93] Correspondingly, Aristagoras' own flight from the action is called a δρησμόν, and takes him to Thrace, which, as the nearby ethnographical section points out (5.6), is the land of both slaves and tattoos (though not of tattooed slaves).[94] In his speech before Lade, Dionysus of Phocaea declares that this is the time for the Ionians to choose whether to be free or slaves or, to be more precise, runaway slaves (δρηπέτησι). We all know their response.[95]

According to Aristotle (*Poetics* 1449a32–4).

Comedy is the representation of morally inferior men (φαυλοτέρων), not however in all manner of evil (κακία), but in the sphere of the ridiculous, which participates of the shameful (αἰσχροῦ). For the ridiculous is some sort of blunder (ἁμάρτημα) and shame (αἶσχος) without pain or destruction (ἀνώδυνον καὶ οὐ φθαρτικόν).

It is doubtful that fifth-century Greeks would entirely concur with this qualified formulation. The iambic and comic tradition appear more than ready to apply laughter to all manner of painful topics, including physical suffering, war, enslavement and destruction.[96] In Herodotus, at any rate, laughter represents an intermittent strand in the fabric of a profoundly serious attempt to reconstruct and understand the past and its significance in the present. Such a reconstruction foregrounds, as in the narrative of the Ionian Revolt, the awareness of short- and long-term *kaka*. But here a self-consciously literary initial comedy balances the final tragedy of Miletus,

---

[91] Schol. Aeschines 2.83 confirms the Greek practice of tattooing runaway slaves. Plato *Laws* 854d proposes the regulation that 'if anyone, slave or foreigner, is caught committing sacrilege, his crime should be written on his face and hands'.

[92] Plut. *Per.* 26.4. Cf. Aristophanes, fr. 71 K-A. Jones (1987)149–50. For an analogy between the Ionian Revolt and the Samian Revolt against Athens, see n. 18 above.

[93] For discussion of this evaluation see Introduction, pp. 21–5 above.

[94] 4.142 (Scythians); 5.126.1 (Aristagoras' flight). The Thracians sell their children for export (5.6.1); in this culture, however, tattoos are a status symbol for the well-born (5.6.2). Asheri (1990) 141–3. For the Thracian ethnography, see Irwin, Ch. 1 above.

[95] 6.11.2; cf. 6.12.3: 'It is better for us . . . even to suffer slavery in the future rather than being subjected to the present one'.

[96] See Halliwell's commentary on this chapter of the *Poetics* (Halliwell (1987) 85).

which moved the Athenian theatre to tears (6.21). The weight Herodotus attributes to the self-serving manoeuvres of two rascally buffoons may represent another concession to the apologetic traditions by which the Ionians themselves preferred to wash their collective hands of any involvement in an episode in their history that almost everyone, rightly or wrongly, considered inglorious. But if Herodotus is often willing to embrace local versions of events, he also inserts them in a broader context and pushes them to their logical consequences, with the result that they occasionally turn against the groups whose interests they were designed to serve.[97] Here, to be sure, the Ionians get their wish and are largely absolved from the moral responsibility for the 'beginning of evil' for themselves and others. This, however, comes at a cost: they are also stripped of initiative, valour, determination, love of freedom and hatred of tyranny. As the central and helpless element in a triptych, between Aristagoras and Histiaeus, between East and West, they bear a striking resemblance to their ridiculous unspoken embodiment, the man with APOSTASIS branded on his head.

---

[97] There are many examples of this practice. In Book 5, see e.g. the way he combines the stories of the two Cleistheneses. But the clearest case is Herodotus' account of the origins of Spartans and Athenians at 1.56–8, where the propaganda traditions of each city lead Herodotus to an ambivalent conclusion: the Spartans were Greek but outsiders to Greece, while the Athenians are autochthonous but of barbarian origin. See Thomas (2001): 222–5, Sourvinou-Inwood (2003) esp. 122–31; Munson (2005) 8–10.

CHAPTER 6

The Dorieus episode and the Ionian Revolt (5.42–8)

Simon Hornblower

My subject is the 'Dorieus episode', chapters 42–8 of Book 5 of Herodotus. They deal with the late sixth-century western adventures of the Spartan prince Dorieus, half-brother of King Cleomenes. This piece of narrative is, remarkably enough if there is anything in the biographical tradition associating Herodotus with Thurii, one of only three main sections in Herodotus which cover west Greek affairs in any detail, using 'west Greek' to mean Italy and Sicily. The others are, first, the story of the Samians at Zancle, the later Messina (6.23–5), and, second, the excursus prompted by the Greek approach to Gelon for help in 480 BC (7.153–71). This ends with material about Rhegium and Taras which Herodotus explicitly and apologetically calls 'an insertion into his account', λόγου παρενθήκη. This general Herodotean parsimoniousness about Italy and Sicily may have prompted Thucydides' contemporary Antiochus of Syracuse (*FgrH* 555) to write a history of the west in Ionic Greek. The choice, by this Dorian writer, of Ionic, the Greek of ethnography down to Nearchus of Krete and beyond, was a way of saying, 'I am doing what Herodotus did not; I am filling a Herodotean gap.'

Herodotus' seven chapters about Dorieus of Sparta are rich and precious.[1] They are positioned roughly at the centre of the nine-book *Histories*, and my object in the present study is to try to locate them in the architecture of Book 5 and of the whole work. In particular I want to develop an idea I have argued for briefly elsewhere,[2] and to try to show that the Dorieus episode is not the irrelevance or παρενθήκη it might at first appear, but is closely tied in both with the Ionian Revolt which takes up much of Book 5, and with

---

[1] At the Cambridge colloquium in 2002 I examined some features not here discussed because I have now published my views about them in a book about Pindar and historical writing: Hornblower (2004) 107–13 (Dorieus and the 'lost clod of earth' in Pindar *Pythian* 4), 299 (on the rival Sybarite and Crotoniate versions at 5.44–5 as a good example of the Herodotean' unadjudicated alternative), and 301–6, on 'derailing individuals'.

[2] Hornblower (2004) 306 and n. 55.

the main narrative generally. The tie-in is, I suggest, effected above all by three comparisons suggested by Herodotus. The first is between Dorieus and his half-brother Cleomenes. The second is between the fates of two cities, Sybaris in south Italy and Miletus in Ionia. The third is between Philippus of Croton and the Athenian Cleinias, great-grandfather of the famous Alcibiades, and I shall argue that Herodotus cleverly brings us down to the time of this inhabitant of the world of Thucydides.

First Cleomenes. That Dorieus is generally a foil for Cleomenes is surely clear, and in particular I believe we are meant to notice that the two half-brothers respond in different ways to appeals from or suggestions by foreigners for military assistance or action. Let us look at the more general aspects first. When Cleomenes famously said to the Athenian priestess (5.72.3) οὐ Δωριεύς εἰμι ἀλλ' Ἀχαιός, 'I am not a Dorian but an Achaean', this, as Macan noted long ago, was a sort of pun as well as a repudiation of programmatic Dorianism: 'I'm not Dorieus' as well as 'I'm not a Dorian'. And the whole section 41–8 is an analepsis inside the story of Aristagoras' appeal to Cleomenes, a ring begun by the words Κλεομένης . . . εἶχε τὴν βασιληίην ('Cleomenes was holding the kingship') and closed by Κλεομένεος ἔχοντος τὴν ἀρχήν ('when Cleomenes was ruling', 39.1 and 49.1). Everything in between is supposed to explain how Cleomenes rather than Dorieus came to be king.

Again, the Pythia's prediction that Dorieus would 'take the place he was sent against' (ἡ δὲ Πυθίη οἱ χρᾷ αἱρήσειν, 5.43) is exactly matched in the next book by the Pythia's prediction that Cleomenes would take Argos, Κλεομένει γὰρ μαντευομένῳ ἐν Δελφοῖσι ἐχρήσθη Ἄργος αἱρήσειν (6.76.1). In both cases the interpretation and execution of the oracle was flawed: Dorieus (on the Sybarite version at least) got distracted at Italian Sybaris and so ended up fulfilling the oracle by taking that place and not Sicilian Eryx, the place he was really supposed to have been sent against and which (it could be claimed) the oracle had had in mind. As for faulty execution, I agree with Harrison that Dorieus did not just mistake the direction he was supposed to go in; there is also a suggestion that he ought to have confined himself to doing what the oracle prescribed and nothing else.[3] Similarly Cleomenes took *an* Argos as an oracle had predicted, but it was the wrong Argos (6.76). Both men were in fact cavalier about oracles and religion; we recall that Dorieus, before going to Libya, did not consult the oracle at all nor carry out any of the usual prescriptions, νομιζόμενα. This means more than oracular consultation. From the Alexander-historians,

---

[3] Harrison (2000) 155.

describing city-foundations remote from Delphi, Dodona or Ammon geo-graphically, we know that games and sacrifices were usual preliminaries.

At this point we *should* glance briefly at the problem of Dorieus' right to the kingship because there is a feature which tends to be neglected. Dorieus belongs to a familiar mythical and historical category; Asheri even calls him a 'stock character, the typical younger son of a noble house who, feeling himself overshadowed, is impelled to seek his fortune abroad at the head of a band of disaffected persons'.[4] Another such in Herodotus, to look no further, is Miltiades of Athens, who left Athens for the Thracian Chersonese because he was 'fed up with the rule of the Peisistratidae' (6.35.3). The Dorieus/Miltiades analogy has often been drawn, not least because both stories pretend that the colonizing expeditions were more unofficial than they really were. (Thus Dorieus asks the Spartiates for a 'band of men' and gets one, not once but twice.) This, however, is not the neglected and puzzling feature I have in mind. That feature is the statement at 42.1 that Dorieus was the finest young man of his age group and that he felt certain that on the basis of manly qualities, ἀνδραγαθίη, he ought to be king. What is odd about this is that it implies an elective view of the kingship, a possibility not as far as we know raised till the time of Lysander in 400 BC.[5] Modern commentators tend to rationalize this away by saying that Dorieus thought on some other grounds that he had a good claim, thus Jeffery said that he was the son of the 'first, true queen'.[6] Maybe so, but that is not what Herodotus says he relied on. Herodotus has in fact softened the oddity in advance by saying (39.1) that Cleomenes was king 'not by ἀνδραγαθίη but κατὰ γένος', 'not by manly qualities but by descent'. In Herodotus, as in Thucydides, negative presentations like this one are always worth watching; the point of this one is to play up the contrast between the brothers. 'Not by ἀνδραγαθίη' at 39 makes no historical sense, given that Spartan kingship did not depend on personal qualities; it makes good literary sense, but only by comparison with Dorieus whom we have not quite met yet. But if as I insist it makes no historical sense and Dorieus had no real claim to the kingship,[7] then the Dorieus story does not after all carry out its ostensible purpose of explaining why Cleomenes came to be king. That is why I want to look for another reason for bringing on Dorieus as foil to Cleomenes.

I find one such reason in the specific contrast I have already mentioned briefly, namely the contrast between the two brothers over their reaction to foreign approaches or suggestions. Before proceeding, we should be careful

[4] Asheri (1988a) 751.   [5] Plut. *Lys.* 24–6, Diod. Sic. 14.13.2–8.
[6] Jeffery (1976) 123.   [7] See Hornblower (2004) 109 and n. 83.

not to fall into the trap of thinking that Herodotus endorsed the view of Dorieus that Dorieus was manly and admirable whereas Cleomenes was not. The problem is in fact one of what narratologists call focalization. What Herodotus says is that Dorieus εὖ τε ἠπίστατο that on the basis of ἀνδραγαθίη, manly qualities, he would get the kingship. The verb ἐπίστα-μαι often means 'I know' in the philosopher's sense of know which implies the truth of the proposition in question, but not always. It is sometimes compatible with unfounded belief or misplaced confidence. There is a clear Herodotean example of this in an earlier book: Syloson on impulse gave his fine red cloak to the unknown guardsman Darius and ἠπίστατο that he had lost his cloak through folly (3.139.3). In fact this is irony because we know already that Syloson did what he did by 'divine chance', θείη τύχη, and we will soon find out that his impulse was not foolish but a good investment in what Tom Wolfe in *Bonfire of the Vanities* memorably called the 'Favour Bank'.

At 5.42, all translators rightly take the word ἠπίστατο to mean Dorieus 'was confident', 'felt sure', felt certain', and regard εὖ as a mere strengthener. This leaves us free to suppose that Herodotus was critical of the pretensions of Dorieus. Like Tacitus in his attitude to Germanicus and Tiberius, as elucidated by Pelling,[8] the historian ostensibly admires the glamorous and impetuous young man Germanicus, but secretly prefers the canny old ruler Tiberius, who understood how to 'consiliis et astu res externas moliri' ('to manage foreign affairs by diplomacy and guile', *Annals* 6.32). As for Herodotus' statement (39.1) that Cleomenes was king not by ἀνδραγαθίη but by γένος, 'descent', this might seem to imply that Herodotus is denying him the quality of ἀνδραγαθίη, and perhaps it does plant that idea in our heads. But a moment's thought will show that there is no such implication. Strictly, all Herodotus is saying is that it was not through this quality but for another and (I would add) more valid reason that Cleomenes was king, with no implication as to whether he possessed the quality or not. That is true whatever Herodotus thought about his mental balance.

Let us now recall the context of the Dorieus episode. The context is an approach by Aristagoras of Miletus, with a speech analysed elsewhere in the present volume by Christopher Pelling (see pp. 187–94). Cleomenes, prompted by the precocious Gorgo, rejects the approach; the Athenians accept it. Who was right? There is no doubt what Herodotus thought: it is easier to fool, διαβάλλειν, thirty thousand people than one man, as he wittily puts it (5.97). The Athenian help of twenty ships is repeatedly called

[8] Pelling (1993).

an ἀρχὴ κακῶν, 'a beginning of evils', and this famously Homeric phrase equates the seductive Ionian orator with the sexually seductive Helen: the ships in which Paris abducted her were ἀρχεκάκους (*Iliad* 5.63).[9] The Ionian appeal to Athens was in virtue of kinship (5.97.2): the Milesians are ἄποικοι, colonists, of the Athenians; but more surprisingly Aristagoras tries the kinship argument on the Dorian Cleomenes as well, when he begs him to 'save the Ionians, ἄνδρας ὁμαίμονας, kinsmen, from slavery' (5.49.3). Euripides at the end of the *Ion* (line 1590) was to make Dorus and Ion half-brothers, and perhaps this is what Aristagoras has in mind. Or did he know that Cleomenes was a half-hearted Dorian? In any case an argument that did not work with Cleomenes worked with the Athenians, who, as David Lewis pointed out to me once, sent the Ionians a commander with the mythically resonant Ionian royal name Melanthios (5.65). This detail forbids attempts to treat the Ionian kinship argument as anachronistic retrojection from the post-479 BC period. C. P. Jones has well expounded the power of kinship appeals,[10] but there were always Greeks who regarded it as a mere try-on. Cleomenes seems to have been one of these; perhaps his attitude to religion was relevant because colonial kinship is essentially a religious notion.

There are both comparisons and contrasts with Dorieus, but I think the contrasts are the more important. The most obvious contrast is that Dorieus, not twice but perhaps three times, gets into a disastrous foreign venture of the sort Cleomenes avoids. 'Perhaps three' because Herodotus does not say whether the Sybarites or Crotoniates were factually correct about whether Dorieus helped Croton. If he did help them, then, as we have seen, he was successful in the short term because Sybaris was destroyed, but it was a longer-term disaster because it used up his favourable oracle, so to speak, and so vitiated his later Sicilian expedition in advance. Herodotus' brevity about the battle in western Sicily should not obscure the scale of the Spartans' own Sicilian disaster a century before the Athenian one: he just says Dorieus and his four co-oikists and their army, an official Spartan army, were 'defeated by the Phoenicians and Egestaeans' (5.46.1; Egesta is a *polis* far in the west of Sicily). Now, between the defeats of Hysiae at the hands of the Argives in 669 BC and Leuctra at the hands of the Thebans in 371 BC, there are not a lot of Spartan defeats of any sort, and Dorieus was responsible for one of them. This is one of the great historical might-have-beens: a solidly entrenched Spartan presence in western Sicily makes the

---

[9] For further discussion of this phrase see Irwin, p. 47 n. 16 above, Munson, pp. 152–3 above, Pelling, p. 182 below and Henderson, p. 305 below.

[10] Jones (1999).

history of much of the fifth century rather harder to imagine. But the strain on manpower would have been serious, and a different sort of Sparta would have been needed to sustain the imperial role, as Cleomenes perhaps saw.

And that may be the answer to the question, why did Cleomenes do nothing to avenge the serious and humiliating Spartan defeat in Sicily? The question is a good one but it is not my question, it was put by Gelon near the end of Book 7, where he says (ch. 158) that the Spartans did nothing to help him against the Carthaginians, nor did they avenge the slaughter of Dorieus son of Anaxandridas when he was defeated by the Egestaeans: for all you Spartans cared (he goes on) the whole of Sicily could have come under barbarian rule. The formulation is interesting: the 'Phoenicians and Egestaeans' of Book 5 have collapsed into just 'the Egestaeans'. These are incidentally Herodotus' only mentions of Egesta or the Egestaeans anywhere and, though from the literary point of view they are two references, they are just one single reference historically. And here in Book 7, unlike in Book 5, it is made clear that the Egestaeans are not Greeks, as we might naturally but erroneously have concluded from the curious Egestaean hero-cult to Philippus of Croton (5.47) – not to mention their famous Doric temple, unnoticed by either Herodotus or Thucydides. They are in fact, as Thucydides would tell us later, Elymians, firmly dealt with in his *Sikelika* (6.2.3) along with Eryx as barbarian *poleis*.

The defeat of Spartans by Egestaeans surely has some advance significance for us when we recall the way the Athenians were sucked into a Sicilian entanglement by these very people a century later. We need not suppose that Herodotus had specific knowledge of the events of 415–413 BC when he wrote up Dorieus; there was after all a first Sicilian expedition by the Athenians in 426–424 BC. Egesta itself does not feature in Thucydides before the 'Sicilian narrative' (Books 6 and 7), but there is an epigraphically attested alliance with the Athenians, the date of which is disputed but which not everyone wants to push down to 418 BC from 458 BC.[11] To return to Cleomenes, I stress that the idea that he might have avenged Dorieus' Sicilian disaster but did not, just as he might have helped Aristagoras but did not, is not spelt out in Book 5, but is made explicit in Book 7, and that is the sort of thing I mean by saying that the Dorieus passage must be read against the *Histories* as a whole.

Dorieus was not the only impetuous Spartan whose death was left unavenged by Cleomenes. His chief co-oikist Euryleon moved south to

---

[11] ML 37 with *SEG* 39.1. One might argue that Herodotus' interest in Egesta tells against a date as late as 418.

take Selinus' colony Minoa, later Heracleia Minoa. He then liberated Selinus itself from the one-man rule of Peithagoras, but set himself up as a tyrant himself and was killed after fleeing to an altar of Zeus Agoraios. Now Selinus was a grand-daughter colony of Megara via Hyblaean Megara, and one wonders how the Megarians back home viewed a Spartan throwing his weight around like this. It is exactly the sort of behaviour the Spartans went in for in, once again, Sicily at the end of the fifth century in the run-up to the Corinthian war of 395–386 BC, ostensibly liberating Syracuse but actually bringing it under the tyranny of Dionysius. This later phase of Spartan policy elsewhere was arguably a cause of the Corinthian war of 395–386 BC, because in Corinth, the mother-city of Syracuse, this interference cannot have been welcome. It is what Isocrates meant when he spoke of the Spartans 'subverting the free governments of Italy and Sicily' (5.99), and here there is no possibility of contamination from later events, because nobody has yet suggested that Herodotus was writing as late as the Corinthian war. For another Spartan getting side-tracked into a disastrous entanglement we may think of Phoebidas' impulsive occupation of the Theban Cadmeia in 382 BC at the invitation of a local faction; he was supposed to be on his way to north Greece about something different.

Let us return to Dorieus: how did he get involved in Libya, then Italy, then Sicily? The Libyan idea is not motivated except in terms of disgruntlement at being passed over; but as has often been noticed this is unconvincing because the expedition looks official – if we are allowed to use that word about any early Greek undertaking. Dorieus 'asked the Spartiates for a force of men', where I agree with Macan that 'Spartiates' is not in apposition to λεών.[12] The motive not explored by Herodotus is perhaps the more respectable and Pindaric motive, the lost clod of earth which gave Sparta a charter to Libya,[13] unless Pindar's version was itself inspired by Dorieus. So Herodotus prefers to present Dorieus as the impetuous younger brother, and to exaggerate his alienation from the regime at home, just as Thucydides will do for Brasidas. Next, Dorieus gets lured into a Sicilian venture by a man from Boeotia, Antichares of Eleon, who has some oracles from Laius or perhaps better Lasus as some editors prefer. If we read Herodotus backwards we will recall that by marked contrast Cleomenes (6.108) had in about 519 BC shrewdly refused an appeal by some other Boeotians, actually Plataeans, on the ostensible grounds that the Spartans were too far off to help, but actually so as to generate πόνοι, trouble, between the Athenians

---

[12] Macan (1895) *ad loc.* That is, it does not mean 'he asked for a force which was to consist of Spartiates'.
[13] See n. 1 above.

and the Boeotians. This was a good piece of 'consiliis et astu' diplomacy. Antichares, the 'returner of favours' is a signifier for both Aristagoras and those Plataeans. Dorieus was easily talked into things by people of this sort; Cleomenes was not.

Dorieus is not entirely persuaded by Antichares, because he goes to Delphi for a second opinion, but like the equally headstrong Cylon in Thucydides (1.126.6), he does not think hard enough about what the oracle really meant. Finally, there is the Sybarite version, according to which Dorieus was sidetracked into involvement on the side of Croton in a local Italian war. This is not the last time a Spartan did something of the sort: Thucydides reports (7.50.2) that Gylippus at a critical moment in 413 BC made the almost incredible decision to waste time helping the people of Cyrene's colony Euesperides, modern Benghazi, against some Libyans they were having trouble with just then. Kinship is again relevant (Sparta-Thera-Cyrene-Euesperides) but again it hardly justifies the diversion. Incidentally, if Dorieus did help Croton, this was not in line with Spartan policy in this century, which was to help Croton's enemies: they lent the Dioscuri to the Locrians for their war against Croton, and so the Locrians won the battle of the Sagra river.[14] But one result of Dorieus' success in elevating Croton was that the Crotoniates were in a position to be, as Herodotus will tell us later in an important passage (8.47), the only western Greeks to fight for the Greek cause at Salamis. They were under the command of the Pythian athletic victor Phayllos of Croton, an epigraphically attested person, in whose honour Alexander sent Croton part of the spoils of Gaugamela (Plut. *Alex.* 34). Cleomenes put down medizers at Aegina, but perhaps, without Dorieus, Croton and Phayllus would not have won glory at Salamis.

More immediately, Croton brings me to my second main point of comparison, that between Miletus and Sybaris. This comparison is expressed very explicitly towards the end of the Ionian Revolt narrative (6.21) where in 494 BC, after the fall of Miletus, the exiled Sybarites do not return the favour paid them by the Milesians in 510 BC when they shaved their heads and went into deep mourning for Sybaris: these cities 'were closely connected by guest-friendship, more so than any we know of' says Herodotus, in a notably strong formulation: πόλιες γὰρ αὗται μάλιστα δὴ τῶν ἡμεῖς ἴδμεν ἀλλήλῃσι ἐξεινώθησαν. The comparison is made in other ways too, by the epic technique of similarity of language: Miletus before the Ionian Revolt was 'specially flourishing', μάλιστα δὴ τότε ἀκμάσασα (5.28) while one of the suitors of Agariste of Sicyon is Smindyrides from, precisely,

---

[14] For this battle see Dunbabin (1948) 358, giving the sources.

Sybaris, a city which was 'specially flourishing at that time', ἤκμαζε τοῦτον τὸν χρόνον μάλιστα (6.127.2): the two formulations could not be
much closer. Now to repeat and insist, the Dorieus episode is framed by
Ionian Revolt narrative; Herodotus needs to feed in Sybaris' destruction
early and emphatically so that it will be in our minds for his account of the
devastating climax to the Ionian Revolt narrative.

There is another and profounder point. The fates of these two great Greek
cities of the west and east Mediterranean are conspicuous illustrations of the
generalization at the beginning of the entire work (1.5.4) about great cities
becoming small. I want to insist on this point: the word 'illustrations' is
perhaps too weak, as if there were dozens of examples in Herodotus of that
generalization. In fact it is not easy to come up with more than a very few
such decisive examples in his *Histories* of the overthrow of very prosperous
old cities and the diaspora of their populations. Even the capture of Babylon
led to a mere change of management, though a violently executed one; and
though Sardis changes hands several times in the *Histories* and is burnt
down once, nevertheless its life as a city goes on right to the end of the
Histories (9.108.1). I concede that there are one or two other cities in the
relevant category; I think of the fate of Eretria and the Eretrians, an explicit
reprisal for Sardis (6.101.3). The tragedy of Miletus and Sybaris – and literal
tragedy is what the Athenian playwright Phrynichus turned Miletus into
(6.21.1) – is deepened because the two cities happened to be close friends,
though one fell at the hands of the Persians, one at the hands of other
Greeks. This latter contrast in turn gives substance to another powerful
chapter (6.98), where the κακά of the three generations Darius, Xerxes and
Artaxerxes are said to have been inflicted either by the Persians or by 'the
leading cities or peoples', κορυφαίων, fighting for supremacy, ἀρχή.[15] This
implies Greeks and is usually taken to mean the Athenians and Spartans.
It certainly embraces them; but I suggest it can take in other places as well,
including and especially the people of Sybaris and Croton disputing for
primacy in Magna Graecia.

In terms of number of lines, the material in the Dorieus section about
Sybaris, a whole page of Oxford text, is right out of scale compared to
the eight words about the historically quite certain defeat of Dorieus at
Eryx, especially given that Herodotus is not sure whether Dorieus helped
the Crotoniates against the Sybarites anyway. But if we then ask how the
western Greeks are relevant to the Persian war, and if so which western
Greeks, the obvious answer as we have seen is not the Sybarites but their

---

[15] For fuller discussion of these κακά see Munson, pp. 149–59 below.

enemies at Croton. But that is not all because there is another way in which the lives and history of the eastern Greeks intersected with the western Greeks. Immediately after the account of the fall of Miletus Herodotus tells us (6.23–5) about how the Samians, long-standing friends of the Spartans, fled west, together with some Milesian refugees, and came to occupy Zancle, the future Messina in Sicily. This story is picked up and corrected on detail by Thucydides in his *Sikelika* (6.4.5–6), one of his only two back-references to the Ionian Revolt,[16] and there is independent confirmation in the form of some Samian coins struck in Sicily.[17] The opportunism of these Samians and Milesians, invited over by the Zancleans whom they end up betraying to Anaxilas of Rhegium, recalls the opportunism of Dorieus and Euryleon in south Italy and Sicilian Selinus.

The Herodotean parallelism between Miletus and Sybaris goes beyond the general truth that great cities become small, important though that truth is: it is also a signifier for a genuine interconnectivity between the east and west Mediterranean. Herodotus needs the Dorieus section to introduce us at length to what will turn out to be a crucial element in this entire complex, the fall of Sybaris. The relation between Dorieus and the rest of the *Histories* turns out to be very carefully managed. We proceed straight from stories about Croton and *Sybaris* to a speech by the *Milesian* Aristagoras, though it is not until 6.21 that the Miletus–Sybaris strands will actually be brought together. The sweep of Herodotus' *Histories* is pan-Mediterranean indeed, and this does no more than reflect the genuine elite mobility and interconnectivity which characterized the world he moved in. Thus we find Callias of Elis, an Iamid seer, on the Crotoniate side in the war with Sybaris (5.44); he is a long way from home, but a poem of Pindar makes his travels a little less surprising than they might otherwise have been.[18] This 'western' Iamid will eventually be balanced by another Elean Iamid seer, Teisamenos, who did the sacrifices for the Greeks at the battle of Plataea (9.33).

I end with Philippus son of Boutacides of Croton, who went to Cyrene after being cheated of his marriage to the daughter of Telys the ruler of Sybaris (ch. 47 is the source for his very mobile and incident-packed career, which continues to be interesting even after his death). From there he set off to join Dorieus 'with his own trireme, manned at his own expense, being an Olympic victor and the most beautiful Greek of his time' (οἰκηίη τε τριήρεϊ καὶ οἰκηίη ἀνδρῶν δαπάνῃ, ἐών τε Ὀλυμπιονίκης καὶ κάλλιστος Ἑλλήνων τῶν κατ' ἑωυτόν). Note the emphatically repeated οἰκηίη, 'his

---

[16] The other is 4.102.2.   [17] Barron (1966) 40–5.

[18] See Hornblower (2004) 304: Pind. *Olymp.* 6 attests other contacts between the Peloponnesian Iamidae and the west.

very own'. He was then accorded a hero-cult at Egesta for his beauty, the only person so to be treated by them; the reason for the heroization is certainly a novel one.

If we move forward three books in Herodotus to the battle of Artemisium in 480 BC, we encounter Cleinias son of Alcibiades, who won the prize for individual valour (8.17): 'He served, all at his own expense, with two hundred men in his own ship', ὃς δαπάνην οἰκηίην παρεχόμενος ἐστρατεύετο ἀνδράσι τε διηκοσίοισι καὶ οἰκηίῃ νηί. There are no other persons in Herodotus of whom this is said. But there is someone in Thucydides, none other than the famous or younger Alcibiades, who has his own ship, τῇ αὐτοῦ νηί in Sicily (Thuc, 6.50. 1, cf. 61.6, ἔχων τὴν ἑαυτοῦ ναῦν). Gabrielsen has tried to argue, with parallels, that 'his own' merely means that he was in charge of it, or that it was his flagship.[19] It is a fatal weakness of Gabrielsen's view that he ignores the literary chime between Thucydides on the younger Alcibiades and Herodotus' description of Alcibiades' ancestor Cleinias.[20] Thucydides' meaning should not be diluted. The ship was indeed Alcibiades' own personal property. I suspect that Herodotus' reference to Cleinias would have had a contemporary resonance for his readers and hearers, familiar as they would have been with the younger Alcibiades' ostentatious possession, which was rather like a private jet. As for Philippus, to return to him, he resembles Alcibiades in more than one way: both men were Olympic victors (see Thuc. 6.16 for Alcibiades), and this joins Philippus and Alcibiades but not Cleinias. The interweaving is nothing if not artful. So Herodotus joins not only east to west Mediterranean, but Persian to Peloponnesian Wars, and the Dorieus episode brilliantly helps to achieve this geographical and chronological elongation.

---

[19] Gabrielsen (1994) 202.
[20] This is all the odder in that he starts his whole book with Cleinias at Artemisium (Gabrielsen (1994) 1); but he does not make the connection.

CHAPTER 7

Aristagoras (5.49–55, 97)

Christopher Pelling

I. PUSHOVERS AND PUTTINGS-ACROSS:
ARISTAGORAS AT ATHENS

πολλοὺς γὰρ οἶκε εἶναι εὐπετέστερον διαβάλλειν ἢ ἕνα, εἰ Κλεομένεα μὲν τὸν Λακεδαιμόνιον μοῦνον οὐκ οἷός τε ἐγένετο διαβάλλειν, τρεῖς δὲ μυριάδας Ἀθηναίων ἐποίησε τοῦτο.

(a) Apparently it is easier to impose upon a crowd than upon an individual, for Aristagoras, who had failed to impose upon Cleomenes, succeeded with thirty thousand Athenians.

(b) It seems to be easier to fool a crowd than a single person, since Aristagoras could not persuade Cleomenes of Lacedaemon, who was all alone, but he succeeded with thirty thousand Athenians.

(Herodotus 5.97.2, tr. (a) de Sélincourt and (b) Waterfield)

If Aristagoras were a website, he would be full of links. The most obvious link here is between the way he played matters at Sparta (5.49–51) and the way he is now more successful at Athens: hence this famous comment that it is εὐπετέστερον – 'easier', or more literally 'more of a pushover' – to διαβάλλειν thirty thousand people than one – not really Waterfield's 'fool' or 'persuade', nor even quite de Sélincourt's 'impose upon', but rather 'put one across'. More on these boldly daring choices of colloquial translation in a moment: but, however we translate them, we shall anyway see that those two words εὐπετής and διαβάλλειν are almost Aristagoras' signature tunes. At Athens Aristagoras has indeed just used εὐπετής of the Persian foe: they are hopeless with shield and spear, and would be such a pushover (εὐπετέες τε χειρωθῆναι εἴησαν, 5.97.1). He had used the same language at Sparta, where he argued that the Persians were easy to beat (εὐπετέως, εὐπετέες, 5.49.3–4) and Sparta could easily (εὐπετέως) make themselves the masters of all Asia: in so doing he was 'putting one across Cleomenes well' (διαβάλλων ἐκεῖνον εὖ, 5.50.2) – though not well enough, as he failed to add the last touch: when Cleomenes asked him about the distances involved, he made the bad mistake of being honest.

Other links go further back. One connects with Aristagoras' earlier persuasive moment, when he urged Artaphrenes to attack the Cyclades at 5.31: there are similarities there with the arguments he will try at Sparta and Athens. 'You can easily (εὐπετέως) attack and take . . .' – not merely Naxos but Paros, Andros, and eventually Euboea: just as at 5.49 Aristagoras' rhetoric will soar a lot further than it would seem to need, a long way past Ionia and all the way to Susa. So Persians can be pressed to westward desires, Greeks to eastward: Aristagoras, rhetorically adept as he is, can obviously argue this either way, and make either argument as attractive as the other.[1] And at 5.31 there is already the creative use of geography and the relaxed approach to distance: Naxos is 'close' to Ionia, and Euboea is 'as big as Cyprus' as well as being 'a total pushover to take', εὐπετέως again.[2] The internal audience there, Artaphrenes, is immediately persuaded: the external audience – Herodotus' contemporary narratees, then all the later narratees too, including us – may be more knowing, picking up the signal that things that are promised as 'easy' have a knack of being very difficult indeed.[3] Then there are the links with Hecataeus, at 5.36 a more genuinely learned figure who also tries to use geography to guide counsel, and does not think in terms of pushovers or ease: and much good does it do him.[4] However wise he may be, he has less impact than Aristagoras' seductive persuasion. This indeed is a charmer, Aristagoras son of Molpagoras, 'Best-speaker son of Song-speaker'.[5]

[1] We have already had one similar westward/eastward mirroring in such 'easy' talk: in Book 3 first Mitrobates chided Oroetes for letting Samos remain free when it would be such a pushover to defeat (3.120.3), then Charileus chided the Samian Maeandrius for not attacking these pushover Persians (3.145.2). The repeat of the rhythm here goes with the other ways in which Maeandrius relates to the Aristagoras episode: cf. pp. 188–9 and 197 below.

[2] On Aristagoras' speech in 5.31 see further Ceccarelli (1996) esp. 50–2: she notes the irony that Aristagoras' big talk (and also Histiaeus' at 5.106, with which it links in various ways) should lead to the invasion of 490 BC, reaching Greece in giant strides and – in line with Aristagoras' promise – reaching in particular Euboea (i.e. Eretria). See Munson, pp. 158–9 above.

[3] Herodotus and Thucydides are here similar: Rood (1998) 34 n. 20. We have just seen such delusive pushovers in a different register, for at 5.20.1 Alexander of Macedon tells the Persians that they can have πολλὴ εὐπετείη of the females at the party – but they too turn out to be not so easy, and indeed not so female, on which see Fearn, pp. 103–4 above. The theme will persist into the later books, where in the final campaign it is the Persians who continue to have false expectations of easy victories (7.211.1, 8.10.1, 8.136.2), when so many of the themes of the Ionian Revolt are recurring with a difference: but note also the neat twist of Artemisia at 8.68β.1, it will be easy – if you *don't* attack.

[4] More on this below, p. 199.

[5] To say this is, of course, not to suggest that either name is fictional. Simon Hornblower points out to me that in the great stephanophoric inscription (Rehm (1914) no. 122) there is a whole clutch of Molpagorai (name or patronymic) at just the right time, in the early fifth century. 'Aristagoras' is again a frequent name: n. 12 below.

There are links going forward as well. One goes to Histiaeus at 5.106–7, when with breathtaking effrontery – not merely in the barefaced travesty of the truth, but also in the boldness in speaking out so directly to Darius – he tells the king that the Ionian trouble was his own fault: had Histiaeus not been 'dragged away from the sea', then all this nonsense could have been prevented. 'Dragged away from the sea' (ἀπὸ θαλάσσης ἀνάσπαστον) is a quizzical way of describing that honeyed offer of Darius which Histiaeus could not refuse (5.24–5); but it captures the hard reality that the offer really amounted to, and points to the way Darius could and would treat other, less notable subjects.[6] However politely it might be wrapped up, Darius' power was still that of a master over a slave. Yet, Histiaeus goes on, there is still time to put this Ionian unpleasantness right: if he is allowed to return, he will 'set in order'[7] everything and even bring Sardinia into Darius' power. Sardinia, Sardis . . . – there are various points here that make Σαρδώ an appropriate button to press,[8] but geographical feasibility is, once again, not one of them. 'Histiaeus in saying this was putting one across Darius (διέβαλλε), but Darius was persuaded . . .' So sometimes it is not so difficult to persuade just 'one man' after all.[9] Themistocles will know as much later, where with his second Sicinnus trick he manages to 'put one across' (διέβαλε, 8.110.1) *both* the Athenians *and* the Persian king as part of the same stratagem. The democracy and the tyrant have ways of being strangely alike.

Other connections go all the way to Book 9. At 9.90 the Greek counter-offensive after Plataea is under way, and messengers come from Samos to

---

[6] In this category see, for instance, the Paeonians with Osborne, Ch. 2 above.

[7] The word is καταρτίσω, already used of such Ionian constitutional correction at 5.28 and 30.1; see also Munson, p. 156 above. There it was the Parians who set Miletus right. In tyrannized Ionia, such 'setting' comes from outside; we have just seen how Athens has re-set herself internally, for good and for ill, with the Spartan external intervention largely misfiring. There are points here that connect with the wider exploration of Greek freedom.

[8] They are explored by Ceccarelli (1996), who also stresses that Sardinia could be figured as a land of Cockayne – and of liberty. For recognition of the wordplay of Sardis and Sardinia see first Macan (1895) I *ad loc.* and Munson, p. 163 above and Henderson, p. 297 below.

[9] Just as Megabazus had persuaded Darius so 'easily' (εὐπετέως) to bring Histiaeus to Susa in the first place, 5.24.1; Megabazus' suggestion was, however, informed not merely by insight (24.1, ὡς εὖ προορῶν τὸ μέλλον γίνεσθαι – 'as though he had a good insight into what was going to happen') but also by goodwill (4.143.2). Darius' own smooth wording to Histiaeus at 24.1 – 'I have considered and find that no one is better disposed than you to me and my affairs' – encourages comparison with Megabazus, whose genuine loyalty and value were so stressed at 4.143; and the similarity of persuasive patterning between the two scenes, as Darius is persuaded first to summon (23–5) and then to despatch (106–7) Histiaeus, continues that comparison. On the triangle between Histiaeus, Megabazus and Darius see also Greenwood, pp. 132–5 above. – This is not the last time we hear of Histiaeus' 'ease': at 6.27 Histiaeus himself does win an easy victory, over the κεκακωμένοι Chians ('in their weakened state', not least because of the movements Histiaeus has started).

Leutychidas at Delos (Samos and Delos are in different ways two alternative halfway lines between East and West).[10] Their spokesman is Hegesistratus, who urges quick action: as soon as the Ionians see you, they will immediately revolt from the Persians, and the barbarians will be – a pushover, εὐπετές again. Leutychidas finds out what the name is – Hegesistratus – and he can recognize a *nom parlant* when he sees one. 'I welcome the omen', he says, and for the moment the Spartans carry on giving the lead. But once *noms* start speaking, the game can go on. The other ambassadors with Hegesistratus were Lampon son of Thrasycles and Athenagoras son of Archestratides: a blend of brilliance, boldness, Athens-like rhetoric, as well as army-leading,[11] many of the strands that are in the air anyway. And Hegesistratus is – son of Aristagoras. True, it is probably a different Aristagoras, as is usually assumed (though this may not be quite certain),[12] but even so it is not rash to sense a strong whiff of Aristagoras in the air: 'save Greeks from slavery and ward off the barbarian . . .' (9.90.2 ∼ Aristagoras at 5.49.3). Will things now be different? Will the roles of Athens and Sparta be different, and will Sparta really be more biddable this time round? Will this be the start of something good rather than bad, ἀρχὴ ἀγαθῶν rather than the κακῶν of 5.97.3, now that a different sort of *archē* is coming to be in point, that of the Athenian empire?[13] Those are good questions, and the final narrative leaves them hanging.

   And we still have another link to come. At 9.116 Artayctes has managed to get from Xerxes the 'house of a Greek man who attacked your land and paid the penalty': Protesilaus. That is how he 'tricked' or 'put one across' Xerxes, and the word is again διαβάλλειν (this time in the middle: that

---

[10] Stadter (1992).

[11] Hegisistratus was also the name of a νόθος ('bastard') of Peisistratus, 5.94.1 – but probably, even with so many *noms* that speak, it would be rash to extract significance from that.

[12] His son Hegesistratus is a Samian (he is sent by 'the Samians' at 9.90, and addressed as 'my Samian friend' by Leutychidas at 9.91): in that case his father was presumably a Samian too. It is perhaps not inconceivable that a son of the Milesian Aristagoras would have found it advisable to seek citizenship elsewhere after the debacle of the Ionian Revolt, but he is rather less likely to have been welcomed. There is nothing in itself unlikely in two men called Aristagoras: the name is frequent around the Aegean islands (*LGPN* I.59); but equally we do not know enough about citizenship rules to exclude the possibility. Cf. Hornblower (2004) 140–1 on the famous Rhodian Dorieus, concluding 'that *déraciné* elite figures like Dorieus moved freely between *poleis* and that in some sense they retained their original identity, just as Phormio the Arcadian from Mainalos calls himself "an Arcadian from Mainalos but (or 'and'?) now a Syracusan" [Paus. 5.27.1]. . . . We might sometimes want to call this lapsed, sometimes lost, sometimes double, sometimes renewed citizenship, but the main message is that with some of the big names in Pindar and Thucydides it does not do to be too formal and legalistic . . .' And Hegesistratus would be a pretty big name too. But, as Simon Hornblower himself points out to me, such double or displaced citizenship is more likely when the two cities are geographically more distant from one another.

[13] This last *archē*-twist I owe to Liz Irwin.

he is working in his own interest is even more linguistically explicit than it had been with Aristagoras); and 'he was always likely to persuade Xerxes εὐπετέως'. So again things may appear so easy, again it is going to end very badly indeed for Artayctes,[14] and again we hear the same words as had been used of Aristagoras at that climactic moment at Athens, except that here it is the 'one' who is so easily persuaded (as other tyrants have been easily persuaded at crucial moments too, rightly or wrongly), not the '30,000' who proved so gullible at Athens. Along with Themistocles at 8.110 (above, p. 181), this is another in that series of points linking Athenian democracy and Persian tyranny as we move towards the narrative's end – here too a sequence in which the grim fate of Artayctes will play a part, but this time for the brutality shown by the Athenians (9.120.4). They are the masters now, or soon will be: and the difference between Greek and Persian masters is looking more and more elusive.[15]

So much for 'pushovers'. The twist of εὐπετής within 5.97.2 itself is a peculiarly neat one, as after all that 'easy' rhetoric the only thing Aristagoras eventually finds easy is – persuasion, not fighting. And so many of our other speakers have found or go on to find the same, whether they are dealing with individuals or multitudes. They are all so easy to διαβάλλειν.

What exactly, though, does that διαβάλλειν mean? It is a difficult word: it receives seven pages in John Chadwick's *Lexicographica Graeca*.[16] It is normally translated by something like 'trick', 'deceive', 'impose upon', 'taüschen', 'ingannare'. Sometimes the comparison is caught with the 'trick' of Phye played by Peisistratus on the Athenians at 1.60, and there is indeed a certain continuity of gullibility between the two passages.[17] Yet there is no suggestion here that Aristagoras says anything *false*: the falsity would only have come in if he had lied about the distances, as indeed Herodotus thinks he 'ought' to have done (5.50.2) – not a strong moralistic 'ought' there, of course, rather an indication of the sort of line that a consistent διαβάλλων would have been well advised to take. That is itself suggestive of the range of the word, a range we have already seen in the passages already quoted.

---

[14] How it ends so gruesomely, and the terminal significance of the memory of Protesilaus, are both deeply suggestive: see esp. Boedeker (1988).

[15] This is a favourite theme of recent scholarship, and was argued clearly and strongly by Fornara as early as 1971: for a particularly sensitive treatment see Dewald (1997). I had my own say in Pelling (1997).

[16] Chadwick (1996) 87–94, mildly refining LSJ which distinguished 'III. *Set at variance*', 'V. *attack* a man's character, *calumniate* . . . 2 *misrepresent* . . . generally, *give hostile information*, without any insinuation of falsehood', 'VI. *deceive by false accounts, impose upon, mislead*'.

[17] Cf. p. 192 and n. 44 below. Nenci (1994) 304–5, however, points out the different texture of the trickery here.

Sometimes it does involve deceit or at least disingenuousness (Themistocles with his Sicinnus trick, or Artayctes with Protesilaus), sometimes a
barefaced twisting of an underlying truth (Histiaeus with Darius), sometimes as at Sparta a rather different type of disquieting persuasiveness. Nor,
indeed, do we need to infer that the disquieting persuasiveness took quite
the same form at Athens as it did with Cleomenes: there is no suggestion,
for instance, that Aristagoras even used his visual aid of the map in Athens
as he had done at Sparta.[18] Nor need we be very sophisticated in looking
for an explanation for that (and so there is no need to tweak[19] an idea
of Lévêque and Vidal-Naquet, and wonder if the Athenians, so used after
Cleisthenes to land-quantification and geometry, would be more at home
with a map, and so Aristagoras avoids using one). We should be more basic
about this: it is not easy to use a small map to make a point to an audience
of 30,000.

So διαβάλλειν, active or middle, is more complex than simply 'trick'. It
basically seems to be to 'throw words around' (that may even be the force of
the δια- and the -βάλλειν) 'in such a way as to wrong' someone: hence my
racy 'put one across'. Its use as a wrestling metaphor is suggestive, whether
or not that has affected the development of its meaning.[20] That naturally
often gives an overlap with the other familiar sense of 'slander', as 'slander'
is also a mode of 'wronging', though a different one: Aristagoras is not
'slandering' Cleomenes at 5.50.2 or the Athenians at 5.97.2. There is also a
strong hint very often of another meaning of the word, 'set at odds', so that
the person wronged is 'put across' someone else: Chadwick comments on
how easily this links with 'denounce', which after all so often also 'makes an
opponent' of someone. Thus at the beginning of Book 3 Amasis sends the
wrong girl up to be Cambyses' concubine, and she eventually tells him so:
'Sire, do you not realize that you have been διαβεβλημένος by Amasis . . .?'
'Deceived', yes, and most definitely now put at odds with Amasis. There
is something similar when the same word comes back with Cleomenes
in Book 6: Demaratus is attacking him (no 'deceit' this time) because of
the circumstances of his birth, διαβάλλω twice (6.51.1, 64.1); then he and

---

[18] I am not here concerned with questions of historicity, but Fehling (1989) 144 clearly overstates in
describing the map as 'clearly an object bordering on the miraculous': see *contra*, succinctly, Dover
(1998) 221–2. Hence the prosaic, practical explanation that I give here is not inappropriate: the story
moves in a realistic register whether or not it is historically true.

[19] Tweak it we must: Lévêque and Vidal-Naquet (1964) 83 = (1996) 56–7 had Aristagoras using his
map at Athens because the Athenians were used to land-divisions from Cleisthenes, and attuned to
the intellectual control of space. That is taken up by Vernant (1983) 222–3 = (1985) 248–9. But there
is no indication that Aristagoras *did* use his map in Athens.

[20] Cf. καταβάλλω with Fraenkel (1950) 400 and n. 2 ('originally derived from the language of wrestling,
but the metaphorical use is quite common').

Demaratus, unsurprisingly, are διαβεβλημένοι, at odds with one another, at 64.1.[21]

That nuance matters at 5.97. Just before this Hippias has been 'doing everything', διαβάλλων the Athenians to Artaphrenes (5.96.1): 'slander' in this case, it seems, or at least verbally 'attacking' (much of what he said was doubtless true enough).[22] The Athenians have responded by sending ambassadors to Sardis, and have taken a hard line themselves with Artaphrenes (so this is very different from their earlier dealings with Artaphrenes at 73, when they were prepared to give earth and water because – suggestively – of their squabbles with Sparta). Therefore the Athenians are well and truly διαβεβλημένοι (97.1) with the Persians, and it was at this καιρός – a δή rubs it in – that Aristagoras reached Athens. *Both* sides have therefore been worked on by διαβολή; words have been thrown around in both Sardis and Athens to wrong the Athenians; Aristagoras like Hippias has 'put one across' them, and the result is that the two sides are indeed already 'set at odds', 'made into opponents'. It is a confluence of circumstances that makes this the right time, rather as earlier it was a confluence of circumstances – συνέπιπτε ('it happened by coincidence', 35.2), συνέπιπτε . . . πάντα ταῦτα συνελθόντα ('it happened by coincidence . . . all these things came together', 36.1) – that meant that Histiaeus' message arrived at precisely the right moment to stimulate Aristagoras himself.[23] When Aristagoras speaks at Athens about 'the' Persian War, τοῦ πολέμου τοῦ Περσικοῦ (97.1), that may be partly because the idea has taken such root in his own mind that it is as good as happening already *for him* (the way Xerxes at 7.8α.2 sees 'Greek land already προσγινόμενον to Persia', it is as if it is already happening);[24] but it is also because it *is* already happening, the war is already looming as a matter of fact and not just perception.

That affects the 'naïveté' that people so often find in 5.97.2. How and Wells comment:

---

[21] Nor is this the only way that the key words and themes of Book 5 come back to haunt Cleomenes: at 6.82.1 he suffers from the ephors' conviction that he could have taken Argos εὐπετέως.

[22] The Peisistratids are still at it on the eve of Marathon: 6.94.1, Πεισιστρατιδέων προκατημένων (at the court) καὶ διαβαλλόντων Ἀθηναίους . . .

[23] And rather as it will be a confluence of different factors that will enable Mardonius to persuade Xerxes to invade Greece – συνέλαβε γὰρ καὶ ἄλλα οἱ σύμμαχα γενόμενα ἐς τὸ πείθεσθαι Ξέρξην ('For at the same time other factors also occurred that assisted him in the persuasion of Xerxes', 7.6.1). Herodotus' narrative certainly develops recurrent patterns which may suggest that *sooner or later* (say) a Persian tyrant will be expansionist or a freedom-loving subject people may act precipitately; but he is also aware of the force of historical contingency in defining when and how this happens. Cf. Hornblower (2004) 301–6. This is a further aspect of his mental world that is not too far from, nor less sophisticated than, that of Thucydides.

[24] Or as Themistocles sees at 8.60β that 'Salamis is surviving', περιγίνεται: Powell (1939a) *ad loc.* called this 'the present of certain futurity'.

'The remark is a glaring instance of the political *naïveté* of Herodotus' (Macan). Throughout he treats the Ionic Revolt as a scheme of desperate adventurers fraught with evils to Hellas (§3, ch. 28, vi.3). Yet on his own showing the conquest of Greece was already projected in the Persian court (iii.134), and Athens in particular was plainly threatened (chs. 73, 96). The action of Athens did but forestall an inevitable attack, and facilitated later the formation of the Delian confederacy (ix.106 n.; viii.3). Her fault lay not in supporting the Ionians now, but in deserting them later (ch. 103). (How and Wells [1912] II.57, on 5.97.2)

'On his own showing . . .': precisely – and that is Herodotus' point: there is a case for Athens to accept Aristagoras' argument, the case that they are already so endangered that they might as well use the opportunity to strike while they have the prospect of good allies.[25] Yet it is *also* so easy to persuade an assembly, to put one across a mass of people: there is no surprise in that view either, nor any great difference from strands visible in Thucydides or in Aristophanes. In one way the ships that are sent to Ionia are indeed what starts all the trouble, ἀρχὴ κακῶν, just as those Homeric ships of Paris were ἀρχέκακοι (5.97.3 ~ *Il.* 5.62–3); in another, the trouble has been coming for years, with a Greek war looming as 'always "the last" – as the biggest aim and the biggest risk', as Huber put it so well.[26] Look at it a different way again, and it may even go back to those Homeric ships themselves. Different ways of looking at it, equally valid ways of looking at it, are intimated by the context itself and by the *Histories* as a whole. And one wider theme of this volume is the way that simple and complex interpretations can readily coexist in Herodotus, with neither invalidating the other.

Athens is now launched on its career of freedom and democracy, and it is clear that Book 5 is submitting all this to critique. We see its strengths: free men will fight so well for themselves that they can soon dominate their neighbours too (5.78.1, cf. 66.1). As Aristagoras arrives, we see its weaknesses too, with this ingrained gullibility.[27] But neither the strength nor the weakness is quite as simple as that. The strength that empowers Athens also so preoccupies them with those neighbourly wars that they are prepared to offer earth and water to the Persian power (5.73, p. 185 above);

---

[25] So fear – rational fear – plays an important part in triggering precisely the eventuality most feared (as Elizabeth Irwin points out to me): that again is close to the conceptual world of Thucydides, in particular his analysis of both Athenian and Spartan behaviour in Book 1. It also recalls Greenwood's analysis of Megabazus and Histiaeus at 5.23–5 (pp. 131–2 above): Megabazus' nervousness is sensible, but when he acts on it he precipitates the Ionian agitation that he fears.

[26] 'Der Kampf gegen die Griechen ist immer "das Letzte" – als größtes Ziel und als größtes Risiko', Huber (1963) 128, comparing 1.153 as well as 3.134 and 150.

[27] Thus e.g. Stahl (1983) 220: 'Ihr Verhalten ist bestimmt von Selbstüberschätzung, Verblendung, und Täuschung'; but Stahl also emphasizes that this is only one side of the democratic coin.

now we are seeing that there are other ways of looking at the gullibility too, and that even if the Athenians are over-persuaded they may still be getting things right. If the debate at Corinth a few chapters earlier showed there were different, incompatible ways at looking at this newborn child of Athens (5.91–4), there are strands in this narrative too that tell in the same direction.[28]

II. READING CLEOMENES: ARISTAGORAS AT SPARTA

Let us go back to those links, especially the ones back to Book 1 and Book 3. What is it about Aristagoras that makes him so extreme an example of that Herodotean feature whereby 'in a technique both powerful and daunting, everything in the *Histories* seems connected to everything else'?[29] This, after all, is a turning point of the whole work. The theme of East and West, 'wrongs done to the Greeks' (1.5.3), was introduced loudly at the beginning of Book 1, and the Croesus narrative had taken the opportunity to show how the future Greek protagonists Athens and Sparta were getting along at the time (1.59–68). Since then, though, Greece has drifted out of focus. A few parts of Book 3 had looked across to the West, especially to Corinth and Samos; there were indeed indications that Greece would figure at the end of Persia's trajectory, that 'always "the last"' again. But still those indications were scattered and muted. Had Herodotus wanted to, he could have interwoven into that book far more of the material that he has preferred to delay to Book 5. There is nothing specially surprising about that technique in itself: it has something in common with ring composition, where initial themes go away and then come back; or with narrative delay, where important material is delayed until it becomes indispensable or has most interpretative value;[30] or simply with the *Iliad* and *Odyssey*, where the beginnings ensure that we never forget Achilles' wrath or the crisis in Ithaca, but still have less *explicitly* on them through large parts of the first half of each poem than we might have done.

What is startling, though, is that as we return to Greece we find so much of the thematic landscape so familiar: those links ensure that we have been here before, or at least somewhere rather similar. That is in part through echoes of those fleeting earlier passages on Greece, and in part through the recall of 'Eastern' material too (as in Aristagoras' exchange

---

[28] See Moles, pp. 263–7 below.   [29] Stadter (2002) 40.
[30] On this, classically, Fraenkel (1950) Appendix A, taking his prime example from Herodotus (1.111–13); on the application of the principle to historiography, Rood (1998) index s.v. 'delay, narrative', and e.g. Pelling (2000) 69, 89–94.

with Artaphrenes). But to recall is also to encourage to compare, and as so often the narrative poses an issue: how much is the same, how much has changed, and – given that we do know where the narrative is pointing, to that 'always "the last"' of the great Greek war – how much do these developments help us to understand not just what is happening now, but what will happen then?

First, Maeandrius, and that shambles of a Samian attempt for freedom at the end of Book 3, when 'it seems that the Samians did not want to be free' (3.143.2), so difficult did they find it to get their act together. Maeandrius, the ex-scribe – and that scribal past will become important at a later stage of the discussion (p. 197) – had decided to give up the tyranny and pronounce *isonomiē*. He is immediately met by suspicion and rejection: 'who are you, then, to give us freedom . . .?' (3.142.5). It all collapses around him. Maeandrius ends at Sparta, trying to corrupt Cleomenes with golden goblets; but Cleomenes proves unbribable, and tells him – or rather gets the ephors to tell him – to get out of town (3.148).

It looks as if something is being set up there. There are surely links backwards with the Constitutions Debate, with its interest in *isonomiē* and Persians 'not wanting to be free' in a different sense from the Greeks.[31] But a reasonably sophisticated reader or listener might already sense that it looks forward too. Maeandrius tries, Herodotus says, to be 'most just of men', δικαιότατος ἀνδρῶν, but does not manage to carry it through (142.1). Cleomenes, a few chapters later, *does* explicitly become δικαιότατος ἀνδρῶν when he gives Maeandrius his marching orders (148.2). In Samos we are seeing the first steps towards freedom, but also the immense danger of fragmentation that freedom can bring and the difficulty these Greeks (at least these Greeks on the halfway line) find in pursuing and practising freedom without also rendering it vulnerable. But it can be a failed first step which will later give way to a more successful alternative – so, again, that reasonably sophisticated narratee would think, knowing as she or he does that the great freedom struggle of 480 BC is looming. And the δικαιότατος ἀνδρῶν play might suggest that Cleomenes and Sparta will eventually bring us to a more organized, prudent, and virtuous equivalent, where the strengths as well as the weaknesses of freedom will be sensed.

Are the expectations of that reasonably sophisticated narratee on the right lines, now that we are returning to Greece and in particular to Sparta? Recall of the previous sequence is certainly primed: Maeandrius and Lycaretus have just figured again in the narrative at 5.27; their themes then come back when Aristagoras, like Maeandrius before him, gives up his tyranny and

---

[31] I discuss these links in Pelling (2002) esp. 152–5.

declares *isonomiē* (5.37.2) – *isonomiē*, so often the operative word when not-being-a-tyrant is in point.[32] This time it seems to work better, and spreads through Ionia, not without some little local nastiness (38.1), but that is only to be expected. There had been 'easy' rhetoric in the air at Samos too, when Maeandrius had been chided for not taking on the Persians when they were such a pushover (οὕτω δή τι ἐόντας εὐπετέας χειρωθῆναι, 3.145.2).[33] Maeandrius had not believed it himself, but he too had known how to use the rhetoric to get others to do the fighting for him, rather as Aristagoras will be a noted absentee from the fighting when the crunch really comes (99.1–2). And the echoes of Maeandrius are certainly loud once Aristagoras has failed in public, and again there is a bid to bribe Cleomenes the individual: it is only his daughter, Gorgo, who is wise and warns him that he is about to be bribed. And once again the corrupter is ordered out of town (5.51.3 ∼ 3.148.2).

Individual bribery therefore fails; but there was something uncannily like 'bribery' also in Aristagoras' *public* rhetoric at 5.49. There is certainly bonding, racial rhetoric there, in Sparta just as there will be in Athens:[34] we Greeks belong together. But the great emphasis in his map scene is not merely on the ease of conquest, but also on the wealth that awaits.[35] Another verbal point is here important, Herodotus' use of ἔχεσθαι: X 'borders on' or 'connects to' Y, but that ἔχεσθαι can equally mean 'get hands on', 'grasp', 'cling to', a rather more aggressive sort of 'connect'. Not merely are Cleomenes himself and the Spartans urged to 'have' – ἔχειν in a more basic sense – all these places which are so rich in slaves and gold and cattle (49.4): Aristagoras also asks them why they should spend their time here struggling with Messenians and Arcadians and Argives, 'people who have *no connection with* gold or silver, things that someone might feel some enthusiasm to fight and die for' (τοῖσι οὔτε χρυσοῦ ἐχόμενόν ἐστι οὐδὲν οὔτε ἀργύρου, τῶν πέρι καί τινα ἐνάγει προθυμίη μαχόμενον ἀποθνήσκειν), when they could take all Asia so easily (εὐπετέως, 49.8): 'hands-on' ideas, as well as 'easy' ideas, once again.

Now Cleomenes has several good lines waiting for him here. He could, most obviously, say 'no gold please, we're Spartans.'[36] If he had had a feeling

---

[32] On this see Vlastos (1953) and (1964) esp. 7–10: more bibliography at Pelling (2002) 135–7.

[33] Cf. n. 1.   [34] As Hornblower stresses, p. 172 above.

[35] So rightly Forsdyke (2002) 532, stressing also that Aristagoras makes a good deal of the 'fertile' quality of the lands on offer: this, she suggests, feeds into the pattern (culminating in 9.122) where soft lands make soft and servile people, and so is another uneasy strand in the rhetoric.

[36] He could, that is, provided we assume that the Spartan ideological link with asceticism and suspicion of wealth was already a commonplace in Herodotus' day. That is doubted by Hodkinson (2000) 19–64, with some reason. But the case of Pausanias at 9.82 does suggest some play with that commonplace: Hodkinson thinks that there 'Spartan austerity is treated as representative of the poverty of Greece

Reading Herodotus

for uplifting language as good as Demaratus has at 7.102–4, he could surely have produced some resonant put-downs, especially in response to those last assumptions about what is worth dying for. He could also point out that all this talk of going to Susa is irrelevant: we are freedom people here, and freeing Ionia does not mean going all the way to Susa. In fact he says none of these things. He puts it off for three days to think about it, and thinking about it he clearly is: Susa clearly has a lot of attractions, hence his question of how long the march would take.[37] Three days is one thing, three months another: that is where Aristagoras ought (Herodotus says) to have continued to διαβάλλειν as he had done before, but he goes wrong by telling the truth (above, p. 183). And even then Cleomenes does not get the Spartan line quite as one would expect. 'This is not a good thing to put to Spartans, wanting to lead them three months' journey away *from the sea,*' 50.3.[38] What we might have expected – what for instance Nenci (1994), 228 glosses him as saying – is away *from the Peloponnese*. These Spartans are more seagoing types than we might expect, or at least than we would expect from the land-hogging Spartan stereotype in Thucydides; just as Cleomenes is more interested and attracted by all this wealth and enterprise than we would expect. Gorgo may be pretty shrewd to sense the possibility that he might after all get bribed if this goes on. δικαιότατος ἀνδρῶν, is he, still? Well, if he is, it is only just.

So in some ways our sophisticated narratee's expectations have come true. This enterprise is regarded in a rather more cautious and mature way at Sparta; freedom's attractions are now more under control. But the way Sparta is behaving, or at least the way this Spartan king is behaving, is still a little off-key. It will turn out less that this is the real thing for which Samos was a failed overture, rather that it is a repeat performance, a more complex but still unsuccessful rehearsal for what we will see later. Perhaps one strand, as Osborne puts it, is to isolate what went wrong this time so

---

as a whole' (20), which is in a sense right, just as Demaratus' praise of the rule of law at 7.104 strikes a note for all Greece as well as Sparta in particular; but just as at 7.104 the element of fear may be distinctively harsh and Spartan ('the Spartan variant of Greek freedom', Raaflaub (2004) 234), so Pausanias' Λακωνικὸν δεῖπνον ('Laconian meal') is importantly extreme as well as 'representative ... of Greece as a whole'. As Hodkinson himself stresses (21–2), the austere image is already clear in Critias, in the *Lacedaemonian Constitution* (DK[6] 88 B 33–4) and perhaps elsewhere (for DK may well be wrong to assign B 6–7 to a verse *Constitution*). We have no reason to assume that those passages of Critias are much, if at all, later than Herodotus' composition. See also n. 53 below.

[37] Nenci (1994) 227 gives him credit for taking time to think it over, and contrasts this with the Athenian impetuosity in deciding straight away: there may be something in that, but I do not think it the main point. The emphasis of Forsdyke (2002) 533 is closer to the one given here.

[38] There is presumably some play here with the associations of Persians with the 'continent', ἤπειρος: 7.141.4, 8.53.1, *al.* But if so the contrast is, as often in the final books, between Persia as the people of the land taking on the Greeks as a people of the sea: that is a point about Greece as a whole.

that we can see what went right in 490 and 480 BC;[39] or perhaps we should put more stress on the way that it only just went right in 490 and 480 BC, and that the glorious achievements then could so easily have turned out the way that the others had done before.

I have so far been implying that Herodotus is playing with familiar stereotypes, disorienting the audience, insinuating the suggestion that national stereotypes are not so fixed and that even if Spartans have come to fit one stereotype now, they have not always been like that. And that, indeed, is what I wish to suggest. But there are several other possibilities. One is to wonder whether, if we find this Sparta and Spartan king not matching our expectations, we ought to question our expectations: is all this to read Herodotus too much under the shadow of Thucydides, to assume that the Thucydidean stereotyping of Sparta – cautious, land-hogging, selfish, unenterprising – is what Herodotus' audience would have been expecting too? (Not that Thucydides is so simple: he does tweak that stereotype, but it is his starting point, memorably expressed at 1.70, and even at the end of the narrative retains its power and value at 8.96.5.) Contemporary listeners and readers would have seen Sparta in action in the Peloponnesian War, behaving in the way that Thucydides went on to articulate so clearly. But can we be so sure that readers would have been so quick to view Sparta through the sort of filters Thucydides went on to make his own?

Yes, I think we can; those stereotypes are not just a Thucydidean construction. Indeed, we can see them later in Herodotus himself. Take 8.132. Messengers come to Sparta, then on to the Greek camp at Aegina (messengers including 'Herodotus son of Basilides', for those who like their *noms* to *parler*):[40] they beg the Spartans to free Ionia. But they only succeed in bringing them to Delos: 'going further was altogether terrifying to the Greeks, and they thought [actually, more interesting – 'they knew by δόξα'] [41] that Samos was as far away as the pillars of Heracles.' Thus the barbarians are stuck at Samos and the Greeks at Delos, both prevented by fear from coming to grips: we have the two halfway lines again, and Sparta

---

[39] Osborne (1996) 322–3: Herodotus' account 'derives from oral traditions which were not only formed after the Persians had taken control of Ionia, but which had adapted themselves to explain why Ionian resistance to Persia failed while mainland Greece resistance was successful . . .' – and Herodotus takes this further and 'brings out by contrast the distinctive features of mainland Greek success'. Not, of course, that Ionian resistance and mainland Greek resistance were exactly comparable: in Ionia this was rebellion against an entrenched power, in Greece opposition to initial aggression.

[40] On Basilides cf. Hornblower (2003) 56.

[41] Cf. Hornblower, (2004) 110 n. 84. For this cf. Powell (1939a) on 8.5.3: he compares also 8.10.2, 25.1, 88.2, 97.2, 136.2.

and the Greeks they lead are here being a good deal more cautious than the Sparta of Cleomenes. Then there are all those hints, and sometimes more than hints (8.3.2, 9.114.2), of the Spartans pulling out around 478 BC and leaving the job of vengeful counter-attack to Athenians. So it is not unreasonable to infer that Herodotus is assuming audience alertness to that cautious behaviour, and bringing out that Sparta, or at least Spartan kings, had not always been that way.[42]

'Or at least Spartan kings . . .': that suggests a second alternative approach, and that is to say that Cleomenes *of course* is off-key: he is going to be mentally unstable, he is already signalled as coming to the throne in a questionable way, there is already a hint that things are going wrong in 5.48: 'for Cleomenes did not rule for long' – hardly true, of course,[43] but that is the sort of thing that happens to questionable kings – 'but he died ἄπαις', childless or rather sonless, 'with just a daughter Gorgo', that Gorgo who at least saves him from being even more questionable a few pages later. So, if this behaviour is unSpartan, might this be a point not about Sparta as a whole, but just about their disturbing king?

No, it might not: this leads us to the second earlier link, that with Book 1. For Aristagoras is not the first to come looking for Greek allies against a Persian threat, nor the first to try Sparta first. Croesus there did the same. And not merely was Croesus interested in looking westwards and investigating possible allies; the Spartans were also very ready to be brought to look east. The Athenian equivalent passage at 1.59–64 has recently been treated by Vivienne Gray and John Moles,[44] and both have brought out that the picture of Athens is not at all what an audience might have been expecting: this is not the story of perpetual smartness and superiority, but a pointer that the Athenians were foolish, tyrannized, weak, and inactive. That reading is convincing – though we should also notice that to explain Athens' weakness Herodotus only has to give the very recent history, that of the tyranny and more particularly the faction which led the tyrants to fall away after their good start; to explain Spartan strength Herodotus has to

---

[42] Cf. also Johnson (2001) 8–9 on Herodotus' presentation of an adventurous Spartan foreign policy in Cleomenes' time; for comments on which, see Henderson, pp. 300–1 below.

[43] Unless Griffiths (1989) 54, followed by Hornblower (2004) 109 n. 82, is right there to emend οὐ γάρ τινα πολλὸν χρόνον ἦρξε to εἰ γάρ τινα . . . . (with 'apodotic' ἀλλά on the model of e.g. 5.39.2 or 9.27.5): cf. Denniston (1954) 11–13 on such a use of ἀλλά, esp. the eleven Herodotean cases he lists at p. 12. I am not convinced: Denniston notes that such protases are usually negative (or in Herodotus effectively so, as at 2.172.5 and 7.11.2), and here it would be conceding a positive point. Also τινα seems strange after εἰ. We would just have expected πολλὸν χρόνον, as at 1.199.5 or 3.124.2: τινα is more natural with the negative ('no long time at all'), for the use with a positive at 2.58 deals with a different order of uncertainty.

[44] Gray (1997); Moles (2002) 37–8, 52.

go much earlier, to talk about Lycurgus and *eunomia*. That technique may itself suggest that this Athenian weakness was only a recent development, something that might be a transient phase.

More relevant is the picture of Sparta given in Book 1, especially the Spartan keenness to get involved: for here too, as with Athens, we may not be finding exactly what we might expect from the later stereotype. The Spartans immediately respond favourably to Croesus' feelers, even though he has not even told them what he wants them to be 'allies' *for* (1.69.1), what they are committing themselves to; they 'were delighted', ἥσθησαν (1.69.3), so often the word used of *tyrants*' responses to some attractive proposal.[45] True, the Spartans did owe Croesus gratitude for a previous benefaction,[46] but their enthusiasm was also – Herodotus is explicit, 1.70.1 – because they were so pleased that Croesus had picked them from all Greece. This time the Spartan involvement does not come to much, any more than the Athenian involvement in the Ionian Revolt comes to much; and that is largely because, Greeks being Greeks, the Spartans are too busy battling away with Argos when the call from Croesus comes, 1.82.1. But even then the Spartans were *keen* to get to Croesus, and were already busying themselves with their ships when the news of the fall of Sardis came, 1.83. That Argive campaign is famously proleptic of Thermopylae, with 300 Spartan warriors and the one survivor too ashamed to live on.[47] Some things do not change. But it is also proleptic of Marathon and the Spartan non-appearance there – but this time the prolepsis would naturally be taken differently: this time it suggests that behaviour (or at least motives) may be going to change, that Spartan non-appearances have not always been for the same reasons, and that Sparta was at that stage as up-and-at-them, especially as up-and-at-the-Persians, as the Athenians later became.[48] The Spartans were equally

---

[45] Flory (1978) 150 and nn. 7–8; Immerwahr (1966) 177 n. 85; Pelling (2002) 140 and n. 56.

[46] And this previous benefaction (1.69.1) is itself suggestive, as Simon Hornblower points out to me. The Spartans were already at Sardis buying or trying to buy gold for a statue: they were clearly offering something in exchange (we cannot know what), and they clearly knew that Lydia was the place to come for gold and had found their way there. Here too these Spartans are different from the later stereotype.

[47] On this see esp. Dillery (1996).

[48] Later in Book 1 this Spartan similarity to the Athenians is replayed in a different form. When Ionians seek their help against Cyrus at 1.141.4 ~ 152.1, the Spartans do indeed refuse – but not because long-distance involvement is not their sort of thing; it is simply that they will not help Ionians (that Greek fragmentation again). Even then they cannot resist sending an envoy to warn Cyrus off any attack on Greeks, for otherwise he will have Spartans to contend with. 'Who are these Spartans?' asked Cyrus then, just as Artaphrenes and Darius now ask, 'who are these Athenians' (5.73.2, 105.1): and his contempt then was for any people who buy and sell in the agora and deceive one another. Indeed, Cyrus 'hurled these insults against all the Greeks' (1.153.2), the Greeks in general: Spartans so far aren't that different, at least in Persian eyes.

willing for a fight with Polycrates at 3.47 – even if once again it does not come to much. (These pre-490 BC Greeks do tend to be all talk and no trousers, especially when it comes to Persian trousers). This is not just a matter of a quirky king who does not remember his Spartan lines; it is also an intimation that Spartan lines and Athenian lines have not always been so very different, or at least have differed in varying ways.

What does that tell us of Aristagoras?[49] He was not stupid to come to Sparta first: his rhetoric would fall on willing ears. Some parts of his argument are well judged as well, especially the emphasis on Sparta's 'prime place in Greece' at 5.49.2, ὅσῳ προέστατε τῆς Ἑλλάδος – a version of the point which went down so well in Book 1 when Croesus chose the Spartans to approach first (1.69.1–70.1, p. 192 above). Other parts of the rhetoric are equally well judged, including the stress on the Persian effeminate dress. This theme too will end up differently in Book 9: the Persians will emerge as not so feminized at all, and if the dress matters, it is only because at Plataea 'they were lightly-clad men fighting hoplites' (9.63.2), a practical rather than symbolic point.[50] But here it is still the right thing *to say*, confronting what had hitherto been a scary Persian aspect – remember 6.112.3, at Marathon where we have the first people daring to stand up to the sight of 'Median dress', ἐσθῆτα . . . Μηδικήν[51] – and turning it into a claim on the Spartan self-image of manly valour. And however many of the themes of 9.122 are there *in nuce* – why waste time fighting these neighbours when you could rule such rich lands (49.8)[52] – Aristagoras is right to think that the Spartans will not be programmed to think as Cyrus would think at 9.122, and assume that badlands are right for them, goodlands not. Possibly even the offer of dress as one of the *targets*, something Spartans might quite like for themselves, is a well-aimed one (49.4). Not all Spartans lacked a taste for the good things of life: it is interesting that Pausanias has recently been dragged into the narrative, not very relevantly, at 5.32.[53]

---

[49] Any treatment of Aristagoras' rhetoric must be indebted to Solmsen (1943), but her treatment concentrated on the speaker and emphasizing how he is undercut; my focus is rather on what the text suggests about his audience. That allows the implication that Aristagoras, however short his rhetoric falls of truth and insight (Solmsen), may not be felt as missing the mark so completely: his gauging of his audience is better than his gauging of historical reality.

[50] Pelling (1997).

[51] Nor is a taste for elegant dress a sign of soft unmanliness: notice 1.135.1, where it is a matter of Persian pride that they wear this Median dress, finer than their own as it is, into battle.

[52] So Forsdyke (cited in n. 35 above).

[53] On Pausanias cf. n. 36 above, and the discussion of Hodkinson there. I therefore agree with Hodkinson that Herodotus' Spartans are not very different from other Greeks in their valuation of wealth; I depart from him in finding this expressively paradoxical.

III. WRITING DOWN PERSIA: ARISTAGORAS' GEOGRAPHY

There is one other link to discuss, and that is with 52, where Herodotus gives his own version of the geography which Aristagoras had just talked about, and does so with rather different emphases. Herodotus here dwells on the distances, and particularly on the big rivers that mean that 'bordering on' (ἔχεσθαι) does not mean it is so easy to 'get your hands on' (ἔχεσθαι) the next country along the way: as Haubold brings out elsewhere, Book 5 is indeed a narrative where different sorts of 'closeness' are played against one another.[54] It is hard not to see Herodotus' geography as a correction of Aristagoras' easy rhetoric, one that uses a more regular geographical style (datives and second persons as well as numbers)[55] – though here, too, different readings of the same material are not out of the question. The word for these massive rivers is 'navigable by ships' (νηυσιπέρητος): they are so big that ships can ply them, these rivers like the Euphrates and the Tigris. No slight barriers, then: but Steiner for instance preferred to lay emphasis on the way that 'ships' could make the rivers crossable.[56] That is possible, though it does rather depend on whether you happen to have a ship to hand. But even in cases where the word does suggest crossability, it tends to suggest also an element of unease. Thus at 1.189.1 νηυσιπέρητον indicates that Cyrus did find the river Gyndes crossable; but the trouble the Gyndes brought also cost him a year's campaigning, and there is a suggestion that this is, cosmically speaking, no coincidence.[57] The Gyndes, ominously, looms as one of these 'boat-navigable' rivers here as well, and Herodotus explicitly reminds us of what happened then ('the Gyndes, which Cyrus once divided into 360 channels', 52.5). A little after the Book 1 episode we also saw Cyrus making use of pre-existing boats and fortifying them when crossing the Araxes (1.205.2) – but that was for the campaign that ended in his death. So even for a Persian king boat-navigable rivers are not easy; and Greeks, even more so, ought to welcome ships for a different sort of theme, one of the sea, rather than as something that they would be crying out for in the middle of a long land-march anabasis. So it is still reasonable to see Aristagoras as stressing ease, Herodotus difficulty. Some may still prefer

---

[54] Haubold, pp. 227–8 below, especially his remarks on the different sorts of 'closeness' in the Aegina–Thebes connection of 5.79–80.

[55] Clarke (2003) 75 n. 17 comparing Scylax §§63, 67, 68, 69, 100. (I owe this point to Tim Rood.)

[56] Steiner (1994) 149.

[57] The *360* channels Cyrus caused to be dug cost him *a year's* campaigning time. Those numbers are not likely to be coincidental.

to think that Herodotus is supplementing Aristagoras' account without particularly correcting it;[58] others will find the supplement so great as to *constitute* correction.[59]

Particularly if Croesus is in the narratee's mind, something metaliterary may also be in the air. It is commonplace, after all, to think that Solon is something of a calque for Herodotus himself, applying his wisdom, born of long travel and θεωρίη (1.29.1, 30.2), to explore temporal change.[60] It may not be so clear what one infers from that – is Herodotus likely to do better than Solon in getting his message over, are his readers and listeners likely to be any more receptive than Croesus? – but at least it does not seem outlandish to think in such terms. Is something similar happening with Aristagoras and Herodotus here? Is there some indication that Aristagoras' oral speech and visual display would be one thing (and the display is an important part of this[61] – notice all those deictics of Aristagoras in 5.49, 'these Ionians here' and so on), Herodotus' text – and *his* 'display', the ἀπόδεξις of the proem – will be another, and can do a better, less misleading job? If there is, that could be combined with Michael Flower's suggestion that this is a warning against panhellenic over-aggression in Herodotus' own generation: do not try this yourself, beware of Aristagoras-like temptation, it is all a bigger prospect than you think.[62]

If there is something metaliterary here, then we have other links too: perhaps to 5.92α.2, where Stadter and Moles find something metatextual in Socles' 'if you knew about tyranny the way we do, you would never be acting like this': Herodotus' readers *will* now, in a way, be able to know about tyranny in the way that Socles knows.[63] Or, more close at hand, possibly to that excursus on the origins of writing, only a little later at 57–61: for 'writing' is one thing that distinguishes Herodotus' presentation

---

[58] In the conference this position was strongly argued by Alan Griffiths and Simon Hornblower; so already Deffner (1933) 66. How and Wells (1912) 21 imply a cruder version of this view in their note on ἐπὶ πλέον, 51.3: 'in greater detail (cf. ii.171.1) such as is given in the next chapters' – so they assume that Aristagoras would have given Herodotus' sort of detail had not Cleomenes shut him up so effectively. That, at least, is not plausible.

[59] Thus Thomas (2000) 235: in conference discussion Carolyn Dewald also agreed. So, effectively, does Munson (2001b) 209–11, though she has Aristagoras display the map at Athens as well as at Sparta.

[60] So e.g. Bischoff (1932) 39; Hellmann (1934) 38, 43–5; Drexler (1972) 25–8; Redfield (1985) 102; Moles (1996); Pelling (1999) 332. Stahl (1975) 5, 7, even describes Solon as Herodotus' 'spokesman'. See Pelling (2006).

[61] Cf. Cambiano (1988), esp. 256–9, and Jacob (1988), esp. 283–9 on the importance of 'showing', 'multiplying the efficacity of the oral message' (Jacob). Maps are indeed rather encyclopedia-like in principle, producing information which the recipient or rhetorician has then to order and control.

[62] Flower (2000) 69–76.   [63] Stadter (1992) 782, Moles (2002) 40.

from Aristagoras', and Aristagoras' own presentation at Sparta was 'graphic' too, with γράφειν in its different sense of a pictorial display. Perhaps, admittedly, it is misguided even to try to seek too many links between that excursus and the surrounding narrative; perhaps that implies an outdated and unquestioned view of 'unity';[64] why not leave this as another θῶμα to play with, a piece of Herodotean ποικιλία, and not strain too much to make it 'relevant'? Perhaps, indeed. But if there is anything at all in the present train of metaliterary thought, then we might at least see if we can connect the themes, even if ultimately we may not be surprised if we cannot.[65] Elsewhere in this volume Vivienne Gray suggests several possible lines of connection: I shall add another here.

For Herodotus, writing starts with the Phoenicians. It moves through various regions, with its common associations with tyranny:[66] this, perhaps, is where we should remember that Maeandrius too was an ex-scribe, a point that Detienne and Steiner have exploited.[67] Is it disquieting too that so much of this centres on Thebes and Boeotia? Many of the names are also uncomfortable, one way or another – Laius, the sinister Skaios, Oedipus, then Eteocles; but then these Phoenician-origin Gephyraioi end at Athens, where all roads around here seem to lead. (Notice that the Theban Melanippus is also to be invited to Athens at 5.67.2.) A movement that starts in Phoenicia and goes through tyranny to Athens has something in common with the movement of the *Histories* as a whole; and there is something of the demythologizing tendency of those first four Phoenician-rich chapters of Book 1 as well – there no metamorphosis into a bull, no Golden Fleece, no divine beauty contest; here no Prometheus, no Palamedes, no Musaeus, even if there is a Cadmus, and it is all on a human level. This is perhaps part of the general absence of the gods and the divine element from the surface of Book 5; in the narrative it is hard to bring in divine action too

---

[64] For salutary questioning cf. above all Heath (1989).

[65] The principle here is similar to that articulated by Silk (2001) 27, in the course of a brilliant discussion of a brilliant target, the *OCD*³ article on 'Literary theory and classical studies' by D. P. and P. G. Fowler. The Fowlers traced – clearly sympathetically – a growing scholarly distrust in 'the belief that all the [textual] "clues" will point to a single coherent picture': Silk replies that 'in life, in literature, as no doubt in much-derided science, it makes more sense to *expect* a single "answer" unless and until we are forced to conclude otherwise.' The present case is one where critics may well disagree whether 'we are forced to conclude otherwise'. I am myself uncertain whether the links Gray or I suggest are enough to indicate the coherence for which I am looking. de Jong (2002) 266 confesses, rather reluctantly, that she cannot see any contextual relevance for the Gephyraioi.

[66] On these associations cf. Hartog (1988) 277–81 = (1991) 286–90, and esp. Steiner (1994); both, admittedly, perhaps overstate the case.

[67] Detienne (1988a) 73–81; Steiner (1994) 173–4, 184.

openly when the disaster of the Ionian Revolt looms so close,[68] and even this distant temporal retrospect is tailored to fit that texture.

If, however, there are these tyrannical associations of writing, what should be made of the way it comes to Athens? It comes there with the Gephyraioi, and the point is made precisely as the Gephyraioi, Harmodius and Aristogeiton, are attacking the tyranny. So, for the moment at least, the implied movement may be that of the last chapter of Steiner's book: once writing becomes established in the city of words, its associations can become more ambivalent and less straightforwardly negative.[69] Writing can be good as well as bad, just as Gephyraioi – and Alcmaeonids – can shed their earlier associations. These Gephyraioi are indeed a 'bridge' between different worlds.[70]

I am not sure about any of this, including the last pun. Perhaps, indeed, this is a bridge too far: perhaps we should after all be prepared to let the digression stand as a 'wonder' in its own right, and abandon that globalizing quest for organicity. But the suggestions are worth further thought.

Let us finally return to that 'correction' of Aristagoras' use of geographical persuasion. What implications are there for the persuasive texture of Herodotus' own text? The obvious and easy inference would be one of distancing from Aristagoras, and of a claim to superiority: Herodotus' presentation is good, perhaps because less subject to Aristagoras-like oral manipulation, perhaps simply because Herodotus is wise and unselfish and Aristagoras is not; and if we bring in the suggestions about writing (we do not have to), this is the equivalent of writing having outgrown its tyrannical stage and reached the more enlightened possibility of exploiting its potential. And the suggestions of Panhellenism and its dangers can be made

---

[68] At the conference this absence of the gods from the surface of Book 5 provoked interesting discussion ('Herodotus' most Thucydidean book', Tim Rood). It is important to emphasize the book's 'surface': Tom Harrison rightly observed that there may be more divine suggestions below that surface.

[69] That can be so even if there are to be hints of the looming 'tyrant city' later in the book (cf. e.g. Moles and Henderson, pp. 263 and 305–9 below): tyrannical associations are first appropriated but transfigured, later the appropriation comes to be more important than the transformation.

[70] How much does it matter that the Gephyraioi are not wholly assimilated even at Athens? For discussion of this cf. Gray, pp. 213–15 below. Their marginality is rather played down at 57.2 – 'the Athenians received them as fellow-citizens on certain explicit terms, with the qualification that they be excluded from a few rights, not very many and not worth relating here' – but it is more stressed at the end of the sequence at 61.2 – 'they have certain rites established at Athens, in which the other Athenians play no part, and their separate cults include a temple and rites of Achaean Demeter.' If nothing else, there may be a hint of the paradox that it was part-outsiders who freed the Athenians of their tyrant – those Athenians who were rightly so indignant when other, more fully-fledged outsiders tried to reimpose the tyranny. Athens, perhaps, is put in its conceptual place, less a site for home-grown constitutional sophistication than one might think . . . (I am again indebted to Elizabeth Irwin for the suggestion made in this last sentence.)

relevant too: Herodotus' text is better equipped than Aristagoras' speech to teach such lessons; and the textuality can add to their persuasiveness, this time with good persuasion rather than bad.

But then one remembers Hecataeus. The narratee may remember Hecataeus even more if, as so many have thought since Jacoby, the writing excursus has some relation to Hecataeus' own treatment of the same topic (for we know that Hecataeus did treat it). Jacoby thought Herodotus was simply lifting it from Hecataeus,[71] Marincola preferred to stay neutral on whether Herodotus was supplementing or correcting Hecataeus;[72] it is worth mentioning that our source for the relevant Hecataeus fragment (*FGrH* 1 F 20, a scholiast on Dionysius Thrax) *contrasts* Hecataeus' version with that of Herodotus. If, as I suspect often elsewhere, Herodotus is implicitly improving on as well as alluding to Hecataeus, then that adds an extra point to any metaliterary suggestions: writing can be bad as well as good, and Hecataeus' writing on this same topic was not wholly accurate.[73] In any case, whether Herodotus is correcting Hecataeus or simply echoing him, the earlier author is very likely in the sophisticated narratee's thoughts intertextually. Perhaps, indeed, all that geography would anyway have been enough to bring Hecataeus to mind.[74]

He is also in even the rather less sophisticated narratee's mind intratextually, from 5.36 and before. At 5.36 Hecataeus figured in the narrative as a historical character, and he had his own lesson to teach, based there too on his catalogue of the Persian empire: do not touch it, he pleaded with his fellow Ionians, it is too big. 'And when he did not persuade them of that, in second place he urged them to gain mastery of the sea . . .', 36.2. The rhythm is the same as that of Croesus again, this time his advice to Cyrus at 1.207, where at an early stage Croesus abandons the obvious implications of his argument, do not attack at all, and moves on to second best, in that case pick the right place for the battle.[75] Nor is Hecataeus any more successful in the advice he gives to Aristagoras in the last chapter of Book 5. Real wisdom, as so often in Herodotus' text, turns out to be extremely elusive: elusive to gain, elusive to transmit. As a historical actor Hecataeus

---

[71] Jacoby (1913) 439.   [72] Marincola (1987) 130 n. 22.

[73] This would therefore be rather along the lines of 2.2.5, where Herodotus' point is surely something like: yes, the Greeks *do* tell many laughable stories [just as Hecataeus so famously said in his proem]; look at this laughable story of Psammetichus, [one told by Hecataeus himself]!' So, effectively, Lloyd (1975–1988) II.8–9; on that proem (*FGrH* 1 F 1) cf. also Bertelli (2001) 80–4, and also Bertelli's interesting remarks about 'agonistic intertextuality' at p. 68 (quoting Assmann).

[74] West (1991) 159 n. 86 suggests that the map, especially described as γῆς ἁπάσης περίοδος, would also point to Hecataeus.

[75] Pelling (2006).

found it difficult to transmit wisdom in oral debate; he found it difficult as an author too, and that is especially clear if Herodotus projects a need to correct him.[76]

Will Herodotus' own writing be able to do better? Perhaps – but there is not much in the text to encourage confidence. The Greeks will do these things, they are so easy to be put upon, they overrate their resources, they are carried away by the prospect of pushovers, and they push too far, too soon, and too hard; and they always will, however much the wise adviser or his text can try to put them off. Or so one could easily think. That would be an even more Thucydidean reading of Herodotus than those that are currently fashionable (for instance Raaflaub's Thucydidean Herodotus in the Brill *Companion*):[77] for Thucydides too may be writing for later generations to understand clearly (τὸ σαφὲς σκοπεῖν) what happened in his own time and what may happen again, but – so scholars often say – there is little in Thucydides' text to make us hope that the readers might do anything about it, or avoid repeating past mistakes.[78] And earlier parts of the paper have suggested a Thucydidean Herodotus in another way, one who plays with national stereotypes, Athenian and Spartan as well as Greek and Persian, and does interesting things with them.

Yet there is one way in which Herodotus remains more unThucydidean, and that is in the way that so many alternative readings are possible. They have been possible here too. Perhaps Cleomenes was a Spartan oddball, perhaps not; perhaps Athens was rash, perhaps sensible; perhaps Herodotus' text can do better than Hecataeus', perhaps not; perhaps the writing excursus goes suggestively with the narrative, perhaps it is just another self-standing wonder. It may be easier to put one across a crowd than an individual, or sometimes it may not. This may not be a text that itself tries to 'put anything across' its readers, but it does put many possibilities to them. The one thing it resists is any notion that learning historical lessons

[76] De Jong (2001) 115 thinks there is also a metahistoriographical dimension to 5.36.2, pointing to the lessons proper study of geography and peoples can give; she does not, though, consider how far the metatextual dimension extends to Hecataeus' lack of persuasiveness.

[77] Raaflaub (2002) esp. 183–6: so already Strasburger (1955) 22 = (1965) 604–5.

[78] This is of course a controversial reading of Thucydides 1.22 (with the usual comparanda, 2.48.3 and 3.82.2), and one that I would only accept myself with some qualification. In Pelling (2000) 102–3 I resist the inference that nothing could ever be done to avoid past mistakes, though applying moral and practical lessons is doubtless difficult: it is simply that there the reader is on his or her own, and that this is not what Thucydides' text is about. Hippocratic works similarly often concentrate on rendering the pathology of a disease intelligible, and the practical therapeutic implications are left for a different type of work. The parallel of Hippocratic practicality opens a vast topic, already much discussed: on the issues see, succinctly, Hornblower (1987) 133–4. I intend to return to this elsewhere. Within Thucydides' own text we see historical agents learning from experience, at least to a limited extent: on this see the thought-provoking paper of Rutherford (1994).

is a pushover. Historical understanding requires constant thought and re-examination; it is a highly provisional business, and every time one thinks and reads again one may come up with something new. And that is the joy of reading Herodotus.[79]

[79] My thanks to Judith Mossman, Tim Rood, Michael Flower, Alan Griffiths, Philip Stadter, Carolyn Dewald, and especially Simon Hornblower for very useful correspondence and comments, several of which I have silently incorporated; and to the Classics department at the University of North Carolina, Chapel Hill, as well as to the Cambridge audience for comments on my own oral 'displays' of earlier versions. The editors have been extraordinarily helpful, but I should mention that Elizabeth Irwin (a) does not share my hesitations about 'unity' (pp. 197–8) and (b) feels that Herodotus' text may itself be 'putting something across' its readers in a deeper sense than I here address.

CHAPTER 8

Structure and significance (5.55–69)

Vivienne Gray

Herodotus 5.55–95 deals with events that laid the foundation for Athens' greatness in the fifth century, namely her liberation from the tyranny that Peisistratus established and his sons Hippias and Hipparchus continued after his death, and the reforms of Cleisthenes.[1] Most of the history of Greece arises in the earlier books of Herodotus' *Histories* as digressions from the main account of the rise and expansion of eastern power; for example, the story of the acquisition of the tyranny at Athens by Peisistratus arises out of Croesus' search for the strongest allies among the Greeks (1.56–64). Herodotus 5.55–95 is another such digression. It takes the form of a flashback (*analepsis*). The arrival of Aristagoras at Athens with his appeal for assistance against the Persians generates it (5.55.1), and the decision of the Athenians to accept his appeal and send ships and troops for the liberation of Ionia closes it (5.97.1–3). Within the digression Herodotus seems to choose material that charts the increase in the strength of the Athenians – presumably because her strength is why Aristagoras chooses to approach her after the Spartans refused him. He says famously at 5.78: *isēgoriē* is an excellent thing, since under tyranny, the Athenians played the coward since they were working for a master, but once liberated they worked for themselves and became far more militarily powerful than before.[2]

However, this larger digression itself contains further digressions from this main story, and some of these are not so obviously focused on the liberation or Athenian growth, nor is their relationship to one another clear. They are rich also in peculiarities, where the amount of space spent on one story or even one aspect of a story seems out of proportion to its

---

[1] Thanks to the editors for the invitation to contribute to the volume and for stimulating feedback.

[2] Of particular relevance are her victories over Calchis and Boeotia (5.74–7), which provoke the statement about the connection of tyranny with weakness and *isēgoriē* with strength (5.78). This equation is repeated in the mouth of Cleomenes when he attempts to reimpose tyranny on Athens in order to weaken her (5.90–5, esp. 5.91.1). See Lateiner (1989) 163–86 on the representation of autocracy. Other references to greatness: 5.66, 5.91.1, 5.97.1.

importance to the whole.[3] Irene de Jong has summarized the structure of this section with some comments on the significance of the parts.[4] I hope in this chapter to examine their structural content and bring out some more of that relationship, particularly in the stories of the killing of Hipparchus and the reforms of Cleisthenes.

Herodotus divides the story of the growth of Athens into two sections by means of 'directional' and 'framing' opening and closing statements.[5] In the first such statement he announces that he will describe the liberation of Athens from its tyrants (5.55.1). After a false start involving the killing of Hipparchus, which he says explicitly did not achieve liberation, and a subsequent long account of the origins of his killers, he announces a return to the theme of liberation in another such statement (5.62.1) and he tells the story of how the Alcmaeonids bribed the Pythia to coerce the Spartans into liberating Athens. There follows the first failed expedition of Anchimolius and the successful one of Cleomenes, during which the Peisistratids were removed from Athens (5.62–5). He then uses another directional statement to announce the second phase: the achievements and sufferings of the Athenians after their liberation down to the arrival of Aristagoras (5.65.5). This begins with Cleisthenes' struggle against Isagoras and his constitutional innovations (henceforth 'reforms'). There follows Isagoras' appeal to the Spartan King Cleomenes, Cleomenes' first invasion and seizure of the Acropolis, then his second assault in alliance with Boeotia and Calchis, and finally his failure to re-install tyranny in Athens.

At the beginning of the first section, a long sentence encapsulating the story of the killing of Hipparchus forecasts the focuses to come in that story: 'When Hipparchus the son of Peisistratus, brother of Hippias the

---

[3] Herodotus' *Histories* take the conflict between Greece and the Eastern powers as their main theme, but stories regularly arise out of that main theme, often as a means of explanation, but other times apparently without much justification, as when the mere mention of a man's name generates other stories in which he was involved. One popular description of these digressions is as footnotes, which implies that they are less important than the main narrative: Lateiner (1989) 19: 'he wanted to distinguish the thematically significant from the inessential'. Gould (1989) more cautiously recognizes 'subordinate' stories that 'have a power and weight out of all proportion to its overt function as an explanatory link in the narrative' (p. 53) in a narrative that loops and eddies like a river (p. 58) – without pronouncing on their significance. Cf. Romm (1998) 26: Herodotus lays claim to the privilege of telling the reader what he wants, untrammeled by the idea of main narrative. De Jong (2002) recently summarizes views on these digressions and explores the *analepsis* as a structural element, finding that Herodotus takes it over from Homer. See also Gray (2002).

[4] De Jong uses Herodotus 5.55–96 as an exemplum of the technique, but her explanation of the digressions is brief. She concludes (265–6) that much of the material would modernly take the form of footnotes, that they enrich the content by providing parallels (Cleisthenes' imitation of his ancestor), and that they exhibit favourite motifs (the dream of Hipparchus), but in the case of the history of the alphabet, finds no relevance to the rest of the narrative.

[5] For framing statements: Immerwahr (1966) 12; Munson (1993); Lang (1984) 2; de Jong (2002) 259f.

tyrant, *seeing a most clear vision in a dream*, is killed by Harmodius and Aristogeiton,[6] *being in their lineage Gephyraioi*, after this the Athenians were tyrannized no less but more than before throughout four years.' The killing that follows is indeed dominated by the vision, which warned Hipparchus of his doom. Hipparchus consults the wise men, but dismisses the warning and then 'goes on the procession in which indeed he dies'. This is all we hear of the killing itself, but we hear much more about the lineage of his killers, which is about four times as long. Herodotus then summarizes the false start in the story of the liberation: 'The vision of the dream of Hipparchus and the origins of the Gephyraioi, to whom the killers of Hipparchus belonged, have been related by me. It is necessary in addition to these things that I take up the topic I started to relate, how Athenians were freed from tyranny' (5.62.1). This is a long false start indeed, in which apparently extraneous elements dominate the narrative of Hipparchus' killing. Why? And why does Herodotus dwell, in the story of the origins of the killers, on how the Phoenician ancestors of the Gephyraioi introduced the alphabet into Greece?

There is similar lack of proportion in how Herodotus describes the reforms of Cleisthenes.[7] He begins with a short statement of the reforms: how Cleisthenes made partners of the *demos*, created ten new tribes in place of the existing four, drove out the names of the sons of Ion, for whom the existing tribes were named, and named the new tribes for local heroes and for Ajax, though he was a foreigner (5.66). He then offers a digression four times as long on the reforms of Cleisthenes' maternal grandfather, the tyrant of Sicyon, whom Herodotus says he imitated in making his reforms (5.67–8). He then restates the reforms of the Athenian, with elaborations that now specify the motive for his reforms: his contempt for Ionians (5.69). The first peculiarity is the focus on the *names* of the tribes at the expense of the new institutions of government, such as we would expect in a modern account of the introduction of democracy; indeed it is only later that Herodotus describes Cleisthenes as the man who established *demokratia* (6.131).[8] But the most striking oddity is the greater space given to the reforms of his ancestor over his own. Obviously, the comparison between the tribal reforms of the two Cleistheneses begins to explain the digression: the Athenian renamed the tribes out of contempt for the Ionians because his ancestor renamed the tribes of the Sicyonians out of hostility

---

[6] I translate the active verb as passive to preserve the Greek word order.
[7] De St Croix (2004) 129–36 notes the peculiarities relating to Cleisthenes' reforms from the point of view of a historian.
[8] Rhodes (1981) 261 believes the word δημοκρατία was not current in Cleisthenes' times.

toward the Dorian Argives; but this is the only point of similarity between the two sets of reforms and there is much more on features that are dissimilar, and these are told at much greater length. Why did Herodotus add this material?

The peculiarities in both accounts can be brought out through contrast with Aristotle.[9] *Athenaion Politeia*, though it regularly uses Herodotus as a major source, omits the dream as well as the digressions on the Gephyraioi and Cleisthenes' ancestor, proving that these are unnecessary for a history of politics. What sort of history is Herodotus writing? It seems odd that he found more interest in the lineage of the killers than in the killing of a tyrant's brother, and more interest in the reforms at Sicyon than those in Athens.

In addition to the structural peculiarities, there is Herodotus' apparent lack of interest in the claims that Hipparchus' death had secured liberation. Many were credited with responsibility for the liberation from tyranny, as Rosalind Thomas has shown,[10] and Harmodius and Aristogeiton were candidates.[11] Herodotus rejects their claims on the grounds that Hipparchus was only the brother of the tyrant, but he makes no attempt to support this with proof or argument, though his display of his inquiry is his regular 'voice-print'. He makes the point elsewhere that the Alcmaeonids were more responsible (6.123), but leaves the case unsupported when he describes the liberation in the narrative. Contrast Thucydides (1.20, 6.53ff.), who is very interested in proving that Hipparchus was only the brother, and that Hippias went on ruling more savagely after his death.[12]

THE GEPHYRAIOI

The dream of Hipparchus

The stories that come in for disproportionate treatment in the killing of Hipparchus are forecast in the opening sentence (above). The vision, and

---

[9] Aristotle gives the only other account of these events. His omissions are the more remarkable because he is heavily dependent on Herodotus for most of his work. See Rhodes (1981) 224–40 on the killing of Hipparchus and liberation, 240–62 on Cleisthenes' reforms = *Ath. Pol* 18–22.

[10] Thomas (2000) esp. 238–82.

[11] Taylor (1981) discusses the traditions about the end of the tyranny in art and literature. There is material as well as literary proof of the honour in which the tyrannicides were held. Taylor (1981) 17: the tyannicides were granted 'important, highly visible privileges'. Herodotus refers to these apparently at 6.109.3 'a memorial such as Harmodius and Aristogeiton do not leave'. Aristophanes, *Knights* 786–7 calls Harmodius noble and *demos*-loving for giving him a cushion.

[12] See *HCT* IV. 317–37.

the lineage of the killers, rather than the actual killing, dominate the space. If the number of words were a guide to the importance of the content, we might conclude that Herodotus is dismissing the incident as one that did not contribute to liberation – perhaps as a snub to those who believed it did.

We would be wrong to draw such a conclusion, I think. Herodotus seems to be presenting Hipparchus' death as a human misfortune of the kind to which he draws frequent attention in his work, and which is exemplified in Solon's view of the human condition. He does not present it as a political action of the kind that the modern historian or even an ancient audience might expect. The vision is a symbol of this and it is literally and figuratively central to the story. Not only does the explicit description of the story as a story about a vision indicate its importance, but its importance is also compounded by the structure of the story. The account is a short story of a recognized kind and its structure takes the form of ring composition, emphasizing the central element. Herodotus first describes the killing, then tells the story of the vision, then returns to a slightly more elaborated restatement of the killing. What then is the function of the central portion, the warning vision? Warning dreams and pronouncements from shrines occur regularly in Herodotus, but to say that it is a favourite motif would be no explanation of its function. Rather, since Herodotus says elsewhere that there are always warnings of this type before *great* disasters (6.27.1), and that is clear from his narrative of, say, Croesus, one interpretation is that the vision enhances the killing, giving it significance as a great action.

It is useful to compare another story of a similar shape in the vicinity to confirm the view that the shortness of this story form does not make it insignificant: the story of the removal of Cleomenes from possession of the Athenian Acropolis (5.72). Here was an event few would want to dismiss, and yet the account of it is very short. A warning dominates this story in the same way the vision dominates the killing of Hipparchus, and statements of the action surround it. Herodotus first outlines how Cleomenes seizes the Acropolis, the Athenians besiege him and he leaves under truce on the third day. He then comments that this was a fulfillment of the pronouncement, and tells the story of this pronouncement: that the priestess warned him that he must leave her temple because entry was not permitted to Dorians. Cleomenes makes his famous response that he was no Dorian, but an Achaean, then Herodotus says explicitly that he ignored the warning, restates the narrative outcome, how he and his Spartans were driven out, and adds an elaboration on the fate of the others who were with him on the Acropolis: the Athenians killed them all.

Both stories are short and dominated by the warning, and both take the form of ring composition, in which statement and restatement of the narrative event surrounds the warning, which is given in flashback. The removal of Cleomenes is a significant political event, just like the killing of Hipparchus, yet they both get short narrative shrift. Cleomenes' assertion that he is no Dorian in contradiction of the priestess is structurally on a par with Hipparchus' decision to ignore the soothsayers and go ahead with the procession: the indication that he ignored a valid warning.[13] Much could be read into Cleomenes' assertion of his identity as a Spartan King with epic Achaean ancestry, but the basic function of the remark is to dismiss a clear warning, as in the case of Hipparchus. The ignored warning makes both the victims representative of the foolish human condition shared by other figures such as Croesus, who also regularly ignores warnings clear to the audience. Taken all in all, then, Herodotus treats both these significant events in a similar way, not to dismiss them, but to present them as events that rise above the merely political to the level of the human condition, possibly with reference to cosmic relations of gods and men.

Herodotus writes in such narrative patterns on the larger and the smaller scale.[14] Some conclusions have been drawn from the comparison with the story of Cleomenes, but they are made even richer by comparison with patterns in Homer, who has been subject to much more analysis than Herodotus and is thus a better guide to how the story functions, and particularly to the idea that a short description of the action itself is no indicator of a lack of significance in the event.

Herodotus' use of Homer's narrative structures is well attested.[15] There are also other examples of the interface between history and epic.[16] It is therefore unsurprising to find that Homer also uses the kind of ring composition found in our stories in dealing with deaths in battle: he narrates the death, then tells stories about the background of the victim, then re-narrates the death, often with elaborations (as also in the case of our stories).[17] What is in the middle (which is the equivalent of the warning in the stories of Hipparchus and Cleomenes) can receive an apparently disproportionate

---

[13] For further discussion of the significance of Cleomenes' *klēdōn* see Irwin, p. 47 above, Hornblower, p. 169 above, and Henderson, p. 307 below.

[14] Immerwahr (1966) for the larger patterns.

[15] See Boedeker (2002) on relations between Homer and Herodotus, esp. 104 on ring composition as a narrative feature, and 107–9 for possible explanation of the significance of their relations. De Jong (2002) 254 also draws attention to the influence of Homer in relation to the *analepsis*. Her remark that 'looking at the Homeric epics as a model has much enhanced our appreciation of its structure' in her own article can be extended to his smaller patterns.

[16] Continuing the observations of Boedeker (2002).

[17] On the Homeric death scenes and the significance of the stories in them: Griffin (1980) 103–44.

amount of literary attention; nevertheless it informs the action far more than any expanded narrative would, in particular by conveying, as scholars have proven, the sense of the pathos of the death of the individual. *Iliad*, 4.473–89 gives us a statement of the death of the lovely Simoeisios, then a longer account about his birth, his mother and her parents and how he did not live to repay his nurture, then a short restatement of his death with grisly detail; it concludes with a quite long simile. Much more space goes on the 'digressions' of background and simile than on the narrative death, and yet this apparent imbalance does not detract from the death; on the contrary, the digression and the simile amplify the pathos of his death.[18] 'The tragic and consistent view of human life is what makes the epic so great. The "obituaries" and the other passages of austere pathos are vitally important for it.'[19] Another instance is the death at *Iliad* 5.541–60 where the act of killing takes up barely two lines, while background and simile take up the rest. The effect is not to detract from the significance of his end, but to enhance it. The significance is the heroic vision of the human condition, particularly how death is inevitable for all the heroes – even Achilles. This is appropriate in a poem devoted to death.

In fact, the Homeric and epic use of the supporting story to create pathos is found as an addition to the story of Cleomenes above, where Herodotus singles out for mention the great achievements of the Delphian, who was bound and put to death after being captured on the Acropolis (5.72.4). The assertion that he could tell many stories of the strength of his *hands* and his *spirit* suggest the pathos of one who was now bound and unable to use his hands or his spirit in his final appearance in life. This Delphian is no major player in the story, but he is a figure imbued with that human and universal significance.[20] The comparison with Homer's way of giving significance to heroic deaths confirms that the structure of Hipparchus' story implies no dismissal of its significance. Rather, the significance is universal, about the human condition rather than politics, just like Cleomenes' removal from the Acropolis. It gives the specific story a universal validity as proof of how the gods work and thus contributes to the larger vision of the relations between gods and men that was also the focus of Homer's epic.

There may have been readers disappointed in the lack of political analysis of the murder, but Herodotus is a philosophical historian interested in the larger significance of the great achievement, and those readers should have

---

[18] See Kirk (1985) *ad loc.*   [19] Griffin (1980) 143.

[20] This application of the narrative structure to others besides Hipparchus shows, of course, if it were needed, that Herodotus is not using the structure to comment on the tyranny's own alleged manipulation of Homer.

appreciated his larger aims. Those who believed that visions did not endow actions with significance were just not on his wavelength. The vision would make those accustomed to his narrative habits and to his mentality dwell on the killing in a way that a more political or more extended description might not.

Herodotus does not speak about Hipparchus elsewhere, but his warning makes the point that he is a criminal and that even the greatest and mightiest will pay for their crimes. The figure in his dream, tall and good-looking (cf. 7.12), calls him a lion in the first part of his prophecy and exhorts him to 'endure his suffering of the unendurable with an enduring heart'. The lion is a dangerous symbol of strength (5.92β.3, 7.180, 7.220 etc.), but he now meets his end. The best heroes endure sufferings, like Odysseus, and this lion will too. The second sentence makes him representative of the general condition of humankind who always pay for their crimes ('none among men will not pay for their injustice'), and makes his forthcoming doom repayment for that injustice. His own particular crimes have not been described, but Herodotus offers more detailed proof of tyrannical injustice elsewhere, in the subsequent description of the tyrants of Corinth, which Socles delivers in order to persuade the Peloponnesians not to reimpose tyranny on Athens (5.92). The idea of the tyrant as a criminal was commonplace. Hipparchus' 'near-miss' decision to ignore the warning (he consulted the dream-men, but then rejected their findings) focuses on another aspect he shares with mankind in general, which is their inability to heed even 'the clearest' warnings. This narrative device also seems to announce the importance of the event, since the near-miss is usually found associated with great events, such as Cyrus' capture of Babylon.[21] Perhaps Herodotus wants us to see that his end was significant, not in relationship to liberation, but to the general fate of mankind that is encapsulated in Solon's advice to 'look to the end' before happiness is assured (1.30–3). The warning gives the tyrant a kind of greatness compatible with portrayals of other aspects of tyrants in the history even though it is a negative kind.[22] Herodotus deals in great deeds, and the greatness of the tyrant makes the illustration of retribution particularly telling. Even the democratic audience was used to the greatness of the tyrant on the tragic stage.

---

[21] Cyrus' capture of Babylon is marked not only by the near-miss (1.191.5), but also by the dilemma and the unresolved motivation (1.190.2–191.1), all of these being devices Herodotus uses to mark significant moments. Another near-miss marks the removal of the Peisistratids from the Athenian Acropolis (5.65.1)

[22] Herodotus can show tyrants to be bloodthirsty monsters where context requires it (5.92), but tragic figures in other contexts (e.g. 3.50–3). Cf. below on 5.65, the expulsion of the Peisistratids.

Herodotus' report of the vision also characterizes Hipparchus' killers as those who give just retribution to great men who commit injustice, preparing the way for their further characterization in the account of their origins.

The origins of his killers

Herodotus frequently moves into a digression from his main storyline by asking the question 'who was this man' and giving background in terms of his lineage, which was of course a basic area of historical research for Herodotus and his predecessors. The killing of Hipparchus generates a question about the origins of his killers in the same way. They have delivered just retribution for crimes committed by the tyrant's brother. Now the φονέεις ('murderers') turn out to be Φοίνικες ('Phoenicians'). The instinct to want to know about lineage and land is found in Artaphrenes' reaction to the arrival of embassies from the new Athenian democracy: τίνες ἐόντες ἄνθρωποι καὶ κοῦ γῆς οἰκημένοι ('who they were and where they were from', 5.73.2).[23] Herodotus shows this interest not only in his main narrative but also in a special form in his catalogue of Eastern forces, where the mention of a particular race regularly gives rise to 'digressions' that chart their origins and their changes of names and territory.[24]

Herodotus presents the digression in two blocks (5.57–61).[25] A first framing statement opens the story of Harmodius and Aristogeiton out into the

---

[23] This phenomenon is found also in Homer: Diomedes, in a more sophisticated context, recites his lineage in answer to the same question from Glaucon in *Iliad* 5.119–211. On this question see Irwin, pp. 69–70 above, Osborne, p. 89 above, and Henderson, p. 293 below. Translations are adapted from Waterfield.

[24] Herodotus 7.61–99. This form of narrative is already found in Homer's *Iliad* 2.484–759. Homer digressed to include stories about those in the catalogue for his own purposes, for example *Iliad* 2.511–16, 657–76, and Herodotus adapts these digressions to his own interests. He regularly describes for each nation he names: their weapons and armour, the names of their commanders, the traditions about the different names they are or have been called. The commanders must of course be named, but the interest in clothing and arms reflects his interest in νόμοι, while his interest in their changing names reflects his interest in the historical process of change and gives him an opportunity to display his research into the different traditions about them. So that we get different traditions about the original names of the Persians, one from the Persians themselves and those who live near them, another from the Greeks; there follows an explanation of why they are now called Persians (7.61). The Medes more abruptly account for their own change of name (7.62). In the case of the Assyrians, the Greeks and the Easterners again differ about the names (7.63). There is also the idea that neighbours are a special source of information about your identity (7.74): 'The Phrygians, as the Macedonians say, were called Bryges as long as they bordered on Macedonia, but changing place to Asia along with their land they changed their name.' Herodotus sometimes gives only the arms and the commanders, but the debate about the names continues through the catalogue: for the Sacae (7.64) and for every nation mentioned in 7.91–5. It recurs in the catalogue of the Greeks who fought at Salamis: 8.44.2, giving the four changes of names of the Athenians.

[25] de Jong (2002) does not describe the internal structure of this particular episode.

story of the origins of their clan, the Gephyraioi: οἱ δὲ Γεφυραῖοι, τῶν ἦσαν οἱ φονέες Ἱππάρχου ('The Gephyraioi – the family to which Hipparchus' assassins belonged', 5.57.1). A description follows of how the Gephyraioi arrived in Boeotia with Cadmus, settled in Tanagra, were expelled by the Boeotians shortly after the Cadmeans were expelled by the Argives, came to Athens, and were given citizenship there, barring only a few privileges that Herodotus deems unnecessary to mention (his way of saying that they were given almost full privileges). A second framing statement opens the story of their clan out to the story of the broader group to which that clan belonged, the Phoenicians who came to Boeotia with Cadmus: οἱ δὲ Φοίνικες οὗτοι . . . τῶν ἦσαν οἱ Γεφυραῖοι ('These Phoenicians . . . among whom were the Gephyraioi', 5.58.1). This dwells on their introduction of the alphabet and also eventually returns to the expulsion of the Cadmeans from Thebes and the Gephyraioi from Tanagra and their journey to other places. Some elaboration occurs in this restatement: that the Gephyraioi established shrines in Athens and these are set apart from those of other Athenians.

The digression is marked by the 'display of enquiry' that Herodotus announced in the preface as one of the main aims of his history: Herodotus' 'voice-print'. This immediately strikes the reader. He presents the account as a conflict between what the clan of Harmodius and Aristogeiton say about their origins, and what he has found by researching: they say they came from Eretria, but he has discovered they came with Cadmus from Phoenicia: ὡς μὲν αὐτοὶ λέγουσι . . . ὡς δὲ ἐγὼ ἀναπυνθανόμενος εὑρίσκω ('As they themselves say . . . but making my own investigations I have discovered', 5.57.1). He narrates their origins and then devotes every detail to proving their origins, 'displaying his research' in a *tour de force* of his tools: oral traditions (*akoē*), personal observation (*opsis*), reasoning (*gnōmē*) and research (*historiē*) as summarized at 2.99.[26] He dwells particularly on their introduction of the letters of the alphabet into Greece (οὐκ ἐόντα πρὶν Ἕλλησι ὡς ἐμοὶ δοκέειν, 'the Greeks did not have them earlier, as it seems to me', 5.58.1), among the many other 'lessons' they gave the Greeks. He pursues the alphabet, I think, because it is the best proof he has found of the Phoenician origins of the Cadmeans. He explains that they gradually changed their language after arriving in Boeotia,[27] and then adapted their alphabet to fit their new language. The Ionians then learned their letters and made further changes to suit Ionic Greek (5.58.1–2). To prove this, he cites the Ionians as a source of information: having acquired the alphabet from the Cadmeans

---

[26] Thomas (2000) shows how interesting Herodotus' methodology can be.
[27] 'Becoming Greek' and changing culture with geography is a common motif: Thomas (2001a) 223–4.

because of their proximity to them, they now call the letters they use 'Phoenician'; Herodotus adds 'most justly' since in fact they did introduce it (χρεώμενοι δὲ ἐφάτισαν, ὥσπερ καὶ τὸ δικαῖον ἔφερε ἐσαγαγόντων Φοινίκων ἐς τὴν Ἑλλάδα, Φοινικήϊα κεκλῆσθαι, 'But they still called the alphabet they used the Phoenician alphabet, which was only right, since it was the Phoenicians who had introduced it into Greece,' 5.58.2).

Herodotus also calls on the Ionians as a source of evidence that they have from a long time back called their writing material *diphtherai* because they once used skins instead of papyrus.[28] The observation that many of the barbarians in his time write on such materials seems to suggest to him, apparently, that the Ionians also learned this from the Phoenicians. The crowning proof is that Herodotus himself has seen these Phoenician letters on victory monuments in the shrine of Ismenian Apollo in Thebes, the heart of Cadmean influence, and they look very like the Ionian ones. In order to fix this proof, he quotes the inscriptions and dates them to the times of Laius and Oedipus, Eteocles and Laodamas, the Cadmean heroes. This takes up a good deal of space in the digression. The final proof that the Gephyraioi are immigrants is found in their separate shrines, the material remains that form the culminating proof of a case in other stories as well.[29] The idea that Greeks were civilized by borrowing barbarian inventions is of course part and parcel of Herodotus' view of their development, as he shows in recounting their numerous borrowings from the highly civilized Egyptians.

We could be satisfied with the observation that Herodotus likes to generate stories of origins, especially involving cultural changes, and that this digression fits the bill, but we could also ask how the story relates to the killing. And what explains Herodotus' selection of detail? It seems unreasonable to assume that he is not making a conscious selection. This selection is evident also in the digression on Cleisthenes' lineage, which is restricted to his maternal grandfather; we find out about Alcmaeon and the male line only in the subsequent account of his family's growth (6.125–31). There must be a reason why Herodotus develops some lineages and leaves others undeveloped, such as those of Isagoras (5.66.1) and the Spartan Anchimolius (5.63.2).

Herodotus certainly has a favourable view of the Gephyraioi. Neither he nor his audience could ignore the privileges and honours that the

---

[28] On this term see also Munson p. 165 n. 87 above.

[29] Consider the material proof of the miracle of Arion: the bronze statue of a man on a dolphin dedicated at Taenarum (1.24.8); also the monuments of Sesostris that prove the extent of his conquests (1.102–3).

tyrannicides continued to enjoy among the Athenians.[30] In the account of the killing, they seem to have struck a blow for justice against tyrannical crime, which seems good. Though they had not killed the main man, and had made his rule harsher in response to his brother's killing, and though the Alcmaeonids were more responsible for the liberation because of their bribery of Delphi to engage the Spartans (6.123.2), Herodotus is evidently not hostile to the idea that the killing was at least a contribution to freedom, since he has the Athenian Miltiades refer to the 'memorials' that Harmodius and Aristogeiton leave behind, in a context in which he is encouraging Callimachus to secure the freedom of the Athenians at the battle of Marathon (6.109.3). There was merit even in killing a tyrant's brother, and the law allowed such killing with impunity. Those who thought they deserved no honour would be satisfied with Herodotus' flat rejection of their claim, but those who honoured them were allowed the recognition that the killing was still an achievement. Herodotus produces a balanced account of their role in the politics of freedom.

Some have argued that Herodotus uses the digression to degrade the Gephyraioi as non-Greek.[31] Less politically, Rosalind Thomas observes that Herodotus likes 'puncturing' myths of lineage, citing other cases of this.[32] However, these negative views run counter to Herodotus' emphasis on their introduction of the alphabet, their other benefactions toward Greeks, and their reception as citizens into archaic Athenian society with almost full privileges, presumably as acknowledgement of these benefactions.[33] Citizenship in Herodotus' times was certainly given to foreigners who benefited the polis. His reference to the 'many lessons' they gave to the Greeks is confirmed in his earlier account of how Melampus introduced many aspects of civilization into Greece, including the rites of Dionysus, which he learned from Cadmus of Tyre and those who came with him to settle in Boeotia (2.49.1–3). Herodotus presents the Egyptians as a special source of instruction for the Greeks, and evidently admires them greatly, so that in presenting the Cadmeans as the authors of other lessons for the Greeks, far from degrading the clan, he is presenting them as admirable.

If we wonder whether being a barbarian in your origins is some kind of slight, in spite of benefactions, we would have to take a dim view of most

---

[30] Taylor (1981) 17: they were granted 'important, highly visible privileges'.

[31] Lavelle (1993) 61. This does not mean that Cadmeans are always presented positively. Said (2002a) 89ff. says that Cadmus becomes the symbol in Cadmean Thebes of barbarianism, in Euripides' view of foreigners.

[32] Thomas (2001a) 126.

[33] However anachronistic the idea of citizenship might be for those early times: Manville (1990) passim.

of the aristocratic clans. As Thucydides observes (1.6.6), if you go far back enough in the history of any Hellenic group, you find barbarian affinities. Herodotus proves even the Spartan Kings to be Egyptian in the maternal line, but it cannot be argued very far that he has a negative view of those kings.[34] It has been argued that writing was a cause of suspicion for Greeks, but there is nothing sinister about the use of the alphabet in this passage. The victory tripods on which Herodotus found the Phoenician letters are very Greek.[35] Perhaps too it is significant that the account refers to their many victory monuments and names Cadmean heroes such as Oedipus. Presumably, when the Gephyraioi said they came from Eretria, they were simply ignorant of their roots, rather than trying to suppress them; they had no interest in dissociating themselves from a group that had given such benefits to Greece and had such illustrious ancestors.

The reason why Herodotus would want to degrade the Gephyraioi might be found in his alleged support for the Alcmaeonids.[36] He attributes the eventual liberation to their bribery of the Delphic oracle, underlines this with confirmation from the Athenians as his source, and seems to view this in a positive light when he mentions it later (6.123). Their own military failures against the tyrants are emphasized, and their responsibility for the arrival of the Spartans, but these just reveal the extent to which they would go against tyranny (πᾶν ἐπὶ τοῖσι Πεισιστρατίδῃσι μηχανώμενοι, 'contriving all that they could against the Peisistratids', 5.62.2). Yet Isocrates shows what a favourable account could be like when he edits out the bribery to restore military credit to the Alcmaeonids. Four times (2.113, 2.315, 2.355, 3.191) he refers to how Cleisthenes 'brought back the *demos* and drove out the tyrants', and turns the bribe into a mere loan from Delphi to finance these operations.[37] The Spartan role is the main focus and their bribery is required for that. It follows that once the Spartan part in the liberation is rejected, so must be the role of the Alcmaeonids in bribing the oracle.

---

[34] Thomas (2001a) 220–2 on Herodotus 6.53. Greeks say Spartan kings were Greek as far back as Perseus, but go no further. Herodotus reasons that Perseus had no human father, but must be counted Egyptian on the side of his mother Danae. The Persians confirm that Perseus was Assyrian and *became Greek* and that the ancestors of Danae were Egyptian (6.54). Herodotus does not describe how these foreigners secured the kingship, but in the course of describing their awards, he likens their practices to those of the Assyrians and Egyptians from whom the traditions said they were descended (6.58.2, 60)!

[35] Steiner (1994) 132 speaks of the inscribed marker as the indication of the oriental tyrant but finds some difficulty in our three tripods (133). Cf. the use of writing in the inscription of the Athenians for their victory over national enemies (5.77.4).

[36] See different views on this in Thomas (1989), Lavelle (1993).

[37] Arist. *Ath. Pol.* 19.4 also ignores the bribery, though he is aware of the Spartans. Fifth-century tradition seems to edit Cleisthenes out of the record: Loraux (2002) 71–2.

In any case, there is no sign of negativity in the lineage of the Gephyraioi; Herodotus' digression goes on from their just killing of Hipparchus to describe their other worthy achievements. This is a regular pattern in his narrative. Consider the sequence of stories about the origins and achievements of Sophanes, who is a killer in the battle of Plataea (9.73–5). The first concerns the achievement of the older inhabitants of his deme of Decelea, the democratic equivalent of the ancestors of the Gephyraioi. We hear of their great achievement in combating the insolent threat that the actions of Theseus posed for the security of Attica, and the honour and security the Spartans gave them for assisting in the recovery of Helen; Herodotus says the Athenians acknowledge this action as 'useful to them for all time'. Next we hear of the two versions of Sophanes' own 'anchored' bravery in the battle of Plataea, then his later great achievement when he killed a pentathlete in single combat, and finally his death as a commander in combat, fighting for his country's control of gold mines, having proved himself a 'good warrior'. Sophanes personifies that happiness and the spirit of his deme in proving useful to Attica throughout his career. The frequent references to events in the history of the Athenian empire beyond the chronological scope of Herodotus' *Histories* give his story an extra dimension. His fame and achievement constitute the special happiness of Solon's Athenian hero, Tellus, who also had an achieving life and a good death in battle (1.30.3–5). The previous story reinforces this message through contrast. There Callicrates, the 'most handsome man in the Greek army', is wounded before battle and carried away without fighting and 'dies a hard death', lamenting not that he has died on behalf of Greece, but that he has not 'used his hand' or gained the glorious achievement he yearned for (9.72). The contrast produces reflection on the importance of achievement: though both Sophanes and Callicrates meet their death, which no warrior avoids, one has a good death in battle after achievement, the other has a poor death without such achievement.

Herodotus' digression on the killers of Hipparchus therefore seems to me to commemorate the great achievements of the clan, in line with the stated agenda of the *Histories* to commemorate great deeds. Herodotus restates this as his main content before his account of Cleisthenes' reforms (5.65.5). These achievements follow on their latest achievement, the killing of Hipparchus. The impression is that they civilized the Greeks and were capable of giving just retribution to tyranny. The emphasis on the status of his killers could also enhance the status of their victim. It is a heroic thought, and one that Herodotus also credits to characters in his own work, that your status as victim depends on your killer's status. Achilles, when he is in danger

of being killed by one whom he considers to be without status, states his
clear preference to be killed by the great Hector, on the grounds that he loses
status as victim if the killer's status is not high (*Iliad* 21.279–83, 'a brave man
would have been the slayer as the slain was a brave man'). Herodotus makes a
character say that if one kills an enemy commander, it is a great achievement,
but even to be killed by one of worth is not a complete disaster, because
of the worthiness of the opponent. Great achievement of course goes hand
in hand with lineage. It is in this conviction that Herodotus explains that
the Alcmaeonids built a better temple than the one they contracted for –
because they were men of wealth and lineage: οἶά τε χρημάτων εὖ ἥκόντες
καὶ ἐόντες δόκιμοι ἀνέκαθεν ἔτι ('They were well off in terms of money
and had been a prominent family for generations', 5.62.3).[38]

The digression has plenty of other interest for readers.[39] As a display of
enquiry, it is a *tour de force*. It is characteristic that while Herodotus displays
his research into lineage and origins, Thucydides reveals the ignorance of
the Athenians about the status of Hipparchus (1.20), associating this with
their acceptance of stories that they did not sufficiently test for veracity:
6.53.2. Thucydides thought that the memory of how the killing had failed
to achieve liberation until the Spartans were called in made the Athenians
fear the emergence of a new tyranny after the mutilation of the Herms and
the parody of the Mysteries (6.53.3). But this kind of political interpretation
seems to be very far from Herodotus' agenda.

Other significant themes could be found, but they are not consciously
developed. The Gephyraioi were of course the kind of people Athens should
honour with citizenship. When we put together the main points of the
story, they could integrate their myth: that Athens welcomes the oppressed,
who seek refuge in their country in flight from their oppressors, repaying
on behalf of all Greeks those who have benefited all the Greeks.[40] This
would make the killers of Hipparchus living proof that the Athenians were
champions of Greeks. Yet it is the Gephyraioi who are the focus of interest
and not the Athenians who received them. The story would have to be
written differently to sustain that interpretation.

---

[38] The compliment to the Alcmaeonids is not backhanded. To focus on how they made the temple
look at the front by dressing it in Parian marble might look like a front, but Herodotus is quite clear:
'they built the temple more finely than the plan, *both in other respects and* in respect of the marble
front.'

[39] Should we try in desperation Herodotus 1.166: the Cadmean victory in which you suffer ruin? This
could be a description of the killing of Hipparchus, since the tyranny got more savage, but none of
the detail supports that either.

[40] This is a theme in the *epitaphios* and Isocrates' eulogies of the Athenians: Lys. 2.11–16, Xen. *Hellenica*
6.5.45–8, Isoc. *Panegyricus* 54–65, with Loraux (1986).

The digression does chart cultural change.[41] It is one of the purposes of the work as a whole to chart the process whereby the small become great and the great small, and Herodotus has a special interest in how cultures change their language with their geographic location. I would see this as an essential message of the digression, but not the explanation of the function of the digression.

A reader might notice how Herodotus is calling attention to the immigrant status of most of the main players in the story of liberation. He calls the lineage of the Alcmaeonids Athenian, but goes on to say that the maternal ancestor of Cleisthenes was Sicyonian (5.62.2);[42] in addition to this there are the Phoenician origins of the Gephyraioi, the Pylian origins of the Peisistratids, and of the earlier kings of the Athenians (Codrus and Melanthus: 5.65.3–4), the 'Carian' origins of Isagoras (5.66.1). To an audience who believed the Athenian claim in Herodotus' time that they were autochthonous, this would appear to be a challenge.[43] Perhaps Herodotus sees the liberation as a release not only from tyranny, but from domination by foreigners? He certainly presents Cleisthenes' subsequent introduction of democracy as a rejection of Ionian ancestry in favour of local origins and heroes, which might be interpreted as part of a move toward autochthony, but he himself had a Sicyonian ancestor, and the rejection of foreigners does not fit the story of the Gephyraioi, since they were evidence that foreigners, far from symbolizing foreign domination, had actually liberated the Athenians from Hipparchus. There are other avenues for the reader's speculation. Pericles' law of 451/450 BC restricting citizenship to those with Athenian parents might make the reader reflect on the place of immigrants in Athenian society, but the different kinds of immigrants presented send a muddied message about their desirability, some of them striking a blow for freedom, others curtailing it. In any case, the citizenship requirements did not extend back into time immemorial, and proof that the Gephyraioi felt no concern about their earlier *immigrant* status is their own claim that they came from Eretria. Of course the idea that the Gephyraioi struck a

---

[41] Hall (2002) emphasizes Herodotus' interest in Hellenicity. See Haubold, Ch. 9 below on the process of historical change depicted in the Aeginetan *logos*. Change is important perhaps in a *logos* where Athens is *becoming* strong.

[42] Paus. 2.18.9 says the Alcmaeonids came to Athens from Pylos in the same wave of refugees as the Peisistratids. Davies (1971) 369 wonders if Herodotus is making them Athenian for reasons of his own or whether Pausanias is just wrong. There seems to me no reason for misrepresentation when Herodotus makes so little of their origins.

[43] Isoc. *Panegyricus* 23–5 develops this claim of autochthony; Herodotus refers to it too: 7.161.3. Athens appears to have changed from claiming to be Ionic to claiming to be autochthonous at the end of the sixth century (first reference to autochthony in Aeschylus 458 BC): Hall (1997) 51–6; Zacharia (2003); Loraux (2000).

blow for freedom might be challenging to an audience with a dim view of foreigners, particularly since Herodotus elsewhere characterizes freedom as a special attribute of Greeks and not of non-Greeks.

There are other ways of reading the lineages in question. In the lineage of the Peisistratids the idea that these kings of the Athenians were undesirable *because foreign* is one possible reading, but their lineage could also demonstrate heroic, and therefore admirable, ancestry. The lineage of the Peisistratids could rather be an appropriate closure as they quit the place, reminding the audience of their heroic status, and how dominating they had been for sixty years.[44] Herodotus confirms their epic lineage through the name of Peisistratus, which proves his Pylian origins, since it is the name also of the Homeric hero. The immigrant status of Codrus and Melanthus may have enhanced their achievement in securing kingship because in other stories this is no mean achievement for foreigners (e.g. 9.34).

THE ACTUAL LIBERATION

When Herodotus returns to the narrative of liberation, the Alcmaeonids use their wealth to bribe the oracle to get the Spartans to liberate Athens after failing to secure the military result themselves. Perhaps the abolition of tyranny was an impulse they had learned from the Gephyraioi, from whom they had earlier received many other civilizing lessons. Herodotus cites 'the Athenians' to validate their bribery (ὡς ὦν δὴ οἱ Ἀθηναῖοι λέγουσι . . ., 'As then indeed the Athenians say . . .', 5.63.1). The Spartans answer the call because they regard the things of the god as 'older' than the things of man, and honour the oracle rather than a friendship with the Peisistratids. Yet they also fail at the first attempt, and at the second take Athens only by a stroke of luck. Herodotus goes out of his way to say that this was a near-miss: καὶ οὐδέν τι πάντως ἂν ἐξεῖλον τοὺς Πεισιστρατίδας οἱ Λακεδαιμόνιοι . . . πολιορκήσαντές τε ἂν ἡμέρας ὀλίγας ἀπαλλάσ-σοντο . . . νῦν δὲ συντυχίη τοῖσι μὲν κακὴ ἐπεγένετο, τοῖσι δὲ ἡ αὐτὴ αὕτη σύμμαχος ('Under normal circumstances, there is no way in which the Lacedaemonians would have got the Peisistratids out of there . . . they would have blockaded for a few days and left . . . What happened, however, was a piece of luck which was as bad for one side as it was helpful to the other,' 5.65.1). The near-miss device often underlines a very great

---

[44] He did not include this lineage in his earlier account of Peisistratus (1.59–64), because there his focus was on the weakness of Athens under tyranny and such lineage was irrelevant.

achievement, and is so used for example to mark the capture of Babylon, where the feast in which the people were engaged was the stroke of luck.[45]

CLEISTHENES

The account of the reforms of Cleisthenes is another case of the ring composition seen in the killing of Hipparchus: two statements of his reforms surround a central digression. In the first statement Cleisthenes is worsted in his power struggle with Isagoras, and he takes the *demos* into partnership in order to gain the ascendancy.[46] He then changes the number of the tribes into which Athenian society was divided from four to ten, drives out the names of the Ionian heroes (which are named), and replaces them with the names of local heroes (which are not) and of Ajax, who is added as a neighbour and friend even though a stranger. Herodotus states his opinion that in making these reforms he imitated his namesake maternal grandfather, the tyrant of Sicyon (δοκέειν ἐμοί, ἐμιμέετο, 'it seems to me he was imitating', 5.67.1), and this generates the much longer digression on the nature of this imitation. He then returns to his starting point and restates the nature of these reforms with some elaboration, adding in particular what has been proved in the digression: that his motive for renaming the tribes was contempt for the Ionians (δοκέειν ἐμοὶ καὶ οὗτος ὑπεριδὼν Ἴωνας . . . ἐμιμήσατο, 'It seems to me that this Cleisthenes also moved by disdain for the Ionians . . . imitated', 5.69.1).

Cleisthenes' imitation of his maternal grandfather could be generally compared to a Homeric simile, where the simile is longer than the action it describes, but comments significantly on it. It is also a proof from analogy, one of Herodotus' preferred methods of establishing the truth, and 'our

---

[45] Here, Cyrus almost fails to capture the city: 1.191.5–6.

[46] προσεταιρίζεται ('to bring into one's club', 5.66.2), a process referred to later as 'attaching the *demos* to his own portion' (πρὸς τὴν ἑαυτοῦ μοῖραν προσεθήκατο 5.69.2). Herodotus makes it clear that this was a power play; cf. Ober (1996). It is an extension of the kind of aristocratic struggle he describes between the dynasts and Peisistratus, but whereas in that case one party when 'worsted' joined another and kept the power at the top (1.59–61), Cleisthenes discovered a new source of power: a population strengthened through liberation (5.78). I am not sure we should think his partnership sinister because of the aristocratic connotations of the word; Munson (2001b) 53. It was undoubtedly beneficial to the *demos*. Herodotus says the *demos* was previously 'pushed away' ἀπωσμένον, by which he seems to imply 'denied participation in power' under the tyranny (5.69.2). Aristophanes, *Lysistrata* 1149–56 confirms that it was tyranny that pushed them away: the Spartans (who liberated the *demos*) replaced the skins the *demos* wore under tyranny with the civic cloak. To say that Cleisthenes previously pushed them away, as some do, would deny Herodotus' later remark that the Alcmaeonids were always in popular favour (6.125–31).

principal tool for illuminating the nature of things'.[47] Herodotus elsewhere
uses analogy in the form of direct imitation to make a point of basic interest
to his historical programme as I read it,[48] and the point he is making in his
comparison of the two Cleistheneses is also an essential part of his historian's
task: to support his opinion that Cleisthenes was motivated to reform
the tribes out of contempt for the Ionians. Herodotus elsewhere deduces
imitation when two practices are similar and the practice of one is older
than the other; also when the practices do not seem home-grown: 2.49, 58.
In this case he emphasizes the sharing of blood and a name (5.69.1); the
shared motives for tribal reform follow as a matter of course. This explains
the very tight focus of the comparison on the ancestor's hostility toward the
Dorians. The focus is signalled by authorial intrusions into the narrative,
a sign of special engagement.[49]

   The digression begins with the statement that Cleisthenes the Sicyonian
was at war with Argos. No detail is provided on this war since it is not
of interest to Herodotus in proving his point. His war simply explains
why he was hostile to everything Dorian, which was synonymous with
everything Argive. There follows a sequence of illustrations of this hostility
and its obsessive extent. First he stopped rhapsodic performances because

---

[47] See on proofs from analogy: Lateiner (1989) 191–6; Thomas (2000) 175–6, 200–11.

[48] The other case of direct imitation arises out of the account of the battle of Plataea at 9.33–4, where
the seer Tisamenus, in holding out against the Spartans for the privilege of citizenship for his
brother as well as himself, imitates Melampus, who held out against the Argives for a kingship to
be shared with his brother. Munson (2001b) 52–64 reads this, along with the comparison of the two
Cleistheneses, as explorations of kingship: the first turns citizenship into a metaphor for the acquisition
of kingly power and advances a view of kingship as informal personal power, while the second raises
questions about tyrannical aspects of the introduction of democracy. My very different view of the
two Cleistheneses is the main focus of this part of the paper, but the comparison of Tisamenus
also seems to me less a disquisition on kingship than an analogical comment on the magnitude
of the battle of Plataea as seen through the eyes of the Spartans. Herodotus announces magnitude
as a measure of historical relevance in his preface, and therefore has a vested interest in proving
the magnitude of the events he describes. Here he proves the Spartans extremely jealous of their
citizenship, then through the analogy enhances this by comparing their unwillingness to share mere
citizenship with the Argives' unwillingness to share kingship; he draws attention to the inequality of
these to make his point even clearer. Their subsequent willingness to share this precious citizenship
with both the seer and his brother before Plataea 'when the mighty fear of the Persian host hung
over them' (9.33.5) then becomes a very great proof of the magnitude of the peril they faced. It was
the only time the Spartans ever granted such a privilege (9.35.1). The comparison comments on that
magnitude in a most interesting way. It also of course forecasts the outcome of the battle and the
future successes of the Spartans.

[49] Contrast the view expressed in Munson (2001b) 52–62, that Herodotus uses the comparison to
indicate the tyrannical tendencies in Cleisthenes and raise questions about the nature of the new
democracy. But this does not explain his selection or presentation of comparative detail, or the
different attitudes he has the two Cleistheneses demonstrate toward their *demoi*, the one ridiculing
them and making them weak, the other taking them into partnership and making them strong; see
below. Munson (*ibid.*, p. 57) says that the *demos* is Cleisthenes' victim as well as his accomplice, but
Herodotus offers no support for the former.

they praised Argos and the Argives. Then he tried to expel Adrastus, a dead hero, an Argive who had inherited the kingship of Sicyon, whose shrine was in the central position of the agora. He requested the permission of Delphi to do this, but he was rebuffed. In spite of this, so great was his hostility that he devised a way of making Adrastus leave on his own account rather than driving him out. So he imported a hero from Thebes to be his rival: Melanippus. His cult was established not in the agora, but in the Prytaneion, because this was 'strongest', i.e. more centrally placed than that of Adrastus. At this point Herodotus says he is 'compelled' to tell us that Cleisthenes chose Melanippus because he was most hostile to Adrastus, members of whose family Melanippus had killed in the saga of the Seven against Thebes (5.67.3: knowledge of the saga is taken for granted; the essential point is the hostility). He also tells us, after briefly describing how Cleisthenes transferred the rituals in honour of Adrastus to Melanippus, that the Sicyonians were 'greatly very much' devoted to the worship of Adrastus, and that he had inherited the kingship of Sicyon legitimately in a crisis of succession (5.67.4). This authorial intrusion culminates in the comment that the Sicyonians celebrated the sufferings of Adrastus in their tragic festivals, honouring him and *not* Dionysus – using negative representation in order to prepare for the shocking way Cleisthenes shared these festivals out between Melanippus and Dionysus (5.67.5). Herodotus seems to impress upon the reader that Cleisthenes flew in the face of the desires of his people – evidently because his hostility toward the Argives was so intense. Finally we come to the main point of resemblance with his namesake descendant: that he changed the names of the Sicyonian tribes. Herodotus explains here too that he 'laughed greatly at' the Sicyonians; for the names he chose to replace the traditional Dorian divisions were those of lowly tenders of animals; he reserved the name of 'rulers' for his own tribe. This culmination of his hatred for things Dorian and Argive carries his contempt for Adrastus over to those who had shown him such respect. They continued with these names for sixty years but then changed back to the Dorian names and named the fourth tribe for one of Adrastus' sons. Herodotus has prepared us for this earlier in referring to the shrine of Adrastus which 'was then and still is' in the agora (5.67.1). Nevertheless, sixty years is the same time as the rule of the Peisistratids, which means that it is shorthand for quite 'a long time'.

The section leading up to this ancestor's tribal reform, which may otherwise seem not relevant to the reforms of the Athenian because it is not about tribal reform, nevertheless establishes Cleisthenes' hostility as his motive for his own tribal reforms. Herodotus is intent on giving as much support as he can to this idea. We understand better the extent of the Athenian's contempt for the Ionians when we understand the extent of his ancestor's hostility to the Dorians. Herodotus proves the imitation not only through the similarity of the reforms, but also through the link of lineage between the two reformers. He emphasizes this link in his ring-composed statements of the reforms because it is likely that one with the same name from the same lineage will do the same kind of thing. It is an example of the power of names as discussed below.

I resist the temptation to take the comparison beyond the motives for tribal reform and see general implications of tyranny in an Athenian demo-cratic reformer being inspired by a tyrannical ancestor. There is no doubt that the Sicyonian is presented as an oppressor of his people. This is evident in his suppression of the reverence in which the Sicyonians held Adrastus,[50] how the Pythian priestess of Delphi addressed him as *leustēr*,[51] and how he laughed at them in reforming their tribes. But the Athenian reformer takes his people into partnership, removes their laughable names, and insofar as he does drive out the heroic sons of Ion, does so with their apparent approval. He uses aristocratic methods and he wishes to increase his per-sonal power, but he has a completely different attitude to the *demos* from that of his ancestor. The comparison in fact makes us reflect on this differ-ence and its more democratic implications.

Moreover, the Athenians under the leadership of Cleisthenes become 'greater' (5.66.1). In keeping with the theme of the increasing strength of the Athenians throughout this part of Book 5, Herodotus presents Cleisthenes'

---

[50] His restriction of the worship of Adrastus is typical of the bad ruler in Herodotus 2.124, 129, where bad government shuts the temples and prevents sacrifice, whereas good government (εὐνομία) opens the shrines and lets people go to their own work and sacrifice.

[51] The Pythia told the Sicyonian when she denied him permission to drive out Adrastus: 'he was king of the Sicyonians, but you are a λευστήρ.' The traditional interpretation of this was that he was an underling, not fighting with spear or sword, and so unworthy. Against this, Ogden argues that stone-thrower is not a military reference, but refers to how Cleisthenes made Adrastus a scapegoat. But Cleisthenes has not yet expelled Adrastus and cannot yet therefore be called that kind of stone-thrower. The reference must be to his previous actions. Aeschylus, *Eumenides* 179ff., makes Apollo associate stone-throwing with killing and destruction and all sorts of awful deaths, and indeed with the Eumenides themselves, and thus suggests a better meaning: that Cleisthenes is being portrayed as a purveyor of this kind of death, the essential bloodthirsty tyrant: 'he was a king *of the Sicyonians*, you are their oppressor' (cf. 5.92 on Cypselus and Periander as such oppressors: Gray 1996). This meaning is made attractive by the involvement of Delphi in both references. Apollo tells the Furies to go out of his shrine and live in the lion's den that suits them better; no god loves their bloodshed. The Pythia may cast the stone-throwing Cleisthenes from her shrine on the same grounds. Sommerstein (1989) *ad loc.* rightly sees stoning as the product of an outburst of wrath rather than a judicial trial. There are frequent images of the *demos* as stone-throwers punishing criminals in undisciplined rage, in not entirely uncomplimentary contexts, but we may be meant to think of the violent and arbitrary punishments Cleisthenes metes out in contrast to the true king who operates a proper judicial system.

tribal reform as a symbolic act of driving out weakness and replacing it with strength, focusing on the change of names involved in the rejection of the Ionian heroes and the adoption of the locals. The change seems to us to conceal some more important effect of tribal reorganization, but for Herodotus, in his two framing statements, the names are central, and the comparison with his ancestor confirms it. He is crediting the reformers with the recognition of the 'power of names',[52] in which names reflect the essence of what they describe: one of his key statements is at 1.139 that the Persians had names that were 'equal' to their physiques and magnificence. The significance of etymology explains why the Sicyonian laughed at his people when he renamed their tribes after animals (swinemen and assmen and pigmen) while reserving the name of 'rulers' for his own tribe;[53] these names make them weak and him strong. The etymology is probably false, but this is irrelevant to how Herodotus is presenting the reforms.

Cleisthenes rejects the Ionian names for the converse reason, that the existing names described underlings and workers rather than warriors. These names were no longer 'equal' to the new military strength of the Athenians, since the physiques and mentalities of menials are not those of warriors.[54] These menial Ionic names must have induced the laughter from others that his ancestor enjoyed in humiliating his people; Cleisthenes removed the stain. It is significant that Herodotus names these Ionian names, but does not name the new tribes Cleisthenes created, except for Ajax the foreigner. The rejected names are the essence.

Herodotus confirms Cleisthenes' 'contempt' for the Ionians when he says elsewhere that even though the Athenians were the best of them, the Ionians were the weakest of the Greek races; and that their weakness was so intolerable that many of them shunned even the *name* 'Ionian' (1.143.3). 'Contempt' is in the same range of feeling as 'shame'. He goes on to refute with gusto the claims of the twelve Ionian cities of Asia to be nobler and

---

[52] See Harrison (1998).

[53] The extent to which he pursues etymology may be seen in his derivation of *theoi* from the idea that they 'dispose' (τίθημι) everything in the world (2.52.1). See Harrison (1998), Plato, *Cratylus* and Barney (2001) on *Cratylus*. *Cratylus* discusses etymologies of a similarly extravagant kind. The belief is that things have the characteristics of the names they bear and the names convey eternal realities, which they 'imitate'.

[54] Plutarch *Solon* 23.4 referred to those who understood the names of the sons of Ion in terms of activities that earned a livelihood: Geleon the farmer, Aigikoras the goatherd, Argades the craftsman and Hoples the hoplite. In another etymology Hoples would derive from the name for beasts of cloven feet: ὁπλή, ὁπλήεις. Euripides *Ion* 1580 derives Aigikoras from the aegis. See the Appendix to Owen (1939). These are the occupations of Perdiccas and his brother when they work as thetes for the Macedonian King (8.137.2). The natural contrast is between people of this kind and people of the ruling kind.

more Ionian than the rest, maintaining that they simply represented the twelve *poleis* they lived in when they were Achaeans in the Peloponnese. Their enslavement to the Persians is particular proof of military weakness.

The increase in the numbers of the tribes to ten, and the creation of 'more out of fewer' is a more straightforward change from weakness to strength: a code for the 'increase of the polis' that was the heart of the Greek understanding of political success. Constitutions breed strength,[55] and the increase in the numbers of tribes and their commanders is part of this.[56]

Herodotus is pulling out the stops to prove that Cleisthenes did act out of contempt for the Ionians and to enhance our understanding of that motive. It may have been controversial. It is believed that Athens found 'Ionianism' an issue of empire; she wished to dissociate herself from its weakness, but had to assert her links with Ionians because they were the heart of her empire; therefore she developed an alternative claim to autochthony but could not entirely afford to reject her Ionian origins.[57] We can only speculate on how contemporary audiences received Herodotus' insistence on their earlier rejection of the name. If they were still ashamed of it, then they might be glad to see their shame assuaged in the formation of their democracy. They might have preferred to forget their Ionian origins altogether, in spite of the usefulness of the link in maintaining influence with their Ionian allies, but Herodotus has been clear throughout that the Athenians were Ionians, for instance in the prelude to the account of the rise of Peisistratus (1.57–8). At least those who were ashamed had the comfort of Cleisthenes' rejection. Others who advertised their Ionianism in the name of empire, and perhaps denied the weakness it was associated with, would not welcome it. Herodotus' reminder of Cleisthenes' anti-Ionianism also gives piquancy to the decision of the Athenians to accept the appeal of Aristagoras. He considers their acceptance to have been an act of stupidity and the beginning of evils for Greeks and barbarians (5.97). They soon

---

[55] As is demonstrated by the weakness of Athens under tyranny, and the spectacular military success of the Spartans produced by the reforms of Lycurgus (1.56–68).

[56] 'Increasing the polis' is standard phrasing for securing its success: Xen. *Hiero* 11.13 summarizes the advice to the tyrant intent on securing this success; cf. Hdt. 8.30.

[57] Euripides wrote a whole tragedy (*Ion*) on this topic, and there he makes the ancestor Ion earth-born, a local in his own right, enshrining the idea of the pure and noble and democratic Athenian identity; he has his sons found the Ionian colonies in Asia to explain that link. Alty (1982) argues that ethnic identity was a factor in politics and that Ionians were seen as inferior to Dorians; our passage is the earliest evidence of this weakness. Hall (1997) 51–6: Athens changed from claiming to be Ionic to claiming autochthony at the end of the sixth century (first reference to autochthony in Aeschylus 458 BC); Zacharia (2003) indicates that the question of Ionianism did not stop with Cleisthenes. See also Loraux (2000).

learned about the weakness of the Ionians (5.97), but this did not prevent them from feeling very great sorrow at the capture of Miletus (5.103) or from championing their cause against the Peloponnesians when they moved to displace them from their homeland (9.106).

A detailed reading of the killing of Hipparchus and the reforms of Cleisthenes indicates that Herodotus writes in narrative patterns that need careful handling and shows how stories that lie outside the main storyline enhance our understanding of its significance. The vision that Hipparchus saw makes his death significant even while underlining his tyrannical injustice, and his killers' noble origins and previous great achievement give him status as their victim while making his elimination a further great achievement. The digression on Cleisthenes' ancestor likewise enriches the meaning of his reforms. The stories may interact in other ways in addition to those suggested in this paper, but the essential point is that the patterns do compel us to investigate the interaction.

CHAPTER 9

Athens and Aegina (5.82–9)

Johannes Haubold

This paper offers a new interpretation of the Aeginetan digression in Herodotus 5.82–9. It argues that the passage does not just provide the background to Athenian–Aeginetan hostilities but also offers an ambitious reflection on the nature of historical change more generally. There have been two detailed analyses of the passage in the twentieth century. Dunbabin discusses its value as a historical source for the Archaic Period, whereas Figueira asks what it tells us about Herodotus' use of sources and the political circumstances of the fifth century that shape his narrative.[1] The present reading differs from its predecessors in that it does not try to reconstruct history or historiographical context, but instead traces the different conceptions of the past that Herodotus interweaves in this passage.

Recent scholarship has asked how Herodotus works with the types of history that were available to him. Critics have focused particularly on the opposition between a distant past and more recent history, each of them characterized by its own rules and purpose. It has been suggested that the earliest past familiar to Herodotus largely corresponds to the 'mythical' events known from epic, tragedy and other traditional narratives; whereas recent history starts roughly with the reign of Croesus and has a more 'realistic' texture. The two kinds of history are separated by what scholars call the 'floating gap' between living memory, usually assumed to go back approximately three generations in an oral society, and a mythical past whose prime function is to provide aetiological reflection on current cultural practice.[2]

Attempts to categorize the different types of history with which Herodotus was working have had the important effect of drawing attention to the divergent textures of reality that cohabit under the roof of *historiē*;

---

[1] Dunbabin (1936–7), Figueira (1985). For an earlier treatment see Macan (1895) II, Appendix 8.
[2] E.g. Thomas (2001b), Bichler/Rollinger (2001) Ch. 2.2, Cobet (2002). The concept of a floating gap goes back to Henige (1974).

and of stimulating research into the ways in which these are combined.[3] Most critics would surely welcome the fact that the reality that underlies Herodotus' account is no longer uncritically assumed to be uniform (i.e. the sum of all that 'is the case'). However, there are worrying signs that new problems may be in store. Concepts such as the 'floating gap' can serve as useful heuristic pointers, yet when pushed too far they threaten to obscure the range of histories and historical registers which we find in Herodotus. This paper looks at one of the passages in which Herodotus combines and reworks some of the approaches he inherited from epic, from divine history near the beginning of time to the history of man and beyond.

THE AEGINETAN DIGRESSION: CONTEXT

I start with some remarks about the context of my chosen passage. Having thrown out the Peisistratids and adopted democracy, the Athenians face war on different fronts.[4] Against the odds, they defeat the Boeotians and Chalcideans. The battered Thebans consult the Delphic oracle on where to find new allies and are told to turn to 'those who are nearest' (οἱ ἄγχιστα).[5] The ensuing assembly dismisses the obvious interpretation: geographical proximity. Instead, it settles for what we might call a 'mythological' explanation: those nearest to the Thebans are the Aeginetans, descendants of Asopus like the Thebans themselves.[6]

The Thebans next send envoys to Aegina (5.80.2): they are given 'the descendants of Aeacus'. Herodotus is vague on what that means in practice but scholars tend to assume that what the Thebans get are cult statues.[7] These they take with them on their subsequent campaign against Athens.[8] Having suffered another setback they return the Aeacids and demand 'men' (ἄνδρες, 5.81.1). The Aeginetans oblige, partly because they are 'elevated on account of their good fortunes', partly because they remember their 'old enmity' towards the Athenians (5.81.2). They send ships that wreak havoc up and down the coast of Attica (5.81.3), and it is at this point that Herodotus interrupts his account to explain what lies behind the enmity between Aegina and Athens (5.82).

The narrative of chapters 77–81 sets up one central question: who is close to whom and for what reasons? That is what the Pythia challenges the Thebans to consider, and straightaway we are reminded of the wider context of our passage, Aristagoras' mission to mainland Greece. Aristagoras, we

---

[3] For a brief account of Herodotean scholarship since Murray (1987 (2001a)), see Luraghi (2001a) 10–15.
[4] Hdt. 5.55ff., 66ff., 77.   [5] Hdt. 5.79.1–2.   [6] Hdt. 5.80.1.
[7] E.g. Nenci (1994) 276.   [8] Hdt. 5.81.1.

recall, has come to Sparta and Athens to look for allies against the Persians.[9] In the context of the looming Ionian Revolt, the question 'who is closest to the Thebans?' has obvious thematic resonance. We are at a crucial point in the *Histories*, a point at which the map of the political world is redrawn, with far-reaching consequences for the rest of the narrative. Who is close to whom matters more in Book 5 than perhaps anywhere else. Notoriously, Aristagoras travels with a map of the world, a potent symbol of the political and cultural realignment that is under way.[10] The problem put to the Thebans in important ways prefigures that faced by the Ionians, and their attempts to cope with it are informed by similar concerns.

The Thebans consider two options, each of them essentially ahistorical. The first amounts to a tautology: those are nearest who are nearest (i.e. in purely geographical terms). The perspective here is ahistorical in a straightforward sense: as the anonymous speaker in the assembly points out, the neighbouring Tanagraeans, Coronaeans and Thespians 'always' (αἰεί) support the Thebans in war. The second, preferred option points to the Aeginetans as relatives of the Thebans. This interpretation turns to the past in order to understand the present. The idea is promising, but it soon becomes apparent that the Thebans' approach to history is not sufficiently sophisticated: the Aeacids can no longer help them.

The second Theban defeat comes about not because the past does not matter in *Histories* 5 but because it matters what *kind* of history one constructs in order to control the present. In the aftermath of the Cleisthenic coup, simple aetiologies no longer suffice. To be sure, at one level the Thebans do make the right choice; Herodotus is careful to point out that Aegina was indeed an obvious ally. However, they do not choose for the right reasons, and as a result fail to secure the kind of support that can help them under the prevailing circumstances. There is an obvious irony in the Thebans' final request for 'men'; we recall that they initially invoked the blood relationship between two *women* (i.e. Thebe and Aegina). Herodotus will return to this point, using the opposition between the genders to striking effect.[11] For now, the Thebans realize that a new approach is needed if they are to stand a chance against the Athenians. And with that new approach comes a new 'map of the world'.

AETIOLOGY AND HISTORY

I said earlier that both options considered by the Thebans are essentially ahistorical. The first simply assumes a permanent present (αἰεί). The

---

[9] Hdt. 5.38ff.   [10] Hdt. 5.49.   [11] See pp. 240–2 below.

second, while acknowledging that a diachronic perspective is important for our understanding of the present world, folds the whole of history into a single point of departure. The sisters Thebe and Aegina mark the very beginning of the societies that are named after them. Things have happened since, and new forces have emerged as a result. The Aeginetan digression explores what these forces are, bridging the gap between the first interpretation of the Thebans, things as they (always) are, and the second: things as they have (always) been. Between these extremes, Herodotus charts a process of gradual transformation. His digression thus turns into a reflection on the nature of history itself, and the factors that determine political and cultural change at different points in time.

In the context of his Aeginetan digression, Herodotus arranges different models of history into a meta-narrative about change through time, from an era where social and cultural change was essentially a matter of transactions between the human and divine worlds to one where it becomes a matter of cultural politics and inter-state relations. We need not assume that Herodotus attached universal value to the model he establishes in the Aeginetan chapters. Still, it can be argued that it acquires paradigmatic force in the special circumstances of *Histories* 5.

Structurally, the Aeginetan digression consists of a series of aetiologies, starting with the institution of a new cult at Epidaurus and culminating in the story of how Athenian women acquired their Ionian dress. The shift in geographical focus (Epidaurus → Aegina → Athens) is matched by a striking shift in emphasis and narrative register. The aetiology of Epidaurian cult reflects epic patterns of crisis and resolution and points back to the very early stages of the universe. When Aegina breaks away from Epidaurus, this is conceptualized in terms reminiscent of the Hesiodic Iron Age: the Aeginetans build ships, abandon justice and, yielding to ἀγνωμοσύνη ('arrogance'), rupture the bond between gods and men by stealing the statues of Damia and Auxesia.[12] The new order is once again enshrined in cult, yet this time the emphasis is on social custom rather than religious function.[13] This tendency is taken to its logical extremes in the story of how the women of Athens acquired their dress: rather than marking a change in the relationship between gods and men, the new dress of the Athenian women marks a change in the relationship between human societies, and between different groups within those societies.[14]

Implicit in the Aeginetan digression, then, is a history of historical change: from the sacred aetiologies of a distant past to cultural politics among present-day human societies. That history is not a rag-bag of

---

[12] Hdt. 5.83.1.   [13] Hdt. 5.83.   [14] Hdt. 5.87.3–88.2.

disparate sources, nor are there any floating gaps to be closed here. Rather, I shall argue that in his digression on how the Aeginetans came to be hostile towards the Athenians Herodotus reworks and expands an already existing model of historical change in clearly articulated stages, each with its own rules and protagonists. Herodotus would have known that model primarily from epic, and so it is epic with which I start.

EPIC AND HISTORY

Much of the Aeginetan digression is modelled on epic, and this is not merely true in the trivial sense that Herodotus uses epic as a quarry for his own historical edifice. Rather, Greek hexameter poetry as a genre provided Herodotus with a model of how the texture of reality changes over time. Greek epic as it had crystallized by the fifth century BC described the history of the universe, from its beginning in Hesiod's *Theogony* to the present as described in the *Works and Days*. Thanks to the dominant Hesiodic and Homeric traditions, that history was relatively uniform by the time Herodotus was active, though it did incorporate a range of different sub-genres. These sub-genres have long been seen to correspond to different stages in the development of the world.[15] In other words, the differences in tone and approach that we find in the texts of early Greek epic correspond to shifts in the nature of historical reality itself.

Perhaps the most important such shift concerns historical agency. In the *Theogony*, history is fundamentally made by the gods. Human beings do occur,[16] but they have little influence on the course of events. This changes in the *Catalogue of Women*, where we witness the making of a composite universe of gods and mortals. History is finally put in the hands of humans in the *Works and Days*. The gods are of course still there, and they do respond to human actions; however, it is human agents such as Perses who decide whether to act justly or not, thereby determining not only their own wellbeing but also the future of entire societies.[17]

The shift from a history of the gods to a history of humans is deeply engrained in epic as a genre, and indeed in the Greek imagination more generally. It is a gradual and complex shift which is never complete and always remains open to modifications. In the following pages I suggest that the Aeginetan digression in *Histories* 5 represents precisely such a modified account of epic history. Like the epic bard, Herodotus is concerned to ground life 'as it is now' in a 'distant' past that is dominated by the gods;

---

[15] E.g. Clay (1989), Ford (1992) and (1997), Graziosi/Haubold (2005).
[16] Esp. Hes. *Theog.* 535ff.   [17] Hes. *Op.* 213ff.

and like his colleagues, the bards, he charts the gradual transformation of divine into human history in an attempt to understand the forces that underlie present-day reality. Moreover, Herodotus too sees this process as structured by recognizable stages, each with its own rules and textures. The two abductions of Damia and Auxesia, the first successful, the second unsuccessful, divide his narrative of Athenian–Aeginetan hostilities into three distinct sections.

EPIDAURUS: GODS

Herodotus starts with a crisis at Epidaurus: the earth does not yield sustenance, and the Epidaurians resort to the Delphic oracle for help.[18] They are told to consecrate statues to the goddesses Auxesia and Damia, which are made of olive wood. The Epidaurians acquire the necessary wood at Athens, in exchange for an annual gift to Athena Polias and Erechtheus. The narrative concludes on a positive note: the earth resumes her life-giving function, while the Epidaurians continue to send their annual tribute.

The setting of this opening section is left vague: Herodotus does not tell us when exactly the Epidaurians suffered their misfortune. There are, however, a number of aspects that point to the distant past, above all the tone of the narrative which at this early stage is very obviously influenced by epic. Herodotus answers the question of how it all started, that epic question *par excellence*, with reference to *Gē*, the cosmic mother in Hesiod and one of the first of the gods.[19] The pattern of divine causation is well known from the *Iliad* (e.g. τίς τ᾽ ἄρ σφωε θεῶν ἔριδι ξυνέηκε μάχεσθαι, 'Who was it among the gods that set them against one another in strife?', *Il.* 1.8); but is here taken to new lengths. Or rather, Herodotus hints that his narrative could have been much longer, that it could or perhaps even should be traced back to the beginning of the universe itself, though he does in fact quickly move on.

Reference to *Gē* anchors Herodotus' *archaeology* of Aeginetan–Athenian relations in a theogonic context. Yet, the most obvious intertext of our passage is not the *Theogony* itself but the *Homeric Hymn to Demeter*, where a failure of crops is resolved by new honours (τιμαί) for Demeter.[20] Unlike the epic narrator, Herodotus offers no explanation of the divine wrath that opens his narrative. To that extent his focus is from the start on the human sphere. However, it is also clear that human activity in the Epidaurian

---

[18] Hdt. 5.82.1. [19] Hes. *Theog.* 117.
[20] Cf. *HHCer.* 305–13 and 460–80. In the hymn with its Olympic perspective the decisive change is wrought not by human cult but by the intervention of Zeus.

chapter merely responds to the will of the gods. As in a *Homeric Hymn*, any change in human culture is seen as a function of divine history.[21]

Divine agency is in fact crucial throughout the section. The earth, or rather Earth, sets things in motion by refusing to yield crops. Delphic Apollo gives the necessary advice. Athena and Erechtheus concede the building materials for the statues, a service for which they are paid with annual sacrifices. Finally, Earth resumes the production of crops, signalling the end of her wrath and with it of the opening narrative. In all this, interaction between gods and men is transparent and communication largely unproblematic. Although the anger of *Gē* is never explained, help is readily available. We note that the Delphic oracle produces not a riddle but a straightforward piece of information (contrast its response to the Theban envoys). When the Epidaurians ask whether to use bronze or stone for the statues they might at first appear to be asking the wrong question. Elsewhere, Herodotean characters make similar assumptions very much at their own risk.[22] In our story, the oracle remains unprovoked: olive wood is what is needed, and the Epidaurians are told as much.

Divine will, and divine communications, largely determine the course of events in Epidaurus. However, there are signs of possible complications. From the interaction between gods and men there results interaction between human societies, specifically Epidaurus and Athens. Two alternative explanations are offered for why the Epidaurians turn to the Athenians for help. The first, which is the one apparently endorsed by Herodotus, emphasizes the sacred nature of the Athenian olive tree. Herodotus further confirms that what is at stake at the beginning of the Aeginetan digression is divine history, the more divine the better. Yet, he also introduces an element of human interpretation and human decision-making, one of the very few in this opening section. The Epidaurians *thought* (νομίζοντες) that the Athenian trees were the most sacred (5.82.2). That is not a controversial view, but it does reflect a process of deliberation that is lacking from Herodotus' second explanation: an unspecified group of informants ('it is also said') suggest that olive trees have not yet spread beyond Attica at the time of our story (5.82.2–3). In some ways this is quite similar to the first explanation. The time when olive trees are only found in Attica brings us back to the moment when Athena became the patron deity of Athens and gave the olive as a gift to the city. That too makes the Athenian olive particularly sacred. Yet, once we have realized the

---

[21] For a discussion of human history as described in the *Homeric Hymns* see Haubold (2001).

[22] Cf. Harrison (2000) 154–6: Dorieus fails to obtain crucial information about his colony at Eryx (i.e. that he was going to die in the process) by failing to ask the right question.

similarities between the two accounts we can better appreciate the main difference between them: the second version minimizes the role of human beings. If olives only existed at Athens there was literally no choice. By contrast, Herodotus hints that human choice – and human agency – is what we ought to be thinking about even at this very early stage in the narrative.

At the end of the Epidaurian section we are left with a new cult which has its roots in a transparent narrative of divine wrath and resolution. So far, human agents have been of minor importance. The transaction between the Epidaurians and the Athenians remains largely a matter of how Damia and Auxesia negotiate their τιμαί vis-à-vis the established Olympian deity Athena. Still, Herodotus does introduce an element of human decision-making when he tells us that the olives of Athens were *thought* to be most sacred, and that this led to the arrangement between Epidaurus and Athens. Already at this point, we are prepared for a possible shift in focus, from gods to men.

AEGINA: MEN

Enter the Aeginetans. They arrive on the scene as part of the old order,[23] but are soon revealed as a force for change. If the first section of Herodotus' digression harks back to theogonic epic, Aegina's emancipation from Epidaurus is reminiscent of the transition to the Hesiodic Iron Age. The pointers are unmistakable: the Aeginetans abandon a system that has so far guaranteed a fair dispensation of justice, a mistake that corresponds closely to the preoccupations of Hesiod.[24] Moreover, they succumb to ἀγνωμοσύνη, not itself a Hesiodic term, but close to the language of instruction that we find in the *Works and Days*.[25] All this starts with the building of ships. Here too Herodotus is drawing on a Hesiodic intertext: in a fragment from the *Catalogue of Women* the Aeginetans are said to have invented the ship:

> ἣ δ' ὑποκυσαμένη τέκεν Αἰακὸν ἱππιοχάρμην . . .
> αὐτὰρ ἐπεί ῥ' ἥβης πολυηράτου ἵκετο μέτρον,
> μοῦνος ἐὼν ἤσχαλλε· πατὴρ δ' ἀνδρῶν τε θεῶν τε,
> ὅσσοι ἔσαν μύρμηκες ἐπηράτου ἔνδοθι νήσου,
> τοὺς ἄνδρας ποίησε βαθυζώνους τε γυναῖκας.
> οἳ δή τοι πρῶτοι ζεῦξαν νέας ἀμφιελίσσας,
> <πρῶτοι δ' ἱστί' ἔθεν νηὸς πτερὰ ποντοπόροιο>[26]

---

[23] Hdt. 5.83.1: τοῦτον δ' ἔτι τὸν χρόνον καὶ πρὸ τοῦ.   [24] E.g. Hes. *Op.* 220ff.

[25] The addressee of the *Works and Days* is repeatedly called νήπιος, 'foolish': *Op.* 286, 397, 633. The opposite is the man who speaks and knows (γινώσκω) justice: *Op.* 280–1. For further comments on ἀγνωμοσύνη see Munson, p. 151 and n. 27 above.

[26] Hes. fr. 205 (M–W).

> And she conceived and bore Aeacus, delighting in horses . . .
> Now when he came to full measure of desired youth
> He chafed at being alone. And the father of men and gods
> Made all the ants that were in the lovely isle
> Into men and wide-girdled women.
> These were the first who fitted with thwarts ships with curved sides,
> And the first who used sails, the wings of a seagoing ship.[27]

Seafaring can be ambivalent in epic. The passage quoted above appears to belong to the same strand in the tradition that evaluates ships positively and sees the Cyclopes, for example, as culturally backward because they do not sail the sea (*Od.* 9.125–30). However, ships can also take on a more sinister meaning. In the *Iliad*, shipbuilding is associated with Paris' fatal trip to Sparta.[28] And the inhabitants of the just city in the *Works and Days* do not sail the sea (Hes. *Op.* 236–7) because they do not have to: the earth bears crops for them (*Op.* 237).

Herodotus combines the Heroic Age account of how the Aeginetans invented the ship with an Iron Age view of seafaring. In so doing, he draws out an important implication of his two intertexts. The *Catalogue of Women* and the *Works and Days* between them provide a model for how historical agency can shift from the divine to the human plane. The settling of Aegina, as described in Hesiod, fr. 205 (M–W), is entirely the work of Zeus. However, once the ants have become human, they start acting of their own accord. In the Iron Age of the *Works and Days*, human beings determine the course of history to an even greater extent. They determine whether to be just or unjust, knowing or foolish, and fare accordingly. Just so, the Aeginetans in Herodotus have taken their fortunes into their own hands. We have here the beginning not simply of a new era in history but, more radically, a new *kind* of history.

The resulting shift in emphasis can be seen in the story of how the Aeginetans acquired the statues of Damia and Auxesia (5.83). Importantly, the theft of the statues is a mere by-product of their disagreement with the Epidaurians. Divine will no longer dictates the making of human culture. To be sure, the Aeginetans too set up a new cult. However, their worship does not focus on humanity's place in the divine order but rather affirms and enshrines their newly gained independence from it. I will discuss the details of the new cult in a moment. First, however, let us consider the

---

[27] Trans. H. Evelyn-White.
[28] *Il.*5.62–3. This anticipates Herodotus' verdict on the Athenian ships as the *archē kakōn* 5.97.3, on which see Index *s.v.*

fact that the Epidaurians had the *same* cult as the Aeginetans (αἰ αὐταὶ ἰροργίαι). Herodotus reports it almost like an afterthought, but it is in fact highly significant. The narrator's perspective on the worship of Damia and Auxesia has changed according to its historical context: what mattered in Epidaurus was the religious function of the statues. What matters in Aegina are the relevant social customs.

By contrast with the Epidaurian section, the cult of Damia and Auxesia is now described in great detail (5.83). We hear of women's choruses performing abusive songs in honour of the goddesses, and we are told of the addressee of those songs, the women of Aegina. The most important point remains implicit: the songs are not primarily addressed to the goddesses. Of course, their ostensible function is still to please or appease them (ἱλάσκεσθαι), yet, rather than improved interaction between gods and human beings the main feature of the cult – and the only one described in detail – is its social structure: ten male *chorēgoi* per goddess; female choruses who tease the local women, never a man. The worship of the Epidaurians has metamorphosed into a custom that is described in strikingly ethnographic terms.

Having lost their statues, the Epidaurians stop sending offerings.[29] The Athenians respond with anger. The word Herodotus uses here is μηνίω, a term that, since epic, refers to the divine wrath that is provoked by a lack of due honours.[30] The refusal of *Gē* to yield crops at the beginning of the Epidaurian section is properly a case of μῆνις, though Herodotus never explicitly designates it as such. How far we have come since the events of ch. 82 can be seen from the displacement of μῆνις to the human sphere. One might say that behind the μῆνις of the Athenians lurks that of Athena, who is being robbed of her offerings. This would indeed be a classic cause for divine anger. However, Herodotus never says that Athena was angry. The gods are no longer central to the narrative.

The Epidaurians live up to their role as just men. When the Athenian envoys arrive they explain the basis of their position: δίκη.[31] The Athenians next send to the Aeginetans, this time asking not for payment but for the statues themselves. The difference may seem slight but is in fact important:

---

[29] Hdt. 5.84.1.

[30] The noun μῆνις is only used of the gods and Achilles. The much rarer verb μηνίω is used of Achilles and Agamemnon. For a discussion of μῆνις in epic see Muellner (1996). Herodotus uses μῆνις and μηνίω of gods (7.197) and heroes (Talthybius: 7.134, 137; Minos: 7.169) and occasionally of humans, but apparently only when he refers to entire societies (Spartans: 7.229; Athenians: 5.84.2, 9.7β).

[31] Hdt. 5.84.1 (. . . ὡς οὐκ ἀδικοῖεν· . . . οὐ δίκαιον εἶναι ἀποφέρειν ἔτι).

by failing to enter into an agreement with the Aeginetans the Athenians do not recognize the new cult as functionally equivalent to that of
the Epidaurians (for good reasons, as we have seen). In fact, the Aeginetans
themselves do not pretend that their worship of Damia and Auxesia is equivalent to that of the Epidaurians. By denying that they have any business
with the Athenians they themselves effectively deny the rationale behind
the making of the statues and hence their original religious function. The
narrator of a *Homeric Hymn* would say that the bond of τιμαί between
Damia/Auxesia and Athena has been broken. The Aeginetans might say
that men, not gods, are what counts now.

THE ATHENIAN EXPEDITION: GODS OR MEN?

There follows a detailed and complex account of how the Athenians tried,
but in the end failed, to recover the statues of Damia and Auxesia. At this
point, the relatively uniform narrative of the opening sections splinters
into competing versions, and the typically Herodotean voice of the critical
enquirer comes to the fore. The basic parameters of the story are as follows:
the Athenians send an expeditionary force with the task of abducting Damia
and Auxesia.[32] The mission ends in a disastrous defeat, with only one
survivor making it back to Athens. One final detail is agreed by all sources:
the decisive battle is accompanied by thunder and an earthquake.[33] The
meaning of these occurrences is contentious, as are a number of other
details. The Athenians know of only one ship, a claim that the Aeginetans
contest with arguments from probability. Moreover, the Athenians assert
that their defeat was brought about by the gods (τὸ δαιμόνιον), whereas
the Aeginetans and Argives put it down to their own superiority. It has
been suggested that the different versions are due to the partisan views of
Herodotus' sources: the Athenians play down their debacle by minimizing
the size of the expedition and the involvement of the enemy. The victorious
Aeginetans and Argives, by contrast, emphasize the size of the invading force
and their own role in bringing it low.[34] This need not be wrong, but there
is more to be said.

What is at stake in the competing stories of the Athenian expedition is
not simply patriotic distortion but above all the question of how to interpret
historical change at all. The incident involving thunder and an earthquake
is crucial in this context, for it frames the events on Aegina not so much as a

---

[32] Hdt. 5.85.   [33] Hdt. 5.85.2, 86.4.   [34] E.g. Figueira (1985) 60.

problem of competing *accounts* but rather as one of competing *readings*. At this point it might be useful to recall what thunder and earthquakes signify in early Greece, and what they signify elsewhere in Herodotus. Archaic and classical Greeks had essentially two ways of reading 'natural phenomena': they could either be taken to point to a specific historical moment, or they could be seen as timeless occurrences which reflect the present order of the universe.[35] In other words, natural events like earthquakes and thunder challenge observers to decide what *kind* of events are unfolding in front of their eyes. Is the universe still evolving and does divine will find expression in unique occurrences? Or has the world taken its final shape? If the former, then phenomena such as thunder and earthquakes say something about the course of history. If the latter, they say something about the (timeless) structure of the universe.

In epic, there is a rule that determines which of these two interpretations applies:[36] before the end of the Heroic Age the world is largely shaped by divine intervention, and 'natural' occurrences tend to reflect specific divine agency. In other words, what appears to be thunder, or an earthquake, is also always a sign and symptom of the unfolding history of the cosmos. By contrast, the post-heroic world depicted in the *Works and Days* and the Homeric similes does not invite this kind of interpretation. Here, events in nature are primarily determined by rules which can be learned and applied generically. For example, weather in these texts is seasonal.[37] Earthquakes tend to happen in certain places.[38] More generally, the cosmos has settled into stable patterns which can be known and should be learned.

There are, then, two ways in which what we call 'nature' can be interpreted in epic, and, as a matter of fact, they correspond to different phases in history. Things are more complicated in Herodotus. Here, ominous occurrences in nature rarely speak for themselves. We may take as an example the earthquake which opened up the Tempe valley in Thessaly. Herodotus reports that the Thessalians attributed it to Poseidon and comments as follows:

---

[35] Thunder: e.g. *Il.* 13.795–800 (generic) vs. *Il.* 20.56 (unique); earthquake: e.g. *Il.* 2.780–5 (generic) vs. *Il.* 20.57–8 (unique). For *Il.* 2.780–5 as referring to earthquakes *cf.* West (1966) *ad* Hes. *Th.* 858; for the similes reflecting the outlook of the *Works and Days* see Edwards (1991) 36.

[36] Graziosi and Haubold (2005), ch. 3 outline the principle as well as discussing real and apparent exceptions.

[37] This is obvious in the *Works and Days*. Seasonal weather in the Homeric similes includes rain and snowfall; *e.g. Il.* 12.278–87 (ἤματι χειμερίῳ).

[38] *Il.* 2.783 (εἰν Ἀρίμοις).

αὐτοὶ μέν νυν Θεσσαλοί φασι Ποσειδέωνα ποιῆσαι τὸν αὐλῶνα δι᾽ οὗ ῥέει ὁ
Πηνειός, οἰκότα λέγοντες. ὅστις γὰρ νομίζει Ποσειδέωνα τὴν γῆν σείειν καὶ τὰ
διεστεῶτα ὑπὸ σεισμοῦ τοῦ θεοῦ τούτου ἔργα εἶναι, καὶ ἂν ἐκεῖνο ἰδὼν φαίη
Ποσειδέωνα ποιῆσαι.

According to native Thessalian tradition, the ravine through which the Peneius
flows was made by Poseidon. This is not implausible, because the sight of this ravine
would make anyone who thinks that Poseidon is responsible for earthquakes, and
therefore that rifts formed by earthquakes are caused by him, say that it was the
work of Poseidon.[39]

Herodotus refuses to be drawn on the question of who caused the earthquake and why. His reading allows both for a generic explanation and one
that sees history as a series of aetiological events which are supervised by
the gods. (We may speculate that this would have been the view taken by
his Thessalian informants.) Elsewhere too Herodotus suspends judgement
on the significance of natural occurrences, though he too does occasionally
interpret them as divine signs. In Book 6 of the *Histories* he describes the
earthquake that struck Delos after being attacked by the Persians:

μετὰ δὲ τοῦτον ἐνθεῦτεν ἐξαναχθέντα Δῆλος ἐκινήθη, ὡς ἔλεγον οἱ Δήλιοι, καὶ
πρῶτα καὶ ὕστατα μέχρι ἐμεῦ σεισθεῖσα. καὶ τοῦτο μέν κου τέρας ἀνθρώποισι
τῶν μελλόντων ἔσεσθαι κακῶν ἔφηνε ὁ θεός.

But after [Datis] had withdrawn his men from the area, Delos was shaken by an
earthquake, which, according to the Delians, had never happened before and has
never happened since, up to my day. This was an omen sent by the god, surely, to
warn people of the trouble that was to come.[40]

Herodotus goes on to explain why he thinks the earthquake on Delos had
to be an omen: Greece was about to suffer more than it had for twenty
generations before Darius. The symbolism of the event is both obvious and
powerful, yet even in this apparently unproblematic case Herodotus still
thinks it necessary to defend his interpretation.[41] More generally, there is
no strict separation between generic events and uniquely significant ones
in Herodotus' universe. For him, divine history does not stop with the
death of the heroes but spills over into the era of 'mortals as they are now'.
Thunder and earthquakes *can* still reflect unique acts of divine intervention,
though they need not always do so. Unlike the epic narrator, Herodotus thus
combines a wide range of histories and historical textures, from sustained
divine planning to the types of events that in epic characterize life among
'mortals as they are now'.

---

[39] Hdt. 7.129.4; trans. R. Waterfield.
[40] Hdt. 6.98.1; trans. R. Waterfield.   [41] Cf. Hdt. 6.98.3.

There are few places in the *Histories* where the tensions inherent in Herodotus' approach become more apparent than when he contrasts the Athenians' interpretation of what happened in Aegina with that of the Argives and Aeginetans: whereas the epic bard knows and tells us how to interpret natural events such as thunder at any given point in time, that certainty has been lost in our passage. Indeed, the Athenian expedition with its conflicting accounts shows all the symptoms of a crisis of interpretation. Is history still primarily controlled by divine will or has divine intervention given way to human agency? Depending on how we answer the question we will be reading two radically different kinds of history. The Athenians see their defeat entirely as a matter of divine intervention. In fact, they explicitly exclude any generic explanations. According to them, the expedition comes to grief because the participants go out of their minds,[42] in other words, their actions cannot be explained in terms of the rules that apply to normal human behaviour. Instead, divine signs render visible the hidden cause of the disaster. The texture and scope of history presupposed here resemble those of the Heroic Age of epic and, even more strikingly perhaps, the world of the *Homeric Hymns*. We may compare the *Homeric Hymn to Dionysus*, where divine intervention, as reflected in divine signs, drives an entire ship crew to madness (ἐκπληγέντες, 50) and eventually to death (52–3). As in Herodotus, there is only one survivor to spread the word.

There can be little doubt, then, about the model behind the Athenian account of their expedition. So, are we returning to a view of history as divine history? Perhaps not. By contrast with the Athenians, the Aeginetans and Argives fight and prevail in the Iron Age. They see the thunder and tremor as incidental to their own initiative (i.e. they simply happen 'at the same time', ἅμα). The Argive force that crosses over from Epidaurus is primarily responsible for the outcome of the episode, not the gods. The point is not that the Aeginetan account is more 'rational' than that of the Athenians. Herodotus in fact finds some of its details improbable. Nor is it enough to call it 'secular' *tout court*. Gods are involved in both cases. The difference is that Aeginetans and Argives subordinate divine agency to that of human beings.

What I have said last is most strikingly borne out by the effect the episode is said to have on the two statues of Auxesia and Damia. According to the Argives and Aeginetans, they fall to their knees as a result of the Athenians' efforts at dragging them off. Human action elicits a divine response. Herodotus doubts the veracity of this part of the story, but nevertheless

---

[42] Hdt. 5.85.2. The Greek word is ἀλλοφρονῆσαι.

reports it in some detail. Once again I emphasize that the Argives and Aeginetans do not exclude divine agency but rather *subordinate* it to human initiative. The distinction is a subtle one but is important for our understanding of the digression as a whole. In order to illustrate my point, let me cite Herodotus' words in full:

ἀποβάντας ἀπὸ τῶν νεῶν τρέπεσθαι πρὸς τὰ ἀγάλματα, οὐ δυναμένους δὲ ἀνασπάσαι ἐκ τῶν βάθρων αὐτὰ οὕτω δὴ περιβαλομένους σχοινία ἕλκειν, ἐς οὗ ἑλκόμενα τὰ ἀγάλματα ἀμφότερα τὠυτὸ ποιῆσαι, ἐμοὶ μὲν οὐ πιστὰ λέγοντες, ἄλλῳ δέ τεῳ· ἐς γούνατα γάρ σφι αὐτὰ πεσεῖν, καὶ τὸν ἀπὸ τούτου χρόνον διατελέειν οὕτως ἔχοντα. Ἀθηναίους μὲν δὴ ταῦτα ποιέειν.[43]

Their account is that the Athenians, disembarking from their ships, when they found that no resistance was offered, made for the statues, and failing to wrench them from their pedestals, tied ropes to them and began to haul. Then, they say – and some people will perhaps believe them, though I for my part do not – the two statues, as they were being dragged and hauled, fell down both upon their knees; in which attitude they still remain. Such, according to them, was the conduct of the Athenians.[44]

In effect, we have here another aetiological narrative: the statues of Auxesia and Damia remained on their knees ever since the Athenians tried to steal them.[45] The image of the two goddesses falling to their knees in front of their abductors is a suggestive one, and we could speculate about its significance in Aeginetan cult. Herodotus does not tell us. Instead, he emphasizes the force used by the Athenians, twice using the word for dragging (ἕλκειν). Moreover, the conjunction εἰς ὅ, 'until', while not establishing a strict causal link, suggests a close connection between the Athenians' physical exertion and the change of posture on the part of the goddesses. Somewhere behind this violent scene there lurks one of the most potent images of the postheroic world of humans: the image of Hesiod's goddess *Dikē* being dragged around by Iron Age man.[46]

ATHENS: WOMEN

My aim in the last section has been to tease out the contrast between an Athenian account that unfolds largely in terms of divine history and an Aeginetan/Argive version in which divine action is provoked by, and mediated through, human initiative. Within the logic of the Aeginetan digression that second version is doubtless the more 'modern' one. Yet, Herodotus finds it suspect in at least one crucial respect, and so for the time being the

---

[43] Hdt. 5.86.3–4.   [44] Trans. G. Rawlinson.   [45] Hdt. 5.86.3.   [46] Hes. *Op.* 220.

crisis of interpretation remains unresolved. It is finally resolved in the last
section of the narrative, which brings yet another shift in geographical focus
and with it an entirely new historical texture. After the Athenian expedition
has come to grief, a lone survivor brings home the news. According to the
Athenians, this man was lynched by the wives of his dead comrades.[47] The
way this is done recalls the female choruses at Aegina: the women form
a circle and, while stabbing their victim to death with pins, teasingly ask
where their men have gone.[48] Abuse there is in both cases. The difference
is of course that the Athenian women's κερτομίη is dead serious. And there
is another point which is of interest here: the Aeginetan choruses never
abused a man. The 'chorus' of Athenian women, by contrast, direct their
aggression specifically at a male victim. Not only are their actions modelled
on the Aeginetans' (and, by implication, the Epidaurians') cult of Damia
and Auxesia; they are cast as an *inversion* of that cult.

By this stage, if not before, it will have become obvious that gender
relations are central to our narrative. We have seen that the Aeginetan
digression as a whole is framed by the Thebans' demand to be given 'men',
and their implicit rejection of the founding sisters Thebe and Aegina.
Herodotus now adds a surprising new twist. From the contrast between
'men' and a heroic ancestry that goes back to two women, he develops a
new kind of history: that of women and their dress.

Much has been written about the role of women in the *Histories*.[49]
Rosselini and Said have looked at their portrayal in the world of Herodotean
ethnography.[50] In this context, women come to represent the propriety or
otherwise of a society's customs. Dewald has taken this argument one step
further, suggesting that women in Herodotus not only act as passive repre-
sentatives of *nomos* but are actively engaged in upholding and transmitting
it.[51] Our passage shows women not so much as the custodians of culture
but as driving forces behind cultural change. Women have long been part
of our narrative, but they have so far remained in the background. In ch. 83
we heard that the cult of Damia and Auxesia featured female choruses, each
led by ten male *chorēgoi*. The action of the Athenian women unleashes the
potential for female agency that has hitherto been dormant, in a way that
recalls the transition from the Epidaurian to the Aeginetan section of the
narrative. There it was human agency more generally that came to the fore
as the narrative unfolded.

---

[47] Hdt. 5.87.2–3.   [48] The episode is briefly discussed in Dewald (1981), Loraux (1985).
[49] For a recent overview see Blok (2002).
[50] Rosselini and Said (1978); cf. also Bichler and Rollinger (2001) 47–50.
[51] Dewald (1981), e.g. p. 99.

The entry of women into the narrative thus follows a pattern established in previous sections. What is new is that it provides a resolution to the interpretative impasse that characterized Herodotus' account of the Athenian expedition. Athenian and Aeginetan/Argive sources quarrelled over whether the debacle of the Athenian expedition was caused primarily by the gods or by men. In the end, the question becomes irrelevant because the 'deed' (ἔργον) of the women is δεινότερον than the misfortune the Athenians suffered in Aegina.[52] δεινότερον can mean 'more powerful', 'more important', as well as conveying a negative value judgement.[53] The word thus spells out what is implied in the dynamic of the sequence: female agency proves decisive. Just how decisive becomes clear once we remember that the term ἔργον is marked in Herodotus. ἔργα in crucial ways constitute Herodotean history.[54] To say that the women of Athens did 'a deed' which was more powerful, δεινόν, than all that went before is to shift historical agency programmatically from gods and/or men to women. Their 'deed' inaugurates a new era, aptly characterized by its protagonists' new clothes.

NEW CLOTHES

The Delphic oracle told the Thebans to seek support from those closest to them. The question of who might be meant soon turned out to be about the nature of history and the forces that drive historical change in the world of *Histories*, Book 5. The Aegina narrative was supposed to clarify matters but has in fact considerably complicated them: we started with divine history (Epidaurus), but soon moved on to the history of man (Aegina). We have now ended up with women, and with the story of their dress.

The new dress of the Athenian women, we are told, is Ionian.[55] It used to be Doric, in fact, 'closest' (παραπλησιωτάτη) to that of the Corinthians. Finally, the theme of 'closeness' re-emerges, but what are we to make of it? There are obvious complications. The fact of their dress alone does not make the Athenian women of Doric origin. Herodotus specifies that all Greek women used to wear the dress that 'we now call Doric' (τὴν νῦν Δωρίδα καλέομεν). Nor are their new clothes unproblematically Ionian.[56] Ionian dress in turn originates in Caria, which makes it seem strangely appropriate to the 'Pelasgian' Athenians.[57]

Things have become complicated in the last section of Herodotus' narrative. In place of a transparent relationship between gods and humans we

---

[52] Hdt. 5.87.3.   [53] LSJ *s.v.* I and II.
[54] See e.g. Asheri (1988b) XVIII–XIX on the opening lines of the *Histories*.
[55] Hdt. 5.87.3.   [56] Hdt. 5.88.1.   [57] Hdt. 1.56–8; 8.44.

are left with a bewildering array of cultural signifiers. Those signifiers are decidedly slippery. 'Doric' and 'Ionian' are of course precisely the kinds of terms that are invoked to form alliances at the time of the Ionian Revolt – Aristagoras will exploit the Ionian connection to win over the Athenians only ten chapters on.[58] However, there are aspects of these identities, and especially the Ionian identity of the Athenians as it emerges from the Aeginetan narrative, which raise unsettling questions: is being 'Ionian' no longer a matter of blood relationship, genealogy rooted in divine history, as it once was in epic?[59] More generally, cultural and political shifts of the most random kind appear to have replaced the certainties of divine history in the last section of the Aeginetan narrative. We now see events driven not by gods but by women – and angry, out-of-control women for that matter. These transgressive dancers and their new, semi-barbaric dress powerfully embody the kind of world with which Herodotus leaves us: a world where divine will has become all but invisible.

In some ways, then, we could not have moved further away from the Epidaurian section of the narrative. And yet, as so often, Herodotus has it both ways: the final shift from men to women, swords to pins, *is* still part of the history of the gods. Indeed, it is only as such that we can properly understand it. After so much debate in the previous section, there is striking agreement about the nature and significance of the events in Athens.[60] Aeginetans and Argives too start manipulating their women's pins,[61] and even their cult practice, as a residual marker of divine history, is affected: the women of Aegina start offering their pins to Damia and Auxesia, not because the goddesses demanded it but for the same reason for which they continue to wear longer pins than the standard Doric ones: κατ' ἔριν τὴν Ἀθηναίων, 'to spite the Athenians'. All this amounts to no less than another dramatic shift in the texture of reality and the nature of historical agency. After the Iron Age of men follows the age of women, of clothes, of cultural politics. And it is no coincidence that in the context of *Histories* 5, this new era also appears as the Age of Athens. We recall that shortly before our passage the Athenians have embarked on a process of cultural and political change that challenges all Greeks, including the Thebans, to rethink the shape of their world. It is this 'redrawing of the map' that eventually leads

---

[58] Hdt. 5.97.2; for a discussion of this passage see Pelling, pp. 179–83 and Munson, p. 155 above.

[59] In epic, the Ionians appear to have been the descendants of Ἴων/ Ἰάων; see West's restoration of Hes. *fr.* 10a.23 M–W. Herodotus complicates this view; cf. 7.94, 8.44 (Ion changed the name of a Pelasgian tribe to 'Ionians'). See also Introduction, p. 32, and Irwin, pp. 83–7 above.

[60] Figueira (1985) 57 suggests that we are dealing with a (biased) Aeginetan account. This may well be true, but the important point is that no one questions it.

[61] Hdt. 5.88.

the Athenians to support Aristagoras and precipitate the world war with
Persia. The Aeginetan digression with its seemingly tangential skirmishes
and squabbles provides crucial reflection on the nature of this process.
Not only does it add to our understanding of what it might mean for the
Athenians to support their fellow Ionians. It also helps us place, and thus
appreciate better, the *kind* of history that unfolds in *Histories* 5.

CONCLUSION

The Aeginetan digression gravitates from the question who is closest to the
Thebans – and the related one who detests the Athenians most – to the
real issue of *Histories* 5: who among the powers of mainland Greece feels
close enough to the Ionians to take on their cause? Herodotus here pre-
empts the outcome of Aristagoras' mission in a characteristically unsettling
way: the Athenians do, and for distinctly problematic reasons. Somewhat
unexpectedly, then, the Aeginetan digression throws light on the nature of
their choice in *Histories* 5.97.3; but it does much more besides.

Herodotus uses the seemingly tangential issue of how the Aeginetans
came to be hostile towards the Athenians to embark on an astonishing
narrative experiment. What is at stake in the Aeginetan digression is no
less than the shifting grammar of history itself. The two goddesses Auxesia
and Damia are crucial in this context. Their cult structures the narrative,
helping us to interpret shifts in the texture of reality not as absolute breaks
but as permutations of divine history.

With the help of the two goddesses, Herodotus sketches out a meta-
narrative of historical change that draws on, but also goes beyond, epic
accounts of the history of the universe. Like epic narrators, Herodotus
looks back to a time where history is transparently and (almost) exclusively
made by the gods. However, the end point of his narrative is not a history of
men (ἄνδρες) and their deeds (ἔργα), as known from Homer and Hesiod,
but one of women and cultural politics, an era where ritual practice turns
into murderous strife and even the most fundamental cultural signifiers
become unstable. The point of this experiment is not, I believe, to force
a unified historical framework onto recalcitrant matter. Rather, Herodotus
combines the epic bard's interest in the shifting textures of the past with
an equally powerful intuition that we are still in important ways in the
same story: thanks to Damia and Auxesia even the messy and ultimately
disastrous contingencies that determine the course of history in *Histories* 5
turn out to be part of the unfolding history of the gods.

CHAPTER 10

'Saving' Greece from the 'ignominy' of tyranny? The 'famous' and 'wonderful' speech of Socles (5.92)

John Moles[1]

Scholarly responses to this most challenging speech[2] fall into diverse categories:

1. Socles' speech is 'incredibly inapt to the occasion'.[3]
2. Herodotus is just using the occasion to tell stories.[4]
3. The speech is a mélange of opposing political traditions: Athenian democratic, Corinthian anti-tyrant, Cypselid anti-Bacchiad and Panhellenic, the latter propagated by Delphi.[5]
4. It exhibits the narrative leisureliness of inserted stories in Homer.[6]
5. It is one of the main statements of Herodotus the tyrant-hater, or – more sophisticatedly – one of the main items in Herodotus' tyrannical template/typology/model.[7]
6. As contextualized, it serves more to prompt reflections about contemporary and recent history than to explain the historical situation of 504.[8]
7. Its moralizing is unintelligent, because what really motivates states is self-interest, as largely applies to Sparta here, and the reinstatement of

---

[1] I am indebted to: respondents at Cambridge and at the Newcastle Classics Research Seminar (23 October 2002); Press readers; Liz Irwin for wonderful kindness; previous discussions (few read at the time of the oral versions); and other contributors. Translations are my own. Space imposes brevity and selectivity.

[2] Representative bibliography: How and Wells (1912) II.50–5; Strasburger (1955) 7–15, 18–19, 22; Andrewes (1956) 45–8; Immerwahr (1966) 194–5; Oost (1972); Hohti (1974); Raaflaub (1979) 239–41; (1987) 223–5; Stahl (1983); Lang (1984) 104–6; Salmon (1984) 186–7; 247–8; Gould (1989) 55–7; Sourvinou-Inwood (1991) 244–84; McGlew (1993) 61–72; Gray (1996); (1997); van der Veen (1996) 68–89; Weçowski (1996); Forsdyke (1999); (2002) 542–5; Johnson (2001); Moles (2002) 38–40; Dewald (2003) 30–2, 35–7; Fowler (2003) 310–13.

[3] How and Wells (1912) II.51, following Macan (1895) I.235.

[4] How and Wells (1912) II.51; Waters (1971) 13–14; Hart (1982) 50–2.

[5] Andrewes (1956) 45–8; Zörner (1971) 261ff.; Oost (1972); Salmon (1984) 186–7; Forsdyke (2002) 542–5.

[6] Gould (1989) 56–7 (though such stories are 'tighter' than traditionally supposed: Alden (2000)).

[7] How and Wells (1912) II.340; Stahl (1983); Hartog (1988) 322–39; Lateiner (1989) 172–9; McGlew (1993) 61–74, Gray (1996); (1997); Dewald (2003) 30–2. Cf. further n. 49 below.

[8] Strasburger (1955) 7–15, 18–19, 22; Raaflaub (1979) 239–41; (1987) 223–5; Lang (1984) 104–5; Stadter (1992) 781–2; Wecowski (1996); Gray (1996) 384–5; Moles (2002) 40.

tyranny at Athens on this occasion would ultimately have entailed less destruction than the toleration of Athenian democracy.[9]

8. Its emotive rhetoric aims to scare the audience into agreement.[10]

9. The apparent inappropriateness of some of the material is only apparent and the oblique storytelling approach matches a tricky diplomatic situation.[11]

Some of these views are diametrically opposed. Others differ only in degree. Some convict Herodotus of incompetence, others of literary opportunism. Some emphasize the oral Herodotus, others the written. Some see the speech as detached from its context, others as fully contextualized. Some are free-standing, others combinable.

My own approach is undergirt by three simple questions: first, how good (by any relevant criteria) is Socles' speech? second, should listeners/readers agree with it? Third, if they do, so what? My answers will incorporate elements of positions 5, 6 (deleting 'more') and 9, as well as new arguments.

The context is complicated.

The speech is the longest single speech in Herodotus. It comes at a crucial historical moment. Pressurized by Delphi (bribed by the Athenian Alcmaeonids), the Spartans liberated Athens from Peisistratid tyranny, even though the Peisistratids were their close friends, 'since they gave greater priority to the interests of the god than those of the men' (63.1–65.5). Worsted in 'dynastic struggle' with Isagoras, the Alcmaeonid Cleisthenes 'took the people into his party' and became dominant (so much, Herodotus implies, for 'Cleisthenic democracy'). Isagoras then appealed to the Spartan king Cleomenes. After the failure of his first intervention with a small band of men, Cleomenes collected a large army in order to punish the Athenian people and to establish Isagoras as tyrant, though he concealed these purposes. This second intervention also failed, partly because of Athenian resistance, partly because of the withdrawal of the other Spartan king and of the Spartan allies, led by the Corinthians, 'giving to themselves the reason that they were not acting justly' (75.1).

Herodotus famously comments (78): 'So the Athenians had grown. Equality of speech (*isēgoriē*)[12] shows not in one thing only but everywhere that it is a worthwhile possession, if the Athenians too were better in matters of war than none of those who lived around them, but when they were

---

[9] van der Veen (1996) 68–89. [10] Romm (1998) 122–3. [11] Johnson (2001) 1–20, 23–4.

[12] Sole occurrence in Herodotus; recent discussions of the political concept: (2004); Balot (2004); Carter (2004); McInerney (2004); translations such as 'equality before the law' (Penguin) and 'democracy' (Forsdyke (2002) 537) are category errors.

freed of tyrants became by far the first. These things show that when held down they deliberately behaved basely, as working for a master, but when they were freed each himself wished to work for himself.'

Interpretation is controversial: is the start of 78 about Athens alone or a generalization that includes Athens? The arguments for the latter reading, strong in themselves,[13] find decisive support in this sequence.[14] Herodotus' reasons for specifying 'equality of speech' as the defining attribute of non-tyrannical states will also become clear. And, since 'equality of speech' covers a wide range of states, the polar opposition between 'equality of speech' and tyranny is not politically simplistic.

Discovering that they had been duped by the Alcmaeonids and Delphi, the Spartans felt doubly aggrieved, having exiled their friends the Peisistratids without securing Athenian gratitude. They were disturbed, too, by prophecies of many misfortunes from the Athenians, and also 'they saw the Athenians growing and not at all ready to obey them, considering that if the Attic race were free it would become of equal weight to their own, but if held down by tyranny weak and ready to obey their rule' (91.1). Unappealing in its aim of subjugating Athens to Spartan rule, this political analysis is, nevertheless, substantially the same as Herodotus' own at 78,[15] almost as if the Spartans have 'read the text' (characteristically a sign of characters' insight).

So the Spartans decided to reinstate the Peisistratid Hippias with the help of their allies. This is the first instance in Herodotus of consultation by Sparta of her allies in the so-called Peloponnesian League and, indeed, the first such recorded consultation in any source. In contrast to the earlier cases, the Spartans are now acting as a united body and they do explain their purposes to their allies. Legendarily laconic (3.46), they make a fittingly brief speech.[16]

Although the majority of the allies were averse to the Spartan proposal, only Socles[17] the Corinthian spoke out against it (his sole appearance in Herodotus), directly addressing the Spartans. Listeners and readers recall that the Corinthians led the allied withdrawal from the assault on Athens

---

[13] Moles (2002) 39 and n. 39 (with bibliography).   [14] p. 255 below.

[15] Some regard such formulations as naive. I use 'Herodotus' of: the historical figure ('Herodotus had fought against tyranny'); the writer of the text ('Herodotus records that . . .'); 'the author's voice within the text', as, here, of direct and (in effect) first-person comment; the larger conclusions that the text seems (to me) to reach (e.g. 'Herodotus condemns the Athenian Empire'); and figures within the text that seem to assume Herodotus' authorial and moral author-ity (e.g. Solon). I am not talking of Herodotus' 'personal views'. Such distinctions are alike elementary, difficult to sustain and widely ignored (even by sophisticated critics).

[16] p. 250 below.   [17] Basic name clear, despite MSS variation (p. 264 below).

and their motive for doing so. Socles' contrastingly long speech argues that it is incredible that the Spartans of all people[18] should propose the restoration of tyranny, than which nothing among humans is more unjust or murderous, a claim illustrated by protracted stories about Corinth's experience of tyranny under Cypselus and Periander. The terms of the claim are followed through – at least to some extent – in the oracular representation of Cypselus as a 'raw-flesh-eating lion' and in the statements that Cypselus 'exiled many of the Corinthians and deprived many of their possessions and by far the most of their lives', that Periander 'at the beginning was milder than his father but when he had associated through messengers with Thrasybulus tyrant of Miletus he became much more *murderous* than Cypselus', and that the Spartans' restoration of Hippias would be 'contrary to justice'.

But, unlike Otanes' speech in the Constitutional Debate of Book 3, Socles' speech does not offer a formal analysis of tyranny: both in form and in content it has strong *muthos* qualities:[19] that is, it includes narrative material which extends far into the past; which has been preserved and disseminated orally; which involves much direct contact with the divine (in the form of oracles); which is constructed out of timeless paradigmatic patterns; and which has a marked 'storytelling' character,[20] and surely, indeed, some 'entertainment value'.[21] There are Homeric motifs at the beginning (the one person who breaks the silence of all)[22] and end (Socles' defiant concluding words, 'know that the Corinthians at least will not agree with you', echo Hera's formula to Zeus at assemblies of the gods when he is enforcing a course of action with which she disagrees: 'do it, but be assured that all we other gods will not approve');[23] the 'folksy' initial, topsy-turvy *adunata* (that is, impossibilist reversals of nature as both illustrations and consequences of allegedly impossible and unnatural human behaviour); the triadic structures of the internal narrative; the generally folkloristic character of the story of Cypselus' birth and survival,[24] sharpened by a more specifically tragic intermyth with the story of Oedipus,[25] by allusion

---

[18] Interpretation controversial: p. 252 below.

[19] Similarly, Herodotus' earlier extended treatment of Periander at 3.48, 50–3: Sourvinou-Inwood (1991) 244–84; Boedeker (2002) 112–14; *pace* Gray (1996): 368–70.

[20] The only other 'storytelling' speech in Herodotus is Leotychides' (6.86): Immerwahr (1966) 122; Johnson (2001).

[21] *Muthos* ~ 'entertainment': Thuc. 1.22.4, etc.

[22] *Il.* 3.95–6; 7.92–5, 398–9; 8.28–30; 9.29–31, 430–3, 693–6; 10.218–19, 313–18; 23.676; Gray (1996) 383; Herodotean parallel at 7.10–11 (Artabanus).

[23] *Iliad* 4.29, 8.8–9, 16.443; Socles imports a significant twist: see p. 249 below.

[24] Similar stories about Cyrus (1.107–30), Oedipus, Perseus, Paris, Romulus and Remus, Jesus, etc.; Aly (1969) 93–5; cf. also pp. 258–9 and n. 70 below.

[25] Vernant (1982a); Said (2002) 127.

to the lion-cub fable[26] and by Dionysiac elements;[27] and folktale elements in the Periander narrative about his quest to retrieve the lost object.[28]

After Socles' speech, Hippias invokes the same gods as Socles, but to contrary effect: the Corinthians above all would yearn for the Peisistratids, when the appointed days came for them to be harmed by the Athenians. Throughout this narrative, Herodotus notes the political exploitation of oracles.

> But the rest of the allies held themselves in silence for a time, but, when they heard Socles speaking freely, each individual among them broke voice and chose Socles' proposal, and bore witness to the Lacedaemonians not to do anything revolutionary concerning a Greek city. These matters were brought to an end in this way. (93.2–94.1)

Modern historians emphasize that this 'end' marked a defining moment in the relations between Sparta and her allies: Spartan power turned out to be limited by the need to secure allied consent. The Homeric 'know that the Corinthians at least will not agree with you' plays a key role here. Whereas in Homer the supreme god Zeus can do what he likes even when all the other gods oppose him, here the Spartans were supreme and even now could presumably reinstate Hippias if Corinth were the only state to oppose this policy, but cannot do so once all the allies oppose them. But there is an eloquent 'gap' in the narrative (the more striking because the Spartans are Socles' direct addressees):[29] although we understand that the Spartans abandoned their proposal, it is left unclear whether they themselves were ashamed, unmoved, or persuaded by Socles' speech. One effect of this 'gap' is to refocus attention on the question of the quality of the speech.[30] Although a majority of the allies always opposed the Spartan proposal to reinstate the Peisistratids, were *all* the allies (93.2 ~ 92.1) now right to applaud Socles? What weight should be given to Hippias' negative response? On one level, as the Peisistratid tyrant whose reinstatement is in question, he is severely compromised; on another, he cites disturbing oracles and he is an expert in oracles. Should the external readership,[31] then, take the same view as the preponderant internal audience?

---

[26] Cf. Aes. *Ag.* 712–36; McNellen (1997) 18.

[27] I think: cf. *Bacchiads* attempting to kill divine baby, lions, raw-flesh-eaters, ambiguous smile, change from gentleness to savagery; Corinthian tyranny and Dionysus: Hdt. 1.23; Pind. *Ol.* 13.18–19; How and Wells (1912) II.341; Salmon (1984) 201–1.

[28] Thompson (1958) 475 (*s.v.* Lost) intrigues; Aly (1969) 93–5.

[29] Fluffed by the Penguin translation's 'the Spartans abandoned their purpose'.

[30] For another see p. 266 below.

[31] The *Histories* are a reading text (Flory (1980); Johnson (1994); Naiden (1999); Moles (1999); Fowler (2001)) and thus primarily so to be interpreted, whatever their oral origins.

Readers are also responding to this sequence under the looming shadow of Persia, the sequence being one of an elaborate series of retrospectives explaining the state of Sparta and Athens when Aristagoras of Miletus came to Greece to seek support for the Ionian Revolt (49, 55, 97).

Plainly, interpretation has much to consider.

Socles *qua* historical or dramatic figure addresses the Spartans directly. The rest of the allies turn out to be indirect addressees – witness their reaction. There is a third audience: Hippias, not directly or indirectly addressed, though alluded to, but who then himself replies to Socles directly. (This deft choreography suggests Hippias' ambiguous *locus standi* in a debate between Sparta and her allies and his desperation when he sees Socles' impact.) Readers of Herodotus form a fourth audience, whose assessment of Socles' performance will be conditioned alike by their own judgements of the performance, by the reactions of the various internal audiences and by any other material factors in the context.[32]

The Spartans had said that they (the Spartans), deceived by fraudulent oracles, had not acted rightly in expelling the Peisistratids, who were their close friends and had undertaken to make Athens subservient, with the result that the ungrateful Athenian people, having become free, had perked up, hybristically expelled the Spartans and the Spartan king, and given a harsh lesson to their neighbours, which others too were likely to have to learn. Consequently, they proposed to repair their error with the help of their allies and reinstate Hippias with 'a common reasoning (*logos*) and a common expedition' (91.3).

The Spartans' tone was conciliatory (as befitting admission of error), since they wanted to win back their allies after the latters' abandonment of the assault on Athens. Their plea that they had not acted rightly is on one level manipulative, since the Corinthians, followed by the rest of the allies, had abandoned that assault precisely because they disapproved of Cleomenes' purpose of making Isagoras tyrant, and their account has other obviously tendentious elements. Nevertheless, five of their stated motives for their change of policy towards the Peisistratids – they had been deceived by false oracles; the Peisistratids were close friends; tyranny would keep Athens subordinate; the freed Athenians were ungrateful; and a free Athens would be ever more dangerous to other Greek states – reflect their real feelings. Several elements in their case (culminating in the plan

---

[32] 'Audience' is variously handled by Lang (1984) 104–6; Gray (1996) 382–4; Romm (1998) 122–3; Johnson (2001).

to 'give back what we took away') argue on a basis of justice. And two of those elements – tyranny would keep Athens subordinate, otherwise Athens would prove dangerous to her neighbours – are politically shrewd.

Socles is described as having spoken 'freely' (93.2). At least some of what he says should controvert the Spartan speech directly. It does. It is not the expulsion of the Peisistratids that was 'not right': their restoration would be an assault upon the whole natural order (92α.2), and the Spartans' summoning of Hippias was a 'great wonder', their subsequent speech 'an even greater wonder' (in the ironic sense of 'something wondrously bad', hence an illustration of the reversals of nature at the start of the speech). The Peisistratids should be seen not as 'friends' but as tyrants, and among humans there is nothing more unjust than tyranny, so that Hippias' restoration would necessarily be 'contrary to justice'. If the Spartans 'took away' things from the Peisistratids, tyrants 'take away' far more from their victims.[33] And whereas the Spartans speciously invoked 'commonness', Socles champions what he terms 'equal governments' (*isokratiai*) and (it seems) 'freedom', emphasizing that within the Peloponnesian League the 'Corinthians *at least* will not approve' of the Spartan proposal. 'Equalness' and 'freedom' should apply in all relevant contexts: internally within the Peloponnesian League, as demonstrated by Socles' very speech (both in the mere fact of its delivery and in the sort of case that it argues); internally within cities, as illustrated by the 'equal governments' of Athens and Corinth, both free of tyranny, and – apparently – of all the other allied states, and externally between cities.

Whereas earlier it is as if the Spartans have read Herodotus, here it is as if Socles has read the Spartans' thoughts, for his espousal of 'equalness' seems to answer Spartan dislike of the prospect of Athens' being of 'equal weight' to themselves (91.1). The Spartans cannot morally or logically impose tyrannies on others while strenuously avoiding tyranny at home. The 'lesson of history' is not the danger of Athenian aggression but the wickedness of tyranny, as illustrated by the stories about the Corinthian and Milesian tyrannies. Socles crowns these stories with a challenging ambiguity: 'such is your tyranny and such are its deeds' (92ζ.4). Here 'your' (Greek 'to you') can connote alternatively: 'let me tell you' (admonitory ethic dative), 'the tyranny you are talking about', and 'the tyranny you yourselves propose to exercise'. The Greek gods[34] are invoked against tyranny: Greece is the 'community' that matters. These direct ripostes to the Spartans' arguments are underpinned by numerous verbal contrasts.

---

[33] See n. 44 below.
[34] For the striking usage cf. 5.49.3 (Aristagoras); 9.90.2 (Hegesistratus); Harrison (2000) 215.

But there are other aspects to Socles' response to the Spartans. His application of the 'topsy-turvy' commonplace to the notion of the Spartans' overthrowing 'equal governments' and 'bringing back tyrannies into the cities' trades on the Spartans' reputation as *the* great opponents of tyranny[35] and thus simultaneously shames them (for making their present proposal) and appeals to their (allegedly) better nature (for them to abandon it). And since appeal to the natural order was often used to underwrite treaties,[36] Socles' use of the 'topsy-turvy' commonplace emphasizes the 'inequality' of Sparta's proposed treatment of her allies. From all these points of view, his extended demonstration of the evils of tyranny is not redundant but intensificatory. But his explanation for the Spartan proposal – that they themselves had never experienced tyranny – palliates its wickedness. He also appeals to Spartan self-interest. If they persist, the Spartans will lose that great reputation and they will also lose the 'commonness' that they seek within the Peloponnesian League. They may even – the genie once out of the bottle – one day suffer tyranny themselves. For tyrannies grow by association: witness the 'association'[37] of Thrasybulus and Periander.

Contrary to the scholarly consensus, therefore, Socles' address to the Spartans is not merely formal: he *is* trying to persuade them (he could not anticipate winning the debate through the allied response alone). Increasingly odd, then, that we are not told how they reacted.

What of the allies as indirect addressees?[38] Socles' championing of 'equal governments' and 'freedom' will naturally appeal. His Corinthian narrative will reinforce their pre-existent dislike of tyranny (already suggested by their withdrawal from the assault on Athens). Thrasybulus and Periander's 'pruning' of 'outstanding citizens' will have particular resonance for those states, like Corinth herself, whose 'equal governments' take the form of oligarchies. Socles' standing-up to Sparta will inspire the other allies to do likewise. More insidiously, Socles' twice-stated formulation of the Spartans' proposal in terms of a generalization (92α 'undoing equal governments you are preparing to bring back tyrannies into the cities'; 92η 'do not establish tyrannies in the cities') raises the possibility that the Spartans may sometime do to others what they now propose doing to Athens.[39] Socles here comes close to modern arguments that the Corinthians' 'real' concern

---

[35] Cf. 92α '*you*, Lacedaemonians'; Thuc. 1.18.1; *contra* Johnson (2001) 8–12, this is the first appropriate occasion for the Corinthians' expressing 'astonishment' at what can be rhetorically represented as dramatically reversing Spartan tradition (despite recent practice).

[36] How and Wells (1912) II.51; Hdt. 4.201.2–3; Dion. Hal. 6.95.

[37] Note the striking: '[Periander] associated with Thrasybulus *by messengers*'. Cf. also 8.142.5.

[38] Gray (1996) 382–5; Johnson (2001).   [39] So already Macan (1895) I.236.

was not with political morality but with power politics, but his position is more sophisticated than those analyses because it links power politics with morality. Although 'friendship' for the Peisistratids was one of the Spartans' motives for their proposal and although they sought the approval of their so-called 'allies' on the basis of 'commonness', 'friendship', 'alliances' and 'commonness' are unstable within tyrannies, because the tyrant by definition pursues his own interests only, as illustrated by Periander's request to Thrasybulus and the practical examples of Cypselus, spared as a baby through the Bacchiads' pity, mass murderer when he became tyrant; of Thrasybulus and Periander, systematic murderers of outstanding citizens; and of Periander, necrophiliac of his wife and stripper of all Corinthian women.[40]

Socles' 'stories' about Cypselus, Thrasybulus and Periander, therefore, function – among many other things – as 'figured speech' (a form of rhetoric which implies a meaning and which can use 'stories'):[41] warning of the dangerous generalizing potential in the Spartan proposal without making this embarrassingly – or even dangerously – explicit. The allies are tacitly invited to detect analogies between their situation and situations within Socles' narratives. Those narratives are consistently concerned with the interpretation of the riddling and the hidden (oracles and necromancy, punning names, the would-be assassins' deceptive visit to the baby Cypselus, Labda's concealment of Cypselus, the corn-chest hiding-place[42] and the would-be assassins' unsuccessful search for Cypselus, Thrasybulus' coded lopping of the corn, Periander's ultimately successful search for the lost object): can the allies interpret/'find' Socles' 'hidden meaning'? What value should *they* put on conflicting and (no doubt) politicized oracles?

The narratives also raise questions about the right balance between speaking, not-speaking, observation and action: the Bacchiads, warned by Delphi of Eëtion's son, were exhorted to 'observe these things well', but it was when the first man 'observed' the baby Cypselus' smile that he was overcome by pity, whereas Labda concealed Cypselus in the place that 'seemed to her least observable'.[43] The Bacchiads, rightly putting the two oracles together,

---

[40] From the point of view of readers, the Spartans' claim that the Athenian people were 'ungrateful' (hence 'friendship' with them could be dissolved) is matched by similar accusations against the people by the Sicilian tyrant Gelon (7.156.3).

[41] 'Figured speech': Ahl (1984); 'stories' in Demetrius 292; in Herodotus: Moles (1996) 270, 279; 'free' or 'frank' speech can include 'figured speech' (Moles (1996) 282 n. 43).

[42] κυψέλη, anciently (cf. Paus. 5.17.5) and mostly today taken as (swanky) 'chest', has also been understood as 'beehive' (Roux (1963); Nenci (1994) 293–4) and 'corn-chest' (Gray (1996) 379). Criteria are: (i) linguistic usage; (ii) 'unobservability'; (iii) ready accessibility to the lame Labda; (iv) safety for a baby. The last is best (cf. also p. 261).

[43] 'Observe' glosses Greek φράζομαι.

'held this matter in silence', but it was the would-be assassins talking at the doors that warned Labda, and then their falsely telling their masters that they had fulfilled their instructions which allowed Cypselus' growth to manhood and tyranny. Conversely, the allies' 'keeping silence' now would connive in the potential growth of Spartan tyranny.

The Corinthian tyrants also 'take things away'.[44] Cypselus takes away from many their fatherland, from many their money and from by far the most their lives. Periander takes away the fatherlands and lives of all those left untouched by Cypselus and having taken everything away from the males, turns his attention to all the women, free and slave alike, from whom in a single day he publicly takes away their clothes, hence also the whole state's last vestiges of shame and self-respect. Will the allies similarly allow the Spartans to strip them of their dignity? For, as everyone knows, 'at the same time as taking off her underclothing a woman also takes off her shame' (1.8). This is the paradigm of Candaules' wife to the nth degree. And by this act the free women are reduced to the same status as slaves. This 'stripping' shows the capricious and grotesque lengths to which tyrants may go to oblige their guest-friends – just as the Spartans are now trying to do for Hippias. Socles intensifies the challenge to the allies' self-respect with the words, know that the Corinthians *at least* will not agree with you.' Note Socles' multi-purpose deployment of 'shame' as a moral and rhetorical weapon against both Spartans and allies: the former to be shamed out of an unjust proposal, the latter to be shamed into opposition to that proposal by the thought of the extreme shame to which tyranny would expose them.[45]

So far, then, Socles' speech seems excellently suited to its complex context, combining direct address to the Spartans with indirect address to the allies, controverting the Spartans' case systematically, mixing in appeals both to their better nature and to their self-interest, establishing the indivisibility of moral and utilitarian considerations and of internal and external tyranny, conveying, while disguising, the most immediately dangerous threat, and tacitly exhorting the other allies to resist the nascent Spartan tyranny.

Several other factors seem to confirm the speech's excellence.

If the speech is to be judged by its results, it is a triumph. Before it, a majority of the allies are opposed to the Spartan proposal (92), but all but Socles keep silence. Socles is the one man brave enough to articulate the silent disapproval of the allies at large. But after the speech, he has

---

[44] This translation glosses a series of verbal relationships centring on the prefix ἀπο-.

[45] *Pace* Hart (1982) 52 and Waters (1971) 14, the end of Socles' narrative could not be less bathetic.

persuaded *all* the allies and not only that: every single one of them now breaks voice[46] in his support: he has literally given them all a voice (with which, indeed, they echo his own climactic phrases). From his 'figured' speech', they have detected the necessity of their speaking out. It is the Spartans who are silent now (if enigmatically so). Doubtless, we should here sense another narrative pattern potent both in myth (e.g. Croesus' son (1.85.4)) and in tragedy (the notorious 'silent figures' of Aeschylus): the climactic and validating speech of the hitherto conspicuously silent.

The speech also embodies some of the wider political values of the narrative. Book 5 is centrally concerned with the struggle between freedom and despotism. Socles supports freedom and speaks 'freely'. Socles' speech and the allies' reaction seem to exemplify Herodotus' own political analysis at 78 and in exact detail. Socles champions 'equal governments' in general against tyranny. Herodotus praises the universal value of 'equality speech'. In speaking freely Socles instantiates that 'equality of speech'. When the rest of the allies break voice in Socles' support, they also instantiate that 'equality of speech'. It is now clear why Herodotus used *that* term in 78. And 'each individual among them' does so, just as when Athens was freed from tyranny 'each himself wished to work for himself' and the result was an increase in corporate growth. Similarly, with the removal of the threat of Spartan 'tyranny', the allies are individually energized to produce the best genuinely 'common' policy, a policy which preserves alike the interests of the individual allied states, of the allies en bloc, of the whole Peloponnesian League, including Sparta, of Athens (spared the reintroduction of tyranny) – in short, of all Greece.

This apparent parallel between Socles' views and Herodotus' can be pursued. This episode seems to have a certain 'meta'-quality: to invite reflections about the status and purpose of the *Histories* itself. There is a speaker and an internal audience or audiences. Socles is a sort of historian of Corinthian history à la Herodotus, even supplying material about Corinth which Herodotus *in propria persona* does not. Socles' observation 'but had you such experience of that thing [tyranny] as we have, you would be *sager* advisers concerning it than you are now' is rightly taken by many scholars as a key statement of the *Histories*' main practical function.[47] And, when Socles makes it, he is assuming the role of 'the adviser', a role sometimes

---

[46] The striking φωνὴν ῥήξας, otherwise only at 1.85.4 – of Croesus' hitherto silent son – and 2.2.3 – of the children isolated by Psammetichus in order to discover the oldest language (Johnson (2001) 7), creates further emphasis.

[47] E.g. Strasburger (1955) 7–14; Raaflaub (1987) 232; Stadter (1992) 782; cf. Thuc. 1.22.4 with Moles (2001) 214–18.

taken by figures within the narrative that are in some sense analogous to Herodotus himself.[48]

Socles' representation of tyranny corresponds in many respects to Herodotus' own typology:[49] the pervasive imagery of unnaturalism, animalism and sexual excess (the topsy-turvydom, eagles, lions, the lame Labda, Periander's necrophilia and stripping of all Corinthian women); tyrants' preternatural skill at reading signs;[50] familial disfunctionalism; illegitimacy both political and quasi-literal; killings and exiles; waste of substance in order to maintain power (Thrasybulus' destruction of the corn; Periander's misuse of his seed; the burning of the Corinthian women's clothes); bad counsel; subjects' loss of initiative and self-respect and virtual enslavement; the problem of succession. Many of these themes also interact, in, as it were, seesaw fashion, with Herodotus' own treatment of Periander in 3.48–53. Periander's interpretation and implementation of Thrasybulus' advice in 5.92, where he kills the prominent citizens, corresponds to 3.48, where he aims to castrate 300 Corcyrean noble youths (even if he does not in fact succeed).[51] 5.92 gives a further layer of explanation to the enmity between Periander and his son, Lycophron, as being also the product of a family curse.[52] Equally, the narrative of 3.48–53 fills out the final impression of sexual nullity left by 5.92. Socles' insistence on the need to resist tyranny also fits Herodotus' belief that tyranny results partly from the passivity of the tyrannised.[53] In short, Socles' superficially loose *muthoi* embody an analysis of tyranny and an analysis which, while undoubtedly emotive, is also detailed, sophisticated, and (apparently) consonant with Herodotus' own.

There are other important echoes of wider Herodotean concepts. The whole narrative of the Corinthian tyranny enacts the Herodotean movements of small things becoming great and vice versa: as an individual Cypselus starts as a baby and then becomes great; as an institution, the Cypselid tyranny moves from smallness to greatness, to – proleptically – annihilation (and within this 'imagery', the child/son *Periander* is 'always already' an 'outsize man').[54]

---

[48] Pre-eminently Solon (1.30–32), with Moles (1996) 263–5.
[49] References in n. 7 above. 'Typology' is a controversial term. Of the scholars cited in n. 7, Hartog and Lateiner come closest to straightforward acceptance of the notion, whereas Gray (1996) stresses adaptation of models to different contexts and Dewald (2003) 47 and 49 claims 'a profound bifurcation' and 'doubleness' between model and practice, at least as regards the Greek tyrants. Nevertheless, all attribute to Herodotus far more 'modelling' than Waters (1971).
[50] Steiner (1994) 128; Gray (1996) 380–1.
[51] This was the subject of Alan Griffiths' paper at the Colloquium.   [52] Said (2002) 127.
[53] 1.59–60; 62.2; 63.1; 96.2–98.3; 3.80.3; 6.11.2; 7.155.2, etc.   [54] van der Veen (1996) 86–9.

So far, then, the case for Socles's speech seems overwhelmingly positive. Are there any negatives?[55]

What, first, of Socles' representation of Periander's tyranny? Historically, of course, it is a travesty.[56] Its *broad* outlines, nevertheless, have to be accepted, partly because, as we have seen, they have so many resonances with Herodotus' own thinking, partly because they form an important element of a case which seems on so many levels to be rightly persuasive. But how does this representation square with the allusion, in the immediately subsequent narrative, to Periander as arbitrator between Mytilene and Athens (95)?

What, too, of Socles' treatment of Cypselus? Socles had claimed that tyranny was supremely *unjust* and described Bacchiad rule as an 'oligarchy', hence, presumably, from a Corinthian point of view in 504 (or the 420s), an '*equal* form of government' (similarly, the oracle given to the Bacchiads addresses 'Corinthians' generically).[57] But Delphi told Eëtion that his son would 'bring justice to Corinth', and justice falling not on 'oligarchs' but on 'monarchical men'. It is true that Socles takes this oracle's meaning to be the same as the earlier one given to the Bacchiads (prophesying the birth of a 'mighty, flesh-eating lion'), that is, that Eëtion's son would overthrow the Bacchiads, but the perspectives both on the Bacchiads and on Cypselus are radically different.[58] Further, the oracle given to Cypselus himself addresses him as 'king'. Clearly, these different oracles reflect anti- and pro-Cypselus and anti- and pro-Bacchiad traditions, as well as the general tendency of oracles to tailor their emphases to individual consulters.[59] It is no doubt also historically true that 'pro-tyrant' oracles provided an apologetic fig-leaf for those who failed to resist tyranny ('the tyrants had the gods

---

[55] For organizational simplicity, I defer consideration of what to many is the greatest negative – the contemporary perspective – until pp. 261–3.

[56] Itself explicable in terms (a) of how folk memory tended to demonize the tyrants over time (Liz Irwin at the colloquium) and (b) of Herodotus' own parallelism between Greek tyrants and eastern potentates.

[57] Notoriously (despite Megabyzus' advocacy at 3.81), Herodotus has little interest in oligarchy *per se* (Giraudeau (1984) 107; Lateiner (1989) 169 n. 18; Dewald (2003) 29–30), whether because as the commonest form of Greek government in his own day it required least explication or because within the historical period of his narrative it created relatively little political disruption.

[58] Cf. McGlew (1993) 63–74. Gray (1996) 374–5 argues that δικαιώσει means (only) 'punish' or 'pass judgement on Corinth without the usual connotations of justice'. But the usage cannot be divorced from the initial 'more unjust' or the concluding 'contrary to justice' and the context implies that the activity involves combating *monarchical* rule, itself, in context, implicitly unjust. Note Gray (1996) 375, conceding '[Cypselus] may have been right to attack the [Bacchiads]'. It is true that this is 'rough justice' (ὀλοοίτροχον . . . πέτρηισι evokes *Il.* 13.137 ὡς ἀπὸ πέτρης: Vernant (1982a) 36 n. 23; Gray (1996) 373), but a *form* of justice it remains. It is also true – and important – that 'chastise' is *another* level of meaning (p. 262 below).

[59] Weçowski (1996) 220–8.

on their side'),[60] and this has been argued to play a role in the present narrative.[61]

But these factors do not in context render the different perspectives less jarring.[62] The narrative also brings out the fact that Cypselus and the Bacchiads were ambiguously related, so that, while on one level he is the typical tyrannical usurper, on another level, he is, quite literally, 'one of the family'.[63] At the least, then, Herodotus (so to speak, as opposed to Socles) is conveying that one man's tyrant can be another man's king and one man's oligarchy another man's monarchy, and reminding us that even tyrants can play a positive role in the imposition of law over previous disorder[64] – even, perhaps, in the development, within ultimately 'equal governments', of 'equality of law'.[65] Arrestingly also, the oracle given to Cypselus ('blessed this man who comes down into my house . . .') and the concluding statement that he 'wove his life successfully to the end' exemplify the Solonian/Herodotean principle 'call no man happy/blessed until he is dead' (1.30–2).[66]

The episode of the baby Cypselus requires particular consideration. He is in the first instance saved by the 'divine chance' of his smiling at the first of his would-be assassins and by the resultant 'pity' of that man and then of all the others as he is passed from hand to hand, and when his mother overhears their conversation as they renew their determination to kill him it is because 'it had to be that evils should spring up from Eëtion's issue'. Is the pity virtuous? On one level, yes, because it contrasts with Cypselus *qua* raw-flesh-eating lion and subsequent mass murderer.[67] On another level, no, because – as often in Greek ethics – it is a source of weakness which prevents the proper 'observation' of the task in hand – an error for which the would-be assassins themselves soon upbraid one another. Nor is it clear whether Socles takes the 'divine chance' in a strong religious sense or 'it had to be' as denoting active divine will.[68] But the reader must consider these at least to be possibilities, especially in conjunction with the oracles given to Eëtion and Cypselus, with the general 'divine child' overtones of this episode[69] and with the arresting detail of the smile (which, since

---

[60] Lavelle (1991) 324.   [61] Wrongly, as I believe.

[62] *Pace* the scholars cited in n. 5.

[63] Sourvinou-Inwood (1991) 266 ('Kypselos is, through his birth, both central and marginal'), 282–3 n. 122; also Murray (1993) 148–9.

[64] Cf. 1.96–100 (Deioces).   [65] Cf. Peisistratus at 1.59.

[66] van der Veen (1996) 75–6; note the contrast with the equally leonine tyrant Hipparchus (5.56).

[67] Cf. Gray (1996) 376.

[68] Discussion of these difficult glosses: Hohti (1975); Gould (1989) 68–78; Munson (2001a) 34 n. 23; (2001b) 42 n. 64; Mikalson (2002) 192–3; (2003) 148–9; Harrison (2003) 231–3.

[69] Immerwahr (1966) 194–5; Johnson (2001) 13; p. 248 above.

newborn babies do not smile, marks the divine child).[70] Does that smile also denote recognition of kinship?[71] But, simultaneously, the smile, while 'divine' and hardly consciously willed by Cypselus *qua* baby, is also deceptive, because it successfully diverts attention from Cypselus *qua* raw-flesh-eating lion, just as the lion-cub in Aeschylus' *Agamemon* beguiles by its soft glance.[72]

There is another complexity. While the Cypselus-baby narrative has its place in a clear chronological sequence, it is also proleptic of the behaviour of the adult tyrant, who characteristically wins power by deception,[73] at the beginning of his rule smiles on all and sundry,[74] and secures his position by dividing the opposition. Within this perspective, the 'divine chance' of Cypselus' smile suggests the capricious 'smile of Fortune', which moves from person to person.[75] Only united action can dislodge such a tyrant (as proleptically conveyed by the would-be assassins' second plan – that 'all should have a share in the murder'). Tyranny also can seem dangerously 'attractive'.[76] This doubleness of temporal perspective in the *muthoi* is also reflected in the notion of the child/son Periander as 'always already' an 'outsize man'.

There are also elements in the wider narrative that give pause. How can 'equality of speech' be the wonderful thing that Socles, the allies, the Athenians and, apparently, Herodotus himself think it is, when the narrative attests its failures as well as its successes? One of the putative tyrants of this very sequence is *Isagoras* (= 'equal/just speaker'). *Aristagoras* (= 'best speaker') is doing well in his efforts to persuade Cleomenes but then makes a crucial error (50.2), and when he resorts to bribery he is seen off by Cleomenes' little girl (51.2). With the Athenian assembly, however, he succeeds, 'for it seems to be much easier to string along[77] many than one, if he was unable to string along Cleomenes the Spartan alone but did do this to thirty thousand Athenians' (97.2). And Athenian 'equality of speech' led eventually to the Athenian Empire, as the context surrounding Socles' speech reminds us. Again, if 'the Greek gods' and 'Greece' generically oppose tyranny, how could Hippias invoke the very same gods as Socles, why did Delphi sometimes favour tyrants such as Cypselus and, later, the Persians, how can the

---

[70] Immerwahr (1966) 195; Johnson (2001) 13; Virg. *Ecl.* 4.60–3, with Coleman (1977) 149; Lateiner (1977) 176 n. 9 is wrong to describe Cypselus' smile as 'innocent': see p. 267 below.

[71] As in Cat. 61.212–13; Virg. *Ecl.* 4.60–3.   [72] McNellen (1997) 18; Johnson (2001) 13–14.

[73] Cf. 1.59 (Peisistratus); 1.96–8 (Deioces).   [74] Johnson (2001) 14 well cites Plat. *Rep.* 8.566d5–e1.

[75] E.g. Ov. *Tr.* 1.5.27; Apul. *Met.* 10.16.

[76] As Herodotus sardonically conveys at 1.29 ('there arrived in Sardis [~ Athens] all the great *sophistai* from Greece who were alive during that time': Moles (1996) 262.

[77] Cf. Chris Pelling, pp. 179–87 above.

Spartans propose to reinstate Hippias and why did so many Greek states either medize or wobble in their opposition to medism?

Is Socles' case therefore 'sapped', 'undercut', 'deconstructed' or 'problematized'? Do these circumstances illustrate 'a profound bifurcation' and 'doubleness' in Herodotus' narrative of tyranny?[78] Irrespective of the general validity of such interpretations of ancient literature, in this case at any rate I think they are wrong, both intellectually and morally (!) – as Socles' own speech teaches us.

In the first place, there is 'the principle of proportional meaning'. A simple illustration: with one or two exceptions, Mahler's nine symphonies drip with angst. There is *some* angst in Haydn's 104 symphonies. But a critical discourse that says that the proportion is the same in both composers perpetrates a gross mathematical error. The number and the seriousness of the factors in favour of Socles' speech heavily outweigh the negatives.

Second, in so far as Socles' speech and its interaction with the surrounding narrative make general claims about the efficacy of 'equality of speech' and 'equal governments', these claims are not undermined when from time to time the practice goes wrong.

Third, in so far as Socles' speech and its interaction with the surrounding narrative champion ideals, these ideals are not undermined when people (or even gods) fail to live up to them. On the contrary, the ideals provide the fundamental touchstone for the evaluation of the failures and themselves remain unchallenged.[79]

It is of course the job of a serious historian to highlight and analyse the failures both of competence and of morality. But because of the principle of proportional meaning the overall emphasis is not: 'there are these general principles but they are continually undermined in practice'; but rather: 'despite the shortcomings in practice, the general principles are the things to aim at.'

Fourth, while Socles' speech and its interaction with the surrounding narrative make factual and moral claims, these claims themselves acknowledge the difficulties of their implementation. Socles' own analysis does not duck hard issues. It emphasizes tyranny's sheer power.[80] It concedes that tyrants can be 'successful' (both Cypselus and Periander are 'blessed'; Cypselus 'brought the thread of his life to an end well'), even attractive (the baby Cypselus), and that tyranny can introduce a sort of justice, even play a part in the long-term development of justice. But the initial attractions of

---

[78] Dewald (2003) 47, 49.   [79] *Pace* the attractive Pelling (1997).
[80] Eëtion is son of 'Have/Get Power'; Cypselus is the 'powerful' lion; finally, Cypselus 'got power over' Corinth.

tyranny will always in the end prove deceptive,[81] hence the mythic power of the lion-cub fable and the systematic demonstration of the progressive moral deterioration of the Cypselid tyranny, culminating in the 'stripping' of the Corinthian women. Any serious analysis of tyranny has to confront its apparent advantages before arguing their ultimate falsity. The Cypselus narrative is not an inconsistency within the overall analysis but a proof of that analysis's intellectual cogency.

Socles' analysis also acknowledges the role of the contingent: the 'accidental factor' which throws things out of what seems to be their natural course, here the 'smile' of the 'divine baby'. Many critics – with an almost indecent lack of discrimination – have leaped upon this apparent manifestation of Herodotus the determinist or pessimist.[82] Even if this is a correct interpretation, it still subserves Socles' general position (as one of those things whose very difficulty reinforces the need to uphold the general principle as far as possible). But I do not think it is correct: the would-be assassins' pity constitutes a failure of 'observation', as they crucially 'misread' the smile; when they reconsider the situation, they speak unwisely in allowing themselves to be overheard; they fail to 'observe' Cypselus' hiding-place; and finally, they tell their masters that they have killed Cypselus, who unsurprisingly then grows up to manhood and tyranny. The narrative acknowledges *difficulty*, not impossibility.

Similarly, while Socles' own performance instantiates 'equality of speech' and 'equality of government', the desired result has to be achieved with effort.

There remains a factor which, on some interpretations, considerably undermines or ironizes Socles' speech. Socles' speech moves beyond the particular to generalizations about tyranny and about its ever-present threat, alike within states, within alliances and imposed on states by other states. The speech is framed by: an allusion to prophecies of many evils the Spartans would suffer from the Athenians (90.2); the Spartans' fear of Athenian growth (91.1); their claim that others besides Athens' neighbours are likely to suffer from Athenian arrogance and power (91.2); and the allusion of Hippias, oracle expert, to prophecies of future Athenian harassment of Corinthians (93.1). Although all these items make sense in the immediate context, emphasizing motivation and political exploitation of oracles,[83] they also coincide with later developments known to Herodotus' contemporaries, and Herodotus did not have to record these items or so arrange

---

[81] Similarly, 1.96–100 (Deioces); 3.80 (Otanes' analysis).
[82] E.g. Dewald (2003) 44, 47; Harrison (2003) 249.
[83] Johnson (2001) 16–17 (resisting any contemporary implication).

them. The sequence thus creates implicit contemporary/recent-past allusions and 'Athens the tyrant city' comes within the interpretative frame.[84]

Socles' own speech intensifies this perspective. Given the framing forward allusions, the speech's evocation of the Herodotean/Solonian principles of 'looking to the end of every thing' and of 'small things becoming great' raises the question: where does the nascent growth (5.66.1, 5.78.1) of Athens fit here? Indeed, from a listener/reader point of view, Cypselus, besides being the historical Cypselus or any tyrant, also actually *represents* tyrannical Athens, currently fluffy lion-cub but destined to mutate into the 'chastiser' of the Corinthians under the 'leonine' Pericles.[85] Herodotus trails this equivalence at 91.2: Athens 'perked up' = Greek ἀνέκυψε: a witty proleptic pun on Κύψελος.[86]

What are the consequences? Certainly, Herodotus signals historical ironies. At *this* meeting of the Peloponnesian League Corinth saved the newly democratic Athens from tyranny; within about 30 years, that 'internal' democracy will be exercising 'external' tyranny; later still, it will inflict 'chastisement' on Corinth; and only recently, at another meeting of the Peloponnesian League, Corinth took the lead in demanding action against Athens the tyrant city. Doubtless, these ironies, combined with the speech's Herodotean/Solonian principles, have *some* causative implication and, *qua* ironies, perhaps suggest *some* limitation in human foresight. Is there more?

It is at this point that one must consider van der Veen's reading, which may be summarized as follows. Socles and the allies had enough information – from Spartan forebodings, based both on their own perception and on oracles, from Athenian behaviour already, and from the oracular interpretations of Hippias – to foresee that the long-term consequences of the preservation, on this occasion, of Athenian democracy, would be worse than those of the restoration of the Peisistratids.[87] Herodotus is here dramatizing one of the great 'might-have-beens' of history (504 offered the last chance for action against Athens). Just as the Bacchiads fluffed the chance

---

[84] Main statements of this 'school': Strasburger (1955); Fornara (1971b); French (1972); Raaflaub (1979); (1987); Stadter (1992); Weçowski (1996); Moles (1996); Munson (2001b) 58; Moles (2002); unconvincing objections in Gould (1989) 116–20; crude misrepresentation in Harrison (2000) 242; nuanced reservations in Fowler (2003) 311–12, though conceding (311): 'I do not dispute the substance of these observations'; the dimension can, of course, be overplayed; to the references in n. 7 add Stahl (1983) 218–20; Dewald (2003) 31, 48.

[85] 6.131, often, and I think rightly, interpreted as figuring Pericles as tyrant: Strasburger (1955) 17; Thomas (1989) 270–1; Moles (2002) 41–2.

[86] Cf. also Gray (1996) 386.

[87] Cf. Herodotus' celebrated lament at 6.98: in the three successive generations of Darius, Xerxes and Artaxerxes Greece suffered more evils than in the twenty generations before Darius, partly at the hands of the Persians, partly at the hands of the leading Greek states, warring over supremacy.

to kill the baby Cypselus, so Socles and the allies fluffed the chance to kill the 'infant' of Athenian tyranny. Herodotus is advocating a form of state-craft which, while not quite oblivious to moral considerations, ultimately privileges cool and long-sighted calculation of interest, a form of statecraft here illustrated by the 'readings' of the Spartans and Hippias, not those of Socles and the allies. (This Herodotus looks very like Thucydides.)

But there are huge objections to these conclusions.

It staggers belief that a historian with such a complex conception of causality and so acute an appreciation of the role of contingency as Herodotus could be saying that this single decision predetermined the course of Greek history for the next seventy years. Further, on Herodotus' view of the innate self-destructiveness of tyranny, reinstatement of Hippias could only have been a stop-gap: it could not have stopped the clock. Most crucially, not only do these conclusions give insufficient value to the intelligence and multi-layeredness of Socles' analysis but they miss its evocation, within a universal model of tyranny, of the threat from Sparta. Had *that* threat been allowed to materialize, there might have been an alternative history just as oppressive and just as disastrous as the history that did occur. Cypselus *qua* baby and lion-cub stands for the tyrannical Sparta that might have been, just as much as for the tyrannical Athens that was to be. It would have been proportionately wrong to 'kill' Athenian democracy at this point, even though that Athenian internal democracy eventually grew into external Athenian tyranny, because democracy as a form of 'equality of speech' or 'equal government' is intrinsically good and does not inevitably lead to empire, because tyrannical intervention in other states is intrinsically bad, and because the essential thing in context was to kill the *Spartan* baby. And finally, eloquent as the framing oracles are, the run of the text gives 'the last word' not to Hippias but to the allies, the many positive implications of whose 'breaking voice' have already been shown. In short, van der Veen is right that his reading is one that the text raises: but the text also shows that it is wrong.

Wrong. If Socles' speech is correct, that wrongness will be both intellectual and moral.

I finish by arguing the centrality of Socles' speech to the purposes of the *Histories*.

The *Histories* begin with the 'unjust deeds' towards the Greeks of Croesus, 'tyrant' of Lydia. That 'injustice' consists in the imposition of a tribute-based empire.[88] The successors of Croesus' empire, the Persian and Athenian

---

[88] 1.5.3–4; 1.6; Moles (2002) 35–6.

tribute-based empires, are, therefore, also unjust. The *Histories* end ominously with Athens, tyrant-city, on the threshold of her unjust and tyrannical empire.[89] Socles' speech comes roughly halfway through the *Histories*, at the centre, or 'crossing', of the narrative, when the Persians, tyrannical imperialists, are 'crossing' into Greece.[90] This 'crucial' speech prevents the reimposition of tyranny in Athens, averts the establishment of Spartan tyranny over the Peloponnesian League, and promotes the freedom of all Greece. Narrative and thematic architecture buttress the strength of the speech.[91] Herodotus' own related polarity between tyranny and equality of speech (78) is one of a series of contrasts between tyranny and various forms of freedom which punctuates and animates key moments in the historical narrative.[92]

That the Corinthians aborted the reinstatement of Hippias, as they had earlier withdrew from Cleomenes' assault on Athens, need not be doubted. Most scholars accept (unenthusiastically enough) the historicity of Socles. But it is not just Socles' speech that speaks: his name also speaks. In a sequence thick with name- and word-plays, *Socles* is doubly significant: So/cles 'saves his own fame' (this being his only appearance in Herodotus) and he 'saves the anti-tyrant fame of the Spartans'. This double action comes within the category of the 'famous deeds of men', whose encomiastic commemoration is the *Histories*' main purpose (*Preface*).[93] And since Socles argues the opposite case to the Spartans', which is 'wonderful' in a bad sense, his own should be 'wonderful' in a good, hence again categorizable among those 'great and wonderful' deeds. Further, his 'advice' counters the 'tyrannical' advice not only of the Spartans but implicitly also the bloodthirsty advice of the outright tyrant Thrasybulus, 'adviser of brazen actions': Socles' advice, then, should be subtle and humane, as the above analysis shows it to be.

If Socles was a historical figure, it is highly improbable that Herodotus had access to his actual arguments.[94] Indeed, Socles' arguments look like Herodotus' own, and not just in the sense that he has invented rhetorically appropriate arguments but also in the sense that he thinks them right, right in general but especially right at this crucial historical and narrative

---

[89] Moles (1996) 271–77; Dewald (1997).
[90] Cf. Emily Greenwood, p. 128 above.   [91] Cf. also Fowler (2003) 315.
[92] E.g. 1.6.1–3; 1.62.1; 3.80.6; 3.142.3; 4.137.1–2; 5.37. .2; 6.5.1; 6.43.3; 6.123.1–2.
[93] Cf. Herodotus' elaborate punning on *Themistocles* as 'rightly named/famed', 'famed for his rightness'): 7.143 with Moles (2002) 44–5; and his simpler punning on *Pericles* (6.131) as 'far-famed': Moles (2002) 41.
[94] *Pace* Salmon (1984) 249.

moment. On either view of Socles' historicity, then, Socles isn't really Socles: he's Herodotus (though of course, if Socles did not exist, Herodotus' 'commemoration' of him piquantly proclaims the inadequacy of 'history as fact'). Socles, then, speaks with unique 'author-ity'.

Those *Histories* name famous deeds and names and – at least sometimes – suppress the names of the authors of infamous deeds.[95] They also incorporate contemporary or recent-past allusions as a device to jolt contemporary listeners and readers into reflection on their own situations and on the connections between those situations and the historical period down to 479. Socles is not only a speaker, he is an adviser, and the reward he himself both advocates and instantiates for virtuous behaviour is 'naming and faming', while the punishment for vicious behaviour is 'naming and shaming'. Paradoxically, however, Socles does some of this implicitly, through the device of 'figured speech'. He challenges his audiences to penetrate his meaning. How does this relate to historiographical tradition?

Later historiography sometimes explicitly states that its function is to commemorate virtuous behaviour and damn vicious behaviour.[96] The former element is effectively explicit in Herodotus (since 'wonderful' deeds include virtuous deeds). The latter is only implicit but it is there (in the device of non-naming the vicious). Later historiography also sometimes explicitly proffers virtuous and vicious behaviour as examples of what to imitate and what to avoid.[97] Later historiography also sometimes explicitly proffers praise for virtuous behaviour and damnation of vicious behaviour as incentives and disincentives for contemporary and subsequent readers.[98] How can such a programme 'work'? In the case of so-called 'contemporary history', the praise and dispraise affects some contemporaries directly and others potentially. In the case of past history, historiography demonstrates that it has the power to determine people's ultimate reputation, hence both contemporaries and people of the future will also eventually come under the verdict of history, as delivered by future historians.

Most modern scholars exclude any such perspectives in Herodotus, emphasizing his commemorative purpose. But, as in Homer, telling stories about the past is not incompatible with moral exhortation of the people to whom those stories are told.[99] In the present case, Socles, *qua* 'historian', opponent of tyranny and adviser, commemorates Corinthian tyranny in

[95] 4.43.7, 1.51.4 and cf. 2.128; Lateiner (1989) 75.
[96] E.g. Diod. 1.1.5.   [97] E.g. Diod. 1.1.2, 4, 5; Liv. *Praef.* 10.
[98] E.g. Diod. 1.1.5; Tac. *Ann.* 3.65.1–2 with Moles (1998), *pace* Woodman (1995).
[99] Cf. the story of Meleager (*Il.* 9.527–605), often adduced as a parallel to Socles' procedure.

order to deter the Spartans from tyrannical action, to encourage the allies to reject both Spartan tyranny and the restoration of tyranny in Athens and to promote a common Greekness. His speech as contextualized makes Herodotus' contemporaries think of their own present and recent past. His speech is also a 'meta'-speech for the *Histories* as a whole and it provides all its listeners, those of the 420s as well as of 504, with the 'experience' of tyranny which should promote 'good counsel'. As they listened to Socles/Herodotus, Herodotus' contemporaries could hardly have failed to remember that Herodotus himself had had direct experience of tyranny and fought against it.[100] Nor do the *Histories* speak only to contemporary listeners or readers.[101]

The 'gap' in the narrative – the failure to record the Spartans' reaction to Socles' speech – prompts the question: what *was* their reaction? They were shamed but were they ashamed? Whatever, they *were* deterred and in that sense they got their reward: the saving, for the moment, of their anti-tyrannical reputation. Was that reputation sustained? What of later Spartans? Sparta's championship of freedom and Panhellenism at the start of the Peloponnesian War looks hypocritical. Archidamus' view that Sparta should seek Persian support against Athens[102] looks cynical. Lysander's decarchies, precisely 'the establishment of tyrannies in the cities', look terrible. Pausanias' intervention into Athens in 403 to overthrow the Thirty and re-establish Athenian democracy looks virtuous. Of course, these last two examples post-date Herodotus, but the plasticity of his historical imagination projects his moral-political judgements into the future. It would be interesting to run Herodotus' account of the events of 506–4 against the year 403.

What of the Corinthians? They covered themselves with glory on this occasion and Herodotus commemorates the fact. But they didn't care when Athens crushed her ally Samos with spectacular brutality[103] and history would take a dim view of *their* desire to destroy Athens in 404.

What of the Athenians? Saved from tyranny on this occasion, they would go on to establish their own tyranny, which in Herodotus' own lifetime and slightly later would grow ever more unjust and murderous (Scione, Melos).

---

[100] The tradition is reasonably solid: How and Wells (1912) I.3–4; for the general theme of the historian's character as an aid to persuasion see Marincola (1997), 128–74, though the claim that 'for Herodotus, the first historian, the only experience in the narrative is that of enquiry' (133) is incorrect: see text and Moles (1996) 264–5, 270. I do not think that this item falls into 'the biographical fallacy'.

[101] 1.5.3–4; Moles (1996) 278–9; Naiden (1999).

[102] Thuc. 1.82.1.   [103] Cf. 9.120.4 with Stadter (1989) 51.

And what of us, silent readers, like the silent Spartan listeners? To do anything like justice to the richness of the *Histories*, we must of course see that they incorporate competing narratives, competing rhetorics, competing realities, competing potentialities, competing growths, and competing readings. But to respond to Socles'/Herodotus' moral challenge, we must also see that among all these competing entities there is a master narrative, a master reading, a master growth, a master potentiality: the one that inscribes freedom as opposed to tyranny. The tyrannical readings and writings of history by Cypselus and Periander (or even Thucydides and van der Veen) are all very clever and demand scrutiny because one has to know how to deal with them, but they are wrong, both intellectually and morally. Implementation of the master narrative poses immense difficulties, but it is an ideal to which we should aspire and it is also an ideal sometimes capable of implementation. For in their eventually victorious struggle against the Persians, the Greeks, albeit hesitantly, fitfully, fleetingly, did achieve that ideal. And so did Socles, which is why Herodotus commemorates him (or invents him).[104]

Children loom large in Socles' speech. Did Herodotus have any children? We don't know, but one child at least he did father (or mother): 'this is the production of Herodotus of Halicarnassus, in order that neither should the things born from men come to an end nor should great and wonderful deeds, some produced by Greeks, some by barbarians, be without name/fame' (*Preface*).

The master imagery (there are others)[105] is biological: 'born from men', 'come to an end' (as of a family dying out),[106] 'production' (as of children),[107] 'Herodotus' (yet again, a *name* speaks: 'the gift of Hera', goddess of marriage). Herodotus' *Histories* is *his* baby, and it was not for nothing that in the ancient world Herodotus himself was named the Father of History. Herodotus' baby had many babies, but one was pre-eminent. Whatever *his* historicity, 'Socles' is ultimately nothing more than the *nom de plume* of '*Hero*dotus', mother-creator of the text of the *Histories* (Socles' quotation of *Hera* is additionally apposite). Socles' 'wonderful' speech itself births, saves, and matures a baby whose virtues far outshine the sinister babyhoods of the Dionysiac and leonine Cypselus, of the potential Spartan tyranny and of the tyrannical Athens that was to be: that is, the 'baby' variously named 'democratic Athens', 'equality of speech' and 'equality of government': the baby

---

[104] Which of course is what I think but cannot prove.
[105] Notably, the 'inscriptional': Moles (1999).   [106] Cf. 5.39.2.   [107] LSJ s.v. ἀποδείκνυμι I.2.

of freedom, a baby to be loved and cherished but – of course – prevented from becoming a bad baby.

Modern scholarship generally maintains a rather embarrassed silence about this matter, but it is right that one contribution to this collection should save the reputation of the *Histories* as a great libertarian text.[108]

---

[108] Cf. Moles (1998) on *Annals* 4.32–5: Herodotus certainly influenced that sequence, which offers many parallels to the Socles episode; I now think Tacitus had actually read Socles' speech and interpreted it as I do. Of course, neither Herodotus' nor Tacitus' ideas of 'liberty' are above criticism.

CHAPTER II

Cyprus and Onesilus: an interlude of freedom (5.104, 108–16)

Anastasia Serghidou

In his *De Herodoti malignitate* (24), Plutarch accuses Herodotus of not treating all the military exploits that he describes with equal interest. He complains that some of the events are narrated in meticulous detail while others are simply omitted. The Ionian revolt is a case in point: for Plutarch it provides an example of Herodotus' mistaken evaluation, and even suppression, of individuals, whole peoples, and events. In general, Plutarch characterizes Herodotus' treatment of the revolt (τὰ περὶ Σάρδεις) as demeaning, epitomized by Herodotus dubbing the Athenian ships sent to liberate the Greek cities of Ionia as the 'beginning of evils':

ὡς ἐνῆν μάλιστα διέλυσε καὶ διελυμήνατο τὴν πρᾶξιν, ἃς μὲν Ἀθηναῖοι ναῦς ἐξέπεμψαν Ἴωσι τιμωροὺς ἀποστᾶσι βασιλέως, ἀρχεκάκους τολμήσας προσ-ειπεῖν ὅτι τοσαύτας πόλεις καὶ τηλικαύτας Ἑλληνίδας ἐλευθεροῦν ἐπεχείρησαν ἀπὸ τῶν βαρβάρων.

He did all in his power to destroy and demean the deed, having the nerve to say that the ships which the Athenians sent to support the Ionians in their rebellion against the king were 'the beginning of evil' because they attempted to free all those fine Greek cities. (4; tr. Bowen (1992))

Of relevance for our discussion of Cyprus is Plutarch's complaint that crucial naval victories, such as that of the Eretrians over the Cypriots in the Pamphylian sea, have been entirely neglected. Here Herodotus is condemned for 'mentioning the Eretrians casually and passing over their great epic achievement in silence' (Ἐρετριέων δὲ κομιδῇ μνησθεὶς ἐν παρέργῳ καὶ παρασιωπήσας μέγα κατόρθωμα καὶ ἀοίδιμον, 24). Of course, it would be perverse to let the tone of Plutarch's critique dictate our interpretation of Herodotus, but nevertheless the substance of his contention, that Herodotus manipulates victories and defeats according to his own historical agenda, does raise pertinent questions about the design of Herodotus' narrative and his rationale in selecting the peoples, events and places that he will cover and in covering them in the manner that he does.

Accordingly, the aim of this chapter is to examine how Herodotus manipulates the role of Cyprus in the Ionian Revolt and how he teases out its
significance for the broader dynamics of his cultural and historical investigation. I will focus on the way in which the historian treats the involvement
of specific city-kingdoms in the Cypriot Revolt and, furthermore, how he
approaches the cultural and political specificity of this island via an ethnographic approach that gives this 'local' conflict a 'panhellenic' scope.

SYMBOLIC GEOGRAPHY AND THE TOPOGRAPHY OF ETHNICITY

Plutarch was right: the successful Ionian naval battle in the sea of Cyprus
(5.112) does take up little space in Herodotus' account of the events of
the Ionian Revolt. However, if, *contra* Plutarch, we shift our attention
to Herodotus' narrative rather than the events *per se*, then Herodotus'
minimal treatment of this event becomes significant in what it reveals of
his ethnographic priorities.[1] I will suggest that Herodotus has subsumed the
Cypriot phase of the Ionian Revolt and the local history and ethnography
of Cyprus within an ideological nexus involving strategies of hegemony
and submission.

Many scholars have studied the significance of Cyprus as a crucial
Mediterranean crossroads in different periods of antiquity.[2] Owing to its
geographical location the island brought together Oriental and Western
traits resulting in a remarkable cultural syncretism.[3] In this context it is
interesting to consider what role the island's ambiguous location and fusion
of cultures plays in Herodotus' narrative. As we shall see in the following
references, Herodotus' narrative focuses on Cyprus' distinctive intercultural
coding, representing the island as an exceptional, liminal space in which
different cultures, both Greek and non-Greek, styles of art, morals, religion
and historical traditions all converged.[4] In treating the island in this way,
the historian's narrative engages with the cultural specificity of Cyprus as

---

[1] On the ethnographic code of Herodotus and his narrative strategies, see Hartog (1988); Dorati (2000);
Thomas (2000); Munson (2001b).

[2] Prehistoric Cyprus saw moments of thalassocracy encouraged by the intense commercial exchange
it established all over the Mediterranean, cf. Karageorghis (2002). On the crucial role of trade in
ethnic identification see Karageorghis (1994) and Knapp (1993). Citium was one of the kingdoms
most involved in trade: cf. Yon (1995) 125–6. For an overview of the topic see Muhly (1986).

[3] On cultural and religious syncretism in Cyprus, see Pouilloux (1995).

[4] On this creative fusion in Herodotus' treatment of Cyprus see Karageorghis (2004). More generally,
the thematic ends to which Herodotus uses geography have been well explored: see, for instance,
Armayor (1985), and Greenwood, pp. 128–9 above. For the conceptual side of Herodotus' geographic
narrative see already Immerwahr (1966); for equivalent approaches in relation to ethnography see
Romm (1992).

it was generally viewed from the vantage point of mainland Greeks of his day.[5]

It is none other than Aristagoras who introduces the idea that Cyprus might constitute a significant coordinate. The vantage point he presents is, however, not one that is entirely Greek. Herodotus' audience is first made to view Cyprus from a perspective other than their own: Cyprus is employed by Aristagoras as a familiar point of reference against which the Persian satrap Artaphrenes can measure the Greek islands claimed to be on offer. While Aristagoras catalogues the various Greek islands – Naxos and the dependent islands, including Paros, Andros and other Cycladic islands (5.31.1–4) – the real emphasis is placed on Euboea, a large and rich island 'not less important than Cyprus and easy to conquer' (οὐκ ἐλάσσονι Κύπρου καὶ κάρτα εὐπετέϊ αἱρεθῆναι). The comparison with Cyprus is likely to be a trope,[6] and, in literal terms at least, Aristagoras' claim about Euboea's dimensions is certainly false. What must be noted, however, is the persuasive force of the analogy with Cyprus.

At the same time, it should also be noted that the introduction of Cyprus into the narrative proper is punctuated by an equivalent offer of another Mediterranean island – this time in the west – namely, Sardinia.[7] The allusion to Sardinia as 'the biggest island of all' (Σάρδω νῆσον τὴν μεγίστην – 5.106.6) occurs in the context of Histiaeus' deceitful speech to Darius. In a ploy to escape Sardis, Histiaeus exploits preconceptions about the prosperous situation of Sardinia, recorded elsewhere in Herodotus' narrative (1.170.2), to emphasize the material gain that he can offer Darius.[8] The motif of prosperous islands that are ripe for political and economic exploitation prepares us for the themes of Cypriot political and economical subjection to Persia and their later aspiration to revolt. No doubt such a topic was also of interest to contemporary audiences, given more recent attempts to bring Cyprus (not to mention another large island in the west) under Athenian influence (see below).

Herodotus' narrative implies a politically encoded version of Cypriot geography: the island serves as a political landmark that indicates an implicit

---

[5] For the traditional liminality of Cyprus, see *Od.* 17.442–4; on Cypriot otherness, see Aesch. *Ch.* 277–90.

[6] Long-standing economic links associated Cyprus with Euboea: Karageorghis (1991) 115–16, and Lemos (2001). It is quite possible that the geographical parallelism between Cyprus and Euboea owes its origins to a history of cultural and economic exchange.

[7] The Cypriot *logos* is conspicuously put on hold for the *logos* that contains Histiaeus' promise to take Sardinia for Darius, in compensation for the destruction of Sardis (5.105.1–108.1).

[8] For his slick pun on Sardo and Sardis, see Henderson, p. 279 below and Legrand (1946) *ad loc.*

ideological frontier opposing East to West.[9] For instance, in a geographical digression on the river Halys in Book One of the *Histories*, Herodotus locates Cyprus as bordering on the Mediterranean fringe of Asia (1.72.3).[10] More relevant here, Aristagoras refers to the eastern part of the Mediterranean sea near Cilicia as 'where Cyprus is' (τούτοισι δὲ πρόσουροι Κίλικες, κατήκοντες ἐπὶ θάλασσαν τήνδε, ἐν τῇ ἥδε Κύπρος νῆσος κεῖται, 5.49.6). It is worth noting that this geographical reference implies an already established map of the *oikoumenē* that privileges islands and one in which Cyprus looms large. The island has a special place in a conception of the known world where wealth, material and agricultural abundance or slave trading are conceived as important constituent elements of political supremacy and economic dominance (5.49). These resources provide the impulse and the arguments for military and political action.

For a contemporary audience, the symbolic geographies of the Mediterranean islands, including Cyprus, would also have been evocative of current political realities, not least Athenian expansionism.[11] Throughout this period Cyprus was an anomaly: although it displayed manifest cultural ties to the Greek world, it belonged firmly to the eastern part of the Mediterranean and as such eluded total Greek political control throughout its entire history, including – most relevant for Herodotus' audiences – that of Athenian *archē*. In terms of the narrative of Book 5, the geographical and cultural liminality of Cyprus furnishes Herodotus with a convenient symbolic counterpart to his treatment of the Ionian Revolt. In contrast to these crude polarities of Greek and non-Greek, Herodotus' account of the Cypriot Revolt against Persian hegemony reveals a more subtle approach to the concept of a clash of cultures and values. Space, time and ethnography structure the historical narrative and underlie the political interrelation of the city-states and wider 'national' concerns presented by the author. The stock narrative of Persian subjugation as a threat to Hellenic ethnicity and autonomy is played out against the sectional, even divisive, histories and identities of the island's local urban centres represented by the distinctive city-kingdoms.[12]

---

[9] On conceptual complexities and significantly blurred geographical categories in Herodotus' narrative see Pelling (1997). On ambiguous geographical bipolarities in Herodotus see Thomas (2000) 80–6.

[10] Munson (2001b) 103 highlights the ethical dimensions of geographical boundaries as typified by the river Halys; on Cyprus as a coordinate in such boundaries cf. 1.79.

[11] Ceccarelli (1993) and (1996); Constantakopoulou (2002); Payen (1997).

[12] Multi-ethnicity and polyvalent culture are crucial indicators of Cypriot local history: see Colombier (1991), (2003) and Serghidou (1995). The island was seen by ancient authors as both a single and a multiple political entity, some treating Cyprus as a *polis*, while others saw it as a kind of micro-continent. These differing conceptualizations testify to competing cultural narratives of unity and fragmentation: see Serghidou (2006). The latter is particularly manifest in the political and ethnic

In the narrative of Book 5 cultural distance between Greeks and Cypriots is established through both cultural and linguistic criteria. An apparent digression, the appearance of the word *sigynnas*, the Cypriot term for javelins, at the outset of Book 5 (5.9) illustrates this point: the word simultaneously marks the Cypriots as participating in, even as they depart from, common Greek usage.[13] This narrative detail serves in various ways to define and foreshadow the cultural specificity of Cyprus against the 'Hellenic' world that will be explored in the chapters to come, and in a sense is a culmination of Cyprus' few appearances in the first four books of the *Histories* where reference to cultural similarity with barbarians has been the norm (1.105, 1.199, 2.79). In contrast, when the Cypriots reappear after their failed rebellion, a year of freedom, is over, it is as a contingent of the Persian army, depicted with Oriental touches that highlight the small differences in their garments from those of the mainland Greeks: Κύπριοι δὲ παρείχοντο νέας πεντήκοντα καὶ ἑκατόν, ἐσκευασμένοι ὧδε. τὰς μὲν κεφαλὰς εἱλίχατο μίτρῃσι οἱ βασιλέες αὐτῶν, οἱ δὲ ἄλλοι εἶχον κιτάρις, τὰ δὲ ἄλλα κατά περ Ἕλληνες ('The Cypriots furnished 150 ships and were kitted out in the following fashion: the kings among them wrapped turbans around their heads, while the others wore tiaras, but with respect to the rest of their clothing they wore the same as Greeks,' 7.90).[14] Safely subsumed once more under Persian authority, Cypriots are defined in this passage in relation to a binary scheme (Greeks/non-Greeks) despite the multi-ethnicity that is operative in the Cypriot Revolt narrative. In the catalogue of contingents, the diverse origins of the many Cypriots appear apparently without consequence: τούτων δὲ τοσάδε ἔθνεά ἐστι, οἱ μὲν ἀπὸ Σαλαμῖνος καὶ Ἀθηνέων, οἱ δὲ ἀπὸ Ἀρκαδίης, οἱ δὲ ἀπὸ Κύθνου, οἱ δὲ ἀπὸ Φοινίκης, οἱ δὲ ἀπὸ Αἰθιοπίης, ὡς αὐτοὶ Κύπριοι λέγουσι ('Of the Cypriots, the following are the many ethnic backgrounds which they claim themselves to have: Salamis and Athens, Arcadia, Cythnus, Phoenicia, and Egypt').

And yet the situation is different in Book 5: Cypriot multi-ethnicity is there an operative, if at times implicit, feature of the Revolt narrative and is mainly revealed through the sector-based history of the Cypriot kingdoms.[15] The varying responses of Amathous, Curium, Salamis and Soli to

---

individuality of each city-kingdom, as will be discussed below: while Herodotus seems to phrase the claim to liberty in terms of Hellenic identity, he is aware of and accepts local diversity, as well as envisaging a Cypriot entity distinct from Greek ethnicity. On the subject of Greek ethnicity and Herodotus see Thomas (2001a).

[13] The *locus classicus* for language as an indicator of Hellenicity is, of course, Hdt. 8.144.

[14] I follow Legrand (1946) 106 n. 2 (with Pollux 10.164) in reading κιτάρις over the Oxford preference for the reading κιθῶνας: the sense required is that of a head-dress. See also Rosen's new Teubner which prints κιτάριας. On the head-dress as a defining feature of cultural difference see Aristagoras in 5.49.3. For further discussion see Petit (2004) 17–18 and Munson (2005) 58–9.

[15] Antoniadis (1981); see also Fourrier (2002).

the revolt, as depicted by Herodotus, reflect and refract a 'topography' of internal and cultural politics in which city-kingdoms defined themselves variously in relation to Hellenicity and Persian rule. It is, therefore, in a sense a 'topography of ethnicity' whereby ethnic differences are mapped out within the larger geographical entity of Cyprus and in relation to the autonomous status of each of the city-kingdoms,[16] which nevertheless had been subject to external rule since the time of Amasis of Egypt (2.182). This topography is ultimately based on Cypriot self-representations which seem to have fostered a fluid attitude to cultural identity since prehistoric times: as Snodgrass has argued, 'no clear line was expected to be drawn in Cyprus, between Greeks and barbarians.'[17] Consequently, this long-established tradition of cultural syncretism poses difficulties for both ancient readers and modern scholars attempting to map the island in terms of Greeks and non-Greeks. In what follows I will explore how Herodotus exploits the multi-locality of Cypriot culture in his narrative of the Ionian Revolt with an account underpinned by sensitivity to the divergent, local Cypriot identities, ambivalently situated between East and West. The diversity of the ethnic origins of the Cypriot cities which Herodotus catalogues (7.90, quoted above) plays a significant role in his narrative.

That the revolt starts with Salamis is appropriate: culturally, it was among the most hellenized city-kingdoms, even if divided in its allegiances. Its fate (a single year of freedom) is raised into disproportionate prominence when told in a Persian War narrative celebrating its (Greek) namesake and motherland, the very island of Salamis. We learn from authors both contemporary with and later than Herodotus that Cypriot Salamis could function as a significant geographical double for its famous mother-city.[18] As such Salamis generates a more elaborate ethnographic discourse than the other kingdoms which corresponds to its pivotal position as a midpoint

---

[16] My discussion draws both on the concept of 'spatialization' formulated by Hodder (1978) and on the implementation of that concept in understanding Late Prehistoric Cyprus advanced by Bolger (1989). Such analysis may be combined with recognition of the extroverted character of Cypriot culture owing to the circulation of material goods through trade during its prehistoric period.

[17] But in Cyprus, there is abundant evidence that Greeks and 'barbarians' mingled freely, and on roughly equal terms. In a system where the definition of Hellenicity is not the central issue, there is no need for restriction and exclusion; see Snodgrass (1995) 116–17.

[18] Salamis was above all the colony founded by Teucer and therefore systematically associated with the Salamis from which Teucer came. He is said to have given his colony the very 'insular' name of Salamis, (ὄνομα νησιωτικόν) after his motherland (Eur. *Hel.* 148–50; Isoc. *Evag.* 18). Both name and the genealogical links inherent in the colony–metropolis relationship guaranteed the continual association of the two localities (e.g. Isoc. *Evag.* 18, ὁμώνυμον ποιήσας τῆς πρότερον αὐτῷ πατρίδος οὔσης); Aesch. *Pers.* 894–6. On Cypriot Salamis as a replica of mainland Salamis, see Serghidou (1995). For the first reference to Salamis in the *Histories*, related to the Cypriot-Salaminian king Euelthon and his relationship to Pheretima, see 4.162.

between the Hellenic past and present, the mythology of its Greek origins and the history of events that constituted a defining moment of Greekness and would shape the present inhabited by the audience of the *Histories*. But that midpoint is the turbulent present of the Ionian Revolt in which Salamis is divided in its ethnic and political affiliations and in its choice between remaining subject to Persia or becoming free (as Greeks). The importance of Salamis at a narrative level lies in the role it played in the Cypriot Revolt. Not only is it the starting point (5.104), but it is also the turning-point that allows the narrative to shift from Cyprus back to the mainland and the Ionians' cause (5.115). While all the Cypriot cities were under siege by the Persians, Salamis, Herodotus says, provided an exception: the people of the town restored Salamis to their former pro-Persian ruler Gorgus.[19] After a year of freedom Cyprus was once more brought into subjection. At this point the Ionians 'lost no time in returning home to Ionia' (5.115.1).

The transitional role of Salamis is substantiated by specific narrative strategies. For example, mythology and genealogical discourse significantly mark an ethnic affinity with mainland Salamis and stress both differences and similarities with ancestral Hellenic traits. Cypriot Salamis is the birth-place of Gorgus and his brother Onesilus, the instigator of the Cypriot Revolt, while the mainland Salamis is enblematic as a crucial battle site in the Greek–Persian confrontation.[20] Within this frame, Athenian 'Salamis' evokes the naval battle that lies in the future of the narrative, the past of the audience, while Cypriot Salamis functions as a (temporary) symbol of Hellenization that challenges the idea of Persian supremacy. However, the shared name points to a more specific narrative significance:[21] while it symbolically introduces a shared theme, that of Graeco–Persian hostility, it also evokes two different stages of Cypriot Salamis' history that furnish conflicting stances in relation to such hostility. On the one hand, read backwards, Cypriot Salamis evokes allegiances with mainland Greece and Athens; on the other hand, reading forward in Herodotus' text, Cypriot Salamis' name is an awkward reminder that the Cypriots will fight on the Persian side in the famous naval battle.[22]

---

[19] This is reminiscent of what happens when Aristagoras turns the deposed Ionian tyrants over to their respective cities (with the exception of Coes, 5.38).

[20] On this parallelism see Pouilloux (1975) and (1976).

[21] On the importance of onomastics in constructing meaning in the narrative of Book 5 see Irwin, Ch. 1 above: it is surely significant that the idea of the same *onoma* having multiple referents is first introduced in Book 5 in connection with Cyprus and the name of her spears (5.9).

[22] Later, in the case of the Salaminian king Evagoras, the Athenians will find it important to honour him as 'a Greek' acting 'on behalf of Greece' (ὑπὲρ τῆς Ἑλλάδος Ἕλλην, *IG* II² 20.17): see Osborne and Rhodes (2003) no. 11.

The Hellenic pedigree of Salamis is matched by that of the kingdom of Soli. Soli's ties with Hellenic culture are embodied in its ancestral king, Philocyprus, whose Hellenic credentials are enhanced by the linking of his name with the Athenian lawgiver, Solon.[23] The parallelism of the cities is striking: in ch. 110 Soli and Salamis are set on a par as alone providing the elite troops which stand opposite the Persians, and both can claim an ancestral connection with Athens symbolized onomastically and eponymously. And yet, there are differences: in contrast to the Salaminian war chariots who turned traitor and the inhabitants of Salamis who are said to have returned their city to the pro-Persian Gorgus, Soli provides an example of a community that resists the Persian attack longest:

Now, as soon as the Ionians who had taken part in the battle off Cyprus heard about Onesilus' death and found out all the major towns in Cyprus were under siege (all except for Salamis, that is, which had been returned to Gorgus, its former ruler), they sailed back to Ionia. The Cyprian town which held out the longest against its besiegers was Soli; the Persians finally captured it in the fifth month of the siege by tunnelling under its defensive wall. So the Cyprians, after a year of freedom, were reduced once more to a fresh term of slavery. (5.115–16; tr. Waterfield)

But if Salamis and Soli represent somewhat different commitments to revolt, they stand in contrast to another Hellenic city, the Argive Curium (οἱ δὲ Κουρίεες οὗτοι λέγονται εἶναι Ἀργείων ἄποικοι, 5.113.1), whose leader (τύραννος), Stesenor of Curium, abandons the revolt, taking his contingent with him. As with Cypriot Salamis' evocation of the future of its mother-city, the passing reference to their Argive origin at the moment of their treachery may gesture towards the medizing of their mother-city, which at this point is still to come (7.151).[24]

Against these cities of Hellenic origin, the ethnically and politically independent Amathous stands out. Herodotus offers no real explanation for the Amathousians' resistance, except perhaps the character of Onesilus who besieges them when they refuse to obey (οὐ βουλομένους οἱ πείθεσθαι ἐπολιόρκεε προσκατήμενος),[25] but behind their unique response is likely

---

[23] Herodotus refers to Solon 19W. The city was alleged to have taken its name from Solon's advice in its refoundation, see Gallo (1976), Karageorghis (1973), and most recently Irwin (2005b) 147–51, esp. n. 101. On Soli and the scholia tradition, see Irwin (1999).

[24] I owe this point to the editors.

[25] This phrase ties the Amathousians to the first characters of Book 5, the Perinthians who 'refused to be subjects of Darius' (οὐ βουλομένους ὑπηκόους εἶναι Δαρείου, 5.1.1), and the last, the Thracians who although 'willing' (βουλομένων) are nevertheless similarly besieged by another instigator of revolt (περικατήμενος, cf. προσκατήμενος, 5.104.3, each word a single time in Book 5), Aristagoras, who will die during his efforts (πόλιν περικατήμενος καὶ βουλομένων τῶν Θρηίκων ὑποσπόνδων ἐξιέναι, 5.126.2).

to lie their traditional claims to autochthony, their independent response capable of symbolizing independent resistance to pan-Cypriot Greek identity.[26] But this is all implicit in Herodotus' narrative as he surprisingly offers no details about their ethnicity or government. Instead, he explicitly identifies Amathous as the site of the bloody revolt, their resistance providing the setting for the narrative of Onesilus (5.114–16) where the instigator of the revolt is killed and disfigured, and where he achieves an afterlife through the award of heroic status.

THE COMPLEXITIES OF CYPRIOT SUBSERVIENCE

It is against the backdrop of the geography and ethnography of Cyprus and the complex relations between the island's city-kingdoms and foreign powers that we need to appreciate the character and actions of Onesilus in Book 5. Any interpretation of Onesilus' actions must engage with the situation of Cypriot subjugation and dependency in the period after Cambyses.[27] When Aristagoras displays the map of the world to Cleomenes in order to illustrate the location and geopolitical significance of the subjugated territories that surround the Ionians, Cyprus is included in a region where tribute has to be paid to the Persians (5.49.6; cf. 2.182).[28] In a speech attempting to persuade the Spartan king of the viability of the success of this revolt, this brief description implies the support that might be expected from others similarly bound in a tribute relationship to the Persian king: a foreshadowing of the Cypriot Revolt. Given the unity that might be expected from a shared grievance, it is striking that when their revolt comes, the collective response heralded in by ch. 108 is quickly qualified by a narrative of internal ethnic and political differentiation.

Other ironies pervade the Cypriot commitment to independence: Cypriot willingness to adhere to the liberation movement of the Ionians is described in terms that echo their previously voluntary submission to

---

[26] On the complexities of the 'Amathousian' identity see Petit (1995) and (2004) 15–17. For the motif of Amathousian autochthony see Ps-Skylax, *Geogr. Gr. Min* 1.77–8. Theopompus also believed that the Amathousians were the descendants of the pre-Greek people of Cinyras (*FGrH* 115 F 103.3). Baurain (1984) discusses the passages of Theopompus and Ps-Skylax extensively and challenges them. Whether Herodotus expects (some) audiences to know this, or whether he is attempting to exclude such a claim from an understanding of the Amathousian response cannot easily be determined, and perhaps he is doing both for different audiences.

[27] In Herodotus' narrative Persian control by Cambyses follows on from the last claim of Book 2 (2.182) that Amasis was the first to make Cyprus a tribute-paying entity.

[28] On tribute as a crucial characteristic of the ancient Eastern economy see Briant (1982) and Briant and Herrenschmidt (1989). On the evocations of Athenian tribute-collecting in Herodotus' narrative see Stadter (1992) 795, Derow (1995) 5 and Fowler (2003) 311.

the payment of tribute. Now Cypriots are viewed as 'volunteers' and companions to the Ionian Revolt, with Amathous singled out as the exception (Κύπριοι δὲ ἐθέλονταί σφι πάντες προσεγένοντο πλὴν Ἀμαθουσίων, 5.104.1). Against the collective action of the Cypriots so framed, the Amathousian stance represents independence, and nothing less than might be expected from a community whose tradition of autochthony stakes out a claim for its distinct status amid Cypriots, at odds with movement towards a single national identity and ruler. And indeed the Cypriot decision to revolt (ἀπέστησαν, 5.104) is otherwise compromised: for after the initial collective decision, it emerges that the decision taken depends upon the power of the local rulers, whose differing claims to Hellenic origins will end up mapping on to differing commitments to persist in revolt. Consequently, the characterization of power is defined by the specific profile and ethnic aspirations of the ruler, and here we are not so far from the situation that obtains in Herodotus' depiction of the Ionian Revolt with its focus on the personalities of Aristagoras and Histiaeus. In contrast to the other Cypriot cities, the Amathousians are significantly given no named ruler; their actions are their own.

HEGEMONIAL TRAITS AND THE CYPRIOT REVOLT

We may step back and consider the cultural, economic, and political coordinates that frame the character of Onesilus. Of course, while this investigation does not aim to reduce Onesilus to a biographical 'portrait-type', one may consider how this historical agent is also portrayed as reflecting all the traits of a 'monarch'.[29] In Herodotus' narrative, he is a character in whose fate political disunity and conflicting allegiances are played out. Herodotus' Onesilus participates in the motif of unification by a single ruler that represents a long local tradition within the history of Cyprus: archetypal characters such as the Homeric Cinyras or later the Isocratean Evagoras are notable literary examples of local resistance to the ethnic and political fragmentation of the island.[30] At the same time, his acts and decisions are also shaped by his political opposition to his ruling brother Gorgus (5.104), and raise questions about his more personal motivations for revolt even as this fraternal discord also functions as a paradigm of the opposing poles that define Cypriot responses to Persian domination.

[29] Hart (1982) 90; See Munson (2001b) 49–50 on the 'monarchical model'.
[30] On the historical portrait of Cinyras see Baurain (1980); on the Homeric Cinyras and the legends related to his reign, see Loucas-Durie (1989), and Serghidou (2006). On Evagoras see Costa (1974); Lewis and Stroud (1979); Walbank (1987); Osborne and Rhodes (2003) 50–5.

Significantly, Herodotus constructs parallelisms between the internal Cypriot conflict and military defeat and the wider Ionian Revolt. In his narrative of the Revolt, Herodotus reveals that the siege of Amathous, undertaken by Onesilus, was not an isolated adventure: the event was foreshadowed by the destructive burning of Sardis, a point emphasized by the repeated collocation of the two events (5.105.1 and 108.1). One may notice that the simultaneity of these events neatly draws together three protagonists: Onesilus, Darius and Aristagoras. Initially, Onesilus functions as a mediator: he intervenes to ask for help and military collaboration from the Ionians for an ambitious operation (5.108.2). Contact is literally and symbolically established between Cyprus and Ionia as the Ionian navy moves to Cyprus. This link appears to dissolve what might be considered to be a geopolitical frontier. Again, geography functions as a medium for sketching difference and liminality, recalling what Pelling refers to above as a 'creative use of geography'.[31] When the Persian troops and the navy approach Cyprus, the 'Key Islands' appear as the frontier to be transgressed, the geographic borders of the island that permit or prohibit the entrance to Cypriot territory, the fictional gate that opens and closes when the historical circumstances demand it.[32]

THE HORSE, THE SQUIRE AND THE REBEL HEGEMON

Herodotus' description of the revolt is generally built upon the image of face-to-face confrontation, mainly based on recurrent scenes of duels.[33] The first scene of the revolt starts with a reference to the main clash that took place in the plain of Salamis. This clash takes the form of a significant *agōn*, including all the heroic elements that highlight the valour and vigour of the hoplite: Cypriot kings give the order to other Cypriots to attack but they take all the necessary precautions to select 'the best' of their groups

---

[31] See Pelling, p. 180 above.

[32] The emphasis put on these islands implies an association of geographical space and onomastics. The name is significant: they are, the very '"keys" of Cyprus' (Φοίνικες περιέπλεον τὴν ἄκρην αἳ καλεῦνται Κληΐδες τῆς Κύπρου – 5.108). The key islands are later mentioned by Strabo (14.6.2); Plin. *NH* 5.35.129 refers to the 'Clidas et Acamanta', the two promontories; Ptolem. 5.14.7: Νῆσοι... καλούμεναι Κλεῖδες; see finally, an epigram of the *Palatine Anthology* (7.738, Theodorida): Κληΐδες Κύπρου δὲ καὶ ἐσχατιαί Σαλαμῖνος.

[33] The elite troops, men of Salamis and Soli, face the Persians; other Cypriots face the other elements of the Persian army, 5.110; Onesilus and his Carian squire face Artybius and his horse, which is trained to rear up at hoplites 5.112. From the point of view of deriving fame from Herodotus' account, the Ionians' decision to engage the Phoenicians at sea (5.109) seems to have been the wrong one: on Herodotus' niggardly treatment of one of the naval battles around Cyprus see Plut. *de mal. Her.* 24 quoted above and the passing references at 5.112.1 and 115.1.

for this mission (Σαλαμινίων δὲ καὶ Σολίων ἀπολέξαντες τὸ ἄριστον ἀντέτασσον Πέρσῃσι, 5.110). In fact, the clash takes an epic turn with the duel between Onesilus and Artybius, the Persian commander who came to Cyprus with strong Persian forces to crush the revolt. Onesilus' decision to set himself against Artybius has symbolic value: Onesilus is one who deliberately (*ethelontēs*, a 'volunteer') decides, contrary to his Cypriot predecessors, to reject subjugation to Persia.[34] His rejection of Persian rule marks a crucial turn in local politics as the face-to-face confrontation implicates two individuals and two nations.

The scene of confrontation focuses on the exceptional skills of Artybius' horse. The entire scene revolves around an extraordinary duel that opposes not a hoplite to a hoplite, nor a hoplite to a Persian 'anti-hoplite',[35] but rather a hoplite to a horse. Thus we observe Onesilus not only being pitted against Artybius, but also against the danger presented by his horse: 'I am told', he says to his Carian armour-bearer 'that Artybius' horse rears, and savages with his teeth and hooves anyone he comes on. Now think a moment, and tell me which of the two – Artybius or his horse – you would rather watch for a chance of striking' (5.111.2). The clash is neither rare nor peculiar in its Herodotean context. In the context of Book 5, this duel sends us right back to the opening *logos*: we are reminded of other extraordinary duels, namely those of the Perinthians and Paeonians which pitted three separate entities in a symbolic and metaphorical opposition: man to man, horse to horse and dog to dog (ἄνδρα ἀνδρὶ καὶ ἵππον ἵππῳ συνέβαλον καὶ κύνα κυνί, 5.1.2–3).[36] This early encounter in Book 5 prefigures the crucial role the horse plays in the encounter between Onesilus and Artybius. At the same time, the role of the horse is supplemented by the role of the armour-bearer – a character apparently equivalent to Oebares, servant of Darius (3.85–8).[37] His knowledge and prudence moderate the dangerous strength and menacing stature of the adversary while he assumes an advisory role by helping his master choose the right way of fighting:

'What I say is, a ruler and a general should fight with another ruler, or another general. If you kill a general, it will be a great thing for you; and if he kills you –

---

[34] Ἀρτυβίῳ δὲ τῷ στρατηγῷ τῶν Περσέων ἐθελοντὴς ἀντετάσσετο Ὀνήσιλος (5.110–11.1)

[35] On Persians as anti-hoplites see Hartog (1988) 44–50.

[36] For further discussion of this duel, see Irwin, pp. 44–56 above and Osborne, p. 89 above.

[37] Legrand (1946) 140 n. 4 likens the Carian squire to the cautious servant of New Comedy, but it is just as likely that Herodotus draws on popular knowledge of the use of squires in the Persian cavalry. Later sources such as Xenophon attest to the close collaboration between the cavalry and their squires in the Persian army: see Blaineau (2004). There is, however, no real compulsion to choose between these Greek and non-Greek portrayals: Herodotus may well be producing a syncretic *logos*; see below on the head of Onesilus.

which God forbid – even death from a worthy hand is only half as bad as it might otherwise have been. You, then, must fight Artybius; we underlings (ὑπηρέτας) will go for our equals – and for the horse. Don't be afraid of his tricks: I promise you, he will never rear up against anybody again.' (5.111.4)[38]

In this extraordinary situation, the nameless Carian squire is made to reflect on the hierarchies that define the social authority of the *hegemon* and the consequent inferiority of the servant. The horse provides the image of an inferior adversary fit only for a person of modest rank, while a king has to battle with a king.[39] The entire scene alludes to the idea of power and submission, implicitly associated with the Cypriot desire for independence and resistance to Persian rule. Although 'subject to' Persia, Onesilus is seen to be equal to his Persian opponent. However, this is no simple narrative about power, since the clash between supposed equals is complicated by the fact that Onesilus relies on the intervention of his armour-bearer who, although a servant, arguably plays the most important part in overthrowing the Persian opponent:

As for both generals, the following is what happened: Artybius on his horse came charging down upon Onesilus, who, according to the arrangement with his squire, aimed a blow at the rider's body; as Onesilus struck, the horse reared and brought his fore-feet down upon his shield and at that instant the Carian swung his curved sword and sheared its feet clean off. The horse fell, and Artybius, the Persian commander, with him. (5.112)

In the next instalment, the scene passes from individuals to localities and multitudes. The narrative goes back to local differences between city-states and turns readers' attention to the heart of the Cypriot problem: the struggle for emancipation set against the tensions between rulers and communities. Thus our attention is turned to Stesenor, 'tyrant of Curium', who 'played traitor' (5.113.1, see above), and those war chariots from none other than Salamis that follow suit (τὠυτὸ τοῖσι Κουριεῦσι ἐποίεον). As a result of this treachery the Persians gain the upper hand (γινομένων δὲ τούτων κατυπέρτεροι ἦσαν οἱ Πέρσαι τῶν Κυπρίων), and the defeat of the Cypriots leads to the death of Onesilus, 'the originator of the Cyprian Revolt', as well as to the death of the ruler of Soli, Aristocyprus, son of Philocyprus 'whom Solon . . . praised in a poem more highly than any other ruler' (5.113.2).

---

[38] All of the translations that follow are taken from the Penguin translation of de Selincourt, revised by Marincola (1996).
[39] For another Herodotean clash that hinges around socio-political equality, see the war between the Scythians and their former slaves: Hdt. 4.3–4.

Here with the kings of Soli, we are reminded of the significance of names: in good Solonian fashion, Aristocyprus ends his life by being the 'best' (*aristeuō*; cf. ἄριστον of 5.110) for Cyprus.[40] The significance of his name foreshadows Onesilus' end, a narrative in which heroization, cultural valorization and civic memory prevail. Moreover, the mention that Aristocyprus elicits of a Solonian poem glorifying his father, Philocyprus, further strengthens the cultural and political impact of the Cypriot claim to a Greek past. While reference to the Solonian poem alludes to the political propaganda of honour and ethnic recognition that can be seen to drive Onesilus' 'national' revolt, the reference to the Athenian poet is also likely to engage with his audiences' take on the contemporary topic of Cypriot emancipation and rejection of Persian rule in the context of Athenian *archē*.[41] At the same time, proper names function as ideological tools: Aristocyprus, 'the best of Cypriots'; Philocyprus, 'the friend of Cypriots'. As in the very first *logos* of Book 5, onomastics emerges as a narrative tool that defines the Cypriot city-kingdoms and their rulers: it marks locations, ethnic identities and rivalries that reflect the complexities of Cypriot emancipation.[42]

'BENEFICENT' HERO

In the aftermath of the defeat, Herodotus tells us that the people of Amathous engage in symbolic retaliation against the leader of the Revolt who was also the besieger of their city: '. . . in revenge for his having laid siege to their town, they severed the head of Onesilus from the dead body, took it to Amathous, and hung it up above their gates' (5.114.1). While we learn nothing about the way Onesilus died, we are informed that this violent decapitation was soon subjected to a positive turn:[43] 'In time it became hollow, and was occupied by a swarm of bees, who filled it with honeycomb. In consequence of this the townspeople consulted an oracle, and

---

[40] The king evokes the paradigmatic Solonian Tellus of 1.30–1: I owe this idea to Liz Irwin.

[41] Waters (1985) 29–30 has pointed out that although Herodotus presents a lengthy treatment of Solon's interview with Croesus in Book 1, the only explicit reference to Solon's poetry (which he dubs 'propagandist') is here in relation to Cyprus. But here it is prudent to wonder about later propaganda which may have been served by narratives of Solon's connection to Cypriot Soli, namely Athens of the 450s on which see Irwin (2005b) 150 n. 101, and see below on Onesilus and Cimon.

[42] Other sources testify to how and why names change in the service of ethnic propaganda in Cypriot ethnography: for more on onomastics and Cypriot ethnicity, see Serghidou (2006).

[43] Onesilus' posthumous 'paradoxical valorization' is most likely connected with the omission of any description of the moment and manner in which he died (Hdt. 5.113; cf. a similar lacuna in the death of Dorieus, Hdt. 5.46, 48). Boedeker (2003) has used Onesilus as an example in her recent demonstration of the 'prosaic' value of these Herodotean omissions which evidently offer a different (e.g. non-Homeric) model of glorious death; on classical models of glorious deaths see Loraux (1986) and Vernant (1982b). See also Bremmer (1983) 107 who calls the episode an example of 'supranormal status for an abnormal death'.

were advised to take the head down and bury it, and, if they wished to prosper, to regard Onesilus thenceforward as a hero, and to honour him with an annual sacrifice. This was done, and the ceremony was still observed in my day . . .' (5.114.1–115.1). The violent decapitation of Onesilus, and the implicit connotations of his unburied body lacking repose, will testify to an ambiguous heroization, both reflecting the tension of the revolt and the internal rivalry of the communities. The infestation by the bees may seem to condemn the act of decapitation when coupled with an oracle that transports Onesilus from infamy to the 'highest honour'.[44] Indeed, Onesilus becomes a hero, and even a god.[45]

The bee-filled skull is an unusual event, and one that prompts the characters of Herodotus' text to solicit an interpretation in the form of consultation of an oracle. Correspondingly, it poses an interpretative problem for readers as to how to frame this event and Herodotus' narrative of it. The event is described in neutral terms (τούτου δὲ γενομένου τοιού-του . . ., 5.114.1–2), and therefore falls short of constituting a proper *thōma* narrative. Instead, the event evokes in modern scholarship the application of two contradictory frameworks by which to understand its significance, one barbarian and one Greek. Hartog and Petit, among others, have fruitfully examined the decapitation of Onesilus and the ritual treatment of his skull in anthropological terms within non-Greek practices dealing with the treatment of dead enemies and the apotropaic qualities of their skulls, a practice with which Herodotus shows himself familiar in conjunction with the Trausi (4.103), figures who appear prominently a second time at the start of Book 5 (5.4).[46] The non-Greek framing of the event is all the more prominent through the further Phoenician and orientalizing associations evident in its infestation by bees.[47] In contrast, others see it in more familiar Greek terms, a 'prodigious' incident attending situations marked

---

[44] So Hartog (1988) 158. Condemnation may be too strong a term: Herodotus does not mention any collective suffering needing to be appeased by proper care for Onesilus' skull (as, for instance, at 1.167). Instead, it is stressed that the oracle was not spontaneous or unsolicited, rather a choice exercised by the Amathousians to respond to the strange occurrence (τούτου δὲ γενομένου τοιούτου – ἐχρέωντο γὰρ περὶ αὐτῆς οἱ Ἀμαθούσιοι – ἐμαντεύθη σφι τὴν μὲν . . .). For human choice exercised in oracular narratives of Book 5, see 5.1.2 and 5.79 (on which see Irwin, p. 52 above and Haubold, Ch. 9 above).

[45] See, for example, Athenagoras of Athens, *Legatio* 14.1: 'Even those who accuse us of atheism for not acknowledging the same gods they know do not agree with each other about the gods: the Athenians set up Celeus and Metaneira as gods . . . the Amathousians, Onesilus . . .'

[46] Hartog (1988) 156–62, Petit (1996) 110–11 n. 102, (2004) 14–15. On the Greek aspects of the Trausi portrayal see Irwin, p. 62 above.

[47] Compare *Judges* 14:8–20 (see Voutiras (2000) 380) which is of broader interest for our passage, as the editors have noted: the Amathousian recourse to an oracle in order to interpret their bee-infested skull is complemented by Samson making the phenomenon of a lion's bee-filled carcass the answer to what he deems an impossible riddle.

by calamities and unfortunate incidents, often diseases, and one that elicits the traditional processes of heroization:[48] within this framework the *logos* is construed as the rationalized process of heroization ordered and sealed by the oracle and the institution of the annual cult that followed: a roughly standard mode of heroization of 'historical persons'.[49] It is this affinity with Greek practice that causes Petit to dub Herodotus here as 'misobarbaros' in portraying the Amathousian act of decapitation as barbarous, and the whole narrative as an example of *interpretatio graeca*.[50]

This no doubt it is, but perhaps it is worth considering that it may be conspicuously so. Our discussion of Herodotus' Cypriot *logos* has explored how he engages with the cultural ambivalence of Cyprus. If this is correct, his narrative of Onesilus' skull may well be designed to provide an example of cultural syncretism, and an implicit invitation to his audience to choose between ways of framing this event: will they see it as comparable to that of the Trausi whom they have just encountered in the narrative (4.103; cf. 5.4), or as something framed in more Hellenic terms, a barbaric act of decapitation eliciting divine response? In neither case will such stark choices be unproblematic if one follows closely the narrative that Herodotus provides us – each will generate paradox: a well-established barbarian practice would require no oracle for interpretation, while, if the event is seen with Greek lenses, there has been no divine disfavour to appease – the oracle is apparently sought without compulsion. The failure to comply with either narrative pattern may well suggest syncretism, and the corresponding cultural ambiguity may be the point of Herodotus' portrayal. Who exactly are these Amathousians? How are we to understand their actions?

The skull filled with bees is something that requires interpretation no less than the career of Onesilus, which may be summed up in his name, the 'useful one': is his name significant? That will depend not only on whom one asks, the Amathousians or other Cypriots, but also when, for the Amathousian verdict on Onesilus changes after the revolt. The besieger becomes the 'beneficent': the Amathousians bring together the phenomenon with a solicited oracle and in essence activate the meaning of his *onoma* to derive the 'benefit' lying in it.[51]

If Onesilus – skull, career, even name – requires interpretation, no less does Herodotus' narrative of the Cypriot Revolt. The strange bee-filled

---

[48] Rhode (1952) 147 (Fr. trans.), Voutiras (2000) 380.

[49] Farnell (1921) 361–72; see also Voutiras (2000) 380, who examines the comparable heroization of Cleomenes. Harrison (2000) 158–64 provides a recent survey of Herodotean examples of heroization.

[50] Petit (2004) 15.

[51] This parallels the success the Paeonians derive from activating the meaning of an *onoma* in conjunction with an oracle: see Irwin, p. 46 above.

skull leaves readers contemplating how they should interpret it. Regardless of whether it is to be seen in a Greek or non-Greek framework – either case generating ambiguities that match the cultural, ethnic and political status of Cyprus itself – there is another framework in which we must see this *logos*, namely Herodotus' narrative itself. For, as Munson's contribution so astutely observes (p. 165 above), heads have had a peculiar function in the wider Ionian Revolt narrative: the fate of Onesilus' head joins that of the ship's captain Scylax (5.33) and Histiaeus' slave (5.35) in punctuating the *termini* of these revolt narratives, ultimately foreshadowing the final head of the narrative, the one that marks the revolt's failure and end, the embalmed head of its decapitated instigator, Histiaeus (6.30).[52]

Here we may return to Onesilus. What clearly characterizes Onesilus is the political role he assumes within the context of Ionian–Persian politics. A historical agent who in life failed to correspond to any mythological heroic figure of the past, in death Onesilus is very much a hero of the present.[53] As a hero of the present, we have considered how his life and heroization require not only a religious, but also a political interpretation that engages with the political and ethnic differences of the communities involved in the revolt. The response of Amathous to his skull illustrates a change in orientation over time, and that orientation most likely reflects an altered response to Persia: famous as the only city to refuse to join in the revolt – the year in which Cyprus was 'free' – the establishment and performance of cult for Onesilus distance the present-day people of Amathous from that medizing past.[54]

We may now turn to how his continued worship reflects on Cypriot complexities that reverberate beyond the more ostensible and narrow temporal confines of Herodotus' narrative. With his final word on Onesilus (ʼΑμαθούσιοι μέν νυν ἐποίευν ταῦτα καὶ τὸ μέχρι ἐμεῦ, 'The Amathousians were doing this and do so even up to my day', 5.115.1), Herodotus brings Onesilus and his narrative down to his audience's present day. Here the continued worship of a figure whose life was defined by leading rebellion against Persia would no doubt evoke for audiences more recent events where ambiguities of Cypriot identity interacted with ambiguities in Cypriot political alignment, that is, the decades of the 450s and 440s with another instigator

---

[52] See Greenwood, p. 143 above. I owe this point about the function of the decapitations to Liz Irwin. For death more generally as a symbolic boundary in Herodotus: see Darbo-Peschanski (1988).

[53] See Vandiver (1991).

[54] Indeed, if one interprets the hanging of the enemy's skull as barbarian, the subsequent burial and sacrifice to it in hero cult re-enacts a change from barbarian/Persian orientation to one that is Greek, perfectly in line with a *post hoc* embracing of the leader of a revolt from Persia.

of revolt from Persia, the figure of Cimon.[55] The direct parallelism of the
two political figures, though not explicit in the *Histories*, helps us to evaluate
Onesilus' role in Herodotus' narrative of the politics of Cypriot emancipation, and the role of his heroization as expressing a commitment to Hellenic
identity.

Cimon uncannily exemplifies a process of heroization parallel to that
of Onesilus. The Athenian commander, inhumed in Attica along with
a number of other illustrious rulers (Paus. 1.29.15), was honoured by a
heroic cult in the Phoenician kingdom of Citium, in Cyprus (Plut. *Cim.*
19.4). The honour attributed to Cimon depends upon the same process of
heroization and civic remembrance as that of Onesilus, though in this case
the cult is founded as a response to pestilence and famine that oppressed
the population. As with Onesilus, the order came from an oracle that
instructed the population to remember Cimon (μὴ ἀμελεῖν Κίμωνος),
evidently considered to be the cause of the calamities. This cult of Cimon
reiterates the process of heroization applied to Onesilus with an Athenian
touch, and the date of its foundation is uncertain, but no doubt a cult
of Cimon would have taken on particular salience in the mid-390s when
Conon took refuge in Cyprus, and both Athens and Cyprus were keen to
represent his actions with a Persian fleet as Greek.[56] In both cases, then,
the establishment of hero cult of an anti-Persian figure – one Salaminian,
one Athenian – can be used to articulate a contemporary political position:
the community who establish this cult distance themselves from their pro-
Persian position of the past, whether that of Amathus in rejecting the revolt
or that of Citium in opposing Cimon; at the same time, they perform their
new commitments to a free Cypriot – that is, Greek – identity.

The parallelism between Onesilus and Cimon alludes to pro-Hellenic
propaganda: both examples of heroization are representative elements of
retrospective anti-Persian propaganda in which ritual from the present seeks
to neutralize and transform how the past is remembered: a historical enemy
becomes a cult hero whose ritual allows the past to be both remembered
and altered. In the case of the Herodotean Onesilus, through the cult of the
only city which resisted the revolt, he emerges as a guarantor of ideological
cohesion and a signifier of a momentary liberty while also reflecting the
local interests of the Cypriot *hegemones* towards Persian expansionism. And
yet, his ambiguous reception in Herodotus suggests an ironic take on that

[55] See Petit (2004) 10, who likewise sees a parallel between the expedition of Cimon in 450/449 and
the siege of Onesilus.
[56] Plutarch chooses to refer to the cult precisely in this context: *Cim.* 19.3. For a brief account of the
history around this event see Osborne and Rhodes (2003) no. 11. I thank Liz Irwin for this point.

post hoc framing. Onesilus does not emerge as a national hero, indeed he is only an Amathousian – that is, a sectional – hero. The particularity of the cult gestures to a more fundamental difficulty at the heart of the Cypriot Revolt and its hero. Just as Cypriot collective action has been characterized and undermined by the sectional interests of the disparate internal politics of each city-kingdom, its hero Onesilus can also be read as an opportunist, exploiting local political differences instead of embodying a real and uniform aspiration to independence.[57]

As such, Onesilus' ambiguous character bears comparison with his fellow instigator of revolt, Aristagoras, whose death his own anticipates (5.126). The parallelism between these two revolt leaders generates comparison of Ionians and Cypriots more widely. Briant demonstrated how difficult it is to use the idea of 'national consciousness', at least at the beginning of the Ionian Revolt, and the same may be said for Cyprus.[58] Herodotus presents a Cyprus that reflects and refracts the agents, collectivities, and events of the main narrative. While the Athenians abandon the Ionians in their efforts to sustain revolt (5.103) in a move that anticipates their kindred Ionians' reaction to Cyprus (5.115), the depiction of the sectional Cypriots allows their revolt, in turn, to foreshadow what is yet to come in the Ionian Revolt when various Ionian contingents will desert to the detriment of the whole (6.14). Interlaced as it is with the story of Sardis (its capture, 5.100–3, announcement to Darius, 5.105–7, and immediate consequences, 5.116), the Cypriot *logos* functions as a microtheme for the exploration of revolt, and its apparent motivations, chief among which was freedom.[59]

Evidently, in the Cypriot case, freedom was only a brief interlude in a history of enslavement: Κύπριοι μὲν δὴ ἐνιαυτὸν ἐλεύθεροι γενόμενοι αὖτις ἐκ νέης κατεδεδούλωντο ('The Cypriots then, freed for one year once again had been made slaves anew,' 5.116). Subjection, whether voluntary or not, is seen to have a circular movement which affects political development on the island. After the description of the last resistance of the kingdom of Soli,[60] Cyprus appears in the *Histories* (7.98) under the command of Xerxes, and represented in the contingent as among the most notable commanders is none other than Gorgus.[61] The Cypriot trajectory in the *Histories* will finish with a moral judgement, first expressed by Artemisia and later

[57] On the elite of Salamis see Briant (1996) 164; and see also Wiesehofer (1990), who explores the possibility of the Cypriot Revolt as the result of Onesilus' ambition and fraternal antagonism.
[58] Briant (1996) 165 and Yon (1981), who examines the difficult question of Cypriot Hellenicity.
[59] I thank the editors for drawing my attention to the parallelism of the two revolt narratives.
[60] See a vivid description of the revolt and the Soli resistance in Burn (1984) 202–5. On the consequences of submission, see Watkin (1987).
[61] Timoanax, the son of Timagoras, is also singled out there.

echoed by Mardonius. Artemisia brands the Cypriots, along with Egyptians, Cilicians and Pamphylians, as 'cowardly slaves' (κακοὶ δοῦλοι, 8.68.2γ). Subsequently, Mardonius blames the defeat at Salamis on Cypriot, Egyptian and Phoenician cowardice (8.100). In focusing on an interlude of Cypriot liberty, Book 5 suggests an alternative: when the Ionians propose revolt to the Cypriot rulers, the latter envisage a 'free Cyprus' (Κύπρος ἐλευθέρη, 5.109.2–3). However, the likelihood of this vision is called into question by the Ionians' reply, which reminds the Cypriots of ancestral slavery: 'And as for you, remember what you as slaves suffered from your masters the Persians, and be brave men' (ὑμέας δὲ χρέον ἐστι, ἀναμνησθέντας οἷα ἐπάσχετε δουλεύοντες πρὸς τῶν Μήδων, γίνεσθαι ἄνδρας ἀγαθούς – 5.109.3). The terms of the Ionians' appeal reflect a Hellenic ideology that privileged heroic vigour and the ideal of liberty.[62] Herodotus' narrative reflects conflicting Greek views about the position and character of Cyprus: out at sea between idealized Hellenic and Persian values and in the middle of competing geographies. As an audience we are left unsure about whether the Cypriot Revolt has been a significant interlude of freedom, or a chance aberration. This fundamental uncertainty provides a perfect double, enacted in miniature, of Herodotus' Ionian Revolt narrative and the brief interlude of Ionian freedom narrated in Books 5 and 6 and that yet to come.

---

[62] But of course this appeal is not without ironies when placed in the context of characterizations of the Ionians on offer in Books 4 and 6 (4.142 and 6.12), and in contemporary fifth-century discourse: see Introduction, pp. 19–25 above and see also Munson, Ch. 5 above.

CHAPTER 12

'The Fourth Dorian Invasion' and 'The Ionian Revolt' (5.76–126)

John Henderson

The Spartans are com–
The Persians are—
The Athenians –

Crossing the line.

Here at *this* book's wind-up, pause to stop-start what we are doing, half-way between reading and reflection {no man's land[1]}. In a rupturous moment that pulls drastically away from its narrated event so as to oblige attention to the project of narration,[2] find a passage that 'lies at the heart of the *Histories* in every way. It is placed very near the centre of the 9-book pedimental structure. As for its content' – ἱστορήτεον.[3]

The build-up to the fanfare of 5.76 will mean circling round, criss-crossing lanes, shunting back and forth until §10. {ἱστορικῶς;}

1. We have it coming to us. Read Herodotus. We must read Herodotus. What this prose epic wants and demands. So what call for writing does this monstrous invention posit or promulgate? What techno-logic (what dynamic?) harnesses all this feverish *work*, commands the onward march of these legion signs by the myriad?[4] There are so many 'great and marvellous feats to record, not least how come Greeks and non-Greeks warred

---

[1] Our editors convened a mighty colloquy, and (besides showing me what I meant, and *could* mean) have given me every encouragement, plus the benefit of their work in progress and wise counsel.

[2] Harrison (2000) 203 highlights 5.76 (with its antediluvian star Codrus – 'Who burned the cakes?') as marked Herodotean irruption of 'the long view': the past *shown* as 'continuous whole' is vindicated by iterability therein. Immerwahr (1966) 151 remarks the rhetorical (form/thought) fabric of momentousness here. Munson (2001b) 213 points straight to the Thucydidean-Herodotean keynote of the lowering of the Spartan threshold from six-century reluctance to campaign beyond the Peloponnese (Hdt. 5.75, 77, 93; 76 → Thuc. 1.23.6, 118.2, ἢν μὴ ἀναγκάζωνται, 'only under compulsion') to eagerness for the fray in 431 BC.

[3] Fowler (2003) 315, on 5.78, 'This celebrated passage lies . . . structure. As for its content, the expulsion of Athens' tyrants resulted in the foundation of the democracy; this is Athens' internal version of the grander theme of the *Histories*, liberation from the threat of Persian tyranny.'

[4] For this *kind* of enquiry, see Derrida (1996).

on each other' (*Preface*).[5] This stylish polemological project is busy staking
out a cosmos impelled by imperialist drives through isomorphism with its
textual articulation, systematically interrogating humanity through conflict of narremes (dialectical clash, told *as* story). 'Imperialism was a *nomos*.'
(T)history follows sovereign empires as they absorb, more than terrain, territories. 'There was an internal dynamic to the rise and fall of empires that
forced them to conform to the ebb and flow of history'.[6] To tell us why?,
ultimately, our Persian stand-ins and spokesmen, who will have been denied
the opportunity to live or read through the hawk debacles and dove car-
nage that lie ahead of them but tell true behind us, will take Herodoteans
all the way back to (re-read) the cardinal moment of Persian ascendancy
through subjugation of the Medes[7] and provocation of Lydian counter-
insurgency (1.73, 75). Straightmen to all-wise/all-conquering/empire-
founding Cyrus, they still serve up commonsense *Machtpolitik* echoing
through the endzone – at, and past, the very end of the *Histories* (9.122.2):

ἐπεὶ Ζεὺς Πέρσῃσι ἡγεμονίην διδοῖ, ἀνδρῶν δὲ σοί, Κῦρε, κατελὼν Ἀστυά-
γην, φέρε, γῆν γὰρ ἐκτήμεθα ὀλίγην καὶ ταύτην τρηχέαν, μεταναστάντες ἐκ
ταύτης ἄλλην σχῶμεν ἀμείνω. εἰσὶ δὲ πολλαὶ μὲν ἀστυγείτονες, πολλαὶ δὲ
καὶ ἑκαστέρω, τῶν μίαν σχόντες πλέοσι ἐσόμεθα θωμαστότεροι. οἰκὸς δὲ
ἄνδρας ἄρχοντας τοιαῦτα ποιέειν· κότε γὰρ δὴ καὶ παρέξει κάλλιον ἢ ὅτε
γε ἀνθρώπων τε πολλῶν ἄρχομεν πάσης τε τῆς Ἀσίης;

Now that Zeus hands supremacy to Persians and to you over mankind by taking
down Astyages, come (you know the land we own doesn't amount to a whole lot
and what there is of it is rough stuff), let's up sticks and move, get outa here and
take over some other land that's better; there are plenty of 'em that belong to the
cities next door and plenty farther away, and if we take one of these we'll have
more admirers. *It's standard practice for men who are running things to behave this
way* – when oh when will a finer chance come along than the moment when we
are running plenty of peoples, the whole of Asia?

For they listened, all the same, when their model emperor denied this plain
unvarnished fact of life, bidding his hardy people stay put, not soften up –
and they '*never never ever will be slaves*' (ibid. 4, . . . ἄλλοισι δουλεύειν).

---

[5] Cf. Lateiner (1989) 14 on the implied promise of state-of-the-art writing (and thinking). The Thucydidean arch-text (1.23.6): τοὺς Ἀθηναίους ἡγοῦμαι μεγάλους γιγνόμενους . . ., 'The Athenians
top my list, their rise to greatness . . .'

[6] Evans (1991) 38–40, 'The imperialist impulse', cf. Hornblower (1987) 30. This is Xerxes' pitch (7.8):
'Men of Persia, I shall not innovate in installing this *nomos* among you, rather I shall continue to
operate it as I have inherited the thing. As I'm told by our elders, *we have never yet rested on our
laurels*, ever since we took over supremacy from the Medes when Cyrus took down Astyages . . .' (see
9.122, below, × 2). He can be heard – but heeded?

[7] This involves Persian *revolt* from Media (1.125.1, 3, ἀπίστασθαι), followed by unsuccessful – one-
sentence – counter-revolt by the Medes against Darius (1.130.2, ἀπέστησαν. Greeks such as Thucydides exact nominal revenge by calling Persians *Medes*). *Revolt* also gets tarred as ephemeral by the
crushed Babylonian and Egyptian uprisings (3.150–9, 7.2.1, 7: ἀπέστησαν).

Who's listening to *them*? Is this Persian, parochial, savvy . . . – can any reader of Greek inhabit the thinking? (Can *any*?) Herodotus' writing situates itself as the requisite technology for registering the vast political economy of militarized space reticulated by Persian might and its accelerating agenda of ventures, on the stocks, in the pipeline, twinkling in the imperial eye.[8] Along its strategic roads, through its express post, this horse-powered organization makes the running. A speeding dromocracy in its wake, in its sights.[9] From a slow-burning – cool – stop-at-home/sit-on-Helot-and-Peloponnese Spartan point of view, the Persian metropolis is 'three months' too far from the Ionian seaboard, whereas Herodotus is here, *un*-fazed, to make mileage for the *Histories* out of conducting us along this communications-transport-information super-highway, '90 days @ 150 stades per diem' (5.50.1–2): 'nothing in this world could beat the Persian pony express for speed'. The whole deal is the breakthrough that *made* them: however many days a journey takes, there are that many mounts and men stationed along the royal road of Persia – '@ 1 horse + 1 human per diem'. Snow, rain, heat, darkness . . . – nothing but nothing can stop these mailmen completing their successive stretches a.s.a.p. (Known in Persian as the *Angareion* run.) This superb engine of hot-shot empire ran at its slickest and smoothest when transmitting, in quickfire succession, the newsflash of Xerxes' capture of Athens, then of his contretemps at Salamis, zenith to nadir post-haste (8.98–9).[10]

---

[8] Egypt is the yardstick of enormity beggaring all memory techniques: e.g. their long bare lists of multigenerational Pharaoh dynasties on the priests' rolls are all that the *Histories* would supersede {transcend}; those vacant signs', the pyramids', orgy of number-crunching; the toll of generations up to 11,340 years – crushing Hecataeus' calculus (2.100–1, 124–8, 142–3). Darius' Persian machine spews out figures for its print-out marvel of satrap organization spilling into *mappa mundi* (3.89–97; 98–117); Scythia computes as telephone numbers in virtual space spinning into cartographic mockery (4.2–15, cf. 46–86; 36–45). *The* sum will be Xerxes' muster of fighting men, of fighting men plus batmen, camp-followers, and all (7.60–80, 184–6: approx. 5,283,320). Cf. Christ (1994) 171, 175.

[9] See Virilio (1986), cf. Der Derian (1998). Thus Asia Minor west of the River Halys is 'a five days' journey if you're travelling fast and light' (1.72.3); speed-merchant Cyrus promised 'he'd get to Media sooner than Astyages would want . . .' (1.127.2); the space-as-time dimensions of Egypt, 'four months by land or water' to plumb the desert (2.5–11); Cambyses' 'three days' of invasion plus 'twelve days' of water-pipeline (3.5, 9); Darius' kingship is figured as cossack ride-out from Persia (3.88.3, 89.3); Scythian cybernauts steer by 'a ship's summertime log' (4.86); 'ten-day hops' space the trek between oases from Egypt to Cadiz, featuring a '30-day leap' to the Lotus Eaters (4.180–4). The crannies and passes, straits and narrows, of Hellas will cramp the style of those dashing lords of the Persian steppes . . .

[10] Terrorists and freedom fighters must resort to inefficient-insecure-under-cover intelligence operations, as when (1) Aristagoras gets the scalp-tingling word to revolt by cropping Histiaeus' messenger ('just tattoo, then wait for the hair to grow back over it again') (5.35), and (2) Sparta gets word of Xerxes' (four-year) build-up for operation Hellas by tablets from Demaratus, whose decipherment depended on the nous of Gorgo daughter of Cleomenes, again – only now, wife of Leonidas (7.239).

This planet is expanding, not shrinking. {The panoptic Caesars' implo-
sion must wait.}[11] Its pioneer explorer and art-of-the-state documentarist
accounts for power, maps dominions, fronts, hot-spots, and targets. Pulling
in distant borders, opening up new horizons, his pages are needed (they
prove it, over and again) to archive and access all accessible archives, they
translate, inter-articulate, network, a heating globe of seething difference
{culture/s}.[12] Insistently stationed at each farthest staging-post and vantage point on the edge of knowable landscape, we press on to world's ends,
guess on into the beyond no empire can yet own.[13] Within the tale, this
Halicarnassian radar operates on a screen powered by Persian-generated
electricity, for all that it speaks its Greek to *any* embryonic superpower, to
all palace watchers, whether close to home or in whatever world to come
way out west.[14]

Every scene/moment hooks up with every other stitched into the book,
insists the telling sentence/moment, and far beyond. Reaching out to stories (to be) told otherwheres, before and since.[15] Knotted to 'our war',
but segueing, too, into the future's sequel and into future sequels. As we
are prodded, reminded to recall, thematize, recoup, and internalize; and
invited, encouraged to project, construe, conjecture, and imagine . . .[16]

2. So, yes, these stories, these imperial stories, frame knowledge along the
way, they power their own way ahead.[17] And then, some place, guns and
narratives will seize up and jam. One rise see-saws into the next fall (1.5.4),

---

[11] For Ika Willis, work in progress.

[12] This book-culture will create the culture it transmits. By transmitting (its) culture.

[13] So Egypt, up to Elephantine vs. beyond (2.29; cf. 2.99); Persia off, through India and Arabia, past
Ethiopia to the blur of the East (3.115); Scythia, up to the Hyper-boreans, and on (4.16); Libya into
the Sahara, then into the dark continent (4.180, 185); Thrace, and its murky back of beyond (5.9).

[14] Thus (1) Darius' forces swoop *instantly* to run down the Ionian-Athenian coalition forces after their
sack of Sardis, then recover the rebel towns 'at a rate of one a day' (5.102; 117), and (2) Darius
discovers 'most of Asia' for geography, by a combination of circumnavigation with invasion (4.44),
cf. Christ (1994). Whose error is it when the Persian master-race rules distance from Persia on a
scale of inferiority (1.134.2)? The vital statistic is the Persians' endemic inter-cultural biddability, so
cultural malleability (1.135): contrast Egyptian and Scythian immunity to otherness (2.79, 91; 4.76.1,
127).

[15] The story withheld: e.g. Cleomenes' fellow ~~liberationist~~, who paid with his life/obliviation in Athens
(5.72.4): 'Timesi-theus of Delphi, of whose deeds of strength and resolution I would have *g-g-great*
tales to tell . . .' (His *name* is plenty great enough? Cf. Lateiner (1989) 59–75, 'Selection: explicit
omission'.)
    Flash-forwards: e.g. 5.32, King Pausanias 'in time to come', when he'd fallen for the 'Dictator of
Hellas' idea; or the book-end anti-climax in footnote 3.160.2 '(The self-sacrificing pretend-deserter
Persian patriot . . .) [W]*hose* son was (would be) the commander in Egypt lined up against Athens
and allies {subjects}, and *his* son was (to be) deserter to Athens from Persia.'

[16] On Herodotean topicality: esp. Raaflaub (1987) 235–7. Pinning him to the late 420s: Blösel (2001)
179–80, esp. 186. The historicality of the *Histories*, however, {farthers} lies *in* history.

[17] See Munson (2001b).

and still the Herodotean world can but narrate it the way it's come to be; the way it is coming to be (itself). *His* Hellas and barbarian Asia clock up marvels to relate, until he calls time, stalls them at the lights, paused ready to plunge on into the re-runs that must, that will, that have already, come his and his reader's way. Through the moment of his inscription and the trajectory of reception, he knows and shows, future convulsions will heave and burst *his* bounds, onto some yet wider screen. Alexander's Macedon {*not* Herodotus' Alexander of Macedon, attempting to ally Athens *with* Persia, 8.141–4, 9.44–6} will play a 'Xerxes' in negative, defeated by *success.* Then, with the incorporation of Egypt, the post-*Roman* world must emerge to trace and re-trace those – its – limits, over and again. The . . . First World's Eastern Front/the Eastern Bloc.

3. 'Same thing' had (will have) already happened, to Persia. To recap: displacement of the Medes put Persia on the map for Hellas (1.73, 130). Fated Croesus' Lydia attempted pre-emptive strike (46) before the drive west brought Cyrus' squadrons to the Ionian seaboard. Which *was* the 'great' barbarian empire? (54, 91: Lydia or Persia – 'leather-clad' Persia, 71). Which, pray, was the 'great' Greek outfit? (56–8: Sparta – 'who? where?' (asked Cyrus), 153.1, or Athens – 'who? where?' (asked Artaphernes, and Darius), 5.73.2, 105.1).[18] Marching south through Egypt under Cambyses was maddening but made sense, just: planted a {Napoleonic} limit to sense, that is, in out-of-it unassimilable upside-down land.[19] Marching north across the Danube, Darius' compulsion, led away from Greece[20] – led nowhere, to endless boundless townless stateless ungraspable unassimilable ~~nowhereland~~.[21] As we (will) have seen, Book 5 showcases might-have-beens of its own. More than any 'theme', these make up the *Histories* and

---

[18] So with the Paeonians (Darius asking) at 5.13.2. For 1.56–8 and the rise of (which? Which political animal? Tyrannized or tyrannous? Isegoric, democratic – *and* despotic, world-conquering?) Athens: Gray (1997).

[19] In Persian mythology, Cambyses *is* {just is, forever} the Δεσπότης ('Master', to Cyrus' 'Father' and Darius' 'Grocer' (3.89.3).

[20] Bent on prioritizing his strike on Scythia, but derailed by Atossa at 3.134, Darius sent 'the first Persians to come from Asia to Hellas' (3.138.4). Bent on prioritizing his post-Ionian Revolt retribution on Greece, and kept by Mardonius from diversion by revolt to Egypt at 7.6, the newly enthroned Xerxes sends an army to crush that, and tools up for war on Athens (nominally), but Hellas (for real: 7.1–20; 138).

[21] 'Scythians – otherwise unlovable – have managed the single most important target for all mankind with the most wisdom: no invader can get away in one piece and if they don't want to be found no one can catch 'em . . . : , ἄμαχοί τε καὶ ἄποροι προσμίσγειν' (4.46.2–3, 'unbeatable – no way through to get in amongst them'). Correspondingly, they cannot relate to compromised, trapped, minnows like Ionians, 'the least men in all humanity, whether free or enslaved' (4.142.3: Scyths would *not* make historians). Clued-up Xerxes knows Greeks are farmers not nomads, so vincible, but can't hear Artabanus' advice (to us) that 'land-'n'-sea' are the enemy of all Armadas (7.50.4; 49).

their history: on the grandest scale, Persian irruption into Hellas would have meant rubbing out a Herodotean history of Persia, to be replaced by (1) imperial monuments planting Persian domination across its provincial satrapies new and old, plus (2) the view from the Greek West, a re-drawn focalization from Sicily and all points away through Thurii to Spain.[22]

4. Very likely, it nearly did, and the shadow scenario would imprint the Mediterranean future. But 'for now', overrunning Hellas jammed, the Ionian shoreline proved unassimilable, and historical narration choked. Between Herodotus' Persian Wars and his recounting of them, the ineluctable onward tramp of empire supplanting empire, opening up ever grander panoramas of peoples, interaction between cultures, and software for systematizing, weighing up, ordering human calculability, bogged down, lost shape, drove itself round the bend, back in its tracks: Athenians are (currently) where Herodotus left them (forever) dangling. So long as Herodotus is read, they are perpetually picking themselves for the new Persians, pushing on for Ionia as if to be a line to hold, or will it be Sardis next,[23] Lydia again, even, will they ever learn, when? And next, will it be, is it, on for Sicily and the West? *Because* formerly Persia's woulda-been 'next' adventure, so it must go, the *Histories* already tell as much. Would Spartans go to war against the new empire? First invading Athens; then moving onto the Aegean. The psychosis of Thucydides' narrative drive – toward Spartan admirals, Persian money, Athens thrust back into Attica, history re-wound. The *Histories* has all this up its sleeve, and none of it can last.[24]

5. Herodotus' story stoppers history's onward expansion toward pansophy: what superpower will ever own all (knowledge-power)? He writes

[22] The pioneer navigator Phocaeans sail for new lives in the Adriatic, Etruria, Spain; sage Bias urges all Ionia to decamp to the 'greatest' island fortress of Sardinia (1.161–70); Dr Democedes of Croton eggs Darius on against Hellas before returning home with the first Persian forces out West, and setting up as Quite Somebody (3.129–37); failing rebel Aristagoras considers melting away to Sardinia before plumping for Thrace – and instant extinction, to polish off our book (5.124.2–126.2).

[23] Which is to say, Sardis *again*, already sacked by Persia (1.84, 88.3), already torched by Ionians all (5.98–102, provoking Persian revenge in Greece, 102.1).

[24] Take *any* scenario where, say, a Spartan troop of marines hits *Samos*, currently destabilizing the area by developing weapons of mass destruction under its dictator, scattering political exiles to lobby for his overthrow (3.39, 44–56; next instalment at 3.139–49, Darius' first scalp: 143.2, 'Not, so it seems, at all keen to be free people . . .'). These very same Samians don't *go away*, not ever. Think of Herodotus noting that he can but *won't* remember to name that certain Samian bandit (4.43.7). Of Thucydides' last book agonizing over self-Samian loyalty to Attic democracy when Athens itself revolted into oligarchy under the 400 in 411 BC, all the way through to a final glimpse of Alcibiades safe in port there in the penultimate chapter (8.108.2). Or take a *Corinth*, perpetually locked in intermittent atrocity with its satellite *Corcyra* (3.48: τὰ Κερκυραϊκά, Thuc. 1.118.1) . . . – but, then, take *every* footprint planted in this textual Hellasia, and we are inevitably reading back forward to the fifth-century present it subtends, and toward the post-Thucydidean episodes, and series, it must envisage. {Read on. Geographies grid temporalities.}

himself into a wall, the paradox of heroism; and casts the future as ironic repetition of momentum frustrated, mistakes unlearned, a mess of uncomprehending blockage. Of course there had been faux pas, always, along the way. Upstarts who didn't see their place, extra players crowding in, briefly, from the wings. When the major powers backslid, there were Scyths and (even) Argos, acting up, for a while or so (1.106, 4.1, 7.20; 1.1, 7.149). Indeed, the repetitious structures that captured the stasis of history as it approached its present fix had also helped block out the frame for measuring the impetus of the expanding past. As the ?Ionian Revolt? serves to crash historical change into the buffers that await runaway democratic Athens, earlier narratives chop and sliver into fragmenting bites of wildly cumulating iteration, time slowed to melodramatic crawl forfeits explicative force, and the pontoon of geopolitics sticks, then busts.

It had gone as mad as Cleomanes, going along with the less-than-historical Scyths' plan for revenge on Persian invasion by breaking into Persia caught in a pincer movement with Sparta marching East from Ionia (6.84). Crazy as Xerxes, crucially, as he outmassed all rivals – you name 'em – Darius' host in Scythia, the Scythian horde that provoked it by flooding into the Asian heartland, Homer's Trojan booklaunch, or the earlier Mysian-Trojan incursion through Thrace as far as the damn Peneus (7.20.2).[25] Xerxes – Xerxes should've dwelt on the message of Cyrus' drive against the Massagetae, Cambyses screwing up in Ethiopia, Darius in Scythia. Athens – Athens should dwell on Herodotus – on (mis)apprehensions acted out by Croesus, by Xerxes. Could any superpower see the aggressor as their own aggression, the rest of the story would give a grandstand view.[26]

6. Blitzkrieg and sortie. Along the warpath of thistory, empires must *ela(un)ein*, or they must *strateuein*, with *epi* + accusative. The road is long, stacked with ethnographical loot by the column.[27] And then comes the wreckoning. Medes vs. Persians, then Persians suppressed by Cyrus. Next up, 'Assyrian Babylon, Bactria, Sacae, Egypt, or Ionian sideshow?' (1.153): Babylon (178–200). So many plans, but the Messagetae would be there for good, and saw him off (201–16). Not, however, before the patriarch dreamed his succession: 'Darius with wings, one shadowing Asia, one Europe', crystallized fantasy of world-domination (209). Cambyses, athwart impossible Egypt (which had once, if inconsequentially, overrun Asia all the way

---

[25] Cf. Immerwahr (1966) 151 on 'AABB' structuration in this quatrain.   [26] *History* –

[27] E.g. Croesus' offerings listed at 1.50–2, 92–3 (as recalled at 5.36), Amasis' at 2.182; Indian goldrush at 3.97–8, tithe of Greek, ~~Persian,~~ spoils at 9.80–1; cf. Redfield (1985). Ruining his chances, Aristagoras maps the Persian world as *such* rich pickings for Sparta (5.49.8).

to Colchis, and on into Europe, to boot, Thracians, Scyths and all).[28] Cambyses, plotting a fleet for Carthage, taskforce to Ammon, espionage in Ethiopia (3.17), but the first declined, the second vanished, and the third reporting the word back that he'd 'never draw a bow this size' (19, 25, 26). Cambyses, in short, crazed, and dead, this implosive ~~conqueror~~'s legacy the reversionary, atavistic, curse on Persians 'if they were *ever* to submit to Medes' (35, 65).[29] Ethiopians were *out there* for good. Babylon comes round again: yet stays re-captured (3.150–9). But Scythia is Darius' bridge too far. Purporting to punish their aggression, but out to conquer for keeps, he is warned to keep to his own patch, and draw the only line he can, at the border (4.1–142). A combative intercontinental map of planet Earth, analeaping forward to incorporate knowledge down to Xerxes' present, is comple(men)ted by failed Persian adventuring in Libya (145–205). The task set for Book 5 was re-trenchment in Ionia. Straightening out the frontier: settlement.

Of campaigns so far, only the Scythian cascade all over Asia[30] has qualified as *esbolē* (1.103.3, 4.1.1, 119.3), along with Darius' response to it and the manoeuvres adopted to counter him there (4.123.1, 125.3–5 – × 4). With one paraded exception, which we come back to momentarily. Now the Paeonians have Megabazus' 'army driven against' them, and are circumvented because on guard against anticipated *esbolē* (5.2.2 vs. 15.1–2 × 2). The Ionian Revolt opens up with Aristagoras 'making a campaign against' Sardis – or rather, *not* campaigning, *if* that means campaigning personally, but staying in Miletus and appointing generals, to go burn the city unopposed, when the wind catches the fire from a thatched roof torched by some soldier or other (5.99). This cue for action motivates Persian revenge, as Darius heeds

---

[28] 2.102–6: dwarfing Darius' conquests (110), and everybody's, Pharaoh Sesostris' fleet and army left, not volumes of history, but a trail of pillars telling the world and his wife that his opponents were all cunts. Back home, berth of the cool, he reverted to true Egyptian type, parcelling out squares of taxable allotment, but crisscrossing the land with dykes to the point of wiping out horse-and-carriage traffic, and all possibility of communications/transport by road (109).

[29] Fittingly, Cambyses showed off his prowess with bow and arrow by shooting his own cupbearer – 'bull's eye!' (3.35). As for Ammon: 'Most Libyans don't give a toss *now* for the king of the Medes, and they didn't then, either' (4.197.1). Herodotus' Libyan *logos* contrives an epitaph for Persian incursion where they cannot belong in classic intonation, after-echoing into Book 5 (205: *literally* on the fate of worm-infested 'Phere-time'): ὡς ἄρα ἀνθρώποισι αἱ λίην ἰσχυραὶ τιμωρίαι πρὸς θεῶν ἐπίφθονοι γίνονται, 'Yea, so it comes to pass for mankind that overdone strong-arm vengeance doth provoke malevolence from the gods.'

Anybody out there (still) listening? (To this warning – and after-echo of Herodotus' origination of the Trojan War, 2.120.5.)

[30] This worldwide spree of chaotic over-running of all Asia right up to Egypt lasted 40 years, modelling '*non*-imperial' ~~geopolitics~~ (1.103–6). Contrast Cyrus' unified dream of pan-Asian tentacles – 'a vine radiating tendrils from one princess fanny' (1.108).

big-talking double-agent Histiaeus to promise *enough* to put the world back to rights, and hand him lucrative tribute from the greatest island there is – Sardinia (*Sardō*), to compensate for *Sardis* (get it: 5.106.6, cf. 6.2.1). Persian grasp of Western geography stops, with their empire, at the coastline of Ionia, their side of the islands, as Lydian Croesus had recognized (4.143; cf. 1.27). A year's flop in free Cyprus is followed up by the Persians smashing the Sardis arsonists, before 'driving the army against' Caria (5.116, 121, 122). Disasters on both sides undo the instigator, and (we saw) we fade in bathos as a sad caricature of Grand Debate on where to hole up proves the option of emigration to Thrace the wrong one. Besieged locals come out under a white flag and do for Aristagoras and his army both. Short and sardionic. The right man, we will have seen, always in the wrong place, or . . . – which way was it round?

The poetics – the metapolitics – of *esbolē* are the subject of this essay and the off-centre passage it approaches.[31]

7. *Éminence grise* Histiaeus' Miletus will face Persian 'armies driving' their way (6.6–7). Now, in the beginning, the Lydian precursors had in fact tried intensely sustained *esbolē* against Miletus, but were bamboozled into signing a treaty (1.14–18 × 5; + 1 for Clazomenae).[32] And at 'the second enslavement of Ionia', Cyrus repeated the formula, granting a treaty to prove his rule (1.169). Now the Milesian feud with offshore Naxos had brought 'Hell to Ionia for the second time of asking' (5.28.1), and will pay the price by capture and transportation of population, while the ringleader and headman Histiaeus is crucified, then decapitated: five years, and the revolt is over.[33] First Croesus (1.6.2, 26);[34] then the Persians, twice: this will be 'the third {completed} enslavement of {onshore} Ionia' (6.32).[35] Punishment of Athens and Eretria for Sardis, and Athens and Sparta for refusing token surrender to his diplomats (then murdering them, so dooming the future present of Herodotus' narration, 7.133–7), inflicts Marathon on Darius, in the process (1) dedicating fateful Plataea to Athens come what may

---

[31] Payen (1997) 133–244, 'Le Discours sur la conquête', esp. 135–62, 'Le Modèle de la conquête', plots the political narratology of *strateuesthai*, *stratēlatein*, etc. (esp. 147 on *stratiēn esballein* = signal to anticipate dramatic scene).

[32] When Athena gains a temple in exchange for Alyattes' recovery from plague, as the price of both Miletus and Lydia gaining both peace and each other as staunch allies, the invaders halt the already eleven-campaigns long waste of time wasting the harvest, simply by believing that *these* (long) city walls contain plenty, not epidemic. No Xerxes could ever sell himself such a pay-off story by buying such simple-mindedness; if (an) Archidamian war cabinet *could* wear it, this cap would fit exactly (an) Archidamnus' self-ironizing style of sophistic attrition (1.17–22).

[33] Cf. Evans (1976). For Ionia as dramatized analysis of rebellion: Forrest (1979). Many rounds later, Persian garrisons are being dislodged from Miletus as Thucydides' chronicle fades (8.109.1) . . .

[34] Cf. Dewald (1999).   [35] Cf. Nenci (1994) 270.

(6.108–111), and (2) obliging the King of Kings to step up revenge for that *esbolē* at Sardis with an 'army campaign against' Hellas multiplied many times over – when . . . the simultaneous call for a 'campaign against' Egypt in revolt proves too much for him, and Xerxes, talked out of Egypt by the need to stop anyone ever even thinking about 'campaigning against' his land, manages to crush the rebels by remote control (7.1–5). Sardis + Marathon on his lips, he drove his myriads west, through *mock-esbolē* into Lydia and Sardis (31.1), through a whole world of troops and crews in review. The 'campaigning army against' Hellas will process along the apparently pacified land route as far as Thessaly, where the Peneus' *ekbolē* blocks the way, mythic landmark of primeval, Titanic vulnerability Before the Flood (128–30). Total conquest of Hellas is in his sights (138.1), and the moment engorges correspondingly. Pressure will build until barring of the *esbolē* at Olympus, shielding all Hellas *inclusive* of Thessaly, is passed up (172.2), while the crossroads *esbolē* at Tempe is bypassed (173 – × 4), and so, finally, history debouches into *the esbolē*, viz. Leonidas', at Thermopylae (175 × 3; 196, 207, 217.2, 8.15.2).[36] The dam breached, all sorts of *esbolai* ensue in and around Thessaly (8.27–34), and the ultimate *esbolē* into Athens finally arrives (8.66.1, 144.5; 9.6, 7.B1, 17.1).

Into Athens-as-Hellas.

Fearful of Athenian–Persian alliance (oracles menaced Sparta with expulsion from their Peloponnese, 8.141.1), Sparta relinquishes the plan to bar the Isthmus,[37] as Athens screws Hellas to the sticking-point for Salamis and then *Plataea*, fateful Attic border village, again, and marked out for every Greek future (7.233.2).[38] In the campaign, too, the Persians will march out via *Decelea* (9.15.1), and *that* hamlet produces *the* Athenian star in the fighting, in accordance with more cherished Athenian lore (9.73):[39]

---

[36] To take *his* hot plunge through this gateway to Hellas, Pausanias emphatically aligns ἐς Θερμοπύλας with τὴν ἐς τὴν Ἑλλάδα Γαλατῶν ἐσβολήν (1.3.5, glossed with ἔφοδος . . . ἐσόδος at 1.4.1, 2), preparing for his last book's splash privileging Galatian bomb over Herodotus' splurge of Persian flop (10.19–23: without *esbolē*; cf. Hutton (2005) esp. 60, 192).

[37] The Spartan colonists of the almost-but-not-quite-island Cnidos had handed Delphi the chance to flag a peninsula as what Zeus had disjoined together and no man shall sunder: in waded the Persians (1.174). This is where Sparta *almost* signed up to handing all the Greek islands over to Persia, plus Hellas up to Boeotia, but admiral Lichas scrapped the deal – and the unholy alliance it cemented between *Sparta* and *satrap* (Thucydides 8.43: cf., finally, 109).

[38] Thus the third time lucky Peisistratid tyranny must begin by invasion from *Eretria* via *Marathon*, 'the first bit of Attica they held', where there congregated from both city and demes Athenians 'embracing tyranny before freedom' (sc. rather than force-marching the length of Attica to Athens to thwart barbarian occupation, 1.62).

[39] See Flower and Marincola (2002) 236–9 *ad loc.* For (the question of) topical relevance: Fornara (1971a) 34, (1981) 149–50, cf. Vandiver (1991) 70–1.

when, long, long ago, the sons of Tyndareus *esebalon* into Attica with a grand army after recovery of Helen, and were levering up whole demes, unable to get intelligence of where she'd been spirited away to, the story goes that the Deceleans (some say Decelus himself) were fed up with Theseus' gangsterism and agitated over the whole of Attica, and so they spilled the whole caboodle to them, leading their way straight to Aphidnae, which some local betrayed to them, those sons of Tyndareus. As a result of this business, the Deceleans have had the honorary freedom of Sparta and grandstand seats reserved for public events there, all the way through till now, and still in force, to such an extent that into the war that befell the Athenians and the Peloponnesians many years afterwards, when the Spartans vandalized the rest of Attica, they kept hands off Decelea.

'The Athenians', Herodotus just mouthed, 'themselves say {are saying? are forever saying or are saying "*right now*"?} that the Deceleans once did some business that is useful for all time', and then comes the ?explanation? . . .

The triumph of Plataea in invaded Hellas, we learn, will coincide with {its reflex and reversal} Mycale, the same day's sea-battle *in Ionia* (90.1: both of them next to shrines of Demeter *of Eleusis*, 101.1). *Milesians* posted to protect a line of retreat rat on Persia, leading survivors back into trouble and gleefully weighing in: this was 'the second Ionian Revolt' (104). Defeated remnants struggle to reach their king at Lydian *Sardis* (107.1). Herodotus means to cease ominously, with the Spartans off home, but the Athenians pressing on to the very doorstep of mainland Asia, stepping all too easily into the role of Oriental Despot by nailing a rogue to a plank and hoisting him aloft to watch his son stoned dead. You are reminded that the victim's ancestor was the one who came up with that commonsense move that failed to persuade Cyrus to shift his master race from their godforsaken hole of a wasteland. Let no Hellene (no Athenian) suppose that Persians be softie pushovers: 'they chose to live in an unpleasant land and rule rather than sow grain on a plain and be some other people's slaves' (122).[40] When we read here at the disfiguring death that the Athenians were led for both the victory at Mycale and the atrocity committed on the person of the rogue Artayctes by the general *Xanthippus*, we are left to project his lineage forward into the career of his son Pericles (affiliated at 6.131.2; Alcibiades' son, and (*the*) Alcibiades' father, Cleinias, served with distinction at Artemisium, 8.17, 'at his own expense . . . on his own ship'). Herodotus' final shot before the final fade sets up Artayctes' Calvary as the significant site for self-condemning hybris by citing rival accounts with locations at 'the headland where Xerxes yoked his crossing' vs. 'the hill above Madytus' (9.120): the impact of all this

---

[40] See Dewald (1997), Flower and Marincola (2002) 311–12. {And look at what happens to Alexander as (because) *he* 'became great' – another over-reaching Great . . . the new king of Persia.}

Reading Herodotus

was systematically prepared in every detail when Xanthippus, Artayctes, and the 'headland between Sestus and Madytus' entered the text at the 'yoking of the Hellespont' for Xerxes' return, when the crucifixion was anticipated in laboured flashforward (7.33, μετὰ ταῦτα, χρόνῳ ὕστερον οὐ πολλῷ . . .). Here at the narrative bridgehead that should divide Asia's spanking Great King from any sane Greek normalcy, this rending editorial punctum drives us between the two halves of the story of Herodotus' second-wave tragic Lydian guest-friend, the oracularly named *Pythius son of Atys*, through whose son's bisected body marched the Persian host (7.27–9, 38–40, πυνθάνομαι at 28.2, 35.1, 37.3; cf. Croesus' political map at 30.2: his son Atys at 1.34–45): making us watch Athenians making Artayctes watch his son stoned to death nails the moral: (all) sons are slaves to (all) tyrants (7.39.1). Herodotus nails the future to the tender mercies of history, of butchery.

8. '*Esbolē* into Attica' in Thucydides' world, of Herodotus' audiences, names the sanction expected from Sparta in case of a rift (1.58.1) and a prosaic, matter-of-fact, routine (114.1–2): 'under the command of King Pleistoanax, they piled into Eleusis and Thria, then advanced no farther before going back home.' Diplomacy now forever runs on arguing the toss over *The* Persian Wars (*ta* goddam *Mēdika*). Thucydides has Peloponnesians muster again, Corinthian tongues wag on; old scores in and out of Herodotus live, tediously, and virulent, loquaciously (Cylon's curse, Cleomenes' curse; the Helot suppliants, Pausanias and the curse of the House of Bronze – featuring Xerxes' whole sick crew, 1.126–38).[41] Grotesque offensive, the gate to war had medizing Thebes over to throttle their hated neighbour's sanctified frontier post, *Plataea*: all Greek history met to be confounded here, in a village. *Both* the No-Surrender principoleis of free Hellas, would you credit, 'now' send for assistance *to Persia* (2.7.1). A village massacre of surrendered Theban captives, civilians evacuated to Athens, and the Spartan confederates hitting the road for their reflex '*esbolē* into Attica' (10). Athens issues them formal marching orders, 'quit their borders before nightfall'. The fateful step, the fateful moment (12.2–3): 'when he was there at the border', the twelfth-hour Spartan ambassador declared, 'This day will throw the disaster switch for Hellenes' (τοῖς Ἕλλησι μεγάλων κακῶν ἄρξει).[42] HiStory hovers on the brink, for Pericles' pep-talk – 'It's throwback stuff' – and expert review of assets (13), for Archidamus' tilt at the border fort Oenoe (18).

---

[41] In Herodotus: Cylon at 5.71, Cleomenes' curse at 5.70.2, 72.1; Pausanias cf. 5.32.
[42] Strictly 'for Hellenes', note, not for Herodotus' Ἕλλησί τε καὶ βαρβάροισι (5.97.3, below, 'Greeks and aliens both').

Finally, in went the Spartan alliance, but no, they stood back from the plain – 'The foe may not contain their fury, may yet come out and fight' (19–20.3). But, no, they'd remembered, fingers crossed, the last time it was about to happen (21.1): '14 years earlier, when the Spartan King Pleistoanax's *esbolē* via *Eleusis* and Thria advanced no farther than that before withdrawal'. After doing their worst, off drove the task force, 'via Boeotia, not the way they *esebalon*, making a mess of Oropus on the way out' (23.3). The same ritual each summer thereafter. Second time and the longest in duration, they did trash the plain, and seemingly sparked off plague inside beleaguered Athens, leaving Peloponnesians unharmed; prompting overtures to Sparta, spurned (47.1, 54.5–57, 59.1–2). Third summer, 'no *esbolē* into Attica', but 'army campaign against' *Plataea*. Protested in vain by the garrison there in the name of Herodotean free Hellas, the full nostalgia trip (71.1; 71.2, 74.2, *Mēdika*). So the three-year siege went on, between annual *esbolai*, despite a partial break-out, until capitulation led to pleas on deaf ears (much, much more on *Mēdika*), and ruthless extermination by kangaroo court reprisals, for Thebes, '92 years since the Plataean alliance with Athens' in Herodotus (Thuc. 3.52–68; Hdt. 6.108). Ten years go by, and history set its watch by 'the *esbolē* into Attica, aka start of the war' (5.20.1). Peace machinations fragmented the Spartan confederacy, with Corinth abhorring the vacuum and Argos filling it. Hinges would come loose, Athens gambles on subduing the greatest island in the West, Sicily, whereupon Sparta realizes the advice of banished Alcibiades to occupy an Attic outpost fort, and enforce year-round blockade: his choice, the {inevitable, Herodotean} *Decelea* (6.91.6; cf. 93.1–2): 'the very thing the Athenians always dread most of all; the war scenario they've never lived through'. The fort, be it noted, that Spartans had engaged to tiptoe around *forever*, stepping over, never treading on – this nest of Attic traitors to Athens. Why did the idea call for some brainbox renegade? Its plusses had long been available to any drawing board in Hellas. And yet, and so, it came to pass, on their next '*esbolē* into Attica', as the crow flies bisecting the Athens–Boeotia highroad (7.18.1, 19.1–3).[43]

9. Nearly all this present-day desecration of Herodotus' narrative of the heroization of resistance to Persian *esbolē* into Hellas/Athens crams into the hermeneutic space which opens out by virtue of the prolonged time-out

---

[43] Decelea (now an Air Force Base and Olympic Training Centre, where Aphidna is first/last toll station on the Greece Insterstate 1 freeway) was a good place to hide Helen away from Peloponnesians in North Attic geopolitics and Thesean lore: cf. Scholia on Homer *Iliad* 3.242 (quoting 'cyclic writers'), Plutarch *Theseus* 32, Walker (1998) chapter 1. Likewise and contrariwise, those experts in the politics of tradition, Nicias and Chilon, both knew that Spartans would always know as they had always known that *their* nightmare scenario was enemy occupation of Cythera: Thuc. 4.53–6 ∼ Hdt. 7.235.

Herodotus calls between Aristagoras' extrusion from the Sparta of the short-lived and catastrophic King Cleomenes and his arrival in democratized Athens,[44] just when Athens is embarking on its adventure in imperialist engrossment to engulf the Aegean islands up to the seaboard of the Persian zone (5.51–97).[45]

The Spartan chieftain responded to overtures featuring grand gestures of extravagant vistas in his visually aided tour of rich pickings strewn across an Asian garden of delights out there by 'going inside', indeed retreating where he could heed the warning of that beady-eyed {Medusan} daughter *Gorgo* of his to 'revolt' (ἀποστάς), by withdrawing further, 'inside a second building', alone, in Sparta, in here (51.2–3). History, remember, is formally held paused at a standstill by Herodotus' own long-distance pacing out of the overland trek from Ephesus to Susa, mapping his own space-time perspective on imperial power: 'three months', Aristagoras rounded the journey down; but wait – ask Histiaeus – from the capital of Persia to the capital of Lydia *was* scheduled as three months, express delivery; whereas a 'three-day' supplement will be needed to get you down the autobahn *from Sardis to the coastline*, or back.[46] Which is where the whole *Histories* campaign plays out megapolitics, shoehorned into the meiotic width of a seashore.

'Bridge people' (*Gephyraioi*) have meantime freed Athens from tyranny by assassinating the tyrant . . .'s brother (55: despite a widespread current misprision, Thucydides endorses, 1.20.1). Rather, these unAthenian-Athenian near-heroes were in fact responsible for bringing writing to Hellas, and they detain us in fully researched, richly decorative, isolation from narrative and civic body alike (5.57–61).[47] This bridge passage[48] to nowhere dynamically related to the future determination of Hellenic culture is a spell of quarantine, before the show is pulled back onto the road with the actual liberation of Athens, four years on, through Alcmaeonid manipulation of the Delphic oracle, when those exiled aristocrats work the piety system to pressurize Sparta into expelling their buddies, these tyrants, without fuss, a gun-boat job needing not even one Spartan King aboard (62–63.1–2).[49] This didn't work either, mind. The tyrants sent for the cavalry, Thessalian allies, and the Spartans lost lives and leader – on this '?first mission?' (63.3–4). There is more to come, there must be (64.1): 'a later, larger, Spartan mission sent to Athens, the appointed general' this time being none other than King 'Cleomenes' himself, 'no longer sea-borne but overland'. The nuisance

---

[44] See Pelling, Ch. 7 above.   [45] See Munson, p. 155 above.
[46] Dovetailing with Cleomenes' 'three-day' mental excursion figuring out his response to the visitor from Miletus (5.49.9): see Pelling, pp. 189–90 above.
[47] See Gray, pp. 210–18 above.   [48] See Greenwood, p. 128 above.   [49] See Forrest (1969).

cavalry were swatted away as 'the *esbolē* into Attica went ahead' (64.2), and Cleomenes plus freedom-fighter locals got to Athens, where a stroke of luck dropped the tyrants' children in their clutches, and a deal saw safe passage out of Attica, with one week's grace, after 36 years of dynasty (64–5). *That* is how Athens was liberated, we learn; now to catch us up to Aristagoras, hotfooting it to Athens, and there any time now (65.5). Post-tyranny Athens feuded between the Alcmaeonid Cleisthenes and some noble {amusingly} called Isagoras, the former {bizarrely} suborning the people by copying his own namesake and maternal grandad, the tyrant Cleisthenes of nowhere special Sicyon, by (1) undoing the old tribe names (only now Ionian, not Dorian), and (2) introducing new ones (but multiplying them from four to ten, not giving the three others rude farmyard nicknames, while dubbing his own 'The People's Champion'). The elder homonym had played the Delphi card {too?}, to *ekbalein* the foe from the city (in his case a hated Argive hero cult, not the clan of local tyrants) (65–8; 67.1). Behave like a tyrant, mess with language and custom, and you deserve tables turned. Isagoras calls in Cleomenes, gossip said his wife's backdoor man, who *ekballei* the {Periclean} Alcmaeonid faction by invoking the *curse of Cylon* (70–72.1). Cleisthenes went like a lamb – like a Peisistratid. But Cleomenes brought 'no substantial band' to Athens to assist in expelling 700 clans, and replacing the Council with 300 Isagorean officials. Which roused resistance, a week-end's refuge in the citadel, and tail-between-legs withdrawal from Athenian territory under truce for Spartans and Isagoras, but mass execution for the rest (72). So *that* is how Athens stayed 'free'.

The moment, though, perdures. Aristagoras might never have arrived. Ancient Greece chose this moment to abolish its history – all but. It was that close a call when Athens, recalling Cleisthenes and the 700 clans, sent ambassadors *to Sardis* (73.1): 'wanting to make an alliance with the Persians, as they knew full well the Spartans under Cleomenes were on the war-path against them'. The governor knew not where on earth this Athens could be, but put on the table the hand-me-down options of 'earth-'n'-water tokens of submission in exchange for alliance, or else scram . . .' There would have been no Herodotus, Herodotus is here to tell us, if the home front hadn't repudiated their agreement to recommend agreement (73.3).

10. Cleomenes mustered the Peloponnesians. Marched off to undisclosed destination. Meant to instal *Isagoras* {'Equal-in-assembly', boom-boom}[50] as tyrant (74.1–2): 'a large-scale mission, this one, for *esbolē into Eleusis*, synchronized with capture of Attic border posts at *Oenoe* and Hysiae, by

---

[50] See Irwin, Ch. 1 above for the political dialectic sloganized through this family of puns.

the Boeotians, and on the other side, various raids from the Chalcideans'. Athens, caught 'in two minds / on two fronts', turned *Eleusis*-wards; the Peloponnesians, meantime, caught 'in two factions', as Corinth at *this* unThucydidean debate refuses to reverse values and instal any tyrant, and the other Spartan King feuds 'at odds' with Cleomenes (*amphiboliē*, 74.2 ∼ *dichostasiē*, 75.2). *This* won't happen again, the Kings falling out on campaign; those army talismen Castor-'n'-Pollux won't ever hit the campaign trail together, either. And so it is, we are lost in this microthematically fundamental paralysis of the moment of suspended narration (ibid.):

τότε δὴ ἐν τῇ Ἐλευσῖνι ὁρῶντες οἱ λοιποὶ τῶν ξυμμάχων τούς τε βασιλέας τῶν Λακεδαιμονίων οὐκ ὁμολογέοντας καὶ Κορινθίους ἐκλιπόντας τὴν τάξιν οἴχοντο καί αὐτοὶ ἀπαλλασσόμενοι,

Then it was, there *at Eleusis*, that the rest of the allies, seeing simultaneously that the Spartan kings were not of the same mind and that the Corinthians were quitting the ranks, were off and gone too, out of there,

and in these disgruntled receding backs a-slumping, so 'asyndetonic' narrative focalization lifts our blinkers to see before our eyes, there are suddenly and without warning thrust upon us the primal bogeymen of Athenocentrist phobia (76):[51]

τέταρτον δὴ τοῦτο ἐπὶ τὴν Ἀττικὴν ἀπικόμενοι Δωριέες, δίς τε ἐπὶ πολέμῳ ἐσβαλόντες καὶ δὶς ἐπ' ἀγαθῷ τοῦ πλήθεος τοῦ Ἀθηναίων, πρῶτον μὲν ὅτε καὶ Μέγαρα κατοίκισαν — οὗτος ὁ στόλος ἐπὶ Κόδρου βασιλεύοντος Ἀθηναίων ὀρθῶς ἂν καλέοιτο —, δεύτερον δὲ καὶ τρίτον ὅτε ἐπὶ Πεισιστρατιδέων ἐξέλασιν ὁρμηθέντες ἐκ Σπάρτης ἀπίκοντο, τέταρτον δὲ τότε ὅτε ἐς Ἐλευσῖνα Κλεομένης ἄγων Πελοποννησίους ἐσέβαλε· οὕτω τέταρτον τότε Δωριέες ἐσέβαλον ἐς Ἀθήνας.

yes indeed, here it is the fourth time they are come against Attica, *Dorians*, they are, twice *esbalontes* on the warpath, twice on the yellow brick road to welfare for the mass of Athenians, first when they colonized Megara, the mission, this, to give it its proper name, that was in the reign of King Codrus, second and third, though, when they came from Sparta launched to drive out the Peisistratids, and then fourth when at this moment Cleomenes led the Peloponnesians here and *esebale* into Eleusis: so this was the moment when *Dorians* for the fourth time *esebalon* into Athens.

---

[51] Commentators remark the momentum given to pondering Herodotus' project by our openly meta-textual passage: Abbott (1893) 74, 'The passage in the text *appears to have been* written before 446 BC, when Pleistoanax invaded Attica'; How and Wells (1912) II.42: '*It is impossible to say* whether this schedule of expeditions was compiled when the events of 446 BC or 431 BC had made Dorian invasions familiar to Athens. In that case the omission of all reference to the doings of Pleistoanax (Thuc. 1.114) and Archidamus (Thuc. 2.10f.) is *remarkable*, especially in view of the mention in 9.73.' Nenci (1994) 270 holds up an early 420s prism. *Historicality*, though, is what comes and goes.

Boeotia and Chalcis have it coming, next, and get it from the new muscle-flexing People's Republic of Attica.[52] *Is-ēgoriē* is *such* a fortifying force to be reckoned with (77–8). But wait on, Arist-agoras. Thebes needed to get back at them, egged on the folk of Aegina to step up their ancient feud with Athens, and this . . . – this both needs telling 'from the very beginning' and can only be told as a feud between the two sides' feuding versions. Athenians sure of their story, Aeginetans only up to a certain point, and winding up to a frankly incredible climax (but suit yourself), before the dreadful murderous dénouement changed women's national costume in Hellas forever, just look around today: you'll see Ionian (– actually, Carian –) not Dorian dress in Athens, and nothing remotely Athenian-looking wearable in Aegina or Argos . . . (79–88).[53]

No, don't believe it when Aegina's olive-wood statues sink to their knees to resist Athenian piracy, but do listen (86.3): *these* twin-set divinities 'Damiē-'n'-Auxesiē' mark the emergence of seaborne Attic power, 'the-swell-of -the-*demos*'.[54] This tide turns, toward 'today''s imperial thalassocracy (97.3):

αὗται δὲ αἱ νέες ἀρχὴ κακῶν ἐγένοντο Ἕλλησί τε καὶ βαρβάροισι.

Boats! This navy spelled 'Trauma Starts Here' for the international community of nations. / Rule Minerva, Minerva rules the waves = 'This Empire of Evil', in any language.[55]

11. Our feud *almost* changed the course of *The Histories*, but before impetuous Athens could ruin the oracled certainty of victory over Aegina after 30 years of patience, the Spartans got in the way and aborted *that* anti-narrative (89–90.1). We have just been here before, but here we are again. Sparta setting out on a mission to instal tyranny in Athens. No Cleomenes, this time. Not in person. The Spartans had learned that {Cleisthenes' clan} the Alcmaeonids had fixed the Delphic oracle. It was a double whammy: they'd expelled their buddies the Peisistratids, *and* they'd only got a kick in the teeth out of it from ingrate Athens. Plus, the triple incentive, oracles

---

[52] Where Herodotus' Chalcis hosts the Greek fleet and sees Persian vessels founder, their crews punching way above their weight at Artemisium (7.83, 89; 8.1), rebel Chalcis would lead a short-lived Euboean revolt from Athens in 446 BC, but as Thucydides' tale runs out of steam, and the remaining Athenian fleet goes down to Peloponnesian ships off Eretria, surviving sailors save their skins in newly – unilaterally declared – independent Chalcis: 'the news of the sinkings caused the worst panic ever known in Athens, Sicilian catastrophe included' (8.95.6, 96.1).

[53] Cf. Figueira (1985) esp. 58 and n. 22, Haubold, Ch. 9 above.

[54] 'Augmentation' of the free 'people' of Athens: 5.66.1, 78, ηὔξηντο, 91.1, αὐξομένους: Thucydidean Corinth and Sparta must force this genie back in its bottle (Thuc. 1.89.1, ηὐξήθησαν, cf. 1.23.6).

[55] This key puncept has been restored to its centrality by ed. Irwin; on the phrase see Index *s.v.*

formerly held in Peisistratid possession but fetched to Sparta by Cleomenes promised Waves of Heap Big Trouble in store for Sparta from Athens. News to them, this tallied with the evidence of their own sore eyes: Athenian expansionism under way; Athenian refusal to kowtow to them. Lo! (91.1):

a free Attic nation would get on a par with their own power, but an Attica held down by a tyranny would be weak and ready to jump to it.

So Sparta (no names) sent for the former tyrant, re-told the story we've heard, 'we drove out our buddies, fooled by fake oracles, handed Athens over to the people and got no thanks for it, but had our men and our king insulted and expelled (*exebale*), by this expansionist state which we must see to before we regret it, give the Peisistratid back what we took from him', is the gist. The allies have been here before, and, again, follow the lead of Corinth, here vociferously plugging the anti-tyranny line, not heeding the warning from Hippias (91–2; 93.1):[56]

Verily I say unto you that *the time will come when* you Corinthians most of all will miss your Peisistratids, *when the appointed day shall come* for their torment by the people of Athens.

The expedition was stopped in its tracks. A ?fifth? ~~Dorian invasion~~ non-episode.[57] The tyrant took up with the Persians at Sardis, Athenian ambassadors there were told to put him back in charge or else. The Athenians had declined, and just decided that this 'No' put them in the position of openly declared enemies to Persia, when . . . –

– when Aristagoras ('Best-in-Debate', huh) finally made it, just in time for us to realize he was just in time to kickstart the 'Ionian Revolt' saga with a docile audience of 30,000 apparently credulous Athenian demodopes greedily lapping up his far-flung drawn-out over-extended big-eyes bait, with those tempting visual aids. Herodotus builds this intervening interval of exponential increase in Athenian importance into an ever-swelling bulk of undigested sallies and considerations, it's getting to be as far/near as Sardis to Susa, as loaded with impact as Ephesus to Sardis, any road. But . . . – the rest will, after all is done and said, be history (93–7).

The Dorians aren't coming –

In the present of narration, Thucydides knows 'Dorian-Ionian' tribalism as factor in Peloponnesian War propaganda to be a card played by Corinth (1.124.1), a hangover superstition that won't stay buried (2.54, 203), a ploy

---

[56] Perhaps the most loudly signalled overlay between Thucydidean and Herodotean reading of the chances of political balance in mainland Greece: Corinth as pivot.

[57] Cf. Immerwahr (1966) 225 and n. 103.

used by Brasidas in Thrace (5.9.1), and a leading edge in picking, thinking, and fighting, sides in the Sicilian theatre of war (3.86, 4.61.2, 6.6.2, 7.5.4, 57–58, fought against by Hermocrates, 4.64.3, 6.77.1, 80.3, 82). Herodotus accepts the potential for disputation – and an opportunity to play off 'Dorian-Ionian' polarization at Sparta (1.142–52). Then gives it a run-out just the telling once, in caricature, when the priestess of Athene Polias {just} shooed Dorians from the adyton – only for crazy-horse Cleomenes to tell her, 'Ah yes, but I'm Achaean' (5.72.3).[58] Herodotus was prepared to trumpet that Spartan mission of tyrant-cleansing in Polycrates' Samos as positively the 'first Dorian campaign into Asia' (3.56.2). That monstrous prophecy of eventual expulsion from Sparta in the shape of Atheno-Persian alliance embraced the Spartans within the *Dorian* fraternity (8.141). Otherwise, Dorians is strictly 'tribal origins' theory terrain, the preliminary lesson for any historian of Hellas (esp. 1.56.1–2):

Next over-reaching Croesus boned up on researching (*historeōn*) which Hellenic states were most powerful friends to acquire. In this researching (*historeōn*) he found the Spartans and Athenians out ahead, the former first of the Dorian nation, the latter of the Ionian.

At once our reader/author in the text insistently smeared this away into dichotomizing Pelasgian vs. Hellenic tribal identity, with geopolitical narrative attached, From the Flood (56–7).[59]

Now Herodotus' *Decelea* will surely implant an arresting button of interpretivity into the text, obliging us to puzzle, split perspectives, stop and multi-frame the *Histories* with all we think or care to know, and then some. It won't level out, excrescent but underpowered. But his *Eleusis* already amounts to a world-beating *locus desperatus*.[60] The place and the passage

---

[58] Cleomenes plays the great conundrum in Herodotus' story – '*not* that long a reign' (5.48.1, considering how this wild card gets to slice up every limb of Greek history, from shin to groin). In his end, it was Hera's priest who debarred him as unclean, when he'd dismembered the wrong Argos (6.82.1–2, αἱρέειν ἂν κατ᾽ ἄκρης τὴν πόλιν), but Athenians knew it was for *esbalōn* and chopping Eleusis to bits (6.75.3) – whereas Spartans explain he just hooked up with Scythians, and simply lost out to the demon drink (6.84.1, ἀκρητοπότην γενέσθαι), when they brought to the table that crazy plan to crush Persia between themselves crossing into Media and *esballein*, and Sparta marching inland from Ephesus (ibid. 2). What *makes* Herodotus back the majority line of retribution for using Delphi to dispose of Demaratus? (6.75.3, 84.3) Sane, ~~sane~~, sane, ideas, people, accounts, and Greek, to span from Ionian Revolt to . . . Sicilian Expedition.

[59] Cf. Hall (1997). Mytho-logical ethnic divisions were available for politics, defaulting or otherwise, *any time*: cf. Gray, Ch. 4 above, pointing to the 'Ionianism' card played in Athens in and around 415 BC.

[60] Editrix Irwin underlines: the memoriously incised version and counter-version of the Eleusinian invasion/counter-coup noted in Macan (1895) I.74 {note on our passage}: 'A certain number of Athenians seem to have been with Cleomenes at Eleusis: Schol. ad Aristoph. *Lysistr*. 273: τῶν δὲ μετὰ Κλεομένους Ἐλευσῖνα κατασχόντων Ἀθηναίων τὰς οἰκίας κατέσκαψαν καὶ τὰς οὐσίας ἐδήμευσαν, αὐτῶν δὲ θάνατον ἐψηφίσαντο, καὶ ἀναγράψαντες ἐς στήλην χαλκῆν

we came for. 'Dorian invasion' proves so vacant an ideological gesture toward a venomous empty sign, it leaps out from the page provocative as a tabloid headline shorn from copy and context. '*This* is a . . . – *momentous moment*'.[61] The specious {pseudo-epical mock-heroics}[62] count to four anticipates anything the Spanish Inquisition could ever come up with, and the Hellenic Python not only poses as diligent embellisher on the spot, but moves directly from this interim totting up to full narrativization of the successor in its train. Two pluses, two minuses, 'fourth time of asking' nobly encircling the ostentatious count.[63]

We never heard from Herodotus of the first item, 'Megara';[64] and his odd mention of good (last) King Codrus, *pro patria non timidus mori*

ἔστησαν ἐν πόλει παρὰ τὸ ἀρχαῖον νέων ('The Athenians occupying Eleusis with Cleomenes had their homes bulldozed and their assets confiscated; death-sentences were passed on them, and they put up a proscription list on a bronze pillar they set up in the city alongside the founda-tional temple').' And points up: the insistence of the image of 'Cleomenes backing out with tail between legs' in the edgy bristling of *Lysistrata* in crisis-soaked 411 BC (273–82: complete with 'six years-since-a-bath' for the short weekend's work in Herodotus); thus Peisistratids, Alcmeonids, Cleomenes at Eleusis, and Artemisia all bunch up here, alongside old favourites like Theseus repelled Amazons (678–9), to resist all-comers, external or intestinal (616–35, 664–78, cf. 1149–58, with Henderson (1987) 202–3). For Cleomenes in 430s propaganda: de Ste Croix (1972) 167. Under what circumstances (when?) could post-civil strife division of the people between Athens and Eleusis be envisaged as a way back to reconciliation and post-defeat renaissance? 403–401 BC.

The Aristotelian *Constitution of Athens* (39.1–2, 40.4; 41.2–) counts out 11 (12?) political milestones in the whole of Athenian history, with the present, for *this* account, dating from *that* archetypal (re-re-)integration of Athens-Eleusis, in 401: (1) Ion's foundation, (2) Theseus, (3?) Draco, (3) Solon, (4) Peisistratus, (5) Cleisthenes, (6) post-Persian Wars Areopagus, (7) Aristides-Ephialtes, (8) The 400, (9) restored democracy, (10) The 30, and The 10, (11) post-bellum democracy. Magnificent, epoch-making, synoptics, here is a fully amplified mantra of counting-out, figured *as* the text, not as textual command to meta-narration. Cf. Henderson (1997) on ostension and (re)counting.

[61] 'A TRULY *HISTORIC* MOMENT'.

[62] As action-narrative of killing for κλέος ('fame'), the entire *Iliad* unpacks (count on it, Sappho knew) *as* the formula | ἀλλ' ὅτε δὴ τὸ τέταρτον ἐπέσσυτο δαίμονι ἶσος | ('| but when fourth time around he charged like a devil |'): (1) pre-figured at 5.436–8: | τρίς . . . | τρίς . . . | ἀλλ' . . . κτλ (theomachy of Diomedes, '| thrice . . . | thrice . . . | – but . . .') (2–4) paradigmatic (thrice) for 16.705, 786, 20.447: | τρίς . . . | . . . τρίς . . . | . . . | ἀλλ' . . . κτλ (passion of Patroclus, '| thrice . . . | . . . thrice . . . | . . . | – but . . .') (5) denouement clinched {4th (?) time around} for 22.208: τρίς . . . (165) | ἀλλ' . . . κτλ (passion of Hector, 'thrice . . . | but . . .': the timeless moment interrupted by the angels 'as in a dream' . . .). Narratologically, the formula unsettles the primal count to climax '1, 2, 3 = *not*-1, *not*-2, but (wait for it) 3' with its uncanny paradox '1, 2, 3 = *not*-x 1–3, ditto, but (wait for it) **4**'. It all counts.

[63] Immerwahr (1966) 151 compares 2.142.4, where the aeons of Egyptian chronicity are imaged as a tetrad of alternating prosperity and decline marked by shifts in the quarter where the sun rises and sets: '. . . and yet Egypt was completely unaltered by the process'.

[64] The story is told in Pausanias' *Attica* (1.39.4–5) Κόδρου δὲ ὕστερον βασιλεύοντος στρατεύουσιν ἐπ' Ἀθήνας Πελοποννήσιοι· ('In Codrus' subsequent reign, there was a Peloponnesian expedition against Athens:') when they'd put on a dull show and were convoying themselves back, they took Megara from the Athenians and handed it over to volunteer Corinthians and other allies to settle. The Megarians in this way changed customs and tongue, turning Dorian: they claim the city's name is from when Car son of Phoroneus was on the throne in the land . . . . So when, in Attic, Corinthian, and Peloponnesian-alliance histories, was the right to (dis)own Megara *not* a live, recrudescent, issue?

(Horace *Odes* 3.19.1–2), one recent, never hooks into the storyboard cited here (5.65.3, cf. 1.147.1, 9.97).[65] Waving this mythology into line as if it could be the most natural thing in the world to superimpose foundation upon *esbolē* and vice versa . . . – fancy that![66]

'Twice on the warpath, twice on the yellow brick road to welfare for the mass of Athenians' is about as brashly unwinsome a saccharine-substitute fake balance as a rhetorician could spike our page with, and spill the plot. The remaining trio cluttered into just the last few pages in history and the *Histories* have it in common that they under- and/or over-achieved. Beyond us to calculate which debacle cost most, in which currency. Beside the point to count, in any case, since this has been told us as a concatenation, false move as response to false move. So through 'now' and 'fourth time around', and on to immediate repetition back in synod at Sparta, distended to fully elaborated rhetorical amplification, and, unsignalled, 'No. 5'. Herodotus knows we know that war and the interests of the Athenian *dēmos*, the Periclean way, amounts to counting the years by Peloponnesian *esbolē* into Attica. Thucydides' entropic cycle of harmless harm by the $JK^\wedge{-}1$ (joules per kelvin) or 'S' (as *our* scientists notate the effect). In the cultural memory of Hellas, violation of Athens' border zone – *esbolē* – could never lose its aura of heroic stop-the-world resistance to global distortion without forfeiting Herodotus, into the bargain. The *Histories* are pledged to halt the march of expansionist empires right here, on the outskirts of Attica: had the Thucydidean re-match already staged its surreal re-make, Dorian-Persian *esbolē* through the looking glass? It's a mindfield.[67]

From Peisistratus' rise to power as generalissimo against Megara, through their mid-fifth-century *Atticism* when Pleistoanax invaded as far as Eleusis, to Pericles' *Megarian decree* sanctions {trade war}, and more revolutionary *Atticism* put down by Sparta's Brasidas in 424 BC . . . (Hdt. 1.59.4; Thuc. 1.103.4; 139.1; 4.66–74).

[65] Ed. Irwin further points out that: (1) self-sacrificing Codrus, starting point of Attic chronography, is talismanic Attic lore stored ready for re-activation as and when: cf. Pausanias (in last note), Lycurgus *Against Leocrates* 84–9, ἐπὶ Κόδρου γὰρ βασιλεύοντος Πελοποννησίοις γενομένης ἀφορίας κατὰ τὴν χώραν αὐτῶν ἔδοξε στρατεύειν ἐπὶ τὴν πόλιν ἡμῶν . . . ('In the reign of Codrus, there being a famine in the land, the Peloponnesians saw fit to mount an expedition against our city . . .'). As and when*ever*, that is, the recursive question is popped: ἐμβαλόντων δὲ τῶν Πελοποννησίων εἰς τὴν Ἀττικήν, τί ποιοῖσιν οἱ πρόγονοι ἡμῶν; ('The Peloponnesians invade Attica, and what do our forefathers do?') That: (2) Alexis fr. 25.12 lists 'Pericles, *Codrus*, and Cimon' as a proverbial litany of political avatars always open for evocation, and accordingly, on that particular comic occasion, being evoked. And that: (3) Herodotus' uncle Panyassis of Halicarnassus is said to have written a patently à propos work, on τὰ περὶ Κόδρον καὶ Νηλέα καὶ τὰς Ἰωνικὰς ἀποικίας, εἰς ἔπη ζ ('*On Codrus, Neleus, and the Ionian Colonies, vols. I–VII*', Suda *s.v.* Πανύασσις).

[66] The Aristotelian *Constitution of Athens* (19–20) knows to weave into the Herodotean tale of Athens between Cleomenes and Cleisthenes (esp. 19.5–6, 20.2–3: Anchimolius' marines, then Cleomenes' first and second battalions), how Attic skolia served to enshrine Alcmeonid martyrdom, and their precursors', perpetrated/perpetuated in the fight to swap tyranny for demarchy (19.3, 20.5).

[67] Cf. esp. Hornblower (1992) and in Ch. 6 above.

The narratologic at work when so many parables and slogans are crammed into the cranium during Aristagoras' cross-country ride in the time-honoured tracks of Spartan boots headed for outer space beginning at the Isthmus, thenceforth into the back of beyond, leads to no critical breakthrough, but waymarks the road to pre-doomed 'revolt', the shore-line of Asia, the borderline of Attica, through the past epic of Hellas to its present sequel*s*.

Next time, these times, this time, an imperial fleet had hoovered up the islands, raced to suppress a revolting Ionia, started dreaming of light-ning strikes to the heartland interior. That unassimilable otherwhere. Try shooting another arrow to the stars, and say after Darius (5.105.2):

ὦ Ζεῦ, ἐκγενέσθαι μοι Ἀθηναίους τείσασθαι.

Almighty God, only grant me to punish the Athenians!

If you want the cap to fit, you must wear it. Every day you say grace, make it another one of those memos-to-self: 'You're the boss? Don't forget to remember the Athenians' (ibid.).[68]

Off the page, off-line –

They*'re on their way now.*[69]

---

[68] Esp. Moles (1996).   [69] *We've seen the enemy. They're* us.

Bibliography

Abbott, E. (1893) *Herodotus. Books V and VI. Terpsichore and Erato*. Oxford.

Ahl, F. (1984) 'The art of safe criticism in Greece and Rome', *AJPh* 105: 174–208.

Alden, M. J. (2000) *Homer beside Himself*. Oxford.

Alty, J. (1982) 'Dorians and Ionians', *JHS* 102: 1–14.

Aly, W. (1969²) *Volksmärchen, Sage und Novelle bei Herodot und seinen Zeitgenossen. Eine Untersuchung über die volkstümlichen Elemente der altgriechischen Prosaerzählung*. Göttingen.

Andrewes, A. (1956) *The Greek Tyrants*. London.

Antonaccio, C. (1998) *An Archaeology of Ancestors. Tomb Cult and Hero Cult in Early Greece*. London.

Antoniadis, L. (1981) 'L'Institution de la royauté en Chypre antique', Κυπριακαί Σπουδαί 45: 29–53.

Armayor, O. K. (1985) *Herodotus' Autopsy of the Fayoum: Lake Moeris and the Labyrinth of Egypt*. Amsterdam.

Armayor, O. K. (2004) 'Herodotus, Hecataeus and the Persian Wars', in Karageorghis and Taifacos (eds.) (2004): 321–35.

Arnold, T. (1830) *The History of the Peloponnesian War by Thucydides*. Oxford.

Asheri, D. (1988a) 'Carthaginians and Greeks', in *CAH* IV²: 739–80.

Asheri, D. (1988b) *Erodoto. Le Storie, Libro I*. Milan.

Asheri, D. (1990) 'Herodotus on Thracian society and history', *Fondation Hardt* 35: 131–69.

Asheri, D., A. Lloyd and A. Corcella (2007) *A Commentary on Herodotus Books I–IV*, ed. O. Murray and A. Moreno. Oxford.

Aupert, P. and M.-C. Hellmann (eds.) (1984) *Amathonte I. Testimonie 1: Auteurs anciens monnayages,voyageurs, fouilles, origines, geographie*. Paris.

Austin, C. and S. D. Olson (2004) *Aristophanes. Thesmophoriazusae*. Oxford.

Austin, M. J., J. Harries, and C. Smith (eds.) (1998) *Modus Operandi. Essays in Honour of Geoffrey Rickman*. London.

Austin, M. M. (1990) 'Greek tyrants and the Persians, 546–479 BC', *CQ* 40: 289–306.

Badian, E. (1982) 'Greeks and Macedonians', in Barr-Sharrar and Borza (eds.) (1982): 33–51.

Badian, E. (1993) *From Plataea to Potidaea. Studies in the History and Historiography of the Pentecontaetia*. Baltimore.

Badian, E. (1994) 'Herodotus on Alexander I of Macedon: a study in some subtle silences', in S. Hornblower (ed.), *Greek Historiography*. Oxford: 107–30.

Bakker, E. J., I. J. F. de Jong, and H. van Wees (eds.) (2002) *Brill's Companion to Herodotus*. Leiden, Boston and Cologne.

Balot, R. K. (2004) 'Free speech, courage, and democratic deliberation', in Sluiter and Rosen (eds.) (2004): 233–60.

Barney, R. (2001) *Names and Nature in Plato's Cratylus*. Cambridge, Mass.

Barr-Sharrar, B. and E. Borza (eds.) (1982) *Macedonia and Greece in Late Classical and Early Hellenistic Times* (Studies in the History of Art 10). Washington DC.

Barrett, D. S. (1979) 'Herodotus' Sigynnai (5.9) and gypsies', *G&R* 26: 58–9.

Barron, J. P. (1966) *The Silver Coins of Samos*. London.

Baurain, C. (1980) 'Kinyras. La Fin de l'âge du bronze à Chypre et la tradition antique', *BCH* 104: 277–308.

Baurain, C. (1984) 'Réflexions sur les origines de la ville d'après les sources littéraires', in Aupert and Hellmann (eds.) (1984): 109–17.

Baxter, T. (1992) *The Cratylus. Plato's Critique of Naming*. Leiden.

Bertelli, L. (2001) 'Hecataeus: from genealogy to historiography', in Luraghi (ed.) (2001a): 67–94.

Bichler, R., and R. Rollinger (2001) *Herodot*. Hildesheim.

Bischoff, H. (1932) *'Der Warner bei Herodot'*. Diss. Marburg.

Blaineau, A. (2004) 'Charge de cavalerie, choc ou esquive: sur un problème rencontré dans l'Hipparque de Xénophon', in Bois (ed.) (2004): 15–25.

Blok, J. (2002) 'Women in Herodotus' *Histories*', in Bakker *et al.* (eds.) (2002): 225–42.

Blösel, W. (2001) 'The Herodotean picture of Themistocles: a mirror of fifth-century Athens', in Luraghi (ed.) (2001a): 179–97.

Boedeker, D. (1988) 'Protesilaos and the end of Herodotus' *Histories*', *ClAnt* 7: 30–48.

Boedeker, D. (2002) 'Epic heritage and mythical patterns in Herodotus', in Bakker *et al.* (eds.) (2002): 97–116.

Boedeker, D. (2003) 'Pedestrian fatalities: the prosaics of death in Herodotus', in Derow and Parker (eds.) (2003): 17–36.

Bois, J.-P. (ed.) (2004) *Dialogue militaire entre anciens et modernes*. Rennes.

Bolger, D. L. (1989) 'Regionalism, cultural variation and culture-area concept in later Prehistoric Cypriot studies', in Peltenburg (ed.) (1989): 142–52.

Bonfante L. and V. Karageorghis (eds.) (2001) *Italy and Cyprus in Antiquity: 1500–450 BC*. Nicosia.

Bondi, S. F. (1990) 'I Fenici in Erodoto', *Fondation Hardt* 35: 235–86.

Borza, E. N. (1990a) 'Athenians, Macedonians, and the origins of the Macedonian royal house', in *Studies in Attic Epigraphy, History and Topography Presented to Eugene Vanderpool* (*Hesperia* Supplement 19): 7–13.

Borza, E. N. (1990b) *In the Shadow of Olympus. The Emergence of Macedon*. Princeton.

Borza, E. N. (1995) 'The symposium at Alexander's court', in *Makedonika*. Claremont: 159–71 (reprinted from *Arkhaia Makedonia* 3 (1983) 45–55).

Borza, E. N. (1999) *Before Alexander. Constructing Early Macedonia (Publications of the Association of Ancient Historians 6)*. Claremont.

Bowen, A. J. (ed.) (1992) *Plutarch: Malice of Herodotus. Text with Translation, Commentary and Notes*. Worminster.

Bowie, A. M. (2003) 'Fate may harm me, I have dined today: near-Eastern royal banquets and Greek symposia in Herodotus', in *Symposium: banquet et représentations en Grèce et à Rome* (Pallas 61). Toulouse: 99–109.

Braund, D. (1998), 'Herodotus on the problematics of reciprocity', in C. Gill, N. Postlethwaite, and R. Seaford (eds.), *Reciprocity in Ancient Greece*. Oxford: 159–80.

Braund, D. (2004) 'Herodotus' Spartan Scythians', in C. Tuplin (ed.), *Pontus and the Outside World*. Leiden and Boston: 25–41.

Bremmer, J. N. (1983) *The Early Greek Concept of the Soul*. Princeton.

Briant, P. (1982) *Rois, tributs et paysans: études sur les formations tributaires du Moyen Orient ancien*. Paris.

Briant, P. (1990) 'Hérodote et la société Perse', *Fondation Hardt* 35: 69–113.

Briant, P. (1996) *Histoire de l'Empire perse de Cyrus à Alexandre*. Vol. I. Paris.

Briant, P. and C. Herrenschmidt (eds.) (1989) *Le Tribut dans l'Empire perse: actes de la Table Ronde de Paris 12–13 décembre 1986*. Louvain and Paris.

Brock, R. (2003) 'Authorial voice and narrative management in Herodotus', in Derow and Parker (eds.) (2003): 3–16.

Brock, R. (2004) 'Political imagery in Herodotus', in Karageorghis and Taifacos (eds.) (2004): 169–77.

Brown, T. S. (1981) 'Aeneas Tacticus, Herodotus and the Ionian Revolts', *Historia* 30: 385–93.

Browning, R. (1961) 'Herodotus v. 4 and Euripides *Cresphontes* fr. 449 N.', *CR* ns 9: 201–2.

Budelmann, F. and P. Michelakis (eds.) (2001) *Homer, Tragedy and Beyond. Essays in Honour of P. E. Easterling*. London.

Burn, A. R. (1984) *Persia and the Greeks: the Defence of the West c. 546–478 BC*, 2nd edn. with a postscript by D. M. Lewis. London.

Cagnazzi, S. (1975) 'Tavola dei 28 *logoi* di Erodoto', *Hermes* 103: 385–423.

Cambiano, G. (1988) 'La Démonstration géométrique', in Detienne (ed.) (1988b): 251–72.

Cameron, H. D. (1970) 'The power of words in the *Seven Against Thebes*', *TAPhA* 101: 95–118.

Carter, D. M. (2004) 'Citizen attribute, negative right: a conceptual difference between ancient and modern ideas of freedom of speech', in Sluiter and Rosen (eds.) (2004): 197–220.

Cartledge, P. (1993) *The Greeks*. Oxford.

Cawkwell, G. (2005) *The Greek Wars. The Failure of Persia*. Oxford.

Ceccarelli, P. (1993) 'Sans thalassocracie, pas de Démocratie? Le Rapport entre thalassocratie et démocratie à Athènes dans la discussion du Ve et IVe siècle', *Historia* 42: 444–70.

Ceccarelli, P. (2005) 'Messaggio scritto e messaggio orale: strategie narrative erodotee', in M. Giangiulio (ed.), *Erodoto e il 'modello Erodoteo. Formazione e trasmissione delle tradizioni storiche in Grecia*. Trento: 13–16.

Ceccarelli, P. (1996) 'De la Sardaigne à Naxos: le rôle des îles dans les *Histoires* d'Hérodote', in Létoublon (ed.) (1996): 42–55.

Chadwick, J. (1996) *Lexicographica Graeca*. Oxford.

Chamberlain, D. (2001) '"We the others": interpretative community and plural voice in Herodotus', *ClAnt* 20: 5–34.

Christ, M. R. (1994) 'Herodotean kings and historical enquiry', *ClAnt* 13: 167–202.

Clarke, K. J. (2003): 'Polybius and the nature of late Hellenistic historiography', in J. Santos Yanguas and E. Torregaray Pagola (eds.), *Polibio y la Península Ibérica*. Vittoria: 69–87.

Classen, J. (1914) *Thukydides*, Vol. II. Berlin.

Clay, J. S. (1989) *The Politics of Olympus. Form and Meaning in the Major Homeric Hymns*. Princeton.

Cobet, J. (2002) 'The organization of time in the *Histories*', in Bakker *et al.* (eds.) (2002): 387–412.

Coleman, R. (1977) *Vergil. Eclogues*. Cambridge.

Colombier, A. M. (1991) 'Organisation du territoire et pouvoirs locaux dans l'île de Chypre à l'époque perse', *Transeuhratène* 4: 21–43.

Colombier, A. M. (2003) 'Quelques jalons pour une histoire de l'identité chypriote à l'époque des Royaumes autonomes', in M. Chehub, Y. Ioannou, and F. Métral (eds.) *Méditerranée ruptures et continuités. Actes du colloque tenu à Nicosie les 20–22 octobre 2001*. Lyons: 139–150.

Connor, W. R. (1993) 'The Ionian era of Athenian civic identity', *PAPS* 137: 194–206.

Constantakopoulou, C. (2002) *The Dance of the Islands. Perceptions of Insularity in Classical Greece*. Unpublished PhD thesis. Oxford.

Cooper, G./Krüger, K. (2002) *Greek Syntax*. Vol. III. Ann Arbor.

Costa, E. A (1974) 'Evagoras I and the Persians', *Historia* 23: 40–56.

Craddock, P. (ed.) (1972) *The English Essays of Edward Gibbon*. Oxford.

Creuzer, Fr. (1869) *Herodoti Halicarnassensis Musae III*. Leipzig.

Croiset, A. (1886) *Thucydide. Livres I–II*. Paris.

Crowther, N. B. (2000) 'Resolving an impasse: draws, dead heats and similar decisions in Greek athletics', *Nikephoros* 13: 125–40.

Darbo-Peschanski, C. (1987), *Le Discours du particulier. Essai sur l'enquête hérodotéenne*. Paris.

Darbo-Peschanski, C. (1988) 'La Vie des morts. Représentations et fonctions de la mort et des morts dans les *Histoires* d'Hérodote', *AION* 10: 41–51.

Davies, J. K. (1971) *Athenian Propertied Families, 600–300 BC*. Oxford.

de Jong, I. J. F. (1998) 'Aspects narratologiques des *Histoires* d' Hérodote', *Lalies* 19: 217–75.

de Jong, I. J. F. (2001) 'The anachronical structure of Herodotus' *Histories*', in Harrison (ed.) (2001): 93–116.

de Jong, I. J. F. (2002) 'Narrative unity and units', in Bakker *et al.* (eds.) (2002): 245–66.

de Romilly, J. (1971) 'La Vengeance comme explication historique dans l' oeuvre d' Hérodote', *REG* 84: 314–37.

de Romilly, J. (1986) 'Les Manies de Prodicos et la rigueur de la langue grecque', *MH* 43: 1–18.

de Ste Croix, G. E. M. (1972) *The Origins of the Peloponnesian War*. London.

de Ste Croix, G. E. M. (2004) *Athenian Democratic Origins and Other Essays*, ed. D. Harvey and R. Parker. Oxford.

Deffner, A. (1933) *Die Rede bei Herodot und ihre Weiterbildung bei Thukydides*. Diss. Munich.

Demand, N. (1988) 'Herodotus and *metoikésis* in the Persian Wars', *AJPh* 109: 416–23.

Demand, N. (1990) *Urban Relocation in Archaic and Classical Greece*. Norman, Okl.

Denniston, J. D. (1954) *The Greek Particles* (2nd edn.). Oxford.

Der Derian, J. (ed.) (1998) *The Virilio Reader*. Oxford.

Derow, P., and R. Parker (eds.) (2003) *Herodotus and his World. Essays From a Conference in Memory of George Forrest*. Oxford.

Derrida, J. (1996) *Archive Fever*. Chicago.

Detienne, M. (1988a) 'L'Espace de la publicité, ses opérateurs intellectuals dans la cité', in Detienne (1988b): 29–81.

Detienne, M. (ed.) (1988b) *Les Savoirs de l'écriture en Grèce ancienne*. Lille.

Dewald, C. (1981) 'Women and culture in Herodotus' *Histories*', in H. Foley (ed.), *Reflections of Women in Antiquity*. New York: 91–125.

Dewald, C. (1985) 'Practical knowledge and the historian's role in Herodotus and Thucydides', in M. H. Jameson (ed.), *The Greek Historians. Literature and History. Papers Presented to A. E. Raubitschek*. Saratoga: 47–63.

Dewald, C. (1987) 'Narrative structure and authorial voice in Herodotus' *Histories*', *Arethusa* 20: 147–70.

Dewald, C. (1997) 'Wanton kings, pickled heroes, and gnomic founding fathers: strategies of meaning at the end of Herodotus's *Histories*', in Roberts *et al.* (eds.) (1997): 62–82.

Dewald, C. (1998) 'Introduction and notes', in R. Waterfield, trans., *Herodotus. The Histories*. Oxford.

Dewald, C. (1999) 'The figured stage: focalizing the initial narratives of Herodotus and Thucydides', in N. Felson, D. Konstan, and T. Falkner (eds.), *Contextualizing Classics. Ideology, Performance, Dialogue. Festschrift for John Peradotto*. Lanham: 229–61.

Dewald, C. (2002) '"I didn't give my own genealogy": Herodotus and the authorial persona', in Bakker *et al.* (eds.) (2002): 267–89.

Dewald, C. (2003) 'Form and content: the question of tyranny in Herodotus', in Morgan (ed.) (2003): 25–58.

Dewald, C., and J. Marincola (eds.) (2006) *The Cambridge Companion to Herodotus*. Cambridge.

Dillery, J. (1996) 'Reconfiguring the past: Thyrea, Thermopylae, and narrative patterns in Herodotus', *AJPh* 117: 217–54.

Dobrov, G. (1993) 'The tragic and the comic Tereus', *AJPh* 114: 189–243.

Dorati, M. (2000) *Le Storie di Erodoto: etnografia e racconto*. Pisa and Rome.

Dougherty, C. and L. Kurke (eds.) (1993) *Cultural Poetics in Archaic Greece. Cult, Performance, Politics*. Cambridge.

Dougherty, C., and L. Kurke (eds.) (2003) *The Cultures within Ancient Greek Culture*. Cambridge.

Dover, K. J. (1998) 'Herodotean implausibilities', in Austin *et al.* (eds.) (1998): 219–25.

Drexler, H. (1972) *Herodot-Studien*. Hildesheim and New York.

Dunbabin, T. (1936–7) ''Εχθρὴ παλαίη', *ABSA* 37: 83–91.

Dunbabin, T. J. (1948) *The Western Greeks. The History of Sicily and South Italy from the Foundation of the Greek Colonies to 480 BC*. Oxford.

Dunbar, N. (1995) *Aristophanes. Birds*, edited with introduction and commentary. Oxford.

Edwards, M. (1991) *The Iliad. A Commentary*, Vol. V. Cambridge.

Errington, R. M. (1981) 'Alexander the philhellene and Persia', in H. Dell (ed.), *Ancient Macedonian Studies in Honor of Charles F. Edson*. Thessaloniki: 139–43.

Errington, R. M. (1990) *A History of Macedonia* (trans. C. Errington). Berkeley.

Evans, J. A. S. (1976) 'Herodotus and the Ionian revolt', *Historia* 25: 31–7.

Evans, J. A. S. (1991) *Herodotus Explorer of the Past*. Princeton.

Farnell, L. R (1921) *Greek Hero Cults and Ideas of Immortality*. Oxford.

Fearn, D. W. (forthcoming, 2007) *Bacchylides. Politics, Performance, Poetic Tradition*. Oxford.

Fehling, D. (1989) *Herodotus and his 'Sources'. Citation, Invention, and Narrative Art* (tr. J. G. Howie; German original 1972). Leeds.

Ferrill, A. (1978) 'Herodotus on tyranny', *Historia* 27: 385–98.

Figueira, T. (1985) 'Herodotus on the early hostilities between Aegina and Athens', *AJPh* 106: 49–74 (reprinted in T. Figueira (1993) *Excursions in Epichoric History: Aeginetan Essays*. Lanham: 35–60).

Fisher, N. (2002) 'Popular morality in Herodotus', in Bakker *et al.* (2002): 199–224.

Fitzpatrick, D. (2001) 'Sophocles' *Tereus*', *CQ* 51: 90–101.

Flory, S. G. (1978) 'Laughter, tears, and wisdom in Herodotus', *AJPh* 99: 145–53.

Flory, S. G. (1980) 'Who read Herodotus' *Histories*?', *AJPh* 101: 12–28.

Flory, S. G. (2004) 'Rev. of Derow and Parker (eds.) (2003)', *BMCR* 2004.02.03, http://ccat.sas.upenn.edu/bmcr/2004/2004-02-03.html

Flower, M. A. (2000) 'From Simonides to Isocrates: the fifth-century origins of fourth-century panhellenism', *ClAnt* 19: 65–101.

Flower, M. A., and J. Marincola (2002) *Herodotus. Histories Book IX*. Cambridge.

Ford, A. (1992) *Homer. The Poetry of the Past*. Ithaca.

Ford, A. (1997) 'Epic as genre', in I. Morris and B. Powell (eds.), *A New Companion to Homer*. Leiden: 396–414.

Fornara, C. W. (1971a) 'Evidence for the date of Herodotus' publication', *JHS* 91: 25–34.

Fornara, C. W. (1971b) *Herodotus. An Interpretative Essay*. Oxford.

Fornara, C. W. (1981) 'Herodotus' knowledge of the Archidamian War', *Hermes* 109: 149–56.

Fornara, C. W. and L. J. Samons II (1991) *Athens from Cleisthenes to Pericles*. Berkeley.

Forrest, W. G. G. (1969) 'The tradition of Hippias' expulsion from Athens', *GRBS* 10: 277–86.

Forrest, W. G. G. (1979) 'Motivation in Herodotus: the case of the Ionian Revolt', *International History Review* 1: 311–22.

Forsdyke, S. (1999) 'From aristocratic to democratic ideology and back again: the Thrasybulus anecdote in Herodotus' *Histories* and Aristotle's *Politics*', *CPh* 94: 361–72.

Forsdyke, S. (2001) 'Athenian democratic ideology and Herodotus' *Histories*', *AJPh* 122: 333–62.

Forsdyke, S. (2002) 'Greek history, c. 525–480 BC', in Bakker *et al.* (eds.) (2002): 521–49.

Fourrier, S. (2002) 'Les Territoires des royaumes chypriotes archaïques: une esquisse de géographie historique', in A. Hermary (ed.), *Hommage à Marguerite Yon, Actes du Colloque international 'Le temps de royaumes de Chypre, XIII-IVe s. av. J. C.' Lyon, 20–22 juin*. Paris. 135–46.

Fowler, D. P., and P. G. Fowler (1996) 'Literary theory and classical studies', in Hornblower and Spawforth (eds.) (1996): 871–5.

Fowler R. (2003) 'Herodotus and Athens', in Derow and Parker (eds.) (2003): 305–18.

Fowler, R. L. (1996) 'Herodotus and his contemporaries', *JHS* 116: 62–87.

Fowler, R. L. (2001) 'Early *historiē* and literacy', in Luraghi (ed.) (2001a): 95–115.

Fowler, R. L. (2003) 'Herodotus and Athens', in Derow and Parker (eds.) (2003): 305–18.

Fraenkel, E. (1950) *Aeschylus. Agamemnon* (3 vols). Oxford.

French, A. (1972) 'Topical influences on Herodotos' narrative', *Mnemosyne* 25: 9–27.

Friedrich, P. (1977) 'Sanity and the myth of honor: the problem of Achilles', *Ethos* 5: 281–305.

Fritz, K. von (1967) *Die griechische Geschichtsschreibung*, vol. I: *Von den Anfängen bis Thukykides*. Berlin.

Frontisi-Ducroux, F., and F. Lissarrague (1990) 'From ambiguity to ambivalence: a Dionysiac excursion through the "Anakreontic" vases', in D. Halperin, J. Winkler, and F. Zeitlin (eds.), *Before Sexuality. The Construction of Erotic Experience in the Ancient Greek World*. Princeton: 211–56.

Gabrielsen, V. (1994) *Financing the Athenian Fleet. Public Taxation and Social Relations*. Baltimore and London.

Gallo, I. (1976) 'Solone a Soli', *QUCC* 21: 29–36.

Garland, R. (1987) *The Piraeus*. London.

Garland, R. (1990) 'Priests and power in classical Athens', in M. Beard and J. North (eds.), *Pagan Priests*. London: 73–91.

Garland, R. (1992) *Introducing New Gods*. London.

Georges, P. (2000) 'Persian Ionia under Darius: the revolt reconsidered', *Historia* 49: 1–39.

Gibson, R. K. and C. S. Kraus (eds.) (2002) *The Classical Commentary. Histories, Practices, Theory*. Leiden.

Giraudeau, M. (1984) *Les Notions juridiques et socials chez Hérodote. Études sur le vocabulaire*. Paris.

Gnoli, G. and J.-P. Vernant (eds.) (1982) *La Mort, les morts dans les sociétés anciennes*. Cambridge.

Goldhill, S. (1990) 'The Great Dionysia and civic ideology', in J. Winkler and F. Zeitlin (eds.), *Nothing to Do with Dionysos? Athenian Drama in its Social Context*. Princeton: 97–129.

Goldhill, S. (2002) *The Invention of Prose* (Greece and Rome New Surveys in the Classics 32). Oxford.

Gomme, A. W. (1956) *A Historical Commentary on Thucydides*. Vol. II. Oxford.

Gontier, P. (ed.) (1995) *Kyprios Character, Quelle identité chypriote? Sources, Travaux historiques* 43/4.

Goodwin, W. W. (1889) *Syntax of the Moods and Tenses of the Greek Verb*. London.

Gould, J. (1989) *Herodotus*. London.

Gould, J. (2001) 'Give and take in Herodotus', in id., *Myth, Ritual, Memory, and Exchange. Essays in Greek Literature and Culture*. Oxford: 283–303.

Gray, V. J. (1996) 'Herodotus and images of tyranny: the tyrants of Corinth', *AJPh* 117: 361–89.

Gray, V. J. (1997) 'Reading the rise of Pisistratus: Herodotus 1.56–68', *Histos* 1: http://www.dur.ac.uk/Classics/histos/1997/gray.html

Gray, V. J. (2002) 'Short stories in Herodotus' *Histories*', Bakker *et al.* (eds.) (2002): 291–317.

Graziosi, B., and J. Haubold (2005) *Homer. The Resonance of Epic*. London.

Griffin, J. (1980) *Homer on Life and Death*. Oxford.

Griffiths, A. (1989) 'Was Kleomenes mad?' in Powell (ed.) (1989): 51–78.

Griffiths, A. (2001) 'Kissing cousins: some curious cases of adjacent material in Herodotus', in Luraghi (ed.) (2001): 161–78.

Hainsworth, J. B. (1993) *The Iliad. A Commentary*, Vol. III. Cambridge.

Hall, E. (1989) *Inventing the Barbarian. Greek Self-Definition through Tragedy*. Oxford.

Hall, J. M. (1997) *Ethnic Identity in Greek Antiquity*. Cambridge.

Hall, J. M. (2001) 'Contested ethnicities: perceptions of Macedonia within evolving definitions of Greek Identity', in Malkin (ed.) (2001): 159–86.

Hall, J. M. (2002) *Hellenicity. Between Ethnicity and Culture*. Chicago.

Halliwell, S. (1987) *The Poetics of Aristotle. Translation and Commentary*. London.

Harder, A. (1985) *Euripides' Kresphontes and Archelaos*. Leiden.

Harrison, S. J. (ed.) (2001) *Texts, Ideas, and the Classics*. Oxford.

Harrison, T. (1997) 'Herodotus and the ancient Greek idea of rape', in S. Deacy and K. Pearce (eds.), *Rape in Antiquity. Sexual Violence in the Greek and Roman Worlds*. London: 185–208.

Harrison, T. (1998). 'Herodotus' conception of foreign languages', *Histos* 2: http://www.dur.ac.uk/Classics/histos/1998/harrison.html

Harrison, T. (2000) *Divinity and History. The Religion of Herodotus*. Oxford.

Harrison, T. (2003) '"Prophecy in reverse"? Herodotus and the origins of history', in Derow and Parker (eds.) (2003): 237–55.

Harrison, T. (2004) 'Truth and lies in Herodotus' *Histories*', in Karageorghis and Taifacos (eds.) (2004): 255–63.

Hart, J. (1982) *Herodotus and Greek History*. London.

Hartog, F. (1988) *The Mirror of Herodotus* (tr. J. Lloyd; French original 1980, second French edn. 1991). Berkeley, Los Angeles and London.

Haubold, J. (2001) 'Epic with an end: an interpretation of *Homeric Hymns* 15 and 20', in Budelmann and Michelakis (eds.) (2001): 23–41.

Heath, M. (1989) *Unity in Greek Poetics*. Oxford.

Hellmann, F. (1934) *Herodots Kroisos-Logos* (Neue Philol. Untersuch. 9). Berlin.

Henderson, J. (1987) *Aristophanes' Lysistrata*. Oxford.

Henderson, J. (1997) 'The name of the tree: recounting *Odyssey* 24.340–2', *JHS* 107: 87–116.

Henige, D. (1974) *The Chronology of Oral tradition. Quest for a Chimera*. Oxford.

Heygi, D. (1966) 'The historical background of the Ionian Revolt', *AAnt.Hung.* 14: 285–302.

Hodder, I. (ed.) (1978) *The Spatial Organization of Culture*. London.

Hodkinson, S. (2000) *Property and Wealth in Classical Sparta*. London.

Hohti, P. (1974) 'Freedom of speech in the speech sections in the *Histories* of Herodotus', *Arctos* 8: 19–27.

Hohti, P. (1975) 'Über die Notwendigkeit bei Herodot', *Arctos* 9: 31–7.

Hohti, P. (1977) 'συμβάλλεσθαι: a note on conjectures in Herodotus', *Arctos* 11: 5–14.

Hornblower, S. (1987) *Thucydides*, London.

Hornblower, S. (1991) *A Commentary on Thucydides*, Vol. I. Oxford.

Hornblower, S. (1992) 'Thucydides' use of Herodotus', in J. M. Sanders (ed.), *Philolakon. Lakonian Studies on Honor of H. Catling*. Athens: 141–54.

Hornblower, S. (1996) *A Commentary on Thucydides*, Vol. II. Oxford.

Hornblower, S. (2003) 'Panionios of Chios and Hermotimos of Pedasa (Hdt. 8.104–6)', in Derow and Parker (eds.) (2003): 37–57.

Hornblower, S. (2004) *Thucydides and Pindar. Historical Narrative and the World of Epinician Poetry*. Oxford.

Hornblower, S., and A. Spawforth (eds.) (1996) *Oxford Classical Dictionary*, 3rd edn. Oxford.

How, W. W., and J. Wells (1912) *A Commentary on Herodotus* (2 vols). Oxford.

Huber, L. (1963) *Religiöse und politische Beweggründe des Handelns in der Geschichtsschreibung des Herodot*. Diss. Tübingen.

Hutton, W. (2005) *Describing Literature. Landscape and Literature in the Periegesis of Pausanias*. Cambridge.

Immerwahr, H. R. (1956) 'Aspects of historical causation in Herodotus', *TAPhA* 87: 247–80.

Immerwahr, H. R. (1957) 'The Samian stories of Herodotus', *CJ* 52: 312–22.

Immerwahr, H. R. (1960) '*Ergon*: history as monument in Herodotus and Thucydides', *AJPh* 81: 261–90.

Immerwahr, H. R. (1966) *Form and Thought in Herodotus*. Cleveland, Ohio (reprinted 1986).

Irwin, E. (1999) 'Solicising in Solon's Colony', *BICS* 43: 187–95.

Irwin, E. (2005a) 'Gods among men? The social and political dynamics of the Hesiodic *Catalogue of Women*', in R. Hunter (ed.), *The Hesiodic Catalogue of Women. Constructions and Reconstructions*. Cambridge: 35–84.

Irwin, E. (2005b) *Solon and Early Greek Poetry. The Politics of Exhortation*. Cambridge.

Irwin, E. (2007) 'The politics of precedence: first historians on first thalassocrats', in R. Osborne (ed.), *Anatomy of a Cultural Revolution. Athens 430–380 BC*.

Isaac, B. (1986) *The Greek Settlements in Thrace until the Macedonian Conquest*. Leiden.

Jacob, C. (1988) 'Inscrire la terre habitée sur une tablette. Réflexions sur la fonction de la carte géographique en Grèce ancienne', in Detienne (ed.) (1988b): 273–304.

Jacoby, F. (1913) 'Herodotus', *REA* Suppl. 2: 205–520.

Jebb, R. C. (1885) *Sophocles, the Plays and Fragments. Part II: Oedipus Coloneus*. Cambridge.

Jeffery, L. H. (1976) *Archaic Greece. The City-States c. 700–500 BC*. London and Tonbridge.

Johnson, D. M. (2001) 'Herodotus' story-telling speeches: Socles (5.92) and Leotychidas (6.86)', *CJ* 97: 1–26.

Johnson, W. A. (1994) 'Oral performance and the composition of Herodotus' *Histories*', *GRBS* 35: 229–54.

Johnson, W. A (2004) *Book Rolls and Scribes in Oxyrhynchus*. Toronto.

Jones, C. P. (1987) '*Stigma*: tattooing and branding in Graeco-Roman antiquity', *JRS* 77: 139–55.

Jones, C. P. (1999) *Kinship Diplomacy in the Ancient World*. Cambridge, Mass.

Kallet, L. (2001) *Money and the Corrosion of Power in Thucydides. The Sicilian Expedition and its Aftermath*. Berkeley.

Kallet, L. (2003) '*Dēmos tyrannos*: wealth, power, and economic patronage', in Morgan (ed.) (2003): 117–53.

Kallet-Marx, L. (1993) *Money, Expense and Naval Power in Thucydides' History 1–5.24*. Cambridge.

Kamerbeek, J. (1984) *Plays of Sophocles. Commentaries. Part VII: Oedipus Coloneus*. Leiden.

Karageorghis, V. (1973) 'Contribution to the early history of Soloi in Cyprus', *AAA* 6: 145–9.

Karageorghis, V. (ed.) (1986) *Acts of the International Archaeological Symposium Cyprus between the Orient and the Occident*. Nicosia.

Karageorghis, V. (1991) *Les Anciens Chypriotes*. Paris.

Karageorghis, V. (1994) 'The prehistory of an ethnogenesis', in Karageorghis and Michaelides (eds.) (1994): 1–9.

Karageorghis, V. (2002) Κύπρος, το σταυροδρόμι της Μεσογείου 1600–500 Π.Χ. Milan.

Karageorghis, V. (2004) 'Herodotus and Cyprus', in Karageorghis and Taifacos (eds.) (2004): 1–9.

Karageorghis, V. and D. Michaelides (eds.) (1994) *Proceedings of the International Symposium Cyprus in the 11th Century* BC. Nicosia.

Karageorghis, V. and D. Michaelides (eds.) (1995) *Proceedings of the International Symposium Cyprus and the Sea*. Nicosia.

Karageorghis, V., and I. Taifacos (eds.) (2004) *The World of Herodotus. Proceedings of an International Conference held at the Foundation Anastasios G. Leventis, Nicosia, September 18–21, 2003*. Nicosia.

Kerferd, G. (1981) *The Sophistic Movement*. Cambridge.

Kirk, G. S. (1985) *The Iliad. A Commentary*, Vol. I. Cambridge.

Knapp, B. (1993) 'Thalassocracies in Bronze Age eastern Mediterranean trade: making and breaking a myth', *World Archaeology* 24: 332–47.

Konstan, D. (1987) 'Persians, Greeks and empire', *Arethusa* 20: 59–73.

Kramer, L., and S. Maza (eds.) (2002) *A Companion to Western Historical Thought*. Oxford.

Kraus, C. S. (2002) 'Introduction: reading commentaries/commentaries as reading', in Gibson and Kraus (eds.) (2002): 1–27.

Kraus, C. S. (ed.) (1999) *The Limits of Historiography. Genre and Narrative in Ancient Historical Texts*. Leiden, Boston and Cologne.

Kühner, R., and B. Gerth (1898–1904) *Ausführliche Grammatik der griechischen Sprache*. Zweiter Teil: *Satzlehre* (2 vols; 3rd edn.). Hanover and Leipzig.

Kurd, P. (1991) 'Knowledge and unity in Heraclitus', *Monist* 74: 531–50.

Kurke, L. (1992) 'The politics of *habrosunē* in archaic Greece', *ClAnt* 11: 90–121.

Kurke, L. (1999) *Coins, Bodies, Games, and Gold. The Politics of Meaning in Archaic Greece*. Princeton.

Kurtz, D. C., and J. Boardman (1985) 'Booners', in *Greek Vases in the J. Paul Getty Museum* (Occasional Papers on Antiquities, 2). Malibu: 35–70.

Lang, M. (1968) 'Herodotus and the Ionian Revolt', *Historia* 17: 24–36.

Lang, M. L. (1984) *Herodotean Narrative and Discourse*. Cambridge, Mass. and London.

Lateiner, D. (1977) 'No laughing matter: a literary tactic in Herodotus, *TAPhA* 107: 173–82.

Lateiner, D. (1982a) 'The failure of the Ionian Revolt', *Historia* 31: 129–60.

Lateiner, D. (1982b) 'A note on the perils of prosperity in Herodotus', *RM* 125: 97–101.

Lateiner, D. (1989) *The Historical Method of Herodotus*. Toronto.
Lateiner, D. (1990) 'Deceptions and delusions in Herodotus', *ClAnt* 9: 230–46.
Lateiner, D. (2005) 'Signifying names and other ominous accidental utterances in classical historiography', *GRBS* 45: 35–57.
Lavelle, B. (1991) 'The compleat angler: observations on the rise of Peisistratus in Herodotus (1.59–64),' *CQ* 41: 317–24.
Lavelle, B. (1993) *The Sorrow and the Pity. A Prolegomenon to a History of Athens under the Peisistratids, c. 560–510 BC*. Stuttgart.
Legrand, Ph. (1946) *Hérodote, Histoires*. Vol. V; 1st edn. Paris.
Lemos, I. (2001) 'The Lefkandi connection: networking in the Aegean and the Eastern Mediterranean', in Bonfante and Karageorghis (eds.) (2001): 215–27.
Létoublon F. (ed.) (1996) *Impressions d'îles*. Toulouse.
Lévêque, P., and P. Vidal-Naquet (1964) *Clisthène l'Athénien. Essai sur la representation de l'espace et du temps dans la pensée politique grecque de la fin du VIe siècle à la mort de Plato*. Besançon (tr. D. A. Curtis as *Cleisthenes the Athenian*. New Jersey. 1996).
Lewis, D. M. (1989) 'Persian gold and Greek international relations', *REA* 91: 227–35.
Lewis, D. and R. Stroud (1979) 'Athens honors King Evagoras of Salamis', *Hesperia* 48: 180–93.
Lloyd, A. B. (1975–88) *Herodotus Book II* (3 vols). Leiden.
Loraux, N. (1985) 'La Cité, l'historien, les femmes', *Pallas* 32: 7–29.
Loraux, N. (1986) *The Invention of Athens. The Funeral Oration in the Classical City* (tr. A. Sheridan). Cambridge, Mass.
Loraux, N. (2000) *Born of the Earth* (tr. S. Stewart). Ithaca.
Loraux, N. (2002) *The Divided City. On Remembering and Forgetting in Ancient Athens* (tr. C. Pache and J. Fort). New York (originally published in Paris, 1997).
Loucas-Durie, E. (1989) 'Kinyras et la sacralisation de la fonction technique à Chypre', *Métis* 4: 117–27.
Luraghi, N. (ed.) (2001a) *The Historian's Craft in the Age of Herodotus*. Oxford.
Luraghi, N. (2001b) 'Local knowledge in Herodotus' *Histories*', in Luraghi (ed.) (2001a): 138–60.
Macan, R. (1895) *Herodotus. The Fourth, Fifth, and Sixth Books* (2 vols). London.
Maehler, H. (2004) *Bacchylides. A Selection*. Cambridge.
Malkin, I. (ed.) (2001) *Ancient Perceptions of Greek Ethnicity*. Cambridge, Mass. and London.
Manville, P. B. (1990) *The Origins of Citizenship in Ancient Athens*. Princeton.
Marchant, E. (1891) *Thucydides. Book II*. London.
Marg, W. (1965) *Herodot (Wege der Forschung*, 26, 2nd edn.). Munich.
Marincola, J. (1987) 'Herodotean narrative and the narrator's presence', *Arethusa* 20: 121–37.
Marincola, J. (1997) *Authority and Tradition in Ancient Historiography*. Cambridge.
Masson, O. (1960) *Inscriptions chypriotes syllabiques*. Paris.

Mau, J., and E. G. Schmidt (eds.) (1964) *Isonomia. Studien zur Gleichheitsvorstellung im griechischen Denken*. Berlin.

Mavrogiannis, T. (2004) 'Herodotus and the Phoenicians', in Karageorghis and Taifacos (eds.) (2004): 53–71.

McGlew, J. F. (1993) *Tyranny and Political Culture in Ancient Greece*. Ithaca.

McInerney, J. (2004) 'Nereids, colonies and the origins of *isēgoria*', in Sluiter and Rosen (eds.) (2004): 21–40.

McNellen, B. (1997) 'Herodotean symbolism', *ICS* 22: 11–23.

Meiggs, R. (1972) *The Athenian Empire*. Oxford.

Mikalson, J. D. (2002) 'Religion in Herodotus', in Baker, de Jong and van Wees (eds.) (2002): 187–98.

Mikalson, J. D. (2003) *Herodotus and Religion in the Persian Wars*. Chapel Hill.

Miller, M. C. (1997) *Athens and Persia in the Fifth Century* BC: *A Study in Cultural Receptivity*. New York.

Moles, J. L. (1993). 'Truth and untruth in Herodotus and Thucydides', in C. Gill and T. P. Wiseman (eds.), *Lies and Fiction in the Ancient World*. Exeter: 88–121.

Moles, J. L. (1996) 'Herodotus warns the Athenians', *PLLS* 9: 259–84.

Moles, J. L. (1998) 'Cry freedom: Tacitus, *Annals* 4.32–35', *Histos* 2. http://www.dur.ac.uk/Classics/histos/1998/moles.html

Moles, J. L. (1999) '*Anathema kai ktema*: the inscriptional inheritance of ancient historiography', *Histos* 3: http://www.dur.ac.uk/Classics/histos/1999/moles.html

Moles, J. L. (2001) 'A false dilemma: Thucydides' *History* and historicism', in S. J. Harrison (ed.), *Texts, Ideas, and the Classics*. Oxford: 195–219.

Moles, J. L. (2002) 'Herodotus and Athens', in Bakker *et al.* (eds.) (2002): 33–52.

Morgan, K. (ed.) (2003) *Popular Tyranny. Sovereignty and its Discontents in Ancient Greece*. Austin: 95–115.

Most, G. W. (1994) 'Simonides' Ode to Scopas in Contexts', in I. de Jong and J. Sullivan (eds.), *Modern Critical Theory and Classical Literature* (Mnemosyne Supplement 130). Leiden: 127–52.

Muellner, L. (1996) *The Anger of Achilles. Menis in Greek Epic*. Ithaca.

Muhly, J. D. (1986) 'The role of Cyprus in the economy of the eastern Mediterranean during the Second Millenium BC', in Karageorghis (ed.) (1986): 45–68.

Munson, R. V. (1993) 'Herodotus' use of prospective sentences and the story of Rhampsinitus and the thief in the *Histories*', *AJPh* 114: 27–44.

Munson, R. V. (2001a) '*Ananke* in Herodotus', *JHS* 121: 30–50.

Munson, R. V. (2001b) *Telling Wonders. Ethnographic and Political Discourse in the Work of Herodotus*. Ann Arbor.

Munson, R. V. (2005) *Black Doves Speak. Herodotus and the Language of Barbarians*. Cambridge, Mass. and London.

Murray, O. (1972) 'Herodotus and Hellenistic culture', *CQ* 76: 200–13.

Murray, O. (1988) 'The Ionian Revolt', *CAH* IV²: 461–90.

Murray, O. (1993) *Early Greece* (2nd edn.). London.

Murray, O. (2001a) 'Herodotus and oral history', in Luraghi (ed.) (2001): 16–44 (reprinted from H. Sancisi-Weerdenburg and A. Kuhrt (eds.) (1987), *Achaemenid History II. The Greek Sources*. Leiden: 93–115).

Murray, O. (2001b) 'Herodotus and oral history reconsidered', in Luraghi (ed.) (2001): 314–25.

Myres, J. (1907) 'The Sigynnae of Herodotus: an ethnological problem of the early Iron Age', in H. Balfour (ed.), *Anthropological Essays Presented to Edward Burnett Tylor in Honour of his 75th Birthday*. Oxford: 255–76.

Nagler, M. N. (1974) *Spontaneity and Tradition. A Study in the Oral Art of Homer*. Berkeley.

Nagy, G. (1996) *Poetry as Performance. Homer and Beyond*. Cambridge.

Naiden, F. S. (1999) 'The prospective imperfect in Herodotus', *HSCPh* 99: 135–49.

Nenci, G. (1994) *Erodoto. La rivolta della Ionia. V Libro delle Storie*. Milan.

Nenci, G. (1998) *Erodoto. La battaglia di Maratona. VI libro delle Storie*. Milan.

Neville, J. (1979) 'Was there an Ionian Revolt?', *CQ* 29: 268–75.

Nicolaou, K. (1976) *The Historical Topography of Kition*. Göteburg.

Ober, J. (1993) 'The Athenian Revolution of 508/7 BCE: violence, authority, and the origins of democracy', in Dougherty and Kurke (eds.) (1993): 215–32.

Ober, J. (1996) 'The Athenian revolution of 508/7 BC', in id., *The Athenian Revolution*. Princeton: 32–52.

Ogden, D. (1993) 'Cleithenes of Sicyon λευστήρ', *CQ* 43: 353–63.

O'Hara, J. (1996) *True Names. Vergil and the Alexandrian Tradition of Etymological Wordplay*. Ann Arbor.

Olson, S. D. (2002) *Aristophanes. Acharnians*. Oxford.

Oost, S. I. (1972) 'Cypselus the Bacchiad', *CPh* 67: 10–30.

Osborne, R. G. (1996) *Greece in the Making*. London.

Osborne, R. G. and S. Hornblower (eds.) (1994) *Ritual, Finance, Politics. Athenian Democratic Accounts Presented to David Lewis*. Oxford.

Osborne, R. G. and P. J. Rhodes (2003) *Greek Historical Inscriptions 404–323 BC*. Oxford.

Owen, A. S. (1939) *Ion*. Edition and Commentary. Oxford.

Parker, R. (1996) *Athenian Religion. A History*. Oxford.

Parsons, P. (1974) '*P. Oxy* 3013', *Oxyrhynchus Papyri* 42. London.

Payen, P. (1997) *Les Îles nomades. Conquérir et résister dans l'enquête d'Hérodote*. Paris.

Pelling, C. B. R. (ed.) (1990) *Characterization and Individuality in Greek Literature*. Oxford.

Pelling, C. B. R. (1993) 'Tacitus and Germanicus', in T. J. Luce (ed.), *Tacitus and the Tacitean Tradition*. Princeton: 59–85.

Pelling, C. B. R. (1997) 'East is east and west is west – or are they? National stereotyping in Herodotus', *Histos* 1: http://www.dur.ac.uk/Classics/histos/1997/pelling.html

Pelling, C. B. R. (1999) 'Epilogue', in Kraus (ed.) (1999): 325–60.

Pelling, C. B. R. (2000) *Literary Texts and the Greek Historian*. London.

Pelling, C. B. R. (2002) 'Speech and narrative: Herodotus' debate on the constitutions', *PCPS* 48: 123–58.

Pelling, C. B. R. (2006) 'Educating Croesus: talking and learning in Herodotus' *Lydian logos*', *ClAnt* 25.1:

Pelling, C. B. R. (2006b) 'Homer and Herodotus', in M. J. Clarke *et al.* (eds.), *Epic Interactions. Perspectives on Homer, Virgil, and the Epic Tradition Presented to Jasper Griffin by Former Pupils.* Oxford: 75–104.

Peltenburg, E. (ed.) (1989) *Early Society in Cyprus.* Edinburgh.

Peradotto, J. J. (1969) 'Cledonomancy in the *Oresteia*', *AJPh* 90: 1–21.

Perlman, S. (1976) 'Panhellenism, the polis and imperialism', *Historia* 25: 1–30.

Petit, Th. (1995) 'Amathous (*Autochthones eisin*) de l'identité Amathousienne à l'époque des Royaumes (VIIIe–IVe siècles av. J-C)', in Gontier (ed.) (1995): 51–64.

Petit, Th. (1996) 'Religion et royauté à Amathonte de Chrypre', *Transeuphratène* 12: 97–120.

Petit, Th. (1998) 'Amathousiens, Ethiopiens et Perses', *Cahiers du Centre d'études chypriotes*, 28: 73–86.

Petit, Th. (2004) 'Herodotus and Amathus', in Karageorghis and Taifacos (eds.) (2004): 9–26.

Petropoulou, A. (1986–7) 'The Thracian funerary rites (Hdt. 5.8) and similar Greek practices', *Talanta* 18–19: 29–47.

Pirenne-Delforge, V. and E. Suàrez de la Torre (eds.) (2000) *Héros et héroines dans les mythes et les cultes grecs.* Liège.

Pouilloux, J. (1975) 'Athènes et Salamine de Chypre', *RDAC* 1975: 111–22.

Pouilloux, J. (1976) 'L'Hellénisme à Salamine de Chypre', *BCH* 100: 449–59.

Pouilloux, J. (1995) 'Chypre entre l'Orient et l'Occident', in Κύπρος απο την Προϊστορία στους Νέοτερους (Cultural Foundation of the Bank of Cyprus). Nicosia: 11–36.

Powell, A. (ed.) (1989) *Classical Sparta. The Techniques behind her Success.* Norman and London.

Powell, J. E. (1937) 'Puns in Herodotus', *CR* 51: 103–5.

Powell, J. E. (1939a) *Herodotus Book VIII.* Cambridge.

Powell, J. E. (1939b) *The History of Herodotus.* Cambridge.

Powell, J. E. (1966²) *A Lexicon to Herodotus.* Hildesheim.

Pritchett, W. K. (1993) *The Liar School of Herodotos.* Amsterdam.

Raaflaub, K. A. (1979) '*Polis Tyrannos*: zur Entstehung einer politischen Metapher', in G. W. Bowersock, W. Burkert and M. C. J. Putnam (eds.), *Arktouros. Hellenic Studies Presented to Bernard Knox.* Berlin: 237–52.

Raaflaub, K. A. (1987) 'Herodotus, political thought, and the meaning of history', *Arethusa* 20: 221–48.

Raaflaub, K. A. (2002) 'Philosophy, science, politics: Herodotus and the intellectual trends of his time', in Bakker *et al.* (eds.) (2002): 149–86.

Raaflaub, K. A. (2004) 'Aristocracy and freedom of speech in the Greco-Roman world', in Sluiter and Rosen (eds.) (2004): 41–62.

Raptou, E. (1999) *Athènes et Chypre à l'époque Perse.* Lyons.

Redfield, J. M. (1985) 'Herodotus the tourist', *CPh* 80: 97–118.

Rehm, A. (1914) *Milet III. Das Delphinion.* Berlin.

Rennie, W. (1909) *The Acharnians of Aristophanes.* London.

Rhode, E. (1952) *Psyché. Le Culte de l'âme chez les Grecs et leur croyance à l'immortalité.* Paris.

Rhodes, P. J. (1981) *Commentary on the Aristotelian Athenaion Politeia.* Oxford.

Robb, K. (1991) 'The witness in Heraclitus and in early Greek law', *Monist* 74: 638–76.

Roberts, D. H., F. M. Dunn and D. P. Fowler (eds.) (1997) *Classical Closure. Reading the End in Greek and Latin Literature.* Princeton.

Rolling, R. (2004) 'Herodotus, human violence and the Ancient Near East', in Karageorghis and Taifacos (eds.): 121–51.

Romm, J. S. (1992) *The Edges of the Earth in Ancient Thought.* Princeton.

Romm, J. S. (1998) *Herodotus.* New Haven.

Rood, T. C. B. (1998) *Thucydides. Narrative and Explanation.* Oxford.

Rosselini, M., and S. Said (1978) 'Usages des femmes et autres nomoi chez les "sauvages" d'Hérodote: essai de lecture structurale', *ASNP* (ser. 3) 8: 949–1005.

Roux, G. (1963) Κυψελή: où avait-on caché le petit Kypselos?', *Revue des études anciennes* 65: 279–89.

Rusten, J. (1989) *Thucydides. The Peloponnesian War. Book II.* Cambridge.

Rutherford, R. B. (1994) 'Learning from history: categories and case-histories', in Osborne and Hornblower (eds.) (1994): 53–68.

Sahlins, M. (2004) *Apologies to Thucydides. Understanding History as Culture and Vice Versa.* Chicago.

Said, S. (2002a) 'Greeks and barbarians in Euripides' tragedies: the end of difference?' in T. Harrison (ed.), *Greeks and Barbarians.* Edinburgh: 62–100.

Said, S. (2002b) 'Herodotus and tragedy', in Bakker *et al.* (eds.) (2002): 117–48.

Sakellariou, M. B. (1990) *Between Memory and Oblivion. The Transmission of Early Greek Historical Traditions.* Athens.

Salmon, J. B. (1984) *Wealthy Corinth. A History of the City to 338 BC.* Oxford.

Sancisi-Weerdenburg, H. (1989) 'Gifts in the Persian Empire', in Briant and Herrenschmidt (eds.) (1989): 129–46.

Sancisi-Weerdenburg, H. and A. Kuhrt (eds.) (1990) *Centre and Periphery. Proceedings of the Groningen 1986 Achaemenid History Workshop, Achaemenid History IV.* Leiden.

Sansone, D. (1985) 'The date of Herodotus' publication', *ICS* 10: 1–10.

Scaife, R. (1989) 'Alexander I in the *Histories* of Herodotus', *Hermes* 117: 129–37.

Schirripa, P. (2004) 'Il confine mobile della Tracia e la fantasia tragica: miti traci a teatro', in id., *I Traci tra l'Egeo e il Mar Nero.* Milan: 65–84.

Seaford, R. (2003) 'Tragic tyranny', in Morgan (ed.) (2003): 95–115.

Scott, L. (2005). *A Historical Commentary on Herodotus 6* (Mnemosyne Supplement 268). Leiden.

De Sélincourt, A. (1996) Herodotus. *The Histories.* New edn., translated by A. De Sélincourt, revised with introduction and notes by J. Marincola. London.

Serghidou, A. (1995) 'L'Altérité du Chypriote dans le discours grec antique', in Gontier (ed.) (1995): 25–39.

Serghidou, A. (2004) 'Herodotus and the rhetoric of slavery', in Karageorghis and Taifacos (eds.) (2004): 179–97.

Serghidou, A. (2006) 'Discours ethnographique et quêtes identitaires en Chypre ancienne', in S. Fourrier and G. Grivaud (eds.), *Identités croisées en un milieu méditerranéen. Le Cas de Chypre.* Rouen: 165–87.

Shear, J. L. (2003) 'Prizes from Athens: the list of Panathenaic prizes and the sacred oil', *ZPE* 142: 87–108.

Shilleto, R. (1880) *Thucydidis II.* Cambridge.

Silk, M. (2001) 'Pindar meets Plato: theory, language, value, and the Classics', in Harrison (ed.) (2001): 26–45.

Simms, R. (1988) 'The cult of the Thracian goddess Bendis in Athens and Attica', *AncW* 18: 59–76.

Sluiter, I. and R. M. Rosen (eds.) (2004) *Free Speech in Classical Antiquity.* Leiden.

Smyth, H. W. (1956) *Greek Grammar* (rev. edn.). Cambridge, Mass.

Snodgrass, A. (1995) 'Cyprus and early Greek history', in Κύπρος απο την Προισ-τορία στους Νεοτερους (Cultural Foundation of the Bank of Cyprus). Nicosia: 99–123.

Solmsen, L. (1943) 'Speeches in Herodotus' account of the Ionian Revolt', *AJPh* 64: 194–207.

Sommerstein, A. (1981) *Aristophanes. Knights.* Warminster.

Sommerstein, A. (1989) *Aeschylus. Eumenides.* Cambridge.

Sourvinou-Inwood, C. (1991) *'Reading' Greek Culture. Texts and Images, Rituals and Myths.* Oxford.

Sourvinou-Inwood, C. (2002) 'Greek perceptions of ethnicity and the ethnicity of the Macedonians', in L. Moscati Castelnuovo (ed.), *Identità e prassi storica nel Mediterraneo greco.* Milan: 173–203.

Sourvinou-Inwood, C. (2003) 'Herodotus (and others) on Pelasgians: some perceptions of ethnicity', in Derow and Parker (eds.) (2003): 103–44.

Stadter, P. A. (1992) 'Herodotus and the Athenian *arche*', *ASNP* (ser. 3) 22: 781–809.

Stadter, P. A. (2002) 'Historical thought in ancient Greece', in Kramer and Maza (eds.) (2002): 35–59.

Stahl, H.-P. (1975) 'Learning through suffering? Croesus' conversations in the history of Herodotus', *YCS* 24: 1–36.

Stahl, J. M. (1907) *Kritisch-historische Syntax des griechischen Verbums der klassischen Zeit.* Heidelberg.

Stahl, M. (1983) 'Tyrannis und das Problem der Macht. Die Geschichten Herodots über Kypselos und Periander von Korinth', *Hermes* 111: 202–20.

Stanford, W. B. (1972) *Ambiguity in Greek Literature. Studies in Theory and in Practice.* New York and London.

Starkie, W. (1909) *The Acharnians of Aristophanes.* Amsterdam.

Stein, H. (1874) *Herodotos. Dritter Band: Buch V und VI.* 3rd edn. Berlin.

Steiner, D. T. (1994) *The Tyrant's Writ. Myths and Images of Writing in Ancient Greece.* Princeton.

Strasburger, H. (1955) 'Herodot und das perikleische Athen', *Historia* 4: 1–25 (reprinted in Marg (1965): 574–608).

Surikov, I. (2001) 'Historico-geographical questions connected with Pericles' Pontic expedition', *Ancient Civilizations from Scythia to Siberia* 7: 341–66.

Tancock, C. C. (1897) *The Story of the Ionic Revolt and Persian War as Told by Herodotus. Selections from the Translation of Canon Rawlinson, Revised and Adapted to the Purposes of the Present Work*. London.

Taylor, M. (1981) *The Tyrant Slayers*. New York.

Thomas, R. (1989) *Oral Tradition and Written Record in Classical Athens*. Cambridge.

Thomas, R. (1993) 'Performance and written publication in Herodotus and the Sophistic generation', in W. Kullmann and J. Althoff, *Vermittlung und Tradierung von Wissen in der griechischen Kultur*. Tübingen: 225–44.

Thomas, R. (2000) *Herodotus in Context. Ethnography, Science and the Art of Persuasion*. Cambridge.

Thomas, R. (2001a) 'Ethnicity, genealogy, and Hellenism in Herodotus', in Malkin (ed.) (2001): 213–86.

Thomas, R. (2001b) 'Herodotus' *Histories* and the floating gap', in Luraghi (ed.) (2001a): 198–210.

Thomas, R. (2003) 'Prose performance texts. *Epideixis* and written publication in the late fifth and early fourth centuries', in H. Yunis (ed.), *Written Texts and the Rise of Literate Culture in Ancient Greece*. Cambridge: 162–88.

Thomas, R. (2004) 'Herodotus, Ionia and the Athenian Empire', in Karageorghis and Taifacos (eds.) (2004): 27–42.

Thompson, S. (1958) *Motif-Index of Folk-Literature*, Vol. VI, *Index*. Copenhagen.

Töpffer, J. (1889) *Attische Genealogie*. Berlin.

Tozzi, P. (1978). *La rivolta ionica*. Pisa.

van der Veen, J. E. (1996). *The Significant and the Insignificant. Five Studies in Herodotus' View of History*. Amsterdam.

Vandiver, E. (1991) *Heroes in Herodotus. The Interaction of Myth and History*. Frankfurt-am-Main.

Vernant, J.-P. (1982a). 'From Oedipus to Periander: lameness, tyranny, incest, in legend and history', *Arethusa* 15: 19–38.

Vernant, J.-P. (1982b) 'La Belle Mort et le cadavre outragé', in Gnoli and Vernant (eds.): 45–76.

Vernant, J.-P. (1983) *Myth and Thought among the Greeks*. London (French original 1965, 2nd edn. 1985).

Virilio, P. (1986) *Speed and Politics. An Essay on Dromology*. New York.

Vlastos, G. (1953) '*Isonomia*', *AJPh* 64: 337–66.

Vlastos, G. (1964) 'Ἰσονομία πολιτική', in Mau and Schmidt (eds.) (1964): 1–35 (reprinted in Vlastos (1973): 164–73).

Vlastos, G. (1973) *Platonic Studies*. Princeton.

Wohl, V. (2002) *Love Among the Ruins. The Erotics of Democracy in Classical Athens*. Princeton.

Von Reden, S. (1995) *Exchange in Ancient Greece*. London.

Voutiras, E. (2000) 'Le Cadavre et le serpent, ou l'héroïsation manquée de Cléomène de Sparte', in Pirenne-Delforge and Suàrez de la Torre (eds.) (2000): 377–94.

Walbank, M. B (1987) 'Athens honours Evagoras', *EMC* 31: 229–33.

Walker, H. J. (1998) *Theseus and Athens*. Oxford.

Wallinga, H. T. (1984) 'The Ionian Revolt', *Mnemosyne* 37: 401–37.

Waters, K. H. (1971) *Herodotus on Tyrants and Despots. A Study in Objectivity*. Wiesbaden.

Waters, K. H. (1985) *Herodotos the Historian. His Problems, Methods and Originality*. London and Sydney.

Watkin, H. J. (1987) 'The Cypriote surrender to Persia', *JHS* 107: 154–63.

Weçowski, M. (1996) 'Ironie et histoire', *AncSoc* 27: 205–58.

West, M. (1966) *Hesiod. Theogony*, Oxford.

West, S. R. (1991) 'Herodotus' portrait of Hecataeus', *JHS* 111: 144–60.

West, S. R. (1999) 'Sophocles' *Antigone* and Herodotus Book Three', in J. Griffin (ed.), *Sophocles Revisited*. Oxford: 109–36.

West, S. R. (2004) 'Herodotus and Scythia', in Karageorghis and Taifacos (eds.) (2004): 73–89.

Westlake, H. D. (1969) 'Irrelevant notes and minor excursuses in Thucydides', in id., *Essays on the Greek Historians and Greek History*. New York: 1–39.

Wiesehofer, J. (1990) 'Zypern unter persicher Herrschaft', in Sancisi-Weerdenburg and Kuhrt (eds.) (1990): 239–52.

Wilamowitz-Moellendorf, U. von (1931) *Der Glaube der Hellenen*, Vol. I. Berlin.

Winton, R. (2000). 'Herodotus, Thucydides and the sophists', in C. Rowe and M. Schofield (eds.), *The Cambridge History of Greek and Roman Political Thought*. Cambridge: 89–121.

Wood, H. (1972) *The Histories of Herodotus. An Analysis of the Formal Structure*. The Hague and Paris.

Woodhead, W. (1928) *Etymologizing in Greek Literature from Homer to Philo Judaeus*. Toronto.

Woodman, A. J. (1995) '*Praecipuum munus annalium*: the construction, convention and context of Tacitus, *Annals* 3.65.1', *MH* 52: 111–26.

Yon, M. (1981) 'Chypre entre Grèce et les Perses. La Conscience grecque de Chypre entre 530 et 330 a.c.', *Ktèma* 6: 49–57.

Yon, M. (1995) 'Kition et la mer à l'époque classique et hellénistique', in Karageorghis and Michaelides (eds.) (1995): 119–30.

Yoshio, N. (1988) '*Isegoria* in Herodotus', *Historia* 37: 257–75.

Zacharia, K. (2001) '"The rock of the nightingale", kinship diplomacy and Sophocles' Tereus', in Budelmann and Michelakis (eds.) (2001): 91–112.

Zacharia, K. (2003) *Converging Truths. Euripides' Ion and the Athenian Quest for Self-Definition*. Leiden.

Zörner, G. (1971) *Kypselos und Pheidon von Argos. Untersuchungen zur frühen griechischen Tyrannis*. Marburg.

Index locorum

Alcman *PMG*
(1.51) 83

Aeneas Tacticus
(31.28.1) 18

Aeschylus
Ag. (712–36) 249
Eum. (179ff.) 222
Pers. (894–6) 274

Alexis
(*fr.* 25.12) 309

Apollonius of Rhodes
(2.99); 4.320 85

Apuleius
Met. (10.16) 259, 260

Archilochus
(19W) 90

Aristophanes
(*fr.* 71 K–A) 166
Ach. (133–73) 55; (133–73) 66; (137–8) 76; (141–50)
   75–6; (159–60) 74; (169–71) 74
Birds (813–15) 93
Eccl. (650) 81
Knights (1111–15) 124; (1316–20) 55; (1341) 75;
   (173–6) 86; (786–7) 205
Lys. (273–82) 307; (616–35) 308; (664–78) 308;
   (678–9) 308; (1149–56) 219
Peace (435–6) 153
Thesmo. (5–6) 8
Wasps (1296) 165; (700) 86; (97–9)
   76

Aristarchus
P. Amherst (II 11) 14

Aristotle
Pol. (1327b27–33) 67
Poet. (21) 60, 85

[Aristotle]
Ath. Pol (19–20) 309; (18–22) 205; (19.3) 51; (19.4)
   214; (23.4); (39.1–2) 308; (40.4) 308; (41.2ff.)
   308

Athenaeus
(345e) 96

Athenagoras of Athens
Legatio (14.1) 283

Bacchylides
(*fr.* 20B) 106

Catullus
(61.212–13) 259

Critias, DK 88B
(33–4) 190

Ctesiphon *FGrH* 688F
(45a2) 67; (55) 85

Demosthenes
(13.24) 121; (23.200) 121

[Demosthenes]
(12.21) 121

Diodorus Siculus
(1.1.2, 4, 5) 265; (1.1.5) 265; (11.37.6) 14, 15;
   (12.27–8) 149; (12.37) 14, 15; (13.52) 14, 15

Dionysus of Halicarnassus
Dem. (51) 80

Dissoi Logoi DK 90
(2.13) 63

Ephorus *FGrH* 70
(22) 76

Euripides
Andr. (170–6) 63
Cresph. (fr. 449N) 62

330

General index

336

Lightning Source UK Ltd.
Milton Keynes UK
UKOW04f1120181217

314558UK00008B/89/P